Transcendental Meditation in Criminal Rehabilitation and Crime Prevention

Transcendental Meditation® in Criminal Rehabilitation ani Prevention has been co-published simultaneously as *Jou Offender Rehabilitation*, Volume 36, Numbers 1/2/3/4 2003.

Transcendental Meditation®
in Criminal Rehabilitation and Crime Prevention

Charles N. Alexander
Kenneth G. Walton
David W. Orme-Johnson
Rachel S. Goodman
Nathaniel J. Pallone
Editors

Transcendental Meditation® in Criminal Rehabilitation and Crime Prevention has been co-published simultaneously as *Journal of Offender Rehabilitation*, Volume 36, Numbers 1/2/3/4 2003.

Routledge
Taylor & Francis Group
New York London

First published by

The Haworth Press, Inc., 10 Alice Street, Binghamton, NY 13904-1580

This edition published 2013 by Routledge
711 Third Avenue, New York, NY 10017
2 Park Square, Milton Park, Abingdon, Oxon OX14 4RN

Routledge is an imprint of the Taylor & Francis Group, an informa business

Transcendental Meditation® in Criminal Rehabilitation and Crime Prevention has been co-published simultaneously as *Journal of Offender Rehabilitation,* Volume 36, Numbers 1/2/3/4 2003.

Cover design by Brooke R. Stiles

Library of Congress Cataloging-in-Publication Data

Transcendental Meditation in criminal rehabilitation and crime prevention / Charles N. Alexander. [et al.], editors.
p. cm.
"Co-published simultaneously as Journal of offender rehabilitation, v. 36, no. 1/2, 2003 and v. 36, no. 3/4, 2003."
Includes bibliographical references and index.
ISBN 0-7890-2036-X (hardcover : alk. paper) – ISBN 0-7890-2037-8 (soft cover : alk. paper)
1. Criminals–Rehabilitation. 2. Crime prevention. 3. Transcendental Meditation. I. Alexander, Charles Nathaniel.
HV9281.T73 2003
365′.66–dc21

2003001531

ABOUT THE EDITORS

Charles N. Alexander (1950-1998), PhD, was Professor and Chair of Psychology, Director of the Division of Crime Prevention, Rehabilitation, and Substance Abuse in the Institute of Science, Technology, and Public Policy, and Director of the Institute for Research on Higher States of Consciousness at Maharishi University of Management, Fairfield, Iowa.

Kenneth G. Walton, PhD, is Associate Professor of Neurochemistry, Senior Fellow at the Center for Natural Medicine and Prevention, and Associate Director of the Division of Crime Prevention, Rehabilitation, and Substance Abuse in the Institute of Science, Technology, and Public Policy, all at Maharishi University of Management, Fairfield, Iowa.

David W. Orme-Johnson, PhD, formerly Chairperson, Department of Psychology, is currently an advisor and research consultant to the Center for Natural Medicine and Prevention, Maharishi University of Management, Fairfield, Iowa.

Rachel S. Goodman, PhD, is Director of the Career Development Center at Maharishi University of Management and is Assistant Professor of Peace Studies and a researcher on the Maharishi Effect in Government, International Relations, and Societal Quality of Life.

Nathaniel J. Pallone, PhD, Editor of the *Journal of Offender Rehabilitation,* is University Distinguished Professor (Psychology), Center of Alcohol Studies, Rutgers University, where he previously served as dean and as academic vice president.

Transcendental Meditation®
in Criminal Rehabilitation and Crime Prevention

CONTENTS

Contributors xvii

Preface xxi

DAVID C. MASON

Circuit Court of St. Louis, MO

Acknowledgments xxv

Foreword xxvii

JOHN HAGELIN

Maharshi University of Management

In Memoriam: Charles N. Alexander, PhD, 1950-1998 xxxi

GERALD T. GEER

Maharishi University of Management

INTRODUCTION AND OVERVIEW

The *Transcendental Meditation* Program:
A Consciousness-Based Developmental Technology
for Rehabilitation and Crime Prevention 1

RACHEL S. GOODMAN

Maharishi University of Management

KENNETH G. WALTON

Maharishi University of Management

DAVID W. ORME-JOHNSON

Maharishi University of Management

ROBERT BOYER

Maharishi University of Management

HIGHLIGHT: A COMMUNITY-BASED SENTENCING PROGRAM FOR PROBATIONERS

The Enlightened Sentencing Project: A Judicial Innovation 35

FARROKH K. ANKLESARIA

The Enlightened Sentencing Project, St. Louis, Missouri

MICHAEL S. KING

Stipendiary Magistrate, Geraldton, Western Australia

SECTION I: THEORY AND REVIEW

Effectiveness of the *Transcendental Meditation* Program in Criminal Rehabilitation and Substance Abuse Recovery: A Review of the Research 47

MARK A. HAWKINS

Maharishi University of Management

Effects of the *Transcendental Meditation* Program on Neuroendocrine Abnormalities Associated with Aggression and Crime 67

KENNETH G. WALTON

Maharishi University of Management

DEBRA K. LEVITSKY

Fairfield, Iowa

SECTION II: ORIGINAL RESEARCH ON REHABILITATION

First Prison Study Using the *Transcendental Meditation* Program: La Tuna Federal Penitentiary, 1971 89

DAVID W. ORME-JOHNSON

Maharishi University of Management

RICHARD M. MOORE

Channel One, Los Angeles

Walpole Study of the *Transcendental Meditation* Program in Maximum Security Prisoners I: Cross-Sectional Differences in Development and Psychopathology 97

CHARLES N. ALEXANDER

Maharishi University of Management

KENNETH G. WALTON

Maharishi University of Management

RACHEL S. GOODMAN

Maharishi University of Management

Walpole Study of the *Transcendental Meditation* Program in Maximum Security Prisoners II: Longitudinal Study of Development and Psychopathology 127

CHARLES N. ALEXANDER

Maharishi University of Management

DAVID W. ORME-JOHNSON

Maharishi University of Management

Walpole Study of the *Transcendental Meditation* Program in Maximum Security Prisoners III: Reduced Recidivism 161

CHARLES N. ALEXANDER

Maharishi University of Management

MAXWELL V. RAINFORTH

Maharishi University of Management

PAUL R. FRANK

Maharishi University of Management

JAMES D. GRANT

Maharishi University of Management

CHRISTOPHER VON STADE

Fairfield, Iowa

KENNETH G. WALTON

Maharishi University of Management

Effects of the *Transcendental Meditation* Program on Recidivism Among Former Inmates of Folsom Prison: Survival Analysis of 15-Year Follow-Up Data 181

MAXWELL V. RAINFORTH
Maharishi University of Management
CHARLES N. ALEXANDER
Maharishi University of Management
KENNETH L. CAVANAUGH
Maharishi University of Management

Consciousness-Based Rehabilitation of Inmates in the Netherlands Antilles: Psychosocial and Cognitive Changes 205

MARK A. HAWKINS
Maharishi University of Management
CHARLES N. ALEXANDER
Maharishi University of Management
FREDERICK T. TRAVIS
Maharishi University of Management
CARL R. T. CAMELIA
University of the Netherlands Antilles
KENNETH G. WALTON
Maharishi University of Management
CHRISTIAN F. DURCHHOLZ
Maharishi University of Management
MAXWELL V. RAINFORTH
Maharishi University of Management

SECTION III: PREVENTING CRIME AND VIOLENCE

Attacking Crime at Its Source: *Consciousness-Based* Education in the Prevention of Violence and Antisocial Behavior 229

CHRISTOPHER JONES
Maharishi University of Management
MAWIYAH CLAYBORNE
Maharishi University of Management
JAMES D. GRANT
Maharishi University of Management
GEORGE RUTHERFORD
Baltimore, Maryland, Public Schools

Preventing Crime Through the Maharishi Effect 257

DAVID W. ORME-JOHNSON

Maharishi University of Management

Preventing Terrorism and International Conflict: Effects of Large Assemblies of Participants in the *Transcendental Meditation* and *TM-Sidhi* Programs 283

DAVID W. ORME-JOHNSON

Maharishi University of Management

MICHAEL C. DILLBECK

Maharishi University of Management

CHARLES N. ALEXANDER

Maharishi University of Management

SECTION IV: TRANSCENDENTAL MEDITATION IN PRISONS AND PRISON SYSTEMS

The *Transcendental Meditation* Program in the Senegalese Penitentiary System 303

FARROKH K. ANKLESARIA

The Enlightened Sentencing Project, St. Louis, Missouri

MICHAEL S. KING

Stipendiary Magistrate, Geraldton, Western Australia

Cost Savings from Teaching the *Transcendental Meditation* Program in Prisons 319

DAVID L. MAGILL

The Enlightened Sentencing Project, St. Louis, Missouri

REFERENCES 333

Index 385

Contributors

CHARLES N. ALEXANDER (1950-1998), PhD, was Professor and Chair of Psychology, Director of the Division of Crime Prevention, Rehabilitation, and Substance Abuse in the Institute of Science, Technology and Public Policy, and Director of the Institute for Research on Higher States of Consciousness at Maharishi University of Management, Fairfield, Iowa.

FARROKH K. ANKLESARIA, a lawyer by training, is Founding Director of the Enlightened Sentencing Project in St. Louis, Missouri.

ROBERT BOYER, PhD, is a clinical psychologist in private practice, and Adjunct Professor in Psychology at Maharishi University of Management, Fairfield, Iowa.

CARL R. T. CAMELIA, LLS, is Associate Professor of Accounting and Management in the Department of Social and Economic Studies, University of the Netherlands Antilles, Curacao.

KENNETH L. CAVANAUGH, PhD, is Professor of Applied Statistics in the School of Business and Public Administration, Maharishi University of Management, Fairfield, Iowa.

MAWIYAH CLAYBORNE, PhD, an educator in the California public school system, has been implementing and evaluating Consciousness-Based education programs in minority settings for the past 15 years.

MICHAEL C. DILLBECK, PhD, is Professor and International Vice President, Maharishi University of Management.

CHRISTIAN F. DURCHHOLZ, MS, was, at the time of his contribution, a PhD degree candidate in the Department of Psychology at Maharishi University of Management, Fairfield, Iowa.

PAUL R. FRANK, MS, was, at the time of contribution, a doctoral student in the Department of Psychology at Maharishi University of Management, Fairfield, Iowa.

GERALD T. GEER, AB, is Adjunct Professor in Writing at Maharishi University of Management, Fairfield, Iowa and is an editor of academic publications.

RACHEL S. GOODMAN, PhD, is Director of the Career Development Center at Maharishi University of Management, Assistant Professor of Peace Studies and a researcher on the Maharishi Effect in Government, International Relations, and Societal Quality of Life.

JAMES D. GRANT, EdD, is Associate Professor of Education and Dean of the College of Arts and Sciences at Maharishi University of Management, Fairfield, Iowa.

JOHN HAGELIN, PhD, is Chair, Department of Physics and Founding Director of the Institute of Science, Technology and Public Policy, Maharishi University of Management, Fairfield, Iowa.

MARK A. HAWKINS, PhD, was, at the time of his contribution, Assistant Professor, Department of Psychology, Maharishi University of Management, Fairfield, Iowa.

CHRISTOPHER JONES, EdD, is Associate Professor of Education and Chair of the Department of Education at Maharishi University of Management, Fairfield, Iowa.

MICHAEL S. KING, LLB, MA, PhD, is Stipendiary Magistrate at Geraldton, Western Australia.

DEBRA K. LEVITSKY, PhD, was a postdoctoral researcher in physiology at Maharishi University of Management, Fairfield, Iowa, at the time of her contribution.

DAVID L. MAGILL, MSCI, is treasurer for the Enlightened Sentencing Project, St. Louis, Missouri, and Vice-President of Engineering, LTDS Corporation, Fairfield, Iowa.

DAVID C. MASON, LLD, is a Judge in the 22nd Circuit Court of St. Louis, Missouri.

RICHARD M. MOORE, BS, works for Channel One in Los Angeles.

DAVID W. ORME-JOHNSON, PhD, formerly Chairperson, Department of Psychology, is currently an advisor and research consultant to the Center for Natural Medicine and Prevention, Maharishi University of Management, Fairfield, Iowa.

MAXWELL V. RAINFORTH, PhD, is Assistant Professor of Statistics at Maharishi University of Management, Fairfield, Iowa, and Biostatistician with the Center for Natural Medicine and Prevention at that institution.

GEORGE RUTHERFORD, PhD, implemented a successful Consciousness-Based education program as principal of the Fletcher Johnson School in Washington, DC, and was, at the time of his contribution, instituting a new Consciousness-Based education program at Thurgood Marshall Middle School in Baltimore, Maryland.

FREDERICK T. TRAVIS, PhD, is Associate Professor of Maharishi Vedic Science and Dean of the Graduate School at Maharishi University of Management, Fairfield, Iowa.

KENNETH G. WALTON, PhD, is Associate Professor of Neurochemistry, Senior Fellow at the Center for Natural Medicine and Prevention, and Associate Director of the Division of Crime Prevention, Rehabilitation, and Substance Abuse at the Institute of Science, Technology, and Public Policy, all at Maharishi University of Management, Fairfield, Iowa.

CHRISTOPHER VON STADE, EdD, works in community mental health in Jefferson County, Iowa, as Executive Director of the Real World Foundation and as Mental Health Treatment Director for ResCare, Inc.

Transcendental Meditation in Criminal Rehabilitation and Crime Prevention. Pp. xxi-xxiv.

Preface

CRIME RISES DESPITE INCREASED INCARCERATION

Thirty years ago, people in this country said, "We've got a crime problem. What are we going to do about it? Let's get tough. Let's put more people in jail." Not one study existed to say that if we put more people in jail, crime would go down. Still, we went ahead with it, only to find out that as incarceration rates rose, so did the crime rate.

Then we said, "This doesn't work. Let's try a few more things." We tried aggression training, education, job training, counseling, and other programs. We jumped into them all, spending billions across the country with nothing to support any realistic expectation of a reasonable return for the dollar.

Throughout these same years, criminality among our poor has risen, recidivism perpetuates, and our cities have become places where we *used* to live. Our state budgets have less and less to do with schools, teachers, and students–and more to do with prisons, prosecutors, and inmates.

STRESS–THE ROOT CAUSE OF CRIMINAL BEHAVIOR

While there are several programs designed to help rehabilitate criminal offenders, their success is inhibited by their failure to provide the essential element of effective rehabilitation–the ability to avoid future criminal acts. The real objective of rehabilitation should be helping people who are at risk develop something *from within* so they can avoid committing the next crime.

For years, I have researched the causes and risk factors for crime. I have participated in numerous civic studies and commissions on crime. In the process, I came upon reports suggesting that dealing with feelings of personal inadequacy, demands of parents and children, demands of peers, the demands of society–together with the helplessness of poverty–combine to create incredible stress. That stress is the root cause of most criminal behavior.

The proof of this is so obvious that it is easily overlooked. Spend a few minutes with a victim of violent domestic abuse and you will learn that the abuse is triggered by something the victim supposedly did that sent the perpetrator into a rage. The trigger event is always something that most of us might be upset, annoyed, or even angered by. But our ability to cope with the stress caused by this tension is sufficient to stop us from lashing out with violence. The perpetrator lacks this ability to cope with stress.

Some people who face what Shakespeare called "the slings and arrows of outrageous fortune" turn to drugs to escape or feel better. Just ask any addict. Most of us, however, can handle the stress of adversity well enough to avoid addiction to drugs. Most, if not all people, deal with feelings of self-doubt and inadequacy. But when these feelings are chronic, too many of our youth turn to gangs or carry a gun or act to exert control over others by violent intimidation.

STRESS-COPING SKILLS–THE MISSING LINK

For most of us, the stresses of life are manageable, either because we have normal stress-coping skills or because we have sufficient external support such as friends, family, co-workers, spirituality, or financial insulation. However, for those who face stresses and who have below normal stress-coping skills and no external support, rationality becomes lost in a whirlpool of fear, hopelessness, anger, and frustration. It results in a person lashing out, demanding respect by intimidation, and abusing drugs or alcohol to numb the mind. It makes suicide seem like the only option available. To counteract this, we must supply what has so far been the missing link in criminal rehabilitation: training offenders to normalize and improve their stress-coping skills.

For the last seven years, I have vigorously studied programs intended to help criminal offenders avoid re-offending. My investigation led me to an unexpected result. After thoroughly studying the research on the Transcendental Meditation (TM) program, I have concluded that this program offers the most significant rehabilitative tool for offenders. The TM program reduces stress, and it does so more effectively than any other technique available. It is an excellent means to help someone achieve self-esteem, self-control, and resiliency from within. It fosters more coherent thinking. And it focuses the mind on life's more constructive possibilities. Transcendental Meditation has been demonstrated to be an effective way to help an offender resist the temptation to re-offend.

In addition to the many scientific studies supporting the use of Transcendental Meditation in criminal rehabilitation, my colleagues and I have seen its benefits for offenders in our courts whom we have placed on probation. These offenders are now demonstrating greater self-esteem and self-control. Their friends and families speak in glowing terms of the changes in the offenders' lives. Never before in our careers have we seen health benefits, families becoming stronger, and people's lives turning around this fast. Our results over the past 2 years have clearly confirmed the scientific research.

WHY TM?

People often ask me, "Why do you do this–why stick your neck out for something like Transcendental Meditation?" I do this because I believe that part and parcel of a criminal justice system that talks so much about punishment has to be a system that talks about prevention, and preparation, and helping the offender avoid re-offending. My colleagues and my probationers know that I can be tough. If I am going to be a tough judge, then it is hypocritical of me to be tough about sending people to jail unless I am just as tough in trying to help them avoid having to go there.

MY CONFIDENCE BORNE OUT

In the first group I sent through the TM program, I took what might be called a softball approach. These were guys who may have had a few minor drug problems. What no one knew is that in the second group, with some of them, I took a risk. Those probationers know how close I was to incarcerating them. Yes, I did stick my neck out. To be perfectly frank, I staked my career on them. Now I am delighted that so many leaders of society and of the criminal justice system are closely watching the Enlightened Sentencing Project because this program worked, even for those high-risk cases.

REHABILITATION FROM WITHIN

TM is a technique that probationers can do on their own, on their own schedule, in their own time. It gives them a comfortable place to go in their own mind, not because they are required to report but because they want to. It makes them feel better. They find themselves getting along better with their families, and their children are easier to take care of. They develop the strength to turn their backs on tobacco, alcohol, drugs, or whatever the problems are.

By increasing stress-coping ability, enhancing clarity of thought, and developing self-esteem, the TM program supplements traditional rehabilitative programs–aggression training, drug rehabilitation, counseling, community service, sex offender programs, and so on. It helps offenders develop their own internal counseling on the streets to support the external counseling received in traditional programs. And in contrast to what some people think, this program is not religious. It does not require any change in a person's lifestyle, beliefs, personal philosophy, or religion.

This volume's deep knowledge about what is needed for effective rehabilitation brings me great fulfillment. Currently, little scientific research supports the programs that prisons are using in their attempt to rehabilitate inmates. Relatively little evidence exists to justify the billions we spend each year on criminal justice. At such a time in our society, this volume appears as a lighthouse of hope. I strongly recommend that every criminal justice professional study this book and take bold action to apply its technology, the Transcendental Meditation program. I am deeply convinced that this will bring an effective and lasting solution to crime as well as to its personal and social traumas.

Hon. David C. Mason, Judge
Circuit Court of St. Louis, MO

Acknowledgments

The guest editors, and Vicki Alexander (on behalf of Charles N. Alexander), express deepest appreciation to Nathaniel J. Pallone, Editor of the *Journal of Offender Rehabilitation*, as well as to all authors and to others who came to our aid to facilitate the final editing and production of the manuscripts. Particularly important were: David and Claudia Magill–who worked beyond the call of duty; Mark Hawkins; Jean Fulton and Sonja Oslund, copy editors, who between them did the lion's share of the copyediting; Phil Tomlinson, who prepared the index; Sharon Starr, whose help in organizing the paperwork was superb; and Kelly Munly, Anna-Carin Johansson, and Paul Frank, graduate students who assisted in formatting, copyediting, entering edits, and other vital tasks. Last, we feel tremendous gratitude to Anthony and Eden Danaher, Steve Guich and Kay Hazen, Warren Berman, Jay Marcus, and the other generous donors who made the last phase of this project possible. We are, of course, most grateful to Maharishi Mahesh Yogi for his 50 years of tireless efforts to make the wisdom of the Vedic tradition available to all people everywhere.

Transcendental Meditation in Criminal Rehabilitation and Crime Prevention. Pp. xxvii-xxix.

Foreword

Crime has increased dramatically in America during the past 50 years and now costs Americans almost $700 billion annually. Despite more than two decades of get-tough policies, the rate of crime in America is high compared to other developed nations. With longer, often mandatory, prison sentences, including three-strikes laws, the United States has the highest incarceration rate in the world, with more than 2 million of our citizens in jail. Of gravest concern is juvenile violent crime, which has spiraled upward during the past two decades.

America's criminal justice system is under constant strain. Courts, police, probation and parole agencies, and prison systems are overworked and have inadequate resources to deal with the high level of crime. Clearly, a get-tough policy is not enough. Effective crime prevention and rehabilitation are essential.

Increasing recognition of the need for prevention has led to experimental approaches such as Drug Abuse Resistance Education (DARE) and midnight basketball. Unfortunately, long-term studies have found no significant reduction in crime and drug abuse from these programs. Indeed, most well-intentioned rehabilitation programs have fallen short of their founders' goals. While some programs appear to work with some offenders some of the time, it is difficult to know which programs to apply to which offender for maximum results.

These approaches have met with limited success because they fail to address the root cause of crime–the epidemic of stress throughout society. During the past two decades, medical science has documented an alarming rise of stress-related illnesses, such as hypertension, stroke, and heart disease. This same build-up of stress is responsible for a similar rise in social illnesses–family disintegration, domestic violence, substance abuse, and crime. The ultimate cause of most stress is the violation of natural law, that is, life-damaging behaviors that cause strain on the individual, the economy, and the fabric of society.

The Transcendental Meditation Program in Criminal Rehabilitation and Crime Prevention offers a profound and holistic approach to solving the problem of crime. It addresses the epidemic of stress and describes solutions based on restoration of natural law in the life of the individual and society. This highly practical knowledge of living in accord with natural law–the same organizing intelligence that governs the universe–has been revived from the ancient Vedic tradition of India and reformulated into a systematic, scientific framework by Maharishi Mahesh Yogi.

The volume describes an approach from within the individual, an approach that allows the individual not only to automatically achieve the physiological and behavioral transformations necessary to produce law-abiding behavior but also to rediscover the inner Self as a silent, peaceful state of Being–a transcendental field of consciousness underlying individuality. The Transcendental Meditation technique and the other Consciousness-Based approaches of Maharishi Vedic Science provide effortless technologies to experience the inner Self, the home of all the laws of nature. Repeated experience of this Self infuses its silent orderliness into all aspects of individual life and society. It is these technologies that are documented in this volume.

The programs presented in this collection offer an effective complement–or a comprehensive alternative–to conventional treatment approaches for crime prevention and rehabilitation. This prevention-oriented approach is the most hard-headed and hard-hitting response to crime available today, because it focuses on scientifically proven technologies that actually work. And the cost of this effective crime prevention and rehabilitation approach is negligible in comparison to the cost of a typical cycle of crime, incarceration, and recidivism, which can last a lifetime. Thus, this comprehensive approach will save billions of dollars in national resources, reclaim vast human resources lost to criminal behavior, and prevent immeasurable pain and suffering in the lives of millions of citizens who are the victims of crime each year.

There is a growing public demand in the area of criminal justice for cost-effective solutions based upon scientifically proven programs that actually work. Obviously, only a scientific approach to reducing crime and stress, and to restoring life in accord with natural law, will fulfill this need. Presented here are the very best of these programs. The theories are well supported in the psychological and sociological literature, rigorously verified through extensive research, and repeatedly field-tested worldwide.

This volume is essential reading for criminal justice professionals, legislators, government officials, and any other citizens seeking relief from the immense burden of crime. It offers a profoundly rewarding direction for action. I can personally attest to the effectiveness, ease of implementation, and deep satisfaction that comes from putting these technologies into practice. In the summer of 1993 in Washington, DC, Maharishi University of Management's Institute of Science, Technology and Public Policy conducted the National Demonstration Project to Reduce Violent Crime. This project significantly reduced violent crime in Washington, DC, and positively influenced social trends. It confirmed and extended the scientific results previously reported on the Transcendental Meditation program.

A truly effective criminal justice and criminal rehabilitation system should be capable of producing a crime-free nation–a nation where citizens live fully in accord with natural law, as well as with national and local law; where people can walk on the streets without fear; and where citizens live and work together harmoniously for their own fulfillment and for the good of the nation. The programs presented in this book offer a lasting solution to the problem of crime, even with a broad definition of this term that includes terrorism and international conflict, and provides a practical means to achieve this goal.

John Hagelin

AUTHOR'S NOTE

John Hagelin, PhD, is founding director of the Institute of Science Technology and Public Policy, Maharishi University of Management, Fairfield, Iowa, USA.

Orme-Johnson
April 4, 2003

In Memoriam

Charles N. Alexander, PhD, 1950-1998

In a photograph that hangs above my writing desk, my good friend Charles N. ("Skip") Alexander and I, all smiles, face each other across a large birthday cake. Skip holds a lit candle in his hand, and he's about to make a wish for me. I'm beaming, leaning forward expectantly. He's about to say, "I light this light, symbolic of pure consciousness, the light of life for all humanity"–and then he'll give his best wishes for my next year.

Skip and I first met in 1968 as undergraduate classmates at Harvard. How can I describe the gift of being his friend for 30 years? He was irrepressible: he lit that same light of life everywhere he went, on every level, and in everyone he touched.

Intellectually, Skip left us a remarkable legacy. His scholarship shattered the accepted psychological paradigm that human development "freezes" at adolescence. He demonstrated that, even in old age, we humans could unfreeze our creativity and rise to fulfillment in higher states of consciousness. His theoretical and empirical research led to more than 90 research articles and several books, with profound practical applications for educational, developmental, and organizational psychology; for drug and alcohol addictions; for criminal rehabilitation; and for world peace. He was the initial facilitator behind all the chapters collected in this volume. Yet despite his brilliance and professional accomplishments, Skip always cared more deeply about the person sitting next to him than about all his own scholarship. He lived his own message; he radiated a goodness, a kindness, a generosity of spirit, and a personal warmth that unfroze the hearts and minds of all who knew him, inspiring them to transcend their limitations and rise to the highest expression of their potential.

When Skip and I first met, he was rooming with classmates of mine from Phillips Exeter Academy, so I visited often. Even then he was a true seeker of higher consciousness, of life's full potential. He majored in psychology to seek out that potential, and two events–neither academic–helped him find it.

I still enjoy claiming seniority among Skip's friends by pointing out that I attended the 1968 Harvard-Wellesley freshman picnic where Skip met his future wife Vicki, his joy and inspiration from that moment onward. Skip told me once that when he met Vicki, she illuminated his future, and everything changed for him. She became his true love, his life, his joy, his inspiration; as a couple, they uplifted and brought insight for 30 years to everyone they met, and the enviable unity they shared supported and shaped Skip's academic success.

During his undergraduate career, Skip also found the Transcendental Meditation (TM)[1] program as taught by Maharishi Mahesh Yogi. In TM Skip discovered a remarkably simple, effortless, and universally applicable technique to unfold the mind's full potential. Here was a technique that allowed anyone to innocently experience consciousness in its pure state as the inner wakefulness at the source of thought–the fountainhead of creativity and intelligence–while simultaneously eliminating the stresses from the body that block the mind's potential from being actualized. He knew he had found his life's work and would become a teacher of TM, and that role was the heart of his heart. Skip and I graduated in 1972, and, together with Vicki, we traveled overseas to La Antilla, Spain, where we trained with Maharishi to become teachers of TM. Years later, traveling across Germany by train to deliver a paper on heart disease at a prestigious conference, Skip was asked by a fellow passenger what he did for a living. Although he was at the height of his academic career as a world-renowned psychologist, Skip answered simply, "I'm a meditation teacher."

In 1981, Skip was back at Harvard getting his PhD in psychology. He and Vicki had just bought a two-story house on Garden Street; they were going to live on the top floor and were looking for renters for the ground-floor apartment. When I returned to Cambridge that year, Skip quickly conscripted me as his first tenant, and I moved in along with the moving boxes. I hoped that in my new quarters I might gain some insight into Skip and Vicki's secrets for a successful marriage. But here's what I discovered: they had no secrets. That was their secret. They lived life so openly, so fully, so truthfully, that there was never any hidden agenda: their thoughts and feelings were all up front for everyone to see.

Skip's irresistible, magnetic personality made him a natural leader, and as a leader he possessed two remarkable qualities. He could unfailingly draw people into his projects by infecting them with his own limitless enthusiasm and with the belief that they were working for a cause greater than themselves. And he could always bypass, overcome, or melt away all the apparent obstacles to his intended purpose. Then, when the obstacles fell away, he always seized the opportunity to expand his projects far beyond their original goals–which, of course, required more recruits to the cause.

I was recruited fairly early in Skip's career, not only as his first tenant but also to help in the final production of his PhD dissertation–an exhaustive examination of the psychological and sociological effects of the TM program on inmates at the state prison in Walpole, Massachusetts. For many nights, our team of about 10 volunteers assembled in my Cambridge offices and typed Skip's drafts, helped design charts, offered editorial suggestions, and recreated everything again and again, all under Skip's cajoling, entreating, perfectionistic guidance. In the meantime, he was writing furiously, expanding his original thoughts in new directions. We would work through the night until 8:00 a.m., when the daytime office shift arrived, and then head off to our regular jobs. As the days wore on and Skip's thesis kept expanding, we all began to wonder if the project would ever end.

So, apparently, did Skip's thesis committee. After he had submitted his fifth or sixth "draft" to them (each draft with a promise that he would be finished soon), I came home one day to find him pacing around in a circle in the living room. "I can't believe it!" he said. "My thesis committee called me today, and they told me, 'Congratulations–you're done.'" He looked at me in bewilderment. "How can they do that?" he said. "I have three more sections to write!"

Skip's PhD work opened up many new directions in psychological research. His thesis, for example, pioneered the study of TM and adult development in prisons. Taken as a whole, more than 30 studies on TM in criminal rehabilitation and substance abuse support his findings that TM reduces psychopathology and increases self-development in inmates, and significantly reduces rate of return to prison after release. In an arena where most experts feel that "nothing works," the TM research offers both a realistic hope and a scientific foundation for true and effective rehabilitation.

While Skip was writing his thesis, his and Vicki's unbounded love for everyone was creating its own ongoing miracle of rehabilitation and upliftment among all their friends. Sometimes, when you were having a bad day, Skip would make everything all right by putting his arm around you and saying, "You're a practically *perfect* person!" And other times, when you held on to an opinion or action he didn't endorse, Skip's face would crinkle into a marvelous expression of bafflement–a mystified, head-shaking look–and he would quiz you deeply in a bemused sort of way, sometimes grilling you mercilessly about your stance. But even when you started to squirm, you didn't mind, because you knew Skip couldn't help himself; his love and concern and interest in you as a person just drove him to it. Skip was constitutionally committed to the truth, in both his personal and professional life. He had to understand, and he had to tell you what he felt he understood, regardless of the consequences–truth always bubbled over in his life.

After Skip finished his PhD, he began branching out in new directions. In his postdoctoral collaboration with Professor Ellen Langer, also at Harvard, he began a research study in nursing homes in the Cambridge area to investigate the effects of meditation and other behavioral approaches in the elderly. This 5-year project ultimately revealed that the elderly could increase both their mental flexibility and their physical health through such procedures. This early project laid the foundation for one of Skip's most significant studies, which demonstrated the beneficial effects of TM on hypertension in elderly African Americans. Due to its importance, this summary of the research was included in the AMA's national newsletter.

Skip also founded an institute for world peace research. He wanted to examine the theory that group practice of the TM program, and the more advanced TM-Sidhi program, could affect social trends in a positive way through a field effect of consciousness. In the early 1980s, only preliminary research on this theory had been done–and in only a few cities around the world. But Skip, never one to think small, decided that he wanted to use this field effect of consciousness in a large "coherence-creating" project to end the then ongoing war in Lebanon. Along with members of the TM organization living in Israel, he set up plans for a 2-month coherence-creating course in Jerusalem, during which time the number of participants could be mapped against war deaths and other indicators.

I was once again conscripted, this time as part of a new team that would help prepare the preliminary research predictions. Skip was confident that the research study would show measurable improvements in a number of social indicators in both Lebanon and Jerusalem. He lodged these predictions in advance with independent review boards of scientists in both North America and Israel, so that no one could claim at the study's completion that other forces had caused the changes.

After the Israel project was completed, Skip and Vicki left Cambridge and moved to Maharishi University of Management in Fairfield, Iowa, where Skip accepted a professorship with the Department of Psychology. Here he was free to pursue his lifelong passion–to take the entire field of psychology to a new level, a level in which pure consciousness is seen as foundational to human experience. In the Vedic tradition of India, pure consciousness is said to be a unifield field that gives rise to the laws of nature that structure both the universe and the individual, the level where all potentialities are possibilities. In this new role, Skip became a true Vedic psychologist, inspiring hundreds of students to actualize their potential.

In 1990, I joined Skip and Vicki on faculty at Maharishi University of Management. I discovered that during the intervening years, they had decided to start a family. Ever the scientist, Skip had conducted several opinion polls among friends about this idea, and found public sentiment running heavily in favor of it. Soon Nathaniel Charles Alexander was born–and then Skip's own psychological training began in earnest.

"Young Nathaniel," as Skip called his son, turned out to have the same irrepressible will and sense of limitless possibilities that had always characterized the father. He also had the infinite energy of youth. One day when Skip and I were having lunch together with Nathaniel at the University's dining hall, Nathaniel announced he was leaving the table. "No, Nathaniel," Skip said, "you've got to finish your vegetables." Nathaniel stood up and marched across the dining hall. Skip looked at me, smiled conspiratorially, and said, "I've got him in the palm of my hand."

As Nathaniel grew bigger, so did Skip's career. Skip still had a dedicated team of recruits working with him throughout the night, but now they were graduate students and professors preparing grant proposals to the National Institutes of Health for research funding. Over several years, the NIH funded projects proposed by Skip and his colleagues to the tune of more than $7 million, because, as always, his research was impeccable in its methodology and revolutionary in its implications–as the papers in this volume reveal.

Even though I lived close to Skip and Vicki at the University, I began to see less of them as Skip started traveling extensively to visit the sites of his research projects nationally and to speak at conferences internationally. His work and its implications for human health, psychology, and the future of society were beginning to gain the global recognition and acceptance they deserved. Prominent leaders across the disciplines–in the fields of medicine, psychology, sociology, education, prison rehabilitation, drug rehabilitation, and peace studies–began to acknowledge that, taken together, Skip's research papers represented some of the most important contributions to the study of human potential.

Skip's success brought great joy to our University community, of course, and I didn't mind his long absences, since our friendship and love had never been much affected by distances in time or space. And soon enough, we had an opportunity to travel full circle with each other.

In June 1997, Skip, Vicki, and I all returned to Cambridge for our 25th Harvard reunion. Skip, who of course saw the event as yet another opportunity to discuss his work and discoveries, had organized a presentation about higher states of consciousness for one of the reunion's workshop sessions, and I attended along with about 30 classmates. Skip gave a superb talk that smoothly integrated his rigorous scientific research, his deep intellectual insight into human potential, and his personable, humorous, accessible speaking style. That night, we all attended the blowout dance organized by the reunion committee, and, after some initial reticence, Skip and Vicki headed out to the dance floor and started rocking out to the fabulous band. Meanwhile, I was seized on the sidelines by a classmate who had attended Skip's lecture. He recognized me as Skip's colleague and was determined to know more about higher states of consciousness. For half an hour, we screamed questions and answers back and forth to each other over the deafening music: "BUT HOW CAN YOU ACTUALLY *EXPERIENCE* PURE CONSCIOUSNESS?" "WELL, WITH TM THE MIND SETTLES DOWN AND TRANSCENDS THOUGHT!" This was the impact Skip always had: he fired everyone up with irrepressible enthusiasm for his profound knowledge about human potential, and in that way he spread the knowledge around the world. When our classmate was satisfied, I turned back to the dance. There were Skip and Vicki, their arms around each other, dancing together and talking to people they hadn't seen in 25 years with the same joy and enthusiasm they always expressed toward all their closest friends. I looked at them and laughed, and thought as always, "What a beautiful, fabulous couple."

Since Skip's death, I have tried to create a wall within myself to shield my heart from its sense of loss. I have failed in this attempt, however, because every thought of Skip creates in me a wave of love that dismantles every wall I try to build. I have no protection against that love–and that is, of course, Skip's gift to me. He was a destroyer of walls, both between and within people. Were he here, he would lead me forward quickly and relentlessly to the truth within me, in all its human complexity, and we would share it as old friends. And then he would reach out to light again for me the light of life–pointing ahead to the higher life within us all, radiant with all its joyous potential. In this way, even in memory, he remains our friend and mentor. We cherish his life and all the ways it blessed and continues to bless us.

Gerald T. Geer

NOTE

1. Transcendental Meditation and TM are registered or common law trademarks licensed to Maharishi Vedic Education Development Corporation and used under sublicense or with permission.

Transcendental Meditation in Criminal Rehabilitation and Crime Prevention. Pp. 1-33.

INTRODUCTION AND OVERVIEW

The *Transcendental Meditation* Program: A Consciousness-Based Developmental Technology for Rehabilitation and Crime Prevention

RACHEL S. GOODMAN
Maharishi University of Management

KENNETH G. WALTON
Maharishi University of Management

DAVID W. ORME-JOHNSON
Maharishi University of Management

ROBERT BOYER
Maharishi University of Management

ABSTRACT Documented effects of the Transcendental Meditation (TM)[1] technique span the fields of psychology, physiology, and sociology. Part One of this article provides the reader with the background for understanding how a simple technique practiced on the level of the mind can have fundamental effects in each of these fields. It also highlights the singular contributions of Charles N. Alexander to developmental psychology, and their significance for rehabilitation of offenders. Part Two introduces each of the articles in this collection, describing practical applications of the TM program and other aspects of the Consciousness-Based[1] approach to rehabilitation and prevention.

KEYWORDS Transcendental Meditation, developmental psychology, Loevinger, Piaget, self development, consciousness

The papers in this volume present pioneering theory and research on an effective, Consciousness-Based[1] approach to crime prevention and criminal rehabilitation: the Transcendental Meditation (TM) program. Over 600 psychological, physiological, and sociological research studies have documented the outcomes of this program, in both general and offender populations, across age, gender, economic status, and nationality (Orme-Johnson & Farrow, 1977; Chalmers, Clements, Schenkluhn, & Weinless, 1989 [vol. 2, vol. 3, and vol. 4]; Wallace, Orme-Johnson, & Dillbeck, 1990). This research has shown development of the innate potential of the individual, including benefits in daily life such as improvements in creativity, health, emotional well-being, and professional efficacy. Moreover, rehabilitation projects with at-risk populations and incarcerated offenders in several countries (e.g., Anklesaria & King, this volume) offer evidence that the TM program provides a positive, multifaceted impact on personal and social factors identified as key contributors to criminal behavior. The remarkable fact that any one program could have such a wide range of benefits deserves explanation. This paper, and on a larger scale this entire collection of papers, offers a comprehensive discussion of the effects of the TM program and the relevance of these effects to rehabilitation and crime prevention.

The collection of papers in this volume was the initiative of Charles N. Alexander, whose professional work encompassed over 100 studies and papers on the effects and benefits of the TM program and the more advanced TM-Sidhi[1] program. Motivated by the benefits experienced by those whom he instructed in the TM technique, Alexander pursued his research based on a deep conviction that all human beings have the capacity to develop their full potential, but that in some individuals the momentum of development has slowed or frozen. He felt that the key to effective rehabilitation was to unfreeze this development through the TM program. He expressed the organizing principle of his work as follows: "If there has been a primary direction to my personal and professional life, it has been this quest for understanding the highest forms of human development and the means for their cultivation" (V. K. Alexander, 2000). He felt that the Vedic science presented by Maharishi Mahesh

Yogi (hereafter referred to as "Maharishi"), founder of the TM program, best accomplishes these goals because: (a) it has a strong developmental orientation, clearly describing the stages of higher states of consciousness and the mechanics of transitions between stages; (b) it provides a model of the architecture of the mind that accounts for the sequence of development and predicts its extension to higher states of consciousness; (c) although the knowledge is ancient, it is scientifically testable; (d) it makes available a uniform set of developmental procedures–the TM and TM-Sidhi programs–that are effortless to practice, require no change in lifestyle or belief, and are predicted to significantly accelerate development; and (e) the TM program is widely available, having now been taught to over 5 million people worldwide, and has generated the largest existing body of empirical research on meditation and human development (Alexander et al., 1990; Alexander, Druker, & Langer, 1990; Alexander, Heaton, & Chandler, 1994; Alexander & Langer, 1990; Alexander, Rainforth, & Gelderloos, 1991; Dillbeck & Alexander, 1989; Orme-Johnson, 2000).

By the early 1980s, only a few studies on the benefits of the TM program in criminal populations had been completed. These studies had focused on such measures as increased autonomic stability, reduced anxiety, and decreased rule infractions. Maharishi had indicated that more comprehensive stages of human development, known as higher states of consciousness or *enlightenment*, are a natural outcome of practice of the TM technique and that anyone, regardless of their current or past behaviors, can experience these states through practice of the technique (Maharishi Mahesh Yogi, 1969, 1972, 1977a).

These higher states are characterized by improvements in comprehension, moral attitudes, and behavior, by increased intelligence and creativity, and by increased harmony in relations with others. According to Maharishi Vedic Science,[1] an individual's problems and suffering can be eliminated as a consequence of developing full potential, referred to as enlightenment. Even in the earlier stages of development through the TM program, which is the primary component of the Consciousness-Based approach to rehabilitation, individuals become more comprehensive in their thinking and behavior. Inappropriate habits, such as substance abuse, begin to disappear (O'Connell & Alexander, 1994). Alexander was a pioneer in this research. His vision was that the higher states of consciousness described by Maharishi are the logical extension of the natural developmental sequence from childhood through adulthood described by Western psychologists. The testable prediction of this view was that development towards higher states could be assessed by stage advances through existing developmental scales, such as the moral reasoning scale of Kohlberg (1969) and the self-development scales of Loevinger and Cook-Greuter (Loevinger & Wessler, 1970; Cook-Greuter, 1990).

Alexander's doctoral dissertation at Harvard was a critical test of his theory. He studied the effects of the TM program on maximum-security prisoners at the Massachusetts Correctional Institution, Walpole (Alexander, 1982). In both cross-sectional and longitudinal designs, he found developmental increases (using Loevinger's ego- or self-development scale), reductions in anxiety and aggression, and increased frequency of experiences of higher states of consciousness (using the States of Consciousness Inventory [SCI], a new scale that he devised for the purpose) (Alexander et al., 1990; Alexander & Orme-Johnson, this volume; Alexander, Walton & Goodman, this volume). In addition, he demonstrated that these inner psychological changes result in reduced criminal behavior, as indicated by lower recidivism rates of TM subjects after release (Alexander, Rainforth et al., this volume).

In the ensuing years, several other studies on the TM program, crime prevention, and criminal rehabilitation were completed by researchers in a variety of correctional settings. Alexander organized this volume to provide a focused review of these studies, in terms of both theory and research. Taken individually, the papers in this volume describe the efficacy of the program in preventing crime and promoting a more balanced, law-abiding life for the offender. Taken together, they provide a compelling argument for the adoption of this cost-effective program in the educational and criminal justice systems.

The first section of this introduction and overview outlines the Consciousness-Based approach to criminal rehabilitation and summarizes Alexander's synthesis of this approach with modern developmental theory. The second section provides an overview of the articles contained in this volume, and their contribution to the field of crime prevention and criminal rehabilitation.

PART ONE: A CONSCIOUSNESS-BASED DEVELOPMENTAL APPROACH TO REHABILITATION AND CRIME PREVENTION

In this section we summarize the main features of Maharishi's Consciousness-Based approach to rehabilitation (Maharishi Mahesh Yogi, 1977a, 1994, 1995b). We describe the TM technique and the mechanics of its effects, summarize evidence that the technique normalizes physiological stress and increases resilience, and discuss how this program reduces addictive behavior. We then provide an overview of Alexander's model proposing that the seven states of consciousness defined in Maharishi Vedic Science extend the developmental hierarchy of stages in Western models of development to states of enlightenment.

Other Approaches to Rehabilitation

Criminal rehabilitation has been elusive because of the multidimensional nature of the precursors leading to criminal behavior, including psychological, physiological, social, ecological, economic, and political factors. For example, a major review of the causes and prevention of violence, conducted by the National Research Council of the National Academy of Sciences (Reiss & Roth, 1993) identified three broad perspectives on the causes of crime: (a) psychosocial influences, related to personality characteristics, including cognitive and perceptual processes, persistent traits, and familial and peer relationships; (b) social-environmental factors, concerned with the relationship between individual aggression and the broader social context; and (c) biobehavioral influences, associated with stress-related and genetic differences in neurophysiological and neuroendocrine function.

Although a U.S. Department of Justice report showed some optimism toward the field of rehabilitation (Sherman et al., 1997b), the complex interdependence of the multiple contributors to crime, most of which have been resistant to change, is acknowledged (Denno, 1990; Ferris, 1996; Ferris & Grisso, 1996; Hillbrand & Pallone, 1994; Raine, 1993). Society has seen many attempts to address these complex causal factors and to find a means to prevent criminal behavior. The most promising of these approaches tailors therapies to each individual offender (Andrews, Bonta, & Hoge, 1990). Although useful for a few, both time and funding for these approaches would be prohibitive to apply on the scale necessary to affect crime rate and the number of offenders within the criminal justice system. To date, no large-scale rehabilitation approach has produced substantial, wide-ranging results with clear economic viability (Sherman et al., 1997b). Moreover, prevention of crime in children and adolescents, which would be even more effective in precluding the massive expenditures and personnel allocation necessary to deal with criminal offenders, also involves multidimensional intervention in childhood. There is a growing frustration and concern about the inadequacy of previous prevention attempts. It is apparent that a multifaceted strategy must be implemented–a technology with the depth and breadth to address the numerous factors said to contribute to criminal behavior. The research presented in this volume, and other research referred to previously, indicates that the TM technique is that technology.

How can a single meditation technique affect so many of the individual and social risk factors for crime? The following sections address this question by describing the nature of the TM technique, the procedure of instruction, its mechanics, and the comprehensiveness of its results.

The Origin and Nature of the TM Technique

The TM technique originates in the ancient Vedic tradition of India, which holds that transcendental consciousness is a fourth major state of consciousness, distinct from waking, dreaming, and sleep (Dillbeck, 1983a; Dillbeck, 1983b; Maharishi Mahesh Yogi, 1969). Researchers have found that the three well-known major states of consciousness (waking, sleeping, and dreaming) are physiologically and psychologically distinct states, characterized by fundamentally different styles of functioning of the nervous system (Jevning,

Wallace, & Beidebach, 1992). Wallace, in his doctoral dissertation at the University of California at Los Angeles, also confirmed through physiological research that transcendental consciousness is a distinct fourth state of consciousness. He termed this state, restful alertness, in which the mind is fully alert and yet the body is experiencing a deep state of restfulness (Wallace, 1970a).

Research has shown that specific periods of transcendental consciousness are associated with reduction of breath rate, decreased heart rate, higher basal skin resistance, and increased EEG coherence in the high theta/low alpha frequencies, which are indicative of a mental state that is wakeful but not actively engaged in thought or perception (Badawi, Wallace, Orme-Johnson, & Rouzere, 1984; Farrow & Hebert, 1982; Travis & Pearson, 2000; Travis & Wallace, 1997; Travis & Wallace, 1999). A meta-analysis of 32 published studies found that practice of the TM technique reduces basal skin conductance, respiratory rate, and plasma lactate (indicative of anaerobic metabolism and activity of the sympathetic nervous system) significantly more than simply resting with eyes closed (Dillbeck & Orme-Johnson, 1987). These physiological changes are indicative of a deeper, more restful state of mind-body functioning during practice of the TM technique than during ordinary eyes-closed rest. Significantly, this meta-analysis also found lower baseline levels of heart rate, respiratory rate, plasma lactate, and spontaneous changes in skin resistance outside of meditation in TM practitioners, compared to nonmeditating controls. This finding suggests that regular TM practice results in a more relaxed style of functioning outside the practice, conserving adaptive resources for use when they are needed to cope with challenging situations.

Instruction in the TM Technique

The TM technique is an effortless, systematic procedure that is practiced for about 20 minutes twice daily, sitting comfortably with eyes closed. Instruction consists of two introductory lectures, a brief personal interview, individualized private instruction, and at least three group follow-up sessions (Roth, 1987). Practice of the technique after instruction is conducive to a variety of prison security environments, probation requirements, and research protocols, as the individual can practice the technique either alone or in a group (Anklesaria & King, this volume).

Moreover, practice of the technique does not involve adherence to specific lifestyles, behaviors, philosophy, or religious beliefs. Thus, it can be introduced easily into various prison settings, whether or not individuals may also be participating in religious groups, psychological treatment, or educational programs.

Mechanics of the TM Technique

During the technique, the mind effortlessly settles down through increasingly quiet levels of thought until it naturally reaches its quietest state, beyond the finest level of thinking. This process is known as *transcending*. When mental activity is transcended, a state of inner silence, called *transcendental consciousness* or *pure consciousness* is experienced. While experiences of transcendental consciousness are spontaneous during the practice of the TM technique, individuals rarely experience this state of the mind in daily life prior to instruction because attention is habitually engaged in thoughts or directed outward through the senses to concrete experiences. The TM technique provides a systematic means of allowing attention to turn inward automatically so that the natural process of transcending can occur. The mind is spontaneously drawn inward by the experience of the increasing charm of more subtle levels of awareness. Therefore, when the correct initial conditions are set during TM practice, the mind is effortlessly drawn to the subtlest level, transcendental consciousness (Maharishi Mahesh Yogi, 1969).

Definition of Pure Consciousness

There are many definitions of the term consciousness, often involving some concept of active states of consciousness, that is, consciousness *of* something. The active states are like waves on an ocean of consciousness, whereas transcendental consciousness is like the settled state of the ocean, when the waves have settled down and the ocean is completely quiet and expansive. Transcendental consciousness is called pure consciousness because it is unqualified. It is *self-referral* consciousness, aware only of itself, as opposed to consciousness that is aware of something outside itself, called *object-referral* consciousness. In our ordinary states of awareness, when we are thinking about something or perceiving something, there is a tripartite division–the knower (oneself), the known (object of perception), and the process of knowing that connects them, all seen as distinct. (In the example, "I see the tree," "I" is the knower, "tree" is the known, and "see" is the process connecting them.) In transcendental consciousness, the "I," in a natural, effortless way, directly experiences its own unified nature as unbounded awareness, beyond the distinctions of knower, known, and the process of knowing. This unified self-referral state actually underlies object-referral consciousness (Maharishi, 1995b).

The Consciousness-Based approach to rehabilitation provides a systematic technology for directly experiencing this level of consciousness, the TM technique. Experiencing this level of consciousness has profound effects on both mind and body, as evidenced by research on changes during practice of the technique and during daily activity. Many other meditation techniques involve concentration or contemplation, both of which keep the mind active, thus not providing the opportunity for experience of transcending (Orme-Johnson & Walton, 1998; Orme-Johnson, Zimmerman, & Hawkins, 1997).

Rest as a Natural Prescription for Stress Reduction

The unique state of restful alertness during practice of the TM technique facilitates removal of effects of stress that are not removed during the ordinary cycle of waking, dreaming, and sleep. The stress of daily living contributes to many of the risk factors associated with criminal behavior, including psychosocial influences, social-environmental factors, and biobehavioral functioning. Stress-related imbalances result when the body's adaptive or coping mechanisms are overloaded by excessive physical and mental experiences (Chrousos & Gold, 1992; Sapolsky, 1992; Selye, 1978; Walton & Pugh, 1995). The pressures of modern living provide a daily overdose of experience that over time can lead to depression, anxiety, and negative self-perceptions in some individuals. These pressures can also lead to problems of psychological and social adjustment (Masten & Coatsworth, 1995), such as school or job failure, criminal behavior, child abuse (Kotch et al., 1997), delinquency (Hoffman & Su, 1997; Hoge, Andrews, & Leschied, 1996), and drug abuse (Agnew & White, 1992; Hoffman & Su, 1997; Paternoster & Mazerolle, 1994). Research using the State Stress Index has shown that the incidence of violent crimes is highly correlated with social stressors, such as high school dropout rate, infant mortality, divorce, unemployment, new welfare cases, and bankruptcy (Linsky & Straus, 1986).

Biochemically, stress-related imbalances may show up as altered levels of neurotransmitters, such as serotonin, and hormones, such as the stress-related hormone cortisol. Reduced levels of serotonin have been linked with impulsive behavior, aggression, and poor mental health (e.g., Coccaro, Kavoussi, Cooper, & Hauger, 1997; Linnoila & Virkkunen, 1992; for review, see Ferris & Grisso, 1996; Walton & Levitsky, 1994; Walton & Levitsky, this volume). Experimental manipulation to increase or decrease the activity of serotonergic systems has been shown to decrease or increase aggression, impulsiveness, depression, and substance abuse, depending on the direction of manipulation (for review, see Walton & Levitsky, this volume). Individuals who exhibit criminal behavior are frequently found to be impulsive, restless, and aggressive; to violate conventional rules, to lack cognitive coping skills, to have weak relationships with work or school; and to exhibit psychopathic deviation and pro-criminal attitudes, beliefs, and thinking styles (Blackburn, 1986; Wilson & Herrnstein, 1985). Such negative emotional states and behaviors are known to result from stressful experiences and their biochemical consequences.

Rest is a standard prescription for many ailments because it appears to activate the body's innate healing mechanisms. Research shows that the TM program promotes deep rest and is highly effective in reducing stress. Fatigue accumulated during the day is removed through a refreshing night's sleep. The TM program provides a more profound state of rest than sleep, one that removes the long-lasting effects of stress accumulated from extreme stress or simply from the pressures of daily living. Studies in the general population have found that the TM program reduces stress-related symptoms and diseases, such as hypertension (Alexander et al., 1996; Schneider et al., 1995), insomnia (Gore, Abrams, & Ellis 1984), addictive behaviors (Alexander, Robinson, & Rainforth, 1994), psychopathology (Brooks & Scarano, 1985; Eppley, Abrams, & Shear, 1989; Gaylord, Orme-Johnson, & Travis, 1989), and a wide variety of other health conditions (Orme-Johnson & Herron, 1997).

Studies on criminal offenders have reported that the program increases autonomic balance (Orme-Johnson & Moore, this volume) and improves biochemical indicators of chronic stress (see Walton & Levitsky, this volume). Other research on criminal offenders has also shown decreased anxiety and neuroticism (Abrams, 1989; Abrams & Siegel, 1978), and decreased hostility and aggression (Ramirez, 1989). Moreover, the effects of this effortless practice, as indicated by statistical meta-analyses of several hundred studies, are significantly more comprehensive and generally more significant than those of concentration, contemplation, hypnosis, biofeedback, or breath control (Orme-Johnson & Walton, 1998), all of which involve some mental or physiological effort. These results point to the efficacy of the practice as a strategy for removing stress-related dysfunctions and thereby eliminating behaviors that appear to be triggered by an overload of stress (Walton & Levitsky, this volume).

Increased Resilience

With continued practice of the TM technique, the individual also becomes more resilient; that is, resistance to the accumulation of stress-induced abnormalities and to inappropriate behaviors triggered by stressful circumstances is increased. Masten, Best, and Garmezy (1990) define resilience as ". . . the process of, capacity for, or outcome of successful adaptation despite challenging or threatening circumstances" (p. 425). They see psychological resilience as involving "internal states of well-being or effective functioning in the environment or both" (p. 426) and also see it as "successful adaptation despite the odds against good development" (p. 426). They indicate that this adaptation may occur in an environment of risk factors that includes poverty, low maternal education, low socioeconomic status, and family instability. These risk factors, according to Masten et al., correlate with lower academic achievement as well as with emotional and behavioral problems, lower work achievement, and possibly trouble with the law. Coping, "by means of human activities, including thought and action" (p. 430) in contrast, would provide internal or external equilibrium as a response to long-term or immediate threats to well-being.

The repeated experience of transcendental consciousness during the TM technique is thought to be the primary factor responsible for the increased adaptability and resilience found in TM practitioners. Transcendental pure consciousness has been described as foundational to thought and action (see section on levels of the mind that follows). As the individual continues the practice of the technique, a more balanced, integrated functioning of the body and increased alertness and awareness of the mind are maintained even in the midst of dynamic activity, and not just during the practice itself. Progressive strengthening of thought and action and development of inner equilibrium have been demonstrated repeatedly (e.g., Dillbeck, Orme-Johnson, & Wallace, 1981; Gaylord et al., 1989; Orme-Johnson & Haynes, 1981; Orme-Johnson, Wallace, Dillbeck, Alexander, & Ball, 1989). Thus, this technique cultivates the qualities associated with resilience to adverse circumstances, contributing to the prevention of initial criminal acts and repeat offenses.

Effects of the TM Program on Addiction

Substance abuse is closely associated with crime, with more than 60% of adult arrestees testing positive for drug use (National Criminal Justice Reference Service, 2000). Like crime, substance abuse is also a multidimensional problem (Harrell, Honaker, & Davis, 1991; Sadava, 1975), and yet the TM program was found to be effective with individuals from a wide range of socioeconomic backgrounds and types of abuse. In 1994, O'Connell and Alexander edited a volume describing the results of research on the TM program and related programs in treating addictions. In a chapter of the volume, Alexander and colleagues summarized the results of quantitative meta-analyses on 198 studies conducted from the 1970s through the early 1990s (Alexander, Robinson, & Rainforth, 1994). In a review of previous meta-analyses of studies in the general population, Alexander et al. concluded that the TM program, relative to other types of meditative and relaxation techniques, "significantly reverses physiological and psychological factors leading to substance abuse" (p. 71), thereby promoting primary prevention.

In a further meta-analysis highlighted in the paper, studies were included that variously involved populations of students, the general population, criminal offenders, drug users and addicts, elderly cigarette smokers, and Vietnam veterans with post-traumatic stress disorder. Alexander et al. concluded from this meta-analysis that the psychological improvements seen in studies on general populations are found also in known substance abusers. The authors indicated that the effect of the TM program on reduction of substance use was significantly larger than the effects of other relaxation, preventive, and treatment programs, and that abstinence from abuse was "maintained or increased over the long term" with practice of the TM program (Alexander, Robinson, & Rainforth, 1994, p. 72). As noted above, these findings are particularly relevant for crime prevention and criminal rehabilitation because substance abuse related to narcotics and many other drugs is itself a crime and is a contributing factor to many other criminal acts.

Alexander's explanation for the efficacy of the TM program in reducing substance abuse is also useful in understanding its role in criminal rehabilitation (Alexander, Robinson, & Rainforth, 1994). Multiple, interacting dimensions of life (e.g., spirit, mind, body, social behavior, and environment) appear to be involved in the emergence of addictive behavior. When one or more of these fundamental dimensions is deficient or imbalanced, people are at risk for adopting addictive behavior as a means to fulfill unmet needs. While conventional treatments of substance dependence often employ several modalities, they may target only surface levels of functioning, such as attitudes and behavior, failing to root out the deeper causes. If the deeper problems are not eliminated, the benefits may be only temporary, with addictive behaviors resurfacing again and again despite numerous attempts at abstinence. This may account for the rapid decline in abstinence rates following completion of most treatment programs.

Prior to embarking on his prison studies, Alexander had seen results of research completed in the 1970s on effects of the TM program on substance abuse, including alcohol, cigarette usage, and illicit drugs, in adolescent and adult populations. Alexander felt that the TM program as a treatment modality for substance abuse was far more comprehensive than conventional treatments because research over the last 30 years has indicated that this Consciousness-Based approach is capable of addressing the whole person. It brings balance to multiple factors associated with addictive behaviors (Chalmers et al., 1989; Orme-Johnson & Farrow, 1977; Wallace et al., 1990). Alexander applied this same understanding to his exploration of the TM program and criminal rehabilitation.

ALEXANDER'S SYNTHESIS OF DEVELOPMENTAL THEORIES AND ITS SIGNIFICANCE FOR REHABILITATION

Alexander designed a model that incorporated developmental stages described by Western psychology in a continuum with the higher states of consciousness delineated in Maharishi Vedic Science. We will first present an overview of Alexander's theory, then describe in some detail the role of the major Western developmental stages in the model, and finally show how the model extends to Maharishi's higher states of consciousness.

The backbone of Alexander's theoretical synthesis is the hierarchy of levels of mind described in Maharishi Vedic Science. In this view, the mind has levels of functioning, which, proceeding from gross to subtle, are: senses, desires, mind (ideation), intellect, feelings, ego, and transcendental consciousness (see Table 1). Although the levels of mind are active throughout the life span, Alexander believed that one's current developmental stage, as described by Western psychology, is defined by one's dominant style of mental functioning. This development occurs sequentially through a natural hierarchy from the surface, sensory level, to the more subtle levels of mind (i.e., the intellect, the ego) similar to the levels of mind described by Maharishi Vedic Science. Alexander further postulated that transcendental consciousness is the next logical step in individual development beyond the ego level. Alexander's model thus proposes that the progression of individual awareness with the practice of the TM technique makes a grand sweep inward, from the senses to transcendental consciousness. In terms of self-development, with practice of the TM technique, each level of the mind becomes infused with transcendental consciousness, promoting attainment of the individual's full potential (i.e., higher states of consciousness, as described on pages 21-24 of this paper, and seen in Table 1).

Table 1: Alexander's Developmental Model[2]

MAHARISHI'S VEDIC PSYCHOLOGY **Levels of the Mind**	***CONNECTING MODEL*** (Alexander et al., 1990) **Developmental Tiers**	***DEVELOPMENTAL PSYCHOLOGY*** (Piaget) **Cognitive Development**	(Loevinger) **Self-Development**
senses ►	Prerepresentation (sensorimotor mode of knowing)	►sensorimotor	Presocial *(undifferentiated individual self)*
desire ►		preoperational ►*object permanence*	Impulsive
mind ►	Representation (symbolic mode of knowing)	concrete operations ►*conservation of quantity*	Conformist *(conventional psychosocial self)*
intellect ►		formal operations ►*conservation of motion*	Self-Aware Conscientious
feeling ►			Individualistic Autonomous
ego ►		►"post-formal" ►operations	Integrated *(differentiated individual self)*
Higher States of Consciousness		**Proposed Milestones of Extended Development**	
transcendental consciousness (Self)			
cosmic consciousness	Postrepresentation (self-referral mode of knowing)	*subject permanence (Self)*	*differentiation of universal Self*
refined cosmic consciousness		*conservation of finest level of all objects*	*profound intimacy between Self and environment*
unity consciousness		*conservation of underlying unity across all its manifestations*	*complete unification between Self and environment*

Table 1 illustrates Alexander's model and will be the basis for further discussion of the model, including Vedic Science's levels of mind, Western developmental theories, and Maharishi's seven states of consciousness.

Levels of Mind in Maharishi Vedic Science

The levels of the mind described by Vedic Science are familiar to Western psychology. These levels constitute the chapter headings of all the major psychology textbooks in the last hundred years (Orme-Johnson, 1988a). Throughout psychology's history, there have been chapters on the senses, desires and motivation, thinking, intelligence, intellect, feelings, and the holistic aspects of the personality or "ego." These categories have remained constant, even though the theoretical understanding of these levels has changed over the decades. The apparent invariance of the levels, and the existence of terminology for these levels of mind in almost every language of the world, also suggest that they are the natural divisions of the human psyche (R. F. Orme- Johnson, 1987).

Although Western psychology has delineated these levels, Maharishi Vedic Science additionally describes them as forming a hierarchical sequence and, most importantly, identifies transcendental consciousness as the subtlest level. Orme-Johnson (1988a) has observed that transcendental consciousness is the "missing chapter from psychology," which is capable of pulling the field together into an integrated whole. A further principle shared by both Western psychology and Maharishi Vedic Science is that deeper or subtler levels of mind have the power to organize and improve the functioning of the more expressed, outer levels. Piaget (1970), for example, pointed out that symbolic, mental representations of the sensory world used in thinking (concrete operations) can organize and increase the utility of sensory-motor processes. Similarly, logical thought of the intellect (formal operations) can organize thinking in powerful ways. Extending this principle to transcendental consciousness, the most basic level of mind, one would predict that it could organize all the other levels of mind, from ego to the senses. Maharishi Vedic Science indicates that through systematic practice of the TM technique, the qualities of transcendental consciousness are incorporated into each level of the mind, progressively refining and integrating the functioning of all the levels (Maharishi, 1969, 1972). The research summarized below strongly supports this fundamental tenet of Maharishi Vedic Science by showing that the TM program does improve the functioning of all levels of mind.

Senses: Referring to Table 1, Alexander's model begins with the level of the senses, through which action is perceived and initiated. A variety of research indicates the TM program improves sensory-motor performance, including the lowering of sensory thresholds (Schwartz, 1989), shortening reaction times (Appelle & Oswald, 1973; Holt, Caruso, & Riley, 1978; Schwartz, 1989), shortening reflex latencies (Wallace, Mills, Orme-Johnson,

Dillbeck, & Jacobe, 1983; Warshal, 1980), shortening the latency and increasing the amplitudes of sensory-evoked potentials (Banquet & LeSevre, 1980; Kobal, Wandhofer, & Plattig, 1975; McEvoy, Frumkin, & Harkins, 1980; Wandhofer, Kobal, & Plattig, 1976), increasing field independence (Dillbeck, Raimondi, Assimakis, Rowe, & Orme-Johnson, 1989; Gelderloos, Lockie, & Chuttoorgoon, 1987; Pelletier, 1974), and improving athletic performance (Reddy, 1989).

Desire: At the next deeper level is the experience of desire, which is the spur to action. Maharishi explains how the mind is fundamental to behavior: "Action is performed on the level of the senses but has its origins at the inception of the thinking process. A thought starts from the deepest level of the mind; it is appreciated on the thinking level, where it takes the form of a desire; desire in its turn expresses itself in the form of action" (Maharishi Mahesh Yogi, 1969, p. 140).

The impulsive, rebellious, and aggressive actions found in individuals at risk for antisocial behaviors such as crime and substance misuse may occur because the individual has not progressed in development beyond stages dominated by desire and the senses. Research has found that the TM program reduces hostility, aggression, prison rule infractions, and recidivism in criminal offenders (Abrams & Siegel, 1978; Alexander, 1982; Ballou, 1977; Bleick & Abrams, 1987).

Mind: The next deeper level is ideation or "the thinking mind," which processes information received from the senses and carries out the ordinary cognitive functions of memory and thought. This level guides the senses and behavior to express the decisions and desires arising from yet deeper levels of mind. Criminal behaviors are usually linked with cognitive dysfunctions, such as disorganized and faulty thinking patterns, poor coping skills, and inadequate decision making (Gibbs, 1991). While some approaches to rehabilitation have attempted to change the content of the mind, the TM program appears successful at enlarging the functional capacity of the mind itself. Cognitive abilities, such as cognitive flexibility (Alexander, Langer, Newman, Chandler, & Davies, 1989), learning and memory (Dillbeck et al., 1981), and creativity (Travis, 1979) are improved by the program.

Intellect: Deeper (more abstract) than the thinking mind is the level of intellect, the discriminating and decision-making faculty, which makes decisions about the contents of the thinking mind. A number of longitudinal studies have found that the TM technique facilitates growth of fluid intelligence compared to controls, even beyond the age range at which such growth typically occurs (Cranson et al., 1991; So, 1995; So & Orme-Johnson, 2001; Tjoa, 1975). Other indications of improved functioning of the intellect include faster choice reaction time (Cranson et al., 1991) and increased principled moral reasoning (Chandler, Alexander, & Heaton, in press).

Feelings: Influencing the most refined functioning of the intellect is the level of feelings or emotions, which incorporates deeper integrative and intuitive processes in discrimination and decision making. Negative emotions (e.g., hostility, anger, fear, anxiety) not only result from other stressful experiences, but also are themselves stressful, giving rise to further distortions of adaptive mechanisms and loss of physical and mental balance (Henry & Grim, 1990; Walton & Levitsky, 1994; Walton & Levitsky, this volume). Such negative emotions are common among prison inmates and may contribute to impulsive and aggressive behaviors, as well as to addictive use of drugs and alcohol. Extensive research indicates that the TM program balances mood naturally in a manner that continues into activities outside of the program (Gelderloos, Hermans, Ahlstrom, & Jacoby, 1990). In non-offenders and offenders and in veterans suffering from post-traumatic stress disorder, the program reduces trait anxiety, depression, and anger (Abrams & Siegel, 1978; Alexander, Walton et al., this volume; Alexander & Orme-Johnson, this volume; Brooks & Scarano, 1985; Eppley et al., 1989). Other studies indicate the TM program effectively increases positive affect, including happiness and well-being (Gelderloos, 1987b), emotional stability (Overbeck, 1982), and capacity for intimate contact, as well as openness to one's own feelings, and spontaneity (Alexander et al., 1991).

Ego: The subtlest level of the individual self is the level of ego, that is, the experiencer or the "I." This level integrates the senses, thinking mind, intellect, and feelings into a holistic subjective experience. This is the active experiencer of the changing values of actions, sensations, perceptions, memories, thoughts, and feelings (Maharishi Mahesh Yogi, 1972; cf., Alexander, Davies et al., 1990; Dillbeck, 1988; Dillbeck & Alexander, 1989). In Western psychology, the terms "ego development" and "self-development" are used to describe the stages of development of the individual's orientation toward self and world, a concept related to self-actualization (Maslow, 1976). Several studies, including longitudinal ones, support the premise that the TM technique promotes ego development. For example, a 10-year study of alumni of Maharishi International University (MIU), renamed Maharishi University of Management in 1995, a midwestern university where the TM program is integrated into the regular curriculum, showed marked increases in self-development compared to samples of alumni from three control universities over the same period who were matched for age, gender, and pretest year (Chandler, 1990). The MIU alumni also had a higher percentage of individuals achieving Loevinger's (1976) two highest levels of self-development than any of 40 other groups surveyed in the research literature. Moreover, a comprehensive meta-analysis indicated that TM program practitioners, after 3 months of practice, increased by 30% on the composite scale of the Personal Orientation Inventory, the most widely used measure of self-actualization. In contrast, other forms of meditation and relaxation showed only a modest influence on self-actualization (Alexander, Rainforth, & Gelderloos, 1991).

Transcendental or Pure Consciousness: Transcendental consciousness is the least excited state of consciousness; it is "pure consciousness" unqualified by thoughts or perceptions. Transcendental consciousness is a fourth major state of consciousness, physiologically distinct from waking, dreaming, and sleeping, and is the self-referral unified state of the knower, known, and process of knowing. In the context of developmental theory, Alexander et al. (Alexander, Heaton, & Chandler 1994) comment:

> The characteristic of all experience in the waking state is that the self, or knower, is experienced as localized in time and space, and separated from the known by the active processes of knowing–perceptions, thoughts, and feelings–which filter or qualify one's experience of self and world . . . A fundamental limitation of the waking state is that the subject of experience is never able to directly know itself . . . All one actually knows is thoughts, perceptions, and feelings *about* oneself as an object (a process which Maharishi calls "object referral") but one lacks immediate, direct experience of one's own inner Being as the 'I' or subject of experience (a process which Maharishi calls "self-referral"). (p. 43)

Alexander and colleagues cite an extensive literature documenting that even brief experiences of transcendental consciousness have momentous developmental effects, motivating one to seek to repeat and stabilize the experience (Alexander, Davies et al., 1990; Alexander, Heaton, & Chandler, 1994; Alexander et al., 1991).

We now turn to a consideration of how Alexander's model explains developmental sequences proposed by Western psychology.

The Developmental Sequence in Western Psychology

Piaget's Theory of Cognitive Development

Piaget has been one of the most influential theorists in creating models of human development–most developmental theories build on his work. He proposed qualitatively distinct stages of cognitive development that emerge through a child's active experience of the world. As Piaget conceived them, the stage-like changes in the structure of a child's thinking are hierarchical in that each successive, more complex stage integrates the earlier stages while reorganizing and transforming them. According to Piaget, the stages form an invariant, irreversible sequence, each stage serving as the necessary condition for the next stage. The beginning point of development corresponds to the level of the senses in Alexander's model (see Table 1).

Senses–Sensory-Motor Stage: The initial stage is the sensory-motor stage (from birth to about age 2), associated with cognitive processing of experiences that are closely linked to sensory functions and overt behavior.

Desire–Preoperational Stage: The next stage is the preoperational stage (from about age 2 to 7) in which cognitive processes related to overt behavior are internalized but are still primarily linked to sensory or physical experiences. Egocentrism ("I want, I need") is the norm.

Thinking Mind–Operational Thought Stage: In the next stage, concrete operations (roughly age 7 to age 11), abstract cognitive operations can be performed on representations of concrete sensory experiences. This is an early form of representational thought. But these abstract cognitive operations or mental representations still cannot be integrated simultaneously into problem solving.

Intellect–Formal Operations Stage: At the next stage, formal operations (age 11 to age 15), higher-order cognition develops, which involves abstract, symbolic, representational thought rather than simple mental representations of concrete sensory experiences. Problem solving at this stage can incorporate exploration of abstract logical possibilities rather than just concrete experiences. This stage is considered necessary for the problem solving of scientific thinking. Formal operational thought, or abstract reasoning, was Piaget's (1972) proposed end state of human development.

Although Piaget's work has contributed profoundly to developmental psychology, other researchers have suggested possible limitations to his conceptual framework. For example, Piaget primarily focused on the cognitive processes usually associated with scientific or academic thought, which were essential to his concept of formal operations. Yet there are other "ways of knowing" that come into play as critical components of mature intelligence in adult life, such as affective functioning, intuition, contextual thinking, and other aspects of the personality important to development (i.e., emotions and socialization), which were essentially unexplored by Piaget (Cook-Greuter, 1990; Alexander & Langer, 1990).

A further limitation of Piaget's theory involves his identification of formal operations as the end point of human cognitive growth. In contrast, several contemporary theories propose adult development beyond formal operations, in an attempt to define the experience of that small percentage of the adult population that has apparently progressed to more developed stages or states and to further describe the extent of full human potential (e.g., Alexander & Langer, 1990; Arlin, 1989; Commons, Richards, & Armon, 1984; Fischer, Kenny, & Pipp, 1990; Maslow, 1976; Sternberg, 1990).

Loevinger's Theory of Self-Development

Of particular interest are the hierarchies of self-development defined by Loevinger and further conceptualized by Cook-Greuter (1990) and the stages of moral development conceptualized by Kohlberg (1973). Alexander used Loevinger's stages in his model to indicate the prerepresentational and representational steps in normal development. He also used instruments based on Loevinger's stages and Kohlberg's moral development to gauge the ability of the TM program to facilitate further development even in adulthood, and even in those populations considered to be resistant to further stage change. These stages of development are useful also because of their descriptions of stages beyond formal operations, to prepare the ground for presentation of the higher states of consciousness described by Maharishi and researched by Alexander in his prison studies.

Loevinger's theory of ego development, which she subsequently termed self-development (Loevinger, 1984), encompasses not only Piagetian cognitive development but also emotional, moral, self, and social development (Loevinger, 1976; Snarey, Kohlberg, & Noam, 1983). Loevinger indicates that self-development represents the evolution of "a person's frame of reference" (Loevinger, 1984, p. 57), how the individual understands or makes sense of his or her world and own self. This concept of self-development encompasses impulse control, character development, conscious preoccupations, cognitive complexity, and interpersonal style. In this theory, self-development proceeds through a "hierarchically invariant" sequence of levels or stages. Development is said to involve a gradual process whereby higher-stage functioning is achieved first in one area and then, gradually, across the entire functional range, until the more advanced level is broadly stabilized and provides the foundation for growth to yet another, higher level (Loevinger, 1984, pp. 57-58). Loevinger's theory posits eight levels of self-development, representing successive degrees of complexity and sophistication in the organization of experience.

The descriptions of Loevinger's stages delineate a sequence envisioned to unfold across childhood and continually into adulthood. The qualities within a stage can refer to experiences most characteristic of adolescents as well as experiences more characteristic of adults. In some individuals, however, development appears to have been arrested and remains predominately at a level more characteristic of adolescents. For example, Noam et al. (Noam, Recklitis, & Piaget, 1991, p. 313) describe adolescents who are delayed in self-development as exhibiting "age-stage dysynchrony," characterized by difficulties in accomplishing adolescent activities "due to a delayed developmental organization." This also might be applicable to the adult whose self-development level is delayed or has not progressed to maturity.

Senses–Presocial/Symbiotic: In Loevinger's hierarchy, the initial Presocial/Symbiotic level (called "I-1"), sensory processes predominate and there is little or no differentiation between sensory experience and the self. This symbiotic level of infancy is not applicable to adult subjects.

Desires–Impulsive Stage: At the next levels, Impulsive (I-2) and Self-Protective (Δ), individuals lack self-control and are primarily concerned with short-term self-gratification. They tend to have difficulty taking the viewpoint of others and conforming to societal conventions. Noam et al. found that delinquency and aggression are associated with these lower stages of development in adolescents (Noam, Paget, Valiant, Borst, & Bartok, 1994). Noam et al. (1991) note that adolescents in the first three stages are "impulsive, have stereotyped cognitive styles, and are dependent or exploitative" (p. 312). Adults at these levels are considered immature, and are more likely to exhibit aggressive, antisocial, and acting-out behaviors, and antagonistic personality traits such as negativity and habitual externalization of blame (Gibbs, 1991).

Intellect–Conformist Stage: With growth to the Conformist (I-3) level, there is a shift from primary concern for physical rewards and punishments to social approval and belongingness in a group. Self-definition stems from membership in the social group. According to Noam et al. (1991), "Individuals at the conformist stages . . . are particularly concerned with interpersonal acceptance and often express their views in clichés and stereotypes" (p. 312). Further growth to the Conscientious (I-4) level involves a growing appreciation of multiple possibilities along with the ability to think about oneself and the world as objects of thought. This representational thought, commensurate with the formal operational stage in Piaget's theory, is often reached by late adolescence. It involves a growing appreciation of, and capacity to follow, societal rules.

Feelings–Individualistic Stage: At the higher, Individualistic (I-4/5) level, concern for individuality, psychological causality, and self-development emerges. This level is associated with increased tolerance for different contexts and the different points of view of other people.

Ego–Autonomous and Integrated Stages: The most advanced levels, Autonomous (I-5) and Integrated (I-6), are characterized by a deep appreciation for the autonomy and identity of self and others. Inner conflict is no longer projected onto other people and the environment but is coped with, and ultimately resolved, by the ability to transcend polarities and integrate ideas that appeared incompatible at earlier levels. Individuals at these levels are inner-directed, self-actualizing, and exhibit greater adaptation and resilience to the stressors that predict criminal behavior. Of particular interest in this context, Noam et al. (1991) point out that "individuals who have reached the 'postconformist' stages of ego development (I-4, I-4/5, I-5, I-6) generally cope with inner conflict through a high degree of self-awareness. They typically show more cognitive complexity and have interpersonal styles that emphasize mutuality and respect for individual differences" (p. 312).

Alexander's research was designed to ascertain whether the self-development of offenders who may have attained only the preconformist and conformist levels could be enhanced, allowing them to rapidly achieve a higher, more self-aware level, and thus become capable of coping with inner conflict in a constructive way and of displaying greater respect for the concerns of others.

The I-5 and I-6 stages appear to involve advanced forms of representational thought beyond Piagetian formal operations. In fact, certain experiences of the highest levels of Loevinger's ego development stages have been described as "postrepresentational" experiences and indicate a self-actualizing, integrative perspective beyond the representational mode of knowing.

Kohlberg's theory and measurement of "moral" development provides another way of considering individual development. Building on Piaget's work, Kohlberg developed a six-stage model of moral reasoning (1973). He defined the stages in terms of changes in "sociomoral perspective," from a viewpoint that is predominately self-interested or self-involved to a perspective that is shared by other individuals in the group or by society as a whole. In recent years, Kohlberg revised his theory to include a higher stage of postformal development similar to Loevinger's two advanced levels (Kohlberg & Rynkarz, 1990). This seventh stage involves a shift in perspective beyond the individual concerns apparent in the first stages. It addresses questions of universal moral significance and culminates experientially in a sense of unity with the cosmos.

In the cognitive domain, such higher development has been called "postformal" because cognition is said to move beyond Piagetian formal operations (Arlin, 1989; Fischer et al., 1990). The term "postconventional" has likewise been used to define advanced moral development (Kohlberg, 1969) and advanced stages of self-development (Cook-Greuter, 1990; Kegan, 1978), because these theorists propose that the individual may no longer be defined or bound by external conventions at the highest stages. Other ego and personality theorists like Loevinger (1976) and Labouvie-Vief (1990) emphasize the importance of psychological autonomy and integration at the higher stages. Characteristics of "wisdom" (e.g., Clayton & Birren, 1980; Kramer, 1990; Orwoll & Perlmutter, 1990) and "self-actualization" (e.g., Maslow, 1976; Pascual-Leone, 1990) are also attributed to the higher levels of human potential.

Theoretical parallels, extensive common terminology, and cross-referencing of each other's work suggest that these theorists are in fact attempting to delineate the same developmental domain. Like earlier developmental stages, postformal or postconventional development, as described by these theorists, encompasses many aspects of human experience, including the evaluative, affective (or emotional), and cognitive components of orientation to self and world. Yet, individuals at these highest levels are thought to be rare. However, as will be seen in Alexander's model as well as in his research (Alexander & Orme-Johnson, this volume; Alexander, Walton et al., this volume), these levels are within the reach of human development, through experience of transcendental consciousness.

Limitations of Western Developmental Theories

Whereas Western theories of development may have been successful in describing the most common stages of human development, they have not provided a technology that can promote the individual's development of higher levels, particularly in adulthood. Current educational practices have been preoccupied with developing the earlier stages, from childhood to adolescence, only up to formal operations, Piaget's highest stage. Research indicates that self-development frequently becomes set by late adolescence (Loevinger,

1976; Loevinger et al., 1985). After this age, self-development is highly resistant to change (Cook-Greuter, 1990). Moreover, literature on criminal offenders has suggested that self-development is often arrested at the earlier stages of development, generally characterized by impulsive, aggressive, self-gratifying behaviors defiant of social conventions. In contrast, Alexander has suggested, and his research has shown, that the TM technique can unfreeze development. In the next section, we consider how the TM technique is able to unfreeze development and develop higher states of consciousness.

The Seven States of Consciousness in Maharishi Vedic Science

1-3. Waking, Dreaming, and Sleeping: Maharishi Vedic Science describes seven states of consciousness, of which waking dreaming and sleep are the first three (Alexander, Davies et al., 1990; Alexander, Heaton, & Chandler, 1994; Dillbeck & Alexander, 1989; Orme-Johnson et al., 1997). In the waking state, the mind is aware of self and surroundings. In dreaming, there is only an illusory awareness of self and an unreal or imagined world. In deep sleep, there is virtually no awareness of self or the world. These states can be distinguished physiologically by differences in brain waves (EEG), muscle tone (EMG), eye movements (EOG), and other parameters. It is established knowledge that the sleep and dream states assist in rejuvenating the mind and body for more effective activity in the waking state.

In the waking state, the individual's attention is on the object of perception, including thoughts, feelings, external environment, and events. From the perspective of Maharishi Vedic Science, all the developmental stages of Western psychology fall within the waking state. The waking state may evolve over the life span through different stages of development, but it is still the waking state.

4. Transcendental Consciousness: As we have seen, the fourth state is transcendental consciousness. In Alexander's model, transcendental consciousness is not a developmental *stage* because in most people it is not yet permanent. Rather, it is a temporary experience or transitory state. At first it is experienced during meditation and possibly at other times. As the individual continues the twice-daily practice, more experience of transcendental consciousness is maintained with the other three states: waking activity, sleep state, or dreaming. Maharishi has described it as the junction point between waking, dreaming, and sleeping (Maharishi Mahesh Yogi, 1972), and there is physiological evidence supporting this view (Travis, 1990; Travis, 1994).

Although the experience of transcendental consciousness is only transitory, at least initially, this experience powerfully promotes the development of higher stages. Moreover, a person does not have to proceed through the sequence of all the developmental levels of waking state before experiencing transcendental consciousness. From age 10 onwards, anyone, at any developmental level, can sit, close their eyes, and experience their own state of transcendental consciousness. This is possible because the practice is very simple and easily learned. At any level of development, the process of transcending and eliminating stress will stimulate further development. Alexander et al. (1990) write:

> Although the process of transcending to experience pure consciousness is said to promote development during any period, Maharishi's Vedic psychology also describes accumulation of stress as a general phenomenon that may hinder or block growth at any point in the life cycle. . . . The process of transcending to a 'least excited' state of pure consciousness during TM appears to 'unfreeze' development by expanding awareness and, in the process, normalizing the nervous system from deep-rooted stresses that block further growth. . . . (p. 299)

Furthermore, Alexander states:

> Regardless of the level at which development 'freezes,' to the extent that the TM program neutralizes stress and stimulates the general process of transcending to deeper mental levels, it should enhance growth across ages and development levels. In other words, though the ultimate goal of such a procedure is the attainment of higher stages of consciousness, it should also stimulate growth through proposed intervening steps en route to that goal. (unpublished work, 1997)

That goal, in Alexander's opinion, was unity consciousness, the highest state of consciousness in Maharishi's seven states of consciousness. In Table 1 we see that the fifth, sixth, and seventh states of consciousness form a sequence of developmental stages in the growth to full potential or enlightenment (the seventh state).

5. *Cosmic Consciousness:* The fourth state is the foundation for the fifth, sixth, and seventh states of consciousness. Maharishi Vedic Science describes the field of pure consciousness as the infinite, unchanging basis of individuality, but in the waking state we are typically unaware of its existence. When, through the TM program, transcendental consciousness is systematically alternated with activity in the waking state, the nervous system becomes habituated to maintaining transcendental consciousness along with waking, dreaming, and sleeping.

When the unbounded inner awareness of transcendental consciousness is maintained throughout the 24-hour daily cycle along with the constantly changing states of daily life–waking, dreaming, and sleeping–a fifth state of consciousness is established (Maharishi Mahesh Yogi, 1969). This fifth state is called *cosmic consciousness* because of its all-inclusive nature. It is characterized by a permanent shift of perception of the knower or self from primary identification with body-mind and other objects of experience, to primary identification with unbounded, pure awareness as the essential nature of the self. Traditionally, transcendental consciousness is referred to as the Self, capital "S" to distinguish it from the individual ego, or small "s" self (Maharishi Mahesh Yogi, 1969). Whereas the *Self* is unbounded awareness, the *self* is identified with localized thoughts, feelings, and perceptions (Alexander et al., 1991). Alexander notes: "In cosmic consciousness, the unbounded Self is said to provide a stable internal frame of reference from which the changing phases of not only waking state but even dreaming and deep sleep can be silently witnessed or observed" (Alexander et al., 1991, p. 200).

Surveys and longitudinal studies have found that frequency of experiences of transcendental consciousness during waking, dreaming, and even sleep increases with the number of years practicing the TM program, and is associated with specific EEG brain wave patterns that may be a psychophysiological indicator of the fifth state of consciousness (Mason et al., 1997; Orme-Johnson, Clements, Haynes, & Badawi, 1977). According to Maharishi Vedic Science, in cosmic consciousness, the physiology is stress-free and consequently functions most efficiently (1969). In this state, action is spontaneously right, which means that it is beneficial for the individual and society. The activity of daily living is enjoyed on a platform of permanent equanimity, inner fulfillment, and happiness. Only at this level is freedom from craving and dependence on sensory gratification fully achieved (Alexander, Davies et al., 1990; Alexander, Heaton et al., 1994; Dillbeck & Alexander, 1989; Orme-Johnson et al., 1997). This is the direction that human experience can take to eliminate the stress-related motivations and behaviors that typically lead to criminal activity.

6. Refined Cosmic Consciousness: Further development of mind and body facilitated by continued practice of the TM technique and Advanced Techniques[1] of the TM program results in a state of consciousness that has been called refined cosmic consciousness (Maharishi Mahesh Yogi, 1972, 1994). In cosmic consciousness, the individual experiences the nature of the inner Self as unbounded and infinite. This experience of inner wholeness is said to provide the natural basis for gaining greater appreciation and knowledge of others. With development of the sixth state, the individual experiences increasingly more refined perception of the outer environment, mediated by psychophysiological changes that support more refined functioning of all systems of the body, including the senses (see Walton & Levitsky, this volume). Behavior becomes increasingly loving and inclusive, continuing to support an ever more encompassing experience of one's surroundings and ever more enriching and nourishing actions toward the entire environment.

7. Unity Consciousness: During the practice of the TM technique, the individual perceives finer levels of the thinking process, until the unbounded nature of the Self is experienced. In this same way, after the sixth state is established, the capacity of the nervous system to perceive finer levels of outward experience becomes deeper, and eventually even the outer values of life are experienced as infinite during the activity of daily life. Maharishi (1997) proposes that human development culminates in a seventh state, unity consciousness. It is based on optimum functioning of the nervous system. Just as in cosmic consciousness there has been a shift to the experience of the essential nature of the Self as unbounded, so, in this highest state, there has been a shift to the perception that all the objects of experience are infinite, eternal, and unbounded in their essential nature. In this way, the gap between the knower, the individual who is perceiving, and the known, that which is being perceived, is bridged.

With reference to Alexander's model (see Table 1), the sequence of cosmic consciousness to unity consciousness represents development of unbounded awareness so that it is experienced on every level (Alexander et al., 1994). Transcendental consciousness is completely an inner experience. In cosmic consciousness the unbounded qualities of transcendental consciousness have become infused at the level of the ego. The individual self is now experienced as an unbounded Self. In refined cosmic consciousness the qualities of transcendental consciousness have permeated all the other levels of mind and have begun to be experienced even on the sensory level. In unity consciousness, the outer environment as well is perceived to be unbounded infinite consciousness. Development is complete. The mind has found its unbounded nature within, and then has evolved to find that everything else in the universe is that same unbounded ocean of consciousness. In that state, there is no inner or outer. Everything is experienced to be the same infinite continuum.

Higher States of Consciousness and Western Psychology

One valuable application of Maharishi's theory of seven states of consciousness is that it provides a systematic taxonomy for classifying experiences of higher states that have been reported in different cultures throughout the ages (D. W. Orme-Johnson, 1988a; R. F. Orme-Johnson, 1987). In Western psychology, for example, the most elevated human experiences have been described as ephemeral peak experiences (e.g., Maslow, 1964). Unfortunately, this has led to the misconception that higher states can be only temporarily experienced rather than stabilized stages of development. From the perspective of Maharishi Vedic Science, the peak experiences described in the West pertain to experiences of transcendental consciousness, or transitory tastes of the higher states of consciousness. In contrast, cosmic consciousness, refined cosmic consciousness, and unity consciousness are fully stabilized higher states that are based on increasingly refined styles of functioning of the nervous system (Maharishi Mahesh Yogi, 1969). They are not moods or conceptualizations of the waking state. They are as different from each other and from the waking state as waking, dreaming, and sleeping are from each other (Dillbeck, 1983a, 1983b; Maharishi Mahesh Yogi, 1969).

Flavell (1970, 1985) described criteria essential to a momentous developmental transition, such as the one major transition from the prerepresentational mode to the representational mode defined by contemporary models. In their chapter entitled "The Vedic Psychology of Human Development," Alexander, Davies et al. (1990) describe how the higher states of consciousness fulfill both Flavell's and Alexander's criteria of momentous developmental transitions that can occur even in adulthood. Among the criteria for stages of development that would qualify as unambiguous indicators of qualitative advancement to higher states of consciousness, Alexander includes the following: (a) the stage should be as far advanced from representational thought as representational thought is from the sensorimotor period of infancy; (b) it would require major neurophysiological maturation; (c) it would resolve the issue of "who is the knower" posed by James (1902/1982), or posed by many as "Who am I?"; (d) it would incorporate previous modes of cognitive functioning subordinate to "an entirely new mode of knowing characterized by expanded capacities"; and, finally, (e) such higher stages should be characterized by greater adaptability, stability, and accuracy, and be more "comprehensive . . . in their knowledge of self and world . . ." (Alexander et al., 1990, p. 289). All of these characteristics describe a momentous development of the individual, both in terms of physiological balance and integration and in terms of greater profundity of cognitive/emotional functioning.

According to Alexander, the higher states of consciousness described by Maharishi fulfill these requirements. Alexander argues that the self-referral mode of knowing characterizing pure consciousness is as far advanced from representational thought as representational thought is from the sensorimotor period; that the wide range of psychophysiological research describes an increase of balance and orderliness in the individual across physiological systems; that the experience of pure consciousness allows the knower to know him/her Self as unbounded awareness, answering the question posed by William James (1902/1982), ". . . *what* is the thinker?" (p. 196); that the mode of knowing characteristic of higher states of consciousness is inclusive of the other states–waking, sleeping, and dreaming–and yet is more comprehensive; and finally, that the higher states are characterized by a more holistic perception of self and world (Alexander et al., 1990).

Natural Law and Rehabilitation

How does this momentous change then resolve fundamental issues of crime prevention and offender rehabilitation? A final concept can be introduced from Maharishi Vedic Science, that of optimum attunement with natural law. Society's goal has been to teach children from an early age to function within the regularly accepted norms of society known as national, state, and local laws, and to attempt to reform individuals who have not been able to function within those laws. Yet Maharishi Vedic Science also describes the higher states of consciousness as promoting action that is in harmony with nature's action. Maharishi (1986a) describes nature's action as evolutionary and orderly. Science has discovered many laws of nature that describe this orderliness of functioning. Quantum physics has described a *unified field* of the laws of nature constituting all forms of matter and energy. This finding of quantum physics has been likened to the field of pure consciousness that can be experienced by every individual and that is foundational to thought and action (Hagelin, 1987). When individuals experience their own pure consciousness they are creating greater coherence and orderliness within themselves, and thus growing in the capacity to act in a more constructive and life-supporting manner. Maharishi (1986a) explains:

> Thoughts and action arise spontaneously. No one wants to suffer. No one wants to be disharmonious. No one wants to do harm to anyone. But somehow, one finds oneself in that difficult situation where one can't avoid doing wrong. That is why the best education will cultivate a habit of working from that totality of natural law, that field which is our own transcendental consciousness, our own unbounded awareness. When we are developing a habit of spontaneously functioning according to natural law, then we are naturally getting out of that old habit where some negativity could arise. All difficulties, suffering, and failures in life belong to violation of the laws of nature. Life according to natural law will always be orderly, evolutionary, and nourishing to everyone. (p. 98)

IMPLICATIONS

There are innumerable factors that might contribute to the violation of lawful behavior. A rehabilitation strategy that attempts to work with each individual by locating the specific circumstances and influences that led to criminal behavior would be impractical because it would involve in-depth, time-consuming, and costly analysis and therapy. The public has shown that it is impatient with such approaches, considering them ineffective and inappropriate, and in contrast, favors tougher laws and longer prison sentences over therapeutic modalities. Yet the search continues for an effective way to alleviate the burden placed on society by unlawful and harmful behavior.

This paper has introduced a Consciousness-Based approach that applies the Transcendental Meditation program to promote crime prevention and rehabilitation. The paper has indicated that through removing stress-related abnormalities and promoting advancement to higher stages of self development, the same individual who has violated the law may become law-abiding. Even those who have not yet committed crimes may be prevented from doing so by early introduction of the technique into the home or educational environment (Dillbeck & Dillbeck, 1997; Jones, Clayborne, Grant, & Rutherford, this volume).

By acquiring the resilience necessary to favor law-abiding avenues for achieving life's goals, children and adolescents embark on a life of achievement rather than a life of crime. By removing stress-related abnormalities on both the physiological and psychological levels, the individual becomes free to choose actions constructive to society, rather than destructive. By attaining advanced levels of self-development, even in adulthood, the individual moves toward development of full potential, irrespective of prior actions. Adoption of the TM program in educational, social-service, probation, and prison settings accomplishes the goal of providing a cost-effective approach that efficiently promotes the behaviors that society would welcome.

PART TWO: ORGANIZATION OF THE ARTICLES

Charles Alexander organized this volume to reflect the variety of interests of those involved in criminal justice. He anticipated that theoreticians and researchers, prison and social-service administrators, judges, police personnel, policy makers, and the prisoners themselves would approach the volume from the vantage point of their own practical concerns and issues. In addition, he wished to address in a comprehensive manner the myriad factors influencing criminal behavior and to show how the TM program affects these factors. He, therefore, called for contributions from practitioners as well as theoreticians to discuss their experience and insight on rehabilitation and prevention using the TM program. Contributors include a judge, a lawyer, psychologists, educators, a neurochemist, a physiologist, and administrators of criminal rehabilitation programs.

The editors have chosen to highlight the successful St. Louis sentencing program for probationers, pioneered by the Honorable David C. Mason (see Preface, this volume), and by Farrokh K. Anklesaria, as an example of a new direction in implementation of the TM program for rehabilitation.

The other contributions to the volume are distributed among several sections based on the primary focus of the papers, including theoretical and review papers in section one; empirical research on prison projects in section two; implementation strategies for preventing crime and violence in education and in society as a whole in section three; case studies on individual offenders and on a national rehabilitation project in section four; and a cost-benefit analysis as the conclusion of the volume.

Highlight: A Community-Based Sentencing Program for Probationers

The paper entitled "The Enlightened Sentencing Project: A Judicial Innovation" describes the pioneering community-based program for probationers spearheaded by Mason and Anklesaria in St. Louis and adopted by five additional judges in the state of Missouri. The paper, co-authored by Anklesaria and Michael S. King, explores the background and establishment of this innovative project, reporting the wide range of benefits of the TM program experienced by over 100 probationers who had committed offenses ranging from drunk driving to manslaughter.

Section I: Theory and Review

Mark A. Hawkins' review paper, "Effectiveness of the *Transcendental Meditation* Program in Criminal Rehabilitation and Substance Abuse Recovery: A Review of the Research," includes a comprehensive summary of 39 studies. The paper describes risk factors associated with the likelihood of criminal behavior and substance misuse, and summarizes research indicating how the TM program successfully addresses many of these factors. The paper includes two accessible tables documenting the study dates, publication information, setting, population, research design and instruments, results, and implications for each study.

A paper contributed by Kenneth G. Walton and Debra K. Levitsky, entitled "Effects of the *Transcendental Meditation* Program on Neuroendocrine Abnormalities Associated with Aggression and Crime," reviews the relationship between neuroendocrine abnormalities and aggression and describes seminal research indicating that the TM program restores normal function to neuroendocrine systems whose function has been impaired by extreme or low-grade stress.

Section II: Original Research on Rehabilitation

Section two contains six empirical papers describing studies in four prison systems. David W. Orme-Johnson, assisted by John Kiehlbauch and Richard M. Moore, was the first to complete a research study on the TM program in offender rehabilitation. The study, entitled "First Prison Study Using the *Transcendental Meditation Program*: La Tuna Federal Penitentiary, 1971," demonstrated that the effects of TM are physiological as well as psychological. After practicing the technique for two months, subjects showed fewer spontaneous skin resistance responses, suggesting less of the internalized fear and anger that generate stress and create long-lasting consequences that reduce adaptability. The study also found that this increased physiological stability was positively correlated with greater mental flexibility (i.e., decreased psychological rigidity and psychasthenia on the MMPI). The study also illustrated an important principle, that the degree of change in the inmates is strongly correlated with the regularity of their practice of the TM technique.

In the first of three papers resulting from Alexander's dissertation research at Harvard, Charles N. Alexander, Kenneth G. Walton, and Rachel S. Goodman describe the cross-sectional aspect of the research, which involved 160 maximum-security prisoners as subjects. The study, "Walpole Study of the *Transcendental Meditation* Program in Maximum Security Prisoners I: Cross-Sectional Differences in Development and Psychopathology," was a multifaceted assessment of differences in self-development and psychopathology between the group practicing the TM program and various control groups. Inmates who had practiced the TM program for an average of 20 months showed improvement in comparison to controls on three factor-analytic components (Development, Consciousness, and Psychopathology) that were derived from 14 individual test scales. The TM group also scored better than nonmembers on key individual test scales, including, among others, Loevinger's self-development scale (the SCT), State-Trait anxiety, the Postconceptual Experience factor of Alexander's State of Consciousness Inventory, and five scales of psychopathology from the SHAPS assessment.

In the second of the three papers derived from Alexander's doctoral dissertation, "Walpole Study of the *Transcendental Meditation* Program in Maximum Security Prisoners II: Longitudinal Study of Development and Psychopathology," Alexander and Orme-Johnson describe the longitudinal study that extended the findings of the cross-sectional study. With 271 maximum security inmates, Alexander compared changes in self-development and psychopathology after an average of 15.7 months' participation in five programs: the TM program, counseling, drug rehabilitation, Muslim, and Christian. For each program, he studied changes in both new participants, who joined their programs at the start of the 15.7-month period, and advanced participants, who had already been participating in their program for approximately 2 years when the study began. The study design and data analysis controlled for overlap of program membership as well as for 19 demographic and criminal history variables. New TM subjects moved from a dependent, exploitive orientation to a greater awareness of norms and goals. Advanced TM subjects made additional advances to a more responsible, self-monitoring, self-respecting, and communicative level of self-development. They also decreased in aggression, in schizophrenic symptoms, and in trait-anxiety (trend), and increased in frequency of experience of higher states of consciousness. This evidence supports Alexander's hypothesis that the TM program "unfreezes" human development through the dual process of transcending and stress normalization, as described in Part One of this introduction.

The third paper of the trilogy, authored by Alexander, Maxwell V. Rainforth, Paul R. Frank, James D. Grant, Christopher von Stade, and Walton, extends the findings of the first two studies to recidivism outcomes. Entitled "Walpole Study of the *Transcendental Meditation* Program in Maximum Security Prisoners III: Reduced Recidivism," this study retrospectively examined recidivism over a 59-month period. Lower recidivism was found in the TM group compared to random-sample controls and pooled-sample controls.

Recidivism was defined in several ways, but the most stringent definition–returns with new convictions–showed the greatest reduction (47%) in the TM group compared to all non-TM inmates. The TM group also had a higher incidence of clean records. The pattern of reduced recidivism for TM program members was maintained in multiple regression analyses that controlled for significant background variables, including institution of release, drug history, and parole versus full discharge.

The next study in this section is a 15-year follow-up study of a paper on effects of the TM program and recidivism (Bleick & Abrams, 1987). Bleick and Abrams tracked 259 subjects released from Folsom and San Quentin maximum security prisons, as well as from Deuel Vocational Institution (medium security), over a 6-year period. The TM subjects closely matched the source population on ethnic background, seriousness of prior convictions, and category of most recent offense. Over 5 successive years after release, rates of new prison and long jail terms in the TM group were 35% to 50% lower than for the controls. In addition, parole outcomes at 1 year, and rap sheet outcomes for up to 6 years, were significantly more favorable for the TM group than for controls, controlling for 28 social and criminal background variables.

The follow-up study included in this volume, "Effects of the Transcendental Meditation Program on Recidivism Among Former Inmates of Folsom Prison: Survival Analysis of 15-Year Follow-Up Data," used the methodology of survival analysis, and controlled for 22 demographic and criminal background variables. The authors, Rainforth, Alexander, and Kenneth L. Cavanaugh, were able to overcome limitations associated with assessing recidivism at the end of a fixed period of at least 3 years. The TM program group not only had a lower re-offending rate than the control group, but the analysis indicated that the TM program produced permanent rehabilitation, as opposed to merely delaying the onset of re-offending. Data also showed the severity of re-offending to be lower for the TM group compared to controls.

In "*Consciousness-Based* Rehabilitation of Inmates in the Netherlands Antilles: Psychosocial and Cognitive Changes," Mark A. Hawkins, Alexander, Walton, Rainforth, and Frederick T. Travis, along with Carl R. T. Camelia and Christian F. Durchholz, report the results of a study in the federal prison on the island of Curaçao, the Netherlands Antilles, conducted from August 1994 to June 1995. The researchers administered standardized tests of recognized psychosocial and cognitive risk factors for criminal behavior to 300 male subjects before and after instruction of the experimental group in the TM program. The tests and subscales resulted in 21 dependent variables, which were reduced by principal components factor analysis to 6 factors. After 4.5 months, significant positive changes were reported for the TM group compared to controls on 2 of the 6 factors–Cognitive Distortion and Intelligence-Related Measures–and a trend toward significance was seen on a third factor, Psychological Well-Being.

Section III: Preventing Crime and Violence

This third section brings together work addressing societal issues in crime prevention. Implementation strategies presented include an education program to eliminate school violence, a national-level project to decrease crime, and an international program to prevent terrorism and international conflict.

The first paper, "Attacking Crime at Its Source: *Consciousness-Based* Education in the Prevention of Violence and Antisocial Behavior," by Christopher Jones, Mawiyah Clayborne, Grant, and George Rutherford, examines evidence that the TM program can be used in the secondary educational system for aiding development of the students' full learning capacity, creativity, balanced health, and harmonious interpersonal relationships. The paper discusses theoretical issues and factors related to school violence; components of the Consciousness-Based education program; examples of successes in private schools and communities; and outcomes for both the children and the teachers. Education can serve as a deterrent to violence when the educational system provides a systematic technology to develop the child's resilience and inner strength. The technique is found to promote the ability to make right choices under adverse circumstances, as exemplified in the responses of young students practicing the TM technique that are contained in excerpts from a case study.

The two other papers in the section, authored by Orme-Johnson and colleagues, examine a unique application of Maharishi's Consciousness-Based technology in the prevention of crime through removal of societal stress. In "Preventing Crime Through the Maharishi Effect," Orme-Johnson reviews research that addresses the problem of crime as a society-wide phenomenon. The 15 studies reviewed provide empirical support for the theory that stress in the *collective consciousness* of society is a fundamental cause of crime. In this view, groups at every level of social organization–family, community, city, state, nation, and world–generate a characteristic collective consciousness to which each individual contributes. This collective consciousness is apparent in the overall quality of life and level of stress in the social group in question.

In this theory, the collective consciousness of a community and its level of stress are held to influence each individual in the community. Crime, terrorism, and outbreaks of national and international conflict are seen as the result of collective stress and strain. Over 40 research studies on the TM technique and the more advanced TM-Sidhi program have shown that these same technologies that promote balancing and nourishing influences for the individual practitioner also serve as an effective strategy on the societal level, to remove and prevent the symptoms of social stress.

In 1974, the first research on lowering stress in society indicated that when 1% or more of a city's population learned the TM program, crime rate decreased in that city. This phenomenon was named the Maharishi Effect.[1] Subsequently, as few as the square root of 1% of the population practicing the more powerful TM-Sidhi program in a group were found to have a similar effect, promoting greater harmony and well-being in society. In addition to crime rate, the Maharishi Effect has been studied at the level of the economy, on governmental effectiveness, and on international relations, as well as with a large variety of other indicators of quality of life.

The final paper in the section, "Preventing Terrorism and International Conflict: Effects of Large Assemblies of Participants in the *Transcendental Meditation* and *TM-Sidhi* Programs," by Orme-Johnson, Michael C. Dillbeck, and Alexander, presents findings of research on the reduction of terrorism and international conflicts. Terrorism and international conflicts are part of the total crime problem, and must be included in any comprehensive approach to crime. Terrorist acts are politically motivated crimes, and wars consist of heinous acts by society as a whole. Outside the context of war, any individual committing the acts typical of war would be punished.

Even on this global level, Maharishi's Consciousness-Based approach to rehabilitation offers a solution. The Orme-Johnson, Dillbeck, and Alexander paper reports reductions in international conflicts and terrorism on three occasions when groups of approximately 7,000 TM-Sidhi program participants (roughly the square root of 1% of the world's population) practiced these techniques together. Reductions of international conflicts ranged from 24% to 36%, and the reduction in terrorism was 72%. These results along with results of more than 40 other studies on a broad range of quality of life indices have inspired researchers and policy makers to create permanent Maharishi Effect groups in many parts of the world.

Section IV: Transcendental Meditation in Prisons and Prison Systems

Theory, research, and program development converge in section four, which provides a macroscopic view of the role of the TM program in criminal rehabilitation. In a case study, entitled "The *Transcendental Meditation* Program in the Senegalese Penitentiary System," Anklesaria and King describe favorable changes to prisoners, guards, and administrators in the prison system of the West African nation of Senegal when 11,000 inmates and 900 correctional officers and prison administrators were instructed in the TM program. Between 1987 and 1989, everyone in 31 of the 34 prisons in Senegal was instructed. Recidivism dropped from 90% in the pre-meditation period to less than 3% after the program was established. Rule infractions also decreased, and medical expenses went down 70%. These were only 3 of the more than 14 benefits described as successful outcomes by the prison wardens. This study illustrates the value of a large-scale implementation strategy and could be seen as a model for a global rehabilitation initiative.

The volume concludes with a compelling paper on the cost effectiveness of the TM program for rehabilitative efforts: "Cost Savings from Teaching the *Transcendental Meditation* Program in Prisons" by David L. Magill. This paper quantifies cost savings to correctional systems and to society resulting from implementation of the TM program. Based on the reduced numbers of new convictions and decreased parole violations found in studies at several maximum security prisons, Magill estimates the cost savings that could accrue from implementing the TM program in prisons. Reduced medical expenses, more manageable prison environments, improved quality of life for staff, and reduced crime rate for society are also estimated and included in the calculations. The bottom-line savings over 5 years for every 1,000 inmates and 100 correctional officers instructed in the TM program is estimated at $31.6 million. This projection implies that instruction of a substantial fraction of the 6 million people under correctional supervision would lead to savings in the tens of billions of dollars.

INVITATION

As has been seen in this introduction, the collection of papers in this volume provides an overview of the theory, research, and applications of the TM and TM-Sidhi programs for crime prevention and criminal rehabilitation. The editors and authors invite you to examine the papers in depth. It is our wish that this collection serve as an impetus for further research and application of these programs for the well-being of the individual and society.

NOTE

1. Transcendental Meditation, TM, TM-Sidhi, Consciousness-Based, and Advanced Techniques are registered or common law trademarks licensed to Maharishi Vedic Education Development Corporation and used under sublicense or with permission.
2. Adapted from Alexander, Heaton, and Chandler (1994).

AUTHORS' NOTES

The authors would like to thank Robert Oates, Patricia Robinson, and Dennis Heaton for their theoretical and strategic input to this paper.

Address correspondence to Rachel S. Goodman, 1000 North 4th Street, S.U. 366, M.U.M., Fairfield, IA 52557 (E-mail: rgoodman@mum.edu).

Transcendental Meditation in Criminal Rehabilitation and Crime Prevention. Pp. 35-46.

HIGHLIGHT: A COMMUNITY-BASED SENTENCING PROGRAM FOR PROBATIONERS

The Enlightened Sentencing Project: A Judicial Innovation

FARROKH K. ANKLESARIA

The Enlightened Sentencing Project, St. Louis, Missouri

MICHAEL S. KING

Stipendiary Magistrate, Geraldton, Western Australia

ABSTRACT The Enlightened Sentencing Project has its origins in the search by Judge David C. Mason, a Missouri circuit court judge, for a rehabilitation program that would benefit offenders appearing before him. The project initiated by Judge Mason is a pioneering, community based rehabilitation program in which probationers are sentenced to learn the Transcendental Meditation (TM)[1] technique and to participate in classes to enhance their understanding of the technique and its benefits. Thus far in this program, six judges in Missouri have sentenced over 100 probationers whose offenses range from drunk driving to manslaughter. Results have been remarkable, with offenders reporting a wide range of benefits. This paper describes the background and establishment of the Enlightened Sentencing

Project. It also reports on the experiences of the participants, judges, and parole officers involved and suggests steps for implementing similar projects in other communities.

KEYWORDS Offender rehabilitation, Transcendental Meditation, community-based rehabilitation, stress reduction, self-development, probationers

Criminology includes a broad range of theories of the source of crime. Each of these theories has its basis in a specific factor, such as rational human nature, physiology, psychology, social interactions, the political and economic structure of society, or combinations of these. The practical result is a variety of prescriptions for prevention of crime that emphasize different approaches such as special deterrence, general deterrence, preventive detention, retribution, rehabilitation, social reform, political reform, and spiritual development. Some of these approaches and rehabilitation programs are being applied today, but the majority of them have little effect. Thus, it is no surprise that many current administrators of criminal justice simply administer the system (Feeley & Simon, 1994; Gottfredson & Hirschi, 1995).

Dominant features of the criminal justice system over the last 15 years have been: (a) calls for the imposition of harsher punishment, including capital punishment, mandatory sentencing, and longer prison terms; (b) truth in sentencing–the concept that offenders actually serve the sentence imposed, without remission or parole; and (c) increased police numbers as a means of deterrence (Di Julio, 1995). However, imprisonment and increasing police numbers are a costly and relatively ineffective means of preventing crime. In 1995 the average annual cost of a maximum-security inmate was $35,000 (American Correctional Association, 1995). The Bureau of Justice Statistics (1994) reported that about two-thirds of state parolees are re-arrested within 3 years of release. Felson (1994, p. 11) estimated that the 15,000 police officers of Los Angeles County could only patrol each location for about 29 seconds each day–hardly enough to adequately prevent crime. There is clearly a need for new directions in the criminal justice system.

Judge David Mason, of the 22nd Circuit Court of Missouri, has long recognized that a new, more effective approach is needed to deal with these basic issues of sentencing and rehabilitation. Mason has a reputation of being a tough judge. He does not hesitate to imprison offenders whose behavior, in his view, deserves such punishment. At the same time, he believes that the circumstances of a particular case and offender may require that greater weight be given to the ideal of rehabilitation rather than to punishment. Like conscientious judges everywhere, he has sought to balance the tough and the compassionate sides of sentencing.

In applying the principle of rehabilitation in sentencing, Judge Mason has emphasized the responsibility of the criminal justice system to provide effective rehabilitation programs. While acknowledging that the effectiveness of most programs has been under question since the mid-1970s, he has not been dissuaded from pursuing the ideal behind rehabilitation.

Prior to his appointment to the 22nd Circuit Court, Judge Mason had served as Assistant Attorney General for the state of Missouri and as counsel advising the correctional authorities in that state. He has had extensive experience with government and community groups exploring crime prevention and rehabilitation programs. His interest in such programs continued following his appointment to the bench. He was particularly interested in programs that could assist offenders deficient in stress-coping skills, a deficiency which he sees as a primary causal factor in their offending.

INVESTIGATING THE TRANSCENDENTAL MEDITATION PROGRAM

Early in 1996 Judge Mason began investigating the Transcendental Meditation program, a stress reduction and self-development program introduced to the West by Maharishi Mahesh Yogi (usually referred to as "Maharishi"). Mason was particularly interested in two aspects of Maharishi's theory of stress and its effects. The first aspect was Maharishi's claim that stress adversely impacts physiological and psychological functioning, inhibiting the ability of an individual to cope constructively with inordinate demands from the environment. Thirty years ago, Maharishi (1968) stated,

> Crime is evidently a short cut to satisfy a craving–a short cut which goes beyond normal and legal means. Crime, delinquency, and the different patterns of antisocial behavior arise from a deep discontent of the mind; they arise from a weak mind and unbalanced emotions. A weak mind is one which lacks balance and a sense of proportion. (p. 219)

Medical research has provided support for this aspect of the theory, especially since the pioneering work of Hans Selye in the 1930s. Today medicine considers stress to be a contributing factor in disorders ranging from insomnia to heart disease (McEwen, 1998ab; Wallace, 1993, pp. 57-58). The understanding of stress as resulting from overloading physiological systems and producing long lasting changes that can increase both mental and physical disease is supported by many recent studies (see for reviews: McEwen, 1998; Seeman, Singer, Rowe, Horwitz, & McEwen, 1997).

The second aspect of Maharishi's theory that impressed Judge Mason was the fact that the TM program could be used to remove weakness of the mind. Maharishi (1968) said, "It has been found that all kinds of tensions are released and that the hard cruel nature of a man changes to one of tolerance and compassion through the practice of Transcendental Meditation" (p. 219).

Judge Mason reviewed the research on the application of the TM program in criminal justice systems of the United States and other countries. He also studied the reviews of other TM research. The practice of the TM technique has been found to produce a profound level of rest and order in the body and mind, dissolving long-lasting effects of stress and alleviating stress-related disorders such as substance abuse (Hawkins, this volume) and anxiety (Eppley, Abrams, & Shear, 1989). In relation to prison inmates, the technique has also been found to reduce aggression and to promote significant psychological development (Alexander, & Orme-Johnson, this volume; Alexander, Rainforth et al., this volume; Alexander, Walton, & Goodman, this volume) and to enhance positive behavior as well as to reduce recidivism (Alexander, Rainforth et al., this volume; Rainforth, Alexander, & Cavanaugh, this volume).

Of the many available criminological theories, Judge Mason was most impressed with those that posit a connection between stress and crime. His review of research and experience of offenders suggested that such theories were perhaps the ones most relevant to a large number of offenders coming before his court. He was impressed that high levels of stress and lack of stress-coping skills were the predominant features of offenders in domestic violence and substance abuse cases.

In a lecture to an audience of judges and lawyers at the Law Institute of Victoria, Melbourne, Australia, in November 1999, Judge Mason suggested that a link exists between stress and violence, whether it be domestic violence, street violence, or barroom violence. He said, "That feeling, that stress that makes you angry and you want to just smack or hit something, we have all experienced. But not all of us are able to deal with that feeling on an equal level. Those of us who can't deal with it through constructive means, do things that lead to incarceration" (personal communication, November 1999). In the same lecture, the judge said: "No matter what their background, some people just don't have the skills to cope with the kinds of things that can cause them to have low self-esteem, to feel bad, to feel stressed. Some people just don't. Then they turn to things like alcohol or drugs."

However, these substances interfere with normal functioning of the mind and body, including the ability to cope with stressful circumstances. When such an individual is confronted with demanding situations, behavioral reactions, such as further abuse of drugs or criminal activity, may result that are inappropriate to the circumstances.

ENHANCING STRESS-COPING SKILLS THROUGH TM

As his understanding of the relationship between stress and criminal behavior grew, so did Mason's interest in finding a rehabilitation program to enhance the stress-coping skills of offenders, one that gave them the inner resources to handle situations in a positive, life-supporting way. Through his review of the research on the TM technique, particularly its ability to reduce stress, Mason became convinced that this approach would be of value in offender rehabilitation.

Judge Mason explains TM this way:

> It's a simple technique that involves two 20-minute periods a day wherein a person gains a very deep level of rest. During this process of deep rest, the physiology becomes normalized, thinking becomes clearer, self-esteem grows, enlightenment of self and others grows, so that by the time people have gone through the process, their ability to deal with the world around them, to deal with the stresses of the world around them, to find some personal peace within, and to express peace without, is greatly enhanced. (personal communication, October 1996)

THE ENLIGHTENED SENTENCING PROJECT

The Early Stages

The Enlightened Sentencing Project began in late 1996, with Judge Mason sentencing the first offenders in St. Louis to practice the Transcendental Meditation technique as a condition of their probation. Since that time, five additional judges have become involved in sentencing offenders to participate in the project, and over 100 offenders have participated, a number that would be much larger except that funding has so far been available only through private donations. Both first-time and repeat offenders, ranging in age from 18 to 61 years (mean = 30), have participated. Offenses include the use and sale of controlled substances, robbery, assault, child abuse, and one murder (after incarceration).

In the early stages of the project, some community groups raised questions as to its validity. They were concerned that the project might be imposing a religious practice (other than theirs) upon probationers. However, after investigating the situation, Mason concluded that their concerns arose from a lack of knowledge about the nature and mechanics of the TM technique. His investigation confirmed what the teachers of the technique had said, namely, that the practice was a purely mechanical one, based on the natural tendency of the mind to seek a state of greatest happiness. Mason could see that no specific belief system or lifestyle was required. He talked with committed practitioners of the TM technique from different religions as well as with practitioners who were not committed to any religion. He also was impressed by the benefits already reported to him by participants in the project. Thus, Mason felt no hesitancy in continuing the project and recommends that it or similar projects be initiated widely.

Sentencing Offenders

For each potential participant in the project, the process begins with an appearance before the 22nd Circuit Court in St. Louis. Individuals either have been charged with a criminal offense and have entered a plea of guilty, or they have been found guilty by trial. If the judge determines that an offender should be placed on probation, then the judge will consider whether placement in the Enlightened Sentencing Project is appropriate for that individual. In the early stages of the project, it was the judge who would suggest the possibility to the offender. However, as the results of the project became known, the suggestion for placement in the project has increasingly come from offenders, their counsel, or probation officers.

Each judge has taken a different approach in determining whether an offender should be placed in the Enlightened Sentencing Project. Judge Mason believes that any probationer could benefit from such placement. Other judges may identify an offender's particular problem, such as substance abuse, that specific evidence indicates could be resolved with the assistance of the TM technique. Once a decision has been made that participation in the Enlightened Sentencing Project is appropriate as a condition of probation, the probationer is directed by the court to attend an introductory lecture describing the TM technique and the requirements of the project. Individuals who agree to continue then attend one or more additional preparatory lectures, as needed, and are interviewed personally by the instructor. Then, on four consecutive days, the participant receives individualized private instruction and three group follow-up sessions. These lectures and instruction sessions comprise the seven-step process of learning the TM technique.

Follow-Up Classes for Probationers

After this initial course, participants continue to attend class sessions twice each week for 13 weeks for further understanding, to verify that their TM practice is going effortlessly, and to receive feedback on their experiences. During that time, participants also receive instruction in a simple breathing procedure and yoga asanas (stretching exercises) that facilitate the process of normalizing the stress-related imbalances in mind and body. These classes include the knowledge necessary for understanding the nature of the TM practice and its ability to automatically free the mind and body of abnormalities caused by stress. After completing the 13-week course, probationers continue to attend monthly classes for the duration of their probation. This follow-up consists of verification of the probationers' practice of the TM technique, the reporting of experiences, and additional instruction in the application and theory behind the technique.

On completion of the 13-week course, a special graduation ceremony is held where participants receive their graduation certificates. (Videotapes of past graduations are available from the authors.) It is usual for a judge to present the graduation certificates. At the October 1999 graduation, the Chief Justice of the Supreme Court of Missouri presided. On a speaking tour in Australia, two of the St. Louis judges reported that, as of that time (September 1999), over 100 offenders had been referred to the Enlightened Sentencing Project, 69 had completed the courses, and of those completing, only 5 had breached their probation.

Nature of the Clientele

Most of the participants in the Enlightened Sentencing Project are poor, illiterate, substance abusers who live in the ghetto areas of St. Louis. Probation Officer Daniel Spring of St. Louis believes that most probationers face significant challenges when they return to their communities, the environments that nurtured their felonious behaviors. "Violence, drug abuse, crime, and poverty create a tremendous amount of stress," he says. "And many offenders have developed self-defeating behaviors to cope with this environment" (personal communication, April 2000).

Unprecedented Regular Attendance

Probationers generally do not attend any type of class with regularity. However, for the TM program and follow-up classes offered by the Enlightened Sentencing Project, this is not the case. Most participants come to TM classes using bus tickets provided by the Department of Probation and Parole. In one case, the probationer, even while recovering from gunshot wounds, received instruction from the Enlightened Sentencing Project.

Probationers become so fulfilled with the TM program that not only do they attend all 26 classes, but they also do not want to leave punctually at the end of class. They often stay until they are finally asked to leave. A St. Louis Probation and Parole Officer explained the response this way:

> Despite the best intentions of officers, the offenders hate being directed to special programs (i.e., drug treatment, aggressive offender groups). Most of the offenders have been in special programs since they were very young. Most begin the Enlightened Sentencing Project reluctantly, but soon they love the meetings. It becomes a time of relaxation, a safe haven where the mood is focused and peaceful. There is cheerful banter

> and the tone is light. The technique of TM is so simple that all offenders are successful. (personal communication, April 2000)

The Department of Probation and Parole has acknowledged that such regular attendance at any rehabilitation program is unprecedented. The assistant director of the St. Louis branch of the Missouri Department of Probation and Parole said:

> Initially the department dismissed the TM program, but now there has been a change. We are seriously looking at the data. The department is particularly impressed that so many probationers have actually come to the entire course and attended the graduation celebrations. We are also impressed with the political support that Enlightened Sentencing Project has. (personal communication, October 1999)

ASSESSING SUCCESS

The results of the Enlightened Sentencing Project have encouraged a growing number of judges in St. Louis to refer offenders. The project has gained the support of judges at all levels of the state judiciary, as well as corrections officials, counsel appearing before the court, legislators, and project participants and their families.

Probationers' Experiences

One of the principal means of assessing the success of the Project thus far has been the experiences of probationers themselves. It is common for them to comment on the ease of the practice and express surprise that such an effortless technique could bring about significant changes in their lives. For example, the following was reported by D.B., age 32:

> I've had excellent experiences right from the start. I was amazed by the effortlessness of the practice. After my very first meditation, I kept saying, "I didn't do anything."–and yet I had experienced all the symptoms of correct meditation: deep physical and mental relaxation and greater calmness after meditation. It seemed as though my body was just weightless. (Graduation Essay, October 1999)

Probationers also consistently report improvements in diverse areas of their lives–work, home, and relationships with other people. They also report a decrease in substance abuse. The following is the experience of C.K., age 24, who says that the practice of the TM program relieved his anger so he was more able to deal with the demands of his environment in a positive way.

> Once upon a time, I was selling drugs by myself because I thought it was easy and fast money. That's how I got caught up. Then I went to the TM program, and I started meditating. It helped me a lot. Now, I don't do drugs anymore. I work in a restaurant. Before, every time I would get mad I would break stuff like dishes, throwing things and fighting with my lady. But after I started meditating, it changed me a lot because I sit down and meditate and it relieves some of the anger. Everybody knew I had had a change. Thank you to Judge Anna Forder for sending me to the TM program. (Graduation Essay, October 1999)

A similar report by S.B., age 36, illustrates the common experience that positive changes in participants are also noticed by their families and friends.

> Dear Judge Autrey: Since I've been practicing TM, my life has become much better. My wife and kids have noticed a lot of happiness in me. I feel I am in control of myself now. My wife and I don't argue and fight as we have in the past. We get along much better now, like we've fallen in love all over again. People that have been knowing me for years see me as a different person. The important thing is not what others think of me, but what I think of me. I have self-esteem now. I don't drink and take drugs now. My behavior has changed. I am more calm. I think and make some good choices now. I feel peace within myself. It was a blessing to be taught TM. I would never have thought something this easy could make such a big difference in my life. I wish that everyone could learn this. My record shows that I have a temper and a history of assaults. But now that I've been doing TM I know how to cope with my temper and not become violent. (Graduation Essay, October 1999)

Judges' Observations on the Enlightened Sentencing Project

Judges referring probationers to the Project also have been pleased with the outcome. They, too, have noticed changes in the probationers and have been impressed by the results reported by probationers and their families. Judge Mason comments:

> While there are many scientific studies to support the use of Transcendental Meditation in criminal rehabilitation, I have the benefits of seeing its effects on offenders I have placed on probation. They are demonstrating greater self-esteem and self-control. Their mothers, girlfriends, and wives speak in glowing terms of the new man in their lives. One offender actually advised another to plead guilty only if assigned to my court so that he might get into the Transcendental Meditation program. In any event, initial reports are better than expected and confirm all the previous studies. (personal communication, May 1999)

Judge Henry Autrey says:

> I have been using Transcendental Meditation as a condition of probation for over a year. And the results are astounding. I have seen my probationers who participate in the TM program grow and develop in ways I have rarely seen in other probationers. They have a positive social attitude. They secure employment. They exhibit responsibility by maintaining positive probation reports. And, as curious as it may sound, they have an emotionally healthy appearance. By this I mean they do not appear to be stressed, anxious, nervous, or restless. These are responsible people with their lives under control as opposed to life controlling them. In short, they have taken responsibility for their lives. As I understand the purpose of probation, such a result is exactly what we in the criminal justice system seek to achieve. (personal communication, November 1999)

Though generally more reserved in her opinions than Judge Mason and Judge Autrey, Judge Anna Forder comments:

> During the past 2 years, the 22nd Judicial Circuit of the State of Missouri, through the Enlightened Sentencing Project, has been using Transcendental Meditation (TM) as a treatment method with persons placed on probation. Thus far, the persons we have placed on probation have performed extremely well. I am therefore convinced that TM can be a very useful tool in the sentencing and rehabilitation of criminal offenders. This makes me want to continue to assign probationers to TM. . . . It is a relief to have TM as an alternative to traditional methods of rehabilitation because after 20 years as a circuit court judge, I have not seen any other significant change in the way that the court attempts to handle law offenders. (personal communication, November 1999)

Cooperation of the Department of Probation and Parole

Cooperation from probation and parole officers is vital for the success of any community-based rehabilitation project. In the early stages of the Enlightened Sentencing Project, a full presentation of its aims and methods was made to the Probation and Parole Office. Offenders initially need encouragement from their Probation and Parole Officer to attend the Enlightened Sentencing Project classes, and officers were requested to encourage the participation of their probationers. Some probation officers have also been active in encouraging fellow officers to support the participation of probationers in the Project. For example, in a letter addressed to his peers, one officer said:

> It has been discovered that PO [Probation Officer] involvement is essential to the success of these clients. Once the clients are instructed in the

technique of TM, they will enjoy it so much that you will not have to urge them to go to classes. Your firm, initial support will be paramount in their success. (personal communication, March 1999)

It is generally the case that if probation officers also practice the TM technique, they will be more active in referring probationers. Officers and probationers then share a common point of reference, making it easier for the officer to promote regular class attendance by the probationer.

TM Instruction for Officers and Families

Experience has shown that offenders benefit greatly from support given by family members and probation officers who also practice the TM technique. One probation officer commented that his own TM practice helped create greater rapport with offenders. He said:

> TM establishes common ground between PO and offender. I get the chance to relate in an open, enthusiastic and caring way. I have been able to do "anti-criminal" modeling. The Enlightened Sentencing Project gives me the opportunity to demonstrate and reinforce vivid alternatives to pro-criminal styles of life. The offenders observe warmth, enthusiasm, genuineness and honesty. (personal communication, November 1999)

It is not only the probationers who benefit when probation officers practice the TM technique. Probation officers themselves face great challenges everyday where, as one St. Louis PO said, they are "poised on the front lines of all social maladies . . . the buffer between the dark underworld and free society" (personal communication, November 1999). Probation officers in St. Louis are required to conduct home visits to their clients in areas of the city where police officers wear bulletproof vests. And POs now carry firearms.

Obviously, this creates great stress for the probation officers. The St. Louis PO continued:

> The caseloads are vast, wages low, and measurable success is ethereal. Offenders know these weaknesses and play off of them for the purpose of perpetuating their learned self-defeating behaviors. Missouri State Probation Officers receive a tremendous amount of valuable training. The education is contemporary and comprehensive. However, it is stress that often capsizes an Officer's resolve and morale. I strongly encourage Officers to become trained in TM. My experience has been positive. I feel connected to my purpose. I feel a connection with the community that I serve. I enjoy being a Probation Officer now more than ever. (personal communication, November 1999)

FUTURE DIRECTIONS

Thus far, the results of the Enlightened Sentencing Project have been encouraging. In particular, this project illustrates the efficacy of community-based rehabilitation using the TM program. By dissolving long-lasting effects of stress that inhibit the efficient functioning of body and mind, this program unfolds the inner potential of the individual, enabling him or her to better cope with life pressures. Practical improvements in the lives of probationers clearly support the theoretical understanding behind the use of the TM program in the rehabilitation of offenders.

Further research on the TM program as a community-based offender rehabilitation program is planned. Although the available statistics suggest a particularly low recidivism rate for participants in the project, there has not been a controlled study thus far. It will be useful to conduct quantitative research on the effects of the practice of TM on probationers in the areas of substance abuse, psychological development, relationships with others, and recidivism.

In common law jurisdictions, judges traditionally maintain a balance between the certainty of precedent and the necessity of changing the law to address social needs. The scope of judicial innovation is limited by the nature and function of the judiciary. Though not a change in the law as such but rather a creative use of existing laws, the Enlightened Sentencing Project is an example of successful judicial innovation to meet a social need.

As Judge Forder has noted, judges of the 22nd Circuit Court of Missouri intend to continue to refer probationers to the Enlightened Sentencing Project. The project serves as a model for future community-based offender rehabilitation programs using the Transcendental Meditation program. Based on the results achieved, it is anticipated that many more offenders will benefit from the holistic development brought about through the practice of the Transcendental Meditation program.

NOTE

1. Transcendental Meditation, TM, and TM-Sidhi are registered or common law trademarks licensed to Maharishi Vedic Education Development Corporation and used under sublicense or with permission.

AUTHORS' NOTES

This paper has drawn from discussions between the authors and judges who are referring probationers to the Enlightened Sentencing Project. In particular, the authors wish to thank His Honor Judge David Mason, His Honor Judge Henry Autrey, and Her Honor Judge Anna Forder for their kind assistance.

Address correspondence to The Enlightened Sentencing Project, 625 N. Euclid Avenue, Suite 228, St. Louis, MO 63108.

Transcendental Meditation in Criminal Rehabilitation and Crime Prevention. Pp. 47-65.

SECTION I: THEORY AND REVIEW

Effectiveness of the *Transcendental Meditation* Program in Criminal Rehabilitation and Substance Abuse Recovery: A Review of the Research

MARK A. HAWKINS

Maharishi University of Management

ABSTRACT This article reviews research on the Transcendental Meditation (TM)[1] program relevant to the treatment and prevention of criminal behavior and substance abuse. Over the past 30 years, 39 studies have been conducted on the rehabilitative effects of the TM program. These studies have involved various populations, including at-risk youth, participants in treatment programs, and incarcerated offenders. A few studies examined the effects of the TM program in the general population on use of alcohol, cigarettes, and non-prescribed drugs. Longitudinal, random-assignment studies with objective measures confirm the results of retrospective studies and other earlier research. Incarcerated offenders show rapid positive changes in risk factors associated with criminal behavior, including anxiety, aggression, hostility, moral judgment, in-prison rule infractions, and substance abuse. The substance abuse studies, taken together, indicate that the TM program reduces substance use as well as a number of the risk factors that underlie substance dependence, particularly anxiety, depression, neuroticism, and other forms of psychological distress. The TM program also produces a wide range of improvements in psychophysiological well-being, as indicated by better psychological health, enhanced autonomic functioning, and improved neuroendocrine balance. The changes in psychological health appear significant for long-term outcomes, as indicated by the lower recidivism rates for parolee practitioners of the TM technique and lower relapse rates for addicts. As a whole, these studies indicate that practice of the TM technique is an effective approach to rehabilitation for individuals prone to criminal behaviors and addictions.

KEYWORDS Substance abuse, criminal behavior, Transcendental Meditation, TM, crime prevention

The societal costs of criminal conduct and substance abuse are well-documented (Bureau of Justice Statistics, 1999a, b; Federal Bureau of Investigation, 1996; Maguire & Pastore, 1998). Although total crime in the United States appears to have decreased each year since 1992, the rate is still high. In 1997, there were an estimated 36,796,000 victimizations. Of these, 9,443,000 were crimes against persons and 27,353,000 were property crimes (Maguire & Pastore, 1998). In the same year, there were 13,175,070 crimes reported in the U.S., of which 1,634,773 were violent crimes–homicide, rape, assault, and robbery. The remainder were property crimes–burglary, motor vehicle theft, larceny-theft, and arson (Federal Bureau of Investigation, 1997).

A high occurrence of crime means a high cost to society, which is reflected in part in government statistics. For example, in 1992, federal, state, and local governments spent $94 billion to administer civil and criminal justice systems–$368 for every resident of the United States (Bureau of Justice Statistics, 1999b, p. 1). At the end of 1996, there were 5.5 million people (2.8% of all U.S. adult residents) on probation, in jail or prison, or on parole. In 1993, it cost federal, state, and local governments almost $32 billion to maintain such an extensive correctional system (Maguire & Pastore, 1998, p. 3).

Alcohol and drug abuse also create major economic costs to society. A study by the National Institute on Drug Abuse (NIDA) and the National Institute on Alcohol Abuse and Alcoholism (NIAAA) estimates that alcohol and drug abuse cost society $246 billion in 1992 (Harwood, Fountain, & Livermore, 1998). Of this total, alcohol abuse and alcoholism accounted for an estimated $148 billion, while drug abuse and dependence cost an estimated $98 billion. Government spending on attempts to control drug abuse is also high. According to the Office of National Drug Control Policy, the federal drug control budget in 1995 was $13.2 billion; state and local drug control budgets in 1991 totaled almost $16 billion (Bureau of Justice Statistics, 1999a, p. 10).

In addition to the economic costs of criminal conduct and drug abuse, there are extensive human costs as well. Substance use is prevalent in North American society. According to the Substance Abuse and Mental Health Administration (SAMHA) National Survey on Drug Abuse for 1996, an estimated 34.8% of the American population 12 years of age or older used an illicit drug and 82.6% used alcohol at least once. Almost 11% reported using an illicit drug and 64.9% reported using alcohol within the past year. Reported use within the previous month was 6% for illicit drugs and 51% for alcohol (Maguire & Pastore, 1998, pp. 69-70). An estimated 15% of Americans are chemically addicted to alcohol or drugs (Yoder, 1990). Each person who is dependent on alcohol or illicit drugs is likely to directly affect family members, friends, or others in an antisocial or criminal manner, compromising the quality of life and causing harm emotionally, financially, and physically to millions of Americans.

Emergency room use and drug-related deaths are other indicators of the extent of human suffering caused by drug abuse. In 1992, the SAMHA Drug Abuse Warning Network (DAWN) estimated 433,493 emergency room episodes involving drug abuse. Medical examiners from 38 metropolitan areas in the U.S. reported 7,532 deaths in 1992 related to drug abuse (Bureau of Justice Statistics, 1999a, p. 31). Concerning the relationship between alcohol/drug abuse and crime, Harwood et al. (1998) estimate that illicit drug and alcohol abuse was responsible for $69.9 billion in crime-related costs in 1992–$57.1 billion for illicit drugs and $12.8 billion for alcohol abuse. These estimates are based on plausible assumptions of the causal relationships between drugs and alcohol and crime.

Considering the financial costs of crime and drug abuse, an effective rehabilitation program potentially could save billions of dollars. Even more importantly, it could save many lives and reduce or eliminate needless suffering for many thousands of Americans.

This article reviews the Transcendental Meditation (TM) program, which has shown promise as an effective rehabilitation method for criminal and drug offenders. The article briefly (a) summarizes the risk factors associated with criminal conduct and substance abuse, (b) reviews the research on effects of the TM technique on these risk factors, and (c) presents tables of the existing studies using the TM technique in rehabilitation settings.

RISK FACTORS FOR CRIME AND SUBSTANCE ABUSE

Researchers and others interested in rehabilitating at-risk youth, juvenile delinquents, adult substance abusers, and criminal offenders have identified a variety of risk factors that may be subject to change through treatment. Prominent among these are: antisocial personality (characterized by egocentric thinking, psychopathology, and/or personality disorders); negative peer associations; interpersonal conflict (e.g., family discord, conflict with significant others); personal distress (e.g., low self-esteem, anxiety, depression, neuroticism, attempted suicide); low level of social achievement (as indicated by marital status, employment status, education, or income); and recent substance abuse. In some correctional institutions, evaluation of such risk factors is used as a diagnostic tool for identifying specific antisocial, addictive, or criminal thinking styles and behaviors susceptible to treatment. Offenders rarely exhibit all the known risk factors, and there are offenders who exhibit none of them (Ross & Fabiano, 1985). Generally, however, the literature indicates an offender will exhibit one or more of the following:

- Greater frequency of substance abuse, and a high percentage of alcohol and drug use associated with criminal acts (Fergusson, Lynskey, & Horwood, 1996; Martin, 1993; Roslund & Larson, 1979)
- Hostility, aggression, violent behavior (Cherek, Moeller, Schnapp, & Dougherty, 1997; Heilbrun, 1979, 1982)
- Impulsiveness (Arbuthnot, Gordon, & Jurkovic, 1987; McDavid & McCandless, 1962; Stanford & Barratt, 1992; White et al., 1994)
- Pro-criminal attitudes, beliefs, and thinking style (Barriga & Gibbs, 1996; Barriga, Landau, Stinson, Liau, & Gibbs, 2000; Field, 1986; Gibbs, Potter, & Goldstein, 1995)
- Negative peer associations (Agnew, 1985; Elliott, Huizinga, & Ageton, 1985)
- Poor performance at work or school (Andrews, 1990; Brier, 1995)
- Poor quality of family life, including marital conflict between parents, large family size, criminality in one or more parents, insufficient supervision, parental indifference, lack of attachment to parents, and inconsistent or harsh discipline, including child abuse (Hindelang, 1973; Hirschi, 1969; Hoge, Andrews, & Leshied, 1996; Patterson, 1982; Rankin & Kern, 1994; Snyder & Patterson, 1987; West & Farrington, 1973; Wilson, 1980)
- Low moral reasoning (Arbuthnot et al., 1987; Blasi, 1980; Jennings, Kilkenny, & Kohlberg, 1983)
- Low self-concept (Arbuthnot et al., 1987; Fitts & Hamner, 1969)
- Low ego development (Loevinger, 1976; Noam, Paget, Valiant, Borst, & Bartok, 1994)
- Inadequate coping or adaptive skills (Field, 1986; Rutter, 1987, 1990; White, 1967; Zamble & Porporino, 1990)
- Mental health problems (Hodgins, Mednick, Brennan, Schulsinger, & Engberg, 1996; Marzuk, 1996; Toch & Adams, 1986)
- Low verbal and performance intelligence (Hirschi, 1969; Hirschi & Hindelang, 1977; Quay, 1987b; West & Farrington, 1973)

ELIMINATING STRESS AND ENHANCING DEVELOPMENT

Generally, recidivism rates for parolees and relapse rates for substance addictions in adults are greater than 50% (e.g., Emrick, 1974, 1975; Hunt,

Barnett, & Branch, 1971; Langan & Cunniff, 1992; Maguire & Pastore, 1995; Marlatt & Gordon, 1985). Concerning the high failure rate of addiction treatments, Greaves (1980) comments that it is too much to expect a substance abuser to give up the pleasurable, stress-relieving effects of the substance in exchange for unguaranteed promises of a better life sometime in the future. He and other authors (e.g., Klajner, Hartman, & Sobell, 1984; Marlatt & Marques, 1977) recommend meditation as a stress-reducing, pleasurable replacement for substance abuse and addiction. Alexander, Davies et al. (1990) suggest that practice of the TM technique unfreezes delayed development and eliminates stress while simultaneously enhancing psychophysiological and psychosocial functioning. As a result of regular practice of this program, populations that are normally resistant to change (such as maximum-security inmates and chronic substance abusers) experience dramatic personal growth that is associated with increased inner contentment and more appropriate social behavior (see Goodman, Walton, Orme-Johnson, & Boyer, this volume; Alexander & Orme-Johnson, this volume; Alexander, Walton et al., this volume).

GENERAL RESEARCH ON THE TM TECHNIQUE

Over the past 30 years, researchers investigating mechanisms and potential applications of the TM technique have focused on a wide range of potential effects in the areas of physical, mental, and societal health. The efficacy of the technique in reducing substance misuse, overcoming addiction, and rehabilitating criminal offenders is impressive but is less surprising when the wide range of its benefits in non-offender populations is examined. Alleviating substance abuse and criminal behavior can be considered only two among the many psychological and physiological outcomes of the TM technique that enhance overall well-being (Alexander, Davies et al., 1990). For example, research on a variety of populations shows that practice of the TM technique results in changes such as the following:

- reduced use of cigarettes, alcohol, and drugs (Alexander, Robinson et al., 1994; A. Aron & E. N. Aron, 1980; Gelderloos, Walton, Orme-Johnson, & Alexander, 1991; O'Connell & Alexander, 1994)
- reduced hostility and aggression (Abrams, 1989; Abrams & Siegel, 1978; R. E. Ferguson, 1989a, b; Gore, Abrams, & Ellis, 1989; Hahn & Whalen, 1989; Ramirez, 1989)
- reduced impulsiveness (Haratani & Henmi, 1990; Marcus, 1977)
- reduced rule infractions among incarcerated offenders (Abrams & Siegel, 1978; Ballou, 1977; R. E. Ferguson, 1989a, b).
- reduced cognitive distortions (pro-criminal thinking errors) (Hawkins et al., this volume)

- improved performance at school in cognitively and economically disadvantaged children (Jackson, 1977; Nataraj & Radhamani, 1989; Overbeck & Tönnies, 1989)
- improved quality of family and social life (E. N. Aron & A. Aron, 1982; Aron, Orme-Johnson, & Brubaker, 1981; Broome, 1989; Marcus, 1977; Suarez, 1989)
- higher levels of principled moral reasoning (Nidich, Ryncarz, Abrams, Orme-Johnson, & Wallace, 1983)
- better overall mental health, as indicated by increased self-actualization (Alexander, Rainforth & Gelderloos, 1991), ego development (Alexander, Walton et al., this volume; Alexander & Orme-Johnson, this volume; Chandler, 1990), and self-esteem (Ramirez, 1989; Turnbull & Norris, 1982; van den Berg & Mulder, 1976)
- improved abstract thinking ability and higher tolerance for ambiguity (Shecter, 1977; So & Orme-Johnson, 2000)
- greater emotional maturity (Aron et al., 1981; Fehr, Nerstheimer, & Torber, 1977b; Ramirez, 1989)
- better overall mental health, as indicated by reduced neuroticism (Abrams & Siegel, 1978; Ljunggren, 1977; van den Berg & Mulder, 1976), reduced depression (Brooks & Scarano, 1985; Ferguson & Gowan, 1976), and reduced anxiety (Eppley, Abrams, & Shear, 1989)
- increased verbal and nonverbal intelligence (Aron et al., 1981; Cranson et al., 1991; So & Orme-Johnson, 2000; Tjoa, 1975)
- increased field independence (Alexander, Walton et al., this volume; Alexander & Orme-Johnson, this volume; Fergusson, 1992; Hawkins et al., this volume; Orme-Johnson & Granieri, 1977; Pelletier, 1974, 1974 April), which has been associated with a greater sense of separate identity and greater discreteness between affect and ideation (Witkin, Oltman, Raskin, & Karp, 1971)
- increased positive affect and cognition (Ahlström, 1991; Gelderloos, Goddard, Ahlström, & Jacoby, 1987)
- decreased biochemical indicators of stress (Jevning, Pirkle, & Wilson, 1977; Jevning, Wells, Wilson, & Guich, 1987; Wallace & Benson, 1972; Jevning, Wilson, & Davidson, 1978; Wallace, Benson, & Wilson, 1971)
- increased physiological balance (MacLean et al., 1997; Subramanyam & Porkodi, 1980)

REHABILITATION STUDIES ON THE TRANSCENDENTAL MEDITATION PROGRAM

The focus of this review is the two detailed tables of existing studies on the effects of the TM program in the field of rehabilitation. Table 1 (studies in prisons) and Table 2 (studies on use of addictive substances) summarize 39 studies from 1969 to 1998. The research in each table is presented in chronological

Table 1: Research on the TM Program and Criminal Rehabilitation

Author(s), Year Research Completed, (Year Published), Location	Study Description	Summary of Results, Limitations, and Implications
1. Orme-Johnson & Moore, 1971, (this volume), La Tuna Federal Penitentiary, Texas, USA	A 2-month, longitudinal, controlled study with offenders in their early 20s to early 30s incarcerated for drug-related crimes, N = 19: 5 regular meditators, 7 irregular meditators, 7 non-meditating controls.	TM Ss decreased in SSRR significantly more than irregular TM Ss ($p < 0.001$) or controls ($p < 0.05$). Regular TM Ss showed significant reductions on two MMPI scales: on scale 7 (Psychasthenia, i.e., obsessive-compulsive behavior, $p < 0.025$) over irregular TM Ss and controls, and on scale 10 (Social Introversion, i.e., increased social outgoingness, $p < 0.05$) over controls. The study used an unfakeable psychophysiological measurement. Physiological stability and psychological health as a result of practice of TM are likely to counter drug use.
2. Ballou, 1973, (1977), Stillwater State Prison, Minnesota, USA	A 10-month randomly-assigned, longitudinal study of incarcerated offenders under treatment for drug dependency and emotional disturbance, N = 66: 30 TM, 36 controls (20 interested in TM and 16 not interested).	TM Ss had reduced anxiety relative to controls ($p < 0.001$) on STAI; two-thirds reduction in prison rule infractions in experimental Ss compared to no change in controls after 10 months ($p = 0.10$); significant increase in positive recreational and educational activities compared to controls after 6 months ($p < 0.01$). Also, reduced use of cigarettes and drugs were reported. Attrition rate of about 30% among experimental Ss. The TM technique appears to be effective in reducing anxiety, rule infractions, and drug use and increasing motivation for self-improvement.
3. Childs, 1973, (1977), USA	Two-month, uncontrolled, clinical study of 5 juvenile offenders (ages 14-17) charged with possession of marijuana who were recruited for the study by court officer.	Cessation or reduction of drug use, decreased anxiety ($p < 0.05$) (TMAS), positive change on self-report and parents' reports on behavior ($p < 0.05$), increased self-regard ($p < 0.05$) (POI). Limited sample size, no controls. TM program appears to be a useful adjunct to juvenile offender rehabilitation programs.

Table 1 (continued)

Author(s), Year Research Completed, (Year Published), Location	Study Description	Summary of Results, Limitations, and Implications
4. Cunningham & Koch, 1973, (1977), Lompoc Federal Correctional Institution, California, USA	A fifteen-week, longitudinal, controlled, multiwave study of 78 incarcerated offenders (mean age = 25), 30 TM Ss and 48 control Ss.	Significant reduction of state and trait anxiety (STAI) after 6 and 15 weeks of TM practice ($p < 0.001$) compared to controls at pretest and to TM Ss own pretest score ($p < 0.001$). Significant decreases in tension and depression (SQ), as well as increases in relaxation and optimism on author-constructed questionnaire. Control Ss were not posttested. The regularity of TM practice correlated to reduction in state ($r = -0.39$) and trait ($r = -0.34$) anxiety.
5. Ramirez, 1975, (1989), Milan Federal Correctional Institution, Michigan, USA	A 2.5-month, randomized, longitudinal study of 68 incarcerated drug-addicted offenders, 19-33 years of age. Nineteen regular meditators, 15 irregular meditators, and 31 controls. Half of TM Ss received ongoing regular drug treatment while other half received TM only.	Regular TM Ss had greatest change, followed by less change in irregular TM Ss, followed by no change in controls. There were strong significant correlations between regularity of TM practice and increased self-esteem ($p = 0.001$) (RSE), emotional stability and maturity (e.g., reduced neuroticism, $p = 0.002$ and depression, $p = 0.008$) (MMPI), and reduced aggression (e.g., indirect hostility, $p = 0.001$, suspicion, $p = 0.0002$, assault, $p = 0.004$) (BDHI). The TM technique appears to be effective in improving mental health in drug-addicted offenders.
6. Ferguson, 1977,1978, (1989a, b) Massachusetts Correctional Institution, Walpole, Massachusetts, USA	A 3-month, longitudinal, uncontrolled study of 25 incarcerated offenders with an average age of 29.	Significant reductions in anxiety ($p < 0.01$ to 0.05) (STAI) and hostility ($p < 0.02$ to 0.05) (BDHI) depending upon grouping according to regularity; improvements in sleep patterns; substantial reductions in rule infractions. Informal reports of decreased drug use were received by prison counseling psychologists and program staff. Follow-up research showed reduced self-reported drug use. Study had a small sample size and lacked control group. The TM program reduces anxiety and hostility in incarcerated offenders.

Author(s), Year Research Completed, (Year Published), Location	Study Description	Summary of Results, Limitations, and Implications
7. Abrams & Siegel, 1976, (1978), Folsom State Prison, California, USA	Longitudinal, cross-validated, 3-month study of 115 incarcerated medium- and maximum-security offenders.	Significant reduction in state and trait anxiety in TM Ss (first and second groups) over controls ($p < 0.001$, $p < 0.001$) (STAI), in neuroticism ($p < 0.001$, $p < 0.01$) (EPI); in negativism ($p < 0.001$, $p < 0.001$) (BDHI); and better quality of sleep ($p < 0.05$, $p < 0.05$). No significant change in smoking. TM is an effective agent for producing a stable and integrated condition of mind and personality in incarcerated offenders.
8. Abrams, 1976-7, (1989), Folsom State Prison, California, USA	Longitudinal follow-up of incarcerated TM practitioners at 6 months (N = 23) and 9 months (N = 14).	Significant continued reductions ($p < 0.05$) in state and trait anxiety, neuroticism, and hostility. Trend to less heavy smoking and less insomnia. Small subject number and lack of control Ss. The TM technique has lasting beneficial effects on personality and behavior.
9. Alexander, Walton, & Goodman, 1982, (this volume); Alexander & Orme-Johnson, (this volume); Alexander, Rainforth et al., (this volume). (All from dissertation of first author), Massachusetts Correctional Institution, Walpole, Massachusetts, USA	Study included three designs: (1) cross-sectional, (2) voluntary, double-blind longitudinal, and (3) retrospective recidivism study. Subjects were 160 maximum- security prisoners.	Cross-sectional: TM Ss scored higher on ego development, lower on anxiety and psychopathy, than interested or non-interested controls. Longitudinal: TM Ss significantly improved over a 1-year period on a measure of self-development ($p < 0.0003$) and showed decreased pathological symptoms ($p < 0.05$) in comparison to wait-list controls and a non-meditating sample. During the 5-year period examined during the study, the recidivism rate of the TM parolees was significantly lower ($p < 0.01$) than four other treatment groups. Rigorously designed study though not randomized. TM is more effective than other prison programs in developing personality and mental health, and reducing recidivism.
10. A. Aron & E. N. Aron, 1982, (1989), USA	A 9-month longitudinal, controlled study of 17 juvenile African American males (ages 13-16) on probation.	Significant reduction of trait anxiety in TM group ($p < 0.05$) (STAI), Ss reported life was "somewhat better" to "much better" since learning TM. Small sample size. Reduced anxiety and better quality of life may support prosocial behavior.

Table 1 (continued)

Author(s), Year Research Completed, (Year Published), Location	Study Description	Summary of Results, Limitations, and Implications
11. Gore, Abrams, & Ellis, 1984, (1989), Vermont State Prisons, USA	Study had 3 designs: (1) 2-week random assignment, partial crossover, (2) 6-month random selection, quasi-longitudinal studies of 179 incarcerated offenders (average age 23), and (3) 4-month randomly-selected, within-group study of 18 correctional officers.	(1) TM Ss showed significant improvement over controls on Paranoid Anxiety, $p < 0.025$ (EPI); Sleep Disturbances, $p < 0.0005$ (SC); Locus of Control, $p < 0.025$ (LC). (2) TM Ss had reduced Hostility, $p < 0.002$ (BDHI), Paranoid Anxiety, $p < 0.0001$, Sleep Disturbances, $p < 0.0001$, and Increased Locus of Control, $p < 0.0001$. (3) Correctional officers showed significant reduction in Hostility ($p < 0.05$), Paranoid Anxiety ($p < 0.001$), and Sleep Disturbances ($p < 0.005$). TM is immediately effective and is beneficial for both prison inmates and staff.
12. Bleick & Abrams, (1987), Department of Corrections, California, USA	Retrospective, archival recidivism study of 259 male felon parolees who practiced the TM program, compared to 259 matched control parolees and to over 37,000 statewide parolees. Study controlled for over 20 demographic variables. Mean age was 33 at time of TM instruction. Followed up to 6 years after release.	TM practitioner parolees had better parole outcomes compared to statewide parolees at 6 months ($p < 0.004$), 1 year ($p < 0.004$), and 2 years ($p < 0.002$) and compared to matched control parolees at 1 year ($p = 0.0007$), 3 years ($p = 0.007$), and 5 years ($p = 0.02$). Self-selected experimental group. Reduced recidivism among TM practitioners is corroborated by beneficial effects of the TM technique on recognized risk factors for criminal behavior seen in other research on incarcerated offenders.
13. Anklesaria & King, 1989 (this volume), Senegal	Anecdotal report, with archival data from one prison, on nationwide implementation of Consciousness-Based rehabilitation in 31 of 34 prisons, involving over 11,000 inmates and 900 administrative and security personnel.	Overall, reports on inmates of marked reductions in insomnia, negativity, rule infractions, escape attempts, aggression, fights, and murders, and a marked increase in positivity, happiness, self-confidence, and social interactions. In one prison which reviewed archives, there was an 81% reduction in rule infractions and a 43% reduction in medical usage after 3 months of TM practice. Reports on personnel included increased self-confidence, self-control, conscientiousness, health, esprit de corps, and respect for superior officers, and reduced absenteeism and disciplinary infractions.

Author(s), Year Research Completed, (Year Published), Location	Study Description	Summary of Results, Limitations, and Implications
14. Hawkins et al., 1998, (this volume), Federal Prison, Curaçao, Netherlands Antilles	A 4.5-month longitudinal, controlled study of 149 incarcerated offenders with an average age of 28 years.	TM Ss showed a significant decrease in Cognitive Distortion factor (p = 0.036, one-tailed) (HIT) and significant increase in Intelligence-Related Measures factor (GEFT and ITT) (p = 0.05), with a trendwise increase on Psychological Well-Being factor (p = 0.082) (MHI). No significant changes on factors Aggression, Impulsiveness, and Psychological Distress. Very low compliance to treatment and high attrition at posttest (not due to self-selection). The TM technique can reduce a risk factor for criminal behavior while simultaneously increasing a protective factor.
15. Rainforth, Alexander, & Cavanaugh, 1998, (this volume), USA	A 15-year follow-up on 247 parolees from Bleick and Abrams' (1987) study. 120 TM and 127 control Ss were matched on parole year, race, offense, prior commitment record, age, and drug use history.	Survival analysis showed parolees who had learned TM had substantially lower reconviction rates (46.7%) compared to controls (66.9%) and took longer to recidivate (3 years compared to 2.7 years). Further analysis of the data using the Cox proportional hazards model controlled for 20 criminal and social history background variables, estimated the reduction at 37% (p < 0.007). TM practice enhances long-term survival of parolees.

EPI = Eysenck Personality Inventory; GEFT = Group Embedded Figures Test; HIT = How I Think Questionnaire; ITT = Zhang's Inspection Time Test; LC = Levenson's Locus of Control Scales; MHI = Mental Health Inventory; MMPI = Minnesota Multiphasic Personality Inventory; POI = Shostrom's Personal Orientation Inventory; RSE = Rosenberg's Self-Esteem Scale; SQ = Shelley Questionnaire; SSRR = spontaneous skin resistance response; STAI = Spielberger's State-Trait Anxiety Inventory; TMAS = Taylor Manifest Anxiety Inventory

order, determined either by the date the study was completed or the date of publication (given in parentheses). The first column gives the author(s), dates, and location of the study. The second column provides the details of the experiment such as design, subject population, and demographic information. The third column summarizes the main results of the study, any limitations of the research design, and the implications of the study for the field of rehabilitation.

Table 2: Research on the TM Program and Substance Use

Author(s), Year Research Completed, (Year Published), Location	Study Description	Summary of Results, Limitations, and Implications
1. Winquist, 1969, (1977), USA	Retrospective survey using a questionnaire designed by Harvard Medical School. Ss were 484 TM program participants between 15 and 30 years of age; 30% were regular drug users 3 months before starting TM (marijuana, hallucinogens, and hard drugs).	83% of respondents completely discontinued drug use, 15.5% reduced drug use by 50%, 1.5% maintained or increased drug use. Retrospective study of highly motivated Ss attending advanced TM course. The TM program significantly reduces usage of various types of drugs, including hard drugs.
2. Benson & Wallace, 1970, (1972), USA	Retrospective survey from 6 months prior to learning TM to 20 months average time meditating. Data analyzed by independent data processing company. Ss were 1,862 TM technique participants between 19 and 28 years of age. Reported on marijuana, hallucinogens, narcotics, amphetamines, barbiturates, hard liquor, cigarettes, and prescribed medication.	Decreased number of drug users in all categories studied. The longer the TM practice, the greater the reduction in use. After 21 months of TM, most Ss (over 90% in most categories) had stopped using and selling drugs, including prescribed drugs. Retrospective study of highly motivated individuals participating in advanced TM courses. Implies that TM technique is attractive to youthful population and that alleviation of substance misuse is a positive side effect of the practice of the TM program.
3. Graham, Peterman, & Scarff, 1971, Canada	Retrospective survey from unspecified period before starting TM up to 3 years after and 2-month within-group longitudinal study; 431 TM Ss in retrospective study, 15 Ss in longitudinal study. Ss between 16 and 30 years of age. Ss reported on tobacco, alcohol, cannabis, hallucinogen, hard drug use.	82.2% of respondents reported cessation or decrease of tobacco use, 93.6% for alcohol, 97.8% for cannabis, 99.3% for hallucinogens, and 100% for hard drugs; 89.3% of respondents attributed reduction to the practice of the TM technique. Retrospective study of self-selected respondents using non-standardized instruments. TM technique leads to spontaneous reduced usage of substances in beginning and long-term practitioners.
4. Brautigam, 1972, (1977), Sweden	Random assignment to matched groups, partial cross-validation study (the second group learning TM after 3 months) with 20 drug users from low socioeconomic backgrounds, ages 17-24. Ss reported on cannabis, hallucinogen, amphetamine, and hard liquor use. Study was from 6-9 months prior to TM instruction until 3-6 months after.	Decreased drug use for TM Ss compared to increased use during 3-month waiting period for control group ($p < 0.01$). Delayed-start TM Ss showed similar decreased drug use over second 3 months. TM Ss also showed significantly increased psychological heath and increased positive use of leisure time. Delayed-start control Ss insisted on learning TM after 3 months instead of the planned 6 months. TM program reduces substance misuse and improves psychological well-being.

Author(s), Year Research Completed, (Year Published), Location	Study Description	Summary of Results, Limitations, and Implications
5. Lazar, Farwell, & Farrow, 1972 (1977), USA	Longitudinal, within-group, recurrent institutional cycle study of 60 TM program participants, ages ranging from 15 to 57. From before TM instruction and at 4 weeks, 8 weeks, and 12 weeks after. Ss reported on tobacco, alcohol, hallucinogen, barbiturate, amphetamine, and narcotic use.	Ss showed reduced anxiety ($p = 0.004$) in both high and low anxiety; reduced drug use of all types ($p = 0.001$); reduced marijuana use ($p = 0.001$); reduced cigarette use ($p = 0.035$); reduced alcohol use ($p = 0.01$); high correlation between decreased anxiety and decreased drug usage ($r = .71$, $p = 0.019$); regular meditators improved more than irregular meditators. Ss were self-selected. The TM program appears to produce initial sharp drop in substance use followed by a continual gradual decline.
6. Dhanaraj, 1973, (1989), Canada	Retrospective survey mailed to 200 randomly selected TM Ss with at least 3 months practice; 108 respondents reported on tobacco, alcohol, cannabis, hallucinogen, amphetamine, barbiturate, and other drug use.	Results showed 37% ceased smoking, 25% stopped drinking, 53% stopped using cannabis, 38% stopped using hallucinogens, 33% stopped using amphetamines, 60% stopped using barbiturates, and 50% stopped using other drugs. 74% credited TM with helping them to quit. Self-selected return of questionnaire, lack of controls, lack of statistical analysis. Substantial reduction in substance use credited to TM.
7. Katz, 1974, (1977), USA	Eight-month, longitudinal, mail-in survey of 150 TM Ss and 110 untreated controls matched by age and gender. Ss reported on substance use (cannabis and alcohol) from 2 months before TM instruction until 6 months after.	For TM participants, greater reductions in use of marijuana ($p < 0.01$) at month 1 and greater reductions at month 8 ($p < 0.006$) versus no consistent change for controls; alcohol use reduced in TM Ss at month 8 ($p < 0.05$). Prevention of marijuana use: significantly less use ($p < 0.05$) at month 8 in TM Ss who were non-users at pretest compared to non-user controls. Self-selected grouping and survey responding. Reductions in substance abuse are correlated with regularity of TM practice; TM acts preventively in non-users.
8. Myers & Eisner, 1974, USA	4-month, longitudinal design with random assignment from a large pool of volunteers. 3 groups: 60 TM Ss, 60 karate participants, and 60 similarly motivated no-treatment controls. Ss reported on marijuana, psychedelic, upper, downer, and hard drug use.	After 4 months, there was a significant drop in one or more categories of substance abuse in the TM participants relative to the controls ($p < 0.05$). The effect was largest with psychedelics, uppers, downers, and hard drugs ($p < 0.001$). No significant reductions were noted in the drug usage of the karate group. No direct statistical comparison between TM and karate groups. People who start TM become less dependent on harmful drugs in comparison to equally motivated controls.

Table 2 (continued)

Author(s), Year Research Completed, (Year Published), Location	Study Description	Summary of Results, Limitations, and Implications
9. Schenkluhn & Geisler, 1974, (1977), Germany	Retrospective questionnaire of drug use from 2 years prior to learning TM technique and monthly drug use reports for 1-year experimental period. Ss were 76 drug users, ages 15-23, attending a program at a crisis aid institute. Data collected by workers of the drug rehabilitation center. Ss reported on cannabis, LSD, amphetamine, barbiturate, cocaine, opiate, prescribed drug, and other drug use.	57.6% reduction of all types of drugs after 12 months ($p < 0.001$), cannabis use reduced 58.2%, hallucinogens reduced 90.8%, amphetamines and barbiturates reduced 96.3%, and opiates reduced 78.1%; 70% of Ss reported no drug use after 9 months practice of TM. Baseline gained retrospectively; no controls. TM has a strong positive effect on drug usage among juveniles.
10. Shafii, Lavely, & Jaffe, 1974, (1974, 1975, 1976), USA	Retrospective survey by independent researchers of 126 TM Ss and 90 peer-selected controls. Ss matched on age, gender, and educational level. TM Ss partitioned by number of months practicing TM: 0-3 months, 4-6 months, 7-12 months, 13-24 months, and 25-39 months. Ss reported on marijuana, alcohol, and tobacco use from 12 months prior to TM instruction and up to 39 months after.	Cessation or reduction of marijuana use in TM practitioners by 50% after 3 and 12 months ($p < 0.05$) and 75% after 36 months ($p < 0.01$) compared to 17% cessation or reduction in controls. Cessation or reduction of alcohol use in TM Ss by 25% after 3 months ($p < 0.05$). Up to 39 months after learning TM, Ss reduced beer and wine consumption ($p < 0.0003$) compared to controls and reduced hard liquor consumption ($p < 0.004$) compared to controls. Cessation of tobacco use by 43% in TM practitioners after 3 months ($p < 0.05$) and by 57% after 6 months ($p < 0.01$) compared to 3% of controls; TM practitioners, during 1-39 months after learning TM, significantly ceased or reduced smoking compared to controls ($p < 0.02$). The longer a person practices TM, the higher probability of discontinued drug, alcohol, and tobacco use.
11. Friend, (1977), USA	Two-year, cross-sectional study with untreated controls of 128 long-term and 27 new TM participants compared to 38 non-meditating, employed adults. Survey study on "work behavior," with deception procedures to disguise the TM aspect of the study. Author-constructed questionnaire regarding length of time meditating, mild and serious illnesses, usage of beer, hard liquor, and tobacco.	Length-of-time of TM practice correlated negatively with beer ($p < 0.03$), mixed drinks ($p < 0.02$), and cigarette consumption ($p < 0.003$) in long-term group, while the new TM and control groups had mostly comparable levels. Correlational study findings not biased by pro-TM attitude. TM reduces need for stimulation and reduces motivation to use substances.

Author(s), Year Research Completed, (Year Published), Location	Study Description	Summary of Results, Limitations, and Implications
12. Ottens, (1975), USA	11-week random-assignment study of 54 college students in three equal groups: TM, a smoking cessation class (SC), and untreated controls. Ss reported on tobacco use.	Groups found to be significantly different at posttest ($p < 0.01$) with a substantial decrease in tobacco use for TM and SC groups compared to untreated controls. TM group received no follow-up and was instructed to smoke as desired. SC group received 6 sessions of a smoking cessation treatment. Study could have benefited from a TM-SC group. TM practice is as spontaneously effective in reducing smoking as a deliberate smoking-cessation program.
13. Monahan, (1975), USA	Clinical evaluation of 12 chronic drug users with strong drug dependency who were instructed in TM program as part of psychiatric drug treatment program. Ss reported on all classes of drugs.	Range of clinical experience: from regular TM meditators who never again experienced craving for drugs and remained abstinent, to irregular TM meditators who slipped back to drug use. Limited sample size. The practice of the TM technique helps a person to progress more rapidly in drug rehabilitation.
14. Monahan, (1977), USA	Retrospective survey research using a mailed survey of 422 students and professionals in the Philadelphia area (264 TM Ss and 158 control Ss). Ss reported on use of all classes of illegal drugs, alcohol, cigarettes, and prescribed drugs from 3 months prior to TM instruction to 3 years or longer after.	Reduced drug use for regular TM practitioners compared to controls: Caffeine ($p < 0.001$), nicotine ($p < 0.01$), soft alcohol ($p < 0.001$), hard alcohol ($p < 0.01$), prescribed tranquilizers ($p < 0.001$), prescribed analgesics ($p < 0.05$), marijuana ($p < 0.001$), hallucinogens ($p < 0.10$), stimulants ($p < 0.05$), sedatives ($p < 0.05$), all prescribed drugs ($p < 0.01$), and all illegal drugs excluding marijuana ($p < 0.05$). Prescribed antidepressants (NS), prescribed sleeping pills (NS), and opiates (NS) all had very small sample sizes. TM practice reduces need for stimulants and promotes a healthful lifestyle, including reduced use of legal and illegal drugs.
15. Throll, 1977, (1989), New Zealand	4-month, longitudinal study of 30 TM Ss and 15 untreated control Ss, 15-20 years of age. Ss reported on alcohol, tobacco, cannabis, hallucinogen, and prescribed drug use.	Significantly improved personality ($p = 0.01$ to .05) (16PF), reduced anxiety ($p = 0.01$) (STAI), substantial reduction in alcohol, tobacco, cannabis, hallucinogens, and prescribed drug use compared to no change in controls. Self-selected groups. TM promotes mental health and reduces health risk factors, such as substance use, in a highly peer-influenced age group.

Table 2 (continued)

Author(s), Year Research Completed, (Year Published), Location	Study Description	Summary of Results, Limitations, and Implications
16. Davies, 1978, Australia	5-month and 10-month longitudinal studies of 45 high school students from 2 schools. 17 self-selected TM Ss and 28 control Ss matched on age, gender, and educational level. Ss had average age of 16. Ss reported on wine and beer, liquor, tobacco, narcotic, amphetamine, barbiturate, analgesic, and prescribed drug use.	Substantial but not significant differences on anxiety (STAI), personality (IPAT), self-actualization (POI) in TM Ss compared to controls. Significant difference in fluid intelligence ($p < 0.01$) in one school. TM participants as a group showed an overall reduction in drug use (hard liquor, marijuana, barbiturates, analgesics and prescribed drugs) in contrast to increase in controls. Small sample size. Experimental group included regular TM practitioners only. TM program reduces drug use in highly peer-influenced population.
17. Geisler, (1978), Germany	26-month longitudinal controlled study of drug consumption with 146 juvenile clients of an outpatient drug clinic. Ss had age range of 14-25.	Regular TM practitioners showed reduced drug use ($p < 0.01$), less neuroticism ($p < 0.05$) (FPI), and improvement in self-evaluation ($p < 0.001$) compared to irregular meditators and controls. Self-selected groups. TM promotes mental health, self-development, and reduced need for stimulants.
18. Taub, Steiner, Weingarten, & Walton, 1978, (1994), USA	2-year random assignment of 120 disadvantaged, chronic alcoholic volunteers, with an average age of 44, into four approximately equal groups: the TM technique, electromyographic biofeedback (EMG), neurotherapy (NT), or regular treatment (RT). Three-month inpatient treatment with follow-up over 18-month period.	After 18 months complete abstainers formed 65% of TM group, 55% of EMG, 28% of NT, and 25% of RT. TM and EMG groups combined compared to NT and RT groups combined had significantly more abstinent Ss at 6 ($p < 0.02$), 12 ($p < 0.057$), and 18 ($p < 0.009$) months. TM Ss improved significantly on 4 of 6 subscales of POMS, EMG subjects on 2. Reliability of daily drinking disposition report in six months follow-up groups was not as accurate as for the subjects studied monthly. TM is an effective and appropriate treatment modality for disadvantaged and chronically addicted populations.
19. Nidich, 1980, (1989), USA	10-week longitudinal study of 51 college students with a mean age of 20.5. 3 groups: 15 Science of Creative Intelligence course participants who also learned TM (SCI-TM), 25 SCI course participants who did not learn TM (SCI), and 11 personal adjustment class participants (PA). Non-users (cannabis or alcohol) were excluded from study.	Reduction in marijuana use by SCI-TM group over SCI group ($p < 0.025$) and PA group ($p < 0.01$); SCI group also reduced marijuana use compared to PA group ($p < 0.025$). Reduction in beer and liquor use by SCI-TM group over SCI group ($p < 0.025$, NS, respectively) and PA group ($p < 0.01$, $p < 0.05$); SCI group over PA group (NS, $p < 0.05$). Greatest benefit results from the practice of the TM technique.

Author(s), Year Research Completed, (Year Published), Location	Study Description	Summary of Results, Limitations, and Implications
20. Bielefeld, 1979, (1989), USA	Survey of 42 drug, alcohol, or gambling addicts, and mental patients in a hospital vocational rehabilitation unit who had learned the TM technique compared to 233 control Ss. (All those who had been discharged from the medical center for at least 2 months were evaluated.)	TM group was more often outpatient than inpatient ($p < 0.01$), more often employed or between jobs ($p < 0.01$), and less often incarcerated or deceased (NS). TM group was self-selected. TM is not just a self-help technique but a meta-support system that helps patients make better use of support systems like vocation.
21. Farinelli, 1981, (1989), Italy	2-year, retrospective, cross-sectional study of 107 TM program participants and 100 peer-selected controls. Surveyed medical history, physical health past and present, present psychological health, relationships, health risk factors, and use of tobacco, alcohol, caffeine, and drugs.	TM Ss reported better physical health ($p < 0.02$ to 0.001), better mental health ($p < 0.001$), better social relationships ($p < 0.001$), lower use of prescribed drugs ($p < 0.02$), lower usage and higher cessation of cigarettes, alcohol, drugs, and caffeine compared to controls (NS). Long-term practice of TM supports better physical and mental health, improves social behavior, and reduces health risk factors.
22. Browne, Fougere, Roxburgh, Bird, & Lovell-Smith, 1983, (1989), New Zealand	Mail survey to 1,289 TM practitioners who learned 3-12 months earlier. Ss had ages ranging between 15 and 65. Males and females were in equal number. Ss reported on physical and mental health, and use of alcohol, tobacco, cannabis, LSD, opiates, and prescribed drugs.	64.5% were regular in their TM practice; only 12% had discontinued. 73% claimed mental health had improved since learning TM ($p < 0.001$) and 50% claimed physical health had gotten better ($p < 0.001$). There were significant correlations between improved mental and physical health and regularity and duration of TM practice ($p < 0.001$). Significant decrease in drug use ($p < 0.001$). Study lacked control Ss. Long-term practice of TM improves mental and physical health and reduces health risk factors.
23. Brooks & Scarano, (1985), USA	A 3-month, longitudinal study with random selection of Vietnam veterans suffering from Post-Traumatic Stress Disorder (PTSD) from the Denver Veterans Center, and random assignment of Ss to TM (N = 10) or conventional psychotherapy (N = 8). Ss had average age of 33.	TM Ss had reduced emotional numbness ($p < 0.025$), anxiety ($p < 0.005$) (TMAS), depression ($p < 0.025$) (BDI), and alcohol consumption ($p < 0.005$) relative to the controls. Study had a limited sample size. TM may reduce substance abuse by relieving psychological distress, as indicated by decreased depression, anxiety, emotional numbness, family problems, difficulty in getting a job, insomnia, and overall PTSD symptoms.

Table 2 (continued)

Author(s), Year Research Completed, (Year Published), Location	Study Description	Summary of Results, Limitations, and Implications
24. Royer, 1989, (1994), USA	Longitudinal cohort study with initial on-site and follow-up mail-in questionnaires. 110 TM Ss and 214 control Ss. Ss reported on tobacco consumption levels, including decreased usage and quitting over 20-24 month period.	81% of regular TM Ss quit or decreased smoking after 20-24 months compared to 55% of irregular TM Ss and 33% of controls ($p = 0.0001$). Used mail-in self-reports on smoking and self-selected groups. Even though it is not specifically a smoking-cessation program, the TM technique is an effective method of stopping or decreasing smoking. This study shows the TM technique can reduce smoking for the long-term, in contrast to other programs that commonly have only short-term effects.
25. Alexander et al., (1993), USA	3-month, longitudinal, controlled study of 45 TM practitioners and 41 control Ss at industrial work site with an average age 36.6 years. Ss reported on cigarette and alcohol use, as well as several psychological tests.	Regular TM Ss showed significant reductions over irregular TM Ss and controls on trait anxiety ($p < 0.01$), job-related worries ($p < 0.01$), cigarette use ($p < 0.05$), hard liquor use ($p < 0.05$); and increases in job satisfaction ($p < 0.05$), general health ($p < 0.01$), quality of sleep ($p < 0.0025$), and effectiveness ($p < 0.01$). TM Ss were self-selected and control Ss were volunteered by supervisors or by self-selection. TM is effective in increasing job effectiveness by enhancing mental and physical health and promoting a healthier lifestyle.

DISCUSSION

As seen in Table 1, Table 2, and in studies cited earlier, the TM technique provides a wide range of benefits to individuals, regardless of their status prior to beginning the technique, and the reviewed studies indicate its effectiveness in reducing criminal and addictive behaviors. Combined with the more than 600 studies on the TM technique (cf., Chalmers, Clements, Schenkluhn, & Weinless, 1989; Orme-Johnson & Farrow, 1977; Orme-Johnson, Wallace, & Dillbeck, in press; Wallace, Orme-Johnson, & Dillbeck, 1990), these results support the theory advanced by the founder of the technique that its effects are on the most fundamental levels of mind and body (Maharishi Mahesh Yogi, 1995a).

Taken together, the results reviewed here indicate that the TM program would be valuable in rehabilitation, either as a sole treatment or as an addition to existing criminal rehabilitation and substance abuse programs. It should be emphasized, however, that these results should not be generalized to other meditation and relaxation techniques. Although several types of meditation and relaxation approaches have been used in the treatment of stress-related illness and behavioral disturbances, the level of effectiveness of these approaches varies widely, and recommendations for the use of a specific technique must take this into account. Both direct clinical comparisons and statistical meta- analyses support the hypothesis that different techniques produce different outcomes (Davidson & Schwartz, 1976; Lehrer, Carr, Deepa, & Woolfolk, 1994; Orme-Johnson & Walton, 1998). Even closely related techniques may differ significantly in effectiveness, as indicated in a variety of meta-analyses (Alexander et al., 1991; Alexander, Heaton et al., 1994; Eppley et al., 1989; Dillbeck & Orme-Johnson, 1987; P. C. Ferguson, 1989; Hyman, Feldman, Harris, Levin, & Malloy, 1989; Kottke, Battista, Defriese, & Brekke, 1988; Tobler, 1986; Wells-Parker & Bangert-Drowns, 1990). Reviewing these findings, Orme-Johnson and Walton (1998) report that effect sizes ranged from extremely weak or nonexistent (e.g., Effect size = −.003) to quite strong (e.g., Effect size = .89). In a meta-analysis of effects on trait anxiety, for example, Eppley et al. found that concentration-style meditation techniques had no effect whatsoever, whereas other meditation and relaxation techniques had varying effects. In this comparison, the TM technique had an effect size from 2 to 8 times greater than other meditation techniques, depending on the grouping of the comparison techniques and how the data were controlled (i.e., whether for expectation effects, duration of practice, experimenter bias, strength of experimental design, and other factors). The existing body of research supports the usefulness of the TM technique in the treatment of criminal offenders and substance abusers.

NOTE

1. Transcendental Meditation and TM are registered or common law trademarks licensed to Maharishi Vedic Education Development Corporation and used under sublicense.

AUTHOR'S NOTE

Address correspondence to Mark A. Hawkins, PhD, Jan Sofat 39, Curaçao, Netherlands Antilles, Dutch Caribbean (E-mail: mhawkinsphd@yahoo.com).

Transcendental Meditation in Criminal Rehabilitation and Crime Prevention. Pp. 67-87.

Effects of the *Transcendental Meditation* Program on Neuroendocrine Abnormalities Associated with Aggression and Crime

KENNETH G. WALTON
Maharishi University of Management

DEBRA K. LEVITSKY
Fairfield, Iowa

ABSTRACT Both chronic and acute stress can cause long-lasting abnormalities in the neuroendocrine systems mediating adaptation. These abnormalities, in turn, are thought to contribute to psychological disturbances such as anxiety, depression, and hostility, and to behaviors such as substance abuse, violent aggression, and criminal acts. This article reviews evidence for neuroendocrine abnormalities in aggression and crime, defines stress as it relates to adaptation and behaviors, discusses stress-induced abnormalities in neuroendocrine systems, and reviews evidence that the Transcendental Meditation (TM)[1] program may reduce aggression and crime in part by removing these stress-induced abnormalities. The TM program appears to reverse or remove both the physiological and psychological disturbances arising from stress, thus strengthening the individual's coping abilities and restoring a sense of well-being. These normalizing effects of the Transcendental Meditation program are expected to enhance an individual's resilience and to promote the ability to fulfill desires in socially responsible ways. *[Article copies available for a fee from The Haworth Document Delivery Service: 1-800-HAWORTH. E-mail address: <docdelivery@haworthpress.com> Website: <http://www.HaworthPress.com> © 2003 by The Haworth Press, Inc. All rights reserved.]*

KEYWORDS Violence, aggression, stress, allostatic load, hostility, coping, meditation

Aggressive behavior has been associated with abnormalities in three principal regulatory systems in the body: (a) serotonin systems, (b) catecholamine systems, and (c) the hypothalamic-pituitary-adrenocortical (HPA) axis. Abnormalities in these systems also are known to be induced by stress, either severe, acute stress or chronic low-grade stress. This article examines the possibility that many of the neuroendocrine abnormalities correlated with aggression and crime are the long-term consequences of stress. This approach to understanding aggression may help to elucidate how the Transcendental Meditation (TM) program is able not only to reverse the effects of stress (Jevning, Wilson, & Davidson, 1978; MacLean et al., 1997) but to reduce risk factors for crime and promote rehabilitation as well (see, for review, Hawkins, this volume; Alexander, Walton, & Goodman, this volume; Alexander & Orme-Johnson, this volume). This review begins with a discussion of neuroendocrine abnormalities associated with aggressive, antisocial behaviors. It then examines evidence that stress is the key factor causing such neuroendocrine abnormalities. Finally, it examines evidence that the TM program can reverse these stress-induced abnormalities, leading to greater resistance to stress, and reduced tendencies toward aggression and crime.

NEUROENDOCRINE ABNORMALITIES IN AGGRESSION

Abnormalities of Serotonin Systems Associated with Aggression

Abnormalities in the central nervous system–in particular, abnormalities in the function of the neurotransmitter serotonin–have been linked with aggression and crime in a large number of studies. Decreased function of serotonin (also known as 5-hydroxytryptamine or 5-HT) is highly correlated with aggression and impulsivity across a variety of experimental paradigms in both invertebrates and mammals (Brown, Botsis, & Van Praag, 1994; Copenhaver, Schalock, & Carver, 1978; Kantak, Hegstrand, & Eichelman, 1985; Katz, 1980).

In humans, the most specific behavioral correlate of decreased 5-HT function appears to be an increase in impulsive (unpremeditated) aggression (Brown et al., 1994). Criminals committing impulsive offenses have lower cerebrospinal fluid (CSF) levels of 5-HIAA, the main metabolite of 5-HT, than those committing non-impulsive (premeditated) offenses, indicating decreased 5-HT function in impulsive offenders. Furthermore, the more extreme the aggression, the more pronounced the deficit in 5-HT function. For example, individuals who commit multiple murders have lower levels of CSF

5-HIAA than do those who commit single murders (Linnoila et al., 1983). Impulsive offenders with histories of attempted suicide, which is considered an act of self-directed aggression, have the lowest CSF 5-HIAA levels of any of the above groups (Linnoila et al., 1983).

Moreover, a variety of statistical studies have found self-directed aggression, such as suicide attempts, to correlate with aggression towards others (Brown et al., 1994; Plutchik & van Praag, 1997). That is, individuals who engage in acts of violence towards others are likely to make suicide attempts, and suicidal individuals are likely to engage in acts of violence towards others (Apter et al., 1990; Brown, Goodwin, Ballenger, Goyer, & Major, 1979; Brown et al., 1982; Lidberg, Ruck, Asberg, Scalia-Tomba, & Bertilsson, 1985; Linnoila et al., 1983). Consistent with this, low levels of CSF 5-HIAA have been found in both categories of individuals, i.e., those with histories of suicide attempts as well as those with histories of outwardly directed violent acts.

Low CSF 5-HIAA likely signifies that less serotonin is being synthesized, released, or broken down in the brain and spinal cord, thus indicating diminished activity of serotonin systems. Correlations between low CSF 5-HIAA and aggression suggest that impaired functioning of 5-HT systems could be a causal factor in violent aggressive behavior. Additional evidence provides more direct support for this hypothesis. For example, an increase of serotonin function, as brought about by certain pharmacological treatments, decreases violent aggression (Broderick & Lynch, 1989; Fuller, 1996). Moreover, treatments that diminish serotonin function, such as depletion of the serotonin precursor tryptophan, increase aggression (Bjork, Dougherty, Moeller, Cherek, & Swann, 1999; Cleare & Bond, 1995; Copenhaver et al., 1978).

Abnormalities of Catecholamine Systems Associated with Aggression

The catecholamines norepinephrine and epinephrine play important roles in physiological regulation through their mediation of a variety of activities of the sympathetic nervous system, the adrenal medullary system, and the central nervous system. Through the secretion of these neurotransmitters, the sympathetic nervous system (SNS) also appears to be involved in the expression of aggressive behavior (Haller, Makara, & Kruk, 1998; Sgoifo, de Boer, Haller, & Koolhaas, 1996). Norepinephrine, for example, has been proposed to affect aggression on three levels: (a) the hormonal level, (b) the level of the SNS, and (c) the level of the central nervous system (Haller et al., 1998). Epinephrine secreted hormonally, and both norepinephrine and epinephrine released from neurons in the central nervous system, appear to mediate preparations for a prospective fight, while the SNS ensures the appropriate cardiovascular reaction (Haller et al., 1998). Neurons equipped with one sub-type of adrenergic receptor–the alpha-2-adrenoceptor–have been hypothesized to be responsible for the start and maintenance of aggression, while neurons equipped with another sub-type of adrenergic receptors–the beta-adrenoceptors–promote a situation-dependent fine-tuning (Haller et al., 1998). It has also been noted that while a slight activation of the central noradrenergic system stimulates aggression, a strong activation actually decreases readiness to fight (Haller et al., 1998). In summary, the systems whose actions are mediated by epinephrine and norepinephrine are hypothesized to prepare the organism to answer the demands imposed by fights (Haller et al., 1998).

A variety of studies have reported that greater levels of aggression are associated with altered levels of adrenergic (i.e., SNS) responsiveness to stressors. In studies of both animals (Sgoifo et al., 1996) and normal humans (Gerra et al., 1997), more aggressive individuals exhibited higher adrenergic responsiveness to stressors than did their less aggressive counterparts. However, other human studies comparing adult criminals with noncriminals have found indications of sympathetic underarousal in the criminal group (Raine, Venables, & Williams, 1995). The apparent contradiction in these findings suggests that criminal behavior in general cannot be explained merely as an amplification of normal levels of a trait of aggressiveness. For example, one general theory of criminal and antisocial behavior argues that criminals are characterized by a poorly developed conscience and a reduced sensitivity to punishments relative to noncriminals, and, furthermore, that reductions in both autonomic and central nervous system arousal are psychophysiological correlates of these deficits (Eysenck, 1977).

Other theories of the role of physiological arousal in criminal behavior have attempted to explain only a specific subgroup of criminals (for example, individuals identified as psychopaths) rather than criminality in general. One such theory argues that underarousal could account for pathological stimulation-seeking in the psychopathic criminal (Quay, 1965), while another suggests that under stressful conditions psychopathic criminals are less aroused than non-psychopaths (Lykken, 1957). It is clear that psychopaths are an unusually disturbed class of individuals and that not all criminals are psychopaths (Hare, 1970). However, both those criminals who fit the description of psychopaths (Kegan, 1986) and those who do not may be developmentally delayed; in this sense, psychopaths may be similar to other criminals with regard to the role of stress in altering adaptive systems and retarding self-development (see Conclusion, as well as Alexander & Orme-Johnson, this volume; Alexander, Walton et al., this volume).

Abnormalities of the HPA Axis Associated with Aggression

The HPA axis also shows abnormalities in aggressive individuals and in aggression-related affective states in both animals and humans. Some of the clearest associations are found in animal studies. In juvenile and adolescent rhesus monkeys, for example, aggression levels were positively correlated with plasma levels of ACTH and cortisol, two key hormones mediating activity of the HPA axis in response to physical and psychogenic stressors (Higley et al., 1992).

Similarly, in human studies, states or behaviors associated with aggression, such as hostility (Baron, 1974; Buss & Durkee, 1957; Costa, Stone, McCrae, Dembroski, & Williams, 1987; Ranchor, Sanderman, Bouma, Buunk, & van den Heuvel, 1997) and alcohol consumption (Gustafson, 1994; Lang, 1993; White, 1997), have been correlated with elevated cortisol secretion. For example, higher plasma cortisol levels were correlated with greater hostility, irritability, and resentment (Gerra et al., 1996). Moreover, in a comparison of urinary excretion of cortisol, a good indicator of HPA axis activity, men with high levels of hostility had a 3-fold larger ratio of daytime to nighttime excretion rates than did low-hostile men (Pope & Smith, 1991). Elevated levels of cortisol also are found in alcoholics previously incarcerated for acts of violence, as compared with either non-violent alcoholics or violent alcoholics who have never been incarcerated (Buydens-Branchey & Branchey, 1992). The absence of elevated cortisol in this latter group, however, may suggest that incarceration itself contributes to the elevated cortisol, consistent with the known association between incarceration and anxiety stress.

Thus, aggression is associated with abnormalities in the serotonin and catecholamine systems and in the HPA axis. Stress, too, of both the acute and chronic variety, is associated with abnormalities in these systems. Before discussing the association between stress and abnormalities in these systems, however, we present a definition of stress and a broader view of how it is linked to behavior and disease.

STRESS, HOMEOSTASIS, AND ALLOSTATIC LOAD– THEIR ROLES IN DISEASE AND BEHAVIOR

Homeostasis

Understanding stress from a physiological point of view is dependent upon understanding the principles of homeostasis and allostasis, two levels of physiological regulation important for optimum health. All life forms possess a variety of means to preserve their integrity (Goldstein, 1995). A fundamental expression of this ability is the tendency towards *homeostasis*, or internal equilibrium. Homeostasis has been variously defined as the fixity of the *milieu intérieur* (Bernard, 1879), "the constancy of the internal environment" (Goldstein, 1995, p. 8), "the staying power of the body" (Selye, 1978, p. 12), "the normal resting state" (Selye, 1978, p. 76), the coordinated physiological processes that maintain most of the steady states of an organism (Cannon, 1939), or a dynamic and harmonious internal equilibrium (Chrousos & Gold, 1992). The latter two definitions, which emphasize the dynamism and complexity of internal regulation, suggest a richer understanding of internal equilibrium than do the former definitions. This richer understanding, which has developed more recently, is termed allostasis, and will be further discussed below.

In addition to concepts of physiological homeostasis, concepts of psychological homeostasis also have been formulated. From ancient Greek culture, Epicurus declared *ataraxia*–imperturbability of mind or tranquillity of soul–to be a desirable state (Chrousos & Gold, 1992; De Witt, 1954). From a modern perspective, researchers have defined psychological homeostasis as the maintenance of the normal mood state of an individual at rest, wherein all emotions would be alterations from this state (Burchfield, 1979). They also have noted the capacity of the psychic apparatus to initiate both psychic and physiologic processes intended to avert dangers and to assure satisfaction of instinctual needs (Engel, 1953). Moreover, it has been noted that when physiological homeostasis is not well maintained, an individual tends to experience psychological distress (Burchfield, 1979). Indeed, in view of the intimate relationship between mind and body, psychological and physiological homeostasis might be hypothesized to be interdependent and to represent two different aspects of a single mind-body system functioning in a state of maximum balance.

Allostasis and Allostatic Load

Recently, the term *allostasis* has been proposed as an extension of the concept of homeostasis (McEwen, 1998a; McEwen & Stellar, 1993; Seeman, Singer, Rowe, Horwitz, & McEwen, 1997; Sterling & Eyer, 1988). Allostasis has been defined as stability through change, i.e., the ability of the body, when challenged, to achieve stability by increasing or decreasing vital functions to a new steady state (McEwen & Stellar, 1993; Sterling & Eyer, 1988). Thus, whereas the concept of homeostasis has traditionally viewed the maintenance of internal equilibrium as a relatively static process, in which physiological variables are maintained at one specific setpoint by local negative feedback mechanisms, the richer concept of allostasis emphasizes that internal regulation is a more complex and dynamically responsive process, in which physiological variables are continuously readjusted toward new setpoints based on a continuous reevaluation of environmental demands. Furthermore, in the allostatic model, this reevaluation of environmental demands is governed ultimately by the brain, whereas in the homeostatic model it is governed only by local feedback mechanisms (Sterling & Eyer, 1988).

Physiological systems that help to mediate the readjustments integral to allostatic regulation include the autonomic nervous system, the HPA axis, and serotonin systems, the same systems identified above as involved in aggression. Additional systems mediating allostatic regulation include the cardiovascular, metabolic, and immune systems. Such systems are termed *allostatic systems*, and the responses mediated by them, *allostatic responses* (McEwen, 1998a).

Three requirements have been identified as essential to a fully adaptive allostatic response (McEwen, 1998a). These are: (a) the allostatic response must be turned on in a timely manner to initiate the appropriate adaptive activity, (b) the adaptive activity must be maintained for a sufficient length of time to deal with the challenge, and (c) the response must be turned off at an appropriate time after the challenge has passed. If any of these three requirements is not adequately met, the result may be chronic underactivity or overactivity of allostatic systems, which in turn leads to an overall imbalance between these systems and their environment, as well as damage to the organism. The sum total of these imbalances and subsequent damage has been termed *allostatic load*, defined more specifically as the cumulative physiologic toll or "wear and tear" exacted on the body through its attempts at adaptation (McEwen, 1998a; Seeman et al., 1997).

This concept of physiologic toll is closely related to the notions of stress, physical disease, and psychological disease; such states have all been understood to be forms of divergence from internal balance and harmony with the environment (Chrousos & Gold, 1992; Walton & Pugh, 1995; Walton, Pugh, Gelderloos, & Macrae, 1995).

Defining Stress and Disease

In both the homeostatic and allostatic models, stress, physical disease, and psychological disease are viewed as states of imbalance, disharmony, or threatened homeostasis (Chrousos & Gold, 1992; Walton & Pugh, 1995). For stress in particular, modern researchers have formulated a variety of definitions to highlight its many different facets. One of the most integrative of these definitions (Elliott & Eisdorfer, 1982) views a stressful experience as having four components–a stressor, reactions to the stressor, consequences of the reactions, and mediators (see Figure 1).

The components of stressful experience, as shown in Figure 1, are defined as follows:

a. The *stressor*–an event of the internal or external environment that produces a physical or psychosocial reaction in an individual;
b. The *reaction*–a transient response of the individual to the stressor–it has been suggested that, by definition, the stress reaction is compensatory in nature (Goldstein, 1995), i.e., for a reaction to qualify as a stress reaction, it must seek to return a state of threatened homeostasis to a state of established homeostasis;
c. The *consequence*–a prolonged or cumulative effect of the stress reactions on the health of the individual's mind, body, or environment–physiological systems activated by stress may either protect and restore (Munck, Guyre, & Holbrook, 1984) or damage the

body; a stress consequence may be either adaptive or maladaptive; it may lead to a state of either greater or lesser psychophysiological integration. Allostatic load–the wear and tear resulting from chronic overactivity or underactivity of allostatic systems–would clearly represent a maladaptive, and thus undesirable, category of stress consequences; it constitutes a physiologic toll exacted on the body that impairs the body's functioning;

d. The *mediator*–conceived to be any additional event or circumstance that acts as a filter or modifier with respect to a potential stressor. The mediator may act on any or all stages in the sequence of stressor-reaction-consequence to produce individual variations in the stress response. Examples of mediators are the presence or absence of genetic defects, the degree of sleep and rest an individual has received, one's psychological predisposition, one's past experience, and the physical or social context in which a stressor is experienced. Mediators explain why potential stressors may produce no apparent stress consequences in some individuals, but significant stress consequences in other individuals. Thus, there appear to be no absolute stressors in life. No specific life event–whether loss of a job or loved one, financial stress, marriage, divorce, job promotion, or any other potential stressor–is experi-

Figure 1: The four aspects of stressful experience, and their interrelationships.

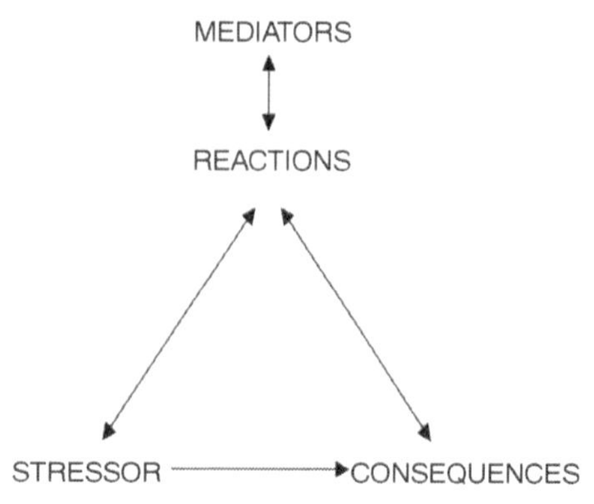

enced by everyone as a stressor of the same degree, nor even, necessarily, as a stressor at all.

Therefore, physiological systems activated by stressors, such as those involved in homeostasis and allostasis, clearly have the capacity not only to protect and restore but also to damage the body (Elliott & Eisdorfer, 1982; McEwen, 1998a; Selye, 1936). Indeed, such systems can themselves be damaged by chronic activation. In the following discussion, three types of these systems will be examined in the context of stress: serotonin systems, catecholamine systems, and the HPA axis.

STRESS-INDUCED ALTERATIONS OF NEUROENDOCRINE SYSTEMS

As described in the previous section, the mechanisms underlying the effects of stress on behavior appear to be identical to those underlying the effects of stress on physical and mental health. Repeated demands on adaptive systems, by experiences which tax those systems, produce wear and tear. This wear and tear takes the form of long-lasting alterations in the structure and function of these adaptive systems. Such alterations generally involve one of the essential features of the allostatic response; that is, they either reduce the ability of a particular allostatic system to turn on its activity, reduce its ability to sustain the activity long enough to meet the challenge, or reduce its ability to turn off the activity at the appropriate time after the challenge has been met. These are the types of changes associated with serotonin, catecholamine, and HPA systems in cases of violent aggression and criminal acts, as noted previously. Some of these stress-related changes are examined in the following paragraphs.

Stress-Induced Neuroendocrine Imbalances in Serotonin Systems

Two characteristics of serotonin suggest that it plays an important role in homeostatic or allostatic processes relevant to health and disease (Verbeuren, 1989). First, serotonin is either synthesized or taken up, stored, released, and metabolized in a wide variety of cells and organs distributed throughout the body. Secondly, serotonin is associated with the regulation of a wide variety of processes. Serotonin neurons probably constitute the most ubiquitous neurotransmitter system in the vertebrate brain, since no region of the central nervous system appears to lack 5-HT innervation (Descarries et al., 1990). Serotonin is distributed in several different cell types in other parts of the body as well. In mammals, significant levels of 5-HT are associated with the enterochromaffin cells of the gastrointestinal mucosa, with pinealocytes in the pineal gland, and with blood platelets. Smaller amounts of 5-HT have been detected in peripheral nerves of the gut and in specialized cells of the heart, lung, kidney, spleen, liver, thymus, thyroid, and blood vessels, as well as in mast cells (Verbeuren, 1989).

In addition to its broad distribution, serotonin has been associated with regulation of a wide variety of processes (Verbeuren, 1989). These processes include sleep, breath rate, pain, body temperature, immune response, EEG synchrony, and psychological states such as anxiety and depression, as well as aggression. In addition, an increase in serotonin metabolism has been associated with the Transcendental Meditation technique (Bujatti & Reiderer, 1976; Walton et al., 1995; Walton, Cavanaugh, & Pugh, in press). While serotonin's roles in these processes are not fully understood, they are likely to be in the mediation of adaptive mechanisms. Indeed, evidence for the involvement of serotonin in physiological adaptation has long existed.

Research spanning three decades suggests that serotonin systems play a central role in the body's attempt to adapt to both acute and chronic changes relevant to stress. In particular, serotonin plays a pivotal role in the regulation of the HPA axis and is involved in the stimulation of ACTH secretion during stress. At the adrenal level, serotonin acts as a local regulator of both mineralocorticoid and glucocorticoid secretion, regulators of mineral and glucose levels, respectively (Lefebvre, Contesse, Delarue, Vaudry, & Kuhn, 1998).

Studies in rodents, for example, have found that an acute challenge produced by intermittent mild footshock (Bliss, Thatcher, & Ailion, 1972; Thierry, Fekete, & Glowinski, 1968) or by immobilization (Curzon & Green, 1968; Curzon & Green, 1969; Kundrotas & Gregg, 1977; Morgan & Rudeen, 1976; Morgan, Rudeen, & Pfeil, 1975; Palkovits, Brownstein, Kizer, Saavedra, & Kopin, 1976) stimulates serotonin turnover in the brain, especially in the cerebral cortex, hypothalamus, and hippocampus (Morgan & Rudeen, 1976; Morgan et al., 1975). Repeated exposure to these or other stressors, however, is associated with decreased turnover of serotonin, especially if either the onset or duration of these stressors is unpredictable (Sherman & Petty, 1980; Sherman & Petty, 1982).

Studies in primates have given similar results. For example, male macaques exposed to chronic stress showed long-term, selective reductions in serotonin activity in the prefrontal cortex as compared to control animals (Fontenot, Kaplan, Manuck, Arango, & Mann, 1995). Macaques in the experimental condition were subjected to chronic stress in the form of frequently reorganized social group membership (i.e., social instability). They were compared with a control, no-stress group that experienced a stable social group membership throughout the study. Furthermore, the animals subjected to this chronic stressor during only the first 14 months of the 28-month study (the "past-stress condition"), showed different changes than did animals exposed to this stressor during only the last 14 months of the study (the "recent-stress condition"). Animals in the past-stress condition had significantly lower 5-HIAA concentrations in the prefrontal cortex compared to those in the no-stress condition and significantly lower 5-HT concentrations in the prefrontal cortex than those in the no-stress and recent-stress conditions. Long-term effects such as these appear to be examples of allostatic load.

The association of chronic social stress with long-term selective reductions in serotonin activity in the prefrontal cortex has been suggested to underlie the association, in human beings, between reduced serotonin function and conditions such as pathological grief and post-traumatic stress disorder (PTSD) (Fontenot et al., 1995). This reduced activity of serotonin systems is similar to the reductions of serotonin activity associated with inwardly or outwardly directed aggression and other hostile behaviors, as described previously.

Stress-Induced Changes in Catecholamine Systems

The locus coeruleus (LC) is the largest nucleus of norepinephrine-containing neurons in the brain (Dahlstrom & Fuxe, 1964). LC neurons project prominently to the brain's fear-anxiety-defense centers in the limbic system (Blanchard & Blanchard, 1979; LeDoux, Cicchetti, Xagoraris, & Romanski, 1990). There they release the neurotransmitter norepinephrine (NE) in response to real or apparent threats to survival (Amaral & Sinnamon, 1977; Aston-Jones & Bloom, 1981; Jacobs, 1986). The LC is believed responsible for one function or a variety of functions, including the regulation of arousal (Jouvet, 1972), vigilance (Aston-Jones, 1985), reward-extinction (Mason & Fibiger, 1978), and fear and anxiety (Redmond & Huang, 1979). A more holistic perspective views the LC as an alarm-aversion system functioning in concert with reward systems to promote survival-maximizing behavior in vertebrates (Redmond & Huang, 1979).

The LC has been proposed by some (e.g., Hartman, Zide, & Udenfriend, 1972) to be an extension, in the central nervous system, of the SNS. The SNS, generally thought of as belonging to the peripheral nervous system, along with the parasympathetic nervous system (PNS) form the autonomic nervous system, which controls the involuntary functions of visceral organs. The coordinated functioning of the SNS and PNS plays a major role in mediating allostatic responses within the body. Increased activity of the SNS is associated with increased arousal, an activated psychic state, and enhanced skeletal muscle activity and tone, while increased parasympathetic activity is associated with drowsiness and sleep, decreased skeletal muscle tone, and decreased motor activity.

When an individual is exposed to physical or mental stress, especially fear, rage, or severe pain, the SNS may become globally activated, in a phenomenon called *mass discharge*. Mass discharge results in a widespread reaction throughout the body, called the *alarm* or *stress response*, which increases the body's ability to perform strenuous muscular activity. In particular, mass discharge of the SNS produces increased values in many physiological parameters, including arterial pressure, blood flow to active muscles, rate of cellular metabolism, blood glucose concentration, muscle strength, mental activity, and rate of blood coagulation (Guyton, 1996).

Several psychophysiological studies using autonomic measurements have provided evidence that SNS activity and responsiveness is chronically increased in patients with PTSD (Blanchard, Kolb, Pallmeyer, & Gerardi, 1982; Malloy, Fairbank, & Keane, 1983). For example, both men and women suffering from PTSD exhibit elevated norepinephrine levels. In addition, male combat veterans diagnosed with PTSD exhibit elevated norepinephrine-to-cortisol ratios (Kosten, Mason, Giller, Ostroff, & Harkness, 1987), while women with PTSD derived from childhood sexual abuse exhibit elevated levels of norepinephrine, epinephrine, dopamine, and cortisol (Lemieux & Coe, 1994).

Stress-Induced Changes in the HPA Axis

The HPA axis is a third major system that both mediates and is influenced by the experience of stress, and is perhaps the most well-studied stress-related regulatory system. The HPA axis is activated by a wide variety of physical and psychosocial stressors that stimulate the adrenal cortex to secrete the glucocorticoid cortisol.

Stressors are thought to increase cortisol secretion when nerve impulses are transmitted from the neurons in the periphery of the body into the brain; ultimately a signal reaches the hypothalamus, which then secretes corticotropin releasing factor (CRF). CRF travels through the bloodstream to the pituitary, where it stimulates secretion of corticotropin (also known as adrenocorticotropic hormone, or ACTH), which then travels through the bloodstream to the adrenal cortex, where it stimulates secretion of cortisol.

Among the different stressors activating this cortisol secretion mechanism are: trauma of almost any type, severe damage to large tissue areas by disease, infection, painful contusion, intense heat or cold, physical restraint, fear, anxiety, apprehension, and injection of norepinephrine and other sympathomimetic drugs, as well as ingestion of most other prescribed and over-the-counter drugs (Antelman, Caggiula, Knopf, Kocan, & Edwards, 1992; Ganong, 1987; Guyton, 1996). The effects of cortisol include the mobilization of energy stores for immediate energy needs, the enhancement of sensitivity of tissues to other stress-related neurohormones, and the inhibition of immune and inflammatory responses. Together, these effects enhance the organism's ability to respond to acute stressors and to restore homeostasis. After the stressor is removed and the initial steps in restoration of homeostasis have been completed, negative feedback mechanisms turn off the heightened secretion of cortisol, thus returning cortisol to its prior level.

Recent evidence suggests that the hippocampus, a portion of the brain's limbic system, plays a key role in the functioning of the HPA axis. The hippocampus has been shown to affect three aspects of HPA-axis activity: the initial cortisol response to stress, the circadian rhythm of cortisol levels, and the feedback inhibition of cortisol levels. The hippocampus has a much greater density of cortisol receptors than do other parts of the brain, and thus has a much greater sensitivity to cortisol (Sapolsky, 1992).

Studies indicate that chronic stress reduces the number of cortisol receptors present in the hippocampus (Sapolsky, 1992; Sapolsky, Krey, & McEwen, 1984b), thus reducing the sensitivity of the hippocampus to feedback inhibition by cortisol. This reduced sensitivity is associated with an impaired ability of the hippocampus to signal the HPA axis to turn down cortisol secretion, consequently producing cortisol hypersecretion (Sapolsky, Krey, & McEwen, 1984a; Sapolsky, Krey, & McEwen, 1986), another neuroendocrine distortion that contributes to the total allostatic load.

EVIDENCE THAT THE TM PROGRAM REVERSES NEUROENDOCRINE ABNORMALITIES

Among the hundreds of studies conducted on effects of the TM program during the last 30 years, several have addressed changes in parameters known to reflect level of stress or function of adaptive mechanisms, including neuroendocrine activity. This section summarizes studies that have produced information on neuroendocrine function, in topical order.

Reversing Abnormalities of Serotonin Systems

Measuring the activity of serotonin systems in humans is challenging because most measuring techniques are invasive and involve some risk to the health of the individual. Excretion rate of 5-HIAA, the main metabolite of serotonin, is one exception. When intake of foods containing serotonin is controlled, 5-HIAA excretion rates can provide meaningful inferences about serotonin activity.

Several studies have investigated correlational or causal relationships between the TM program and 5-HIAA excretion. While further longitudinal, random-assignment studies are warranted, results of studies completed thus far allow for the possibility that the TM program can cause an increase of 5-HIAA excretion, both acutely (during the practice itself) and longitudinally, countering the apparent effect of chronic stress to reduce serotonin activity. The first of these studies tested effects of a single TM practice session on 5-HIAA excretion in experienced practitioners (Bujatti & Reiderer, 1976). The TM group showed a larger increase in 5-HIAA excretion during the practice session than did controls during a comparable period of eyes-closed rest. The TM group also had higher levels at baseline, that is, before starting the practice session. These findings suggest the possibility that activity of serotonin systems is increased by the TM technique, both acutely by each practice session, and also cumulatively, at least in these experienced practitioners. Because subjects were not randomly assigned to the TM and non-TM groups, however, this study did not eliminate the possibility of some preexisting difference between groups that could explain group differences in serotonin activity.

Higher 5-HIAA excretion rates in long-term TM subjects (with regular TM practice for a mean of 8.5 years) compared to non-TM controls was confirmed in another cross-sectional study (Walton et al., 1995). In this study, the difference between the two groups was greater during the night or sleeping hours than during the day or waking hours. Similar patterns were found in both men and women.

The only longitudinal study testing the hypothesis that regular practice of the TM technique increases the rate of 5-HIAA excretion was conducted in young men (Levitsky, 1998). Volunteer subjects were randomly assigned to the TM program group or to a control stress-reduction group. The controls received a didactic, stress-education approach having the same number of meetings with the instructor as did the TM group and also having an activity (keeping a diary of experiences) that occupied time twice daily, thus controlling for instructor attention and timing structure of the TM program. Excretion of 5-HIAA in the TM group increased significantly (by 29%, $p = .03$) in the overnight period (2200 to 0600 hours), after 4 months of twice-daily practice. However, because overnight excretion also increased slightly for the stress-education group (13%, $p = .22$), the posttest difference between the two groups only trended toward significance ($p = .09$). Indeed, because removal of the effects of stress by the TM program is thought to be a cumulative process, the effect of the 4 months of practice in this study was expected to be less than that observed after long-term practice of the technique (Walton et al., 1995).

Results to date, then, are consistent with an ability of the TM program to reverse long-lasting effects of chronic stress on activity of serotonin systems, as reflected in the excretion rate of 5-HIAA. Because serotonin is also produced in other cells of the body besides the serotonin neurons of the brain and spinal cord (Verbeuren, 1989), the functional meaning of reduced urinary excretion of 5-HIAA remains to be fully elucidated. Estimates of the portion of the body's 5-HIAA originating from the brain range between 10-15%. Regardless of the cells of origin of the excreted 5-HIAA, however, our laboratory has found, and will be publishing, results showing highly significant inverse correlations between urinary excretion of 5-HIAA and measures of aggression, anger, anxiety, and depression, as well as a direct correlation of this measure with leadership ability (Walton & Pugh, 1994). The reversal of effects of stress on 5-HIAA excretion is, therefore, likely to be meaningful in relation to rehabilitation and crime prevention.

Reversing Abnormalities of Catecholamine Systems

Catecholamines play an important role in mediating SNS activity and have been used as direct measures of SNS activity. SNS function also may be assessed through a variety of measures other than catecholamines themselves. For example, effects of the TM program on the SNS have been assessed through functional measures such as skin resistance, blood lactate levels, and blood cholesterol levels, as well as through more direct measures such as levels of catecholamines or catecholamine metabolites, or through the sensitivity of receptors for these neurotransmitters. Overall, results of these studies indicate that the TM technique reduces somatic arousal, increases alertness, and increases autonomic stability, in comparison with eyes-closed rest (Cooper & Aygen, 1979; Dillbeck & Orme-Johnson, 1987; Mills, Schneider, Hill, Walton, & Wallace, 1990; Orme-Johnson, 1973; Wallace & Benson, 1972; Wallace, Benson, & Wilson, 1971).

Skin resistance, an easily accessible measure of SNS activity, has been investigated in practitioners of the TM program using at least two distinct parameters: basal skin resistance and the galvanic skin response. Basal skin resistance (BSR) is defined as the skin's resistance to the flow of electrical current, and appears to reflect the level of stress or anxiety experienced by an individual (Katkin, 1965). In a statistical meta-analysis of studies published through 1985, a significantly greater increase in basal skin resistance was observed during the TM technique than during eyes-closed rest (Dillbeck & Orme-Johnson, 1987). This observation is consistent with a reduced level of activity of the SNS during practice of this technique.

The second measure of skin resistance investigated in practitioners of the TM program is the galvanic skin response (GSR; also called sympathetic skin response or SSR). GSR is a transient fluctuation in BSR, and is considered to be a reliable indicator of SNS function. GSR may be measured either as it arises spontaneously (i.e., independently of ambient noise or movements by the subject), or as it is evoked by various stimuli.

The frequency of spontaneous GSRs is one way of defining the lability, or stress level, of an individual (Katkin & McCubbin, 1969); this frequency is known to rise when a person is angry or fearful (Ax, 1953) or when levels of norepinephrine or epinephrine increase (Silverman, Cohen, & Shmavonian, 1959). Stimulants (Greiner & Burch, 1955) and a variety of environmental stressors (Katkin, 1965; Katkin, 1966; Silverman et al., 1959; Zuckerman, 1964) also have been shown to elevate the frequency of spontaneous GSRs.

Moreover, in a given situation, some individuals, referred to as *stabiles*, consistently maintain lower spontaneous GSR than others, referred to as *labiles*. Furthermore, stabiles are better able to withstand stresses (Burch, Cohn, & Neuman, 1942; Silverman et al., 1959; Zuckerman, 1964), better able to cope with environmental pressures (A. Alexander, Roessler, & Greenfield, 1963), and less impulsive on motor tasks than labiles (Lacey & Lacey, 1958). In addition, stabiles have quicker perceptions than labiles (Hustmyer & Karnes, 1964), and are less conditionable to aversive stimuli (Martin, 1960;

Spence, 1958; Stern, 1966; Stern, Stewart, & Winokur, 1961). In the meta-analysis by Dillbeck and Orme-Johnson (1987), individuals practicing the TM technique for some time showed significantly lower baseline frequencies of spontaneous GSR prior to a TM session than comparison subjects did prior to simple eyes-closed rest. This finding is consistent with a wide variety of studies showing a significant reduction in trait anxiety in practitioners of the TM program (Eppley, Abrams, & Shear, 1989) and suggests that the TM program might be capable of changing individuals from labiles to stabiles.

A second physiological parameter used to assess effects of the TM program on the SNS is blood lactate. Blood lactate is a reliable indicator of SNS function because its production is stimulated by norepinephrine, one of the principal neurotransmitters of the sympathetic system. Moreover, when patients with anxiety neurosis are placed under stress, they show a large rise in blood lactate. In addition, such patients, and some normal subjects, experience anxiety attacks upon receiving lactate infusions (Pitts, 1969). As summarized in the meta-analysis by Dillbeck and Orme-Johnson (1987), practitioners of the TM program display a greater decrease in blood lactate during the practice, and a lower blood lactate level outside of the practice, than do controls practicing eyes-closed rest.

A third parameter that has been used to assess the effect of the TM program on the SNS is vanillylmandelic acid (VMA). VMA is a metabolite of the neurotransmitters epinephrine and norepinephrine, and its rate of urinary excretion can be taken as an estimate of turnover of these two sympathetic neurotransmitters and, thus, as an indication of sympathetic activity in the body. A preliminary study found that college students practicing the TM technique for an average of 8.5 years showed a statistical trend toward lower urinary excretion rates of VMA than did a similar group of college students not practicing a systematic technique for stress reduction (Walton et al., 1995). This result suggests a generally lower level of sympathetic activity in the TM group. Similar, but statistically significant, results were recently obtained when excretion rates of the two transmitters themselves (rather than their metabolites) were studied in TM practitioners compared to controls (Infante et al., 2001).

A fourth parameter used to assess the effect of the TM program on the SNS is adrenergic receptor sensitivity. Receptors are macromolecules found on the surfaces of neurons and other cells. Each receptor type binds a specific neurotransmitter; this binding in turn causes these receptors to initiate appropriate responses within the cell. *Adrenergic* receptors are those that bind epinephrine or norepinephrine. Adrenergic receptors are divided into subtypes by virtue of their relative binding affinities for different neurotransmitters and by the kinds of physiological changes they mediate. The so-called alpha-1, alpha-2, beta-1, and beta-2 adrenergic receptors are well-known examples. Cellular receptors are known to be dynamic, that is, their physical properties change in response to various stimuli and physiological conditions. One such dynamic property of receptors is their *affinity* for, or strength with which they bind to, particular neurotransmitters. This affinity can vary between high and low, reflecting increased or decreased ability of the given receptor to bind to the neurotransmitter. Thus, receptors in their high-affinity state allow neurotransmitters to produce a greater influence on the body than do receptors in their low-affinity state. Mills et al. (1990) found that long-term practitioners of the TM program had a lower percentage of high-affinity beta-adrenergic receptors than did individuals not practicing any systematic behavioral technique. Such reduction in high-affinity beta-adrenergic receptors is one possible mechanism by which the TM program could reduce sympathetic nervous system activity. Another possible mechanism is a reduction in catecholamine release. Consistent with this mechanism, Infante et al. (2001) reported that morning (0900 hours) and evening (2000 hours) norepinephrine levels and evening epinephrine levels in blood plasma were significantly lower in 19 practitioners of the TM program as compared to 16 controls. Plasma levels of norepinephrine are thought to be due primarily to spillover from SNS neuronal release. Plasma levels of epinephrine, on the other hand, are due mainly to SNS-stimulated release from the adrenal medulla. A reduction of plasma catecholamines by the TM program is also supported by the observation of reduced excretion of VMA, the major metabolite of norepinephrine and epinephrine, in 22 practitioners of this program compared to 33 controls (Walton et al., 1995).

Other studies involving smaller numbers of subjects reported either no differences in catecholamines (Michaels, Huber, & McCann, 1976; Cooper et al., 1985) or a variety of differences that were dependent on behavioral conditions preceding sample collection (Lang, Dehof, Meurer, & Kaufmann, 1979). The negative findings may have been due to the small number of subjects (lack of statistical power), different collection times, or other methodological differences.

There are other important findings related to the mechanisms of these changes. As covered in the next subsection, a variety of studies show lower cortisol in subjects practicing the TM technique (Bevan, 1980; Jevning, Wilson, & Davidson, 1978; MacLean et al., 1997; Walton et al., 1995). Because cortisol and other glucocorticoids facilitate the formation of high-affinity beta-adrenergic receptors (Davies & Lefkowitz, 1980; Davies & Lefkowitz, 1981; Stone, Eqawa, & Colbjornsen, 1989), lower levels of cortisol in the TM subjects may have been the immediate cause of the smaller number of high-affinity adrenergic receptors found in the Mills et al. study (1990).

Reversing Abnormalities of the HPA Axis

Effects of the TM program on the HPA axis have been assessed primarily through measures of cortisol, aldosterone, and dehydroepiandrosterone sulfate (DHEAS), three hormones secreted by the adrenal cortex. Altered kidney function, as indicated by excretion rate of a variety of electrolytes, is another sign of stress-induced long-term changes in the HPA axis. Effects of the TM program on this indicator also have been studied. The results obtained with these measures indicate the TM program reverses the stress-induced long-term alterations in regulation of this axis, as elaborated in the following sections.

Effects on Cortisol Levels

As noted above, cortisol is secreted by the adrenal cortex in response to either physical or psychogenic stressors. The cross-sectional study by Walton et al. (1995) comparing healthy college students not practicing a systematic technique for stress reduction with a similar group practicing the TM technique found a higher 24-hour urinary excretion rate of cortisol in the non-TM group. This group difference reached twofold in men during the 16-17 hours of waking and was significantly higher in the non-TM group during the sleeping hours as well. The lower rate of 24-hour cortisol excretion in the TM group suggests that these subjects experienced a lower average level of HPA activation throughout the day as compared to the non-TM group.

Results consistent with these findings were later reported in a prospective, random-assignment study of the responses of healthy young men to a sequence of stressors in the laboratory before and after 4 months' practice of either the TM program or a cognitive stress management program (MacLean et al., 1997). In this study, subjects assigned to TM, but not those assigned to the cognitive stress management program, showed a pretest-to-posttest decrease in both the basal level of cortisol in blood plasma and the average cortisol level across the entire stress session. Cortisol responsiveness to stressors, however, increased in the TM group compared to the cognitive group.

This decrease of baseline cortisol from pretest to posttest in the TM group is similar to the results found in earlier studies on smaller numbers of subjects (Bevan, Young, Wellby, Nenadovic, & Dickins, 1976; Jevning et al., 1978; Werner et al., 1986). Because chronic stress in animals increases baseline glucocorticoids (e.g., Akana et al., 1992), the significant reduction of baseline cortisol seen in the MacLean et al. (1997) study is consistent with a reversal of effects of prior chronic stress.

Moreover, the increased cortisol response to acute stressors exhibited by the TM group after 4 months of practice is also opposite to the effects of chronic stress seen in animal studies. Studies on non-human primates and rodents have found that one of the effects of chronic stress is a decreased cortisol responsiveness to acute stress (Brooke, de Haas-Johnson, Kaplan, Manuck, & Sapolsky, 1994; Sapolsky, 1990; Sapolsky et al., 1986; Sapolsky, Zola-Morgan, & Squire, 1991).

Effects on Aldosterone and Kidney Function

The cross-sectional study by Walton et al. (1995) found that differences between the TM group and controls in excretion of the mineralocorticoid aldosterone followed a pattern similar to that of cortisol. Aldosterone is an adrenal steroid hormone involved in salt retention and other aspects of kidney function. Effects of the TM program on aldosterone excretion and kidney function, although more complex to understand, also suggest that the TM program may produce a reversal of long-lasting abnormalities arising from stress. Stress-induced increases of ACTH and other hormones that stimulate glucocorticoid secretion also produce a transient increase in aldosterone secretion. One of the normal functions of aldosterone is to increase retention of sodium ions at the level of the kidney, a useful effect when dietary salt intake is low. However, stress also increases voluntary salt ingestion, an effect mediated by increases in ACTH and cortisol, which act on brain neurons to increase salt appetite (Denton et al., 1984; McEwen, Lambdin, Rainbow, & De Nicola, 1986). This stress-induced increase in both the ingestion and retention of salt causes a rise in sodium concentration in the blood. As a result, water must be imbibed to maintain the appropriate concentration of sodium in the blood. In turn, this water consumption rapidly increases the total volume of blood and, therefore, blood pressure (Guyton, 1991).

The body cannot long survive excessive increases in blood pressure, and seeks to adapt to these increases. One adaptation that has been observed is the development of resistance to the usual sodium-retentive effects of aldosterone, a condition called *aldosterone resistance* or *mineralocorticoid escape* (Gonzalez-Campoy, Romero, & Knox, 1989). Thus, while the ordinary effect of aldosterone is to reduce sodium excretion, under chronic stress, high aldosterone levels can coexist with high sodium excretion. But the adaptation in kidney function that allows sodium to be excreted at a higher rate allows other electrolytes to be excreted at a higher rate as well. For example, losses of calcium and zinc can also occur, which can degrade the function of other systems in the body (for further discussion, see Walton et al., 1995).

Evidence suggests that these stress-induced abnormalities of salt intake and kidney function are also reversed by the TM program. Walton et al. (1995) found that each of these ions was excreted at a significantly lower rate in the TM group than in the control group. Furthermore, in the random assignment longitudinal study described previously (Levitsky, 1998), excretion rates of these ions were significantly reduced after 4 months in the TM group, relative to the stress-education control.

Effects on DHEAS and on the Ratio of DHEAS to Cortisol

Excretion of DHEAS, often classed as an anabolic steroid, with functions somewhat opposite to those of cortisol, tends to follow a pattern also opposite to that of cortisol and aldosterone in comparisons between TM and non-TM groups. DHEAS is the sulfated derivative of dehydroepiandrosterone

(DHEA), an anabolic steroid secreted by the adrenal gland. These two substances are easily interconverted, with DHEAS thought to be primarily a storage form of DHEA. The levels of these substances decline steadily with age and are sometimes used as markers of aging. Stress also reduces their levels, apparently through an inhibitory effect of elevated cortisol on their production (Parker, 1991). Thus, higher levels of DHEAS and of the ratio of DHEAS to cortisol can be used as indicators of a low current or low prior level of chronic stress (Opstad, 1992; Ozasa, Kita, Inoue, & Mori, 1990).

Several studies have reported evidence that the TM program increases DHEAS and the DHEAS-to-cortisol ratio. Two studies have reported higher DHEAS in women who practiced the TM program long-term (Glaser et al., 1992; Walton et al., 1995). For men, however, only those in the oldest age range showed significantly higher levels. Walton et al. (1995) also examined DHEAS-to-cortisol ratios, finding them higher in both men and women who practiced the TM program than in control subjects of the same age. In a randomized trial of effects of the TM program on HPA axis function in prisoners in the Netherlands Antilles, the DHEAS/cortisol ratio was found to increase significantly over a 4.5-month period in the TM group, compared to the control subjects (Walton, Alexander, Camelia, Hawkins, & Durchholz, 2001). The ratio of DHEAS to cortisol may be a more sensitive measure of chronic stress than measures of cortisol alone (Opstad, 1992; Ozasa et al., 1990; Walton et al., 1995). Therefore, this result suggests that the prisoners practicing the TM program experienced a reduction of chronic stress and that the HPA axis was functioning more normally in this group after 4.5 months than in the controls, consistent with psychological results from the same study (see Hawkins et al., this volume).

CONCLUSION

In this article we sought to show that neuroendocrine abnormalities associated with aggression and crime are sufficiently similar to those arising from stress to conclude that stress could be their origin. Both classes of abnormalities, those associated with violence or crime and those arising from stress, involve the neuroendocrine systems mediating adaptation. Challenges or stressors in the environment, whether acute or chronic low-grade, can create long-lasting consequences referred to as allostatic load, a type of wear and tear on adaptive mechanisms that limits an individual's ability to adapt. The stressors that can lead to these abnormalities include most or all risk factors for crime, whether these factors are acutely threatening or are long-term societal conditions. We suggest that loss of adaptive or coping ability can render a person less resilient, that is, less able to resist the factors that may lead them to seek illegal shortcuts to satisfaction of needs and desires, or to vent negative emotions in an aggressive or violent way.

If the TM program removes or reverses such abnormalities, as the research described here suggests, then the result of practicing this program would be a more optimal functioning of adaptive mechanisms. This possibility fits comfortably with research described in other papers in this collection suggesting the TM program increases resilience (see Goodman, Walton, Orme-Johnson, & Boyer, this volume; Alexander, Walton, et al., this volume; Alexander & Orme-Johnson, this volume).

Masten, Best, and Garmezy (1990) define *resilience* as ". . . the process of, capacity for, or outcome of successful adaptation despite challenging or threatening circumstances" (p. 425). They envision psychological resilience as involving "internal states of well-being or effective functioning in the environment or both" (p. 426). These authors conclude that resilient adaptation can occur even in the type of high-risk environment characterized by family instability, high poverty level, and low maternal education, all of which correlate with trouble with the law. The ability of the TM program to strengthen adaptive mechanisms, therefore, is entirely consistent with a progressive strengthening of resilience.

This ability of the TM program to strengthen adaptation and resilience appears to be mediated by a natural tendency of the human body not only to preserve its integrity, as held in the concept of homeostasis, but also to progress towards dramatically higher functional states, such as those associated with the higher states of consciousness discussed in other contributions in this collection (e.g., Goodman et al., this volume; Alexander, Walton et al., this volume; Alexander & Orme-Johnson, this volume). Alexander's theory of the role of the TM program in rehabilitation (see Goodman et al., this volume) thus appears to be further supported by findings in the realm of neuroendocrine physiology.

NOTE

1. Transcendental Meditation and TM are service marks registered in the U.S. Patent and Trademark Office licensed to Maharishi Vedic Education Development Corporation and used under sublicense.

AUTHORS' NOTE

Address correspondence to Ken Walton, Maharishi University of Management, FM1005, Fairfield, IA 52557 (E-mail: kwalton@mum.edu).

Transcendental Meditation in Criminal Rehabilitation and Crime Prevention. Pp. 89-95.

SECTION II: ORIGINAL RESEARCH ON REHABILITATION

First Prison Study Using the *Transcendental Meditation* Program: La Tuna Federal Penitentiary, 1971

DAVID W. ORME-JOHNSON

Maharishi University of Management

RICHARD M. MOORE

Channel One, Los Angeles

ABSTRACT This repeated-measures study investigated effects of the Transcendental Meditation[1] technique on physiological and psychological variables in 17 prison inmates. After practicing the technique for 2 months, inmates showed increased stability of the autonomic nervous system, as indicated by fewer spontaneous skin resistance responses (SSRR), $p < .001$. They also showed reductions in rigidity, obsessive thoughts, and compulsive behavior, as indicated by two scales on the Minnesota Multiphasic Personality Inventory (MMPI), decreased Psychasthenia (MMPI scale 7, $p < .025$), and decreased Social Introversion (MMPI scale 10, $p < .05$). Regularity of practice correlated significantly with the percentage decrease in SSRR ($r = .74$, $N = 12$, $p < .01$). In turn, decreased SSRR correlated with decreased Psychasthenia ($r = .68$, $p < .025$). This correlation between increasing stability of the autonomic nervous system and reductions in rigid or obsessive thoughts and compulsive behavior is consistent with studies in other populations. The results of the present study suggest the Transcendental Meditation program improves integrated function of the frontal lobes of the brain in a manner useful in rehabilitating offenders.

KEYWORDS Autonomic nervous system, social introversion, compulsive behavior, frontal lobes, Transcendental Meditation, rehabilitation

The concept of using the Transcendental Meditation technique for prison rehabilitation arose when the authors were returning with friends from a weekend Transcendental Meditation program Residence Course in Las Cruces, New Mexico. During a Residence Course, participants add extra practice sessions of the Transcendental Meditation program (beyond the ordinary one in the morning and one in the evening) and receive knowledge about the principles underlying the program; together, these deepen the restful and revitalizing effects of the program. As we drove past La Tuna Federal Penitentiary and all eyes gazed out at the prison, there was a silence in the car. Suddenly, we all seemed to have the idea simultaneously that prison inmates could, in essence, be on a Residence Course all the time.

We called the warden and arranged to meet with him and with John Kiehlbauch, then the prison psychologist. We presented the research from Wallace's 1970 *Science* article showing that the Transcendental Meditation technique produces an integrated physiological response that is the opposite of the pattern produced by stress (Wallace, 1970a). We also presented the results from research then in progress showing that practitioners have greater autonomic stability and recover faster from stressful stimulation than do controls (Orme-Johnson, 1973). Kiehlbauch was interested, and we planned a 2-month longitudinal pilot study in which we would administer both the MMPI and a polygraph test for autonomic stability.

METHODS

Subjects

The 17 subjects who volunteered for the study were male inmates of La Tuna Federal Penitentiary near El Paso, Texas, who had been incarcerated for narcotics-related crimes and who were participating in the Narcotics Rehabilitation Act (NARA) program at La Tuna. Fifteen subjects were in their early 20s, and two subjects were in their early 30s; approximately half were of Mexican-American origin, a quarter were Black, and a quarter were Caucasian.

Apparatus

Measurements of SSRR were recorded on a Lafayette polygraph with silver-silver chloride contoured electrodes, 4 × 6 cm on the palm and 1.5 × 2 cm on the middle finger.

Procedure

In early June 1971, the inmates from the NARA program attended an introductory lecture on the Transcendental Meditation program at the prison. Twelve who planned to start the program and five who did not plan to start but were willing to serve as controls were given the MMPI the following week, and phasic electrodermal activity was measured. After electrodes were attached, each subject sat resting in a chair with eyes open for a 5-minute adaptation period followed by a 10-minute measurement period. Physiological measures at pretest and posttest were taken while subjects were awake with eyes open, not during practice sessions of the Transcendental Meditation program. The equipment and two experimenters were in the same quiet room as the subject. The subject was seated so he could not see the equipment but could easily be observed by the experimenters. Only electrodermal responses over 100 ohms in amplitude that were not correlated with the subject's movements or external noise were scored as spontaneous.

The following week, prisoners planning to start the Transcendental Meditation technique were instructed through the standard 4-day course. They were asked to practice the technique 20 minutes twice a day. Transcendental Meditation program subjects met with their instructor for a few minutes each day for 2 weeks and weekly after that for verification of their practice. Over the 2-month period of the experiment, experimental subjects and controls engaged in the same daily prison routines, except that the experimental subjects practiced the Transcendental Meditation technique and attended the verification sessions. To maintain an equal degree of acquaintance with all subjects, the experimenters did not meet with the experimental or control subjects during the time between measurements. Two months after Transcendental Meditation program instruction, subjects from both groups were retested on the MMPI and on the physiological measures. After physiological measurements were taken, the Transcendental Meditation subjects filled out a questionnaire on their regularity of practice. At the time of recording and scoring of SSRR, the experimenters did not know whether a subject had practiced the Transcendental Meditation program regularly or not. All tests were one-tailed since the hypotheses were directional.

RESULTS

Spontaneous Skin Resistance Responses

Of the 12 meditators posttested, five were found to have meditated regularly. Regularity was defined as meditating at least 60 out of the optimal 120 times during the two months. There were five regular meditators, seven irregular meditators, and seven controls.

Table 1 shows that all groups decreased in SSRR on posttesting, probably a laboratory adaptation effect, but the percentage of decrease was significantly greater for regular meditators than for irregular meditators ($t = 4.92$, $p < .001$) or for control subjects ($t = 1.89$, $p < .05$). The higher mean level of SSRR for regular meditators at pretest was not statistically significant, but they did have a significantly lower level at posttest than irregular meditators ($t = 3.18$, $p < .005$). This suggests that the greater reduction in SSRR in the regular meditators can not be attributed to a regression towards the mean.

For basal skin resistance, there were no significant differences between groups on pretest or posttest. The correlation between the number of meditations during the two months and the percentage of decrease in SSRR was $r = .738$, $N = 12$, $p < .01$. Thus, the greater the regularity of meditation, the greater was the increase in autonomic stability.

MMPI

At pretest the three groups showed similar MMPI profiles, with peaks on scales 4 (Psychopathic Deviate) and 9 (Hypomania), a pattern characteristic of

Table 1: Electrodermal Measurements Before and After Two Months of Transcendental Meditation Practice

		Spontaneous Skin Resistance Responses (responses per 10 minutes)			Basal Skin Resistance (Kohms)	
Group		Pretest	Posttest	Difference	Pretest	Posttest
Regular Meditators	Mean	48.8	6.6	42.2	18.0	14.0
	S.D.	29.1	5.4		11.1	3.8
Irregular Meditators	Mean	28.7	17.9	10.8	19.7	12.4
	S.D.	12.5	6.5		11.4	4.8
Nonmeditators	Mean	34.0	11.7	22.3	12.6	*
	S.D.	27.3	13.0		13.4	*

narcotics addicts (Hill, Haertzen, & Glasser, 1960; Olson, 1964). This combination indicates an aggressive personality and the tendency to act out impulses in a socially unacceptable way.

At pretest there were no statistically significant differences among groups on any of the subscales of the MMPI, although initially the regular group did tend to show a lower *K* score, suggesting a more frank attitude towards answering the questions. The level of *K* on posttesting was almost identical for the regular and control groups, and none of the differences among groups on *K* scores were statistically significant, suggesting that the subjects' attitudinal sets towards taking the test were not significantly different.

The regular group decreased more than the control group on scale 7 (Psychasthenia, obsessive-compulsive behavior, $t = 2.53$, $p < .025$) and on scale 10 (Social Introversion, $t = 2.22$, $p < .05$). The regular group also decreased more than the irregular group on scale 7 ($t = 2.14$, $p < .05$). The decrease in scale 10 indicates an increase in social ease and tendency to outgoing behavior in the regular group.

A significant correlation of $r = .68$ was found between the magnitude of decrease on scale 7 and magnitude of decrease on SSRR ($p < .025$, $N = 12$). This relationship suggests that an increase in physiological stability was accompanied by an increase in behavioral flexibility in the Transcendental Meditation group.

Subjective Reports

The subjective reports of Transcendental Meditation program subjects were favorable. All reported increased relaxation, a reduction of tension, and greater mental clarity.

DISCUSSION

This longitudinal study replicates cross-sectional results showing that practice of the Transcendental Meditation technique increases autonomic stability (Orme-Johnson, 1973). The significant correlation between regularity of practice of the Transcendental Meditation program and degree of increase in stability suggests that the prisoners who participated in the program benefited in proportion to the regularity of their practice of the program. Even those subjects who were moderately regular (practicing the Transcendental Meditation program half the recommended frequency is considered minimal participation in the program) showed measurable physiological and psychological benefits.

Decrease on scale 7 of the MMPI suggests reduced rigidity, reduced obsessive thoughts, and reduced compulsive behavior, or conversely, increased flexibility of thinking and action. The significant correlation between changes in scale 7 and changes in autonomic stability suggests an interesting psychophysical relationship, that is, a tendency of increased autonomic stability to covary with increased behavioral and cognitive flexibility.

Subsequent to this study, a meta-analysis of 32 physiological studies has confirmed that practice of the Transcendental Meditation program increases autonomic stability, as indicated by increased basal SR and decreased respiratory rate and plasma lactate during the practice and decreased SSRR, respiratory rate, heart rate, and plasma lactate outside of the practice (Dillbeck & Orme-Johnson, 1987).

The present results are especially interesting in the context of the reported electrodermal hyporeactivity of subjects with antisocial behavior. Studies indicate that psychopathic, delinquent, hyperactive, and aggressive individuals are as if frozen autonomically, showing lower tonic levels of skin conductance, smaller amplitude autonomic responses to stimulation, slower recovery of the skin resistance response, and fewer SSRR (Fowles, 1993; Hare, 1978). In this view, the antisocial individual has an unresponsive autonomic nervous system and, therefore, does not display the conditioning considered by some to be necessary for becoming socialized through learning from repeated mistakes (Damasio, Tranel, & Damasio, 1990). Such freezing of the autonomic nervous system is held to be the physiological substrate of the unfeeling, cold-hearted criminal who experiences no anxiety or behavioral inhibition to curb criminal behavior (Hare, 1978).

A wide range of evidence indicates that the autonomic stability resulting from practice of the Transcendental Meditation technique is quite the opposite of the antisocial pattern described above. In the present research, increased autonomic stability was correlated with increased cognitive and behavioral flexibility. Whereas antisocial individuals show lower levels of tonic electrodermal activity (Fowles, 1993), in the present study, tonic electrodermal activity did not change significantly in the Transcendental Meditation group. Whereas psychopathic inmates tend to show slow electrodermal recovery from stimulation (Hinton, O'Neil, Hamilton, & Burke, 1980), Transcendental Meditation subjects tend to show more rapid recovery (Brooks & Scarano, 1985; Gaylord, Orme-Johnson, & Travis, 1989; Goleman & Schwartz, 1976; Orme-Johnson, 1973) and decreased emotional numbness (Brooks & Scarano, 1985). Whereas subjects with a criminal record tend to show a lack of electrodermal responses (Raine, Venables, & Williams, 1990a), Transcendental Meditation subjects generally show a larger amplitude of electrodermal and heart rate responses (Goleman & Schwartz, 1976).

The kind of stability produced by the Transcendental Meditation program appears to be based on reduced stress, or noise, in the system and hence increased integration rather than freezing of the system. Whereas damage to the frontal lobes has been found to disrupt autonomic functioning and to increase sociopathic behavior (Damasio et al., 1990), the Transcendental Meditation program has been found to increase frontal lobe coherence and improve behaviors mediated by the frontal lobes, including moral reasoning (Dillbeck &

Araas-Vesely, 1986; Dillbeck & Bronson, 1981; Dillbeck, Orme-Johnson, & Wallace, 1981; Gaylord et al., 1989; Levine, 1976; Nidich, Ryncarz, Abrams, Orme-Johnson, & Wallace, 1983; Orme-Johnson & Haynes, 1981; Orme-Johnson, Wallace, Dillbeck, Alexander, & Ball, 1989). Indeed, a meta-analysis of studies on self-actualization found that practice of the Transcendental Meditation program increases reactivity of feelings, spontaneity, capacity for warm interpersonal relations, affective maturity, integrated perspective on self and the world, and resilient sense of self (Alexander, Rainforth, & Gelderloos, 1991). These personality changes are associated with positive behavioral changes, including decreased recidivism (Alexander, Rainforth et al., this volume; Bleick & Abrams, 1987; Rainforth, Alexander, & Cavanaugh, this volume).

This pilot study suggests the utility of the Transcendental Meditation program as a rehabilitative modality and points out the value of regular practice of the program for maximum effectiveness. At La Tuna prison, regular practice was difficult to maintain due to crowding and the prison schedule. Yet, even under those conditions, this pilot experiment supports our original speculation that prison inmates could be enjoying the benefits of a Transcendental Meditation program Residence Course all the time.

NOTE

1. Transcendental Meditation and TM are registered or common law trademarks licensed to Maharishi Vedic Education Development Corporation and used under sublicense with permission.

AUTHORS' NOTES

The authors wish to thank John Baudoux, Gene Spiegel, and Steve Boggs, teachers of the Transcendental Meditation program, for generously contributing their time and energy to this project, and John Bristol, PhD, then of the Department of Physiology at the University of Texas at El Paso, for technical support. A special thanks to John Kiehlbauch, PhD, who was Prison Psychologist and director of the Narcotics Rehabilitation Act (NARA) program at La Tuna Federal Penitentiary at the time of the study. His efforts made the study possible, and he conducted the MMPI component of the study.

Address correspondence to David Orme-Johnson, 191 Dalton Drive, Seagrove Beach, FL 32459 (E-mail: davidoj@emeraldcoast.com).

Transcendental Meditation in Criminal Rehabilitation and Crime Prevention. Pp. 97-125.

Walpole Study of the *Transcendental Meditation* Program in Maximum Security Prisoners I: Cross-Sectional Differences in Development and Psychopathology

CHARLES N. ALEXANDER
Maharishi University of Management

KENNETH G. WALTON
Maharishi University of Management

RACHEL S. GOODMAN
Maharishi University of Management

ABSTRACT Effective rehabilitation of repeat offenders is a way to prevent crime. The Transcendental Meditation (TM)[1] program is an especially promising approach to offender rehabilitation because evidence indicates that this program promotes improvements in both mental and physical health that support law-abiding behavior. The present cross-sectional study of 160 maximum-security prisoners at the Massachusetts Correctional Institution, Walpole, is a multifaceted comparison of differences in self-development and psychopathology between the TM group and various control groups.

Inmates who had practiced the TM program for an average of 20 months had improved scores relative to controls on 3 factor-analytic components derived from 14 individual test scales. Differences were highly significant for all 3 components (Development, Consciousness, and Psychopathology) when TM group members ($n = 46$) were compared with all nonmembers ($n = 114$) or with only the nonmembers interested in learning the technique ($n = 63$). These controls who were interested in learning did not differ on any of the 14 variables from those not interested ($n = 51$).

Compared to nonmembers, members of the TM group also showed improved test scores on key individual test scales, controlling for relevant demographic variables. These scales included Loevinger's Self-Development scale ($p < .0005$); the Postconceptual Experience factor of Alexander's State of Consciousness Inventory (SCI, $p < .01$); Intimacy Motivation ($p < .05$), as measured by the Thematic Apperception Test; State-Trait Anxiety ($p < .001$); and 5 scales of psychopathology from the Special Hospitals Assessment of Personality and Socialization (SHAPS)–Psychopathic Deviation ($p < .01$), Anxiety ($p < .05$), Aggression ($p < .05$), Tension ($p < .05$), and Introversion ($p < .05$)–while remaining within the normal range on the SHAPS Lie and Extroversion scales. These outcomes, along with the outcomes of related longitudinal and recidivism studies, identify the TM program as an effective tool for promoting the psychological health and personal maturation necessary for lasting rehabilitation of maximum-security inmates.

KEYWORDS Rehabilitation, consciousness, psychopathology, crime prevention, self-development, postconceptual experience

The United States has a seven times greater detention rate than western European countries, yet its violent crime rate continues to be higher (International Criminal Police Organization, 1994; United Kingdom Prison Service, 1994). Estimates of the annual costs of crime in the United States run in the $700 billion range (Gest, 1994), and the plight of victims and their families has never been worse (Miller, Cohen, & Wiersema, 1996). Although overall crime rates have declined in recent years, crime among juveniles continues to increase, with a doubling of the rate expected in the next decade (Office of Juvenile Justice and Delinquency Prevention, 1993, 1996). Violence in childhood and adolescence predicts criminal violence in adulthood (Denno, 1990). It is no surprise, therefore, that preventing crime has become a national priority, leading to a recent comprehensive study under the Department of Justice to evaluate the efficacy of crime prevention programs at the family, school, community, and other levels (Sherman et al., 1997b).

Among the most persistent concerns in crime prevention is how to deal with repeat offenders. The first delinquent acts of repeat offenders tend to occur during childhood or adolescence (Denno, 1990; Wolfgang, Thornberry, & Figlio, 1987), and this pattern continues into adulthood. In a study of 3,995 young parolees, 66% were rearrested for a serious new offense within 6 years (Beck & Shipley, 1987). A study of 79,000 felons released on probation found that 43% were rearrested for a felony within 3 years (Langan & Cunniff, 1992). Society's increasingly punitive response to this revolving-door phenomenon–such as California's three-strikes-and-you're-out law–has not reduced crime (Sherman et al., 1997). In fact, due to the costs of building new prisons and maintaining the larger number of inmates, such measures have drastically increased the funding required to support the criminal justice system, jeopardizing resources for public education and other programs that may be key to prevention (Greenwood et al., 1994; Peck & Jones, 1985).

In principle, prevention through rehabilitation could serve an important role in reducing crime. Unfortunately, however, research results over the last 30 years indicate that effective rehabilitation programs are rare. Two large *meta-analyses* (a combined statistical analysis of many separate studies) covering effects of treatment programs in juvenile delinquents and adults have found average effect sizes of .17 standard deviations, which is quite small (Lipsey, 1992), and .38 standard deviations, which is a moderate effect (Lipsey & Wilson, 1993). Overall, then, rehabilitation approaches have had modest effects. Perhaps such results are to be expected. Evidence indicates that the individuals most likely to commit crimes, particularly violent crimes, have suffered deep mental and physical stress early in life, usually originating from dysfunctional family influences (Henry, Caspi, Moffitt, & Silva, 1996; Raine, 1993). Rehabilitation of such individuals is likely to require treatments capable of promoting recovery from the effects of stress, that is, treatments that promote more optimal levels of mental and physical health.

Recent advances indicate that encouraging results are obtained when a client's specific psychological needs are addressed. A small cadre of researchers has long held that studying the psychological characteristics of criminals has produced promising leads toward effective rehabilitation (e.g., Andrews & Bonta, 1994; Gendreau & Ross, 1987; Palmer, 1975, 1978). Andrews, Zinger et al. (1990a) concluded that clinical sensitivity and a psychologically informed perspective on crime are crucial elements missing from most rehabilitation programs. This perspective is also taken in the Department of Justice (DOJ) report (Sherman et al., 1997b), which indicates that interventions may work if tailored to the needs of particular clients. MacKenzie (1997, p. 9-1) states, "The important issue is not whether something works but what works for whom."

Although reports of a low-to-moderate success rate for rehabilitation programs have sent policy makers a discouraging message, the possibility should not be discounted of finding a highly effective program for the majority of inmates. Lack of effectiveness in many rehabilitation efforts may be due largely to the inability of these programs to address the myriad contributors to crime. Many of these contributors fall in the category of stressors, such as low socioeconomic level, family dysfunction, and other adverse social or environmental conditions (Denno, 1990; Ferris & Grisso, 1996; Hillbrand & Pallone, 1994; Raine, 1993; Reiss & Roth, 1993). A program that promotes healing of the mental and physiological damage resulting from stress might overcome the self-destructive behavior patterns that many repeat criminals exhibit. In any event, it is clear that a universally effective rehabilitation program would have to deal on a fundamental level with a wide range of dysfunctional cognitive, emotional, and behavioral patterns in the individual that can lead to criminal actions.

A CONSCIOUSNESS-BASED APPROACH TO REHABILITATION

The current study investigates a promising rehabilitation approach–the Transcendental Meditation (TM) program. Previous studies in both offender and non-offender populations have found that the TM program reduces multiple factors thought to increase the likelihood of committing crime. These include anxiety, aggression, addictions and other psychological factors as well as physiological factors (for review, see Hawkins, this volume; Walton & Levitsky, this volume). Based on these studies, we propose that the TM program will produce a wide variety of beneficial effects in any population, even incarcerated maximum-security criminals. Because the TM program operates at a basic level, it is expected to simultaneously alleviate biological, psychological, and developmental conditions known to contribute to criminal behaviors. Furthermore, it is hypothesized to do so irrespective of the specific factors and background leading to the criminal behavior of any individual offender.

Although there are other treatment modalities associated with the TM program, the core component is an effortless, natural technique that, when systematically practiced, produces beneficial effects on both the cognitive and physiological levels (see Alexander, Rainforth et al., this volume; Hawkins, this volume; Walton & Levitsky, this volume). The systematic practice of the TM technique promotes the experience of transcendental or pure consciousness. This state of restful alertness has been proposed as a fourth major state of consciousness, with a psychophysiological signature fundamentally distinct from the other three major states–waking, dreaming, and sleeping (Mason et al., 1997; Travis & Wallace, 1997). Research has indicated that this deep state of rest alleviates stress-induced imbalances and their symptomatic effects, including hypertension (Alexander et al., 1996; Schneider et al., 1995), insomnia (Abrams & Siegel, 1978), psychopathology (Brooks & Scarano, 1985; Eppley, Abrams, & Shear, 1989; Gaylord, Orme-Johnson, & Travis, 1989), and other health-related conditions (Orme-Johnson, 1987; Orme-Johnson & Herron, 1997) as well as addictive behaviors (for a review and meta-analysis of research on the TM program and addictions, see Alexander, Robinson, & Rainforth, 1994; for a society-level analysis of the effects on addictions, see Orme-Johnson, 1994; for a more detailed discussion of transcendental consciousness, see Goodman et al., this volume).

The research in the present study was completed in 1982. It explores the impact of the TM program on self-development and psychopathology in a maximum security prison population. One of three from the original project (see also Alexander, Rainforth et al., this volume; Alexander & Orme-Johnson, this volume), this study investigates whether practice of the TM technique by prison inmates leads to (a) more rapid self-development, (b) increased experiences of major states of consciousness said to be higher than waking, sleeping, and dreaming (see Alexander, Davies et al., 1990; Alexander, Rainforth, & Gelderloos, 1991), and (c) reduction of psychopathological conditions. Self-development has particular relevance for the study of effective rehabilitation strategies because higher stages of self-development are more resilient to the negative psychosocial factors or stressors that can increase crime (Alexander, Davies et al., 1990; Hoge, Andrews, & Leschied, 1996; Luthar, 1991; Masten, Best, & Garmezy, 1990; Noam, Paget, Valiant, Borst, & Bartok, 1994; Noam, Recklitis, & Paget, 1991).

SELF-DEVELOPMENT AND ITS MEASUREMENT

The concept of self-development may be unfamiliar to many who are involved in criminal rehabilitation, particularly at the adult level. We, therefore, include a brief introduction that will help to explain the relevance of this topic (for a more detailed treatment, see Goodman et al., this volume). Self-development is a broad-based concept covering several dimensions that impact criminal behavior, especially impulse control, character development, capacity for personal relationships, and cognitive development. Persons at different stages of self-development are at greater or lesser risk for committing crimes, with those at higher levels of development showing more resilience in dealing with the many conditions that can lead to crime.

Self-development has been conceived of and evaluated in a variety of overlapping ways. For example, correlations have been found between the measure of self-development used in the present study, which is a version of Loevinger's Sentence Completion test, and other measures of development, including moral development (Kohlberg, 1969; Kohlberg & Kramer, 1969; Rest, 1975), social development (Selman, 1978), and cognitive development (Fischer, 1980). Thus, the approach chosen for this study may be representative of these other frames of reference.

Loevinger (1976, 1979) regards her validated, conceptually comprehensive measure as a direct way of delineating the customary orientation of self and world. Her test instrument is semi-structured and projective, making it difficult to falsify, and it can be scored with high reliability (Hauser, 1976). She has indicated that the development through the stages and transitions of her hierarchy, though sequentially similar in everyone, may occur at different rates and end at different levels across individuals.

Loevinger's scheme can be simplified into three major levels: Preconventional, Conventional and Postconventional (see Table 1). Each level contains several stages of development, which vary along dimensions of impulse control, conscious concerns, and interpersonal and cognitive styles (Noam et al., 1994). From descriptions of these stages, it can be seen that people at lower levels are likely to be more susceptible to factors leading to criminal behaviors. For example, individuals at the Preconventional level (main stages: Impulsive and Self-Protective) have difficulty taking the viewpoint of others and tend to be egocentric or self-centered. This level, shared by many adolescents, is based on a needs-gratification frame of reference in which actions tend to be impulsive, concepts tend to be dichotomous, interpersonal relations are dependent and exploitative, and awareness of inner states is minimal. Individuals at this level are either unaware of or have difficulty conforming to the conventions, rules, or laws of society.

The next level is the Conventional level (Conformist, Self-Aware, Conscientious). Adults typically reach this level, and the transition from Preconventional to Conventional often occurs by late adolescence. Individuals at the Conventional level exhibit a growing appreciation of the conventions or rules that govern interpersonal relations and society and also display capacity to conform to those rules. However, at the lower end of this level, conformity can be limited to the distorted rules of a gang or the local criminal community. At the more mature end (Conscientious stage), individuals exhibit the capacity for self-criticism and formulation of ideals and long-term goals. These individuals are self-respecting, communicative, and responsible in relating to others.

The Postconventional level is the most mature type of functioning in Loevinger's framework. All its stages involve an inner-directed or self-actualizing frame of reference, and individuals at this level of development (Individualistic, Autonomous, Integrated) are rare. Loevinger considers these individuals to have extraordinary flexibility in adapting to demands and coping with external or internal conflicts. Such people are tolerant of ambiguity, have a differentiated sense of unique self, experience inner fulfillment, and tend to live lives grounded in deep moral principles. At this level, interpersonal relationships tend to involve mutual respect for and acceptance of individual differences. The stages at the Postconventional level–from this description alone–can be seen as more likely to engender resistance to common crime-promoting factors than the stages in either of the levels described previously. Empirical evidence supports this conclusion.

Table 1: Some Milestones of Loevinger's Self-Development Scheme

	Stage	Impulse Control, Character Development	Interpersonal Style	Conscious Preoccupations	Cognitive Style
Preconventional	Impulsive (I-2)	Impulsive, fear of retaliation	Receiving, dependent, exploitative	Bodily feelings, especially sexual and aggressive	Stereotyping, conceptual confusion
	Self-Protective (Δ)	Fear of being caught, externalizing blame, opportunistic	Wary, manipulative, exploitative	Self-protection, trouble, wants things, advantage, control	
Conventional	Conformist (I-3)	Conformity to external rules, shame guilt for breaking rules	Belonging, superficial niceness	Appearance, social acceptability, banal feelings, behavior	Conceptual simplicity, stereotypes, clichés
	Self-Aware (I-3/4)	Differentiation of norms, goals	Aware of self in relation to group	Adjustment, problems, opportunities (vague)	Multiplicity
	Conscientious (I-4)	Self-evaluated standards, self-criticism, guilt for consequences, long-term goals and ideals	Intensive, responsible, mutual, concern for communication	Differentiated feelings, motives for behavior, self-respect, achievements, traits, expression	Conceptual complexity, idea of patterning
Postconventional	Individualistic (I-4/5)	*Add:* Respect for individuality	*Add:* Dependence as an emotional problem	*Add:* Development, social problems, differentiation of inner life from outer	*Add:* Distinction of process and outcome
	Autonomous (I-5)	*Add:* Coping with conflicting inner needs, toleration	*Add:* Respect for autonomy, interdependence	*Add:* Vividly conveyed feelings, role conception, self-fulfillment, self in social context	*Add:* Increased conceptual complexity, toleration for ambiguity, broad scope, objectivity
	Integrated (I-6)	*Add:* Reconciling inner conflicts, renunciation of unattainable	*Add:* Cherishing of individuality	*Add:* Identity	

Note: *Add* means in addition to the description applying to the previous level. Descriptions of development stages are cumulative after the conscientious (I-4) stage. Adapted from Loevinger–early stages and some descriptors eliminated for space (1976, pp. 25-26).

SELF-DEVELOPMENT IN CRIMINAL REHABILITATION

The time it takes to pass through Loevenger's levels varies with the individual, so adults may be found at any particular stage. The transition from Preconventional to Conventional typically occurs during adolescence. Self-development typically slows or stops by late adolescence or the end of formal education (which in the case of at-risk adolescents may be early). Older adolescents who have not reached a Conventional level are socially immature and, therefore, at greater risk for criminal behavior and related psychopathologies (Kasdin, 1987; Noam et al., 1984; Noam, Paget, Valient, Borst, & Bartok, 1994). Adolescents and adults at this Preconventional level are more likely to exhibit aggressive (Recklitis & Noam, 1990) and antisocial (Frank & Quinlan, 1976) behaviors. They also exhibit personality traits such as low affect control, negative affect expression, acting-out behaviors, and the tendency to externalize blame (Browning, 1986; Gold, 1980; Kegan, 1982; Loevinger, 1979) that predispose to crime and are common among inmates (af Klinteberg, 1996; Blackburn, 1996; Dodge, Price, Bachorowski, & Newman, 1990; Weekes & Morison, 1993). Conversely, individuals with the highest levels of development are more resilient; they do not succumb as readily to the types of stressors that predict crime (Hoge, Andrews, & Leschied, 1996; Luthar, 1991; Masten, Best, & Garmezy, 1990; Noam et al., 1994; Noam, Recklitis, & Paget, 1991).

Self-development slows dramatically in most people once adulthood has been attained (Loevinger et al., 1985). In prisoners, who tend to be resistant to change regardless of treatment (Sechrest, White, & Bronn, 1979), the rate of self-development is expected to be even slower. However, a large body of evidence now indicates that the TM program promotes self-development in many populations, including development of underlying biological systems, and suggests it should do so in prisoners as well (Alexander, Davies et al., 1990; Jevning, Wallace, & Beidebach, 1992; Mason et al., 1997).

ENHANCING SELF-DEVELOPMENT

Several studies have indicated that the TM program enhances self-development in college graduates and other populations. For example, a recent 10-year longitudinal study investigated the effects of the TM program in alumni from four universities who were matched on age, gender, and date of testing. Results of Loevinger's Sentence Completion test indicated that subjects practicing the TM program advanced significantly in self-development compared to the control groups (Chandler, Alexander, & Heaton, in press).

Self-actualization, another construct for evaluating psychological development, has been examined in many studies. A comprehensive meta-analysis of self-actualization studies (Alexander, Rainforth, & Gelderloos, 1991) found a three-times larger effect size for the TM program than for other interventions (effect size of .78 standard deviation units vs. .27 standard deviation units for the other methods tested).

These results suggest that continued practice of the TM program facilitates advancement through the stages of self-development in adulthood. If self-development could be accelerated in inmates, there would be less recidivism due to their greater ability to function in a manner acceptable to society. Level of self-development was tested in the present study not only by the Loevinger instrument but also by the States of Consciousness Inventory, which estimates the degree of experience of higher states of consciousness (Alexander, 1982; Goodman et al., this volume).

Higher States of Consciousness–Expected Long-Term Outcome of Practicing TM

The TM program was derived from the ancient Vedic tradition by Maharishi Mahesh Yogi (hereafter "Maharishi"), an Indian scholar and teacher (Maharishi Mahesh Yogi, 1969). He holds that the state of transcendental or pure consciousness attained during practice of the TM technique is a normal state accessible to anyone. This state is proposed to be a fourth major state of consciousness, higher than the three commonly experienced states (sleeping, dreaming and waking). But this fourth state is rarely experienced without the aid of an effective technique.

Further development of higher consciousness is available, as discussed in Alexander, Davies et al. (1990) and Goodman et al. (this volume). Such higher states are described in the Vedic tradition as well as in other ancient traditions (Shear, 1990). Although the occurrence of higher states of consciousness in modern cultures is rare, such states are now being confirmed by scientific investigation (Alexander, Davies et al., 1990; Mason et al., 1997; Travis & Pearson, 2000; Travis & Wallace, 1997; Travis & Wallace, 1999). A life-span model proposed by Alexander, Davies et al. (1990) holds that the four higher states identified by Maharishi are a natural culmination of human development and a natural extension of the sequence of stages delineated in Loevinger's scheme.

Stress-Related Imbalances Reflected in Psychopathology and Criminal Activity

Stressful circumstances can be a major contributor to criminal activity (e.g., Ferris, 1996; King, 1996; Raine, 1996). Evidence indicates that psychopathology can arise from stress-related dysfunction of hormonal and neuroendocrine systems. Research indicates that the TM program is useful not only in preventing but also in reversing these dysfunctions (for reviews, see MacLean et al., 1997; Walton & Levitsky, 1994, this volume; Walton, Pugh, Gelderloos, & Macrae, 1995).

Stress-related alterations in neuroendocrine functions occur when the pressure of an experience overloads the individual's coping mechanisms or adaptive processes (Walton & Levitsky, this volume; Chrousos & Gold, 1992; McEwen, 1998a; Orme-Johnson, 1994; Sapolsky, 1992). Factors such as poverty and social disorganization contribute to increased risk of personal distress (Cohler, Stott, & Musick, 1995) and can lead to depression, anxiety, distress, negative self-perceptions, disorganization of psychological functioning, and problems of social adjustment (Masten & Coatsworth, 1995), including criminal activity and school or job failure.

Stress also increases the psychopathology typically associated with violence and crime. Individuals exhibiting criminal behavior are frequently found to be impulsive, restless, and aggressive. They tend to violate conventional rules and procedures; to lack cognitive coping skills; to be weakly tied to settings such as school and work; to exhibit psychopathic deviation, including procriminal attitudes, beliefs, and thinking styles; and to show other signs of negative affect, such as depression, anxiety, and tension (Andrews & Bonta, 1994; Blackburn, 1975, 1986; Wilson & Hernstein, 1985).

The ability of the TM program to prevent or reverse such effects of stress has never been examined in concert with self-development and experiences of higher states of consciousness in the same offender population. Thus, the Special Hospitals Assessment of Personality and Socialization (SHAPS) and other scales most likely to be relevant to this population also were administered in this study to gauge the possible effect of the TM program on psychopathology.

HYPOTHESES

The following three hypotheses guided the present study: (a) compared to control groups, inmates practicing the TM program will show decreased psychopathology, as indicated by questionnaire measures of psychoticism, hostility, aggression, depression, and psychopathic deviation; (b) compared to control groups, inmates practicing the TM program will show enhanced personality development, particularly as indicated by measures of ego- or self-development, moral reasoning, and cognitive development; and (c) compared to control groups, inmates practicing the TM program will show increased reports of higher states of consciousness, as indicated by scores on the State of Consciousness Inventory (a special instrument developed for this study), and similar measures.

METHODS

Subjects

The subjects, 160 adult male inmates from the Massachusetts Department of Corrections system, were drawn almost exclusively from the state's maximum-security institution, the Massachusetts Correctional Institute (MCI), Walpole. According to self-report demographics collected on the subset of men who completed the Personal Questionnaire ($n = 124$), 50% of the sample were Caucasian, 41% African American, and 9% Hispanic. The mean age (SD) of the sample was 28.6 ± 5.7 years and the mean years of formal education was 11.4 ± 2.2. Thirty-five percent were Catholic, 28% were Protestant, and the remainder were Muslim or Other. Inmates had served an average of 37 months of their current prison terms; they had served a total of 70.3 months when prior incarcerations were included. Armed robbery was the most serious current offense for 35% of the inmates. The next most frequently occurring crimes were murder (21%), some form of assault (7%), and manslaughter (6%).

MEASURES

Self-Development

Self-development was measured by the Washington University Sentence Completion Test, an empirically derived, 36-item test developed by Loevinger and colleagues (Loevinger, 1976; Loevinger & Wessler, 1970), which has been examined for validity (Loevinger, 1993; Novy et al., 1994). The test version employed was Form 11-68 for men. Scoring to obtain the Total Protocol Rating (TPR) for ego stage was done on 133 protocols by an independent rater blind to group status. A second rater blind to group status scored a subset of 102 protocols. The correlation between ratings of the two scorers was high (r = .93).

Cognitive Development

The following tests evaluated cognitive development: (a) the Mill Hill Vocabulary Scale, a short-form, group-administered vocabulary test, significantly correlated with score on the Progressive Matrices Test (Raven, 1965), employed here to assess comparability of the groups at pretest; (b) the Group Embedded Figures Test, a measure of flexibility of closure and field independence, both cognitive-perceptual skills (Witkin et al., 1974); and (c) the Plant Problem, a performance measure of the ability to logically include and exclude variables on a multivariable problem, a competence fundamental to Piaget's highest stage of formal operational (abstract) thinking (Kuhn & Brannock, 1977).

Moral Development

Moral development was measured by a short-form, three-dilemma version of the Defining Issues Test (DIT). Derived from the work of Kohlberg (Kohlberg, 1969; Kohlberg & Kramer, 1969), this test is a structured, group administered, standard measure of recognition and preference for different levels or stages of moral reasoning. Specific moral issues are rated and ranked in terms of their perceived importance in making decisions about moral dilemmas (Rest, 1975). The DIT is most reliably scored for percentage of principled moral reasoning employed, that is, percentage of responses at Stage 5 and 6 in

Kohlberg's system (Goodman et al., this volume). The short form correlates highly with the longer six-dilemma form.

Development of Consciousness

Development of consciousness was measured by two instruments. The first was the State of Consciousness Inventory (SCI), a structured questionnaire psychometrically modeled after Rest's Defining Issues Test but directed toward measurement of major states of consciousness as defined by Maharishi in light of the Vedic tradition (see Alexander, Davies et al., 1990; Goodman et al., this volume). The three scales representing waking state were constructed to reflect normal, neurotic, and psychotic experiences of waking consciousness, in accord with criteria set forward by Eysenck and Eysenck (1975) and Spitzer and Endicott (1975). Three scales representing higher states of consciousness were constructed according to criteria described by Maharishi (1969). All items were edited to remove jargon as well as to control for word length and imbalances in social desirability. The goal was to make the items comprehensible and meaningful regardless of an individual's philosophical orientation. A misleading items scale (MIS), following the criteria of Rest (1975), also was incorporated; misleading items were intended to be high sounding but were actually meaningless or nonsensical.

In the context of this study, a principle component factor analysis employing an orthogonal rotation was performed (Harman, 1976). This reduced the SCI scales–Differentiated Postconceptual, Integrated Postconceptual, Unified Postconceptual, Normal Waking State, Schizophrenic, and Neurotic–to three factors that accounted for 89% of the variance (Alexander, 1982). These were: (a) a Postconceptual Experience factor on which the first three scales loaded at > .50; (b) a Neurotic Waking State factor on which the Neuroticism and Normal Waking State scales loaded at > .50; and (c) a Schizophrenic experience factor on which the Schizophrenic scale alone loaded at > .50. Only those items with loadings greater than +.50 were used in computing scores for the factors, using the transformed (z) scores from each scale.

The second scale for measuring development of consciousness was the Tellegen Absorption Scale (TAS). The TAS was a 34-item scale developed by Tellegen and Atkinson (1974) for measuring one's ability for total mental absorption in the current object of attention, an ability said to be related to higher states. This measure correlated at $r = .39$ ($p < .001$) with the SCI Postconceptual Experience factor, consistent with its proposed relatedness to higher states.

Psychopathology and Motivation

Psychopathology and motivation were measured in three ways. The first was the SHAPS, a multi-scale questionnaire measuring various aspects of personality and socialization, with an emphasis on the types of psychopathology exhibited by populations who were either hospitalized or in correctional institutions. The SHAPS scales were empirically derived from the MMPI to avoid the psychometric deficiencies of the regular clinical scales (Blackburn, 1975). Construction of six of the scales is described by Stein (1968). The remaining scales are: Impulsivity, Psychopathic Deviation, Lie (Blackburn, 1971), Anxiety (Welsh Anxiety), and Extroversion (Giedt and Downing Extraversion). The latter two scales were previously determined to be representative of neuroticism and introversion-extroversion personality factors, respectively (Blackburn, 1971).

Though Blackburn (1975) indicated that the SHAPS scales were constructed to minimize the psychometric problems associated with clinical MMPI scales, it was nevertheless found that the eight SHAPS psychopathology scales were intercorrelated (r = .23 to .85). Some scales were highly correlated (e.g., impulsivity and aggression, r = .85; depression and tension, r = .81) and showed highly similar patterns of correlations with the other SHAPS scales. In this study, SHAPS scales were thus reduced, via principal components factor analysis with an orthogonal rotation, to three factors that accounted for 82% of the variance. The three factors were labeled: (a) Secondary or Neurotic Psychopath (40% of the variance), for which SHAPS Depression, Anxiety, Tension, Psychopathic Deviation, Hostility, Impulsivity, and Aggression loaded highly (i.e., > .40); (b) Primary Psychopath (21% of the variance), for which Impulsivity and Aggression loaded positively and Lie loaded negatively (> .40); and (c) Depressed Introvert (21% of the variance), for which Introversion, Depression, Anxiety, and Tension loaded positively and Extroversion loaded negatively. Similar factors have been identified repeatedly in the experimental psychopathology literature (Megargee, 1972; Megargee & Bohn, 1979; Widom, 1978).

The second instrument used to measure psychopathology was the State-Trait Anxiety Inventory. It was a questionnaire measure of State (i.e., immediate anxiety) and Trait (i.e., chronic anxiety) levels (Spielberger, Gorsuch, & Lushene, 1970). This inventory is well known and has been verified in many populations.

Motivation was measured by the Thematic Apperception Test (TAT). Need for Power (Winter, 1973) and Intimacy Motivation (McAdams, 1979) are coding systems empirically derived in accord with the experimental arousal-of-motives paradigm used by McClelland and colleagues (McClelland, 1961, 1975; McClelland, Atkinson, Clark, & Lowell, 1953) in scoring the TAT for social motives. Need for Power was scored by two raters, with an interrater reliability of .90. Need for Intimacy Motivation was scored by McAdams, developer of the measure.

Demographics and Group-Joining Behavior

Demographics and group-joining behavior were measured by a personal questionnaire specifically designed for this study (Alexander, 1982).

DESIGN AND PROCEDURES

Design

Prior to the present research intervention (which began in May of 1978), the TM program had been taught for approximately 2 years at the MCI, Walpole, which was the only maximum security facility in the state of Massachusetts. Of the estimated 119 men who learned the TM program during that period, some 50% still resided during the period of this study either in MCI, Walpole, Southeast Correctional Center (a medium security site) or Norfolk County Jail (also medium security). Of these residents who had learned TM, approximately 77% participated in the testing.

Those who volunteered for testing and those who did not had similar regularity of practice rates initially, according to the records of the TM instructors. However, 24% of the tested and 30% of the non-tested TM subjects were drop-outs from the program (i.e., had not practiced in the 2 months previous to self report). Of these dropouts, tested TM subjects dropped out after an average of 6.2 months (presumably a long enough period of time to gain at least some effects from the practice), while non-tested TM subjects dropped out after a comparable or slightly longer interval.

This present study (Part I) presents the results of the initial testing of the members of the TM program group (mean length of practice, 20 months; n = 46) compared to control groups who were interested (n = 63) and not interested (n = 51) in learning TM. These control groups were formed to determine possible effects of self-selection, that is, whether prisoners who were interested in learning TM had discernible differences in personality characteristics from those who were not. Similar comparisons were done for members of various other program groups already structured in the prison and their interested versus not interested controls. The overall research project at MCI, Walpole, extended into two other studies as well. The second study (see Alexander & Orme-Johnson, this volume) introduced the TM program to new subjects and repeated key measures used in Part I on all subjects. The third study (see Alexander, Rainforth et al., this volume) investigated recidivism in all subjects who had been released.

Procedures

Though random assignment to groups was not possible, efforts were made in both this study and the longitudinal study to approximate double-blind conditions. Testers were blind to program status; although the inmates obviously knew in which program they were participating, they did not know that testers had any connection with their program. For testing, subjects were initially contacted by letter. They were invited to participate in a research study on personality and development in prisoners for $8 per two sessions of 2 to 3 hours each.

All testers ($n = 10$) were blind to the program affiliations of the subjects during the test sessions. Subjects were informed that their names would be removed from tests and replaced with a number to insure privacy. Also, no individual scores or tests would be available to the Department of Corrections. On that basis, subjects then completed an Informed Consent Form.

The Personal Questionnaire requested background demographic information. It also asked subjects to indicate which of nine programs in the prison they had been members of in the past, were currently active in, planned to join, or did not plan to join. Tests were scored blind with respect to the subjects' group-joining status. Data on group-joining status permitted comparisons to be made between the TM group and the other program groups. For all programs, subjects were assigned to an *interested* condition only if they explicitly stated an intent to join. If explicit intent was not expressed, subjects were placed in the *not interested* category for the program in question.

PROGRAMS

Because members of the TM program were compared with members of eight other programs in the prison, brief descriptions of each program are given here. Table 2 contains the classification of subjects by program activity level, as ascertained from the self-report pretest information on program joining.

Transcendental Meditation Program

The TM program was taught to inmates in the same fashion as it is taught to the general public. Instruction involves seven steps, which are spread over 5 or 6 days. Each step lasts 1 to 1.5 hours, except for a personal interview, which usually takes 10 to 15 minutes. The seven steps are as follows: (a) Introductory Lecture, focusing on the effects and benefits that might be expected from practice of the program based on scientific research and past experience; (b) Preparatory Lecture featuring information on the origin and nature of the program as well as details necessary for personal instruction; (c) Personal Interview, usually held immediately after the Preparatory Lecture, allowing the instructor to become acquainted with the pupil and the pupil to ask any personal questions; (d) Personal Instruction, in which each student meets privately with the instructor to learn the practice of the TM technique (the student's first actual session practicing the technique); (e) First Day's Checking, a group meeting for all pupils who learned the technique on the same day, occurs on the day following Personal Instruction and offers further information about correct practice of the TM technique built around the students' own experiences so far and any questions regarding their experiences; (f) Second Day's Checking, following the same group structure as the First Day's Checking but going more deeply into the mechanics and results of the practice of the technique, again

Table 2: Number of Active Members and Dropouts in Different Programs

Program	Total Members	Active Members[a]	Dropouts[b] (%)	
TM	46	35	11	(24%)
AA	44	20	24	(54)
Reachout	25	16	9	(36)
Black Muslims	25	16	9	(36)
Christian Groups	32	13	19	(59)
College	43	24	19	(44)
CASH Drug Rehabilitation	24	15	9	(38)
Counseling	17	11	6	(35)
Political Caucus	25	15	10	(40)

Note. [a]Active members reported participating at least 1-2 times per month.
[b]Dropouts reported no activity during the last 1-2 months.

based on experiences of individual students; and (g) Third Day's Checking, following the same structure as the First and Second Day's Checking, focusing on the positive changes at the subjective level.

In addition to this seven-step structure, participants had an optional weekly meeting available to further discuss their experiences, investigate the mechanics of the technique, and to gain deeper intellectual understanding of the principles governing the technique. Once a month an inmate could have his practice individually checked to insure correctness. The overall emphasis was on individual practice (20 minutes, morning and evening) not on these group meetings. In fact, only a relatively small subset regularly attended meetings. However, the impression of instructors was that many students practiced quite regularly (10 to 14 times per week) even though they rarely attended meetings.

Alcoholics Anonymous

This program followed procedures described by the national Alcoholics Anonymous (AA) organization (Alcoholics Anonymous, 1955). Inmates ran the organization; they brought in AA speakers from the community and held group meetings twice weekly. Outside speakers and inmates discussed alcohol and its effects. Once a month, families of alcoholics met with inmates as a follow-up program to work on the problem together.

Reachout

The Reachout program engaged inmates in counseling youth from various community programs. Inmates ran the organization under the close supervision of counseling staff from the Department of Legal Medicine (DLM). Reachout staff, in consultation with DLM counselors, periodically held sessions to prepare prescreened men to become counselors for delinquents. Their work with youth involved individual and group counseling techniques.

Muslims

The American Muslim Mission is considered part of the World Community of Islam. This organization is held to be a moderate, theologically motivated group. This program was run by inmates. High religious values and a rigorous personal routine, including regular prayers and reading of the Koran, are emphasized. A mosque was established, and members prayed up to five times per day.

Christian Organizations

The Christian organizations maintained a fundamentalist orientation, with leadership provided by ministers and other individuals and groups from outside communities. The leadership described the purpose of these organizations as evangelical. Their aim was to establish religious discipline and values in the inmates. Charismatic prayer meetings were held once or twice weekly. Bible study groups were held, and inmates were encouraged to read the Bible and pray regularly.

College Programs

Two or three college-level courses were offered each semester through either the University of Massachusetts or Bunker Hill Community College. Inmates had to have graduated from high school or completed the pre-college GED (equivalent to high school diploma) program offered within the institution to participate in the college courses. Offerings included mathematics and English, as well as other beginning college courses, and classes typically met twice per week.

CASH (Can Anyone Save Humanity) Drug Rehabilitation

CASH is an organization based on a self-help philosophy that utilizes group settings for drug rehabilitation counseling, especially for rehabilitation from use of hard drugs. During the pretest time period, the program was primarily run by inmates who were receiving ongoing training and supervision from outside consultants. However, the inmate orientation director of the prison was responsible for intake procedure. After an orientation meeting, members would commit to a 4- to 5-month basic group therapy program that met several times per week. Participants were encouraged to commit for an even longer term and to become trained as facilitators. Facilitator training involved 1 hour per week of individual attention plus an hour or more per week with a group.

Political and Community Caucus Groups

Inmates ran political and community caucus groups to promote interfacing with the community to discuss criminal justice issues, promote inmate-community relations, and provide an avenue for personal and political exchange among inmates as well as between inmates and the community. Group meetings were held at least once a month, with the opportunity for more frequent involvement.

Department of Legal Medicine (DLM) Counseling

Although housed in Department of Corrections institutions, the DLM is under the auspices of the Massachusetts Department of Mental Health. At the time of pretest, almost all counseling was conducted on an individual basis. Counselors used an eclectic style–primarily insight-oriented or supportive therapy. Inmates typically attended once per week for an hour. During intake, the counselor and inmate contracted to meet for a given length of time–from less than a month to 1 year or more. Crisis-oriented counseling was provided, but inmates only received good time credit for ongoing involvement.

DATA ANALYSIS

In view of the sizable number of dependent variables (14), the chance of committing a type-one error when considering these variables separately was substantial. Thus, a principal component factor analysis involving all dependent variables was performed to reduce the number of variables and to permit a more comprehensive test of overall effect. This involved normalization of scores from the many different measurement scales (with their arbitrary units) to z scores (standard deviation units). Results of this and other types of analysis are presented in the Results section.

RESULTS

Demographic Outcomes

Members of the TM group did not significantly differ from those who were interested in TM or those not interested in TM on the 10 self-report pre-incarceration demographics: age, intelligence quotient (IQ), education, occupational status, father's occupational status, race, seriousness of crime, number of siblings, birth order, and religious affiliation. Another demographic variable, months served in prison for the current offense, was not a self-report item but was objectively determined from prison records. TM group members had currently served significantly more months in prison (*M* = 50.4) than those who were interested but did not learn (*M* = 32.2) and those not interested (*M* = 31.8). This was due, in part, to the fact that to qualify as a TM group member, the inmate had to have begun the TM program at least 6 months earlier. Members of some other programs also had been in prison significantly longer than nonmembers (i.e., AA, Reachout, Christians, College, Political Caucus) and for periods comparable to that for the TM group, again due, in part, to the minimum membership requirement of 6 months. Months currently served in prison did not, however, correlate significantly with any outcome measure. Members of the TM group had not been previously incarcerated more frequently than those interested or not interested (*M* = 1.35, 1.66, and 1.6, respectively). Also, the subgroup of inmates interested in the TM program did not differ significantly from those not interested on any demographic, except membership in the Protestant faith. Those interested were more likely to be members of the Protestant faith (27%) than those not interested (13%).

According to demographic self-report, the TM, Counseling, and Christian groups were the least self-selecting programs along major demographic divisions. The College program was the most self-selecting; members were significantly higher than those interested and those not interested in joining on IQ, prior educational attainments, and father's occupational status. (IQ refers to pretest score on the Mill-Hill Test.) Members of the College group also had fewer siblings and were more likely to be first born than those interested and not interested in joining the College program. Since more-affluent families also tend to be smaller in size, the sibling result may contribute to an overall demographic profile, suggesting that inmates who joined the College programs tended to be higher in socioeconomic and educational status than those who did not.

The next most self-selective program, the Muslims, tended to have younger members than those of other groups. Muslims were also predominantly black and non-Catholic. Members of the Muslim group had committed more serious crimes and had a lower occupational status on the street than nonmembers. Members of the drug rehabilitation program (CASH) also tended to be black and younger than nonmembers. The Political Caucus group, as well, had a higher percentage of blacks than did the nonmember segment of the sample. Reachout members had committed more serious offenses than nonmembers.

In addition to the lack of significant differences on the self-report demographics among the TM group, and those interested and not interested in joining, interested subjects did not significantly differ from subjects who did not express an interest in joining on any of the test measures. Moreover, in general, across all programs, interesteds did not diverge significantly from not interesteds.

Factor Analysis of Test Measures

There were 14 test measures and 8 other programs to which the TM program was being compared. Therefore, a principal component factor analysis with a varimax rotation (Harman, 1976) was performed to reduce the probability of type-one errors and to identify whether there was a fundamental factor structure underlying the dimensions and factors. The 14 test variables were reduced to three factors that accounted for 48% of the variance in test scores (see Table 3). This effectively reduced the number of primary comparisons from 504 to 27, of which 1.35 would be expected to reach significance at the $p = .05$ level from chance alone. The factor analytic procedure also served to eliminate test-scale redundancy and to simplify interpretation of results. The three factors identified were: (a) a Psychopathology factor–accounting for 24% of the test variance and defined by high scores on the State-Trait anxiety scale and on the three SHAPS psychopathology factors; (b) a Developmental factor–accounting for 13% of the variance and characterized by high positive scores on developmental measures (ego, moral, and cognitive) as well as on field independence and participation in avocational businesses; and (c) a Consciousness factor–accounting for 11% of the variance and defined by a high Absorption

Table 3: Factor Loadings from Principal Components Analysis of Test Measures[a]

	Factor 1 (24%) Psychopathology		Factor 2 (13%) Developmental		Factor 3 (11%) Consciousness
.920	Secondary psychopathology	.571	Formal operations	.762	Absorption
.818	Depressed introversion	.566	Field independence	.644	Post-conceptual experience
.796	Trait anxiety	.553	Principled moral reasoning	(.371	Intimacy motivation)
.734	Primary psychopathology	.533	Self-development	(−.331	Need for power)
.724	State anxiety	.510	Participation in avocational businesses in prison		

[a]Factor loadings of the 14 pretest measures via principle component factor analysis, giving 3 orthogonal factors (with associated variances). Scales were loaded at > .50. (The 2 motive measures, intimacy motivation and the need for power, loaded most highly on Factor 3, but did not make the .50 cut-off and were not included when calculating the score on this factor.)

score, indicating capacity for episodes of total attention and self-altered experience (Tellegen & Atkinson, 1974), and by a high frequency of self-reported, postconceptual experience on the SCI.

Although the positive loading of Intimacy Motivation (.37) and the negative loading of Need for Power (−.31) were not high enough to warrant inclusion in the Consciousness factor scale (cutoff for loadings was .50), these results do suggest that the Consciousness factor is consistent with descriptions of highly developed human functioning advanced by other researchers (e.g., Bakan, 1966; McAdams, 1979). For further discussion, see Alexander (1982).

APPARENT EFFECT OF THE TM PROGRAM ON THE PSYCHOPATHOLOGY, DEVELOPMENTAL, AND CONSCIOUSNESS FACTORS

The results obtained in the cross-sectional comparison of members of the TM group (who had been practicing the TM technique for an average of 20 months) with the interested and not interested groups were clear-cut. The TM group scored significantly lower on the Psychopathology factor than did all nonmember categories, with *effect sizes* (Cohen's effect size, d) ranging from −.75 to −.90 ($p < .001$; see Figure 1). This group also scored significantly higher on the Developmental factor than all nonmember categories, most notably compared to the interested group ($d = .72, p < .001$) and the total nonmember group ($d = .65, p < .001$). On the Consciousness factor, the TM group also scored significantly higher than did all nonmember categories, with effect sizes ranging from .49 to .82 ($p = .05$ to $< .01$). Furthermore, active members of the TM group (i.e., those who practiced at least once or twice per month in the month prior to pretest) scored higher on this factor than did all nonmembers ($d = .62$, $p < .01$). Consistent with this result, regularity in the TM program correlated significantly with the Consciousness score ($r = .46, p < .05$).

Due to the manner in which factor analysis deals with missing data, 159 of the 160 subjects classified by TM group membership received scores on the Developmental factor, 125 on the Psychopathology factor, and 117 on the Consciousness factor. Of the 124 subjects classified for the eight other programs, 124, 121 and 108 of the subjects were assigned scores on the three factors, respectively. Hence, data loss was minimized. Furthermore, when only the 124 TM-group subjects who completed the Personal Questionnaire were included in the analysis, the results were highly similar in effect sizes and p values to those previously described above for the larger number of subjects.

Comparison of outcomes from the TM program with outcomes resulting from the other programs also showed large differences. For the three factors (Psychopathology, Developmental, and Consciousness), the TM program was the only one in which members scored significantly and consistently better than all nonmember categories (Figure 1). Only two other programs showed

Figure 1: Comparisons of the Three Principal Factor Scores Across the Nine Program Groups

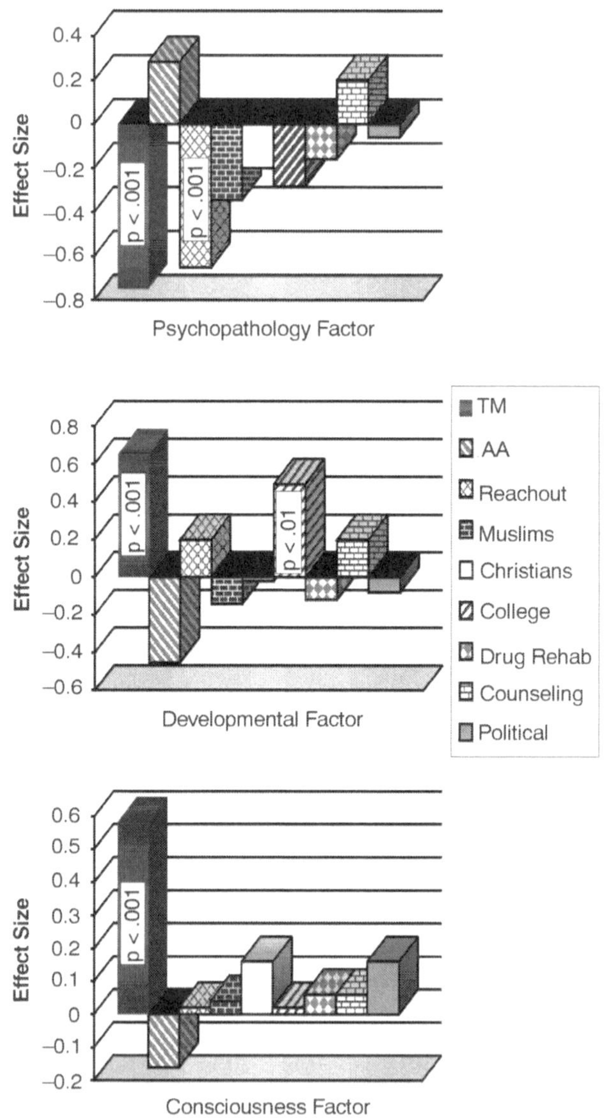

significant effects of membership, and these showed effects on only one factor. Reachout program members scored significantly lower than all nonmember categories on the Psychopathology factor, and College program members scored significantly higher than nonmembers on the Developmental factor.

These apparent effects of the Reachout and College programs are likely related to selection bias. The Reachout organization prescreened interested inmates to exclude those who were considered too deviant (i.e., too high on psychopathological symptoms) to be trusted in the counseling of youth. According to the self-report data, membership in the College program was the most self-selecting of all, selecting for inmates high in demographics correlated with developmental level.

Because there was some overlap of membership in different programs, analyses of covariance were run to test the possibility that overlap with Reachout or with College could explain the significant differences in the Psychopathology and Developmental factors, respectively. When membership in these programs was the covariate, the difference between the TM program and controls remained highly significant for all three factors (see Alexander, 1982). The difference in the Psychopathology factor for Reachout when TM membership was the covariate also was significant, but the difference for College was not.

TEST OF SPECIFIC PREDICTIONS FOR SELF-DEVELOPMENT

Loevinger's Self-Development Scale

The level of development on this scale was surprisingly high. The modal stage in this sample of prisoners, the Self-Aware level (I-3/4; see Table 1), was the same as the modal stage in adult American culture as a whole (Holt, 1980; Loevinger, 1976). Thirty-two percent of the inmate sample scored below I-3/4, 41% scored at the I-3/4 level, and 36% scored above I-3/4.

Examination of self-development by level of membership in the TM program (i.e., TM group member, interested in TM, or not interested in TM) showed that, proportionately, the interested and not interested groups contained over three times as many men at the preconventional level as did the TM group (Figure 2). Proportionately, approximately twice as many prisoners in the TM group fell in the postconventional (≥ I-4) range, relative to those in the interested and not interested groups. In tests for significant differences, demographic variables that might be related to self-development in a way that could confound the levels of TM treatment were adjusted for statistically. Based on empirical studies of demographic correlates of self-development (Loevinger, 1976, 1979), the following were selected as relevant covariates–age, education, race, and occupational status (both of the inmate and his father). Religion (separate dummy coding of Protestant and Catholic) and months currently

Figure 2: Stacked Percentage Distribution of Developmental Stage for the TM Group, the Controls Interested in TM, and the Controls Not Interested in TM

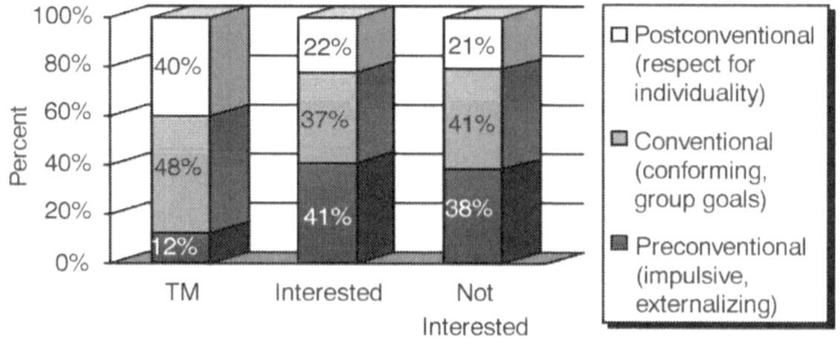

served were added because they discriminated between levels of membership in the TM group. Finally, seriousness of crime was included because it is a major variable for classification of inmates, as described in the correctional literature (Lipton, Martinson, & Wilks, 1975; Sellin & Wolfgang, 1964).

Following convention (Loevinger, 1979), self-development was entered as an ordinal variable (I-2 = 0 ... I-6 = 10). The omnibus F for analysis of variance, controlling for the 9 covariates, indicated a significant difference between the adjusted means on Loevinger's Self-Development for the 3 groups (TM member, interested, and not interested; $F = 6.27$, $p = .003$). A one degree of freedom contrast (Kepple, 1973) on the adjusted, unweighted means was performed with the prediction that TM group members would score significantly higher than the interested and not interested groups (contrast weights assigned were 2, −1, −1). The contrast, as well, proved highly significant ($F_{1, 121} = 14.00$, $p < .00025$). Comparison of the adjusted Self-Development levels of the 3 groups indicated that the mean score for the TM group was 1.12 and .86 steps higher than the scores for interesteds and not interesteds, respectively. TM group members were, on the average, approximately midway between the Self-Aware (I-3/4) and the Conscientious stages (I-4), whereas the interested and not interested groups fell approximately midway between the Conformist (I-3) and the Self-Aware levels (I-3/4).

TEST OF PREDICTIONS ON OTHER VARIABLES

Cognitive and Moral Development

Differences on individual variables were tested using one-tailed analysis because predictions were made for each of the individual variables comprising the three factors. The TM group members did not score higher than the interested group or the not interested group on principled moral reasoning, as measured by the Defining Issues Test. However, the active TM member subgroup scored .51 and .59 steps higher than the interested and not interested groups, respectively, on Kuhn's measure of level of cognitive development (solving a natural experiment problem requiring use of the formal operational isolation of variables scheme). There was a statistical trend toward a positive effect associated with the TM group relative to the various nonmember categories ($d = .24$ to $.30$, $p = .10$).

Development of Consciousness

The TM group scored significantly higher on the SCI Postconceptual Experience factor than did all nonmember groups. The active TM member subgroup, especially, scored higher than the combined nonmember groups ($d = .80$, $p < .001$). Also, regularity of practice of the TM program correlated at $r = .54$ ($p < .001$) with this Postconceptual Experience factor. (Regularity was scored on an ordinal scale: 5 = 10-14 TM sessions/wk, 1 = no practice during the last month.) Tellegen's measure of absorption correlated at $r = .39$ ($p < .001$) with the SCI Postconceptual Experience factor. TM group members showed a trend towards a significantly higher score on Tellegen's scale ($d = .28$ to $.39$, $p < .10$), when compared to the nonmember categories.

Reduction of Negative Affect

The TM group scored significantly lower on the secondary or Neurotic Psychopathology factor ($d = -.65$ to $-.95$, $p < .005$) and on the Depressed Introversion factor ($d = -.58$ to $-.77$, $p < .005$) than did all nonmember groups. The TM group members also were significantly lower than most nonmember groups ($d = -.45$ to $-.63$, $p \leq .05$) on the Primary Psychopathology factor.

The TM group scored significantly lower on both State Anxiety ($d = -.77$, $p < .005$) and Trait Anxiety ($d = -.87$, $p < .001$) than the interested group, and showed similar differences when compared with the other nonmember groups. The TM group also scored significantly lower than the interested group on the six individual SHAPS psychopathology scales (Depression, *effect size* = $-.77$, $p < .005$; Psychopathic Deviation, *effect size* = $-.67$, $p < .005$; Anxiety, *effect size* = $-.58$, $p < .025$; Aggression, *effect size* = $-.49$, $p < .025$; Tension, *effect size* = $-.49$, $p < .025$; Introversion, *effect size* = $-.49$, $p < .025$; Impulsivity, *effect size* = $-.41$, $p < .05$ and Hostility, *effect size* = $-.34$, $p < .05$). The Lie score ($M = 5.5$, out of 11) was within the normal range for SHAPS (Blackburn, 1975). Scores on the Lie and Extroversion subscales were somewhat higher in the TM group than in the nonmember categories but not significantly so.

Motivation Scores

On the TAT measure of intimacy motivation, which is an approach behavior or indication of positive affect (McAdams, 1979), the TM group scored significantly higher than the interested group ($d = .49$, $p < .025$), all nonmembers ($d = .41$, $p < .025$), and the not interesteds ($d = .39$, $p < .05$). Also, active TM group members trended higher than all nonmembers ($d = .32$, $p < .10$). On the TAT subscale Need for Power, 135 of the 137 inmates chose the exploitative type of imagery (Winter, 1973). There was no significant difference on intensity of Need for Power in the comparison between the entire group of TM members and all categories of non-TM members. Nevertheless, within the TM group, there was a highly significant inverse correlation between regularity of practice and Need for Power ($r = -.47$, $p < .01$). Moreover, the most regular meditators (10 plus meditations per week) did score significantly lower than all non-TM members ($p < .05$).

Internality and Self-Differentiation

On field independence as measured by the Embedded Figures Test, there were higher scores in TM group members than in the nonmembers who were interested ($d = .37$, $p < .05$). But the effect size when compared to the not interested group was substantially smaller (.20), so that the comparison with all nonmembers was only a trend ($d = .26$, $p < .10$). In light of Rock's (1975) finding of a qualitative change in self-reflection at the I-3/4 Transition, the apparent shift of the TM group to an I-3/4 or Self-Aware level of self-development is especially indicative of movement toward a self-differentiated, internal frame of reference.

Behaviors

Engagement in avocational businesses is an independent activity undertaken by some of the inmates; it is not considered an institutional group program as such. Avocational businesses include woodworking projects, pottery, and so forth. They are, essentially, private enterprises set up by an individual or a small group of men to deploy or develop skills and earn additional income. There is no formal group structure provided for the men, and, generally, sustained engagement in an avocational business requires self-initiative.

The TM group was significantly more likely to engage in avocational businesses within the institutions than was either the interested control group ($d = .54$, $p < .025$) or any of the other nonmember groupings ($d = .58$ to $.80$, $p < .005$). Post-release behaviors are reported in the retrospective recidivism study (Alexander, Rainforth et al., this volume).

DISCUSSION

The outcomes of this cross-sectional study support the hypothesized higher level of self-development and lower level of psychopathology in the TM group as compared to a variety of control groupings. In summary, the key findings are as follows. The 14 subscales tested were examined by principle components analysis, giving rise to 3 factors accounting for 48% of the variance in test scores: a Psychopathology factor, a Developmental factor, and a Consciousness factor. Using these factors, the TM group was compared with two control groups who were either interested or not interested in beginning the TM program. The TM group was also compared with 8 other treatment groups. The TM group scored significantly better than the interested and not interested groups on all 3 factors. Also, factor scores for the TM group compared favorably with those of the 8 other prison programs, with the TM group scoring the lowest of all the program groups on the Psychopathology factor and highest on the Developmental and Consciousness factors. Only the TM group showed significant differences from its control groups on each of the three factors when demographic covariates and overlap of membership were statistically controlled.

Individual Measures

Results on individual measures were similar to those on the factors. The TM group scored significantly lower than nonmembers on psychopathology measures, including State-Trait Anxiety and 5 scales of psychopathology from the SHAPS, while TM group scores on the SHAPS' Lie and Extroversion scales were within the normal range. On Loevinger's Self-Development test, the TM group scored substantially higher than the interested and not interested groups ($p < .0005$), controlling for relevant demographic covariates (i.e., IQ, education, time of testing, and religious orientation). However, the interested controls were virtually identical in Self-Development level to the not interested controls, providing evidence that subject self-selection had no significant influence on the findings.

Key distributions of subjects at different levels of Loevinger's Self-Development scale indicated that more than three times as many inmates in the interested and not interested groups fell in the low (Preconventional) range relative to the TM group. At the other end of the scale, nearly twice as many in the TM group scored relatively high, that is, in the Postconventional range, compared to the interested and not interested groups. In terms of higher states of consciousness, the TM group scored higher on the Postconceptual Experience factor of Alexander's SCI and on TAT-measured Intimacy Motivation than did the total nonmember group.

These cross-sectional findings are consistent with the basic premise of the TM technique: Systematic practice of the technique, resulting in experience of the underlying state of pure awareness, enhances individual development and alleviates stress-related imbalances. Such a result suggests that this Consciousness-Based[1] approach to rehabilitation provides an effortless, natural, and universally applicable method for reducing risk factors for crime. No other study has reported such a wide range of effects due to a single program.

STRENGTHS AND WEAKNESSES OF THIS STUDY

The logic of any cross-sectional study is that significant differences between members and nonmembers of a group, especially those nonmembers interested in joining the group, reflect underlying treatment effects. The cross-sectional differences found in this study between TM group members and nonmembers were robust. The results showed that significant differences were sustained whether TM group members were compared to the interested controls, the not interested controls, or the total nonmember group. This provides evidence against self-selection as a significant factor in the observed differences. Also, the TM program group differed significantly from the nonmember groups on all 3 test factors. Conversely, when demographic variables and overlap of membership were controlled for, only one of the other eight program groups (Reachout) significantly differed from its nonmember control groups on any factor (Psychopathology), and this difference was clearly due to the restriction of membership to only the healthiest individuals. In addition, the TM program group had the smallest number of drop-outs (24%) of any of the programs, yet significant results were obtained whether or not those who dropped out of the practice were included in the statistical calculation. Finally, among those who had not started the TM technique, the group interested in TM and the group not interested in TM did not differ from each other on any demographic or test variable, except that those interested were more likely to be members of the Protestant faith than those not interested (27% membership and 14% membership, respectively).

This study also has shortcomings. First, a cross-sectional design alone cannot establish causality. Also, group membership for this phase of the larger study was completely self-selected, and there was some membership overlap in different groups. However, each of these weaknesses was largely overcome by adding a longitudinal component (Part II of the larger study) that gave results similar to those of the present study (Alexander & Orme-Johnson, this volume).

OTHER RESEARCH SUPPORTING THE FINDINGS IN THIS STUDY

The outcomes described in this study uphold the stated hypothesis–that inmates practicing the TM program would show reduced psychopathology, increased self-development, and increased experiences of higher states of consciousness. The outcomes also are consistent with results of previous and later studies on effects of the TM program. Results of other studies, partly from non-offender populations, include enhancement of self-development, facilitation of cognitive and moral development, increased internal frame of reference (e.g., increases in field independence, internal locus of control, self-acceptance, self regard, and self-actualization), and increased engagement in constructive work and positive social behaviors. A number of studies have shown reduced psychopathology, including reduction of highly negative impulses and increase of impulse control, reduction of negative affect (i.e., anxiety, depression, neuroticism, irritability, hostility, and anger), and increased cooperative behaviors and affiliative orientation. Evidence that the TM program increases development to higher states of consciousness includes increased tendency toward self-actualization (i.e., more frequent peak experiences, enhanced self-concept, and enhanced self-awareness) and correlations between experiences of higher states of consciousness and improved intelligence, creativity, and mind-body coordination. Many of these findings are described elsewhere in this volume (Goodman et al., this volume; Hawkins, this volume; Hawkins et al., this volume).

Also the outcomes of Parts II (Alexander & Orme-Johnson, this volume) and III (Alexander, Rainforth et al., this volume) of the larger study directly support the conclusion of the present study. Part II showed significant changes in the same variables as found to be different in this cross-sectional study. And the reduced rate of recidivism in the TM group, as reported in Part III, is consistent with the proposal that these changes in psychopathology and development are important for the reduced recidivism rate. Thus, the conclusion arrived at in Part I–that these cross-sectional differences reflect effects of implementing the TM program in a prison setting–becomes even more compelling.

NOTE

1. Transcendental Meditation, TM, and Consciousness-Based are registered or common law trademarks licensed to Maharishi Vedic Education Development Corporation and used under sublicense.

AUTHORS' NOTE

Address correspondence to K. Walton, 1000 North 4th Street, FM 1005, Fairfield, IA 52557 (E-mail kwalton@mum.edu).

Transcendental Meditation in Criminal Rehabilitation and Crime Prevention. Pp. 127-160.

Walpole Study of the *Transcendental Meditation* Program in Maximum Security Prisoners II: Longitudinal Study of Development and Psychopathology

CHARLES N. ALEXANDER

Maharishi University of Management

DAVID W. ORME-JOHNSON

Maharishi University of Management

ABSTRACT We studied longitudinal changes in self-development and psychopathology over a 15.7-month period (SD = 4.4 months) in 271 maximum-security prisoners who were participating in either the Transcendental Meditation (TM) program, counseling, drug rehabilitation, or Muslim or Christian groups. For each program, new and advanced participants were compared with (a) subjects interested in participating who were delayed from starting, (b) subjects who were not interested in participating, and (c) subjects who dropped out. Only regular participants in the TM program changed significantly. Controlling for pretest scores, overlap of membership, and 19 demographic and criminal history factors, both new and advanced TM members who were regular in their practice increased more than one step in Loevinger's ego development scale, while drop-outs, delayeds, and not interesteds remained relatively unchanged ($p < .00025$). On the average, after 15.2 months of practice, new TM subjects moved from the Conformist, I-3 level, a dependent, exploitative orientation, to the Self Aware transition level, I-3/4, modal stage of American adults, which is characterized by a greater awareness of norms and goals. Advanced TM subjects (20 months regular practice at the beginning of the study) were at the Self-Aware stage at pretest, but after 13 additional months of TM practice, they grew to the next stage (Conscientious, I-4), which is more responsible, self-monitoring, self-respecting, and communicative. TM subjects also showed significant reductions in aggression ($p < .05$), especially those who meditated at least twice a week ($p < .005$). In addition, they showed reduced schizophrenic symptoms ($p < .05$), decreased trait-anxiety ($p < .10$, trend), and increased frequency of postconceptual experience of higher states of consciousness ($p < .01$), but did not significantly differ on either of the misleading items scale.

KEYWORDS Rehabilitation, Transcendental Meditation, psychopathology, crime prevention, ego-development, Maharishi Vedic Psychology

This is the second of three papers based on a doctoral dissertation from Harvard University (Alexander, 1982), testing the ability of the Transcendental Meditation (TM)[1] technique to rehabilitate maximum security prisoners. The first paper presents a cross-sectional study (Alexander, Walton, & Goodman, this volume), this paper reports the longitudinal results, and the third paper presents the recidivism results on meditating inmates after release (Alexander, Rainforth, Frank, Grant, von Stade, & Walton, this volume).

The theoretical perspective informing this research holds that effective rehabilitation can be achieved only by programs that stimulate development of the individual to higher stages of ego or self-development. In this view, individuals at risk for crime tend to be frozen at an immature level more typical of adolescence. As expressed in the terminology of Loevinger's system of stages of self-development (Loevinger, 1976; Alexander, Walton et al., this volume), antisocial and aggressive behavior is found more frequently in adults stationed in the Preconventional level and in the early stages of the Conventional level (Frank & Quinlan, 1976; Recklitis & Noam, 1990). Preconventional behavior is often impulsive and self-centered, with minimal awareness of one's own inner motivations and feelings. Preconventional thinking tends to be in terms of simplistic, black-and-white dichotomies with no shades of gray. Interpersonal relations are dependent and exploitative. The preconventional person is either unaware of, or has difficulty conforming to, the conventions, rules, or laws of society.

As self-development grows to the Conventional level, the sense of self becomes increasingly differentiated from the environment, providing individuals with the ability to see themselves in the perspective of the bigger picture of society. They begin to more clearly appreciate the long-term consequences of behavior, begin to develop long-range goals, and grow in the ability to fulfill desires with fewer inner and outer conflicts. The Conventional level has three substages, Conformist, Self-Aware (or Conscientious-Conformist), and Conscientious. Criminals frequently score at the Conformist level, which in their case may mean conforming to the distorted rules of their gang or local criminal community. The next step, the Self-Aware stage, represents a qualitative change in self-reflection, that is, people begin thinking about who they are and what they are doing. The Self-Aware stage is indicative of a transition in the direction of acquiring a self-differentiated, internal frame of reference as the basis of morality (Rock, 1975). The Self-Aware stage is considered a transition to the Conscientious stage. At the Conscientious stage the individual has the capacity for self-monitoring and can formulate ideals and long-term goals. Such people tend to be self-respecting members of the community who are communicative and responsible to others.

Previous research has found that it is very difficult to change self-development in adults using Western psychological approaches (Loevinger, 1985). Our search for effective means to facilitate continued stage development in adulthood led us to try an approach from the ancient Vedic tradition of India as brought to light by Maharishi Mahesh Yogi (Alexander, Davies et al., 1990; Alexander & Langer, 1990; Dillbeck & Alexander, 1989; Goodman, Walton, Orme-Johnson, & Boyer, this volume; Orme-Johnson, Zimmerman, & Hawkins, 1997). We hypothesized that practice of the TM technique would promote self-development in prison inmates through a dual process of transcending and the release of deep rooted stresses (Alexander, 1982). Transcending allows the activity of the mind to settle from its usual incessant activity into the silent level of transcendental consciousness, the Self. Physiological research indicates that experiences of transcendental consciousness correspond to a unique fourth major state of consciousness (Jevning, Wallace, & Beidebach, 1992; Wallace, 1970a; Wallace, 1970b). Transcendental consciousness has been distinguished from ordinary waking, dreaming, and sleeping on 20 psychophysiological dimensions (Alexander, Cranson, Boyer, & Orme-Johnson, 1987). It is generally a state of complete quiescence and integration of all branches of the nervous system, including periods of respiratory suspension and increased EEG coherence (Badawi, Wallace, Orme-Johnson, & Rouzeré, 1984; Dillbeck & Bronson, 1981; Dillbeck, Orme-Johnson, & Wallace, 1981; Farrow & Hebert, 1982; Gaylord, Orme-Johnson, & Travis, 1989; Levine, 1976; Nidich, Ryncarz, Abrams, Orme-Johnson, & Wallace, 1983; Orme-Johnson, 1977; Orme-Johnson & Haynes, 1981; Travis & Pearson, 2000; Travis & Wallace, 1997; Travis & Wallace, 1999).

The profound physiological rest gained through transcending sets the initial conditions for the body's self-repair mechanisms to normalize long-lasting effects of stress. A wide range of evidence indicates the TM program normalizes effects of stress, including reduction of stress hormones (Jevning, Wilson, & Davidson, 1978; Jevning, Wilson, & Smith, 1978; Walton & Levitsky, 1994; Walton, Pugh, Gelderloos, & Macrae, 1995; MacLean et al., 1997), decreased resting levels of heart and respiration rates, decreased plasma lactate, fewer spontaneous skin resistance responses (Dillbeck & Orme-Johnson, 1987), decreased blood pressure (Alexander et al., 1996; Schneider et al., 1995), decreased anxiety (Eppley, Abrams, & Shear, 1989), and reductions of over 50% in medical care utilization (Herron, Hillis, Mandarino, Orme-Johnson, & Walton, 1996; Orme-Johnson, 1987; Orme-Johnson, 1995). In our prison study we used self-report measures of transcendental consciousness and other higher states of consciousness to indicate transcending, and we used measures of aggression, anxiety, and schizophrenic experience to index reversal or normalization of effects of stress.

Our study was a recurrent, institutional cycle design (Campbell & Stanley, 1966). The cross-sectional component compared subjects who had already been practicing the TM program for approximately 20 months with other groups on 14 developmental and stress-related measures. The control groups consisted of subjects interested in learning the TM technique, of subjects not interested in learning the TM technique, and of subjects participating in eight other prison programs. The other programs were Alcoholics Anonymous (AA), Big Brothers/Reach Out (programs to train inmates for the counseling of youth offenders), Black Muslims, Christian fellowships, the college program, drug rehabilitation counseling, group therapy counseling, and political caucuses (programs that permit interfacing with the community to discuss criminal justice). A factor analysis reduced the 14 measures to 3 factors, a Psychopathology factor (loading on anxiety and psychopathology), a Developmental factor (loading on ego, moral, and cognitive development, field independence, and participation in avocational businesses), and a Consciousness factor (loading on capacity for episodes of total attention, and a high frequency of self-reported experiences of higher states of consciousness). The cross-sectional study found that the TM group scored the lowest of all the program groups on the Psychopathology factor and highest on the Developmental and Consciousness factors, controlling for demographic covariates and for overlap of membership in other prison programs.

The purpose of the longitudinal follow-up was to determine if the main findings of the cross-sectional testing could be replicated and extended (i.e., recycled over time). Table 1 summarizes the findings of the cross-sectional study and gives the predicted results of the longitudinal study.

Table 1: Stages of Ego Development and Their Characteristics, Showing the Results of the Cross-Sectional Study and the Predicted Results of the Longitudinal Study

Stages of Development	Characteristics	Results of the Cross-Sectional Study	Predicted Results of the Longitudinal Study
3. Preconventional Impulsive (I-2), Self-Protective (Δ)	No stable sense of self, impulsive, opportunistic, conflicts with society.		
4. Conformist (I-3)	Conforms to external rules, often of one's peers or local group ("the gang"); dependent; exploitive.	Interesteds and Not Interesteds in TM fell midway between the Conformist and the Self-Aware levels.	
5. Self-Aware (Conscientious-Conformist, I-3/4)	Begins to differentiate self in relation to the group and to society. Awareness of norms and goals. The modal stage in adult Americans.	TM group scored midway between the Self-Aware and the Conscientious stage.	New TM subjects will develop from below the Self-Aware stage to the Self-Aware stage, while controls delayed from starting TM and not interested will remain at their original developmental level.
6. Conscientious (I-4)	Self-monitoring, long-term goals, self-respecting, communicative, responsible.		Advanced TM will shift, on the average, one developmental stage from the Self-aware level to the increasingly Self-differentiated Conscientious stage.
7. Postconventional (I-4/5 to 6)	Highly established sense of self and respect for others, deeply principled, flexibility in resolution of conflicts, harmony with society.		Advanced TM already stationed at the Conscientious stage will transition to Postconventional levels.

Note: Also refer to Table 1 in Alexander, Walton et al., in this volume, for the levels of character development, interpersonal style, conscious preoccupations, and cognitive styles of these milestones of Loevinger's self-development scheme.

METHODS

Subjects

The subjects were inmates of the Massachusetts Correctional Institution, Walpole, a maximum-security facility for male offenders. Demographic profiles reported for subjects were based on Department of Corrections (DOC) records. As a check on the general reliability of DOC records, we determined the intercorrelation of a subset of seven pretest self-report variables used in the cross-sectional study and DOC demographics that were coded in a similar fashion (age, race, seriousness of crime, years of education, number of prior incarcerations, number of months currently served, number of months since last transfer). Correlations between paired self-report and DOC records for the given demographics were quite high, ranging from r = .440, $p < .001$ (on number of prior incarcerations) to .93, $p < .001$ (on age at pretest). The average correlation for the seven variables was $r = .61$ (SD = .189), and the means were highly similar. DOC computerized records allowed us to classify all subjects on 47 demographic and criminal history variables.

All inmates in the sample were male: 49.5% white, 45.5% black, 5% Hispanic. The median age range was 26-29 years; the median education was ninth grade. The religious affiliations of the inmates prior to their incarceration (some men converted, particularly to the Islamic faith, during incarceration) were: 49.5% Catholic, 37.5% Protestant, and 13% other (including Greek Orthodox, Muslim, Jewish, or no religious affiliation). Inmates had served 62 months (median) of their current sentence by posttest; the minimum current sentence of the sample was 10-12 years (median); the total number of prior incarcerations (juvenile and adult) was 2 (median). Armed robbery was the most serious current offense for 33% of the sample; murder was committed by 28.2% of the inmates; rape by 7.8%; burglary by 4.8%; manslaughter by 3.9%, and unarmed robbery by 3.9% of the sample. The remaining 18.4% was divided among 15 other offense categories. The median age of the inmates at first arrest was 14 years. At the time of the current incarceration, 58.2% of the sample was single, 18.4% divorced, 16.5% married, and 6.8% was separated or widowed. The occupation of most of the sample when on the street had been some form of manual labor (61.8%) or the provision of relatively unskilled services, for example, enlisted soldier, janitor, or gas station attendant (22.6%). The job of longest duration held by the inmates was 5-6 months (median). Of the sample, 58.25% were known drug users, and 36.9% of the inmates had been specifically identified as heroin users. Information on drug abuse was obtained by the DOC from the probation department. An inmate was categorized as a drug user if he had been arrested for narcotic offenses or if he admitted to drug use.

Representativeness of the Sample

Our sample was compared to the Walpole prison population as a whole (n = 630) on 10 parameters that were available at the time of the study. On 8 of the 10 parameters (i.e., number of incarcerations, minimum sentence, age at pretest, marital status, occupation, education, drug use, and age at first arrest), our posttest sample did not significantly deviate from the Walpole population. The average percentage difference between the posttest sample and the Walpole population on these eight characteristics was +/−3.80% (SD = 2.08). On two characteristics, the posttest sample did significantly deviate from the population: on a subcategory of offense type and on racial composition. The percentage of murderers in the overall posttest sample (28.6%) was significantly higher than in the population (19.7%) ($Z = 2.169$, $p < .05$). However, this difference does not represent a conceptually meaningful departure of the sample from the population (19.7%) because at pretest the percentage of murderers in our sample (20.6%) was highly similar to that of the population. The difference at posttest was due to attrition from pretest to posttest of the proportion of the sample composed of non-murderers, because the non-murderers were released sooner. With regard to race, at posttest (and pretest) our sample contained proportionally fewer white inmates (49.5%) than did the larger Walpole population (63.5%) ($Z = 3.140$, $p < .01$). Within the posttest sample, however, the proportion of whites in the meditating (50.9%) and nonmeditating (48%) subsamples was similar. Hence, race would be unlikely to affect the internal validity of our treatment outcome findings.

PROGRAMS

Transcendental Meditation Program

The TM program was taught to inmates using the same seven-step procedure that is used worldwide for the general public (Roth, 1987). Most of the steps last approximately 1-1/2 hours and are spread over 5 or 6 separate days. They are: (a) an Introductory Lecture on the benefits; (b) a Preparatory Lecture on the origin and nature of the program; (c) a brief Personal Interview, usually given immediately following the Preparatory Lecture; (d) one-on-one Personal Instruction, in which the student is taught the standardized TM technique; (e) First Day's Checking, a group meeting that covers the basics of meditation for all pupils who learned the technique on the same day; (f) Second Day's Checking, focusing on the mechanics of stress normalization; and (g) Third Day's Checking, a vision of enlightenment–the goal of meditation.

An optional weekly meeting was available to members to further discuss their experiences and the mechanics of the technique and to provide a deeper intellectual understanding of the principles governing the technique. Once a month an inmate could have his practice individually checked to insure correctness. The emphasis was on individual practice (20 minutes morning and evening), not on these group meetings. Only a relatively small subset of the members regularly attended meetings. However, the impression of instructors was that many students practiced quite regularly (10 to 14 times per week) even though they rarely attended meetings.

For purposes of conceptual clarity and to reduce the sheer number of statistical comparisons (and hence the likelihood of some of the results being due to chance), it was decided to reduce the number of comparison programs to be evaluated at posttest. In advance of the posttest data analysis, the following four programs were selected that, for purposes of comparison to and control of TM treatment effect, appeared most relevant on theoretical and methodological grounds.

Department of Legal Medicine (DLM) Counseling

The Transcendental Meditation program is conceived of by its advocates as a personal or self-development program (Maharishi Mahesh Yogi, 1972) and a psycho-therapeutic or adjunctive therapeutic program (Bloomfield & Kory, 1976). Therefore, it seemed appropriate to exclude those programs lacking explicit self-development or therapeutic goals and to include those groups that have been viewed as conventional or community alternatives to therapeutic or self-development programs. Individual (DLM) counseling offered the most conventional approach to therapeutic change within the prisons.

The TM program and DLM counseling both advocate an individual approach to personal development. The former is considered a totally self-regulative procedure that once learned requires no further supervision from instructors (Roth, 1987), and the latter takes place between individual client and therapist and does not involve group or community support. TM focuses on the release or normalization of stress and development of so-called higher states of consciousness. Counseling emphasizes coping with conflict and the development of maturity or ego strength. The two approaches do of course differ in their specific methods and definition of goal states. A comparison of the similarities and differences in outcomes of the two programs, given that both are operating with sufficient program integrity (Quay, 1977), would prove informative.

Although housed in DOC institutions, the DLM was under the auspices of the Massachusetts Department of Mental Health. Counselors used an eclectic style–primarily insight oriented or supportive therapy. Inmates typically attended once per week for an hour. During intake, the counselor and inmate contracted to meet for a given length of time, which could range from less than a month to 1 year or more. Crisis-oriented counseling was provided, but inmates only received good time credit for ongoing involvement.

CASH (Can Anyone Save Humanity) Drug Rehabilitation

The CASH drug rehabilitation program, like the AA program, offers therapies alternative to the individual counseling approach. Both rely upon a self-help group or community of fellow drug users as the therapeutic vehicle. They have a specific goal of coping with drug addiction, and they both claim that underlying transformation in the attitudes and self-concept of the individual is a prerequisite to coping with the drug abuse problem.[2] We selected CASH over AA as our alternative therapy comparison group for several reasons. First, the kinds of drug abuse problems (and hence the clientele) handled by CASH were more general. CASH offered a more intensive follow-up program. Finally, the DOC was interested in evaluating CASH because the Massachusetts Department of Mental Health had been funding it but lacked means for evaluating the program's effects.

The CASH program was primarily run by inmates who were receiving ongoing training and supervision from outside consultants. However, the inmate orientation director of the prison was responsible for intake procedure. After an orientation meeting, members would commit to a 4-month to 5-month basic group therapy program that met several times per week. Participants were encouraged to commit for an even longer term and to become trained as facilitators. Facilitator training involved 1 hour per week of individual attention, plus an hour or more per week with a group.

Christian Organizations

Finally, there were alternatives to therapy, such as participation in religious organizations, that served similar or complementary therapeutic functions (Sarbin & Adler, 1970). It would seem that the mechanisms that mediate the effects of fundamentalist religious groups would be consistent with those that operate in alternative therapies like AA. Both require personal commitment and exert normative group pressure; both involve persuaders that promise resolution of conflict, acceptance by the group, and alignment with a higher purpose as a consequence of proper attitudinal and behavioral change. In fact, both AA and CASH at times rely upon religious or quasi-religious values, especially those drawn from Christianity, to support their worldview and practices. In a sense, involvement in a revivalist religious organization would simply represent an intensification of commitment to a more complete world (and otherworldly) view whose rituals, traditions, and beliefs have accrued legitimacy over a longer period of time. Conversion to that worldview might involve an even more thorough overhaul of personal beliefs and a pervasive lifestyle change; the latter would typically include involvement in proselytizing activities that strengthened the legitimacy and power of the group and one's commitment to it. Tart (1975), Katz (1981), and Maslow (1962) suggest that religious organizations that also provide spiritual practices or regimens may facilitate transformation directly through those practices as well as via group support mechanisms.

The Christian organizations maintained a fundamentalist orientation, with leadership provided by ministers and other leading figures and groups from outside communities. The leadership described the purpose of these organizations as evangelical. Their aim was to establish religious discipline and values in the inmates. Charismatic prayer meetings were held once or twice weekly. Bible study groups also were held, and inmates were encouraged to read the Bible and pray regularly.

Muslims

In addition to the fundamentalist Christian Organization, we selected a Muslim group, the American Muslim Mission (a.k.a. World Covenant of Islam), to represent another religious alternative to therapy. Although the underlying organization of the two groups is in some respects quite similar (e.g., regular meetings for reading the Bible or Koran to reformulate worldview, encouragement of proselytizing activity, adoption of codes of behavior), in other ways the two groups obviously differed. For example, the Christians solicited members across racial groups while the Muslims appealed almost exclusively to blacks. Also, the Muslims, in principle, engaged in a rather rigorous set of spiritual practices, including prayer or meditation to Allah five times daily, while the Christian regimen was less demanding in terms of personal practices. On Fridays, Juma prayer service was mandatory for practicing Muslims.

The American Muslim Mission is considered part of the World Community of Islam. This organization is held to be a moderate, theologically motivated group, not to be confused with the militant Black Muslims of the early 1970s. This program was run by inmates, and a mosque was established for prayer.

MEASURES

Measures were selected to tap: (a) development as conceptualized in the West (Loevinger's Washington University Sentence Completion Test of Ego Development); (b) development as it is conceptualized in the Vedic tradition of India (Alexander's States of Consciousness Inventory); and (c) psychopathology (trait anxiety, Short-form Special Hospitals Assessment of Personality and Socialization, SHAPS) (Blackburn, 1971; Blackburn, 1975). These measures were chosen to assess the predicted mechanisms by which TM practice is said to foster development, i.e., experiences of higher states of consciousness (such as transcendental consciousness) and the release of deep-rooted effects of stress.

A smaller number of measures was administered at posttest. At pretest, several men had complained about the length of the testing sessions, and the number of subjects who completed different measures varied considerably. It was crucial methodologically to maximize the number of subjects who would participate in posttesting. Therefore, it was decided to substantially reduce the size of the posttest battery such that all tests could be easily completed within one test session as opposed to two, and yet inmates would be paid the same amount, $8.00, for their participation. Reduction of number of tests administered was also indicated, because prior reduction of the 14 initial measures to 3 principal factors suggested substantial redundancy among tests. Finally, the DOC preferred a shorter retest schedule to reduce the time demand of the staff who would have to oversee the retest procedure.

The posttest schedule followed the same sequence used in the pretest:

1. Informed Consent Form.
2. Loevinger's Washington University Sentence Completion Test (SCT) for men (the same form–Form 11-68–was administered at pretest).
3. Short-form Personal Questionnaire: focused only on program-joining behavior and required checking off of regularity in different programs. The short form was presented in a grid-like format with the various programs presented down the left side of the page and degrees of regularity of attendance indicated across the top of the page.
4. Spielberger's Trait Anxiety Form: STAI Form X-2, which was also presented at pretest; the State-Anxiety Form, STAI Form X-l, was not administered at posttest.
5. Short-form Special Hospitals Assessment of Personality and Socialization (SHAPS): aggression and lie SHAPS scales only, with items presented in random order.
6. Short-form State of Consciousness Inventory (SCI): a subset of items and categories of experience were selected that, on conceptual grounds (and in terms of clarity and readability of items), appeared to most meaningfully represent the states of consciousness described on the long-form SCI. The short form reduced the SCI from 108 items and 9 categories of experiences (12 items describing experiences for each category) to 36 items and 6 categories of experience (6 items per category). Each category was followed by a first-person account of typical experience of that category (e.g., experience during the dreaming state) in five different stages or states of consciousness (Alexander, 1982). Also included for each category was a high-sounding but actually misleading or nonsense item describing experience of that category. The five states of consciousness were as follows: (a) postconceptual experience, level IVc (pertaining to Unity Consciousness, the seventh and highest of Maharishi's Seven States of Consciousness); (b) postconceptual experience, level IVa (pertaining to Cosmic Consciousness, the fifth of Maharishi's seven states); (c) normal adult waking state experience; (d) neurotic adult waking state experience; and (e) schizophrenic adult waking state experience.

   Postconceptual experience, level IVb, pertaining to Refined Cosmic Consciousness (also called God Consciousness), the sixth of Maharishi's seven states, was not represented in the SCI short form. It was believed that the items in IVb may be more indicative of conventional religiosity than of the higher state of consciousness they were selected to represent.

PROCEDURES

Pretesting took place from May 1978 to March 1979, and the process of posttesting took place from October 1979 to August 1980. Posttesting was extended over almost as many months (10 months duration) as the pretesting (11 months duration). The average number of months from pretest to posttest was 15.7 (SD = 4.4). Posttesting was completed when each pretested subject had been canvassed at least twice but no more subjects came for testing.

After each subject completed all posttests, he then met individually with a tester. Together the subject and tester reviewed the subject's reported program-joining behavior on the personal questionnaire, clarifying and augmenting the score sheet as required. At posttest, pretest self-report information was supplemented by the relatively detailed posttest self-report interview. This was necessitated in part by the fact that the DOC institutional records for the months in which inmates participated in the various programs and hence received good time credit toward parole did not specify degree of regularity of participation within the month. Private reports on dates of participation for some members by the program directors of the Muslims, Christians, and TM program were also obtained. The DLM individual counseling staff's records were up-to-date and regularly reported in the DOC records, so private reporting was not required for that program.

Posttesting occurred after 13-17 months of TM practice for the new meditators. TM subjects from the cross-sectional study who were already meditating were also restudied to see if continued practice of the TM program produced additional improvement. This was the regular advanced TM group. At posttest they had been meditating an additional 13 months, for a total of approximately 33 months of TM practice.

Statistical Design

Though change over time is typically represented in terms of gain scores, analysis of covariance with pretest scores as the covariate is generally believed to provide a more precise and hence more powerful analysis of relative change in the experimental group compared to the control groups (Campbell & Stanley, 1966; Judd & Kenny, 1981). Though our quasi-experiment did not permit us to gain such control by experimental methods, analysis of covariance allowed us by statistical methods to adjust observed group means to the means (unweighted adjusted means) that "would have been obtained had the subjects within groups and the groups themselves been equated on the control variable" (Kepple, 1973, p. 480).

To evaluate longitudinal change, we generally adhered to the following data-analytic strategy. One-way analyses of variance were performed to determine the effect of each program treatment factor (independent variable) on each posttest measure (dependent variable) with pretest as the covariate (control variable). Only those subjects who received both a pretest and a posttest score on the given measure were included in the analysis. Membership in each treatment program was divided into six mutually exclusive categories or levels on the basis of pooled information sources on program-joining behavior: active advanced member; drop-out (or stopped) advanced member; active new member; drop-out (or stopped) new member; delayed from starting (until after posttest); and not interested in joining the program. Active indicates that the member participated in the program at least once or twice a month during the two months prior to posttest. Drop-out or stopped indicates that the subject dropped out more than two months prior to posttest. Advanced members of all programs joined their programs on the average 25.8 months (SD = 5.4) prior to the pretest. New members joined their programs on the average 1.8 months (SD = 2.1) after the pretest.

For purposes of longitudinal analysis, subjects were assigned new member status if they joined the program less than 4 months before the pretest (though most subjects began after the pretest date); the range of mean starting dates for the programs was: + .09 months after pretest to + 5.24 months after pretest. Because we typically could not specify when within the month the subject began the program (due to crudeness of monthly records), the records should be accurate within one month.

The last TM course to be taught prior to our initial pretest had taken place some 8 months earlier, so we considered members of that earlier group to be advanced practitioners by the pretest date. Therefore, the 4-month cut-off seemed an appropriate marker for dividing the TM group into advanced and new members. Also, it permitted all subjects to be classified. We then applied the same cut-off to the other programs. Given that the average length of participation of advanced members in the other programs (range: 23.37–34.67 months) was even higher than for TM (20.00 months), the grouping of subjects with 4 or fewer months participation with the new members seemed appropriate for the other groups as well. Even with this addition of members, the new member groups were smaller than the advanced member groups for the other programs.

The most significant adjustment we made was for the pretest score, which is assumed to totally mediate effect of assignment of subjects to conditions. Nevertheless, as an additional precaution we also covaried or adjusted for: overlap of membership in the program being evaluated with active membership in the four other programs (active member = 1, other = 0); demographics and criminal history variables on which advanced, new, or nonmembers significantly differed from one another (omnibus F, $p < .10$, two-tailed); and for additional demographics and criminal history variables significantly correlated (partial correlation, $p < .10$, two-tailed) with the given outcome posttest (adjusted for pretest score). In addition to a reduction of the error term, such an approach should control for initial demographic differences between groups that may have been responsible for outcome differences, rather than the supposed treatment effect. We initially explored some 47 demographics that the prior correctional and relevant testing literature suggested may have a mediating effect on test outcomes.

The final step involves the testing of hypotheses about differences that should be obtained between group means (levels of the given treatment factor). The method of planned comparisons or contrasts is particularly suited to this task of prediction. The contrasts procedure permits comparisons between group means by the multiplication of the means by a set of coefficients or predictor weights and an algebraic summation of these weighted means (Kepple, 1973). A multiple degrees of freedom omnibus F only identifies a significant result for all the group differences taken together; it does not specify the nature or magnitude of the differences between particular groups (or levels of the factor). Contrasts provide a means of decomposing the omnibus F's overall sources of variance of df > 1 into single df F-tests that make specific predictions. The computational formula for comparisons between means based on unequal sample sizes we employed is given by Kepple (1973).

We performed contrasts on the means of the one-way ANOVAS adjusted for relevant covariates. Contrast weights (coefficients) must sum to zero. A contrast with the predictor weights (1, 0, 1, 0, −1, −1) describes the general form of our predictions about the TM program: active advanced (+1) and active new members of TM (+ 1) will display significantly higher adjusted mean scores in the predicted direction on outcome measures than delayeds (−1) and not interesteds (−1), while advanced (0) and new TM drop-outs (0) will score between active members and nonmembers. As indicated earlier, a contrast on the adjusted means is considered a more sensitive measure of differential treatment effect or change over time than a contrast on simple gain scores.

Because all contrasts to be performed on the TM program were planned in advance–predicting specific outcomes consistent with cross-sectional findings–one-tailed tests were employed.

We predicted that other programs would not produce significant treatment effects. Nevertheless, at least some advocates of each of these programs would have made the same positive predictions for their treatment that we made for the TM program. Therefore, the statistical tests for the other programs were also one-tailed in the therapeutic direction; otherwise, the TM program would have been given a statistical advantage in producing significant results.

In all cases, the tests for the lie scale, misleading items scale, and normal waking state factor remained two-tailed, because there is no simple directional prediction of the relationship between these measures and therapeutic change that would be applicable across all programs and all developmental levels.

RESULTS

Demographic Characteristics of the Groups

Forty-seven DOC pre-incarceration and current test-related demographics were initially considered. An exploratory correlation matrix was generated, and 18 highly redundant variables were eliminated. Principle component factor analysis with iterated communalities was applied to further reduce the remaining 29 variables to 10 highly interpretable variables that accounted for 66.5% of the variance. The variables were: (a) seriousness of crime, (b) repeat offender, (c) Catholic/Caucasian, (d) time of intervention interval, (e) single status, (f) young drug user, (g) divorced, (h) sibling order, (i) maximum security level prison, and (j) occupational status (Alexander, 1982).

The TM subjects were the least self-selecting of the tested prison programs. There were no significant differences between advanced (long-term) members, new members, controls delayed from starting the TM program, and subjects not interested in learning TM. Interestingly, there were proportionally more non-whites in the advanced TM group than in the new TM group. However, the proportion of whites in the pooled new and advanced TM groups (48%) was highly similar to the proportion in the pooled non-TM group (51%).

Demographically, the most self-selecting group was the Muslims, who tended to be black (95%), younger, single, less likely to be divorced, and of lower occupational status. The Christian group tended to be Protestant, black, and single, and new Christian members who were pretested earlier had a longer duration between pretest and posttest relative to advanced or new members.

The minimum sentence of the TM posttest sample was significantly shorter than that of the non-TM posttest sample ($t_{100} = -2.835$, $p < .01$, $r = .27$). Minimum sentence, however, was not significantly ($p < .05$) correlated with any psychological test outcome. Moreover, on the seriousness of crime factor, of which minimum sentence was a component part, the posttest TM sample score was slightly, though not significantly, higher than for the non-TM posttest sample.

Program Sample Sizes and Drop-Out Rates

As would be expected, the drop-out rate among the advanced or long-term members was higher than for the relatively new members in each program. Presuming a gradual process of attrition, members who began less recently should be less likely to have participated at least once or twice a month during the last two months prior to retesting (the criterion for *active* membership). At posttest, the TM program had the lowest drop-out rates for both advanced and new members–as it did for advanced members at pretest (see Table 2).

Based on unweighted means, the average number of months minimally regular between pretest and posttest for currently active, advanced members across programs (M = 9.97, S.D. = 2.8) was almost five times higher than for current drop-outs (M = 2.00, S.D. = 2.8). Excluding new Counseling subjects, the currently active new members of the other programs for which there was information had been involved over twice as long (M = 11.5, S.D. = 2.4) as the drop-outs (M = 4.9, S.D. = 2.1). For Counseling, length of involvement for drop-outs was almost as high (4.4 mo.) as among active new members (5.7 mo.). An empirical and conceptual problem in classifying the Counseling members is that a drop-out may, in fact, be a successful graduate of the program. Therefore, we analyzed the results of Counseling members two ways: one treating ongoing Counseling members as active members and the nonactive members as drop-outs, the other treating those no longer in Counseling as graduates who should perform better than nonmembers, with current active members scoring between the two.

Overlap of Program Membership

Inmates received good time credit towards parole for active participation in programs. Initially, it appeared that inmates shopped around but actually remained active in only a few programs (Alexander, 1982). In any case, the degree of overlap of active membership among these five programs did not reach statistical significance.

Table 2: Number of Subjects Classified as Members in Five Prison Programs at Posttest

Program	Total Members	Advanced Active[a]	Advanced Stopped[b]	New Active[a]	New Stopped[b]
TM	50	13	11(45.3)[c]	19	7(26.9)[c]
Christian	63	12	31(72.1)	13	7(35.0)
Muslim	38	8	21(72.4)	5	4(44.9)
Drug Rehab.	41	7	21(75.0)	6	7(53.8)
Counseling	79	12	39(76.5)	12	16(57.1)

a Active = minimally, once or twice/month last 2 months
b Stopped = stopped more than 2 months ago.
c Percentage (%) of drop-outs.

Attention to overlap in membership that includes drop-outs can be misleading. For example, inmates who joined TM were more likely than non-TM inmates also to have joined Drug Rehabilitation ($r = .33$, $p < .001$), yet the subjects who remained active in TM were unlikely to have remained active in Drug Rehabilitation ($r = -.176$). A similar relationship was observable between the Christian organization and Drug Rehabilitation. Because we were particularly interested in the effect of active membership in programs on psychological test outcomes, it seemed more appropriate to adjust for overlap in active membership alone rather than general membership, which included drop-outs.

Self-Development

Advanced active and new active TM group members scored substantially higher in self- or ego development at posttest (controlling for pretest score) than did the delayed group and the not interested group ($F_{1,76}$ 14.34, $p < .00025$, $r = .3984$) (see Table 3). The contrast employed (1, 0, 1, 0, −1, −1) was conservative because it essentially required an outcome in the predicted direction for both new active and advanced active TM subjects (or a very large effect for one category).

It could be claimed that an apparent TM effect on ego development is created because drop-outs are not included in the active TM categories. In our contrast, drop-outs are assigned a zero weight because it is assumed that when subjects no longer engage in the practice, they will stop achieving additional gains. An alternative explanation would be that drop-outs might not have undergone change. If this were the case, the overall TM effect would be highly inflated. To address this criticism, an additional, highly conservative contrast was performed. Drop-outs were, essentially, pooled with active members via weighted means, and all TM members were contrasted with nonmembers. If drop-outs had not undergone substantial improvement, then their inclusion in the TM group should attenuate the TM effect but not remove it entirely (if the actives had indeed changed significantly). In fact, pooling drop-outs with actives attenuated but certainly did not remove the TM effect on ego development ($F_{1,76} = 6.533$, $p < .01$, $r = .28$) (see Table 3). The effect size (r) was decreased by approximately 30%. Of course, an argument could also be made in the opposite direction, that it is justified to pool drop-outs with nonmembers. Put simply, the logic of this contrast (2, −1, 2, −1, −1, −1) would be that if you don't take a pill (the treatment), it won't work and that any initial effects of the pill would be subject to complete reversal. The contrast (2, −1, 2, −1, −1, 1) yielded a highly significant result ($F_{1,76} = 23.70$, $p < .000005$, $r = .488$). The latter effect (r) was approximately 20% greater than that for the initial prediction.

To explore our specific longitudinal predictions, an examination of mean change scores (adjusted for demographic controls) is appropriate. Though easier to interpret, change score analysis should yield results that are slightly less

Table 3: Contrasts on the ANCOVA Comparing Active TM Program Members to TM Drop-Outs and Nonmembers on Seven Outcome Measures After a Long-Term Treatment Intervention

OUTCOME VARIABLE (Posttest Score)	MEMBERSHIP IN TRANSCENDENTAL MEDITATION PROGRAM[a]					
	Advanced Active[b]	Advanced Stopped	New Active[b]	New Stopped	Delayed	Not Interested
EGO DEVELOPMENT						
M	6.308	5.375	5.167	4.000	4.176	4.519
SD	1.843	0.518	0.985	1.500	2.215	1.673
ADJ.M'[c]	5.862	4.553	5.750	4.144	4.479	4.757
N	13	8	18	7	17	27
contrast weights	*# covariates*	*df*	*F*[f]	*t*[g]	*Significance*	*r*
(1, 0, 1, 0, −1, −1)[d]	8	1,76	14.34	3.19	< .00025	.3984
(13, 8, 18, 7, −18.5, −18.5)[e]	8	1,76	6.53	2.56	< .01	.2813
AGGRESSION						
M	13.375	12.667	15.500	17.429	16.529	17.762
SD	7.855	5.686	6.630	6.051	6.186	6.730
ADJ.M'[c]	13.732	16.4 77	13.638	16.168	15.899	17.417
N	8	3	14	7	17	21
contrast weights	*# covariates*	*df*	*F*[f]	*t*[g]	*Significance*	*r*
(1, 0, 1, 0, −1, −1)[d]	9	1,55	3.19	1.79	< .05	.2341
(8, 3, 14, 7, −16, −16)[e]	9	1,55	2.12	1.46	< .10	.1928
TRAIT ANXIETY						
M	35.600	37.333	37.143	38.857	42.235	40.300
SD	11.501	8.733	10.227	12.335	10.311	9.385
ADJ.M'[c]	38.151	39.187	35.468	37.403	41.273	39.986
N	10	6	14	7	17	30
contrast weights	*# covariates*	*df*	*F*[f]	*t*[g]	*Significance*	*r*
(1, 0, 1, 0, −1, −1)[d]	9	1,70	2.29	1.51	< .10	.1781
(10, 6, 14, 7, −18.5, −18.5)[e]	9	1,70	2.43	1.56	< .10	.1830
LIE						
M	5.000	5.000	4.571	3.857	3.588	4.333
SD	2.507	2.646	1.828	2.795	1.661	2.536
ADJ.M'[c]	4.925	4.547	4.956	4.625	3.451	3.846
N	8	3	14	7	17	2.1
contrast weights	*# covariates*	*df*	*F*[f]	*t*[g]	*Significance*	*r*
(1, 0, 1, 0, −1, −1)[d]	8	1,56	3.18	1.78	< .10	.2318
(8, 3, 14, 7, −16, −16)[e]	8	1,56	3.22	1.82	< .10	.2366

	MEMBERSHIP IN TRANSCENDENTAL MEDITATION PROGRAM[a]					
OUTCOME VARIABLE (Posttest Score)	Advanced Active[b]	Advanced Stopped	New Active[b]	New Stopped	Delayed	Not Interested
POSTCONCEPTUAL EXPERIENCE (SCI)						
M	3.918	3.018	3.732	2.623	2.788	2.788
SD	1.372	1.378	0.935	0.809	1.047	0.814
ADJ.M[c]	3.594	2.769	3.731	2.726	3.038	3.010
N	10	5	14	7	17	27
contrast weights	*# covariates*	*df*	*F*[f]	*t*[g]	*Significance*	*r*
(1, 0, 1, 0, −1, −1)[d]	8	1,66	6.47	2.54	< .01	.2989
(10, 5, 14, 7, −18, −18)[e]	8	1,66	2.34	1.53	< .10	.1849
NORMAL WAKING STATE (SCI)						
M	3.924	4.140	3.652	3.386	3.921	3.542
SD	1.115	0.590	1.023	1.145	0.772	0.914
ADJ.M[c]	3.774	3.600	3.726	3.459	4.108	3.899
N	10	5	14	7	17	27
contrast weights	*# covariates*	*df*	*F*[f]	*t*[g]	*Significance*	*r*
(1,0,1,0,−1,−1)[d]	9	1,65	.959	.979	NS	.1206
(10, 5, 14, 7, − 18, − 18)[e]	9	1,65	2.11	1.45	< .25	.1774
SCHIZOPHRENIC EXPERIENCE (SCI)						
M	2.167	2.822	1.964	1.889	2.601	2.181
SD	0.921	1.323	0.906	0.595	1.003	0.815
ADJ.M[c]	2.007	2.302	2.284	1.973	2.669	2.389
N	10	5	14	7	17	27
contrast weights	*# covariates*	*df*	*F*[f]	*t*[g]	*Significance*	*r*
(1, 0,1, 0, −1, −1)[d]	12	1,62	3.03	1.74	< .05	.2159
(10, 5, 14, 7, − 18, − 18)[e]	12	1,62	3.79	1.95	< .05	.2388

[a] Advanced = began Transcendental Meditation (M) 20 months before pretest. New = subjects who began TM 16.6 months prior to posttest. Delayed = interested at pretest but delayed from starting till after posttest. Not interested = not interested at pretest and did not subsequently join.

[b] Active = at least once or twice/month during 2 months prior to posttest. Stopped = dropped out more than 2 months prior to posttest.

[c] Posttest score adjusted for these covariates: pretest score; overlap with active membership in other programs (active member = 1, other = 0); demographics on which advanced TM members differed (p < .10) from new or nonmembers (i.e., security level of prison, months between pre- and posttest, race); additional demographics correlated (p < .10) with each outcome posttest score adjusted for pretest score (see Alexander, 1982, Table U).

[d] Contrast (1, 0, 1, 0, −1, −1) predicts Active TM members (Adv. and New) differ significantly in the predicted direction from nonmembers (Delayeds and Not Interesteds) and that Drop-Outs score between the two.

[e] Contrast weighted by TM subgroup sample sizes: predicts that TM members (actives and drop-outs) differ from nonmembers in the predicted direction.

[f] F contrast on the ANCOVA performed on the adjusted means (note c).

powerful than, but consistent with, those based on ANCOVA pretest adjustment procedures (Judd & Kenny, 1981). In this case, the effect size (r) associated with the change score analysis ($F_{1,77} = 22.056$, $p < .00001$, $r = .472$) was only 3.3% smaller than that produced by the pretest adjustment method for the same contrast. In fact, consistent with the findings produced by pretest adjustment, change score analyses yielded significant results (or trends) for all other outcome measures as well. Nevertheless, on the few measures for which active TM members had particularly high scores at pretest, the levels of significance for the change score analyses were somewhat attenuated due to regression effects associated with the change score procedure.

For the subjects who completed both the pretest and posttest, the unadjusted group mean for the advanced active TM was 5.308 (S.D. = 1.182) at pretest and 6.308 (S.D. = 1.843) at posttest. The unadjusted mean change score for active, advanced TM was + 1.000 (S.D. = 1.291), and the adjusted mean change score was + 1.092 steps. The unadjusted group mean for the new active TM at pretest was 3.944 (S.D. = 1.626) and at posttest was 5.167 (S.D. = .985). The unadjusted mean change score for new active TM was 1.222 (S.D. = 1.666) (adjusted mean change = 1.238). Hence, the adjusted mean change score over the approximately 15-month intervention period was slightly higher than one full step of ego development for both advanced active and new active TM subjects.

Highly consistent with our recycle design, the mean of the new active TM group at posttest (5.167) is just slightly lower than the mean for the advanced active TM group at pretest (5.308); and the advanced active TM group progressed a further step during the current intervention period (6.308). On the average, the new active TM subjects evolved from a Conformist (I-3) to a Self-Aware transition stage, and the advanced active TM group shifted from the Self-Awareness transition level to the Conscientious stage of self development (see Figure 1).

The drop-out group and the nonmember (delayed and not interested) group remained relatively unchanged from pretest to posttest. The slight, and statistically nonsignificant, decrease in scores among the drop-out group and delayed controls is unlikely to represent a meaningful regression in development. All else being equal, due to testing effects (e.g., boredom with task), adult subjects often tend to score somewhat lower upon retest with the Sentence Completion Test (though the effect is most salient over short-term retest periods) (Loevinger, 1979).

It is somewhat misleading, however, to imagine that, individually, all of the new active TM subjects were uniformly stationed at the Conformist level at pretest, or that consistently all new and advanced TM subjects went up one step between pretest and posttest. Finer grade analysis of individual change scores for new and advanced members, reveals a different and richer pattern of change than would have been discerned from examination of group means alone.

Figure 1: The pretest and posttest unadjusted group means on the Loevinger's ego development scale for the New Active TM, Advanced Active TM, Drop-out, Delayed, and Not Interested groups after the 15 month (approx.) intervention. Consistent with our recycle design, the New Active TM group evolved from the Conformist to the Self-Aware stage, and the Advanced TM group evolved from the Self-Aware to the Conscientious stage. There were no significant changes in Drop-out, Delayed, and Not Interested groups.

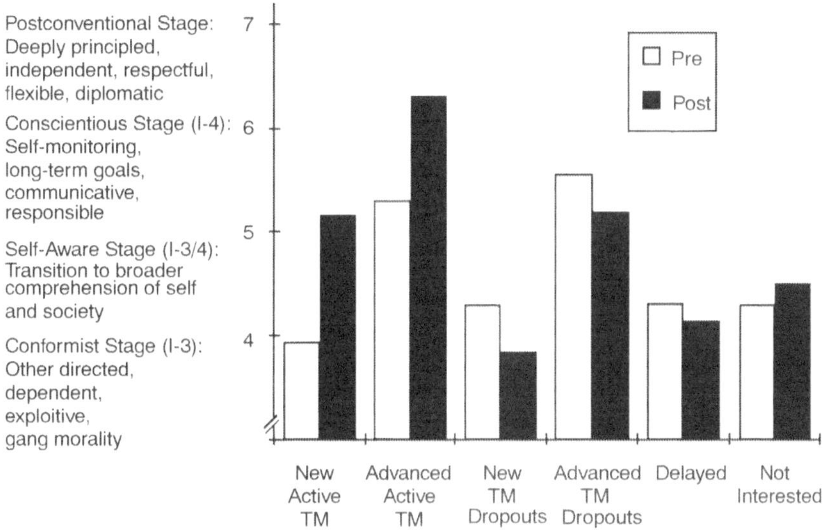

Whereas 10 of the 18 new active TM group members began below or at I-3, only 2 active TM subjects remained below the Self-Aware level (I-3/4) after the intervention period. No active TM subjects actually resided at the Conformity stage after the intervention. Therefore, most new active TM subjects who went up, in fact, increased by two or more steps. In the new TM group, 12 of 18 (67%) progressed at least one step. The most common patterns of change were from the Self-Protective Conformist Transition (Δ/3) to the Self-Aware Transition (I-3/4) (+ 2 steps); from the Conformity level (I-3) to the Conscientious Stage (I-4) (+ 2 steps); from the Self-Protective Stage (Δ/3) to the Self-Aware Transition (+ 3 steps); from the Self-aware transition to the Conscientious Stage (+ 1 step). There was clearly an I-4 or Conscientious Stage ceiling among practicing new TM group members. At the posttest, all but 2 in the new TM group scored at either I-3/4 or at the I-4 Stage, with no subjects scoring above I-4.

Among the advanced active TM group members, 8 of 13 (62%) advanced one or more steps. Five advanced one step; 3 advanced 2 or more steps. The most common pattern of change was movement from I-3/4 to I-4 (+ 1 step). Again, there appeared to be some developmental (or environmental) pressure to stay at or below the Conscientious level. Three of the subjects who remained developmentally stationary from pretest to posttest were I-4; the other 2 were I-3 and I-3/4. Nevertheless, 3 subjects who began at an I-4 plus level did progress to still higher stages. Two subjects attained the developmental endpoint of Loevinger's system, moving from I-4 and I-4/5, respectively, to her Ego Integration (I-6) position. One subject shifted from the Conscientious Stage (I-4) to the Individualistic (I-4/5) transition level.

The State of Consciousness Inventory (SCI)–TM Results

Members of the advanced active and new active TM groups scored significantly higher on the Postconceptual Experience factor (controlling for pretest scores) than TM nonmembers ($F_{1,66} = 6.47$, $p < .01$, $r = .2989$) (see Table 3). The Postconceptual Experience factor score represents the average frequency of experiences of the SCI items that compose the SCI factor I during the month prior to testing. The mean change scores (adjusted for demographics) for the advanced active and new active TM groups were .572 (S.D. = .976) and .399 (S.D. = 1.126), respectively. The unadjusted posttest means for the advanced active and the new active TM group were 3.918 and 3.732, respectively. This would suggest that active members were beginning to have postconceptual experiences more than "some of the time" (approx. 10%) and close to "often" (approx. 33%). Though it could be claimed that self-report of active members may be inflated due to their expectation of change on higher-state-like experiences, active members scored no higher on the adjusted, face valid, misleading items scale than did nonmembers ($F_{1,165} = .0629$, n.s.). Apparently, the active TM group did not simply respond to items that sounded good if they did not correspond to their actual experiences. SCI instructions do not cue the subject that any particular items embedded in the form refer to special positive experiences (see Alexander, 1982, Appendix 4 and Appendix 6-6, for SCI item descriptions).

Because drop-outs scored relatively lower on the Postconceptual Experience factor (though not significantly lower than nonmembers), the contrast that pooled drop-outs and active TM members attenuated the TM effect ($F_{1,66} =$ 2.336, $p < .10$). When drop-outs are pooled with nonmembers, the TM effect is increased comparably ($F_{1,66} = 12.78$, $p < .0005$, $r = .4027$). No subject in the entire sample reported experiencing a stabilized postconceptual experience stage across the 6 categories of experience on either SCI factor I or the face valid Differentiated (Cosmic Consciousness, IVa) and Unification (Unity Consciousness, IVc) postconceptual experience scales.

As predicted, the advanced active and new active TM groups did not significantly differ from the delayed group and the not interested group on the posttest Normal Waking State factor controlling for pretest score ($F_{1,65}$ = .9586, n.s.). The new active and advanced TM groups did score significantly lower on the adjusted posttest Schizophrenic Experience factor than did nonmembers (delayed and not interested groups), whether drop-outs were excluded in the membership category ($F_{1,62} = 3.031$, $p < .05$) or included ($F_{1,62} = 3.787$, $p < .05$) (Table 3).

The results for the TM groups were much the same on the original conceptually based SCI scales generated by experts as they were on the empirical SCI factors reported above (Alexander, 1982, p. 221).

Aggression, Trait Anxiety, and Lie Scales–TM Findings

The adjusted posttest aggression score was significantly lower for advanced active and new active TM groups than for the delayed and not interested ($F_{1,55} = 3.19$, $p < .05$, $r = .2341$) (see Table 3). The result was somewhat attenuated when drop-outs were pooled with active members ($F_{1,55} = 2.123$, $p < .1928$). Interestingly, when a more stringent requirement for inclusion in the active TM category was set (practice of the program at least twice/week during the past 2 months), a more dramatic TM effect was detected ($F_{1,55} = 7.304$, $p < .005$, $r = .3849$).

There was a trend toward reduction in Trait Anxiety on the adjusted posttest for the advanced active and new active TM groups ($F_{1,70} = 2.29$, $p < .10$, $r = .1781$) that was maintained when drop-outs were included in the TM membership category ($F_{1,70} = 2.43$, $p < .10$, $r = .1830$). Examination of the adjusted posttest means suggests that, relatively, the advanced active TM group did not change as much from pretest to posttest as the new active TM group or even the drop-out new TM subjects. This could in part have resulted from a floor effect or lower limit on Anxiety level within the prison. At pretest, the active TM group ($M = 37.600$) was already scoring at the normative level for undergraduate males ($M = 38.0$, $N = 253$) and well below the norm for prison inmates at a federal correctional institute in Tallahassee, Florida ($M = 45.0$, $N = 212$) (Spielberger, Gorsuch, & Lushene, 1970). Though the advanced active TM group mean change score was only -2.00, the advanced active TM group still had the lowest absolute group mean at posttest ($M = 35.60$). If a floor effect were present, it would not be eliminated by adjustment for pretest, which only controls for regression effects. The contrast (0, 0, 2, 0, −1, −1), essentially removes the advanced active TM group from the direct comparison. In this case, the new active TM group scored significantly lower than nonmembers (the delayed and not interested groups) when adjusting for pretest score ($F = 2.7897$, $p < .05$, $r = .1958$). The actual effect size difference between the two contrasts is quite small but sufficient for the latter to attain statistical significance. Decreased anxiety has been replicated in many other prison studies (Dillbeck & Abrams, 1987) and in studies with the general population (Eppley et al., 1989).

The ANCOVA performed on the change score indicated that all six categories of TM membership declined on mean lie score from pretest to posttest. The ANCOVA on the change score (adjusting for demographic covariates) did not reach significance ($F_{1,56}$ = 1.3195, n.s., r = .1517).

Test Outcomes for Other Programs

On the five outcome measures for which directional predictions were made, there was not one significant positive outcome ($p < .05$, one-tailed) for active members compared to nonmembers in the four other programs (see Alexander, 1982, Tables 26-29). Also, when all members (active and drop-out) were compared to nonmembers for the four groups, there were no significant findings in the predicted direction. Lack of findings was clearly not influenced by some kind of negative response bias of members in the other groups relative to their respective nonmember comparison groups. In none of the four groups was there even a statistical trend toward lower scores among active members or all members (active and drop-outs) than among nonmembers on the lie scale. In three of the four programs (with the exception of Counseling), the lie scores of active members at posttest, controlling for pretest, were actually slightly–though not significantly–higher than for nonmember categories.

On the Normal Waking State factor (for which no prediction was made), active Counseling members actually scored significantly higher than nonmembers ($F_{1,67}$ = 4.489, $p < .05$, two-tailed, r = .2506). In addition to the four normal waking items there are four pathological items that composed the Normal Waking State factor. Also, we know that the original unrotated Normal Waking State posttest factor, in addition to correlating highly with the rotated Normal Waking factor (r = .803), also correlated positively with the rotated Schizophrenic Experience scale (r = .280) and quite negatively with the rotated Postconceptual Experience factor (r = −.527). Finally, not only did the active Counseling group score higher on the Normal Waking factor but they also scored higher on the three measures of pathology. The above sources of information taken collectively suggest, in retrospect, that the Normal Waking factor is at least in part colored by the psychopathology of everyday life. Even some of its so-called Normal Waking state items suggest a personality that becomes easily absorbed or overshadowed by environmental stressors; as Selye (1974) explains, stressors may be subjectively experienced as either positive or negative. For example, SCI (18) states, "During an intense situation, I forget myself and get totally involved in the emotions triggered by the incident." SCI (24) says, "If I visually perceive an enjoyable or disturbing event, I find the image or event remains in my mind and comes back when I pursue other thoughts" (see Alexander, 1982, Appendices 5-1 and 6-6, for Normal Waking Items). Intensive Counseling could constitute just such an absorbing and sometimes unsettling experience that makes salient both internal and external sources of conflict or stress.

Interestingly, when we treated subjects no longer in Counseling as graduates rather than drop-outs (Contrast: 0, 1, 0, 1, −2), somewhat of a reversal of the above pattern took place. There was no trend toward Counseling graduates scoring significantly higher than nonmembers in ego development ($r = .0457$, n.s.) (see Alexander 1982, Table 26). Counseling graduates were significantly lower than active members ($F_{1,57} = 4.6427$, $p < .025$, $r = .2744$), and they evidenced a trend toward a higher Postconceptual Experience level than did nonmembers ($F_{1,67} = 1.757$, $p < .10$, $r = .1599$); there was no such trend for active members compared to nonmembers ($r = .0484$, n.s.).

Active Drug Rehabilitation members scored significantly higher in adjusted posttest Schizophrenic Experience than did nonmembers (the delayed and not interested groups) ($F_{1,60} = 2.786$, $p < .05$, $r = -.2106$) (see Alexander, 1982, Table 27); the result was not maintained when drop-outs were added to the membership category ($r = -.0027$, n.s.). Also the total membership in Drug Rehabilitation (actives and drop-outs) was significantly higher in trait anxiety than the nonmember contingency ($F_{1,68} = 5.0779$, $p < .025$, $r = -.2637$), but the finding did not reach significance when only active members were compared to nonmembers ($r = -.052$, n.s.).

The active TM group compared to the nonmember group substantially increased on the developmental measures of consciousness and ego stage and decreased on the 3 indices of psychopathology. What is immediately evident in a visual comparison of treatment effects is that the profiles of the other four programs strikingly differ from that of the TM program. The effect sizes are smaller, and, to a certain extent, a reversal of the TM pattern is observed: the programs tend to score relatively higher on the pathological than on the developmental indices. Though the effect sizes are indeed rather small, the direction and magnitude of the effects is somewhat similar between the Christian and Muslim religious groups (with the exception of the negative Muslim association with Anxiety) and between the individual Counseling and Drug Rehabilitation counseling groups (with the exception of a negative association of Drug Rehabilitation with Aggression). Compared to their respective nonmember comparison groups, active membership in the two counseling programs is positively associated with score on the developmental indices, whereas membership in the religious groups is negatively associated with score on the developmental indices. Both counseling and religious groups tend to be slightly more elevated (above $r_p = 0$) on the pathology indices than their respective comparison groups (in 10 of 12 cases).

One should bear in mind in interpreting these results that our nonmember contrast groups are variable and based on either unweighted or weighted means for the delayed and not interested groups (for TM and Drug Rehabilitation, respectively), or on a pooled nonmember category (for Christians, Muslims, and Counseling). Also, in Figure 2, only the new Muslim members are

Figure 2: The treatment effect size (i.e., partial correlation of active membership vs. nonmembership in five programs) controlling for pretest, overlap of active membership, and significant demographic covariates. It can be seen that the TM practice increased ego development and postconceptual experience and decreased trait anxiety, schizophrenic experience, and aggression. The other programs did not have a significant effect on any variable, and in some cases, resulted in a trend in the wrong direction.

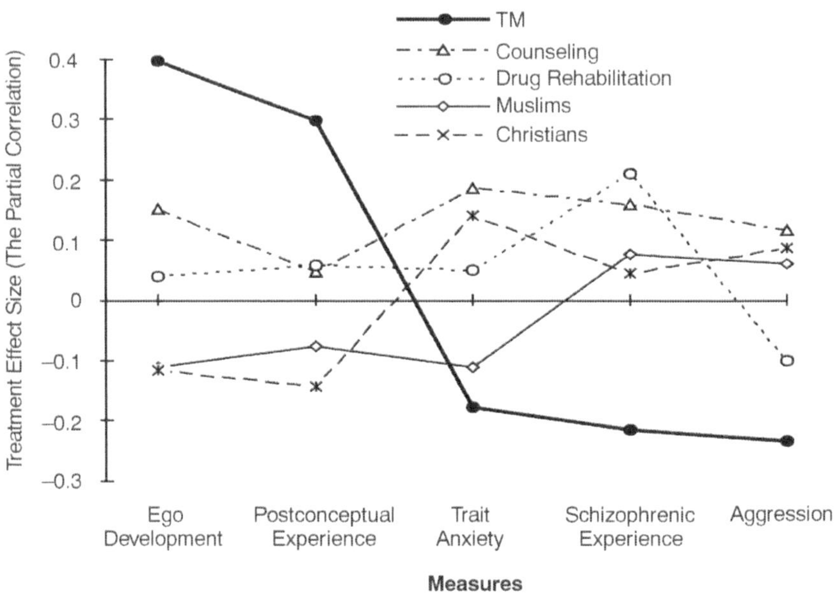

represented in the Muslim Contrast because of the potentially confounding interaction effect of active TM membership with advanced active Muslims. Certainly, however, in terms of the overall comparison of the TM program effect to that of the other four programs, the outcome is unambiguous. Active TM members scored higher in the predicted direction than did the active members of the other programs compared to their respective nonmember groups, on every outcome measured. A comparison of partial correlations for nonindependent samples indicates that there was at least a trend ($p \leq .10$, one-tailed) toward the TM effect being significantly greater in the predicted direction for 14 of the 16 effect size comparisons (assuming that after adjustment for overlap in active membership, the correlation among membership groups is zero). The two exceptions were that active TM members did not score significantly lower than the active Muslims on Anxiety nor than active Drug Rehabilitation members on Aggression, compared to their respective nonmember groups (see Figure 2). Half of the effect sizes (8 of 16) were significant at least at $p < .05$ (one-tailed). The test of the differences between correlations is not a very powerful test, and relatively large differences in effect size are necessary for the result to reach significance.

Attrition

Experimental attrition, as stated earlier, was relatively low (range: 29-31% depending on the measure). As far as we can determine, no subjects refused to posttest because of their dissatisfaction with the programs in which they participated. The main reasons for failure to retest had to do with the release of men from prison or their transfer to institutions having lower levels of security. Even those incarcerated subjects who did not retest (with the exception of one man) claimed that they were interested in retesting but that factors outside their control, such as visits from outside or conflict with work schedules, interfered with their ability to actually do so.

One way to check on whether the pretest subjects systematically differed from those who completed both the pretest and the posttest was to determine whether their pretest scores differed from the pretest score of subjects who also completed the posttest. After all, pretest score on a given measure, more than any other variable (including treatment affiliation), tends to be the best single predictor of outcome score on the same measure (Judd & Kenny, 1981). We found that the subjects who completed the pretest did not significantly vary ($p < .10$, two-tailed) from the subjects who completed both the pretest and the posttest on any of the 7 outcomes (see Alexander, 1982, Table W, Appendix 1).

For the TM program specifically, we also found that TM group members (advanced and new pooled) who retested did not significantly differ ($p < .10$, two-tailed) from those who did not retest on the seven outcome measures. Further, TM nonmembers (delayed and not interested groups) who retested did not significantly differ on the 7 outcome measures from the TM nonmembers who did not retest (see Alexander, 1982, Table X, Appendix 1).

Length of Time Active in Programs

The number of months between pretest and posttest was quite comparable between programs. Also, the number of months from initial membership in a program to pretest (and posttest) was relatively similar across programs, with the exception of advanced Muslims, who were members of their group for a longer period of time (34.67 months from start to pretest) than advanced members in other programs. With respect to number of months of active participation in programs (at least once or twice/month) between pretest and posttest, there was some disparity among programs. We already indicated that the TM program had the lowest recent drop-out rate of the five programs. Also in terms of total number of months of active participation between pretest and posttest, the new active and advanced TM groups participated for more months (M = 13.79 and M = 13.69, respectively) than active new and advanced members in other programs. New active Counseling and advanced active Drug Rehabilitation were regular for the least number of months (M = 5.67 and M = 6.43, respectively) in comparison to other groups.

In general, the effect size (*r*) and direction of the correlation between length of involvement in programs (from pretest to posttest) and change score was consistent with the ANCOVA results on adjusted posttest scores for active vs. nonmember groups in the various programs (cf., Alexander 1982, Tables 22, 27-29 with Table 30). These correlations were based only on the association between length of participation in program and test change scores for the subset of the subjects that had joined the program. Membership was pooled across active and delayed, advanced and new categories, and length of participation alone was taken as the independent variable. No adjustments were made for demographic covariates or other variables.

For the TM program, with the exception of Trait Anxiety, all predicted outcomes were in the same direction as on the ANCOVA contrasts. The correlations between months regularly in TM practice and the main variables of interest– ego development and level of postconceptual experience–were positive and significant ($r = .303$, $p < .025$) ($r = .230$, $p < .10$).

For the other programs, the number of months of program participation was negatively associated with outcomes. Number of months regularly in Drug Rehabilitation was associated with a significant decrease in ego development ($r = -.375$, $p < .025$), and a significant increase in Schizophrenic Experience ($r = .338$, $p < .025$) and Normal Waking Experience ($r = .31$). Change in test outcomes appears relatively uncorrelated with length of participation in Counseling. The Muslims were the only other program for which length of participation in the program was associated more with positive than negative consequences. Inmates who participated longer in the Muslim group decreased significantly in self-reported aggression ($r = -.367$, $p < .05$). Whereas the Muslims as a whole did seem to benefit from longer participation in their program, there was no significant difference in months of active membership between TM subjects and the Muslims. Therefore, the greater improvement in the TM group compared to other programs cannot be explained in terms of longer participation in the program, because the Muslims had practiced just as long, and length of practice of the other programs was, if anything, negatively correlated with benefits.

DISCUSSION

The results of the longitudinal follow-up replicate and extend the cross-sectional findings, showing that TM practice increases self-development and postconceptual experiences, and decreases aggression, schizophrenic symptoms, and trait-anxiety. This gain in a population otherwise recalcitrant to change is consistent with our hypothesis that the TM program may act to "unfreeze" human development in adulthood. It supports the hypothesis of a two-phased mechanism underlying developmental changes through the TM technique: stress release reversal of effects of stress (decreased psychopathy), and transcending (increased experiences of transcendental consciousness).

Inmates actively participating in the other four programs (Counseling, Drug Rehabilitation, Muslims, Christians) did not change significantly on any measure, and in some cases there was a tendency to change in an adverse direction. The results could not be explained by the demographic covariates of crime, or by attrition, or by differences in the lengths of membership in the different programs.

The average increase of more than one step in ego development in the inmates practicing TM in the present study is unprecedented in the literature. Overall, the stage of self-development (ego stage) has been shown to be very stable in adults (Loevinger, 1985). Several interventions have succeeded in facilitating ego development among students (e.g., Sullivan, 1975), but these interventions have not fared as well in adults. No change was reported for adult teachers after engagement in a two-quarter, intensive educational curriculum to promote self-development as measured by Loevinger's system (Sprinthall & Mosher, 1978). In another study, an organizational development training program based on ego development apparently promoted a modest rise in mean self-development level for subjects initially below Conformity (I-3) but did not facilitate developmental change beyond the Conformist level (study by Lasker described in Loevinger, 1979). Prisoners in both the new active TM and advanced active TM groups made advances beyond the Conformist stage. In a study by Torbert in adults, a Boston College MBA program was restructured to reflect an action inquiry climate. Although 10% of the students had advanced two stages, the average stage progression for all MBA students was only .1 (Torbert, 1994).

Our prison inmates who undertook the TM program changed as much or more after a little more than a year of intervention than college students generally do after four years of college. According to some longitudinal studies, students typically change 1/2 stage (equivalent to one step in our coding system) during college (Loevinger et al., 1985). Previously there had been little evidence of further ego development in adulthood after 20 years of age, as measured by Loevinger's system.

It has been discovered that Self-Aware (I-3/4) is the most commonly occurring self-development level among Americans (Holt, 1980; Loevinger, 1979). The new active TM group started below the modal level of Americans (Conformist, I-3) and caught up to the modal level (Self-Aware) in one year. The advanced active TM group, starting at the modal level, increased yet another stage (to the Conscientious stage I-4) after another year of TM practice. This indicates that in less than three years of the TM program, these maximum security prisoners actually rose to a higher level of development than is typical of the American public. Remarkably, the changes in the new and advanced meditators took place at an age–median 26-29 years–at which self-development is typically believed to have halted. Also the inmates' formal level of education was quite low–median = 9th grade (though educational programs were available in the prison). Certainly the prison was not, on the whole, a rich or stimulating environment likely to facilitate stage change, according to Kohlberg's criteria for environmental catalysts (Kohlberg, Kauffman, Scharf, & Hickey, 1974). Controls delayed from starting the TM program and inmates not interested in joining the program showed no evidence of ego development during the intervention.

It is also unlikely that the prison staff, as a whole, operated at a post I-3/4 self-developmental level, which occurs with relative infrequency in non-college level subjects (Holt, 1980). At least on Kohlberg's related measure of moral reasoning development, under normal conditions, guards and other prison staff typically do not operate from a sufficiently higher level of moral reasoning than inmates to stimulate the latter's moral development (Kohlberg et al., 1974; Scharf & Hickey, 1976).

Loevinger conceptually sets the Conscientious stage (I-4) parallel to Kohlberg's *Democratic contract* stage 5. Stage 5 represents principled moral reasoning, in which the subject can take a prior-to-society perspective and interpret the law in terms of the spirit and underlying principles in which it was generated, not as a set of intractable rules to which one must conform. At the Self-Aware (I-3/4) level there is already said to be a lessening of the subject's adherence to the group and a recognition that exceptions to rules are tolerable and that one does not always have to conform to group expectations (Rosen & Nordquist, 1980). At the Conscientious stage (I-4), consciousness of self is said to have developed sufficiently to permit the adoption of self-evaluated standards. "Major elements of what is generally understood as the adult's conscience are present, such as long-term goals that are self-evaluated and not imposed, a sense of responsibility for the consequences of one's own actions, and differentiated self-criticisms" (Rosen & Nordquist, 1980, p. 1155).

The Conscientious (I-4) position is postconventional, in the sense that at I-4 one is capable of criticizing conventions, but the sense is that what is being criticized is an already internalized set of values, standards, or concepts. The conscience itself is some kind of internalized voice or amalgamation of voices from prior identifications into an ego ideal with which the self in part identifies. It is only when one begins to gain an awareness of the self that is independent of internalized concepts or identifications–an awareness of awareness itself unmediated by prior thoughts or symbols–that postconceptual self-differentiation at the Cosmic Consciousness level begins to take place.

We suggest that Loevinger's postconceptual levels of Individualistic, Autonomous, and Integrated (I-4/5- I-6) reflect a transition to the postconceptual (see Alexander, Walton et al., this volume, Table 1). It is striking, given the relatively low developmental starting point of prisoners, that two in the advanced TM group shifted to Loevinger's highest Ego-Integration position (I-6) and a third shifted from the transition level (I-4/5) to the Autonomous stage (I-5). Individuals at this level of development have extraordinary flexibility to adapt to demands and to successfully resolve external or internal conflicts. They have a stable, differentiated sense of unique self on the basis of which they can appreciate the uniqueness of others. Knowing who they are, they are not threatened by differences in others, and interpersonal relationships are based on mutual respect. In the dominant culture, even among college graduates, the percentage of the population at Loevinger's I-6 is less than 1% (Holt, 1980; Loevinger, 1979). In our small sample of advanced active TM inmates, 2 of 13 subjects (or 15.4%) had already attained to stage 6. This is a small sample. However, a subsequent study with young adults replicates and extends this finding (Alexander, Heaton, & Chandler, 1994; Chandler, 1990). This 10-year longitudinal study found that at pretest, 9% of the graduates of Maharishi University of Management scored in the highest Autonomous (I-5) and Integrated (I-6) stages of Loevinger's stages, whereas at posttest 38% scored at these levels. This is the highest group average of the 40 studies reported in the literature. Only 1% of graduates from three other colleges scored at these levels at either pretest or posttest, similar to what has previously been reported in the literature. Moreover, a further study of 45 males with over 10 years of TM experience used modified instructions sensitive to potential high-level responders and found 87% were above the highest level typically reached by adults (the Conscientious level). The majority of TM subjects had reached the final two stages (Autonomous and Integrated), which are characterized by balanced growth of affect and cognition and enhanced self-actualization (Alexander, Davies et al., 1990).

We have already explored a variety of alternative explanations that might have accounted for the positive outcomes of active TM members on the self-development scale and other measures. We have attempted through statistical means to control for overlap of program membership, demographic self-selection, the effect of active vs. drop-out status, total number of months engaged in the practice, and experimental mortality or attrition from the pretest to posttest.

One further alternative explanation warrants consideration: the creation of positive expectancies for treatment outcome (Smith, 1975, 1976). A number of factors mitigate against this likelihood:

1. The ego development scale is particularly resistant to attempts at faking good (Redmore, 1976).
2. Approximately halfway though the intervention period the TM program lost its funding. Hence during the critical months prior to

retest, TM members received virtually no exposure to high expectancy creating contingencies or positive group support.

3. External integrity of treatment did not break down for the other programs, but active members in the other programs did not significantly increase in ego development.

For these and other (see Alexander, 1982) reasons, differences in positive expectancies are not likely to have caused the different outcomes observed.

Effectiveness of the TM Program

The relativist reader might still ask, why would a meditation technique derived from an Eastern philosophical tradition promote development in Westerners or promote change in a self-development scale that clearly measures milestones in development in accordance with a Western psychological-philosophical (even middle-class) tradition? Our response is as follows: As claimed by Loevinger, her stages should, in fact, correspond to a universal deep structure of self-development independent of philosophical beliefs and fundamental to the development of the self in different cultures.

Lower stages of self-development have been articulated in great detail within the Western psychological-cultural tradition. The Western tradition has focused its cultural efforts on construction of developmental support technologies during the first part of the human lifecycle. Particular attention has been paid to formal schooling devoted to the articulation and amplification of language and symbolic systems in the service of the development of formal or conceptual thought. Less attention has been paid to the possibility of hierarchical transformation in self-development in adulthood. This development corresponds to cognitive development beyond the formal operations level, the level of logical thought, which is defined as the highest developmental level by Jean Piaget, often said to be the father of modern developmental psychology.

In the Eastern traditions, and particularly in the Vedic tradition as expounded by Maharishi, higher states of self-development (i.e., higher states of consciousness) have been articulated in great detail, and less attention has been paid to development within the first period of human life (Maharishi Mahesh Yogi, 1969). The Eastern traditions have focused their cultural efforts on the specification and amplification of post-language or postconceptual systems like meditation in the service of the development of higher states of consciousness beyond formal operations.

We propose that the milestones charted in adult consciousness development within Maharishi's seven states of consciousness simply represent the potential, logical, and empirical extension of normal self-developmental stages described within Western systems (Alexander, Davies et al., 1990; Goodman et al., this volume; Orme-Johnson, 2000). A minority of native Western mystics within the larger cultural tradition of the West have described a strikingly similar phenomenological terrain of inner states to that presented in Eastern texts (Dupre, 1980; Hicks, 1980; Huxley, 1945; James, 1929) and in Maharishi's system in particular.

If Eastern and Western descriptions of underlying self-development are, in fact, continuous with one another, and if TM practice is a universal developmental technology applicable across cultural tradition and developmental stage, then it is not surprising that application of the TM technique to an adult population at relatively low levels of ego development would result in the subsequent catalyzing of development in that population through intervening developmental levels en route to higher states of consciousness.

Further research on these inmates found that these internal changes had long-term behavioral consequences, as indicated by a 33% reduction in recidivism (return to prison) rate among the TM inmates released from prison over a 3.5-year period, in comparison to all members of the four other programs (Alexander, Rainforth et al., this volume). Similar reductions in recidivism have been replicated in maximum security prisoners in both Folsom and San Quentin prisons and in medium security prisoners in Deuel Vocational, all in northern California (Bleick & Abrams, 1987). Given that the present results are cross-validated by over 600 studies showing holistic physiological, psychological, and social development (e.g., Chalmers et al., 1989; Orme-Johnson & Farrow, 1977; Wallace et al., 1990), we recommend that the TM program be implemented and evaluated on a large scale in our criminal justice system.

NOTES

1. Transcendental Meditation, TM, and TM-Sidhi are registered or common law trademarks licensed to Maharishi Vedic Education Development Corporation and used under sublicense or with permission.

2. The results of this longitudinal study were presented to the Annual Meeting of the American Psychological Association, Los Angeles, August, 1981.

3. The TM program was initially introduced and funded at Walpole under a drug abuse prevention grant. Several studies had indicated that practice of the TM technique was associated with reduction in drug abuse (Orme-Johnson & Farrow, 1977, pp. 491-555). Advocates of the TM program also proposed that internal transformation of the individual provided the basis for the solution to the drug abuse problem, but the claimed methods for facilitating the change (the stress release and transcending mechanisms during the TM technique) were strikingly different from the social or group mechanisms of change employed by the alternative drug rehabilitation programs. Nevertheless, it could be maintained that individuals who join the TM program also undergo some form of value reorientation and are subject to the same kinds of social pressures that create inflated expectations and promote "self-reconstitutive" processes in the alternative therapy groups. If general mechanisms such as normative group pressure or attitude training were sufficient to explain TM's effect, then we might expect those programs that explicitly rely upon such procedures to produce similar results.

AUTHORS' NOTES

The motivational research component of this study was funded by an NSF Grant (No. BNS 76-80965) to Professor David McClelland. Generous private donations were provided by James Sinclair, Gil Younger, Dr. and Mrs. Keene Dimick, Steven and Gillian Foster, Dr. Samuel and Merrian Schuster, and Susan Otto Gore.

Address correspondence to David Orme-Johnson, 191 Dalton Drive, Seagrove Beach, FL 32459 (E-mail: davidoj@emeraldcoast.com).

Transcendental Meditation in Criminal Rehabilitation and Crime Prevention. Pp. 161-180.

Walpole Study of the *Transcendental Meditation* Program in Maximum Security Prisoners III: Reduced Recidivism

CHARLES N. ALEXANDER
Maharishi University of Management

MAXWELL V. RAINFORTH
Maharishi University of Management

PAUL R. FRANK
Maharishi University of Management

JAMES D. GRANT
Maharishi University of Management

CHRISTOPHER VON STADE
Fairfield, Iowa

KENNETH G. WALTON
Maharishi University of Management

ABSTRACT Part III of the Walpole Prison Study builds on the earlier longitudinal and cross-sectional findings in Parts I and II that reported reduced psychopathology and accelerated psychological development in members of the Transcendental Meditation[1] prison program. Part III is a retrospective investigation of recidivism among 286 inmates released from Walpole prison, who were followed for up to 59 months. The sample comprised all subjects from the following sources who had been released six months prior to data collection: (a) all inmates who had learned the TM program at Walpole; (b) random samples of four other prison programs at Walpole (counseling, drug rehabilitation, Christian, and Muslim); (c) a random sample of the Walpole inmate population; and (d) subjects who were tested longitudinally in the prior Walpole studies. The rate of return to prison for a stay of 30 days or more was 32% among inmates who practiced the TM technique compared to 48% for a combined control group comprised of members of four other prison programs. This represented a proportionate reduction in recidivism of 33%, which was statistically significant (p = .042). Separate comparisons showed that the TM group also had lower reincarceration rates than each of the four other programs, with proportionate reductions in recidivism ranging from 29% to 42% (p = .007 to .073). In addition, the TM group compared to all non-meditating subjects had a lower rate of reincarceration due to new convictions (47% lower, proportionately; p = .045) and a 27% proportionately lower rate of reincarceration/warrant for arrest (p = .069). The pattern of reduced recidivism for TM program members was maintained in multiple regression analyses, controlling for background and release variables (e.g., parole vs. full discharge, institution of release, drug history). These findings are consistent with the proposition that the reduced psychopathology and accelerated psychological development resulting from the TM program are responsible for reductions in criminal behavior.

KEYWORDS Transcendental Meditation, recidivism, maximum security prisoners, corrections, treatment, evaluation

The United States has the highest incarceration rate of any developed nation, with almost 2 million inmates in prisons and jails (Beck, 2000). The recent explosion of the U.S. prison population is largely due to stiffer sentencing laws, such as mandatory life terms for three-time felons, tough penalties for drug offenses, and the trend towards sentencing juveniles as adults. As Cullen and Gendreau (1989) have pointed out, the current punitive emphasis of criminal justice policy is a reaction to the view that "nothing works" in the field of rehabilitation, a view promulgated by a highly influential research review by Martinson (1974). Subsequently, more careful syntheses of the research using meta-analytic techniques have identified a subset of rehabilitation programs that are effective (Andrews, Zinger et al., 1990a; Lipsey, 1992). Lipsey (1992) found that rehabilitation programs reduce recidivism by approximately 5 percentage points on average, with wide variation in the efficacy of treatment approaches–the most effective being oriented towards improving life skills of offenders. A group of Canadian rehabilitation researchers (Andrews, Zinger et al., 1990a) have shown that substantial reductions in recidivism can be achieved. However their approach is limited to high-risk offenders and requires appropriate classification and assignment of offenders to treatment. Also, meta-analyses by Lipsey and by Andrews, Zinger et al. focused primarily on juveniles,[2] a population that is presumed to be more malleable and less recalcitrant to reform efforts than adult offenders.

Only ten controlled evaluations of the effects of prison rehabilitation programs on recidivism were published from 1995 to 2000: fewer than two studies per year.[3] Yet there is a need to continue to seek a more effective means of rehabilitating offenders. This need is apparent for several reasons. First, problems caused by the exploding U.S. inmate population (e.g., overcrowding of prisons, escalating burdens on state budgets) have brought about renewed interest in alternatives to longer incarceration as a way to decrease crime rates (Harland, 1996). Second, even with longer prison terms, most prisoners are eventually released and may commit new offenses if they are not successfully rehabilitated. Thus, society must confront its decision to ignore the need for rehabilitation. Third, as long as rehabilitation is not fully effective, new treatment approaches must be sought. The need to improve rehabilitation outcomes is underscored by the fact that each year 31 million people in the United States are victimized by crime (Miller, Cohen, & Wiersema, 1996), and most crimes are committed by a minority of habitual, high-rate offenders (Moffitt, 1993; Piper, 1985). Finally, there is a need to seek ways to maintain effects of rehabilitative treatments after incarcerated offenders are released into the community (Field, 1998).

Most rehabilitation approaches attempt to help offenders to reform through external factors such as discipline, counseling, or training programs. The novel approach evaluated in this study is in direct contrast to these conventional approaches. It is based on a self-development program that aims to facilitate spontaneous behavioral improvement from within. This program involves individual practice of the TM technique, an easily learned mental technique that is said to alleviate psychological stress, promote orderliness and clarity of thinking, and foster integration and growth of the personality (Maharishi Mahesh Yogi, 1966, 1972; Roth, 1994). Use of the TM technique in rehabilitation has been proposed as a means to reduce the stress and emotional turmoil at the root of aggressive and antisocial behavior; the TM technique also reduces the tendency to think in narrow, self-serving ways by culturing more self-aware, purposeful, and orderly processes of thinking (Iyer, 1977; Goodman, Boyer, Walton, & Orme-Johnson, this volume; Hawkins et al., this volume). The goal is to enable offenders to spontaneously behave in a more orderly, law-abiding manner (Maharishi Mahesh Yogi, 1977b).

Numerous studies have shown neurophysiological and biochemical changes during practice of the TM technique that are opposite to the effects of stress, as well as lasting effects outside of the practice on physiological variables, personality traits (measured by standardized tests), cognitive function, and behavioral outcomes (Wallace, 1970a, 1986; Alexander, Davies et al., 1990). Physiological changes include increased integration of brain function (as measured by EEG coherence), reductions in biochemical correlates of stress (i.e., lower basal values), and more adaptive physiological responses to stressors, as well as a range of improvements in physical health (Dillbeck & Bronson, 1981; Dillbeck & Orme-Johnson, 1987; Goleman & Schwartz, 1976; Orme-Johnson, 1987). Enduring psychological effects include reductions in trait anxiety, anger, and depression, improvements in intelligence and comprehension, increased cognitive flexibility, higher levels of principled moral reasoning, internalization of the locus of control, and development of a healthier self-concept (Eppley, Abrams & Shear, 1987; Brooks & Scarano, 1985; Cranson et al., 1991; Shecter, 1977; Alexander, Langer et al., 1989; Nidich, Ryncarz, Abrams, Orme-Johnson, & Wallace 1983; Nystul & Garde, 1977; Alexander, Rainforth & Gelderloos, 1991). These cognitive and personality changes apparently lead to behavioral improvements, as indicated by changes such as growth of prosocial attitudes, increased warmth of interpersonal relations, enhanced job performance, and decreased abuse of alcohol, cigarettes, and illicit drugs (Brown, 1976; Marcus, 1977; Alexander, Swanson et al., 1993; Alexander, Robinson, & Rainforth, 1994).

Previous reviews have inferred from this research (which has mainly been conducted on the general population) that the TM program leads to decreases in the major risk factors associated with criminal behavior (Hawkins, this volume). Consistent with these findings, 13 evaluations of the TM program in correctional institutions have shown improvements in the psychology and behavior of inmates, including reductions in hostility and anxiety and fewer prison rule infractions (Dillbeck & Abrams, 1987; Hawkins, this volume).

The present study is the third in a series of investigations on the effects of the TM program that were conducted at Massachusetts Correctional Institution, a maximum security prison in Walpole, Massachusetts. Part I was a cross-sectional study (Alexander, Walton, & Goodman, this volume), comparing individuals who had been practicing the TM program for 20 months to subjects who had not learned the technique. The TM group was significantly lower on state anxiety, trait anxiety, depression, neurotic psychopathy, and impulsiveness. They also scored significantly higher on the Sentence Completion Test (SCT), a standardized measure of self-development, psychological maturity, and integration, which is highly resistant to attempts to "faking good" on responses. Part II was a longitudinal study (Alexander & Orme-Johnson, this volume) that investigated changes over a 13-17 month period in subjects who had been pretested in Part I. The subjects already practicing the TM program from the cross-sectional study and inmates who learned the TM program after the pretest were compared to control subjects who did not learn the technique. Both TM groups decreased in aggressiveness and trait anxiety and showed significant gains on the SCT self-development scale relative to controls. The improvements on SCT in these two studies suggested that practice of the TM program promotes psychological development from immature levels characterized by impulsiveness and conformity to peer pressure, to more mature levels in which individuals are more conscientious and capable of self-criticism.

No matter what psychological effects a program may produce for the individual, the ultimate indication of rehabilitation to the corrections community is whether the man or woman returns to prison (Sechrest, White, & Brown, 1979). The logical next step of the research is to determine if there are enduring post-prison effects of these programs on recidivism. Only two other studies have systematically investigated the effects of the TM program on criminal recidivism, both of which were conducted on inmates released from the Folsom and San Quentin prisons as well as Deuel Vocational Institution in California (Bleick & Abrams, 1987; Rainforth, Alexander, & Cavanaugh, this volume). A third study, a case study, was conducted on the entire prison population of Senegal (Anklesaria & King, this volume).

The present follow-up study investigated recidivism rates over a 59-month period among inmates who learned the TM technique compared to other inmates who had not been instructed. A key objective of the study was to control for membership in a rehabilitation program, which may reflect a variety of factors other than the treatment itself. These non-specific factors associated with program participation presumably include motivation to amend behavior patterns, support from other group members, and attention from trainers or group leaders. It was hypothesized that recidivism would be lower for the TM program in comparison to other prison programs and that this effect would persist after controlling for demographic and criminal-history variables.

METHODS

Subjects and Research Design

This retrospective follow-up study is an ex post facto analysis of archival data. The inmates included in the analysis were sampled from, or exhaustively represent, four different sources: (a) all 152 inmates who had learned the TM technique at Walpole State Prison; (b) random samples from four Walpole prison programs–Counseling, Drug Rehabilitation, Christian, and Muslim (690 subjects, approximately 172 per program); (c) a random control sample of 225 inmates drawn from the Walpole population; and (d) 81 nonmembers of the TM prison program (interested and not-interested) who participated in the cross-sectional longitudinal psychological testing for Parts I and II (see Alexander, Walton et al., this volume; Alexander & Orme-Johnson, this volume). The different prison program random samples were drawn from the complete program membership lists extending from 1975 to mid-1980. The control sample was randomly selected from Massachusetts Department of Correction lists of all inmates present in Walpole on the first of January 1977, 1978, and 1979. To ensure similar dates of program involvement, only those inmates who had been involved in a program after July 1976 (the month the TM program started at Walpole) were included in the program random samples. To be included in the study, inmates must have been released from prison before December 1, 1980–6 months prior to data collection. Approximately 30% of the entire sample had been released before this date.

The four other rehabilitation programs provided comparison groups in the earlier cross-sectional and longitudinal studies at Walpole. These programs were selected on the basis of their aims to promote self-development, in parallel to the TM program. The drug rehabilitation program was based on a self-help philosophy, the individual counseling program was insight-oriented, while the Christian and Muslim programs aimed at spiritual development. Whereas the TM program involves twice-daily practice of a meditation technique, the Muslim program emphasized prayer several times per day. The drug rehabilitation and Muslim programs were run by inmates. All programs involved weekly meetings as well as the members' commitment to participate, and all were concurrently active while the TM program was being offered at Walpole.

The selection procedures from the above four sources provided 286 research subjects. Among these, 53 had learned the TM program, 143 attended counseling, 74 participated in a drug rehabilitation program, 96 belonged to a Christian organization, and 53 took part in Muslim religious activities. These subgroups overlapped due to participation of inmates in multiple programs. The other program groups, after excluding subjects in the TM group, contained the following numbers of subjects: counseling–117; drug rehabilitation–56; Christian–78; Muslims–40. Effects of the TM program were determined by comparisons with a pooled control group of all subjects who did not practice the TM program, with the four other programs separately, and with a combined program sample comprising subjects in at least one of the other programs.

Data Collection

The primary recidivism outcome in this study was return to prison for 30 days or more; this is the same definition used by the Massachusetts Department of Correction (Metzler & Wittenberg, 1980). Second, because a released convict can be returned to prison for minor violations of the conditions of parole, as well as for new criminal activity, recidivism was more stringently defined as conviction and return to prison for a new criminal offense. Data were also collected on a third measure of recidivism: return to prison or warrant issued for re-arrest; former inmates did not meet this definition if they had totally clean records.

Recidivism data were obtained from the Massachusetts Department of Correction through June 1980. The master card file and inmates' institutional folders provided release date, type of release (full discharge or parole), date of return to prison (if applicable), reason for return (parole infraction or new conviction), and whether a warrant for the releasee's arrest had been issued. The inmate folders provided information on the following background variables that had been identified as potential predictors of recidivism in the research literature: age at first arrest (Metzler & Wittenberg, 1980), drug abuse (Metzler & Wittenberg), time on longest job (Metzler & Wittenberg), prior adult incarceration (Hoffman & Beck, 1974), age at release (LeClair, 1977), type of crime (Sechrest et al., 1979), race (Smart, 1979), and institution of release (pre-release or other; LeClair, 1978). Subjects were followed for a maximum of 59 months after release.

There was no missing information on either recidivism status or prison program membership. The only variables on which there were missing data values were age at first arrest (6 cases missing), prior commitment (1 case), race (2 cases), and drug abuse history (6 cases).

Statistical Analyses

Investigation of the effects of rehabilitation programs must consider whether the treatment groups differ on demographic variables that have been associated with crime and recidivism. The TM and control groups were compared on subject background variables using the chi-square test for differences in proportions. For this analysis, continuous variables were first dichotomized using cut-off values close to the sample median. Similar tests were performed to compare members and non-members of other rehabilitation programs on background variables.

Tests for differences in proportions were also applied to the analysis of recidivism outcomes. These tests compared outcomes for the TM and control groups on the three recidivism measures over the entire follow-up period, based on the proportion who recidivated in relation to all subjects. The same statistical procedure was applied to compare return-to-prison outcomes for the TM group to members of the other four rehabilitation programs.

To permit direct comparisons between the TM group and non-meditating control subjects at specific follow-up times, rates of return to prison were calculated at six-month intervals, from 6 months through 30 months. This provides information on recidivism rates for inmates who had been released for similar amounts of time. These rates were calculated by dividing the number of inmates who had recidivated before the endpoint of interest by the number of inmates at risk. For example, the inmates at risk at 12 months included only those who had been released at least 12 months prior to data collection. The recidivism rate at 12 months is the percentage of these inmates who were returned to prison before 12 months. An inmate who was released 15 months prior to data collection and who returned to prison 9 months after release would be counted as a non-recidivist at 6 months and a recidivist at 12 months, but would not be counted at 18 months or later endpoints. Because the number of inmates at risk diminishes as the length of the release period increases, recidivism rates were only calculated up to 30 months.

An alpha level of .05 was used for all statistical tests. P-values for the effects of the TM program on recidivism outcomes were one-tailed, in view of the directionality of the hypothesized effects. All chi-square statistics for between-group comparisons were converted to Z-statistics, because the comparisons involved only one degree of freedom. To permit comparison with other studies, Glass effect sizes and phi coefficients (tetrachoric correlations) were calculated as statistical measures of the magnitude of treatment effects, based on the recidivism rates for the TM and comparison groups.[4] To represent the practical significance of treatment outcomes, the proportionate reductions in recidivism were calculated by the formula:

> 1 − (% recidivism rate in the TM group / % recidivism rate in the comparison group).

To check whether results obtained from the analyses of the return-to-prison outcomes may have been affected by other variables, multiple regression analyses were performed to control for differences between treatment groups and for key predictors of recidivism, including background variables, release type (parole versus full discharge), and time since release. Multiple regression procedures provide a means of assessing the independent contribution of each program, while "holding constant" the contribution of other variables. In these analyses, the dependent variable was the dichotomous return-to-prison outcome over the entire follow-up period.[5] Membership in each of the rehabilitation programs (including the TM program) was dummy-coded as a separate independent variable, thus taking participation in multiple programs into account. The other 10 independent variables were the same set of background and release variables on which the groups were compared (see above). Covariates from among this latter set of variables were retained in the regression model only if they were statistically significant predictors of recidivism. T-statistics obtained from the regression for each of the rehabilitation program variables were converted to point-biserial correlations (Cohen & Cohen, 1975, p. 465) to provide a measure of the magnitude of the treatment effect of each program relative to the untreated condition. Since the dependent variable is dichotomous, these effect size indicators have the same interpretation as a tetrachoric correlation coefficient obtained from a chi-square statistic for a 2 × 2 contingency table. To assess the influence of these variables on the analyses of treatment effects, the regression analyses were repeated both including and omitting all background and release variables.

RESULTS

Comparisons on Background Variables Associated with Recidivism

Table 1 compares subjects in each rehabilitation program on background variables that previous research has found are predictors of recidivism, as well as on type and timing of release. The variables that significantly predicted recidivism in the present study were age at release and type of release (parole

Table 1: Background and Release Variables Associated with Recidivism

Variable	TM (n = 53)	Counseling (n = 143)	Drug Rehab (n = 74)	Christian (n = 96)	Muslims (n = 53)	Controls (n = 78)
Race (% white)	57%	63%	37%	51%	15%	69%
Median Age at First Arrest	15.29	14.50	13.77	14.67	13.37	14.70
Median Age at Release†	29.25	26.97	27.40	27.59	27.07	28.12
Longest Job > 4 mos.	66%	56%	47%	56%	45%	53%
Drug Users*	74%	71%	85%	74%	79%	69%
Prior Adult Commitment	77%	79%	77%	83%	74%	82%
Person Offense†	85%	72%	76%	70%	77%	77%
Paroled *†	79%	87%	85%	82%	91%	91%
% Released Before 6/79*	79%	60%	72%	65%	76%	67%
% Released Before 12/77*	6%	10%	18%	7%	19%	10%
% Released Prerelease*	30%	34%	27%	33%	34%	38%

*–Significant association with recidivism in this study.
†–Significant association with TM group membership.

versus full discharge). There were no significant differences between the TM group and the non-meditating controls on race, age at first arrest, employment history, drug abuse, prior adult commitment, or release date. Significant differences between groups were found on offense type (offense against the person: $p = .022$), percent paroled (as opposed to fully discharged: $p = .048$), and age at release ($p = .008$). These variables were controlled for in regression analyses on the recidivism outcomes reported below. Type of release was the only variable on which the groups differed that also significantly predicted recidivism in this study.

There were also significant differences between members of the other programs compared to nonmembers, as follows: drug rehabilitation members had more prior commitments than the remainder of the sample ($Z = 4.05, p < .001$). The proportion of black members was higher in the Muslim ($Z = 7.18, p < .001$) and drug rehabilitation programs ($Z = 4.05, p < .001$), while the Counseling program had a higher percentage of white members ($Z = 2.40, p < .02$).

Recidivism in the TM Program Group Compared to Control Groups

Inmates who participated in the TM program experienced lower recidivism rates than the comparison groups. Over the entire follow-up period, rates of return to prison were lower in the TM group (32%) compared to the combined sample of members of the other four programs (48%). This difference was statistically significant ($Z = 1.725, p = .042$). Over the same time frame, rates of reincarceration due to new convictions were also lower in the TM group (11.4%) than in the combined control groups (21.7%), which also was a statistically significant reduction ($Z = 1.694, p = .045$). Also, the percentage of releasees either with a warrant for arrest or who were returned to prison, or both, was 41.5% in the TM group compared to 56.5% in the pooled control groups. This difference was a statistical trend ($Z = 1.482, p = .069$). In terms of percentage reduction, the TM group was 33% lower than the combined-programs sample on return-to-prison outcomes, 47% lower than all non-meditating controls on new recidivism convictions, and 27% lower than all non-meditating controls on return-to-prison/warrant for arrest outcomes.

Figure 1 compares the TM program with each of the four other comparison programs (Christian, Counseling, Drug Rehabilitation, and Muslim) on rates of return-to-prison over follow-up period as a whole. The results were statistically significant for the comparisons of the TM program with the Counseling ($Z = 1.826, p = .034$), Drug Rehabilitation ($Z = 2.447, p = .007$), and Muslim programs ($Z = 2.2072, p = .014$), and reached a statistical trend with the Christian program ($Z = 1.455, p = .073$). Proportionately, reductions in recidivism ranged from 29% for the Christian group to 42% for drug rehabilitation. There were no significant differences among the other programs on rates of return to prison.

The above analyses were based on comparisons of overall recidivism rates regardless of when inmates were released and, therefore, did not take into ac-

Figure 1: Reincarceration Rates for the TM Group and Members of Four Other Rehabilitation Prison Programs at Walpole Prison

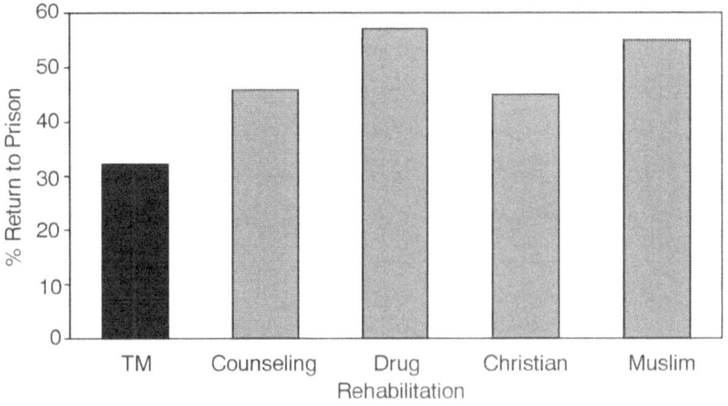

count variation in follow-up times. Figure 2 shows that the rates of return-to-prison for the group practicing the TM program were consistently lower than for the combined control group at all endpoints from 6 months to 30 months. (This was also true at later time points, which were not shown because the number of subjects with longer release times was small.)

Multiple Regression Analyses of Prison Program Membership for Recidivism, Controlling for Background and Release Variables

Four of the eleven inmate characteristics entered into the multiple regression were significant predictors of return-to-prison. In descending order of the magnitude of their contribution to explaining variance of the dependent variable, these predictors were: (a) paroled vs. full discharge ($t(274) = 3.13$; $p = .002$), (b) length of time released ($t(274) = 2.75$; $p = .006$), (c) pre-release institution ($t(274) = 2.48$; $p = .014$), and (d) drug history ($t(274) = 2.30$; $p = .022$). Paroled inmates recidivated more often than fully discharged inmates; inmates released for fewer months recidivated less often; and men released directly from Walpole, Concord, Norfolk, and Southeast Correction Center recidivated less often. Men with a reported drug history recidivated more than those without.

Table 2 displays the results for the five program variables obtained from the multiple regression analysis of return-to-prison outcomes. The two columns on the left show the results of controlling for the four background and release

Figure 2: Reincarceration Rates by Time Since Release, for the TM Group and Members of Other Rehabilitation Programs Combined

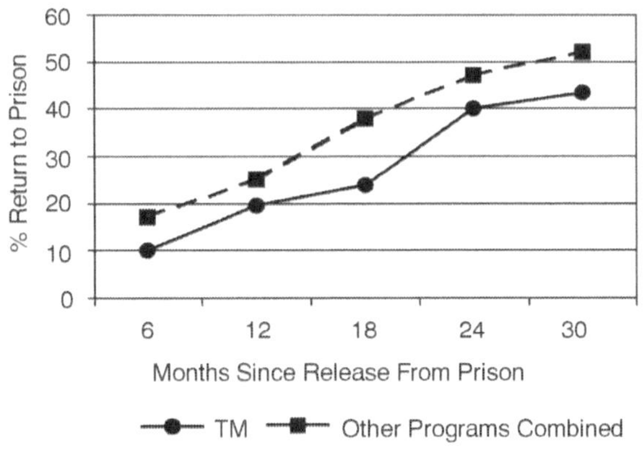

variables that significantly predict recidivism. The two columns on the right show the results when these control variables are dropped from the regression analysis. These two analyses yielded very similar results for the effects of the five program variables, as indicated by the magnitude of the point-biserial correlations (r_{pb}). The TM program was found to significantly lower recidivism in both analyses ($p = .027$, when controlling for the predictors of recidivism; $p = .029$, when not controlling). The magnitude of the treatment effect indicated by rpb was slightly higher when the background and release variables were included in the analysis. The other four rehabilitation programs were not found to have significant effects. In fact, the negative point-biserial correlations for the other rehabilitation programs (compared to no treatment) indicated that participation in these programs was associated with slightly higher return-to-prison rates. Very similar results were obtained from including all ten background and release variables in the regression (see Alexander, 1982).

DISCUSSION

In this study, it was found that recidivism rates among inmates instructed in the TM program were significantly lower than in comparison groups. Proportionately, over the follow-up period as a whole, the reincarceration rate was 33% lower in the TM group than in the combined sample from the four other prison programs. Among the three outcome measures examined, the largest

Table 2: Recidivism Results for Multiple Regression Analysis of the TM Technique and Other Rehabilitation Programs, Controlling versus Not Controlling for Background and Release Variables

	Controlling for background and release variables that significantly predict recidivism		Not controlling for background and release variables	
Program	*t*-statistic	r_{pb}	*t*-statistic	r_{pb}
TM program	1.95	.117*	1.92	.114*
Counseling	−1.03	−.062	−1.27	−.076
Drug rehabilitation	−.61	−.037	−1.36	−.081
Christian	−1.03	−.062	−.75	−.045
Muslims	−.42	−.025	−1.06	−.063

*$p < .05$

proportionate reduction of 47%, for the TM group relative to the pooled control group, was seen on the measure that employed the strictest definition of recidivism–new convictions. This finding is important, because inmates released on parole may be returned for technical violations of the terms of parole, and this may not reflect a relapse to serious criminal behavior. The TM group was also proportionately lower than the controls, by 26%, when recidivism was defined most broadly as return-to-prison or warrant-for-arrest. The reductions in all three outcome measures for the TM program indicate improvement in a range of post-release behaviors and suggest that the effects are robust across different ways of measuring recidivism.

The effect of the TM program on reducing the rate of reincarceration was significant when controlling or not controlling for different background variables, when controlling or not controlling for time of release, when using different comparison groups, and when controlling for participation in other programs. Thus, the findings of this study are consistent and do not depend on how the data were analyzed. Because 90% of the control subjects in the study were randomly selected from the prison population at Walpole and because the subjects in the TM group were similar to other inmates, it is likely that the study conclusions can be generalized from the subjects in this study to a broader population of maximum security prisoners.

Random assignment to different treatment conditions was not possible in this study. Numerous obstacles, ranging from inmate attitudes and research ethics to administrator perspectives and institutional regulations, complicate the use of random assignment in the prison setting. Because subjects self-selected into rehabilitation programs, it is conceivable that this led to differences between the groups on key factors that could account for the more favorable outcomes in the TM group. Compared to the remainder of the sample, the TM group members were committed more often for offenses against the person, were older at release, and had a higher percentage of parole as opposed to discharge; these differences were statistically significant. Among these variables, only parole versus discharge predicted recidivism rates, which was not a preexisting variable that was ascertainable when subjects began to participate in the various prison programs. Moreover, because all 11 background and release variables collected in this study were controlled for by entering them in the multiple regression analysis, it seems unlikely that any of these variables can explain the lower return-to-prison rates in the TM group.

It is plausible, though unlikely, that other demographic variables could account for the results in this study. In the earlier, cross-sectional study at Walpole (Alexander, Walton et al., this volume), a check was performed on the similarity of the members of the TM group who had already been practicing the TM program to members of the other groups of inmates in the study who were classified as interested or not interested in learning the TM program. All three groups were similar on age, race, number of siblings, birth order, IQ, education, occupation, father's occupation, and seriousness of crime. Also, two other studies reported that the TM program reduced recidivism rates of former prisoners after statistically controlling for 26 background variables, including key predictors of recidivism (Bleick & Abrams, 1987; Rainforth et al., this volume).

It is important to consider time of release when analyzing recidivism data, because inmates who were released earlier had more opportunity to commit new offenses, and hence would be expected to have higher recidivism rates. Although tests for difference in proportions did not take into account variations in time of release, which could potentially have led to misleading results, this explanation was ruled out by further statistical analysis. Time of release was controlled for in the multiple regression analysis. Also, the TM group had consistently lower reincarceration rates than the combined programs sample at all follow-up times from 6 months to 30 months. When time of release was controlled for through these direct comparisons, the average reduction obtained over the 6-30 month period was somewhat attenuated (but still favorable) compared to the 33% obtained in the analysis that did not control for time of release. In any case, a slightly higher proportion of subjects in the TM group had been released for over 1 year, which would have given them a higher chance of recidivating.

Comparisons with Other Rehabilitation Programs

An important influence on changing behavior of inmates may be motivation to participate in rehabilitation programs. Group joining motivation as a general variable was controlled for in this study by comparison between inmates who were sufficiently motivated to join different Walpole programs. Four other programs were selected because, like the TM program, they aimed to foster psychological or spiritual development and involved ongoing commitment of their participants. The TM program had lower reincarceration rates than the combined program sample, showing that recidivism was reduced compared to the average of the four other programs.

Another possible confounding factor is participation in multiple rehabilitation programs. The TM program might appear to reduce recidivism, even if, in fact, it were ineffective, if proportionately more of the TM group than the controls participated in other programs that were effective. However, the rates at which members of the TM group participated in the other four programs were closely similar to the rates of participation among inmates not in the TM group. Participation rates in the four other programs for members of the TM group versus nonmembers were: counseling (49% vs. 50%), drug rehabilitation (34% vs. 24%), Christian (34% vs. 31%), and Muslim (24% vs. 16%). Such small differences could not account for the lower recidivism in the TM group. Moreover, the multiple regression analysis explicitly controlled for overlap among programs by separately coding the membership of each program. In this analysis, the effects of the TM program were statistically significant when compared to the entire sample, while the other four programs all had nonsignificant effects in the negative direction.

In the comparisons with the combined program sample, a larger control group was used to increase the statistical power. However, even in the comparisons with the other four programs separately, the reduction for the TM program was statistically significant relative to the counseling, drug abuse, and Muslim programs, and a statistical trend relative to the Christian group. The more favorable outcomes for the Christian program than for the other three control programs may be due to their members of the Christian program being released later (on average). That reincarceration rates for the other programs did not significantly differ from each other supports the validity of pooling data from subjects in the other programs into a combined control group.

Program integrity has been recognized as a major factor mediating the impact of correctional programs (Quay, 1977). To the degree that a program's integrity has been diminished one would expect reduction in the rehabilitative impact. Implementation of the TM program was privately funded, and this funding was lost early during the experimental period, with the result that the support structure for the program was virtually eliminated. Because the TM technique is practiced on an individual basis, an inmate can continue it alone, and as long as he practices the program regularly it should yield the predicted results (Cunningham & Koch, 1976). Nevertheless, research has indicated that when dealing with populations having special needs (e.g., institutionalized psychiatric patients or prisoners: Glueck & Strobel, 1975; Ellis, 1979) a program support structure is instrumental for ensuring regularity of the practice of the TM technique by clients. When statistically significant results are still obtained despite an attenuation of the treatment effect, there must be a strong relationship between the treatment variable and the outcome variable (Prentice & Miller, 1992). That the TM program group has substantially lower recidivism in spite of loss of its program integrity suggests that, had this not occurred, the results of the study might have been even stronger.

Comparison with Other Studies

Even with the aforementioned constraints on implementing the TM program at Walpole, the magnitude of its effect on recidivism compares favorably with other studies. The 33% proportionate reduction on the primary recidivism measure (not controlling for time of release or other predictors) was slightly larger than the corresponding 30% reduction in recidivism in the long-term follow-up of the California TM study (Rainforth et al., this volume). (However, the two studies in California are not directly comparable to those of the current study because they applied different criteria for recidivism.) Statistical measures of the magnitude of treatment effects on reincarceration rates (ES = .33, phi= .16) were as large as those for the most effective type of treatment for adult offenders identified in Lipsey's (1992) meta-analysis. Although these effect sizes were based on an analysis that did not control for length of follow-up, subject background, and release variables, the multiple regression analysis indicated that controlling for these variables made little difference to the estimated treatment effect. A more conservative estimate of the effect of the TM program in the present study is obtained when the comparison group is the general Walpole sample, but even then the effect size (ES = .24, phi = .118) is larger than those for the majority of treatment categories in Lipsey's meta-analysis. Given these findings, it would appear that, despite the aforementioned constraints on continued implementation of the TM program at Walpole, the observed effects were of a magnitude that is of practical significance.

The results for the comparisons of the TM program with other rehabilitation programs in this study are consistent with meta-analyses that have shown larger effects of the TM program relative to conventional treatments. For example, the ability of the TM program to reduce the intake of alcohol, cigarettes, and illicit drugs is substantially larger than for standard substance-abuse treatment and prevention programs (Alexander, Robinson & Rainforth, 1994). The TM program also produces larger reductions of trait anxiety and larger increases in psychological health than other forms of meditation and relaxation (Eppley, Abrams, & Shear, 1989; Alexander, Rainforth, & Gelderloos, 1991).

It is encouraging that positive results were found for the TM program in maximum security prisoners, a population that has generally been found to be recalcitrant to programs designed to bring about rehabilitation. The findings of this study are consistent with a theoretical model that was tested in Parts I and

II of the larger study at Walpole (Alexander, Walton et al., this volume; Alexander & Orme-Johnson, this volume). This model posits that criminal behavior arises when psychological and social development has been prematurely arrested and that regular practice of the TM technique can stimulate a restarting or acceleration of development. Consistent with this model, the inmates in the earlier Walpole studies showed levels of development equal to or lower than the population median, but those who learned the TM program showed impressive gains on a holistic measure of self-development. These findings are indicative of major developmental advancement beyond the impulsive and conformist styles of thinking that characterized inmates who did not practice the TM program.

Explanation of Treatment Effects

Rehabilitation programs that have been previously identified as effective are based on either multi-modal treatment approaches (Lipsey, 1992) or on targeting treatment according to the level of risk and treatment needs of offenders (Andrews, Zinger et al., 1990a), or on both. Given that the TM program does not conform to either of these approaches, it may seem surprising that recidivism was substantially reduced in this study and that the magnitude of the reduction was generally larger than that typically reported for other rehabilitation programs. To understand these findings, it is necessary to consider the TM technique in further detail.

According to its founder Maharishi Mahesh Yogi (1969, 1972), the TM program enables the mind to settle down, with the result that the ordinary active level of thoughts and perceptions is transcended and the inner nature of consciousness at the basis of the mind is experienced. Research on the TM program has characterized this experience as a restfully alert state of mind and body, and has distinguished it from the ordinary waking, dreaming, and sleep states on over 20 psychophysiological parameters (Alexander & Boyer, 1989). On the basis of the enduring effects of the TM program observed outside of the practice, it has been proposed that this experience facilitates an optimal style of mental and physical functioning (Wallace, 1986).

This experience of an optimal style of mental and physical functioning is proposed to represent a deeper level of consciousness that is natural, but is not fully developed without an appropriate technique that fosters it. (A useful parallel can be made to language acquisition. Language acquisition is natural, but is only fully developed in the right environment.) The experience facilitates restructuring and integration of the personality from the most fundamental level of the mind (Alexander, Rainforth & Gelderloos, 1991; Alexander, Davies et al., 1990). This understanding of how the TM program could have distinctive effects on the personality of an offender is testable and has been supported by considerable research (see for review, Goodman et al., this volume). Profound changes in the way an offender comprehends situations and views himself in relation to others might be expected to have far-reaching effects on his reactions to situations and on his behavior in general. This hypothesis of a fundamental shift to a different mode of functioning is supported by the psychological and behavioral changes found in other studies of the effects of the TM program on prisoners, by the dramatic changes in level of self-development among practitioners of the TM technique reported in the previous Walpole studies (Alexander & Orme-Johnson, this volume; Alexander, Walton et al., this volume), and by reductions in recidivism reported in this study.

Hence, although the TM program is a single treatment modality, its impact on a broad set of causal factors involved in the development of criminal behavior (Hawkins, this volume) can be understood in terms of holistic improvements in mental functioning and psychological maturity. Effective rehabilitation programs affect not only the behavior but also the thinking of offenders (Izzo & Ross, 1990). The thinking of offenders becomes more orderly and constructive through practice of the TM technique because this technique improves the very quality of the mind within which thoughts arise. Such holistic effects could account for the findings of the present study. The TM technique is not targeted or matched to specific treatment needs of offenders.

The previously reported ability of the TM program to remove or reverse the effects of stress also provides an explanation of how the program could significantly impact behavior. Chronic exposure to stress is known to have a pervasive effect on health, performance, and behavior (Selye, 1978; Maclean,1978). Empirical research has strongly implicated the negative effects of stress on the functioning of the nervous system as a major factor underlying habitual patterns of violent behavior (Sapolsky, 1996; Raine, 1993; Walton & Levitsky, this volume), and other research has implicated psychosocial stress as a factor in the onset of criminal behavior (Agnew, 1992; Vaux & Ruggerio, 1983). The TM program has been found capable of redressing intense effects of stress, as seen in patients with post-traumatic stress disorder (Brooks & Scarano, 1985), which suggests that even deeply rooted effects of stress could be treated when the TM technique is practiced regularly over a period of time. Although the TM technique is a mental practice, its lasting influence in counteracting the physiological effects of stress may account for enduring improvements in the behavior of offenders.

If rehabilitation treatments are to permanently modify behavior, then presumably treatment effects must carry over into the everyday lives of offenders (Field, 1998). There is evidence that inmates continue to practice the TM technique on their own several years after instruction (Bleick & Abrams, 1987), which would increase the likelihood of enduring changes in behavior patterns.

CONCLUSION

Further research on the TM program in criminal offender populations should be conducted to confirm the effects on recidivism and to control for a wider range of variables. Future studies should provide structure for follow-up and support for regularity of the inmates' practice (both while incarcerated and after release) and should investigate the relationship of post-release outcomes to regularity, to variables that have previously been shown to be affected by the TM program, and to changes in factors that are known predictors of outcomes. Ideally, future studies would be based on stronger research designs and would randomly assign subjects to participate in the TM program or comparison treatments. Another important question that future research may address is whether the TM program could enhance the effectiveness of other rehabilitation programs, thus leading to greater reductions in recidivism than have hitherto been achieved. The most successful rehabilitation programs identified so far deliver service to high risk offenders targeting modifiable criminogenic risk factors while matching treatment to the offender's learning style and rehabilitative needs (Andrews, Zinger et al., 1990a). Whereas this approach relies on appropriate assessment of risk of recidivism, requires correct classification of offenders into treatment programs, and is limited to high-risk offenders, implementation of the TM program is not subject to these requirements or restrictions. The evidence to date from the present study and other studies of the TM program in prison settings suggests it is a promising tool for achieving behavioral change, either alone or in combination with certain other approaches.

NOTES

1. Transcendental Meditation and TM are registered or common law trademarks licensed to Maharishi Vedic Education Development Corporation and are used under sublicense or with permission.

2. Lipsey (1992) included only studies in which the majority of subjects to whom treatment was applied were juveniles. Of the study findings analyzed by Andrews, Zinger et al. (1990a), 85% were juveniles.

3. A series of computerized searches was performed on the Social Science Abstracts, PsycInfo, PAIS, and ArticleFirst databases, specifying the keywords: offender AND rehabilitation, prison AND rehabilitation, prison AND treatment, corrections AND treatment.

4. Glass effect sizes were calculated using Cohen's (1988) arcsine transformation. Phi coefficients were calculated assuming equal numbers of subjects in the treatment and control groups.

5. Conducting multiple regression analyses with a dichotomous dependent variable such as recidivism violates a basic statistical assumption of the regression model–that the dependent variable is normally distributed. However, numerous empirical studies have shown that multiple regression with a dichotomous dependent variable yields valid results despite violation of the assumption (Cohen & Cohen, 1975).

AUTHORS' NOTE

Address correspondence to Maxwell Rainforth, Maharishi University of Management, DB1134, 1000 North 4th Street, Fairfield, IA 52557-1134 (E-mail: rainforth@mum.edu).

Transcendental Meditation in Criminal Rehabilitation and Crime Prevention. Pp. 181-203.

Effects of the *Transcendental Meditation* Program on Recidivism Among Former Inmates of Folsom Prison: Survival Analysis of 15-Year Follow-Up Data

MAXWELL V. RAINFORTH
Maharishi University of Management

CHARLES N. ALEXANDER
Maharishi University of Management

KENNETH L. CAVANAUGH
Maharishi University of Management

ABSTRACT This study examined recidivism rates over a 15-year period among former inmates who learned the Transcendental Meditation (TM)[1] program at a maximum security prison in California. Recidivism outcomes for participants in the TM program were compared with those of matched controls using survival analysis, a general statistical technique for analysis of failure processes. With recidivism defined as rearrest leading to felony conviction, the TM group had a 46.7% recidivism rate during the follow-up period compared to 66.7% for the controls. Survival analysis, using a variety of statistical models and controlling for 22 demographic and criminal background variables, showed that this decrease was statistically significant. Survival analysis based on the Cox regression model indicated that risk of recidivism was reduced by 43.5% (p = .0008). The most appropriate model for the data was found to be a split population Weibull model allowing for immunity to relapse. This model indicated that 58.1% of the TM group versus 73.7% of the control group would eventually re-offend (p =

.01). These long-term differences in recidivism outcomes between groups remained significant while covarying for salient factor scores (a predictive index of recidivism risk), age at first arrest, and participation in prison education and group therapy programs. Moreover, the split population survival model indicated that the TM program resulted in permanent rehabilitation, rather than merely delaying the onset of re-offending. A measure of severity of re-offending also was lower for the TM group compared to controls (p = .023). Furthermore, TM subjects who also took group therapy showed a total effect size for reduction of recidivism that was greater than the sum of effect sizes for subjects with TM alone and group therapy alone–a synergistic effect. These results indicate that lasting rehabilitation can be achieved using the TM program. Further, the results indicate the TM program can be used to advantage with certain other rehabilitation programs and may enhance their effectiveness.

KEYWORDS Transcendental Meditation, rehabilitation, recidivism, repeat offenders, maximum security prisoners, survival analysis, long-term follow-up

Despite the prevailing political climate advocating "getting tough on crime," the need for effective rehabilitation is persistently voiced. There is a "fervently expressed but ill-defined demand by criminal justice professionals, policy makers, and the general public for correctional options that work" (Harland, 1995, p. xiii). Aside from the suffering, fear, and property loss that offenders cause to the community, the exorbitant costs to taxpayers of incarcerating prisoners calls for more effective means to deal with offenders. In California, for example, the prison population was 6.6 times higher in 1999 than it was in 1980, the cost per inmate is $20,758 per year, and the total budget of the California Department of Corrections is $3.9 billion (Petersilia, 1994; California Department of Corrections, 1999). Dramatic increases in the prison population have also occurred in the United States as a whole. In 1995 there were over 1 million state and federal prisoners–four and a half times the number from 20 years earlier (United States Census Bureau, 1998). The criminal justice system, including prison, jail, probation, and parole programs, contains over 5.5 million individuals (United States Census Bureau, 1999).

Part of the problem is the high recidivism rate among offenders. Two-thirds of those sentenced to probation are rearrested within 3.5 years (Petersilia,

Turner, Kahan, & Peterson, 1985). Among former prison inmates, 62.5% are arrested for a felony or serious misdemeanor within 3 years of release, and 41.4% are returned to prison or jail (Beck & Shipley, 1989). Recidivism rates increase sharply with length of prior criminal record: in the United Kingdom, 30% of inmates are reconvicted after 2 years if they have no prior record, but this rate rises to almost 90% with five or more prior convictions (Phillpotts & Lancucki, 1979).

The other articles in this volume have presented evidence showing that the Transcendental Meditation (TM) program reduces effects of stress and other risk factors for criminal behavior, and moreover that practice of this program can profoundly reform the psychology and behavior of offenders. For policy makers, however, the most informative criterion of the success of a rehabilitation program is lower recidivism–fewer offenses committed after release by the group that received treatment (Maltz, 1984).

To date 18 studies have investigated the effects of the TM program in prison settings (see reviews by Dillbeck & Abrams, 1987; Hawkins, this volume). These studies have consistently demonstrated improvements in the behavior, personality, and health of inmates; they show reduced aggression and hostility, fewer prison rule infractions, reduced anxiety, decreased social introversion and psychopathology, improved sleep, and reduced cigarette use.

Several of these studies used random assignment or other strong controls in the research design. For example, Ballou (1977) randomly assigned 50 volunteer inmates to either the TM program or a wait-list control group who would learn the technique later. Levels of anxiety were significantly reduced over 10 weeks in the TM group compared to both the wait-list controls and subjects not interested in learning the TM program. Also, there was a significant decline in prison rule infractions in the TM group relative to matched controls, comparing the 10 months the TM program was implemented to the 10 prior months. Seventy percent of those trained in the TM program were still meditating regularly 1 year after instruction.

Two previous studies have examined the effects of the Transcendental Meditation program on criminal recidivism. In a retrospective study of inmates released from a Massachusetts maximum security prison (Alexander, 1982; Alexander, Rainforth et al., this volume), a group who had learned the TM program (N = 53) was compared to a control group (N = 233) of inmates who did not practice the TM technique. Recidivism, which was defined as return to prison for 30 days or more, was examined over a 3-year period. The recidivism rate in the TM group was proportionately lower than the control group by 33%. This reduction remained significant after controlling statistically for time of release and 8 predictors of recidivism identified by previous research.

A second study of released inmates who had learned the TM program (Bleick & Abrams, 1987) tracked 259 inmates for 6 years after release and compared their recidivism rate with that of matched controls. Subjects were adult male felons from three California prisons of which two were maximum security (Folsom and San Quentin Prisons) and the other a high-medium security (Deuel Vocational Institution). The TM subjects were similar to the population of other inmates in the same prisons on the following characteristics: percentage who were African-American, seriousness of prior commitments, and category of the most recent offense. Over 5 successive years after release, rates of new prison sentences and long jail terms in the TM group were 35% to 50% lower than for the controls (43% lower on average). Moreover, controlling for 28 social and criminal background variables by stepwise regression, parole outcomes at 1 year, and rap sheet outcomes up to 6 years were significantly more favorable for the TM group than for controls.

The present research examines subjects from the Bleick and Abrams study who were at Folsom Prison, tracking their re-offending rates for up to 15 years after release. Recidivism rates over the entire follow-up period are examined using survival analysis, a general statistical technique for analysis of failure processes.[2] This approach overcomes the limitations due to assessing recidivism at the end of a fixed time period (e.g., after 3 years), which can be misleading if treatment effects vary over time or due to omitting subjects with shorter follow-up times (Maltz, 1984). In contrast, survival analysis makes use of all follow-up times, taking account of both the time until relapse and the rates of relapse. Potential biases due to insufficient follow-up time to observe relapse are minimized through appropriate adjustment of statistical calculations for such cases of truncated follow-up times (which are designated as *censored* observations). Like regression models, survival analysis models can statistically control for predictors of recidivism. As in the Bleick and Abrams (1987) study, in the present research it was hypothesized that the TM group would be lower than the controls on multiple measures of recidivism after statistically adjusting for key predictor variables.

METHOD

Subjects and Data Collection

From 1975 to 1982, a total of 153 male inmates at Folsom Prison volunteered to learn the TM program. By October 1982, all had been paroled. For each TM subject, a non-meditating control subject was selected from the Folsom Prison records by matching closely on parole year, race, and offense, and matching approximately on prior commitment record, age, and history of drug abuse. For both subjects in a matched pair, the date on which the experimental subject learned the TM technique was taken as the date of entry into the study. Because the California Department of Corrections (CDC) discards records for deceased parolees, subjects who were deceased at time of data collection in 1991 were excluded. Subjects also were dropped if they were: paroled out of state or to Federal custody, serving a parole violation at time of entry into the study, found not guilty of the offense for which they were incarcerated, or if either their parole date or re-arrest date was missing. These criteria led to inclusion of data on 248 subjects, 120 of whom had learned the TM technique and 128 of whom were controls.

After matching, additional demographic and subject background variables for both groups were retrieved from CDC files. These variables were: ethnicity, marital status, educational attainment (grade level by standardized test), IQ, employment history, military service and discharge, alcohol and drug abuse history, age at first arrest, age at first commitment, age at parole, prior commitment record, months served during term under consideration, and CDC rule violations prior to entry into the study. These variables included the most commonly cited predictors of recidivism (e.g., review by Pritchard, 1979). Voluntary participation in three prison self-improvement programs (education, vocational training, and group therapy) was included, as well, as a way of addressing the motivational factor involved in volunteering for instruction in the TM technique. An overall index of recidivism risk, the salient factor score [the 1981 revised version (Hoffman, 1983)], was computed for each inmate. The U.S. Parole Commission uses this scale as an actuarial device for assessing parole prognosis. It is based on 6 criminal history variables: number of prior convictions, number of prior commitments, age at current offense, commitment during past 3 years, parole/probation violation at time of offense, and prior drug offense convictions. Scores on this predictive scale range from 0 to 10, with 0 signifying high risk.

Recidivism outcomes for the period up to 1991 were obtained from post-release criminal records, or "rap sheets," maintained by the California Justice Department's Bureau of Identification.

Data Analysis

Dependent Variables

Follow-up time for each subject commenced from his date of release (i.e., parole date). The primary criterion for recidivism was re-arrest (subsequent to release from the term served at the time of study entry) leading to re-conviction of a felony. The event markers (re-arrest) used in this definition of recidivism were obtained from the standardized database maintained by a state agency, thus providing a more reliable recidivism measure than parole violation (Maltz, 1984); also, these event markers more closely approximate the actual date of recidivating than do the date of prosecution, reconviction or reincarceration (Maltz, 1984). Moreover, recidivism was deemed to have occurred only if a new felony conviction officially confirmed that a serious offense was committed.

These primary recidivism outcomes were on a dichotomous scale (i.e., 1 for a new offense, otherwise 0 at each time point). A secondary analysis examined severity of outcomes on a graded scale, which was coded annually from the rap sheet data: 0 = clean (no reconviction or parole revocation); 1 = misdemeanor, parole revocation, or insanity suspended sentence; 2 = nonviolent felony; 3 = violent felony. These outcomes indicate the most serious offense to date since release.

Independent Variables

The main independent variable was treatment (TM vs. controls). Other independent variables indicated whether or not subjects participated in each of the three other treatment programs (education, vocational training, or group therapy). To control for potential predictors of recidivism and to statistically control for any differences between groups that may have remained after matching, all available subject and criminal background variables were analyzed as covariates.

Statistical Procedures

This section provides a technical description of statistical calculations used to obtain the results of this study. The reader who is not technically oriented may proceed directly to Results section.

To provide descriptive statistics for recidivism rates over time, the proportions recidivating in the TM and control groups were calculated as a function of time using the product limit method (Collett, 1994). Statistical significance of differences between the two groups were assessed using Cox proportional hazards regression (Cox, 1972; Cox & Oakes, 1984). Cox regression analysis yields an estimate of the relative reduction in risk of recidivism due to treatment, thus providing a single measure of the magnitude of the treatment effect. It also provides a statistical test of the treatment effect that is equivalent to the non-parametric log-rank test when there are no covariates other than the treatment variable. Congruent with the matched pairs design, this analysis was applied to the dichotomous recidivism outcomes, covarying for treatment and stratifying on subject pairs. Effects of all variables were examined using two-sided significance tests at the 5% alpha level.

In addition to these descriptive and non-parametric analyses, which made no assumptions about the distribution of relapse times, a formal statistical modeling approach to the data was also taken. The purpose of this approach was, first, to describe accurately the time course of treatment effects and, second, to permit accurate statistical control over predictors of recidivism by including them as covariates in the model. For the Cox regression model to be an accurate statistical description of the data, it is necessary that the relative risk, defined as the ratio of the hazard functions of the two groups, be independent of time. This assumption was shown to be invalid for the present data set by including a time dependent covariate in the Cox regression model (Collett, 1994; Dixon, 1992). (The relative risk from the Cox model is, nevertheless, still a valid indicator of the average reduction in recidivism over the entire follow-up period.)

Several authors have pointed out that standard survival models are often inappropriate for recidivism data because a positive proportion of the population is immune to relapse over the long-term, whereas standard models predict eventual failure by all individuals (Maltz, 1984; Schmidt & Witte, 1989; Maller & Zhou, 1996); that is, empirical data suggest that a percentage of former inmates will never reoffend, and this is incompatible with the standard survival analysis models. This pattern seen in other studies seemed to apply to data for the current study: time plots of the percentage recidivating in the TM and control groups showed that both of the curves leveled out to horizontal asymptotes below 100%. In such situations, the proportional hazards assumption of the Cox regression model may not be valid. Instead, a good fit to the data can be obtained from a *split population* model, which distinguishes two types of individuals in the population: those who will relapse and those who will never relapse (Schmidt & Witte; see also Maller & Zhou, who refer to these as "long-term survivor" models).

A split population model based upon the Weibull distribution was found to provide an adequate description of the data for the TM and control groups. Models of this type require few assumptions and are easily interpretable. Moreover, they provide sufficient flexibility to describe a wide variety of patterns for the time course of recidivism. This versatility is on the basis of three model parameters: the percentage of releasees (Ω) who will eventually recidivate (or probability of eventual relapse for any given individual), the scale parameter (λ), which specifies the relapse rate among releasees who eventually reoffend, and a shape parameter (γ) which determines the manner in which the reoffending rate increases or decreases with time. [In such a model, the cumulative proportion recidivating at time t is given by $F(t) = \Omega\ (1 - exp(-\lambda t^{\gamma}))$, where $0 \leq \Omega \leq 1$, $\lambda > 0$ and $\gamma > 0$ are the model parameters, and *exp* is exponentiation to the power of e, the base of the natural logarithm function.] If $\Omega = 1$ then 100% of the releasees will eventually reoffend, if followed for a sufficient length of time. If $\gamma = 1$ then among eventual reoffenders the conditional reoffending rate is constant, but if $\gamma < 1$ reoffending rates start off high but taper off over time; $\gamma > 1$ implies increasing reoffending rates. Thus a value of Ω close to 1 coupled with a high value of λ corresponds to a high rate of reoffending, while a low value of γ indicates that the majority of new offenses tend to be committed soon after release.

Potential predictors of recidivism were incorporated in the model according to the method recommended by Maller and Zhou (1996).[3] This method links the parameters of the split population Weibull model to covariates $X_1 \ldots X_k$ via the equations:

$$\Omega = 1 - 1/(1 + \exp(a_1X_1 + a_2X_2 + \ldots + a_kX_k)),$$
$$\lambda = \exp(b_1X_1 + b_2X_2 + \ldots + b_kX_k),\ \gamma = \exp(c_1X_1 + c_2X_2 + \ldots + c_kX_k).$$

These equations express the parameters of the survival model as nonlinear functions of linear combinations of the predictors.[4] This approach controls for the effect of the covariates and enables predictions regarding their combined influence to be generated from the model; this is analogous to the way predictions are derived from standard regression-type models.[5]

By applying this method, model parameters were statistically adjusted for differences between the groups on the covariates, in a manner closely resembling the procedure used to calculate adjusted group means from analysis of covariance models.[6] This approach takes account of variability of the values of the covariates across subjects and statistically controls for differences between treatment groups. Note that a positive value for a coefficient associates an increase in the value of the covariate with an increase in the value of the corresponding model parameter. Therefore, positive values for the coefficients of the covariates with respect to Ω and λ indicate increased risk, and negative values with respect to γ indicate earlier occurrence of relapse.

A split population Weibull model was fit to the observed data by maximizing the log-likelihood function using the Newton-Raphson iteration method, as described by Maltz (1984). Visual inspection and quantitative analysis indicated that this model provided a good description of the data. Time plots for the TM and control groups showed that predicted cumulative recidivism rates from the model were close to the rates estimated from the data by the product-limit method; furthermore the model predictions fell within the 95% confidence intervals based on the Kaplan-Meier estimates (Collett, 1994) for virtually the entire 15-year follow-up period. To further test the appropriateness of the Weibull distribution for describing the observed pattern of relapse times in this study, the standard log minus log plot test (Collett, 1994) was modified by first dividing the estimated values for the survivor function (i.e., relapse-free proportion of releasees) at each time point by the estimate of Ω from the model (the estimated proportion of releasees who will eventually recidivate). The resulting values estimate the survivor function for the recidivant fraction of the population of releasees. Consistent with a Weibull model, plots (for the TM and control groups) of the logarithm of the negative logarithm of the conditional survivor functions versus the logarithm of the relapse times were both very close to a straight line.[7] Tests for the significance of covariates in the model were performed using the log-likelihood test (Collett).

Outcomes on the graded recidivism scale were examined by repeated measures analysis applied to yearly follow-up data. To utilize all available data, given the variability of the follow-up times, this analysis was performed using the restricted maximum likelihood approach (Dixon, 1992), which permits estimation of the model under the assumption of ignorable missing data (Rubin, 1976). Because the outcomes in this analysis were a cumulative measure of the worst recorded behavior by each subject since release (analogous to the cumulative percentage recidivating based on the primary outcome), the dependent variables rise over time as new offenses are committed; a sharp upward trend indicates a rapid rate of reoffending. Therefore, to compare the time dependency of relapse behavior in the two groups, linear and quadratic trends were tested for using orthogonal trend components in the repeated measures analysis (Winer, 1971).[8]

Effects on the primary recidivism outcome were evaluated by survival analysis on a MicroVax 3400 using BMDP programs 1L and 2L, specially written Pascal routines, and the SURFIT software package for IBM-PC compatible computers (Maltz, 1990). Severity of recidivism was investigated using BMDP program 5V.

RESULTS

Subject Characteristics

Table 1 shows the comparability of the two groups on demographic and criminal background variables. The average age was 37.4 at entry into the study and 39 upon release. The subjects were 45% African American or Hispanic; they showed an 8th grade educational level on standardized achievement tests, and 95% had a history of drug and/or alcohol abuse. They had an average of 2 prior violent felony convictions, had served an average of 1.7 prior prison commitments, and, at study entry, had served 3 years out of the current commitment of 4.7 years. The offenses for which releasees were reincarcerated were: homicide–16.1%, robbery–35.1%, assault–9.3%, theft–12.1%, sexual offense–5.6%, drug offense–17.4%. The average follow-up time after release from prison was 12.2 years.

There were no significant differences between the TM and control groups on any of the matching variables, which implies that the groups were statistically similar on these key characteristics. Statistically significant differences were found between groups on the salient factor score and on participation in educational and group therapy programs. To statistically control for these differences, these variables were included as covariates in analyses of treatment effects reported below. No significant differences were obtained on any other subject profile variables.

Primary Recidivism Outcomes

Figure 1 shows the cumulative proportion recidivating over time among releasees from the TM and control groups. Cox regression analysis yielded a relative risk of .565, indicating that, averaged over the follow-up period, the recidivism risk was 43.5% lower for the TM group than for controls. This ob-

Table 1: Characteristics of Subjects in the TM and Control Groups

	TM[b]	Controls[b]	Difference[a] (F or χ^2)
Subject Profile			
Ethnicity (black/Hispanic)	45.0% ± 50.0%	45.3% ± 50.0%	0.00
Married	42.4% ± 49.6%	36.5% ± 48.3%	0.88
Age at entry to study	37.9 ± 6.5	36.9 ± 6.9	0.95
Educational attainment (grade level on test)	8.6 ± 1.7	8.1 ± 2.1	3.46
IQ range (% above average)	36.2% ± 48.3%	30.1% ± 46.0%	1.01
Dishonorable military discharge	10.0% ± 30.1%	13.3% ± 34.1%	0.65
Employment prior to offense (at least 6 months)	67.0% ± 47.2%	66.4% ± 47.4%	0.01
Substance abuse history	93.3% ± 25.0%	96.1% ± 19.5%	0.95
Criminal Background			
Age at first arrest	15.6 ± 4.5	15.1 ± 3.7	0.86
Age at first conviction	19.2 ± 6.5	18.0 ± 4.9	2.65
Prior prison terms	2.3 ± 1.8	2.4 ± 1.8	0.35
Prior violent felony convictions	2.2 ± 2.1	2.2 ± 1.8	0.02
Current commitment (yrs)	5.0 ± 2.9	4.4 ± 3.2	2.08
Years served prior to study	2.8 ± 2.8	2.9 ± 2.8	0.04
CDC rule violations prior to study	2.7 ± 6.6	1.6 ± 6.5	1.47
Salient factor score	3.1 ± 2.6	2.1 ± 2.3	11.62*

[a]Dichotomous variables were analyzed by the χ^2 test; all other variables were analyzed by the F-test.
[b]Data are expressed as means ± S.D. Data for dichotomous variables are expressed as percentages.
* $p < .001$

served difference was statistically significant in the case-control analysis (p = 0.0024) and in the direct comparison of the two groups (Z = 3.36, p = .0008).[9]

Lower recidivism rates for the TM group were also obtained from survival analysis using the split population Weibull model with covariates. An initial model was fitted with covariates for effects of the TM program on all 3 parameters of the split population Weibull distribution, excluding other covariates. The results for this model are displayed in Table 2, in which the columns indicate: the covariates in the model, the parameters of the split population Weibull distribution to which these are applied, the model estimates for the coefficients of the covariates, and the Z statistics from the log-likelihood test for the significance of the covariates.

Interpretation of the results in Table 2, based on the signs of the coefficients and their relationship with the survival distribution parameters, is as follows.

Figure 1: Cumulative Proportion Over Time of Subjects in the TM and Control Groups Who Were Rearrested and Reconvincted of Felony

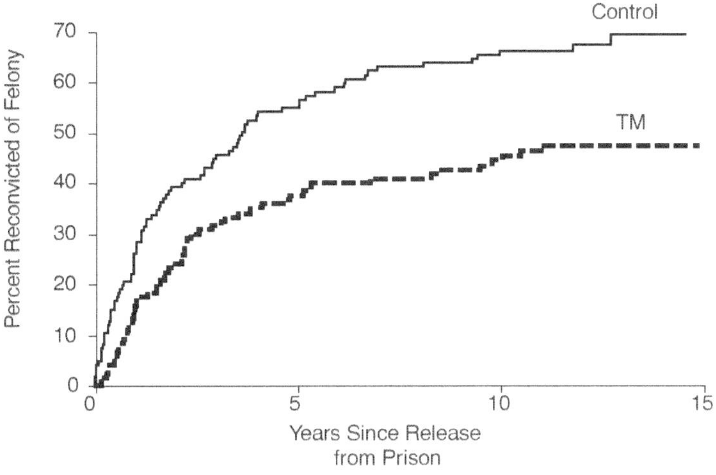

For the TM group compared to controls, the percentage of releasees who recidivated over the long term was significantly lower (Ω = 48.3% vs. Ω = 70.3%; Z = 2.89, p = .004); also among reoffenders the rate of reoffending was lower for the TM group than for controls (λ = .315 vs. λ = .428) and reoffending tended to occur later in time (γ = .971 for the TM group vs. γ = .802 for the control group).[10] However, because these effects on the rate and shape parameters (λ and γ) were not significant, they were omitted from the models for subsequent analyses. In the lower half of Table 2, these differences between the TM and control groups, with respect to proportion of long-term recidivists, are expressed by three widely used indicators of the magnitude of the treatment effect: the Glass effect size (d = .452) expresses the difference in outcomes between groups in standard deviation units, the coefficient ϕ = .224 represents the correlation between group membership and recidivism status, while the odds ratio (OR = .394) indicates that degree to which the control subjects were more likely than the controls to recidivate.[11]

Next, analysis controlled for key variables by including them as covariates in the split population Weibull survivor model. To assess effects of the TM technique on long-term recidivism while statistically adjusting for differences between the groups, education, group therapy program participation, and the salient factors scores were applied as covariates to the Ω parameter. Following

Table 2: Split Population Survival Model Results for Primary Recidivism Outcome, Covarying for TM Participation

Covariate	Parameter	Coefficient	Z
Constant	Ω	0.862	
TM vs. controls	Ω	−0.931	−2.89*
Constant	λ	−0.848	
TM vs. controls	λ	−0.307	−1.18
Constant	γ	−0.221	
TM vs. controls	γ	0.191	1.16
Long-term recidivism rate Ω for each treatment condition:			
	Controls	0.703	
	TM	0.483	
Treatment effect size:			
	Standardized difference, *d*	0.452	
	φ coefficient	0.224	
	Odds ratio, OR	0.394	

* $p < .005$

a stepwise model-building procedure, additional covariates were applied to any of the model parameters if the log-likelihood test showed that this led to significant improvement in model accuracy.

The resulting model is shown in Table 3. The coefficients in the table indicate the role of each covariate in predicting recidivism. The probability of eventual recidivism (Ω parameter) is significantly predicted by the salient factor score ($p = .01$), educational attainment ($p = 4 \times 10^{-10}$), and age at first arrest ($p < .004$); higher scores on these variables predicted lower risk. Participation in the TM and group therapy programs was significantly associated with lower probability of eventual recidivism ($p = .048$ for TM; $p = .01$ for group therapy), while education programs did not produce significant changes ($p > .11$). For the rate of relapse among eventual recidivists (λ parameter), the only significant predictor was the salient factor score ($p = .015$); a high score indicated slower rates of reoffending. The temporal distribution of relapse among eventual recidivists (γ parameter) was related only to number of previous prison commitments ($p < .0006$). Adjusting for the effects of the covariates, the long-term rates of recidivism (Ω parameter) were 58.1% in the TM group and 73.7% in the non-TM group. These percentages correspond to a Glass effect size of .331 standard deviations and to a φ coefficient of .165, which indicate the magnitude of the treatment effect adjusted for the covariates.

Table 3: Split Population Survival Model Results for Primary Recidivism Outcome, Covarying for TM Program Participation, Between Group Differences, and Significant Predictors of Recidivism

Covariate	Parameter	Coefficient	Z
Constant	Ω	8.598	
TM vs. controls	Ω	−0.704	−1.98*
Group therapy	Ω	−1.076	−2.59**
Educational programs	Ω	0.611	1.58
Salient factor score	Ω	−1.862	−2.57*
Educational attainment	Ω	−0.631	−6.25****
Age at first arrest	Ω	−0.118	−2.90**
Constant	λ	−0.806	
Salient factor score	λ	−1.027	−2.44*
Constant	γ	0.161	
Prior commitments	γ	−0.110	−3.45***
Covariate-adjusted Ω for each treatment condition:			
	Controls	0.737	
	TM	0.581	
Treatment effect size:			
	Standardized difference, *d*	0.331	
	φ coefficient	0.165	
	Odds ratio, OR	0.495	

* $p < .05$ ** $p < .01$ *** $p < .001$ **** $p < .0001$

Because the TM program and group therapy both significantly reduced recidivism, further statistical investigation examined the manner in which they acted alone and in concert. To examine effects of the TM program in the absence of group therapy, while controlling for effects of key variables, subjects identified as not satisfactorily completing a course in group therapy were omitted from the analysis. Since the estimated treatment effect would depend on the control variables used in the analysis, to permit comparison with the analysis on the entire sample, the same covariates were retained regardless of whether they were still significant in the subgroup analysis. The effects of the TM program are still significant for this subgroup if a one-tailed test is used ($p = .043$). The reduced significance level reflects the 21% reduction in the number of subjects in this analysis and not an attenuation of the treatment effect: the effect sizes for the TM program in this subgroup are virtually identical to those obtained in the analysis of the entire sample.

Also, the effect of group therapy alone was analyzed on data from the non-TM subjects, using the same covariates as before. In this analysis group therapy was not significant. However, when subjects who learned the TM technique and also took group therapy were compared to subjects receiving neither treatment, highly significant treatment effects were obtained (p = .001). In this analysis of the combined treatments, effect sizes (d = .978, ϕ = .469) were greater than the sum of the effect sizes for TM alone (d = .321, ϕ = .159) and group therapy alone (d =.335, ϕ = .165).

Secondary Recidivism Outcomes

Figure 2 shows outcomes on the graded recidivism scale (at 3, 6, 9 and 12 years after release) by offense severity. The shading within the bars on the chart shows the proportion of subjects in the TM and control groups who committed new offences at different severity levels: parole violations and misdemeanors (least severe; top portion of the bar), nonviolent felonies (middle portion), and violent felonies (most severe; bottom). The total height of each bar represents offenses of all types. At each of the follow-up times and at all levels of severity, the rates of reoffending were lower in of the TM group than in the control group. (Except at 12 years, there were fewer parole violations and misdemeanors in the control group than in the TM group, but the overall reoffending rate was greater than in the TM group, even after 12 years. Apparently, 12 years after release, subjects in the control group who initially had less severe offenses had progressed to more serious crimes.) As shown in Table 4,

Figure 2: Recidivism Outcomes by Level of Severity in the TM and Control Groups at 3, 6, 9, and 12 Years After Release

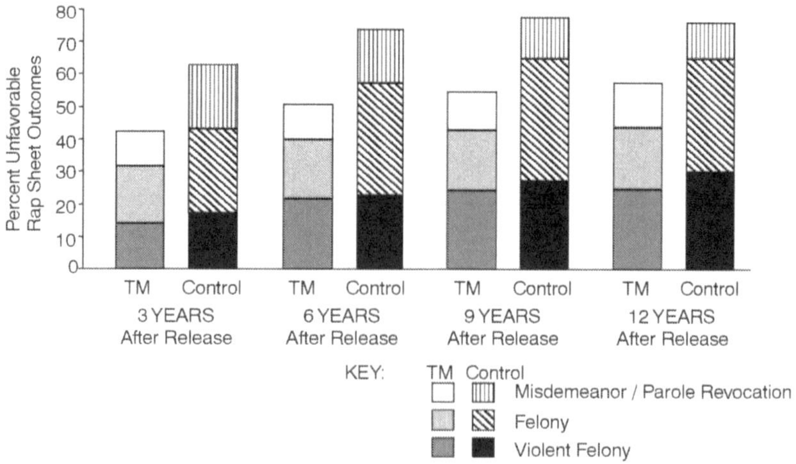

Table 4: Effects of Treatment on Graded Recidivism Outcome–Results of Repeated Measures Analysis with Orthogonal Trend Components

Model Component	Coefficient	Asymptotic Std. Error	Z
Constant	2.5426	0.2669	9.53***
Covariates			
Salient factor score	−0.6817	0.2379	−2.87**
Educational attainment	−0.1403	0.0300	−4.68***
Trend variables			
Linear	0.0368	0.0043	8.48***
Quadratic	−0.0034	0.0005	−6.65***
Treatments			
TM	−0.1421	0.0626	−2.27*
Education	−0.0560	0.0662	0.85
Group therapy	0.1347	0.0753	−1.79[a]
Treatment x Trend Interactions			
TM x Linear	−0.0023	0.0037	−0.60
TM x Quadratic	0.0009	0.0004	2.02*
Ed x Linear	−0.0038	0.0040	−0.93
Ed x Quadratic	0.0005	0.0005	−0.99
GT x Linear	0.0091	0.0045	−2.01*
GT x Quadratic	−0.0006	0.0005	1.06

[a]$p < .10$ * $p < .05$ ** $p < .005$ *** $p < .0001$

these differences in the seriousness of reoffending were statistically significant. Repeated measures analysis over the first 12 follow-up years,[12] covarying for salient factors scores, group therapy, and educational program participation, showed there was a significant reduction across all time points due to TM program participation ($p = .0037$).

Orthogonal trend analysis showed significant linear and quadratic trends across treatment groups, indicating, as expected, that new offenses were being committed but that reoffending tapered off over time. There was a significant interaction between TM program participation and the quadratic trend ($p = .048$), which indicated that the time course of relapse differed between the two groups.[13] However, there were no significant main effects or interactions with linear trends for group therapy or education programs.

Similar results were obtained when the repeated measures analysis was extended to consider all potential predictors of recidivism as covariates. A step-wise, model-building approach, including covariates if they were significant in the model, led to the inclusion (in the model reported in Table 4) of educational attainment as an additional control variable. The main effect for TM program participation was again statistically significant (p = .023) as was the interaction between TM and the quadratic trend (p = .044). There also was a significant interaction between the linear trend variable and participation in group therapy (p = .045), indicating that this treatment also reduced the rate at which new offenses were committed. No other main effects or interaction terms were significant.

DISCUSSION

The results of this study indicate that recidivism rates among inmates who learned and practiced the TM program were substantially reduced over an extended period after release from prison. Significant differences between the TM and control groups were sustained even when statistically controlling for all available predictors of recidivism.

Compared to the majority of prison program evaluations, the average follow-up period of 12 years employed in this study is unusually long (Maltz, 1984, p. 74). The reduced rates of reoffending over this period clearly indicate that the effects of the TM program are enduring over the long term. Statistical analysis over the entire follow-up period, by survival analysis and repeated measures analysis, avoids potential biases inherent in more traditional approaches to program evaluation based on outcomes at the end of a fixed follow-up period. This statistical approach also permits detailed analysis of the time course of reoffending, which was found to be lower in the TM group at all follow-up times.

Statistically significant differences were found between the TM and control groups using various techniques of survival analysis, including the nonparametric log-rank test, the Cox proportional hazards regression, and split population survivor models with covariates. Construction of split-population survival models with covariates provided accurate descriptions of the time course of relapse while controlling for key variables. This technique is a comparatively recent innovation that has been applied in few other recidivism studies, which takes into account the important fact that after release many former prisoners maintain clean records over the long term. Statistical significance was obtained regardless of distributional assumptions or the choice of covariates to be included in the model. The results indicated that the probability of an inmate eventually recidivating was lower if the inmate had practiced the TM program while in prison.

Reductions in recidivism were obtained using two different approaches to quantifying outcomes. Results from survival analysis of the dichotomous recidivism outcome variable were consistent with repeated measures analysis of the severity of reoffending on an ordinal scale. Thus, the findings of this study were further cross-validated by examining the data using a variety of statistical methods, showing the results to be robust and not dependent on any one particular method of analysis.

Validity of the findings is enhanced by the use of official records obtained from the California Department of Corrections. By defining rearrest leading to reconviction of felony as the primary recidivism outcome, the analysis was based on firm evidence of reoffending, as close as possible to the dates that new offenses were known to have occurred. Of course, only a small fraction of actual crimes lead to arrest and reconviction (Maltz, 1984), and so it is likely the released offenders in this study committed a greater number of new offenses than were recorded. This is a concern for virtually all studies of recidivism, since they generally also rely on official data. It is not a problem, however, if we assume that actual rate of offending is governed by a random process and that this is independent of the rate of detection of offenses by law enforcement agencies. In this case, arrests still proportionately reflect actual offenses; compared to actual offenses, the random pattern of arrests is "thinned out" in time but is governed by the same type of random process (Murray & Cox, 1979, p. 49).

Alternative Explanations

Selective loss of data to follow up might conceivably account for the results, even though the reasons (including subjects moving out of state and the CDC policy of discarding a subject's records upon his or her death) were not related to criminal behavior. The 19% loss of follow-up data seems acceptable, considering the length of the follow-up period. Also, if data loss or attrition had grossly altered the constitution of the TM and control groups, one might anticipate that this would lead to significant differences between the groups on the variables on which the groups were originally matched. However, this was not the case; the means of the matching variables were very similar. Moreover the earlier Bleick and Abrams study (1987) included the same subjects but tracked them for only 6 years. Consequently, in this prior study the level of data loss was lower, but still the TM program was found to significantly reduce recidivism. Therefore, it seems unlikely that data loss can account for the differences between the TM and control groups.

Another potential limitation on inferences drawn from this study is the use of an ex post facto, case-control research design, which in theory does not rule out all alternative explanations for the results. The only way to address this rigorously is through random assignment of subjects to treatment conditions, which was not feasible due to such pragmatic constraints as the rules of prison administration and the desire of inmates to participate; it is well known that "true experiments are the exception in correctional research" (Maltz, 1984).

Evidence from other research suggests that lack of random assignment need not pose a serious threat to the conclusions of this study. Several meta-analyses on the efficacy of offender rehabilitation programs found that the magnitude of treatment effects was affected only slightly by research design strength (e.g., Andrews et al., 1990; Lipsey, 1992). (In fact, Lipsey found higher effects in studies with random assignment compared to studies without it.) Similarly, the magnitude of effect of the TM program was affected little by excluding poorly designed studies from three statistical meta-analyses of effects of the TM program on trait anxiety, self-actualization, and substance abuse (Eppley, Abrams, & Shear, 1989; Alexander, Rainforth, & Gelderloos, 1991; Alexander, Robinson, & Rainforth, 1994). Consistent with these research findings, previous random assignment studies on prisoners have reported improvements in behavior and personality traits (Ballou, 1977; Ramirez, 1989).

Moreover, either by matching or by statistically adjusting, the study controlled for variables that have been frequently identified in the literature as important predictors of recidivism. These controls covered such key factors as age, race, marital status, educational and employment background, history of substance abuse, criminal record, and age at release. Significant differences between the TM and control groups persisted after adjusting for an extensive list of variables. In the split population Weibull model of the primary outcome, covariates were applied to the distribution parameter that appeared to be most affected by the TM program; only after their influence was taken into account was the influence of the program deemed significant.

Another key factor to be considered is that subjects self-selected to learn the TM technique, and thus, improvements relative to controls may reflect motivational differences. Presumably motivation would be a factor in inmate participation in other optional prison programs designed to rehabilitate them. Although participation in group therapy did reduce recidivism, vocational programs made little difference, and educational programs were associated with a noticeable (but statistically insignificant) increase in recidivism. Therefore, participation per se in conventional programs did not reduce recidivism. Moreover, effect sizes for the TM program were similar for analyses based on the entire sample and analyses which omitted group therapy subjects, even though subjects in the latter analysis were likely to have had less motivation to improve. Also, the Abrams and Siegel (1979) study at Folsom, which used a matched, wait-listed control design to control for motivation, is directly relevant to the present research. That these authors were able to replicate their findings within the same setting strongly suggests that effects of the TM program on prison inmates are not due to extraneous factors. Thus, it is unlikely that the apparent effect of this program is merely due to the subjects' expectations or motivation to improve.

Maltz (1984) points out that when a program evaluation examines the efficacy of the rehabilitation process, as well as the final outcomes (e.g., recidivism), it yields deeper insights concerning treatment mechanisms and greater confidence in the attribution of outcomes to treatment as the cause of the outcomes. In this regard the present evaluation is bolstered by the 18 previous studies of effects of the TM program, which included assessment of personality and behavioral variables (for a review see Hawkins, this volume).

Given that effects of the TM program are said to accrue from regular practice (Maharishi Mahesh Yogi, 1972), one may ask whether the inmates in this study continued to practice the TM program regularly. Consistent with the outcomes of this study, in the earlier study at Folsom that included the same subjects (Bleick & Abrams, 1987), the majority of subjects instructed in the TM technique continued to practice it while in prison for several years after beginning the practice. Four to seven years after instruction, 37% of subjects were still practicing the technique at least once a day. Data on regularity of practice after release from prison was not readily available in the present study.

Lower recidivism can be due to either permanent rehabilitation or merely delayed onset of reoffending. Thus, it is interesting that results from the split population Weibull survivor model indicate that the TM program effected permanent change in the behavior of inmates. This is evident from the fact that significantly lower values were observed for the TM group on the Ω parameter (indicating the probability of eventually reoffending), but not on the λ parameter (indicating the rate of relapse among those who eventually reoffend). It is plausible that the program's effect was realized even before the inmates were paroled. Ample evidence indicates that even a few months of regular practice of the technique is sufficient to induce significant changes in personality and behavior variables of inmates (Dillbeck & Abrams, 1987). For example, in the Walpole prison study (Alexander & Orme-Johnson, this volume; Alexander, Walton et al., this volume) impressive gains in ego or self-development were achieved in the TM subjects, and these were reflected in substantially lower recidivism rates (Alexander, Rainforth et al., this volume).

Broader Implications

Compared with recidivism outcomes for other offender rehabilitation programs, the magnitude of the reduction seen in this study is practically important. The effect size reported in Table 3 (.33 standard deviation units) is slightly higher than the average effect size obtained by Lipsey (1992) for the most effective type of rehabilitation programs for adult offenders ("skill-oriented" programs: ES = .32). Given that this comparison is made to the 17 best out of 202 non-juvenile programs in Lipsey's meta-analysis (i.e., the top 8% of his primary studies), it is apparent that, by the standards of the field, the reduction achieved in the present study is relatively large. Considering that the TM technique was formulated as a means of self-development and was not specifically designed to rehabilitate offenders or to directly target risk factors for criminal behavior, these results are quite striking. Completion of at least 2 months of group therapy also led to significant reductions in rearrest and reconviction of felony (even though effects of group therapy on the severity of recidivism scale were less pronounced) and is likewise supportive of the effects of "treatment from within" approaches. The results of this study on the comparative effects of standard treatments is consistent with Lipsey's summation that group counseling produces modest reductions in recidivism while effects of educational and vocational programs are negligible.

The evidence from this study concerning the implementation of the TM program alongside other treatments in correctional settings may be of great practical interest. The effect of the TM program and group therapy together was greater than the sum of the separate treatment effects, suggesting synergistic effects of the treatment combination. In fact, the effect size for TM plus group therapy combined (ϕ = .47) was larger than the mean effect size (ϕ = .32) for appropriately targeted treatments–the most effective rehabilitation programs identified in the literature, according to the meta-analysis of Andrews et al. (1990). That implementing the TM program might enhance the efficacy of standard treatments is consistent with Ballou's (1977) finding that inmates who learned the TM technique doubled their number of educational, recreational, and vocational activities, and tripled the number of hours spent in those activities.

The synergistic effects obtained when both the TM program and a conventional treatment were used may reflect the broad range of effects of the TM technique on reducing stress, improving learning ability, and decreasing risk factors associated with criminal behavior (Hawkins, this volume). These changes would be likely to enhance the offender's flexibility to change behavior, as well as to improve the capacity to learn new skills and new ways of coping with situations that previously led to illegal behaviors. Such potential benefits, along with decreases in factors that predict reoffending, could substantially boost effects of standard rehabilitation treatment.

Ideally, future studies of the TM program in correctional settings will examine effects on recidivism, using prospective designs for comparing the program with alternate treatments and random assignment of subjects to conditions. In addition to use of behavioral history variables, dynamic criminogenic factors (e.g., self-development, social skills) should be assessed at baseline and longitudinally so that their effects can be taken into account as predictors of recidivism and potential moderators of treatment outcomes. Generalizability of treatment effects to the larger prison population was limited in this study due to the voluntary participation of subjects in the TM program and in group therapy. Inclusion criteria that are less self-selective should be used in the future (e.g., by providing stronger incentives to participate) so that subjects who would not otherwise be interested in the treatment programs are encouraged to participate. (However, in a large-scale project in Senegal, implementing the

TM program on a mandatory basis led to marked improvements in prisoners' behavior and lower return rates to prison [Anklesaria & King, 1993b, this volume-b].) Perhaps subjects could be offered more favorable parole outcomes if treatment participation led to documented improvements in their behavior. Follow-up should include meetings with program instructors not only while in the prison programs but also after release, to verify continued compliance. In view of the consistency of the results of this study with the earlier study of practice of the TM program by inmates in California prisons, it would seem that reliable conclusions can be based on shorter follow-up times.

However, in view of the staggering costs of crime–close to $700 billion in the United States each year to victims, businesses, and government (Gest, 1994)–and also the poor track record of most existing rehabilitation programs, it would seem unethical to wait for future research before implementing programs that many existing studies have found to be especially promising. The fact that the present study was on the most recalcitrant individuals–felons at a maximum security prison who had multiple prior convictions–suggests that implementing the TM program might be an effective solution to one of the tough realities of criminology: that a small percentage of offenders commits the majority of crimes (Moffitt, 1993; Piper, 1985). If so, it may be possible to lower crime rates without incarcerating a large number of repeat offenders for the remainder of their lives.

In any case, because most offenders are eventually released into society, the need for rehabilitation cannot be ignored. Given the history of problems and unfortunate circumstances surrounding virtually every habitual offender, if rehabilitation is to have anything more than a superficial impact on their lives, something must be done to remove the deeply rooted effects of stress and the inner turmoil they experience. Over 600 studies on the TM program have shown its efficacy for improving the quality of life for the individual and society. Its ease of implementation and the magnitude of its effects suggest that the TM program would be highly cost effective (Dillbeck & Abrams, 1987; Magill, this volume). For purely pragmatic reasons, it would seem in the interest of society to adopt this program in correctional settings.

NOTES

1. Transcendental Meditation, TM, and TM-Sidhi are registered or common law trademarks licensed to Maharishi Vedic Education Corporation and used under sublicense or with permission.

2. Survival analysis is applied to the analysis of time intervals from the beginning of observation until a failure event (e.g., failure of a mechanical device, death of an individual, onset of a disease). Individuals can be said to fail rehabilitation treatment when they commit new crimes. In this context, "survival" refers broadly to the freedom from failure and describes the status of an individual at a particular point in time or over a certain time interval.

3. Maller's method expresses the long-term recidivism percentage as the inverse logit of a linear combination of the covariates, and the recidivism risk as the exponential of a linear combination of the covariates. Covariate models in logistic regression and survival analysis based on the exponential distribution are included as special cases of the long-term survival model with covariates. Models of this type can easily be fit by modifying the Newton-Raphson procedure for fitting models without covariates, as described by Maltz (1984), by specifying the appropriate first and second partial derivatives of the model parameters.

4. These functions constrain the parameters to take only their proper values ($0 \leq \Omega < 1$, $\lambda > 0$ and $\gamma > 0$) while allowing the coefficients (a_i, b_i, c_i) to be chosen freely over all possible positive, zero, or negative values.

5. The class of split population Weibull models generalizes several conventional methods of analyzing recidivism data, such as logistic regression analysis and survival analysis based on exponential covariate models with the proportional hazards property. Maller's method expresses the long-term recidivism percentage as the inverse logit of a linear combination of the covariates, and the recidivism risk as the exponential of a linear combination of the covariates.

6. Adjusted values of the split population Weibull distribution parameters for the TM and control groups were calculated from the linear combination of the covariates, in which the coefficients were the fitted values for the model, and the value of the covariates other than treatment were set equal to their sample means (pooled across groups). The value of the treatment variable was set to 1 for the TM group and 0 for the control group. This procedure has the effect of statistically equating the values of the parameters for each group on all covariates other than treatment.

7. In addition to the analyses reported using the split population Weibull model, we also attempted to model the data in the present study by means of split population models based on the exponential, log-logistic, and log-normal distributions. All of the candidate models appeared to provide a reasonably good fit to the data, based upon visual inspection of predicted cumulative recidivism rates from the model versus the estimated rates from the data by the product-limit method. However, the split population Weibull distribution appeared more appropriate to the characteristics of the data and provided a better fit.

8. Whereas standard repeated measures analysis procedures require the restrictive compound symmetry assumption to be met with respect to the covariance structure of the dependent variables (Maxwell & Delaney, 1990), the procedures used in this study relaxed this assumption to allow a banded structure of the covariance matrix (Dixon, 1992).

9. Cox regression analysis also found significant differences between treatment groups ($p < .046$) while covarying for salient factor scores, educational attainment, marital status, rule violations, and participation in education and group therapy programs while in prison. The first four of these covariates were selected as recidivism predictors from among all subject background variables, using the stepwise option for Cox regression analysis applied to the control group. The last two covariates were included in the Cox analysis of treatment effects to control for differences between groups. This analysis yielded a relative risk of .684, indicating that the overall reduction in recidivism rates due to the TM program was 31.6% during the entire follow-up period, statistically adjusting for the covariates.

10. These parameter values imply that, among releasees who recidivate, 27% from the TM group do so in the first year after release compared to 35% from the control

group. These percentages are calculated from the cumulative Weibull distribution, $1 - exp(\lambda t^{\gamma})$, where λ and γ are the Weibull distribution parameters, and t is time (1 year in this case).

11. The Glass effect size was calculated from the long-term recidivism percentages in the two groups using Cohen's (1988) arcsine transformation. The log-odds ratio is given directly by the model as the coefficient of the treatment variable with respect to the Ω parameter, which in Table 2 is $-.931$. The odds ratio is found by taking the exponential of this value to the base of the natural logarithm function, *e*. It represents the reduction as a result of treatment in the odds of reoffending (i.e., the probability of recidivating divided by the probability of not recidivating) relative to the control condition. An odds ratio of 1.0 indicates no treatment effect, and an odds ratio below 1.0 indicates that recidivism was lower in the experimental group than the control group.

12. The repeated measures analysis was performed on annual data for the first 12 years because the majority of releasees were followed for at least that long. After 12 years, the majority of subjects have missing data on the dependent variable.

13. The difference in the time course of relapse for the two groups was clearly seen graphically in a time plot of means of model estimates for means of the dependent variable for each follow-up year. The significant main effect for TM participation reflects the fact that the time curve of means for the TM group was lower at all time points than the corresponding curve for the control group. The significant interaction between TM participation and the quadratic trend is reflected in the slightly smaller downward curvature in the curve for the TM group. This was because, in the earlier follow-up years, the control group curve rose more steeply than the curve for the TM group, after which both curves tapered off to horizontal. This indicates a faster rate of reoffending in the first few years after release for the control group.

AUTHORS' NOTES

The authors are grateful to Catherine Bleick, in conjunction with Robert Dickover and others at the California Department of Corrections, for collecting the data; to Folsom Prison and the CDC for permitting the program to take place; and especially to the TM teachers for their largely volunteer time in teaching the TM program to the inmates.

Address correspondence to Maxwell V. Rainforth, Maharishi University of Management, 1000 North Fourth Street, Fairfield, IA 52557.

Transcendental Meditation in Criminal Rehabilitation and Crime Prevention. Pp. 205-228.

Consciousness-Based Rehabilitation of Inmates in the Netherlands Antilles: Psychosocial and Cognitive Changes

MARK A. HAWKINS
Maharishi University of Management

CHARLES N. ALEXANDER
Maharishi University of Management

FREDERICK T. TRAVIS
Maharishi University of Management

CARL R. T. CAMELIA
University of the Netherlands Antilles

KENNETH G. WALTON
Maharishi University of Management

CHRISTIAN F. DURCHHOLZ
Maharishi University of Management

MAXWELL V. RAINFORTH
Maharishi University of Management

ABSTRACT The objective of the present study is to test the effects of practice of the Transcendental Meditation (TM)[1] technique on recognized psychosocial and cognitive risk factors for criminal behavior. The study was conducted at the federal prison on the island of Curaçao, Netherlands Antilles, from August 1994 to June 1995. The 300 male subjects (experimental group = 149, control group = 151) were predominantly of African descent and ranged in age from 16 to 62 ($M = 28.2$, $SD = 8.4$). Standardized tests were translated from English into Spanish and Papiamentu (the native language of most subjects) and showed 90% word-to-word accuracy in reverse translation. Twenty-one dependent variables were reduced by principal components analysis to 6 factors. Univariate analysis of covariance for effect of group on factor change scores showed significant positive changes in the experimental group on 2 of the factors, Cognitive Distortion ($p = 0.036$) and Intelligence-Related Measures ($p = 0.05$). It showed a trend toward significance on the factor Psychological Well-Being ($p = 0.082$). These changes were obtained despite low compliance with treatment and high involuntary attrition. An intent-to-treat approach was used, in which all subjects for whom data are available are included. As has been seen in prior research (Hawkins, this volume), these limited results indicate that the practice of the TM technique can simultaneously reduce a risk factor (cognitive distortion) and increase a protective factor (field independence), supporting the assertion that the TM technique rehabilitates offenders by positively affecting overall human development.

KEYWORDS Transcendental Meditation, TM, risk factors, rehabilitation, human development

Since the 1940s, scientists have attempted to identify risk factors that predict criminal behavior. The seminal work by Glueck and Glueck (1940) on a cohort of 1,000 juvenile delinquents in Boston identified a variety of characteristics that correlated with antisocial or criminal behavior. Research since that time has generally replicated and extended these early findings (Andrews & Bonta, 1994). Researchers have also identified protective factors–personality characteristics that protect the individual from developing psychopathy and antisocial behavior (Rolf, Masten, Cicchetti, Nuechterlein, & Weintraub, 1990). There is considerable overlap between risk and protective factors. For example, if low self-esteem contributes to antisocial behavior, an increase in self-esteem may be viewed as increasing a protective factor (high self-esteem) or reducing a risk factor (low self-esteem). The current study measured a number of psychosocial or cognitive correlates of criminal conduct in incarcerated offenders to test the effectiveness of the Transcendental Meditation (TM) technique in reducing the risk of continued criminal conduct.

Curaçao is a small island 40 miles off the coast of Venezuela and is the largest and most populated of the five islands of the Netherlands Antilles (Central Bureau of Statistics, 1996). In 1993, the population of Curaçao was 144,057. The male population of the federal prison on Curaçao at the time of the study (1994-1995) was 474. Compared to the United States, in which 7 out of every 1000 people are incarcerated (Maguire & Pastore, 1995), 3 out of every 1000 people on the island of Curaçao were incarcerated at the time of the research project. Crime data for 1993 (Central Bureau of Statistics, 1996) showed that the overall crime level on Curaçao was 5,010 offenses per 100,000 people. This is comparable to the 5,483 offenses per 100,000 people in the United States for the same year (U.S. Department of Justice, 1996). Although there is no empirical support for the assertion, Curaçao law enforcement professionals stated that the high levels of burglary and robbery on the island (which actually exceed per capita levels for the United States) were due to a large extent to cocaine addiction. The prison's director and chief supervisor both estimated that 80% of the inmates were incarcerated for drug-related crimes.

In January 1994, researchers in the Psychology Department of Maharishi University of Management (M.U.M.) in Fairfield, Iowa, were contacted by Carl Camelia, a professor at the University of the Netherlands Antilles (U.N.A). Camelia had organized a large-scale rehabilitation project using the TM technique at the federal prison on the island of Curaçao. Research on this project was a collaborative effort between the University of the Netherlands Antilles and Maharishi University of Management (M.U.M.). The instruction of the TM technique was funded by the Ministry of Justice of the government of the Netherlands Antilles because of growing concern over the high level of drug use on the island and the high rate of recidivism at the prison.

Three investigators from M.U.M. and one from U.N.A. conducted psychosocial, cognitive, psychophysiological, and biochemical research from August 1994 until June 1995 (Camelia, Alexander, Hawkins, Durchholz, & Walton, 1995; Durchholz et al., 1995). The current study is the first of a four-part, multifaceted study, which focused on the research question: Will Maharishi's Consciousness-Based[1] approach to rehabilitation promote emotional, personality, cognitive, and behavioral development in incarcerated offenders? Practice of the TM technique was predicted to foster positive changes in aspects of psychosocial and cognitive functioning that have been identified either as risk factors or as protective factors for criminal behavior. Specifically, the experimental subjects were expected to increase in protective factors (increased psychological well-being; improved social interaction; greater self-esteem; increased field independence–a direct measure of cognitive style and an indirect measure of internal frame of reference, coping ability, and fluid intelligence; and improved neurophysiological functioning as indicated by a faster inspection time–a cognitive measure highly correlated with nonverbal intelligence). The experimental subjects were expected to decrease in dynamic risk factors (reduced psychological distress, reduced cognitive distortion, reduced hostility and aggression, and reduced impulsiveness).

A Consciousness-Based approach to rehabilitation is perhaps best characterized as a psychophysiological, developmental model. Maharishi (1972) defines stress as an abnormality on the chemical, structural, or mechanical level that is lodged in the body due to an overload of experience. Physical, mental, emotional, or ego-related overloads create stress. Whatever the origin of the overload, however, the lasting abnormality is always on a physiological level. It creates an abnormal or suboptimal style of physiological functioning that adversely affects mental performance, resulting in an anxious, hostile, criminal, or otherwise-stressed mind. Variations of Maharishi's overload-of-experience definition for stress have been independently advanced by contemporary stress researchers (e.g., Holroyd & Lazarus, 1982; Sapolsky, Krey & McEwen, 1986; McEwen, 1998b) who see stress as a key factor in a person's real or perceived ability to adapt to challenging situations.

With this understanding of the Consciousness-Based approach to rehabilitation, it can be hypothesized that reduction of stress (i.e., normalization of functioning of the nervous system) and development of consciousness would have far-reaching effects in the field of criminal and drug rehabilitation. Thirty-nine studies conducted in the United States on normal and criminal populations provide substantial support for this hypothesis and have shown the TM technique to be successful in reducing substance use or abuse, creating positive changes in criminal offenders, and reducing criminal recidivism (cf., Hawkins, this volume).

All empirical research on the effects of the TM technique in correctional settings has taken place in the United States. Over the past 25 years, however, there have been more than 100 projects worldwide utilizing the TM technique in correctional facilities. These projects have produced a large volume of anecdotal information on the effectiveness of the TM technique as a rehabilitation method in different cultural settings (Anklesaria & King, 1993a). More empirical investigations in settings outside the United States are needed. The present and associated studies (Camelia et al., 1995; Durchholz et al., 1995; Walton et al., this volume) represent attempts to address this need.

METHODS

Study Design

This study is part of a multifaceted evaluation of the Transcendental Meditation technique in a correctional setting. It differs from most previous research on the TM technique in criminal rehabilitation because of its larger sample size, use of two non-fakeable cognitive performance measures, use of two tests for socially desirable responding (lie scales), and use of tests specifically chosen to measure constructs considered as risk or protective factors for criminal behavior.

Randomized Study Design

The study was originally conceived as a stratified-randomized, longitudinal, single blind, controlled, cross-validation study on the effects of the Consciousness-Based approach to rehabilitation. It was to last 9 months. The random assignment to treatment or control groups was stratified (matched) on the variables of age (6 categories: subjects in their teens, 20s, 30s, 40s, 50s, 60s) and type of crime (2 categories: violent or nonviolent). The delayed-start controls were to cross over to form a new experimental group after 4.5 months. However, because of security concerns arising from a renovation project that unexpectedly began during the experiment, there were insufficient subjects available for the second posttest, and the final stage of the research was canceled. Therefore, the cross-validation aspect of the study was lost.

Upon review of the data after completion of analysis, it was decided that data from the randomized subjects would not be separately reported. This was due to several reasons: (a) 21% of the 152 subjects of the random-assignment study did not pretest; (b) among the 120 randomized subjects who pretested, 37% of those randomly assigned to learn the TM technique subsequently chose not to learn; and (c) an additional 32.5% of the randomized subjects were not posttested due to unforeseen early releases because release dates provided by the prison's Office of Records were inaccurate. With the loss of almost half of the randomized subjects, the effect of randomization to equal groups at pretest was essentially nullified, and these subjects were added to the non-randomized subjects for analysis. Possible pretest group differences in the non-randomized subjects were statistically tested.

Non-Randomized Subjects

The non-randomized subjects (N = 300) included the randomized subjects who were pretested in August or September 1994 (N = 120), 28 subjects who dropped out of the experimental group before instruction in TM, 34 self-selected volunteers who had expressed interest in the TM technique at the time of pretest of the randomized subjects but had not initially wanted to be involved in the research, and 118 self-selected subjects who were pretested in January or February 1995 and posttested in May or June 1995, up until the project was halted. All subjects, whether randomly assigned or self-selected, had initially expressed interest in learning the TM technique.

Subjects

The subjects ($N = 300$) were male volunteers from the inmate population of the federal prison on Curaçao, Netherlands Antilles. The inmates in the prison were predominantly medium security inmates, housed in the main prison in 5 cellblocks. Of these 474 inmates, 10 were maximum-security inmates, housed in a segregated section of one of the cellblocks, and 70 were minimum-security inmates, housed in three army-style barracks in a compound adjacent to the prison. As indicated by country of birth from prison records, 84% of the inmates were from the Netherlands Antilles, 6% were Colombian or Venezuelan, and 10% were other national origins (African, American, Dutch, French, Italian, Surinamese, and a number of Caribbean nationalities). The age of the subjects ranged from 16 to 62, with an average age of 28.2 and a standard deviation of 8.4 years. Occupations of the inmates, as indicated by prison records, included: skilled workers (45%); unskilled laborers (13%); retail employees (11%); and a mix of students, professionals, and miscellaneous occupations (4%). Twenty-seven percent of the inmates were recorded as unemployed/no occupation.

Subjects were divided into two groups. Group 1 ($N = 149$) included all inmates who had learned the TM technique. Group 2 ($N = 151$) included all inmates who were originally interested in learning but did not learn. Female inmates ($N = 14$) and subjects who were not interested in learning the TM technique ($N = 13$) were excluded from the study because they were not sufficiently numerous to form separate control groups.

Test Instruments

Self-report test instruments were specifically compiled to test for many of the psychosocial correlates of criminal thinking and behavior. Two cognitive performance tests also were used. The tests and test subscales produced 21 dependent variables. Three demographic variables, 3 control variables, and the dependent variables were used to determine group differences at pretest. The independent variable was the attendance at group practice of the TM technique.

Description of Independent Variable

Frequency of Meditation (FREQ)

FREQ was derived by calculating the average weekly attendance at group meditation for the period from the week of instruction in the TM technique until (and including) the week of the posttest. An inmate who had shown leadership and responsibility at the beginning of the program and had been a great help as a translator and researcher-inmate liaison recorded attendance.

Description of Demographic Variables

Age (AGE)

Ages were calculated at time of pretest from the date of birth on the computer printout provided by the prison records office.

Type of Crime (CRTYPE)

CRTYPE was a binomial category of nonviolent crimes (burglary, larceny, motor vehicle theft, drug trafficking) and violent crimes (murder, rape, robbery, aggravated assault). Crime types were categorized according to the Federal Bureau of Investigation's Uniform Crime Report (U.S. Department of Justice, 1996). The data for CRTYPE were derived from the computer printout records provided by the prison's Office of Records and translated from Dutch to English by a local lawyer.

Level of Educational Achievement (EDUC)

EDUC indicated the highest level of educational achievement that the inmate had attained. The information was obtained by interviewing each subject during pretesting. In the Netherlands Antilles, the educational system is the same as the Dutch system. Educational levels in the study were transposed to equivalent levels in the American system. The educational levels were (1) primary school, (2) partial or completed vocational school, and (3) partial high school or higher.

Description of Control Variables

Expectancy Question (EXPECT)

A one-item Expectancy Question (Alexander et al., 1996) was used to test for equivalency at pretest between the experimental and control groups on expectancy of benefits from the practice of TM. The question asks: "Overall, how much do you expect to improve from practicing the Transcendental Meditation technique? (Circle one)." The scale is a semantic differential scale with numerical values of 0 to 10 and bipolar descriptors of *Not at all* (0) to *A great deal* (10).

Socially Desirable Response Set (SDRS)

The SDRS (Hays, Hayashi, & Stewart, 1989) is a modified version of the Marlowe-Crowne Social Desirability Scale (Crowne & Marlowe, 1960) and indicates whether subjects are presenting themselves honestly. One improvement over earlier versions of this scale was the expansion of options to facilitate responding. Hays et al. changed two options (*True* and *False*) to a 5-point numerical scale continuum from *Definitely True* (1) to *Definitely False* (5). However, only the extreme values (1 or 5) of the numerical scale are used for each of the 5 items, to polarize the social desirability of the responses. Any item that is answered 1 or 5 is given a score of 1; other scores are assigned 0. Out of a score of 5, a 3 or higher indicates the presence of socially desirable responding.

How I Think Questionnaire Anomalous Responding (HITAR) Subscale

The HITAR subscale (Barriga & Gibbs, 1996; Gibbs, Barriga, & Potter, 1996) is a lie scale, to determine if subjects are simply giving socially desirable responses. Six possible responses range from *agree strongly* to *disagree strongly*. Items were scored 6 through 1 accordingly, with the positively worded items reverse-scored. Anomalous responding is indicated by the size of the score. The higher the subscale score, the greater the degree of anomalous responding, with 3.5 indicating the presence of socially desirable responding.

Psychosocial Dependent Variables

Mental Health Inventory (MHI)

The MHI is an indicator of overall mental health–both psychological distress and well-being (Veit & Ware, 1983). The test uses a 6-point Likert-type scale with both descriptors and numerical values, ranging from *All of the time* (1) to *None of the time* (6). Every question contains the phrase *during the last month* to remind subjects to answer according to how they have been feeling recently.

Buss-Durkee Hostility Inventory (BDHI)

The BDHI (Buss & Durkee, 1957), according to reviews (e.g., Biaggio & Maiuro, 1985, p. 72), "is probably the best known and most frequently used inventory of its kind." The inventory contains 8 subscales (assault, indirect hostility, irritability, negativism, resentment, suspicion, verbal hostility, and guilt), with a total of 75 items, and uses a true or false response option. Only the four aggression subscales (assault, indirect hostility, verbal hostility, and irritability) were used in the present study to reduce the size of the test packet.

Barratt Impulsiveness Scale (BIS)

The BIS (Barratt, 1959, 1965; Patton, Stanford, & Barratt, 1995) has undergone many revisions since 1959 in an effort to more closely measure the various components of the trait of impulsiveness. The most current version (BIS-11) was used in this study. The BIS uses a four-item response scale with four headings (*Rarely/Never, Occasionally, Often, Almost Always, Always*); under each, subjects may blacken an empty square. In the present study, four of the six subscales of the BIS were used (attention, cognitive instability, motor impulsiveness, and perseverance). The other two subscales, self-control and cognitive complexity, were judged to be resistant to change by treatment.

How I Think Questionnaire (HIT)

The HIT (Barriga & Gibbs, 1996; Gibbs et al., 1996; Gibbs, Potter, & Goldstein, 1995) is a test designed to measure cognitive distortions in antisocial youth. Cognitive distortions are considered to be thoughts, attitudes, or beliefs that are self-serving, rationalizing, or otherwise nonveridical; they have been described previously in the literature on juvenile delinquency and adult criminal conduct (e.g., Samenow, 1984; Sykes & Matza, 1957; Yochelson & Samenow, 1976, 1977). The HIT has four subscales. The primary cognitive distortion is the subscale labeled Self-Centered. There are also three secondary cognitive distortions (Assuming the Worst, Blaming Others, and Minimizing/Mislabeling), which are used to neutralize feelings of guilt or remorse. The HIT uses a balanced 6-point Likert response scale from *agree strongly* to *disagree strongly*. This study is the first to use the HIT with a mixed population of adults and juveniles.

Self-Esteem Scale (SE)

The self-esteem measure (SE) in this study is a two-item scale used by Alexander et al. (1996) in an investigation of the effects of the TM technique on hypertension in elderly, inner-city African Americans. The two items–"How often do you feel good about yourself?" and "How often do you feel bad about yourself?"–used a 5-point Likert response scale from *very often* to *never*. Since the scale was so brief, the two SE items were embedded in the Mental Health Inventory as item numbers 13 (bad) and 20 (good).

Behavioral Inventory (BI)

The BI is a 12-item questionnaire modified from Childs' (1977) questionnaire for juveniles and their parents to be more representative of an incarcerated subject population. Behaviors such as rule infractions, performance at work and school, and poor quality of interaction with family were added to the inventory. The inventory used a 6-point Likert-type scale with both descriptors and numerical values that ranged from *never* (1) to *always* (6). As with other tests, the subjects were asked to indicate how they behaved during the past month.

Data Scoring

Data were analyzed by one of three methods: (a) averaging the values for each subscale's items (BDHI: four aggression subscales; BIS: four subscales; MHI: three psychological distress subscales and two psychological well-being subscales; and HIT: four cognitive distortion subscales), (b) averaging all items of a test (SE, BI), or (c) calculating the test score (SDRS).

Cognitive Dependent Variables

One of the cognitive performance measures was administered to the subjects in a group (Group Embedded Figures Test). The other was administered individually (Zhang's Inspection Time Test).

Group Embedded Figures Test (GEFT)

The GEFT (Witkin, Oltman, Raskin, & Karp, 1971) is a modification of the examiner-administered Embedded Figures Test (EFT). It is a perceptual-motor measure of field dependence-independence (psychological autonomy) that requires the subject to locate and trace a previously seen simple figure within a larger complex figure. The EFT and its related tests are among the most popular tests of cognitive function (LaVoie, 1984) because field independence has been correlated with intelligence. For example, Arthur and Day (1991) showed a significant correlation (r = .62) between performance on the Group Embedded Figures Test and Raven's Progressive Matrices, a measure of general intelligence. In this study, GEFT is used as a direct measure of field dependence/independence and as an indirect measure of stability of internal frame of reference and nonverbal intelligence. The GEFT was administered to all eligible inmates.

Data Scoring

The GEFT was scored by adding up the correct responses in Part Two and Part Three of the test booklet, for a possible total number of 18. A response was judged to be correct if the simple figure was clearly and completely outlined within the complex figure, without any other lines drawn.

Zhang's Inspection Time Test (ITT)

Inspection time (IT) was first conceived as a measure of speed of information processing by Vickers, Nettelbeck, and Willson (1972). The most commonly used inspection time test, which consists of two vertical lines of differing lengths connected across the top and presented tachistoscopically by light-emitting diodes or on computer screen, requires subjects to identify on which side is the longer line. Researchers critiquing IT have repeatedly expressed concern about the use of apparent motion cues by test subjects (Chaiken & Young, 1993; Egan, 1993; MacKenzie & Cumming, 1986). This study used Zhang's ITT, which employs a novel IT discriminative stimulus–a 3 cm by 3 cm square with one side randomly missing. This is hypothesized by Zhang (1991) to eliminate apparent motion cues. During Zhang's ITT, a brief visual cue (+) is presented 800 msec before each stimulus presentation. After presentation, the square is masked by a solid square. The subject's task is to use 1 of 4 letters that appear on each side of the solid square to identify the side that was missing.

Inspection time, as measured by other versions of IT tests, has been highly correlated with intelligence (Kranzler & Jensen, 1989). Zhang (1991) and So (So & Orme-Johnson, 2000) found Zhang's ITT correlated with nonverbal intelligence in Chinese subjects. So also reported that the practice of the TM technique over a 15-month period significantly improved IT performance and increased intelligence in school children, as measured by Cattell's Culture Fair Intelligence Test.

Data Scoring

Inspection time was scored using the computer-generated IT score from Zhang's ITT. For the IT program, the Parameter Estimate Sequential Test (PEST) computer program is used to control the IT task and measure the subject's IT performance (Taylor & Creelman, 1967). Briefly explained, Zhang's ITT calculates inspection time based upon the speed and accuracy of the responses: the more accurate the responses, the faster the stimulus is presented. As the accuracy reduces, so does the speed of presentation. After many cycles of increasing and decreasing accuracy/speed, the program computes an average inspection time. The IT score is given in milliseconds to 5 decimal places.

Test Administration

With the exception of the HIT, the self-report measures were collated into a test packet that inmates in groups of 20-30 completed in one sitting of approximately 1 hour. As a break from the test packet, the Group Embedded Figures Test was conducted after half an hour and at the conclusion of the GEFT, subjects completed the test packet. The GEFT was conducted according to the standard instructions (Witkin, Oltman, Raskin, & Karp, 1971), except that instructions were given in English, Papiamentu, and Spanish. After the test packets were handed in and it was confirmed that all questions had been answered, the subjects returned to their cellblocks.

The ITT was administered individually to subjects in the afternoon; on days when group testing did not take place, it was administered in the morning. The test was given using an AST Bravo NB portable computer and a Samtron 15-inch color monitor, with the subject placed approximately 50 cm from the monitor screen. Subjects arrived in groups of 3. One subject was seated at the computer and given a sheet of instructions for the ITT. After the subject had read the instructions, comprehension was verbally confirmed. A practice run was conducted. Successful completion of the practice run was followed by the test. The time to complete the test varied from 10 to 30 minutes. After completion of the ITT, the subject did the HIT questionnaire. While the other 2 subjects waited to take the ITT on the computer, they were given the HIT questionnaire to complete. The HIT, the longest test in the packet, took about 20 minutes.

The same protocol was used at pretest and posttest. Getting subjects to test individually proved more difficult than to come in groups, and the researchers were unable to test the same number of subjects on IT ($N = 155$) and the HIT ($N = 198$) as they were able to test on the test packet ($N = 313$) before their scheduled departure.

Statistical Analysis

The statistical analysis comprised four stages, utilizing both univariate and multivariate analysis.

Stage One (Univariate Analysis)

Since the demographic variables CRTYPE and EDUC were categorical and used ordinal scales, the Pearson chi-square test of independence was performed on them to determine if the experimental and control groups were different at pretest. Analysis of variance (ANOVA) was performed on (a) the demographic variable AGE; (b) the 3 control variables: EXPECT, SDRS, and HITAR; and (c) the 21 dependent variables (BDHI: four subscales; BIS: four subscales; MHI: three psychological distress subscales and two psychological well-being subscales; HIT: four cognitive distortion subscales, SE, BI, GEFT, and ITT) to determine if the experimental and control groups were equivalent at pretest.

Stage Two (Multivariate Analysis)

A principal components analysis of standardized pretest scores ($N = 313$) of the 21 dependent variables was conducted using the averaged scores for each inventory subscale or test, a correlation matrix, varimax rotation, and pairwise deletion. The cutoff point for the inclusion of a variable on a factor was set at $\geq \pm 0.4$.

Stage Three (Univariate Analysis)

From the results of the principal components analysis, pretest and posttest factor scores were created from the standardized data by taking all variables that loaded significantly on a certain factor at $\geq \pm 0.4$, weighting them according to their factor loading, and summing them. Then, analysis of covariance (ANCOVA) was performed on the factor change score (posttest factor scores minus pretest factor scores) to determine which factor change scores showed significant change at the .05 level according to treatment grouping. Probability levels are reported as one-tailed due to the directional hypothesis of the study. The pretest factor score, demographic variables, and control variables were included as covariates if they significantly predicted the posttest factor score in a stepwise linear regression. However, if the analysis of covariance showed that a covariate was not significantly predicting the factor change score (.05, two-tailed), it was dropped and another ANCOVA was run. In the stepwise linear regression, EDUC and HITAR were not used because these data were unavailable for 40% of the subjects.

Stage Four (Univariate Analysis)

Separate ANCOVAs were then performed on the dependent variables comprising each significant factor change score to determine which dependent variables were contributing most to the change in the factor.

RESULTS

Descriptive Statistics

Experimental Group, Independent Variable Descriptive Statistics

The average weekly attendance at group meditation for Group 1 ($N = 149$) was uncharacteristically low, only 1.5 times per week, with a standard deviation of 2.3. However, all subjects who were instructed in the TM technique were included in the experimental group, regardless of degree of compliance.

Demographic, Control, and Dependent Variables

Number of Subjects Pretesting and Posttesting

Half the subjects were lost (from 300 at pretest to 149 at posttest) due to unforeseen early releases and the stoppage of the project on June 6, 1995, while posttesting was in progress. Numerous attempts were made from June 6 to July

21, 1995, to resume posttesting. However, the correctional officers' union was firm in its resistance, citing security concerns.

Inferential Statistics

Tests of Independence

The Pearson chi-square test of independence showed no significant differences between groups at pretest for CRTYPE ($\chi^2 = 0.000$, $p = 1.000$) and EDUC ($\chi 2 = 4.909$, $p = 0.086$).

Analysis of Variance

The univariate analysis of variance for effect of group for the demographic variable AGE ($F = 0.005$, $p = 0.943$), the 3 control variables of EXPECT ($F = 0.077$, $p = 0.781$), SDRS ($F = 0.196$, $p = 0.659$), and HITAR ($F = 0.145$, $p = 0.704$), and the 21 dependent variables showed that there were no significant differences between groups at pretest. Among the 21 dependent variables, F-ratios and significance levels ranged from $F = 2.587$, $p = 0.109$ to $F = 0.025$, $p = 0.875$.

Principal Components Analysis of Dependent Variables

Expert factor analysts recommend a combination of approaches when determining how many factors to extract (Gorsuch, 1974; Harman, 1976). The criteria for choosing the number of factors to be extracted in this study (based on Hair, Anderson, & Tatham, 1987) were the latent root criterion (the Kaiser-Guttman rule), scree-tail test, percentage of variance accounted for, simplicity of factor structure, and interpretability. Using these criteria, five-, six-, and seven-factor principal components matrices were extracted from the 21 dependent variables. The scree-tail test (Cattell, 1966; Cattell & Vogelman, 1977) suggested the five-factor solution; the Kaiser-Guttman eigenvalue-greater-than-one rule (Kaiser, 1956) suggested the six-factor solution; and the seven-factor solution was extracted for the simplest factor structure. All three solutions fulfilled the criterion of percentage of variance accounted for ($\geq 60\%$). Using a $\geq \pm$ 0.4 cutoff point for inclusion in a factor, and in consideration of the criteria mentioned above, the six-factor solution was judged to have: (a) the second-most simple factor structure (only one multiple loading) and (b) the highest interpretability. The seven-factor solution had the simplest factor structure (no multiple loadings) but had one factor that was difficult to interpret. For these reasons, the six-factor solution was selected over the seven-factor solution. The matrix for the six-factor solution is shown in Table 1.

Table 1: ANOVA of Factor Change Score for Factor 1 (Cognitive Distortion) (N = 74)

Source	Sum of Sq.	df	Mean sq.	F-ratio	P-value
Group	17.558	1	17.558	3.369	0.036
Error	375.199	72	5.211		

Note: All *p*-values for ANOVAs and ANCOVAs are given as one-tailed, due to the directional hypotheses. None of the potential covariates significantly predicted a changed score.

Factor Headings

The factors of the 6-factor solution were labeled (1) Cognitive Distortion (CD), (2) Psychological Distress (PD), (3) Aggression (AGG), (4) Impulsivity (IMP), (5) Intelligence-Related Measures (IRM), and (6) Psychological Well-Being (PWB). The six-factor solution has 3 factors (1, 3, 4) that are composed of the subscales or first-order factors of a questionnaire (e.g., Factor 1 was composed of the four subscales of HIT). Factors 2 and 6 are composed of second-order factors of the MHI (Psychological Distress and Psychological Well-Being, respectively), with SE and BI also loading on Factor 6. Thus, the principal components analysis confirms that these inventories' subscales are testing the same or related constructs. Factors 1 through 4 showed acceptable or nearly acceptable internal consistency (.67 to .94); factors 5 and 6 did not (.53 and .33, respectively).

Analysis of Variance of Factor Change Scores

Univariate analysis of covariance (ANCOVA) of weighted factor change scores was conducted on the six factors using the demographic variables AGE and CRTYPE, the control variable SDRS, and the pretest factor scores as covariates only when they significantly predicted the change score. The ANCOVAs are shown in Tables 1 through 6. In the first factor, Cognitive Distortion, the experimental group ($N = 35$) had a least squares mean reduction of −0.291 standard deviations, and the control group ($N = 39$) had a least squares mean increase of 0.684, indicating a significant reduction ($p = 0.036$) in cognitive distortion in the experimental group. In the second factor, Psychological Distress, the experimental group ($N = 77$), with a mean change of −0.164, differed only slightly from the control group ($N = 72$), which had a mean change of −0.110. Similarly, the experimental and the control groups were virtually the same for the third factor, Aggression, with the experimental group moving

Table 2: ANCOVA of Factor Change Score for Factor 2 (Psychological Distress), Covarying for the Pretest Value and Age (N = 149)

Source	Sum of Sq.	df	Mean sq.	F-ratio	P-value
Group	0.109	1	0.109	0.039	0.422
PD (Pre)	73.700	1	73.700	26.270	0.000
AGE	22.384	1	22.384	7.979	0.005
Error	406.793	145	2.805		

Table 3: ANCOVA of Factor Change Score for Factor 3 (Aggression), Covarying for the Pretest Value and Socially Desirable Responding (N = 149)

Source	Sum of Sq.	df	Mean sq.	F-ratio	P-value
Group	0.178	1	0.178	0.060	0.403
AGG (Pre)	86.993	1	86.993	29.578	0.000
T1SDRS	22.443	1	22.443	7.631	0.006
Error	426.463	145	2.941		

Table 4: ANCOVA of Factor Change Score for Factor 4 (Impulsiveness), Covarying for the Pretest Value (N = 149)

Source	Sum of Sq.	df	Mean sq.	F-ratio	P-value
Group	0.077	1	0.077	0.034	0.427
IMP (Pre)	140.641	1	140.641	61.612	0.000
Error	333.270	146	2.283		

Table 5: ANOVA of Factor Change Score for Factor 5 (Intelligence-Related Measures) (N = 74)

Source	Sum of Sq.	df	Mean sq.	F-ratio	P-value
Group	1.827	1	1.827	2.790	0.05
Error	47.160	72	0.655		

Note: None of the potential covariates significantly predicted change score.

Table 6: ANCOVA of Factor Change Score for Factor 6 (Psychological Well-Being), Covarying for the Pretest Value and Age (N = 149)

Source	Sum of Sq.	df	Mean sq.	F-ratio	P-value
Group	3.325	1	3.325	1.967	0.082
PWB (Pre)	43.140	1	43.140	25.523	0.000
AGE	14.695	1	14.695	8.694	0.004
Error	245.084	145	1.690		

in the direction of reduction (−0.017) and the control group moving in the direction of a slight increase (0.053). In the fourth factor, Impulsiveness, both groups moved in the direction of reduction. The experimental group had a mean change of −0.101 and the control group had a mean change of −0.146. On the fifth factor, Intelligence-Related Measures, the experimental group ($N = 35$) showed a significant change ($p = 0.05$), with an increase of 0.103, compared to the control group ($N = 39$), which had a mean reduction of −0.211. For the sixth factor, Psychological Well-Being, the experimental and control groups showed a trend towards a significant difference ($p = 0.082$), with an experimental group mean increase of 0.027 and a control group mean decrease of −0.044.

Analysis of Individual Dependent Variables that Comprised Significant or Trendwise Factor Change Scores

Among the variables that comprised the factors, three variables showed almost significant changes: two of four variables on the factor Cognitive Distortion, HITAW ($F = 2.437$, $p = 0.062$) and HITBO ($F = 2.687$, $p = 0.053$), so it appears that although no single subscale was significantly different between groups, the HIT total was. One of the four variables making up the factor Psychological Well-Being, SE, showed a trend toward significance ($F = 2.574$, $p = 0.055$).

In the analysis of the dependent variables comprising the Intelligence-Related Measures factor (ITT and GEFT), the lack of even a trend towards significance spurred a deeper analysis. Recall that the GEFT was administered in groups and the ITT was administered individually, along with the HIT. When looking at the between-group differences of the subjects who tested on the GEFT, there were no significant changes on the GEFT ($N = 137$, $F = 0.787$, $p = 0.189$) or on the smaller number of subjects who also tested on the ITT ($N = 85$, $F = 0.109$, $p = 0.372$), *but who did not necessarily test on the GEFT*. However, when the between-group differences in GEFT scores were analyzed for subjects who tested on the ITT, that is, for those subjects who took the GEFT in a group and who also came individually to do the ITT and the HIT, the GEFT scores were significantly higher in the experimental group at posttest ($N = 58$, $F = 5.82$, $p = 0.01$). In this subgroup, the ITT scores still were not significantly different between groups ($N = 58$, $F = 0.260$, $p = 0.306$). Therefore, the highly significant change in the GEFT scores in a subgroup of the experimental subjects accounted for the significant change in the Intelligence-Related Measures factor for the entire experimental group. This subgroup was also the only group of subjects tested on the HIT and the only to demonstrate a significant reduction in cognitive distortion.

DISCUSSION

The present study is strengthened by its controlled, longitudinal design and sample size. This study showed a significant growth in field independence, as measured by the GEFT, a non-fakeable cognitive performance measure, echoing randomized studies showing similar results with the GEFT (e.g., So & Orme-Johnson, 2000; Pelletier, 1974). Results on a non-fakeable measure indicate they are due to more than socially desirable responding or expectation effects, although socially desirable responding or demand characteristics associated with learning the TM technique may have influenced the self-report measures. The study controlled for socially desirable responding with two lie scales (SDRS, HITAR). Linear regressions showed that socially desirable responding did not significantly correlate with the subjects' responses, with the exception of the BDHI. Analysis of variance on pretest variables indicated that the experimental and control groups came from the same population sample. Comparison of pretest values indicated that self-selection did not cause the groups to differ at pretest on the demographic, control, or dependent variables.

The study was confounded by high attrition rates due to unexpected early releases and the stoppage of the project, which precluded completion of posttesting with many subjects. It must be emphasized that this attrition was involuntary. The reason given by the executive committee of the guards' union for halting the project was concern about security over the size of the group going to the group meditation hall for both meditation and testing. Offers by the researchers to test under higher security, such as offering to test inmates in very small groups, were repeatedly rebuffed.

The compliance to treatment in this study was uncharacteristically low. The average weekly attendance for subjects who were attending group meditation at all was 5 times per week. For the entire experimental group, when nonparticipants were included, the average attendance at group meditation was only 1.5 times per week. The frequency of attendance at group meditation does not indicate how often subjects might have meditated on their own. However, the researchers assumed that subjects would not be meditating in their cells due to overcrowded, noisy conditions. In some cases, six to twelve inmates occupied cells originally designed to accommodate four, which would likely lessen the opportunity and intention of inmates to practice on their own in the cells.

Despite decreasing statistical power due to loss of subjects at posttest and poor compliance with the treatment, significant differences were found between experimental and control groups on Cognitive Distortion ($p = .036$) and Intelligence-Related Measures ($p = .050$). A trend toward significance was found on Psychological Well-Being ($p = .082$).

Reduced Cognitive Distortions

Cognitive distortions, or thinking errors, are indicative of developmental delay and pro-criminal thinking, attitudes, and beliefs. Barriga, Harrold, Stinson II, Liau, and Gibbs (2000) determined that self-serving cognitive distortions predicted externalizing antisocial behavior, and a relationship between cognitive distortions and antisocial behavior has been clearly established by other researchers (refer to Gibbs et al., 1995, for a review). Barriga (1996) showed that cognitive distortions mediate the path from moral reasoning to externalizing behavior. Cognitive-developmental theory stresses the primacy of cognition in the motivation of prosocial or antisocial behavior (Kohlberg, 1984).

Viewed from this cognitive-developmental perspective, how does the practice of the TM technique reduce cognitive distortions, even when cognitive distortions are not being targeted by the treatment? It has been proposed (Alexander, Davies et al., 1990) that the practice of the TM technique unfreezes or accelerates human development, providing an opportunity for greater unfolding of inner potential–from deeper structures and functions to the more superficial or expressed aspects of the personality. These functions and structures include ego, as indicated by ego development and self-actualization (Alexander &

Orme-Johnson, this volume; Alexander, Walton, & Goodman, this volume; Chandler, 1990; Chandler, Alexander, & Heaton, in press); affect, that is, greater sensitivity to one's own feelings and to those of others (Baer, Nidich, & Abrams, 1989) and capacity for intimate contact (Hjelle, 1974; Nidich, Seeman, & Dreskin, 1973); desire, as indicated by reduced drug use (Alexander, Robinson, & Rainforth, 1994); intellect, i.e., increased intelligence (Cranson et al., 1991; So & Orme-Johnson, 2000); ideation, i.e., greater orientation to positive values (Gelderloos, Goddard, Ahlstrom, & Jacoby, 1987); perception, i.e., greater perceptual acuity (Dillbeck, Assimakis, Raimondi, Orme-Johnson, & Rowe, 1986; Martinetti, 1976; Pelletier, 1974, 1974 April); and behavior, as indicated by improved work performance and job satisfaction (Alexander et al., 1993; Friend, 1977).

From the perspective of Maharishi's Consciousness-Based approach to rehabilitation, cognitive distortions arise from developmental delay. Developmental delay, in turn, arises largely from accumulated stress in the body, which hampers the proper development or functioning of the nervous system. A properly functioning nervous system is balanced, adaptable, and stable (Alexander, Robinson, Orme-Johnson et al., 1994; Walton & Levitsky, 1994). When limitations are placed on consciousness as a result of improper functioning of the nervous system, the thinking and behavior of an individual become distorted.

Regular practice of the TM technique promotes the experience of unbounded awareness during the practice of the technique and, due to a less stressed, more balanced functioning of the nervous system, maintenance of expanded awareness during activity (Maharishi Mahesh Yogi, 1963/1995). Consequently, thinking and behavior are motivated from deeper, more expanded, undistorted levels of awareness.

Intelligence-Related Measures

Both inspection time and field independence are considered intelligence-related measures (Brand & Deary, 1982; Juhel, 1991; Nettelbeck, 1987: Witkin et al., 1971). Zhang's Inspection Time Test (ITT) and the Group Embedded Figures Test (GEFT) have been correlated significantly with intelligence as measured, for example, by Raven's Progressive Matrices (Arthur & Day, 1991; Zhang, 1991). Since both inspection time and field independence have been correlated with intelligence, an improvement in either one may indicate a growth of intelligence. The experimental group improved on the Intelligence-Related Measures factor. Analysis of the difference between ITT and GEFT indicated that the significant change on this factor was due to changes in field independence and not inspection time (IT), although So and Orme-Johnson (2000) showed significant improvement in both IT and intelligence. Consequently, the discussion of this factor is primarily with regard to field independence and the GEFT.

Previous research has repeatedly shown the practice of the TM technique to increase intelligence, even in adult populations (e.g., Aron, Orme-Johnson, & Brubaker, 1981; Cranson et al., 1991; So & Orme-Johnson, 2000; Tjoa, 1975). According to conventional wisdom, however, individuals stop growing in intelligence by late adolescence. Researchers have identified level of intelligence as a protective factor for youths at high risk for juvenile delinquency (Kandel et al., 1988; White, Moffitt, & Silva, 1989). Therefore, increases in intelligence in a criminal sample may indicate the development of a protective factor that would improve the chances of successful reintegration into society upon release from prison.

Increased field independence (articulated cognitive style) is considered to be indicative of a more stable internal frame of reference. Witkin et al. (1974) report that subjects who score higher on tests of field independence also show a more stable internal frame of reference and are less susceptible to peer pressure. Improvements on embedded figures tests indicate broader comprehension combined with the ability to focus more sharply. From the perspective of the growth of consciousness, the awareness becomes more unbounded as pure consciousness is infused into the nature of the mind. At the same time, due to the increased orderliness and clarity of mind, one is able to focus more attentively on objects of perception and to perceive with greater acuity (Dillbeck, Assimatis et al., 1986; Martinetti, 1976; Pelletier, 1974, 1974 April). Improvement on this factor indicates that the meditating subjects in the present study may have expanded their awareness and developed a stronger internal frame of reference.

Psychological Well-Being and Social Behavior

The experimental subjects also showed a trend toward significant change on the Psychological Well-Being factor. The results indicate that the practice of the TM technique positively influenced the emotional ties the inmates felt to family and friends, increased general positive affect, increased self-esteem, and increased prosocial behavior. Subsequent analysis on these four variables indicated that self-esteem was the measure most responsible for the change in this factor. This finding is supported by previous research showing that the TM technique increases well-being (Haratani & Henmi, 1990), improves family relationships (Broome, 1989; Suarez, 1989), and increases self-esteem (Nystul & Garde, 1977).

Aggression, Impulsiveness, and Psychological Distress

Although significant results were seen in the 3 factors already discussed, the Aggression (AGG), Impulsiveness (IMP), and Psychological Distress (PD) factors did not show significant changes. These results do not confirm prior research on the TM technique. Previous TM prison studies using the

Buss-Durkee Hostility Inventory (BDHI) have found reductions in aggression (Abrams, 1989; Abrams & Siegel, 1978; Alexander & Orme-Johnson, this volume; Alexander, Walton et al., this volume; R. E. Ferguson, 1989a, 1989b; Gore et al., 1989; Ramirez, 1989). In these previous studies, however, compliance with the recommended TM program was higher than in the present study.[2] Previous research also shows that significant results were seen using the BDHI after 3 months, a shorter treatment period than in the current study (Abrams, 1989; Abrams & Siegel, 1978; R. E. Ferguson, 1989). Therefore, it is more likely that the lack of results in this study was due to poor compliance rather than to insensitivity of the test to treatment effects or brevity of treatment period.

Previous research with the TM technique and the Mental Health Inventory (MHI) indicates that the second-order factors Psychological Well-Being and Psychological Distress are sensitive to the changes brought about by the technique (Alexander et al., 1997). On the other hand, the Barratt Impulsiveness Scale (BIS) has been used primarily as a diagnostic tool, providing insufficient data to determine sensitivity to treatment effects.

A meta-analysis by Eppley, Abrams, and Shear (1989) clearly shows the practice of the TM technique to be highly effective in reducing anxiety compared to other meditation and relaxation techniques. Other research on the TM technique has reported a normalization in impulse expression (Penner, Zingle, Dyck, & Truch, 1974) and a reduction in depression (Fehr, Nerstheimer, & Törber, 1977a). Given the low level of compliance (1.5 meditations per week, on average), the significance of observed effects may rely upon the relative sensitivity to change of the measures used. It may be that the BDHI and MHI (and possibly the BIS), although capable of discriminating meditating subjects from non-meditating subjects when the TM subjects are meditating regularly, were not sensitive enough to discriminate between groups at such a low level of compliance.

Generalizability Issues

Generally, the controlled, longitudinal design of the experiment appeared to control for possible threats to internal validity. However, the fact that results were seen primarily in a subgroup of the experimental group requires some explanation (refer to Hawkins, 1998, for a detailed discussion). When comparing the subjects who came individually to be tested on the HIT and the ITT at both pretest and posttest ($N = 74$) with those subjects who came only to the group testing at both pretest and posttest and did not test individually on the HIT and the ITT ($N = 75$), there were between-group differences on CRTYPE ($\chi^2 = 3.923$, $p = 0.048$) and EDUC ($\chi^2 = 7.152$, $p = 0.028$).

The subgroup of subjects who came for individual testing represents the subjects who came to test individually *first*–not subjects who came versus those who refused to come. This is because at pretest the individual testing took longer than anticipated and the researchers had to return to the United States before individual testing was complete, and during the posttest that occurred after the second 4.5-month period (see Procedures), the project and research were halted prematurely. In this situation, it is not known if the remaining subjects would have come for individual testing had there been more time. One may conjecture that those subjects who came first were more motivated. Alternatively, they simply may have had more time available, a possibility not systematically examined.

It is likely that we see significant differences in the factors Cognitive Distortion and Intelligence-Related Measures, a trendwise difference in Psychological Well-Being, and nonsignificant differences in the factors Aggression, Impulsiveness, and Psychological Distress due to an interaction between low compliance with treatment, differential sensitivity of the measures to treatment effects, and possible differences in the susceptibility of the tests to socially-desirable responding. On the other hand, significant changes on the GEFT, a non-fakeable cognitive performance test, were seen in a subgroup of the experimental group. Because the changes in cognitive distortion (HIT) and field independence (GEFT) were seen only in a subgroup of the population sample, generalizability of these results remains questionable, although there is inconclusive evidence that the subgroup came from a different population than the larger group of subjects.

CONCLUSION

Despite the low compliance with treatment and the loss of subjects at posttest, significant or trendwise results were obtained for 3 out of 6 factors. These results indicate the ability of Consciousness-Based rehabilitation to unfold the inner potential of incarcerated offenders, allowing them to think from a more expanded, less distorted level of awareness, supporting actions that are more prosocial and lawful. The reduction in cognitive distortion and the increase in field independence seen in these offenders support earlier research on incarcerated offenders, indicating that the practice of the TM technique can reduce risk factors for criminal behavior and increase protective factors. These results indicate that the TM technique deserves greater consideration as a treatment modality in the field of corrections.

NOTES

1. Transcendental Meditation, TM, Maharishi University of Management, and Consciousness-Based are registered or common law trademarks licensed to Maharishi Vedic Education Development Corporation and used with permission.

2. Regular, twice daily practice of the TM technique (14 times a week) is recommended for maximum benefit. A review of previous prison studies using the TM tech-

nique that reported regularity of meditation (Orme-Johnson & Moore, this volume; Cunningham & Koch, 1977; Ballou, 1977; Childs, 1977; Ramirez, 1989; R. E. Ferguson, 1989a, 1989b; Abrams & Siegel, 1978; Alexander & Orme-Johnson, this volume; Alexander, Walton et al., this volume; Bleick & Abrams, 1987) showed that 75-80% of experimental subjects meditated eight or more times a week during the treatment period. In the present study, only 8% of the experimental subjects meditated eight or more times a week and only 25% meditated more than four times a week.

AUTHORS' NOTE

Address correspondence to Mark Hawkins, PhD, Jan Sofat 39, Curaçao, Netherlands Antilles, Dutch Caribbean (E-mail: mhawkinsphd@yahoo.com).

Transcendental Meditation in Criminal Rehabilitation and Crime Prevention. Pp. 229-255.

SECTION III: PREVENTING CRIME AND VIOLENCE

Attacking Crime at Its Source: *Consciousness-Based* Education in the Prevention of Violence and Antisocial Behavior

CHRISTOPHER JONES
Maharishi University of Management

MAWIYAH CLAYBORNE
Maharishi University of Management

JAMES D. GRANT
Maharishi University of Management

GEORGE RUTHERFORD
Baltimore, Maryland, Public Schools

ABSTRACT This paper presents the thesis that Consciousness-Based[1] education, including the practice of the Transcendental Meditation (TM)[i] technique, can be a highly effective tool for reducing or eliminating violent behavior in schools. After reviewing current approaches to preventing violence in schools, the authors review the factors contributing to the unique effectiveness of the Transcendental Meditation program. Central to this effectiveness is the program's ability to simultaneously deal with multiple causes of crime and violence. The paper reviews research demonstrating that practice of the technique reduces 23 identified risk factors for crime in four broad categories–physiological, psychological, and sociological circumstances and substance abuse. The paper concludes with a review of prior implementation of this program in educational and other settings as well as a discussion of the steps for implementation in new educational settings.

KEYWORDS School violence, meditation, rehabilitation, crime prevention, Transcendental Meditation (TM)

In the literature on crime and prevention, the role of education has received surprisingly little attention. Education and crime can be seen as two extremes on a continuum that might be called socialization or training for citizenship. At one extreme is the educated person who has learned, among other things, how to achieve his or her desires while still serving the common good. At the other extreme is the person who has not learned how to reconcile individual desires with those of society, who may even be rebelling against the society and what it represents.

As evidence for the connection between education and crime prevention, one can point to the reciprocal relationship between factors that lead, on the one hand, to educational success and, on the other, to illegal behavior. Most of the factors that lead to success in school–for example, good social skills; a supportive family environment; a stable, focused mind; and good abstract reasoning ability–are considered protective factors preventing violent or illegal behavior. Conversely, those factors that are considered risk factors for criminal behavior–for example, poor social skills, a dysfunctional family, difficulty focusing and paying attention, and poor abstract reasoning ability–all represent risk factors for school as well. To put it simply, success in school is associated with a lower risk of criminality, just as failure in school is associated with higher risk (Herrnstein, 1995).

While some researchers have studied the relationship between low school achievement and criminal behavior (Moffitt, 1993; Farrington, 1991) or the effect of violence prevention programs in the schools (Drug Strategies, 1998), no one seems to have focused in detail on the role of education in crime prevention. It may be that this connection is so deeply held as to be undeniable, yet it bears articulation: education is one of the most powerful long-term weapons in the hands of a community in its battle against crime and other antisocial behavior. In the long run, it would be hard to conceive of a better crime prevention program than to strengthen one's local school. A corollary of this principle is that the school board members in a community should be the community's most outspoken and active agents in the battle against crime.

John Dewey, America's preeminent educational theorist, articulated this connection between education and constructive social behavior when he wrote the following:

> I believe . . . that education is the fundamental method of social progress and reform. . . . all reforms which rest simply upon the enactment of law, or the threatening of certain penalties, or upon changes in mechanical or outward arrangements, are transitory and futile. . . . By law and punishment, by social agitation and discussion, society can regulate and form itself in a more or less haphazard and chance way. But through education society can formulate its own purposes, can organize its own means and resources, and thus shape itself with definiteness and economy in the direction in which it wishes to move. (Dewey, 1889/1964, p. 437-438)

THE PROBLEM

Dewey's noble sentiments notwithstanding, traditional public education has not lived up to its potential for crime prevention, much less social renewal (Counts, 1932; Tyack, 1974). It has not been effective in educating youths in the manner Dewey and other educational reformers had hoped. As a result, schools have become the victim, even sometimes the unwitting accomplice, of social problems like crime.

The extent of the problem can be illustrated by the fact that the number of juvenile homicides tripled between 1984 and 1994 (Gergen, 1996) or by the fact that a U.S. Department of Justice study found that "1 in 5 juvenile arrestees carried a gun all or most of the time" (Bilchik, 2000). Even though a precipitous drop in violent and property crimes in 1995 and 1996 was heartening, the U.S. education community was shaken by a spate of school shootings during 1998 and 1999 in Philadelphia, Mississippi; Jonesboro, Arkansas; Springfield, Oregon; and Littleton, Colorado.

In a July 1998 conference of state attorneys general reported in *The Denver Post*, Mike Moore–newly elected president of the Association of State Attorneys General–expressed his concern. He said that school violence had moved over the past two years from an inner-city, gang-related phenomenon to an increasingly rural and random occurrence. As an illustration of the widespread nature of school crime, the attorney general of South Dakota, Heidi Heitkamp, reported at the same conference that she had conducted an informal poll in one of her state's schools. She asked children in a school-wide assembly to stand up if they had ever seen anyone in school with a gun. She told the conference that "every kid in the school stood up" (in Lofholm, 1998, p. B4).

The problem is not that the school violence prevention approaches are completely ineffective. Indeed, there is evidence that some approaches have positive effects on specific aspects of violence (Tolan & Guerra, 1994; Sherman et al., 1997a,b,c). The problem lies rather in two well-established facts: (a) there are many causal factors in crime (American Psychological Association, 1993; Gibbons, 1986; Reiss & Roth, 1993) and (b) the causes that have been identified are deeply rooted (Wilson, 1995). Because crime has many causes, programs addressing only one contributing factor are incomplete. Because crime is deeply rooted, approaches that try to reduce crime by having students read, think about, and discuss their behaviors are also unlikely to get at the unspoken and less tractable sources of behavior, sources that lie beneath words and thinking.

THE THESIS

One approach to preventing crime not only addresses these two major weaknesses, but also extends beyond other school-based approaches: Consciousness-Based education. Consciousness-Based education does not target a single cause of crime. Rather, it addresses the root cause of the many forms of immoral and antisocial behavior–stress and lack of full development of the individual.[2] Because Consciousness-Based education affects physiological and psychological functions that underlie behavior, it is capable of promoting individual growth more powerfully and deeply than purely intellectual approaches. Consciousness-Based education need not replace programs that target more specific sources of violent behavior (e.g., conflict resolution programs). Rather, we suggest that Consciousness-Based education is a necessary component of any comprehensive approach to violence prevention in a community. This is because Consciousness-Based education is a scientifically supported program of stress-reduction and development that works simultaneously on the individual and societal levels to prevent crime and antisocial behavior.

THE TARGET OF CRIME PREVENTION PROGRAMS

By definition, crime is any behavior for which the society has chosen to impose sanctions, from the violent acts against persons to so-called victimless and white-collar crime. Even among crimes against persons, criminologists distinguish many varieties, such as situational, relationship, predatory, and psychopathological. Because we are focused here on two related causes of crime that are shared by most types of crime–stress and lack of maturity–we have intentionally chosen to treat all forms of crime together. This unified perspective is consistent with research indicating that individuals who have committed a wide variety of crimes show improvements due to Consciousness-Based education.

Most educators are inclined to take a broad view of crime. In school, they must deal with a wide range of behavior–from life-supporting action that promotes society on the one hand to life-damaging, antisocial action on the other. Educators try to civilize, to culture, in short, to move all students as far on the continuum toward positive, life-supporting behavior as possible. From this perspective, educators are in constant battle with all behavior that is antisocial, immoral, even rude, because it degrades the social fabric. Bullying or harassment, for example, though in most cases not illegal, must be curbed because it degrades the society of the school and the larger society for which the student is bound. And bullying arises largely from the same psychological and physiological factors as crime. If we educate students in the direction of prosocial and moral behavior, we will be assured of progress toward a crime-free environment. If we address only crime, we may be forever struggling just to keep violence at bay.

EXISTING EDUCATIONAL APPROACHES TO CRIME PREVENTION

Current school-based approaches to crime can be grouped into three broad categories according to their emphasis: physical constraint, social services, and conflict resolution curricula.

Approaches Based on Policies of Constraint and Punishment

In searching for solutions to the escalation of public school violence, many educators have embraced get tough measures resembling those used to control crime in the society at large. The prevailing ideology here is that the best way to lower violence in schools is to find, detain, and exclude any students who have the potential for committing violent acts. As a result, schools may come to resemble prison lock downs more than places for learning. Some of the more commonly taken measures include metal detectors at school entrances, barbed wire fences, zero tolerance policies, and police officers and security guards to monitor student behavior during school hours. In addition, school personnel are trained to maintain an attitude of toughness and control towards violent behavior and its precursors. Incidents arising in the school are more likely to be referred to the criminal justice system than to be dealt with by school personnel (Noguera, 1995).

A variant of this approach is the establishment of alternative learning centers for violent and disruptive youths. In Texas, for example, a 1996 law gave teachers the right to permanently remove chronically disruptive students from the classroom (Rose, 1996). Rather than being expelled from school altogether, these students are assigned to an alternative center for periods that range from 30 days to a year.

The track record of get tough policies in schools leaves much to be desired. One major drawback is that the use of coercion and control interrupts learning and may actually promote mistrust and resistance. Not only do such programs fail to eliminate violence, but the manner in which they are undertaken may itself foster an aggressive backlash (Noguera, 1995). In addition, get tough programs by themselves tend to ignore the psychological and physiological risk factors associated with violent behavior. They often neglect the issue of rehabilitation or education.

Approaches Based on Increasing Social Services and Counseling

Approaches in this category seek to improve school safety by increasing, integrating, and coordinating school-based service delivery, especially mentoring and counseling. Specific strategies center around school-based teams of professionals (including police and probation personnel), gang councils and/or intervention groups, and police partner programs to council at-risk youths. After-school tutoring or study programs and weekend and summer activities may also be used to provide interesting and safe alternatives to "street life" (Morley & Rossman, 1996). Examples of the social service approach include Cities in Schools, Inc., a national program seeking to provide comprehensive school-based services for children and adolescents at-risk for delinquency, and Drug Abuse Resistance Education (DARE), the most widely used program for drug-use prevention (Ennett, Tobler et al., 1994). DARE is available in more than 50% of all school districts in all 50 states (Wysong, Aniskiewicz, & Wright, 1994). Begun in 1983, this organization promotes an antidrug message and gives skills to help preadolescents resist the enticement of drugs. Delivered by trained police officers, DARE attempts to build students' self-esteem and resistance to peer pressure, to increase students' affiliation with school, and to delay the onset of experimentation with drugs and alcohol. Unfortunately, a controlled study of the long-term effects of DARE found no significant differences between the experimental and control groups (Dukes & Stein, 1997). This finding supports the observation that the effects of most drug-use prevention programs diminish quickly after the program ends (Hunt, Barnett, & Branch, 1971).

Approaches Based on Curriculum

Curriculum-based programs seek to enhance school safety by modifying existing courses or introducing new curricula. Curricular enhancements may focus on personal skills, the law regarding drugs or violence, violence prevention training, conflict resolution programs, peer mediation, and antidrug or antigang components (Morley & Rossman, 1996; Carruthers, Carruthers,

Day-Vines, Bostick, & Watson, 1996). According to the National Institute for Dispute Resolution (NIDR), there are several thousand conflict resolution and peer mediation programs in schools nationwide (NIDR, 1993). One example is Students for Peace (SFP)–a comprehensive violence prevention program for middle schools funded by the Centers for Disease Control and Prevention from October 1993 to September 1996. SFP addresses personal, behavioral and socio-environmental factors as part of its strategy (Orpinas et al., 1996).

In general, research on curricular approaches to violence prevention, assessing what does or does not work, is in its early stages. In a recent empirical review of violence prevention programs, Tolan and Guerra (1994) identified 36 approaches. The researchers found some evidence supporting about one-third (13) of those approaches. Five other approaches did not appear to be effective; eight had unclear or mixed results; and ten had not been tested. Some experts have taken the position that traditional measures of objective testing, records review, portfolios, and self-assessment are insufficient. They believe that an effective means for evaluating conflict resolution curricula has not yet been developed (Carruthers et al., 1996). This is an extreme position. Yet most researchers would agree that, based on research, it is too early to make substantial judgments about the effectiveness of many curriculum-based programs.

Consciousness-Based education and its core practice, the Transcendental Meditation technique, have been thoroughly tested in prisons, in schools, and in large sociological studies (cf., Hawkins, this volume; Orme-Johnson, this volume). In addition, while the application of Consciousness-Based education is considered a complete program in and of itself, its implementation does not preclude the use of the other strategies mentioned above. Indeed, it is likely that Consciousness-Based education would enhance the effectiveness of those strategies by alleviating stress and developing students' latent abilities.

CONSCIOUSNESS-BASED EDUCATION

At least since William James' introduction to the study of psychology (James, 1890), consciousness has been understood to be thought and perceptual experience. James, in fact, introduced the notion that consciousness could be found only as a backdrop for experience and had no independent existence. However, over the span of history, many people have glimpsed dimensions of consciousness that transcend thought content. Reports of these experiences describe a serene, yet dynamic, state where consciousness is aware only of itself. Numerous great educators, writers, and statesmen–for example, Plato, St. Augustine, Jean-Jacques Rousseau, Emerson, Thoreau, and Ionesco, to name a few–have described such experiences clearly in their writings. Plato held that this experience brought knowledge of the Good. Emerson referred to it as the Oversoul. Ionesco simply called it the certainty of being. Most of these writers attributed great significance to the experience of pure consciousness and identified it as their true Self (Pearson, in press).

From these descriptions, it is apparent that the experience of pure consciousness is widely, if not universally, available across cultures and in different times. However, most individuals who have written of this experience have not had a method for systematically attaining or culturing it. As it happened, history favored India as the land in which pure consciousness, as well as its benefits to life, were most carefully explored and explained. In the Vedic tradition of India,[3] long before recorded history, technologies for making the experience of the pure state of consciousness readily accessible to anyone were also well known. Systems were developed for applying these technologies to every area of life, including health, architecture, government, defense, and education. These technologies and this system of education were all but lost to popular culture, even in India, until Maharishi Mahesh Yogi[4] revived them again in their original form and effectiveness as Vedic Science (for a more complete discussion of the history of this science, see Domash, 1977, and Chandler, 1987). The chief goal of Consciousness-Based education is the development of the consciousness of the student–of his or her innate intelligence and creativity–so that every facet of life is enriched at once.

The core practice of Consciousness-Based education is the Transcendental Meditation technique. It is a simple mental procedure for systematically gaining the experience of pure transcendental consciousness and bringing the orderliness of this state into daily life. The technique involves no concentration or contemplation. It is taught in a uniform way around the world, and to date more than 5 million people from different cultures and professions have been instructed in the practice. The technique works on the basis of innate capabilities of the human nervous system and, therefore, requires no change in lifestyle or belief. It is not a religion, nor does it involve any religious practices. As long as one follows the simple instructions, it is not even necessary to believe in the effectiveness of the practice to gain its benefits. Due in part to the standardized teaching of the technique and in part to the immediate benefits that it brings, the Transcendental Meditation technique has become the most thoroughly researched self-improvement program in the world.

The Transcendental Meditation (TM)-Sidhi program is an advanced practice based on the Transcendental Meditation technique. Most of the benefits found with the practice of the Transcendental Meditation technique have been demonstrated in even greater degree with the added practice of the TM-Sidhi program.

As we will see in more detail below, the benefits for education of the Transcendental Meditation and TM-Sidhi techniques are manifold. In general, they have been shown to reduce stress, develop the student's latent mental potential, accelerate development, and have a positive measurable effect on society at large. Specific studies supporting these findings are cited in the research section of this article (see also Goodman, Walton, Orme-Johnson, & Boyer, this volume; Hawkins, this volume).

In addition to the practice of the Transcendental Meditation and TM-Sidhi techniques, Consciousness-Based education includes three other elements that are meant to complement the traditional curriculum at all levels of schooling.

- The Science of Creative Intelligence (SCI), an interdisciplinary science of consciousness based on Vedic Science that provides a framework of ideas from which to understand the relationship between the subject matter found in school and one's own inner nature.
- A prevention-oriented health education program that helps one understand, among other things, the value of diet and daily routine in effective learning and development.
- A Consciousness-Based faculty development program to prepare teachers to use classroom teaching strategies that support the rapid, holistic growth of the student.

These three elements along with the Transcendental Meditation technique form an integrated program of ideas and practices that has been implemented in a variety of settings, ranging from exclusive private schools to urban schools with at-risk children. Some of the effects of this implementation are discussed below.

RESEARCH ON THE TRANSCENDENTAL MEDITATION TECHNIQUE RELATED TO CRIMINAL RISK FACTORS

An extensive scientific literature exists on the Transcendental Meditation technique. More than 600 studies have been conducted at over 200 independent institutions.[5] A portion of this research focuses on Consciousness-Based education per se (for reviews of this area, see Dillbeck & Dillbeck, 1987; Nidich & Nidich, 1992; and Jones, 1989). Another segment has addressed the use of the TM technique in the prevention of crime (for reviews, see Marcus, 1996; Dillbeck & Abrams, 1987; and Hawkins, this volume) while yet another segment of the research addresses rehabilitation of chronic alcohol and drug abuse (for reviews, see Alexander, Robinson, & Rainforth, 1994; Gelderloos, Walton, Orme- Johnson, & Alexander, 1991; and Hawkins, this volume).

Criminal behavior is a complex social phenomenon influenced by both individual and social forces. Programs that focus on a specific risk factor or rehabilitation modality have had a degree of success. But when dealing with such an intransigent phenomenon as crime, with its multiple causes, one must look for rehabilitation programs that can effectively deal with numerous factors simultaneously. Twenty-three identified risk factors for crime (in four broad categories) are discussed below, and the effects of the Transcendental Meditation technique on each are examined.

Physiological Factors

The physiological perspective (also known as the medical model) identifies abnormalities in chemistry and structure of the physiology that contribute to criminal behavior. These abnormalities may have their origins either in heredity or in the environment. Family studies, twin studies, and adoption studies of criminal behavior have suggested a significant heritability of criminal tendencies. For example, the conviction of one's biological father for a crime is a stronger predictor of one's own conviction than is the conviction of an adopted father (Mednick, Gabrielli, & Hutchings, 1984).

What specific physiological factors have been correlated with criminal tendencies? Physiological and neurophysiological studies have found high levels of arousal in the autonomic nervous system of criminals. Research has also found a general dysfunction in those parts of the central nervous system responsible for executive control. The following specific variables have been found to be related to criminal behavior: complications in delivery as a newborn; frontal lobe dysfunction; decreased skin conductance; high levels of testosterone in males; reduced levels of 5-hydroxyindoleacetic acid (5HIAA, a metabolite of serotonin) in the spinal fluid; reduced levels of autonomic reactivity; and poor conditioning of autonomic responses. Overall, the composite picture that emerges from research on the physiology of a person prone to criminal acts is a veneer of quiescent dullness over a disorderly and easily excitable internal state. Such an individual neither learns easily from experience nor is capable of controlling impulses that arise in emotions.

In contrast to this picture, practice of the Transcendental Meditation technique creates in the individual a restful but highly alert, stable internal state in the autonomic nervous system. This alert, stable internal state then persists in activity after meditation. Studies have shown, for example, that when subjects come out of meditation, they exhibit both increased relaxation and increased sensitivity to external stimuli (Orme-Johnson, 1973). Prospective, controlled studies also show that regular practice of the Transcendental Meditation technique leads to greater resistance to stressful stimuli, a reduced threshold for excitement, and more rapid habituation (or learning) from novel events. Overall, the picture that emerges from research on Transcendental Meditation shows a person who is more quiet yet more alert on the inside and more energetic, more dynamic on the outside–a clear contrast to the dull yet highly volatile physiology of the criminal. Research on the Transcendental Meditation technique with regard to drug use and other physiological variables is summarized in Table 1.

Table 1: The Transcendental Meditation Technique and the Physiology of Criminal Behavior

Established Risk Factors	Benefits of the Transcendental Meditation Technique
Increased threshold for engagement, low reactivity[a]	Reduced threshold for engagement, increased reactivity[b]
Frontal lobe dysfunction[c]	Increased coherence in brain wave activity across the cortex[d]
Reduced levels of 5-hydroxyindoleacetic acid (5HIAA) in cerebrospinal fluid[e]	Increased 5HIAA in urine samples[f]
Poor conditioning to external stimuli[g]	More rapid habituation to stressful stimuli[h]
Use of alcohol and illegal drugs[i]	Reduced use of prescribed and non-prescribed drugs[j]

[a] Raine, Verebles, & Williams, 1990a; Raine, & Jones, 1987
[b] Friend, & Maliszewski, 1978
[c] Raine, Verebles, & Williams, 1990b
[d] Banquet, 1973; Hebert & Lehmann, 1977; Levine, 1976
[e] Kruesi et al., 1992; Higley et al., 1992
[f] Walton, Pugh, Gelderloos, & Macrae, 1995; Walton & Levitsky, this volume
[g] Herrnstein, 1995
[h] Orme-Johnson, 1973
[i] Miczek et al., 1993; Goldstein et al., 1989
[j] Gelderloos et al., 1991

Psychological Risk Factors

Stress has been identified as a broad causal factor in criminal behavior (Marcus, 1996), with stress defined as any environmental demands beyond the individual's current coping ability. Research indicates that stress in childhood and adolescence plays a large role in the development of criminal behavior (Agnew & White, 1992; Weatherburn & Lind, 1997). Whatever risk factors may be present in the physiology of the individual at birth, the degree of stress that the individual encounters (or, inversely, the support that he or she receives) either compensates for or accentuates them.

A number of psychological factors in early life have been correlated with later criminal behavior. These include anxiety and hyperactivity, attention deficit disorder (ADD), moderately low levels of intelligence, dishonesty, high impulsiveness and risk-seeking, poor peer relations skills, and a variety of abnormal personality factors identified broadly as the antisocial personality. Research on the Transcendental Meditation technique indicates growth in directions exactly opposite to those associated with criminal psychology. Regular practice of the technique significantly reduces anxiety, increases intelligence and learning ability, and promotes balance in the personality, all as measured by standardized personality inventories and measures of self-actualization. In addition, regular practice also contributes to growth of moral judgment, as measured by Kohlberg's moral judgment interview, Rest's defining issues test, and Higgins' Moral Atmosphere Interview. Thus, research indicates that most of the psychological factors related to criminal behavior can be reduced or reversed through regular practice of the Transcendental Meditation program. These findings are summarized in Table 2.

Sociological Factors

Broadscale sociological studies have found a high correlation between social stress and crime. Linsky and Strauss (1986) found moderately high correlations (from .45 to .69) between an index of stress at the state level and various categories of crime. The stress index is derived from 15 measures, including indicators of economic stress (e.g., business failures), family stress (e.g., divorce rate), and other social indicators (e.g., level of high school dropouts). The study's authors conjecture that as the incidence of stressful life experience increases in society, individuals with criminal tendencies are more likely to act on those tendencies.

The Chicago School of Sociology has attempted to look more deeply into the interplay of social factors in crime, which is also referred to as the ecology of crime (Barak, 1994). The leading theory to arise from this approach is social disorganization theory. From this perspective, criminal activity is an outgrowth of a weakened social fabric. Society is weakened by family functioning factors, such as poor parental management methods, low emotional cohesion, or inadequate family coping skills (Tobin & Guerra, 1994). It is also influenced by broader demographic factors such as unemployment, poverty, ethnic heterogeneity, residential mobility, and urbanization (or population density). The weakened social fabric may be evidenced in sparse local friendship networks, unsupervised peer groups, and low organizational participation (Sampson & Groves, 1989). It has also been recognized that crime and social disorganization have a mutually reinforcing relationship. As social disorganization contributes to crime, crime also contributes to social disorganization (Barak, 1994).

To date, considerable research has focused on the sociological impact of the Transcendental Meditation technique and the more advanced TM-Sidhi program, especially when practiced in groups. The theory behind this research holds that there is a reciprocal relationship between individual and collective or societal consciousness. (The quality of a society's consciousness is comprised of the quality of consciousness of each of the individuals in that society.) Researchers have sometimes referred to the quality of national consciousness as the national mood. Eminent sociologists such as Durkheim

Table 2: The Transcendental Meditation Technique Related to the Psychology of Criminal Behavior

Known Risk Factors	Benefits of the Transcendental Meditation Program
High anxiety and psychological stress[a]	Reduced anxiety[b]
Low intelligence[c]	Increased intelligence[d]
Low academic achievement[e]	Improved academic achievement[f]
Antisocial personality;[g] poor peer relations skills[h]	Increased capacity for warm interpersonal relationships;[i] increased sensitivity to feelings of others;[j] reduced hostility[k]
High impulsivity[l]	Reduced impulsivity[m]
Low ego strength and self-regard[n]	Increased self-concept and ego strength[o]
Earlier than usual risk taking behaviors, including drugs and alcohol[p]	Reduced use of alcohol and non-prescription drugs[q]
Dishonesty[r]	Increased level of moral judgment[s]

[a] Farrington, 1989; Spergel, 1966
[b] Eppley, Abrams, & Shear, 1989
[c] Lynam, Moffitt, & Stauthamer-Loeber, 1993
[d] So, 1995
[e] Moffitt, 1993; Farrington, 1991
[f] Kember, 1985
[g] Hare, 1970
[h] Pepler, King, & Byrd, 1991
[i] Nidich, Seeman, & Dreskin, 1973
[j] Marcus, 1977
[k] Abrams & Segal, 1978
[l] White et al. 1994; Krueger, Schmutte, Caspi, & Moffitt, 1994
[m] Haratani & Henmi, 1990; Candelent & Candelent, 1975
[n] Milner, 1998; Spergel, 1966
[o] Turnbull & Norris, 1982; Chandler, 1990
[p] Herrnstein, 1995
[q] Alexander, Robinson, & Rainforth, 1994
[r] Happel & Auffrey, 1995
[s] Nidich & Nidich, 1989b; Nidich, Ryncarz, Abrams, Orme-Johnson, & Wallace, 1983

(1897/1951) have attempted to define the essential nature and motivating factors in collective consciousness, yet they did not attempt to confirm their views through empirical means.

The Transcendental Meditation and TM-Sidhi programs systematically cultivate transcendental consciousness in the individual, irrespective of national setting or cultural background, thus developing coherence [as indicated by EEG measurement (Travis & Wallace, 1999) and phenomenological analysis (Travis & Pearson, 2000)]. Over 40 empirical studies, using a variety of rigorous statistical methods, have indicated a positive effect of the Transcendental Meditation and the TM-Sidhi program on several sociological variables. These include crime rates, accident rates, violent deaths, war conflict, and the Misery Index (which mathematically combines unemployment and inflation levels), among others (cf., Orme-Johnson, this volume). When a predicted level of participation is reached–1% of a community practicing the Transcendental Meditation technique or the square root of 1% practicing the TM-Sidhi program together in a group–a measurable influence of positivity has been observed.

Many variables with known contribution to social stress and disorganization are affected. Table 3 summarizes the benefits of the practice of the Transcendental Meditation and TM-Sidhi techniques on several of the sociological risk factors for criminal behavior.

The sociological benefits of the Transcendental Meditation technique in reducing social stress are particularly relevant to schools, since schools are themselves communities which can experience both social strain and its consequences. Researchers in the sociology of education have referred to this social aspect as the *school climate*, the social whole that is more than the sum of its parts. Research by Nidich and Nidich (1992), using the Moral Atmosphere Interview, indicates that a school climate can be positively influenced by the practice of the

Table 3: The Transcendental Meditation Technique Related to the Sociology of Criminal Behavior

Known Risk Factors	Benefits of the Transcendental Meditation and TM-Sidhi Programs
High unemployment[a]	Decreased inflation and unemployment[b]
Family dysfunction[c]	Greater marital satisfaction[d]
High violence and crime in the environment[e]	Reduced crime rates;[f] reduced war conflicts[g]
High social stress[h]	Improved quality of life in society[i]

[a] McCarthy & Hagan, 1992
[b] Cavanaugh, King, & Ertuna, 1989
[c] Farrington, 1991; Quay, 1987a
[d] Aron & Aron, 1982; Chen, 1984
[e] Sullivan, 1995
[f] Dillbeck, Banus, Polanzi, & Landrith, 1988; Dillbeck, Cavanaugh, Glenn, Orme-Johnson, & Middlefeldt, 1987
[g] Davies & Alexander, 1990
[h] Linsky & Strauss, 1986
[i] Dillbeck et al., 1987

Transcendental Meditation technique. In addition, many of the other studies on the sociological effects of the Transcendental Meditation technique used subject groups who were practicing in the context of a school or university environment (for review, see Orme-Johnson, this volume). Results show that a school sponsoring the practice of the Transcendental Meditation technique by groups of students, or young adults, can have positive influences on its own social climate as well as on the society surrounding the school.

Alcohol and Drug Abuse

Alcohol and other drugs are estimated to account for 54% of violent crimes in the United States (Hazelden Foundation, 1991). Many of the risk factors for crime discussed previously are also risk factors for alcohol and drug abuse. These include physiological considerations, such as depleted levels of serotonin; psychological considerations, such as depression, anxiety, and low self-esteem; and social considerations, such as peer pressure, family dysfunction, and lack of social cohesion (Alexander, Robinson et al., 1994). The extent of the connection between substance abuse and crime and violence justifies selecting substance abuse as a risk factor for independent consideration.

More than 20 research studies have confirmed that practice of the Transcendental Meditation technique has a positive influence on substance abuse. The most significant of these, a statistical meta-analysis of 198 independent treatment outcomes, found that the Transcendental Meditation technique produced a significantly larger reduction in tobacco, alcohol, and nonprescription drug use than standard substance abuse treatments and standard prevention programs (Alexander, Robinson et al., 1994). In addition, relapse rates for individuals who learned the Transcendental Meditation technique were significantly less than with other programs. Whereas the effects of conventional programs typically fall off within three months, the effects of the Transcendental Meditation technique increase over time, with total abstinence from tobacco, alcohol, and nonprescription drugs ranging from 51% to 89% over an 18- to 22-month period (Alexander, Robinson et al., 1994).

In summary, the research in Table 4 indicates that the Transcendental Meditation technique, the core of Consciousness-Based education, is a health-producing intervention with a comprehensive array of benefits for the individual and society. These benefits appear uniquely suited to counter the complex personal and social factors that underlie criminal behavior.

APPLICATIONS OF THE TRANSCENDENTAL MEDITATION TECHNIQUE TO PRISONS

In the United States, the Transcendental Meditation technique has been taught at Folsom State Prison in California; the Federal Correctional Institu-

Table 4: The Transcendental Meditation Technique Related to the Causes of Drug and Alcohol Abuse

Known Risk Factors	Benefits of the Transcendental Meditation Technique
Reduced levels of neurotransmitters such as serotonin[a]	Increased levels of serotonin[b]
High anxiety and psychological stress[c]	Reduced anxiety[d]
Depression[e]	Reduced depression[f]
Low self-esteem[g]	Increased self-esteem[h]
Negative peer pressure[i]	Increased inner locus of control[j]
Lack of social cohesion[k]	Increased social harmony as measured by greater cooperation and reduced crime and violence[l]

[a] Tennant, 1985; Walton & Levitsky, 1994
[b] Walton & Levitsky, 1994
[c] Swaim, Oetting, Edwards, & Beauvais, 1989; Long & Scherl, 1984; Wills & Schiffman, 1985
[d] Eppley, Abrams, & Shear, 1987; Alexander, Swanson, Rainforth, Carlisle, Todd, & Oates, 1993
[e] Paton, Kessler, & Kandel, 1977
[f] Brooks & Scarano, 1985
[g] Steffenhagen, 1980
[h] Childs, 1973; Turnbull & Norris, 1982
[i] Baumrind, 1985; Oetting & Beauvais, 1987; U.S. Department of Health and Human Services, 1991
[j] Alexander, Rainforth & Gelderloos, 1991; Nidich et al., 1973; Seeman, Nidich, & Banta, 1972
[k] Clarke & Saunders, 1988; U.S. Department of Health and Human Services, 1991; Long & Scherl, 1984
[l] Orme-Johnson, Alexander, Davies, Chandler, & Larimore, 1988; Orme-Johnson, 1992

tion in Milan, Michigan; Walpole Prison in Massachusetts; Stillwater Prison in Minnesota; La Tuna Federal Penitentiary in New Mexico; the Federal Correctional Institution in Lompoc, California; and several institutions in the Vermont system of corrections. In addition, the technique has been used in prison programs internationally, such as in Senegal–where the Transcendental Meditation technique and the Science of Creative Intelligence were introduced to 11,000 inmates and 900 correctional officers throughout the prison system. The effectiveness of these programs has been reviewed elsewhere in detail (Dillbeck & Abrams, 1987; Anklesaria & King, this volume). Still, it is worth highlighting a few of the findings here. If the Transcendental Meditation technique can successfully rehabilitate hardened criminals, it is reasonable to expect that it would reduce criminal behavior in at-risk or disruptive children.

In addition to research on the risk factors summarized in previous sections, two prison studies looked at recidivism among parolees who were taught the Transcendental Meditation technique as compared with those who learned more traditional rehabilitation techniques. Traditional techniques included such things as prisoner education, vocational training, counseling, drug rehabilitation, and psychotherapy. One study (Bleick & Abrams, 1987) found that 34.5% of the parolees who received traditional prison techniques were arrested again after an average of 6 years, as compared with 19.8% from the TM group–a relative difference of more than 40%. A 15-year follow-up of these subjects (Rainforth, Alexander, & Cavanaugh, this volume) found that the risk of recidivism over the entire 15-year period was reduced by 43.5% in the TM-group (46.7% convicted of new felonies vs. 66.7% in the control group). A similar study conducted at Walpole Prison found a relative difference of 48% (Alexander, 1982; see also Alexander, Rainforth et al., this volume).

Huge changes occurred in many of the prisoners who learned the Transcendental Meditation technique. One inmate at San Quentin said the following:

> I have spent years of my life with nothing but drugs and penitentiaries to fill my shallow mind. Who would ever think that I would find inner peace at a place called San Quentin? TM gives a person something that nobody can take away. That something is an inner peace and a discovery of one's "Self." (Maharishi University of Management, 1993, p. 9)

Both the experimental studies and the practical experiences of prison wardens and guards indicate that the Transcendental Meditation technique can be effectively applied in the prison setting. If it can be effectively applied in these highly stressful environments, with individuals whose behaviors are already well on the wrong side of the law, consider the effect and cost-savings that could be realized with in-school programs for children still only at risk. This potential is expressed powerfully by a 38 year old convict who recently began practicing the Transcendental Meditation technique as a condition of his parole by Judge David Mason of Missouri. After the convict's first meditation, he made the following comment:

> I have to admit I was skeptical at first . . . but now I see [meditation] as something substantial and real. When I meditate, I feel like the stillness of a man standing at the center of a hurricane. Everything is whirling around him, but at the center he is silent.
>
> If I had learned this twenty years ago, my whole life would have been different. I was a young man. I was scared. I had no idea where to turn. (personal communication, October 1996)

Research has indicated that Consciousness-Based education can provide students with the physiological and psychological protection needed early in their lives and, at the same time, give them understanding of their own personal development. Together, protection and understanding can prevent the fear and lack of direction that many young students report, especially in urban environments.

CONSCIOUSNESS-BASED EDUCATION IN EDUCATIONAL INSTITUTIONS

Over the years, most research on Consciousness-Based education has been conducted either at Maharishi University of Management (M.U.M.–formerly Maharishi International University) or Maharishi School of the Age of Enlightenment (M.S.A.E.), both in the United States. In other countries several studies indicate that these results can be replicated in other settings.

Maharishi University of Management

Maharishi University of Management in Fairfield, Iowa, founded in 1971, was the first institution to implement Consciousness-Based education in a comprehensive way. The University currently offers 11 undergraduate majors, 5 master's programs, and 3 doctoral programs. The doctoral programs include physiology, management, and Maharishi Vedic Science. The University currently enrolls students from more than forty countries.

The motto of the University is "Knowledge Is Structured in Consciousness," meaning that the quantity and quality of knowledge a student gains depends upon the depth and quality of his or her consciousness. All staff, faculty, and students participate in group practice of the Transcendental Meditation technique twice daily–first in the morning before breakfast and again before dinner in the evening–in facilities specifically designed as meditation halls. As a result of morning practice, teachers and students come to class with the restful alertness, wakefulness, and focus characteristic of the Transcendental Meditation technique. As a result of afternoon practice, they are able to turn to evening homework, again fresh and ready to learn.

The benefits of the Transcendental Meditation technique extend beyond the classroom. Students also report dramatically increased rates of personal growth and development. Indeed, as mentioned above in the review of research, numerous studies have demonstrated long-term, cumulative effects in the direction of self-actualization (see the meta-analysis by Alexander, Rainforth, & Gelderloos, 1991). Consistent with these results, a study of University alumni found dramatic and unprecedented gains in ego development when compared with three groups of alumni from traditional universities. The Maharishi University of Management alumni both began at a higher level than the three schools that, together, constituted the control group, and made greater progress over the test period. At posttest, 38% of the M.U.M. subjects scored at the highest autonomous and integrated levels on the main measure of ego development, compared with 1% among the controls. In the normal adult population, approximately 1% would score at these levels (Chandler, 1990). In addition to the study of ego development, other longitudinal studies of M.U.M. undergraduates have found increases in fluid intelligence and field independence, both factors thought not to develop after late adolescence (Dillbeck, Assimakis, Raimondi, Orme-Johnson, & Rowe, 1986; Cranson, Orme-Johnson, Gackenbach, Jones, & Alexander, 1991), and increased psychological health (Gelderloos, 1987a). Studies in Cambodia and China (So, 1996) have replicated the increases in fluid intelligence. A cross-sectional study of University students also found high levels of moral development using Rest's Defining Issues test, as compared with controls from another college (Nidich & Nidich, 1989b). Despite the fact that the student body at Maharishi University of Management is more diverse than at most other universities, it is remarkably free from intercultural tension or conflict. The regular group practice of the Transcendental Meditation technique, together with study of the Science of Creative Intelligence, combine to create a uniquely harmonious, yet focused, environment for learning. Student outcomes assessments indicate that students score well on nationally standardized tests of academic content. Students are acquiring the traditional knowledge necessary for graduate school or work, but they are not experiencing the usual stress that college study entails (Jones, 1989). Research on intelligence, moral development, and ego development indicates that Consciousness-Based education develops the student's latent creativity and intelligence beyond what is found through the standard system of education. These results suggest that Consciousness-Based education should be considered as a powerful addition to other methods of addressing crime and antisocial behavior.

Maharishi School of the Age of Enlightenment

Three years after the founding of the Maharishi University of Management, a number of faculty established a school to apply, at the elementary and secondary levels, the same principles and practices of Consciousness-Based education that had been piloted and developed at the University. The aim was to create a seamless education, kindergarten through PhD, that brought the knowledge of consciousness, as well as its benefits, to education. This system was designed to support the rapid realization of the individual's potential as well as the ability to act in accord with natural law.[6] In the more than 20 years the Maharishi School of the Age of Enlightenment has been in operation, it has achieved the same level of recognition for its innovative approach to education as has the University.

The school's approach to education has been summarized fully by Nidich and Nidich (1987, 1992; see also Nidich, Nidich, & Rainforth, 1986). It combines the same essential elements described above for Consciousness-Based education, though significantly adapted for younger children. Beginning in kindergarten and first grade, the children are taught basic knowledge about consciousness–its source deep within the mind, its range through all the disciplines, and its goal in the development of one's full potential. In first grade, for example, children learn, as a basic principle, that it is the nature of life to grow (that growth is fundamental to existence). They see this principle in the growth of a seed into a tree, in their own physical growth, in the development of a star system, in the pursuit of learning by their own mind. In short, the children see a few fundamental principles reflected in all the subjects they study. These principles help to unify knowledge, and they enable students to relate anything they learn to their own practice of meditation and to their own growth as a person.

The practice of the Transcendental Meditation technique, combined with the study of the Science of Creative Intelligence, has led to student outcomes and school achievements that are remarkable in their scope and caliber. Research on the school has shown, for example, that students make significant gains relative to age norms on the Iowa Tests of Basic Skills and the Iowa Tests of Educational Development over the course of nine months and over one and a half years (Nidich, Nidich, & Rainforth, 1986; Nidich & Nidich, 1989a). In other research on cognitive functioning, students in this system of education–compared to matched controls–have shown higher levels of field independence (Gelderloos, Lockie, & Chuttoorgoon, 1987) and of cognitive development, as measured by a series of Piagetian conservation tasks (Warner, 1986). Warner also found higher levels of information processing, reflectivity, and cognitive flexibility in the M.S.A.E. students as compared with matched controls.

Nidich and Nidich have extensively examined the social development levels of students at M.S.A.E. (Nidich & Nidich, 1987, 1992), using the Moral Atmosphere Interview developed by the Harvard Center for Moral Development. This measure requires students to respond to dilemmas according to what they, as individuals, should do, what they would do, and what others in the school *should* and *would* do. The M.S.A.E. students were compared with two of the most academically and socioeconomically advanced Just Community Schools (JCS), using the results of a study by Higgins, Power, and Kohlberg in 1981. These JCS schools were designed around the development of a just, moral community. One school was located in a suburban community just outside of Boston (JCS#1); the other was located in an affluent suburban community near New York City (JCS#2). Table 5 summarizes the results of this comparison, indicating that there is a higher percentage of prosocial choice among the M.S.A.E. students and greater congruence between what the children say they ought to do and what they would do when confronted with a real-life dilemma.

TABLE 5: Percentage of Students at Maharishi School of the Age of Enlightenment (M.S.A.E.) and Just Community Schools (JCS) Responding in a Prosocial Manner to All of the Dilemmas

	M.S.A.E.	JCS#1	JCS#2
Number of students	24	15	18
Prosocial choice for self	71%	60%*	50%*
Prosocial behavior for self	79%[a]	44%*	47%*
Prosocial choice for others	83%	60%**	67%*
Prosocial behavior for others	83%[b]	33%**	50%*

Note: From "Holistic Student Development at Maharishi School of the Age of Enlightenment: Theory and Research" by S. Nidich and R. Nidich, 1987, *Modern Science and Vedic Science*, 1(4), p. 455. Copyright 1987. Printed with permission.

[a] The differences in prosocial behavior for self between M.S.A.E. and JCS#1 and between M.S.A.E. and JCS#2 are significant at the $p < .05$.

[b] The differences in prosocial behavior for others between M.S.A.E. and JCS#1 and between M.S.A.E. and JCS#2 are significant at $p < .01$ and $p < .05$, respectively. No significant differences were found between the two Just Community Schools.

* $p < .05$
** $p < .01$

Published research does not capture the full extent of the impact of M.S.A.E. on its students. Other outcomes assessment and statewide competitions give a richer picture of the students' accomplishments. In the 1998-99 school year, for example, students from grade 9-12 scored in the 99th percentile on the Iowa Tests of Educational Development–both nationally and in Iowa. Individuals and groups from the school have won first place in state competitions in speech, spelling, Odyssey of the Mind (an international competition in improvised creativity), the American Junior High School Mathematics Exam, the history fair, and many areas of artistic achievement. In seven of the last eight years, M.S.A.E. students have won at least one of the two first prizes in the state science and engineering fairs. In sports, as well, the students have excelled, capturing in recent years state championships in tennis and golf.

Taken together with the more formal research studies, these achievements indicate that something unique and effective is taking place in the school. M.S.A.E. has a liberal admissions policy and an exceptionally high percentage of students on scholarship, as compared with other private schools. Longitudinal research on academic performance has shown that when new students enter the school, they score at about the national average (Nidich, 1989a). This implies that school factors rather than entry characteristics are responsible for the students' high level of success. These achievements encourage consideration of the applicability of this approach for other schools, particularly urban public schools. Two such examples follow.

Consciousness-Based Education with At-Risk Students: Newark, NJ

A carefully documented project applying Consciousness-Based education to children at risk was conducted through a social service agency in Newark, New Jersey. Most of the children in this project came from single parent homes, many of them living with relatives rather than parents.

Thirty children from the experimental group and 32 matched controls were pretested on several measures of cognitive and personal development (analytical intelligence, self-concept, performance on a computer task, and general intelligence) and followed over a 45-week period. The experimental group learned and practiced the Transcendental Meditation technique (or a variant of the adult technique for children under the age of 10) outside of school at the social service agency. They were posttested again at the end of the time period by testers blind to group membership. After the 11-month period, the experimental group did significantly better than the controls on all the measures except the computer task which showed no difference.

In addition to the quantitative data collected, videotaped interviews were conducted with the children (Dillbeck & Dillbeck, 1990) that speak more directly to the benefits they experienced. The children are remarkably articulate in noting the connections between a more stable and alert internal frame of reference and improved functioning in activity. A few of the interviewer questions and the unrehearsed answers appear below.

Ten-year-old girl:

Q. What happened when you started TM?
A. My work got better, my teacher said I improved, I had a lot of compliments, and I got a lot of money [from my parents].
Q. Why do you think that happened?
A. Because it helps you to relax. You could take your mind off things once you meditate for even 2 minutes. It helps you relax. You can get everything done.

Ten-year-old boy:

Q. What happened when you started TM?
A. I feel my body's growing, and I feel my heart's like turning into a new person.
Q. How does this happen?
A. When I'm mad, I meditate and it makes me, like, express better, and I won't get hyper or nothin' like that when I'm mad.
Q. Why do you suppose that happens?
A. . . . Well, 'cause sometimes when I get in trouble, when I meditate I just feel better.

Ten-year-old girl:

Q. What happened when you started TM?
A. My grades improved, and my manners and my behavior. Since I started meditating, I'm more relaxed, and I'm more interested in learning.

Nine-year-old boy:

Q. And what happened to you when you started meditating?
A. I just got calmer. [pause] I didn't have as much fights.

Ten-year-old girl:

Q. Have you noticed any difference in the children in your SCI [Science of Creative Intelligence] class and the children who don't take SCI?
A. Yes. Well, for instance, the kids at [the SCI class] don't pick on me. See everybody at my school picks on me a lot about my weight, but nobody here ever does that.

Nine-year-old girl:

Q. Have you noticed any difference in the children in your SCI class and the children who don't take SCI?
A. Well, they're happier and they don't fight as much as they usually do. When they do, they like play around.

These comments by the children illustrate some of the spontaneous changes that occur when students begin a Consciousness-Based education program, even in a complex and challenging urban environment. Many of these changes, such as reduced fighting and anxiety, directly address the factors discussed above as risk factors for criminal behavior.

Consciousness-Based Education with At-Risk Students: Washington, DC

Another Consciousness-Based education project with at-risk students was undertaken in Washington, DC. In a public elementary-middle combination school, 80% of the staff began the Transcendental Meditation technique, and approximately 25% of the students learned the practice. The effects of this project were similar to those found in New Jersey. Fights dropped considerably, and visitors remarked on the feeling of harmony and order that dominated the school climate. The Maslach Teacher Burnout Inventory, a measure of teacher stress, found statistically significant reductions in teacher burnout as compared with teachers from another elementary school in the same vicinity.

In interviews with 18 randomly selected students, all indicated that they enjoyed their practice of the Transcendental Meditation technique. Fifteen said they had noticed changes in themselves as a result of the practice, and 16 indicated that they noticed positive effects on their schoolwork. Their most interesting comments came in response to the question: "Do you feel that the TM program has been good for the students at your school? And, if so, have you noticed changes in the school compared to before the program was begun?" The responses include the following.

Thirteen-year-old girl:	"Yes, nobody at our school gets hurt or killed now."
Thirteen-year-old boy:	"Yes, some people get real hyper–[the TM program] calms you down, lets you think and lets you remember things way back."
Twelve-year-old boy:	"Yes, they used to be real bad last year, most kids were bad, and when they started meditating, the badness get knocked out of them."
Twelve-year-old boy:	"Yes, because they don't fight like they used to. Before more kids start to meditate last year, but the year before last they used to fight almost every day. Now we hardly have no fights no more."
Fifteen-year-old boy:	"Yes, a lot of fighting has been stopped and a lot of kids getting along with each other more better. Two years ago there were a lot of fights–different fights–a lot of brutal fights."
Thirteen-year-old girl:	"Yes, because a lot of the kids change–half of them have a real decent attitude. [Before] It was terrible."

All but one of the students felt that the program had been good for their school, and even he was very appreciative of the benefits of the practice for himself; he just hadn't noticed any changes in his friends. In general, the dominant impression from the interview tapes was that violence at the school had been significantly reduced. Tardiness had replaced violent crime as the number one problem.

IMPLEMENTATION OF CONSCIOUSNESS-BASED EDUCATION

It is not necessary to use all of the components of Consciousness-Based education described in an earlier section to bring about significant student and teacher improvements. The two basic components–the Transcendental Meditation technique and the Science of Creative Intelligence course–can be covered in school in one period a day. In this period, students practice their meditation in a group and study the unifying principles of the Science of Creative Intelligence and the health education curriculum. The national organization that teaches the Transcendental Meditation technique in schools (the Consciousness-Based Education Association) recommends that there be an additional quiet period set aside in school for a second meditation practice, to ensure that all students practice the technique twice every day. The Consciousness-Based Education Association also recommends faculty development for all those involved in facilitating the Transcendental Meditation technique and SCI in their classrooms, to help fully integrate the existing faculty into the new program.

In most settings where Consciousness-Based education has been implemented, program administrators have started by teaching the Transcendental Meditation technique to teachers, school administrators, and parents who are leaders in the community. This helps develop a steering group of individuals who are familiar with the practice from their own personal experience. When the program is ready to be offered to students, it is best to start with older students in the school who are role models for the younger ones. Beyond this, the greater the number of students who start, the greater the positive effects on the school environment.

CONCLUSIONS

We have presented here the most significant evidence in support of the thesis that Consciousness-Based education–even the Transcendental Meditation technique alone–can be a highly effective tool by which schools can reduce, and even eliminate, violent and criminal behavior. Because the causes of crime are complex–physical as well as mental, social as well as individual–a holistic program is needed to adequately prevent crime. Consciousness-Based education is such a program. As has been shown, this program alleviates the student's stress, develops his or her latent abilities, enhances his or her overall personal development, strengthens prosocial judgment, improves academic performance, and contributes in a direct way to a positive school climate. While Consciousness-Based education can be effective in itself, there is also no reason that it cannot be used with other conflict-resolution and violence prevention programs.

Research on the effects of Consciousness-Based education on school crime is only in its early stages. However, compelling research already exists to show that the core technology–the Transcendental Meditation technique–can, by itself, dramatically impact drug and alcohol abuse, criminal behavior (including recidivism), and most of the risk factors tied to crime. In addition, research and outcomes assessment conducted at institutions where Consciousness-Based education has been applied suggest that many additional benefits should accompany the predicted reduction in school violence and antisocial behavior. These include such things as improved standardized test results and success at educational competitions. The potential impact of the approach is substantial for schools burdened with crime as well as those confronted with antisocial or disruptive behavior.

Eliminating crime, violence, and antisocial and disruptive behaviors represents only a small fraction of the capability of education. Schools have the power to create moral individuals who have learned to fulfill their own desires while simultaneously serving the good of society at large. Research on the Maharishi School of the Age of Enlightenment and Maharishi University of Management indicates that, when educators set their sights on such a target, applying the technologies for development of consciousness that are now available, schools can become the agents of progress and social reform that John Dewey and other leading theorists have envisioned.

NOTES

1. Transcendental Meditation, TM, TM-Sidhi, Vedic Science, and Science of Creative Intelligence and Consciousness-Based are service marks registered in the U.S. Patent and Trademark Office, licensed to Maharishi Vedic Education Development Corporation and used under sublicense.

2. By *stress*, we refer to the physiological or psychological strain caused by events or environmental factors beyond one's coping ability. In this view, even positive events, such as winning a prize, can cause stress if they overload the machinery of perception and cognition. But more typically, we are referring to frustration, disappointment, or losses that are beyond one's capacity to understand and effectively negotiate. *Full development* can be defined as simply the use of one's full mental capacity. It is well accepted that human beings use only a fraction, perhaps 5%-10%, of their full mental capacity.

3. The Vedic tradition generally refers to the body of knowledge in India dealing with Veda. *Veda* is the Sanskrit word for knowledge, and thus the *Vedic tradition* is that tradition responsible for the understanding of the nature and scope of knowledge. It is as diverse as the Western disciplines, with correspondingly many branches and applications.

4. Maharishi is an Indian teacher who began teaching the Transcendental Meditation technique in 1957. He was the favored student of Brahmananda Saraswati, the most recent in a long line of teachers known as the Shankaracharya tradition. This tradition is widely regarded in India as the custodian of the Vedic knowledge and technology of consciousness.

5. Four hundred thirty (430) of these studies have been collected in 5 volumes of research: *Scientific Research on Maharishi's Transcendental Meditation and TM-Sidhi Program, Collected Papers*, Vols. 1-5, (Orme-Johnson & Farrow, Vol. 1, 1977; Chalmers, Clements, Schenkluhn, & Weinless, Vols. 2-4, 1989; Wallace, Orme-Johnson, & Dillbeck, Vol. 5, 1990).

6. Action in accord with natural law is Maharishi's expression for action based upon self-knowledge. For Maharishi, the individual self is also the source of all the laws of nature, which govern physical phenomena; therefore, action based upon one's self is also action in accord with the source of natural law. It is consistent with the tradition in legal philosophy, going back to the Stoics, known as natural law theory.

AUTHORS' NOTE

Address correspondence to Chris Jones, Department of Education, Maharishi University of Management, 1000 North 4th Street, Fairfield, IA 52557 (E-mail: cjones@mum.edu).

Transcendental Meditation in Criminal Rehabilitation and Crime Prevention. Pp. 257-281.

Preventing Crime Through the Maharishi Effect

DAVID W. ORME-JOHNSON

Maharishi University of Management

ABSTRACT Criminologists view crime as a multidimensional problem that is best prevented by programs that strengthen informal social control, which is the internalized propensity of the individual to find rewarding behavior patterns within the law. This paper introduces the theory and research on crime prevention through the Maharishi Effect, a powerful mechanism of increasing informal social control by increasing coherence and decreasing stress in the most holistic level of society, its collective consciousness. A review of 15 published studies conducted on city, state, national, and international levels finds strong evidence that crime is reduced and quality of life is improved when 1% of a population practices the Transcendental Meditation (TM)[1] program. This is termed the Maharishi Effect. This review also finds that crime is reduced and quality of life improved when groups the size of the square root of 1% of a population practice the more powerful TM-Sidhi program together in one place. This is called the Extended Maharishi Effect. Theoretically, such a transformation is made possible by the ability of the TM and TM-Sidhi[1] programs to provide direct experience of the unified field of natural law in the simplest form of human awareness, transcendental consciousness, which brings life in accord with natural law. This program is easily implemented and highly cost effective as a primary protective factor against crime. *[Article copies available for a fee from The Haworth Document Delivery Service: 1-800-HAWORTH. E-mail address: <docdelivery@haworthpress.com> Website: <http://www.HaworthPress.com> © 2003 by The Haworth Press, Inc. All rights reserved.]*

KEYWORDS Crime prevention, Transcendental Meditation, Maharishi Effect, consciousness, informal social control

For as long as statistics have been kept, the homicide rate for American cities has been higher than for comparable cities in other countries. Today, our cities continue to be the most violent in the world. In the 1960s, the overall crime rate in America began accelerating. Since 1985, homicides committed by youths have increased 50% for white males and 300% for black males. Most other industrialized nations also have seen major increases in crime, at least in property crime. The general worldwide rise appears to be due to the erosion of cultural, family, and community values (Wilson, 1994). Crime is a multidimensional epidemic that involves virtually every area of society–the criminal justice system, health, education, social welfare, and the economy (Bureau of Justice Bulletin, 1993). A recent major review concludes that in order to prevent crime, we have to address basic issues about the fundamental structure of society (Sherman, 1997a).

OVERVIEW OF CRIME PREVENTION APPROACHES

The responsibility for reducing the national crime load has been given to the Department of Justice (DOJ), which spends over $3 billion annually for crime prevention programs. Congress has mandated independent scientific evaluations of these programs to create a knowledge base from which it can evolve rational policies to guide the flow of national funding (Freeley & Sarat, 1980; Sherman et al., 1997). However, according to reviews, after 25 years and $100 million in grants, the majority of these evaluations are so inconsistent and poorly controlled that it is not possible to conclude which crime prevention programs work and which do not (Rubinstein, 1977; Sherman, 1997a).

Nevertheless, criminological research and theory have given a definite direction to prevention programs. The majority of people are prevented from committing crimes by what criminologists call informal social control–each person's internalized bonds to family, community, and the nation that steer the individual away from criminal behavior and towards a rewarding life in society (Sherman, 1997b; Tittle & Logan, 1973). As informal social control breaks down, government has to create formal social controls to maintain order in society: more laws, police, and prisons (Black, 1976; Wilson, 1994). The large volume of crime in our society indicates that informal, internal social control has broken down considerably, forcing Congress to funnel 75% of crime prevention funds into police and criminal justice programs. These are necessary in order to cope with the immediate and present danger of crime, but they are only crisis management, not true prevention.

A recent major review of research in this area recommends that crime prevention programs should be multitiered and address many levels of society–family, community, schools, labor markets, policing, and criminal justice simultaneously (Sherman et al., 1997). This is because risk factors for crime are highly interdependent (Hope, 1995; Orme-Johnson, 1994; Sherman,

1997b). High-crime communities, domestic violence, chaotic schools, unemployment, and high-crime locations, for example, all interact to increase the likelihood of crime. Risk factors at all levels of society need to be changed into protective factors, such as strong parental attachments to children, consistent disciplinary patterns for children (Hirschi, 1969), watchful and supportive communities (Braithwaite, 1989), good marriages, strong schools, and viable employment opportunities (Sampson & Laub, 1993).

Evaluating what works at each level of society is complex because programs with the same name may differ in actual content; also, implementation of programs may differ from one area to another. A program that works in one community may not work in another (Sherman et al., 1997). Certainly we need to determine which are the best formal social-control programs for coping with the current crime problem. But to most effectively prevent future crime, we need to know which programs are best for developing internal, informal social control.

Review of Research on External Formal Social Control

In general, the most cost-effective strategy for external social control seems to be focusing police on serious offenders and on high crime areas (Sherman et al., 1997). Police practices that work include extra police in high-crime areas, police units focused on serious repeat offenders, arrests of employed suspects for misdemeanor domestic violence, and proactive enforcement of drunk-driving laws. Promising police programs include patrols to detect illegally carried handguns and zero-tolerance enforcement of minor violations.

Research indicates that the following police programs do not work: random patrols of entire beats, more rapid response to 911 calls, neighborhood watch, arrests of some juveniles for minor offenses, arrests of unemployed suspects for domestic assault, arrest crackdowns at drug markets, and community policing programs (such as recreation) with no clear focus on crime (Sherman et al., 1997).

Prison programs, like police programs, seem to work best when they focus on the serious offender. But generalized fear-based programs are less effective than rehabilitation programs that develop informal social controls. Incapacitation of high-rate, serious repeat offenders works.

Prison programs that do not work include boot camps using military basic-training models; other harshness programs, like Scared Straight and shock probation; and community-based alternative sanctions lacking treatment programs and services. Similarly, school programs based on fear arousal and moral appeal appear to be ineffective (Sherman et al., 1997).

Another formal social-control program that appears to work is control of criminogenic commodities, such as alcohol, cash, and firearms in public places (e.g., airports and transit systems) (Cook, 1995). Yet programs such as gun detectors that safeguard areas where advantaged people congregate, such as airports, may detract from investing time and funds to make high-crime areas safe (Sherman, 1997b). Safety guards, lights, fences, cameras, and alarm systems are of unknown effectiveness (Sherman et al., 1997). Also, such practices may only divert crime to other areas rather than decrease the overall crime rate (Barr & Pease, 1990).

Perhaps the greatest drawback to formal social control is that it turns the nation into a fortress society (Sherman, 1997a), which–in its extreme–is totalitarianism. Clearly, as a democracy, we must find ways to foster informal social control as our first line of defense against crime.

Review of Research on Informal Social Control

Arguably, community policing efforts to increase police legitimacy in minority poverty areas may fall within the realm of informal social control. Research shows that such programs are promising. Research also shows positive results from prison programs that help offenders cope with their problems, such as prison-based therapeutic community treatment of drug-involved offenders and structured rehabilitation programs focused on individual risk factors (Sherman et al., 1997).

School-based programs that work include those that clarify and communicate norms about expected behavior, such as anti-bullying campaigns, those that teach the necessary cognitive skills for social adaptation, those that teach self-control, and those that improve overall school organization so that schools can carry out their primary mission of teaching basic skills (Sherman et al., 1997).

There is also strong evidence that pulling young people into the labor market for legitimate work prevents crime (Gottfredson, 1985; Sampson & Laub, 1993), and the Job Corps appears to reduce crime in its clients. There is also contrary evidence from the Department of Labor indicating that job training does not reduce crime in high-risk youth (Sherman, 1997a). In principle, however, behavioral research has shown that punishing the unwanted behavior while at the same time providing a positively reinforcing alternative is a powerful means for reducing antisocial behaviors. If people have an alternative channel to fulfill their desires that is not punished, they will quickly go for the non-punished alternative.

A congressional mandate has called for emphasis on youth crime and on the risk factors in the family, school, and community environments that contribute to it. Although crime usually begins in adolescence, evidence indicates that it is better to start prevention programs at an earlier age. One review found that adolescent prevention does not work for high-risk youth in high-crime areas (Harrell, 1996). However, parent-training strategies for troublesome preadolescent children do work, and home nurse visitations in early infancy are effective in preventing delinquency (Sherman et al., 1997).

Despite such successes, there is a major limitation of even the promising family, school, and community crime prevention programs. They are least likely to take hold and work in urban high-crime, poverty communities where they are most needed. How to make these programs work is a major task of crime prevention research (Sherman, 1997a).

A NEW APPROACH TO CRIME PREVENTION: INCREASE COHERENCE IN COLLECTIVE CONSCIOUSNESS TO INCREASE INFORMAL SOCIAL CONTROL

The present paper addresses crime prevention through a radically new approach, albeit one with ancient roots. It aims at strengthening informal social control from within the very fabric of society itself by creating coherence in collective consciousness. *Collective consciousness* is defined as a common field of consciousness that links all individuals in society (Dillbeck, Cavanaugh, Glenn, Orme-Johnson, & Mittlefehldt, 1987; Maharishi Mahesh Yogi, 1977a; Orme-Johnson, 1994; Orme-Johnson, Alexander, Davies, Chandler, & Larimore, 1988).

Collective Consciousness in the Social Sciences

It bears keeping in mind that while contemporary social theory views human beings classically as ontologically separate individuals, the longest tradition of philosophical thought in the West–the idealist tradition–has maintained, at least implicitly, the connection of human beings on the level of consciousness. In principle, strengthening that connection could be a means of reducing crime.

Several of the founding theorists of the social sciences have proposed concepts of collective consciousness, although practical applications of this idea to reducing crime have not been developed to date. Gustav Fechner, who pioneered the study of sensory thresholds (psychophysics), described a unity or continuity of a general consciousness underlying the discontinuities of consciousness associated with each individual, accessible in principle simply through lowering the threshold of conscious experience (James, 1898/1977). William James, considered to be the father of American psychology, suggested that the brain may serve to reflect or transmit this preexisting universal field of consciousness, which is the transcendental, infinite continuity underlying the phenomenal world. James argued that the facts of experimental neuroscience could just as well support this transmission model as the more commonly held paradigm that consciousness is produced *de novo* in each individual brain (James, 1898/1977). Psychology, however, has not developed this theory into an empirical science with practical applications.

Emile Durkheim (1897/1951), a founder of modern sociology, proposed that individuals in society are unified by an underlying *conscience collective* (pp. 307-320). He described this collective consciousness as the mind of society, created when "the consciousness of the individuals, instead of remaining isolated, becomes grouped and combined" (p. 310). Durkheim believed that suicide rates could be explained by the quality of collective consciousness, and–in principle–so could crime. But he did not suggest any ways to improve collective consciousness in order to reduce suicides or other problems.

It is unfortunate that these various views of collective consciousness have not entered the mainstream of the social sciences because a wide range of human experience has been left unexplained. Experiences of field effects of consciousness are commonly reported, such as the feeling that someone, even at a distance, is directing attention at you, only to find out that this is, indeed, the case (Schlitz, 1996). Other examples include: an intuition or dream about a relative or friend that turns out to be true; the thought to call someone and, when the phone rings, it is that person; and prayer for someone diagnosed with a terminal illness who gets better. Over the years such phenomena have been experimentally investigated with increasing methodological rigor, and small but statistically reliable results have been found (Dossey, 1989; Radin, 1998; Schlitz, 1996). Could it be that the matrix of attentional vectors from stressed individuals coursing throughout society creates a collective milieu that aggravates crime and other problems? It is our everyday experience that we feel the quality of a family's consciousness when we enter the home, of a city's consciousness when we enter the city, or of the country's consciousness when we cross the national border. Could stress in family, city, national, and world consciousness influence the crime rate and other social problems? The concept that field effects of consciousness influence individuals in society may challenge a purely materialist worldview, but it accords with the statements of many monumental thinkers of the new physics, who have ascribed to consciousness a fundamental role in natural law.

Collective Consciousness and Modern Physics

Sir Arthur Eddington, who provided experimental confirmation of Einstein's General Theory of Relativity, suggested that "The idea of a Universal Mind or Logos would be, I think, a fairly plausible inference from the present state of scientific theory; at least it is in harmony with it" (cited in Dossey, 1989, p. 125). Could there be a way to bring human life into harmony with what Eddington calls the Universal Mind, to organize life in society into a synergistic, harmonious, crime-free, problem-free system? Let us consider what impelled several leading scientists of our time to postulate a connectedness between mind and physical reality.

The divergence of science from strict materialism was motivated by a startling discovery. It was found that at the quantum level, concrete matter is an abstract, unmanifest reality–a wave function, that has no concrete location nor other specific physical properties. However, when consciousness enters the picture to make an observation or measurement, the wave function collapses to manifest the concrete, specific, material reality of our familiar world (Farwell, 1996). Commenting on this discovery, Eugene Wigner (1967), Nobel laureate and pioneer of measurement theory, wrote:

> When the province of physical theory was extended to encompass microscopic phenomena, through the creation of quantum mechanics, the concept of consciousness came to the fore again: it was not possible to formulate the laws of quantum mechanics in a fully consistent way without reference to the consciousness. . . . It may be premature to believe that the present philosophy of quantum mechanics will remain a permanent feature of future physical theories; it will remain remarkable, in whatever way our future concepts may develop, that the very study of the external world led to the conclusion that the content of consciousness is an ultimate reality . . . [P]hysicists have found it impossible to give a satisfactory description of atomic phenomena without reference to the consciousness. (pp. 172, 186)

Max Planck, who discovered the quantum phenomenon and is held to be the father of quantum mechanics, directly stated: "I regard consciousness as fundamental. I regard matter as derivative from consciousness" (cited in Klein, 1984). Over time this view has been similarly expressed by other eminent physical scientists, for example, Sir Arthur Eddington's "mind stuff" and Wolfgang Pauli's "unity of all being" (cited in Dossey, 1989, p. 124). In a review article on quantum mechanics appearing in *Scientific American*, French physicist Bernard d'Espagnat summarized the field by stating, "The doctrine that the world is made up of objects whose existence is independent of human consciousness turns out to be in conflict with quantum mechanics and with the facts established by experiment" (1979, p. 158). If consciousness is intimately connected to the objects of the world, does our consciousness also create direct influences on society that could impact on the crime rate?

Erwin Schroedinger, who received the Nobel prize for his development of the Schroedinger equation, the most widely used mathematical tool in quantum theory, wrote: "Mind has erected the objective outside world of the natural philosopher out of its own stuff" (Schroedinger, 1958/1967, p.131). Schroedinger continued, "The reason why our sentient, percipient and thinking ego is met nowhere within our scientific world picture can easily be indicated in seven words: because it is itself that world picture" (ibid, p.138). Supporting this view, modern neuroscience recognizes that size, shape, color, texture, visibility, and all other qualities of an object of experience are not uniquely determined by the external world but are features of subjective experience (Farwell, 1996; Farwell & Farwell, 1995). Hundreds of experiments have shown that even ordinary human consciousness exerts a small but statistically reliable direct influence at fundamental levels of natural law. For example, attention can actually change the outcome of random processes, even those generated by quantum mechanical events (Farwell, 1996; Jahn, Dunne, Nelson, Dobyns, & Bradish, 1997).

One more development in modern science needs to be noted before we explore the relevance these advances in physics may have for crime prevention. This is the discovery of the unified field of natural law. The evolution of science has always been in the direction of discovering increasingly more unified levels of natural law. For example, electricity and magnetism, once thought to be two different forces, were found to be different aspects of the electromagnetic field. Einstein was guided by the deep intuition that the most fundamental level of nature is a single unified field, and superstring theory has authenticated his vision by proposing a unified field theory capable of uniting all the force and matter fields (Schwarzschild, 1985; Waldrop, 1985). The relevance of these streams of knowledge for improving the human condition, including crime prevention, has been brought to light by Maharishi Mahesh Yogi (Maharishi Mahesh Yogi, 1977b, 1986a, 1996).

Collective Consciousness in Maharishi Vedic Science

Whereas modern science has provided an intellectual understanding of the unified field of natural law, Maharishi Vedic science provides the direct experience of the unified field in the simplest form of human awareness, the state of least excitation of consciousness, transcendental consciousness. Because the unified field is the source of order in nature, the nervous system that directly experiences this field becomes habituated to function in accord with this holistic basis of all laws of nature, thus reducing and eventually eliminating problems, including crime.

The practical, applied program for experiencing the unified field of consciousness and bringing life in accord with natural law employs as its basis the Transcendental Meditation (TM) technique, which allows the mind to settle from its active phases of thought and perception to its ground state of transcendental consciousness. In Maharishi's (1977a) words:

> The Transcendental Meditation technique is an effortless procedure for allowing the excitations of the mind to settle down until the least excited state of mind is reached. This is a state of inner wakefulness with no object of thought or perception, just pure consciousness aware of its own unbounded nature. It is wholeness aware of itself, devoid of differences, beyond the division of subject and object–transcendental consciousness. It is a field of all possibilities, where all creative potentialities exist together, infinitely correlated yet unexpressed. It is a state of perfect order, the matrix from where all the laws of nature emerge. (p. 123)

As a result of the repeated direct experience of the unified field in the state of transcendental consciousness, the individual's life becomes completely evolutionary and life supporting (Maharishi Mahesh Yogi, 1994). With regard to modern criminological theory, the unified field can be said to be the ultimate source of informal social control–self control from within that puts the individual in harmony with the environment and society without need for recourse to external coercion.

Maharishi (1972) explains with a simple analogy how the experience of the unified field of nature's intelligence at once strengthens individuality and brings individual life into harmony with society. He states:

> When sap is supplied, each different leaf and petal is enriched, but at the same time, the unifying value, the area where all the petals and leaves meet, is also strengthened. Thus the green becomes more green; the red becomes more red. The sap strengthens and supports diversity, while integrating all aspects into a unity. When the petals become enlivened, then the unity of the petals, the flower as a whole, is fresh and bold. Whole and parts are developed simultaneously. (Lesson 10)

Over 600 studies conducted in 200 universities and research institutes suggest that practice of the TM program strengthens the diverse qualities of individuality, while at the same time it unifies the individual with society (Chalmers, Clements, Schenkluhn, & Weinless, 1989; Orme-Johnson & Farrow, 1977; Wallace, Orme-Johnson, & Dillbeck, 1990). In terms of reducing risk factors for crime, the effects of the TM program on the individual include reduced stress (Eppley, Abrams, & Shear, 1989; Walton & Levitsky, 1994; Walton & Levitsky, this volume), increased serotonin–low levels of serotonin are correlated with criminal aggression (Bujatti & Riederer, 1976; Walton & Levitsky, 1994; Walton & Levitsky, this volume); reduced hostility, aggression, and recidivism in prison inmates (Abrams & Siegel, 1978; Bleick & Abrams, 1987; Orme-Johnson, 1981); reduced substance abuse (O'Connell & Alexander, 1994); increased job satisfaction and productivity, and improved relations with supervisors and co-workers (Schmidt-Wilk, Alexander, & Swanson, 1996); happier marriages (Aron & Aron, 1982); improved school climate (Nidich & Nidich, 1988); accelerated cognitive and personality development (Alexander et al., 1990; Alexander, Rainforth, & Gelderloos, 1991; Cranson et al., 1991; Alexander & Orme-Johnson, this volume); increased academic achievement (Nidich & Nidich, 1989a; Nidich, Nidich, & Rainforth, 1986); and improved police effectiveness (Anklesaria & King, 1993a). (Also, see other papers in this volume.)

In Maharishi Vedic science, the changes produced in the individual spread throughout society through the field of collective consciousness. Maharishi (1977a) describes collective consciousness and its reciprocal relation to the individual as follows:

> Just as the quality of consciousness of an individual determines the quality of his thought and behaviour, so also there exists another type of consciousness for a society as a whole: a collective consciousness for each

> family, city, state, or nation, having its own reality and the possibility of growth. The quality of the collective consciousness is a direct and sensitive reflection of the level of consciousness of its individual members. . . . Enriched collective consciousness further enriches individual consciousness. It is through the mutual enrichment of individual and collective consciousness that an ideal society is born. (pp. 91, 138)

In this view, stressed individuals contribute stress to collective consciousness, which influences everyone else in society and increases the probability of crime and other problems. The more stressed the individuals in society are, the more stressed the collective consciousness becomes. This typically results in a more totalitarian state needed to maintain some semblance of order in society. On the other hand, when individuals experience transcendental consciousness, which is the unified field of natural law, their contribution to the collective consciousness becomes more coherent. As a result, society becomes increasingly integrated by intrinsic, internal control, which arises from the most fundamental level of order in nature, the unified field.

One more principle needs to be mentioned before turning to research testing this theory in the arena of crime prevention. This is the principle that coherence is more powerful than incoherence, which is found throughout nature. Applied to crime, this principle means that only a relatively few individuals functioning more coherently can overcome the incoherent influence of the stressed elements in the population. Coherent elements of a system exert an influence proportional to their number squared, whereas the effect of the incoherent elements is only proportional to their number. From this, Maharishi estimated that when the number of people practicing the TM program exceeded only a small fraction of the population–on the order of 1%–an influence of coherence would spread throughout society. This prediction has been experimentally verified many times; it was named the Maharishi Effect in honor of Maharishi (Borland & Landrith III, 1977; Orme-Johnson, 1994). A review of research on the Maharishi Effect follows.

In 1976, with the introduction of the more advanced TM-Sidhi program, a more powerful effect was expected (Maharishi Mahesh Yogi, 1996). Whereas the TM program allows the mind to settle to transcendental consciousness, the TM-Sidhi program trains the mind to think and act from transcendental consciousness, propagating waves of coherence throughout society. Research on the individual has shown that the TM-Sidhi program results in a wider distribution within the brain of the brain's response to sensory input, as well as an increase in the amplitude of cortical and brain stem responses to somatosensory stimuli (Lyubimov, 1992; Petrenko, Orlova, & Lyubimov, 1993). When added to the TM program, the TM-Sidhi program produces acute and long-term increases in EEG coherence (Orme-Johnson, Wallace, & Dillbeck, 1989; Travis & Orme-Johnson, 1990), particularly in those parameters of EEG coherence that are correlated with creativity, concept learning, moral reasoning, and neurological efficiency (Dillbeck, Orme-Johnson, & Wallace, 1981; Jedrczak, Toomey, & Clements, 1986; Nidich, Ryncarz, Abrams, Orme-Johnson, & Wallace, 1983; Orme-Johnson & Haynes, 1981). One aspect of the TM-Sidhi program is Yogic Flying, in which electroencephalogram (EEG) coherence is maximum at the point of liftoff, and alpha wave activity is sustained, indicating stabilization of the integrative effects of transcendental consciousness in activity (Orme-Johnson, 1988b; Orme-Johnson, Clements, Haynes, & Badawi, 1977; Travis & Orme-Johnson, 1990). The TM-Sidhi program integrates and rejuvenates the entire mind/body system, as indicated by enhanced neurological efficiency (Wallace, Mills, Orme-Johnson, Dillbeck, & Jacobe, 1983), improved efficiency of concept learning (Dillbeck, Orme-Johnson et al., 1981), increased sensitivity and balance of endocrine systems (Werner et al., 1986; Walton, Pugh, Gelderloos, & Macrae, 1995), and reduced physiological indicators of biological aging (Jedrczak, Beresford, & Clements, 1985). Moreover, research has found that when a group practicing the TM-Sidhi program together in one place exceeds the square root of 1% of the population, there are measurable effects of crime reduction in the larger society, a phenomenon known as the Extended Maharishi Effect (Dillbeck et al., 1987; Hagelin, 1987; Maharishi Mahesh Yogi, 1986a; Orme-Johnson et al., 1988).

EMPIRICAL RESEARCH ON THE MAHARISHI EFFECT

This review is a primary evidence analysis of published research on the Maharishi Effect and the Extended Maharishi Effect. The following 15 studies summarize the published research on the reduction of crime and improved quality of life in society through the Maharishi Effect. Studies 1 through 9, and 12 are on cities and metropolitan areas, studies 10 and 11 are on the state or provincial level, and studies 12 through 15 are on the national and international levels. Studies 1 through 3 are epidemiological, the study of the distribution and determinants of crime prevalence (MacMahon, Pugh, & Ipsen, 1960). In this case, epidemiological means the comparison of areas in which more people learned the TM program with areas in which fewer people learned. Studies 4 through 15 involved either experimentally changing the number of meditators in an area and observing the subsequent changes in crime rate and quality of life or using time series analysis to study the relationship between naturally occurring changes in the group size of the TM-Sidhi program participants and changes in crime rate. Trends, seasonal effects, other periodicities in the data, and influences of other variables were controlled using Box-Jenkins autoregressive integrated moving averages (ARIMA) time series analysis (Box & Jenkins, 1976; McCleary & Hay, Jr., 1980). Whereas studies 1 through 3 focus on the Maharishi Effect, which is the change in crime due to 1% of the population learning the TM program, studies 4 through 15 consider the Extended Maharishi Effect, the effects of a group of the square root of 1% of a population practicing the more powerful TM-Sidhi program, including Yogic Flying (Maharishi Mahesh Yogi, 1986a).

Studies on the City and Metropolitan Level

1. Twenty-Four U.S. Cities–A Retrospective Study

This study examined all 24 cities in the United States with populations over 10,000 in which 1% or more of their populations were practicing the TM program by 1972. These experimental cities were compared to 24 control cities selected by an independent investigator prior to collection of the last several years of data. Matching variables were total population, college population, and geographic region (Dillbeck, Landrith, III, & Orme-Johnson, 1981). In the control cities, less than 0.7% of the population had learned the TM technique. Stepwise discriminant analysis showed that 1% cities and control cities were similar on per capita income, percentage of persons aged 15 to 29, stability of residence, percentage unemployed, and percentage of families with incomes below poverty level. The two groups of cities did differ on median years education and pre-intervention crime rate slope, which were controlled statistically by analysis of covariance.

The study examined change in the Federal Bureau of Investigation (FBI) total crime index in 1973, the year after the 1% cities reached 1%, as well as the change in crime-rate trend for 6 years from 1972-1977. Change in crime rate in 1973 was assessed as the difference in the actual 1973 crime rate from the level predicted by linear regression on the 6-year pre-intervention baseline period from 1967-72. Change in crime-rate trend was assessed by comparing the slope of regression on the post-intervention period with the slope for the pre-intervention period.

In 1973, there was a significant (24%) decrease in crime rate in 1% cities relative to controls ($p < .001$). In addition, the post-intervention slope of the crime trend for the 1% cities decreased, compared to an increase in the slope in the control cities ($p < .025$). During the post-intervention period, the mean slope of change in crime rate for the 1% cities was not significantly different from zero, while the slope for the control cities was significantly greater than zero ($p < .0001$). This result indicates that the crime rate continued to increase in the control cities, but was arrested in the 1% cities.

Because this study took place in a period when cities of this size were increasingly complying with FBI standards for reporting to the Uniform Crime Report index, a second analysis was conducted on a reduced sample of twenty 1% and twenty control cities, eliminating all cities showing a sudden increase in crime that might have been an artifact due to a change in police reporting procedures. The results for this reduced sample were similar to those for the whole sample: a 22% decrease in crime in 1% cities in 1973 compared to an increase of 2% in control cities ($p < .005$) and a reduction of 89% in crime-rate trend in the 1% cities compared to an increase of 53% in control cities ($p < .05$). In addition, a significant correlation was found between the percentage of TM-program participants in each city in 1972 and the crime rate change in 1973 ($r = .53, p < .001$) as well as between percentage of TM program participants and the crime trend (change in slope, $r = .41, p = .01$). This study demonstrated that the Maharishi Effect is immediately apparent in the crime rate and is also apparent as a long-term effect that persists over many years. The study also found that the effects of the meditators were independent of the influences of major demographic variables known to alter crime rates.

2. One Hundred and Sixty U.S. Cities–A Causal Analysis

Causality implies lagged correlation, i.e., the cause should precede the effect in time (McCleary & Hay, Jr., 1980). One type of causal analysis, called cross-lagged panel correlation, compares the synchronous correlation (the correlation between two variables at the same time) with the lagged correlations (the correlation of a variable with another variable at earlier and later times). The hypothesis that A is causing B is supported if variations in A are followed in time by correlated changes in B, whereas changes in B are not followed in time by correlated changes in A, assuming that the synchronous correlations at both time periods are equal (Kenny, 1979).

Crime data are readily available for cities only on a yearly basis, so rapidly changing processes cannot be studied using these data. However, because the TM program–once begun–is practiced twice a day on an ongoing basis, yearly data are expected to capture the dynamics of the prediction that rising numbers of TM participants will cause a decline in crime rate in subsequent years. This prediction was tested in a stratified random sample of 160 U.S. cities, with 40 cities in each of four population groups: greater than 250,000; 100,000 to 250,000; 50,000 to 100,000; and 25,000 to 50,000 (Dillbeck, Banus, Polanzi, & Landrith, III, 1988). This sample comprised 25% of the total urban population of the U.S. (1970 census) studied over the 15-year period 1964 to 1978. As before, FBI total index crime data were used.

For each city, a trend line was calculated that represented changes in crime rate from 1964 to 1971, before significantly large numbers began practicing the TM program in the U.S. The trend line was projected from 1972 to 1978 to predict what the crime rate would have been had the earlier trend continued. The trend of increasing crime seen from 1964 to 1971 was predicted to continue in the period from 1972 to 1978 in cities with low percentages of TM participants. However, in the cities with high percentages of TM participation, the slope of the crime-rate trends was predicted to decline below the previous slopes. Partial correlations were used to control for 10 specific social variables known to influence crime: median years education, percent unemployed, per capita income, percent of families in poverty, stability of residency over 5 years, median age, percent over age 65, population size, population density, and ratio of police per population. The assumption of stationarity was tested and upheld.

Except for one, in which the difference was essentially zero, the crossed-lagged differences were each in the direction that would be predicted by the hypothesis of TM program causality (p-values ranging from < .01 to .05). Because some of the smaller cities in the random sample could have been part of a larger metropolitan area, a second cross-lagged panel analysis was conducted using Standard Metropolitan Statistical Areas (SMSAs).

3. Eighty U.S. Standard Metropolitan Statistical Areas (SMSAs)– A Second Causal Analysis

Using the same causal analysis as above for the 16-year period from 1964 to 1979, a second study was conducted on a random sample of 80 SMSAs that constituted 55% of the SMSAs in the U.S. with over 200,000 population. This sample included 47% of the total metropolitan population of the U.S. The results were essentially the same as with the cities: a stable causal structure was found that supported the hypothesis that the Maharishi Effect reduced crime rate. Both raw correlations and partial correlations, which controlled for other variables known to influence crime, showed that level of TM participation predicted reduced crime in subsequent years ($p < .01$ for each year). The magnitudes of the correlations of TM leading to crime decrease were small, an average of −.22, accounting for 5% of the total variance. However, a correlation of this magnitude is equivalent to an improvement of 17.6% in a dichotomous outcome variable (e.g., cure rate) due to a treatment (Rosenthal & Rubin, 1982).

4. Union Territory of Delhi–Decreased Crime (1980-1981)

A study in India involved time series analysis of the impact on crime rate in New Delhi of a group of TM-Sidhi program experts attending a course in Vedic Science there from November 1980 to early April 1981. The impact of the group was assessed on a time series comprising 304 observations of daily crime totals for Delhi from June 1980 to March 1981. After weekly, monthly, and other cycles and trends were removed from the time series, the estimated impact of the group was highly statistically significant ($p < .0001$), indicating a decrease in crime by 11% from the pre-intervention average. The size and statistical significance of the intervention parameters proved to be highly robust to alternative specifications of the noise model. This reduction in Delhi's crime rate could not be accounted for by changes in governmental policies. A detailed analysis by an Indian police official showed that there were no changes in local police policy, no special drives on crime, no systematic transfer of police staff, and no apparent change in the number of criminals through externment or court clearance (Dillbeck et al., 1987).

5. Metro Manila Region–Decreased Crime and Death (1979-1981)

A study in the Philippines found that a group of approximately 400 TM and TM-Sidhi participants, who regularly practiced their program together as part of their jobs, had a significant positive effect ($p < .025$) on a monthly quality-of-life index. The index was comprised of crime totals, fetal deaths, and other deaths, the most unambiguous indicators of quality of life available for study in this experiment (Dillbeck et al., 1987).

6. Metro Manila–Decreased Crime (1984-1985)

The second study in the Philippines was on the weekly time series of crime totals for Metro Manila's 8 million population from December 31, 1982, to March 7, 1985. A large group of approximately 1,500 teachers of the TM program who also practiced the TM-Sidhi program went to Manila, principally in August and September 1984, because of a demand for the TM program in rehabilitation and educational settings. There were more than 300 TM and TM-Sidhi program participants, the square root of 1% of Manila's population, in the city during the experimental period from August to January. Impact-assessment analysis indicated that crime decreased significantly during the experimental period by 12.1% ($p < .005$) (Dillbeck et al., 1987).

7. Washington, D.C.–Decreased Violent Crime (1981-1983)

Maharishi University of Management (then called Maharishi International University) opened a branch campus in Washington, D.C., called the College of Natural Law. This was for the expressed purpose of creating coherence in the nation's capital. A study using the transfer function approach of time series analysis supported a causal relationship between participation in the group practice of the TM and TM-Sidhi programs at the College of Natural Law and decreased violent crimes in Washington over the 2-year period of the study. Alternative explanations in terms of weather, changes in police coverage, demographic shifts, or increases in neighborhood watch programs could not account for the results (Dillbeck et al., 1988). When the College of Natural Law had to move from Washington, a move which began in 1986 and ended in 1987, the homicides in Washington, D.C., increased drastically to become the highest in the nation in 1990.

8. Merseyside, England–Decreased Crime (1988-1991)

A time series analysis on monthly crime data and a coherence-creating group practicing the TM-Sidhi program showed a phase transition to decreased crime in March 1988 when the group size exceeded the predicted threshold of the square root of 1% of the population. The crime rate fell by 16% in Merseyside ($p = .00006$), whereas during the same period in the rest of England and Wales, it increased by 20%. Merseyside moved from the third highest crime rate of all metropolitan areas in the U.K. to the second lowest area. There were 170,000 fewer crimes in Merseyside than expected over the 3.5-year experimental period, and the projected savings to the government was 850 million British pounds (Hatchard, Deans, Cavanaugh, & Orme-Johnson, 1996).

9. Washington, D.C.–Decreased Violent Crime (1993)

This study was a prospective experiment in which a group of approximately 4,000 participants in the TM and TM-Sidhi programs assembled in Washington, D.C., from June 7 to July 30, 1993. The hypothesis that levels of violent crime in the District of Columbia would fall substantially below the predicted crime trend during the demonstration project was posited with a 27-member Project Review Board comprised of independent scientists and leading citizens. The Board approved the research protocol and monitored the research process. The District of Columbia Metropolitan Police Department (DCMPD) provided weekly crime data from a database used for their FBI Uniform Crime Reports. The study statistically controlled for the effects of weather variables, daylight, historical crime trends and annual patterns in the District of Columbia, as well as trends in neighboring cities.

Time series analysis of 1993 data showed that homicide, rape, and assault (HRA) crimes dropped significantly during the demonstration project, corresponding to increases in the size of the group. The maximum decrease was 23.3%, $p < 2 \times 10^{-9}$ (24.6% using a longer baseline, with 1988-1993 data, $p < 3 \times 10^{-5}$), coincident with the peak number of participants in the group during the final week of the assembly. No significant decreases in HRA crimes were found during the same period in each of the 5 previous years. Nor could the effect of the coherence-creating group on reducing HRA crimes be accounted for by additional police staffing. The results for HRA crime were highly robust to alternative time series model specifications and showed that the effect of the group size was cumulative and persisted after the demonstration project ended. Calculation of the steady-state gain, based on the time series model, predicted that a permanent group of 4,000 coherence-creating experts in the District would have a long-term effect of reducing HRA crimes by 48% (Hagelin, Rainforth, Orme-Johnson, Cavanaugh, & Alexander, 1999).

It should also be noted that another major purpose of the project, which was lodged in advance, was to create coherence for the national government. During the project, a floundering Clinton administration suddenly began to make progress. On July 18th, journalist Sally Quinn (1993) wrote in *The Washington Post*:

> Well, in case anyone hasn't noticed, Washington is in a lull, at least from the vantage point of the inmates. . . . [T]he Clinton administration appears to have revived. . . . But such a swift reversal of political fortune is not easy to account for. The inmates may logically wonder whether Clinton really turned things around or if something else is going on . . . almost mysteriously and almost overnight, in the face of government distress . . . (p. C1)

This change was also observed from inside the White House. Clinton's special assistant and White House press secretary, George Stephanopoulos (1999), wrote of that period that by the Fall of 1993, the Clinton White House had found its footing. It held the Middle East peace ceremony, passed NAFTA and the Brady bill, got its economic plan through, and had proposed the centerpiece of our domestic agenda: health-care reform. Time series analysis showed that, coincident with the onset of the demonstration project, President Clinton's approval rating increased ($p = 5.29 \times 10^{-8}$), media positivity increased towards him ($p = .01$), and all five available indicators of social stress in the District decreased [i.e., emergency psychiatric calls ($p = .009$), hospital trauma cases ($p = .02$), complaints against the police ($p = .01$), accidental deaths ($p = .05$), and a social stress index comprised of these four variables ($p = 3.22 \times 10^{-5}$; Goodman, Orme-Johnson, Rainforth, & Goodman, 1997)].

Studies on the State and Provincial Level

10. The Ideal Society Campaign–An Experimental Study

The first publicly announced, prospective experimental research on the sociological effects of groups collectively practicing the TM-Sidhi program was undertaken in the summer of 1978, as part of a project called the Ideal Society Campaign held in 20 countries. In the U.S., a group of approximately 300 teachers of the TM program went to the state of Rhode Island, with part of their objective being to teach the TM program to 1% of the population.

By the beginning of August 1978, only about 5,045–half the required num ber of 1% of the population–had been instructed in Rhode Island. This included those who previously had learned the TM technique. However, the 300 TM teachers who went to Rhode Island practiced the TM-Sidhi program together in small groups in various cities throughout the state. This added influence was calculated to be sufficient to create coherence for a population of 532,000. This, together with the 5,045 TM participants, was predicted to exceed the threshold for creating a transition to improved quality of life in Rhode Island's entire one million population (Dillbeck et al., 1987).

This prediction was evaluated using time series analysis of a composite index of eight variables for 7 years of monthly data from 1974 to 1980. Because the group was there in 1978, the analysis included data for more than 2 years after the experimental period. The eight variables were FBI total crime, motor-vehicle fatality rate, motor-vehicle accident rate, death rate, per capita beer consumption, per capita cigarette consumption, unemployment rate, and degree of pollution (particulates). To control for the possibility that the quality of life generally improved in that region of the U.S., the quality of life in Rhode Island was contrasted with that of a nearby state of similar population, Delaware.

Time series analysis found that during the Ideal Society Campaign, the quality of life in Rhode Island significantly improved ($p < .01$). A significant but less pronounced improvement continued after the intervention ($p < .01$). These results indicate that direct intervention of a large group of participants in the Transcendental Meditation and TM-Sidhi programs improves the quality of life on the state level. Quality of life was assessed using not only the FBI total crime index but also two major crime risk factors–unemployment and alcohol (beer) consumption–as well as a variety of other measures that indicated a general increase in coherence in society.

11. Puerto Rico–Decreased Crime (1984)

A time series analysis of the impact of a TM-Sidhi group of more than the square root of 1% of Puerto Rico's 3.4 million population ($n = 185$) from April to June 1984 showed a decrease of 543.1 crimes per month ($p < .025$) during the group's presence in the territory, compared with the mean of the series at other times. The police department had established an air-to-ground surveillance system using helicopters, patrol cars, and motorcycles in May 1980, but an impact-assessment series analysis of this program showed that its effect on crime was statistically insignificant. There was no other apparent alternative explanation for the effect of the TM-Sidhi group (Dillbeck et al., 1987).

Studies on the National and International Levels

12. Israel–Decreased Crime and Improved Quality of Life in Jerusalem and in Israel as a Whole, and Decreased War Intensity in Lebanon (1983)

This project was designed by the late Charles N. Alexander as a critical experimental demonstration of the Maharishi Effect on armed conflict in a major trouble-spot area, the civil war in Lebanon. The experiment created a group of resident Israeli TM and TM-Sidhi experts in Jerusalem at an arbitrarily chosen time (July and August 1983) to test the effect of the group on crime and quality of life in Jerusalem and in Israel as a whole as well as on the war in Lebanon. The major hypotheses and the proposed categories of measurements were lodged in advance of the experiment with a group of research scientists in the

U.S. and Israel. Upon arrival in Israel, the authors met with Israeli scientists to finalize selection of a smaller subset of measures.

The analysis of the project used all of the non-redundant daily time series data available at the time the researchers left Israel in the fall of 1983; these included eight social indicators: (1) crime in Jerusalem, (2) crime in Israel as a whole, (3) automobile accidents in Jerusalem that involved personal injury, (4) fires in Jerusalem, (5) a stock index of all freely traded stocks on the Tel Aviv stock exchange, (6) a national-mood scale derived from content analysis of a major newspaper, (7) reported war deaths of all factions in the Lebanese war, and (8) a war-intensity scale of the Lebanese war derived by newspaper content analysis.

The critical thresholds of TM-Sidhi program participants needed for Jerusalem, Israel, and Lebanon were calculated at 65, 122, and 197, respectively, which took into account the number of practitioners already in the area. The size of the experimental group actually fluctuated between 65 and 241 during the experiment.

Time series transfer function analysis indicated that crime decreased by 7.4% in Jerusalem ($p = .023$) and by 4.1% in Israel as a whole ($p = .022$). When the TM-Sidhi group was largest, an impact on the war in Lebanon was seen, as evidenced by decreases in war deaths ($p = .019$) and war intensity ($p = .0045$; Orme-Johnson et al., 1988). This result of decreased war in Lebanon due to groups practicing the TM-Sidhi program has been replicated seven times (Davies, 1988; Davies, Alexander, & Orme-Johnson, 1988).

For the study in Israel, the effects were generally stronger on composite quality-of-life indices than for individual measures such as crime. The overall composite index of all variables showed an increase of 1.69 standard deviations ($p < .0001$). The observation that the results for the indices were stronger than for the individual variables suggests the presence of a common influence of coherence acting on all the variables at once. In the presence of such an influence, the common variance would be enhanced due to an averaging out of the random components across measures. This result supports the hypothesis that the TM and TM-Sidhi techniques operate to create coherence on a fundamental, unifying level of natural law (Orme-Johnson, Alexander, & Davies, 1990; Orme-Johnson et al., 1988).

13. United States–Decreased Index of Homicide, Suicide and Motor Vehicle Fatalities (1979-1985)

This study assessed the influence of the group practice of the TM and TM-Sidhi programs at Maharishi University of Management (Fairfield, Iowa) on reducing violent death in the U.S. due to homicide, motor vehicle accidents, and suicide. The major period of the study was from 1982 to 1985, during which time the size of the group in Iowa was frequently larger than the square root of 1% threshold for the U.S. The last year for which violent fatality data were available at the time of the study was 1985. A secondary analysis was also conducted over the period 1979 to 1985, which included the inception of the group practice at Maharishi University of Management in 1979.

Box-Jenkins time series analysis–using the impact assessment approach on a weekly aggregate index of homicide, motor vehicle accidents, and suicide–indicated a statistically significant decline in violent deaths (31 fewer deaths per week, $p < .0001$) in the week immediately after the group of TM-Sidhi participants exceeded the predicted threshold of the square root of 1% of the U.S. population (1,500 in 1979 and 1,550 by the end of 1985). When the number of participants in the group was considered as a continuous variable, time series transfer function analysis indicated that increased TM-Sidhi group participation was associated with a significant decline in violent deaths that began in the same week and increased in magnitude during the following weeks. The steady-state gain associated with these effects indicated a decrease of 5.5% in violent deaths due to these causes when the TM-Sidhi group exceeded the square root of 1% of the U.S. population. A reverse transfer function analysis indicated that changes in the violence index did not lead to changes in the number of TM-Sidhi participants, supporting a conclusion that the TM-Sidhi group has a causal effect of reducing violent deaths in the U.S. (Dillbeck, 1990).

14. Canada–Improved Quality of National Life: Improvements on a Weekly Index Including Homicide, Suicide, and Motor Vehicle Fatalities (1983-1985); Improvements on a Monthly Index Including Homicide, Suicide, Motor Vehicle Fatalities, Cigarette Consumption, and Worker-Days Lost in Strikes (1972-1986)

This study used the same weekly measure of national violence (homicide, motor vehicle accidents, and suicide) for Canada as had previously been used for the U.S. in the study described above. It found that during the weeks from 1982 to 1985 in which the size of group practice of the TM-Sidhi program at Maharishi University of Management in Iowa reached the square root of 1% of the combined population of the U.S. and Canada, violence decreased in Canada ($p < .01$). A simultaneous reduction of fatalities due to all other accidents also occurred ($p < .005$). This study also measured a monthly index of quality of life for Canada for 1972 through 1985, consisting of violent fatalities, cigarette consumption, and worker-days lost in strikes. When the predicted threshold for the combined U.S.-Canada population was reached by the Maharishi University of Management group, there was a significant improvement in the quality of life in Canada on this index ($p < .001$; Assimakis & Dillbeck, 1995).

15. Decreased International Terrorism (1983-1985)

Terrorism is crime committed for political purposes, often on the international level. This study was of the impact of three large assemblies approaching the square root of 1% of the population of the world (n = 7,000). The dependent variable was the number of casualties and injuries due to international terrorism, obtained from the Rand Corporation data bank for 1983-1985 and aggregated into 5-day periods. Using time series intervention analysis to estimate the combined effects of the assemblies, the study found a significant reduction in terrorism after the beginning of the assemblies ($p < .025$). The study also found significant decreases in international conflicts during the assemblies, as indicated by content analysis of major newspapers (Orme-Johnson, Dillbeck, Alexander, Chandler, & Cranson, 1989; Orme-Johnson, Dillbeck, & Alexander, this volume). This worldwide influence of coherence has been named the Global Maharishi Effect. Other research has replicated decreased international and domestic armed conflict through the Extended Maharishi Effect (Davies, 1988; Davies et al., 1988; Orme-Johnson et al., 1988; Orme-Johnson, Dillbeck, Bousquet, & Alexander, 1989).

DISCUSSION

A recent major review of crime prevention research proposed that research in this area should address three major questions (Sherman et al., 1997). In the context of the Maharishi Effect, these questions are:

1. What are the independent effects of the Maharishi Effect?
2. What conditions are required for the Maharishi Effect to work?
3. What is the cost effectiveness of the Maharishi Effect?

What Are the Independent Influences of the Maharishi Effect?

The results of the 15 studies reviewed previously far exceed the criteria currently being applied to determine crime prevention approaches that work. The current definition of what works in crime prevention is "at least two confirming studies at a moderate level of methodological rigor, with the preponderance of other evidence supporting the same conclusion" (Sherman et al., 1997, Appendix: Research Methods, pp. A-4, A-6). The sample sizes of all studies on the Maharishi Effect are much larger than for other research on crime prevention. All studies on the Maharishi Effect are at least at the city level, whereas no previous crime prevention studies have reached the city level (Sherman et al., 1997). The Maharishi Effect studies typically cover substantially longer periods of time than previous research, up to 15 years (Dillbeck et al., 1988). All Maharishi Effect studies either used a control group or statistically controlled for other variables known to influence crime; appropriate, state-of-the-art inferential statistics were used to draw quantitative conclusions and causal inferences. The measurement variables were objective, publicly available data, usually FBI Uniform Crime Report statistics. Although reported crime is known to underestimate actual crime, this source of error can be considered constant across baseline, experimental, and control conditions and should not affect the overall conclusions, especially when results have been replicated many times.

In the context of previous research on crime prevention, which has shown limited effectiveness and generality (Sherman et al., 1997), these are truly remarkable findings. An eminent reviewer of the research on the Maharishi Effect, with 30 years of experience in academic study, teaching, and writing in the field of international relations, stated:

> The claim can be made plausibly that the promised practical societal impact of this research significantly exceeds that of any other ongoing social-psychological research program. For this reason alone, the research along with the theory that informs it deserves the most serious evaluative consideration by the social science community. (Edwards, 1990, p. 3)

Because empirical facts without a theoretical context do not constitute science, implicit in a consideration of the independent effects constituting the Maharishi Effect is a consideration of its theory. As we have seen, the proposition of a universal field of consciousness underlying nature is in accord with the leading edge of quantum field theory. The influence of individuals on others at a distance is an action-at-a-distance phenomenon. Physics explains action-at-a-distance, such as radio or gravitation, in terms of fields–in these cases, by the electromagnetic (EM) and gravitational fields, respectively. What field might mediate the action at a distance evident in the Maharishi Effect? Low level EM fields do influence biological systems, including the human nervous system (Adey & Bawin, 1977). However, the EM radiation emitted by the human nervous system appears to be of orders of magnitude too small to be detected by another human at a distance (Orme-Johnson et al., 1988). The other fundamental force fields–the strong and weak interactions and gravitation–are also of inappropriate scales to mediate direct effects between humans. Hagelin (1987) has proposed that the Maharishi Effect is mediated by the agency of the unified field due to the intrinsically nonlocal structure of space-time at this scale.

Hagelin (1987) points out that if the effect is mediated by the unified field, it will not necessarily fall off as a precise function of the inverse square of the distance from the source, as is the case with other known fields. There are, however, known distance-related differences in the influences associated with the Maharishi Effect. For example, crime decreases in cities with 1% or more practicing the TM program but not in other cities (Dillbeck, Landrith, III et al., 1981). The Vedic tradition at the source of the TM and TM-Sidhi programs notes these distance effects. For example, the Yoga sutras of Patanjali (trans. 1912/1978), of thousands of years antiquity, state: "*Tat sannidhau vairatyagah*"

(Yoga-Sutra, 2.35). This is translated by Maharishi Mahesh Yogi (1996) as follows: "In the vicinity of Yogic influence–unifying influence, integrating influence, coherent and harmonious influence–conflicting tendencies do not arise" (p. 11).

In this model, the reduction of crime in the Maharishi Effect occurs in part because the effectiveness of all other programs of crime prevention is enhanced. Studies have shown that the action-at-a-distance effects of the TM and TM-Sidhi programs reduce risk factors for crime, such as unemployment and inflation (Cavanaugh, 1987; Cavanaugh & King, 1988; Cavanaugh, King, & Ertuna, 1989; Cavanaugh, King, & Titus, 1989). Changes in other risk factors include reductions in alcohol consumption and divorces as well as improvements in quality of life variables, such as suicides, the number of civil cases reaching trial, cigarette consumption, pollution, traffic fatalities, infectious diseases, and all-cause mortality (Dillbeck et al., 1987; Orme-Johnson & Gelderloos, 1988). Research on crime prevention has found that school programs that change the overall climate of the school are more effective than piecemeal approaches (Sherman, 1997a). The Maharishi Effect expands this holistic approach to the most holistic level of society, its collective consciousness, which influences all risk factors at once.

What Conditions Are Required for the Maharishi Effect to Be Seen?

Because the Maharishi Effect is based at a fundamental level of natural law that is self-sufficient, not depending on anything outside of itself, the Maharishi Effect is independent of specific external conditions. The only requirement is that 1% of the population practices the TM program or a group equal to or larger than the square root of 1% practices, the TM-Sidhi program together in one place. For example, research has shown that the Maharishi Effect is independent of the local culture, as indicated by its effectiveness in such diverse locations as the U.S., India, Puerto Rico, Canada, and the Philippines (see the Empirical Research section for references).

Research on other crime prevention modalities has found that the effectiveness of crime prevention programs in one area is conditional on informal social control by other institutions, such as the home, schools, and community. Unfortunately, previous crime prevention programs have been least successful in the high-crime populations that need them the most (Sherman et al., 1997). In contrast, the results found in the Maharishi Effect studies, involving action-at-a-distance or field effects, can involve high-crime areas without the necessity of going there. In all the studies on the Maharishi Effect, it was not the criminal population that was meditating, yet crime decreased.

A case in point is the demonstration project in Washington, D.C., a location that was known as the murder capital of the world in 1993. During the project, experts in the TM-Sidhi program from over 50 countries came to D.C. and remained meditating in their hotels. Yet assaults, rapes, and homicides decreased by 23% in the city at large. This effect was predicted in advance and could not be explained by changes in police activity, weather patterns, or other variables. In addition, other indicators of social stress decreased in Washington and the national government became more effective (Hagelin et al., 1999).

The potential ethical concern about influencing other people at a distance without their consent or even their knowledge is not a real issue because everyone in society is always influencing everyone else through collective consciousness anyway. The real issue involves the kind of influence one has, whether stressed or coherent. Is it ethical to stress everyone else in society when there is a means available to reduce the individual's stress and create coherence? Is it responsible to allow any government to flounder in a milieu of collective incoherence, wasting billions of dollars ineffectively fighting problems, when coherence can easily be created, that brings support only to useful undertakings?

Intentionality might pose another potential ethical concern. It needs to be pointed out that there is no intention on the part of the individual practitioners of the TM and TM-Sidhi programs to have any particular kind of influence. The meditators do not wish for crime reduction or for anything else during these techniques. They merely practice an innocent procedure that allows the mind to settle to transcendental consciousness, held to be the unified field of natural law. As a by-product of individuals directly experiencing the unified field, coherence is created in the individual and in society. The unified field works out an influence that fully supports the life of everyone in society, as only its infinite organizing power could.

What Is the Cost Effectiveness of This Approach to Reducing Crime?

The cost of crime in the U.S. in 1990 was estimated at $200 billion. This includes $80 billion in federal, state, and local government expenditures for the criminal justice system (Bureau of Justice Bulletin, 1993; Congressional Budget Office Report, 1990), police, and corrections (Cohen, 1990). It also includes another $120 billion in victims' expenses for medical care and lost property (Cohen, 1990).

The crime decrease due to the Maharishi Effect and Extended Maharishi Effect will depend on the percentage of the population involved. The studies reviewed above have used groups near the minimum requirement, that is, 1% TM-program participants in a population or the square root of 1% of a city, state, or country for a TM-Sidhi group. The mean reduction in crime under these conditions for all the studies was approximately 15%. However, the reduction of crime due to a full-fledged crime prevention program based on the Maharishi Effect research is estimated to be much greater, a 50% reduction of crime (Orme-Johnson, 1994). A full program would entail positioning TM and TM-Sidhi groups in three tiers: city, national, and world (Maharishi Mahesh Yogi, 1986b).

One proposal is to establish groups of approximately 1,000 in 50 major U.S. urban areas, along with a group of approximately 10,000 (in excess of the square root of 1% of the world's population and six times the square root of 1% of the national population) in Washington, D.C., to take care of the national and international levels. Based on the changes observed in prior research on the Maharishi Effect, the projected long-term cost benefit of such a program would be over $600 billion annually, resulting from its effects in reducing crime, stimulating the economy, reducing health care costs, and decreasing expenses associated with automobile accidents (Orme-Johnson, 1994). If every participant in the project were to receive a good salary (according to the national standard of living), and if facilities were built or rented for group practice of the TM and TM-Sidhi programs, the cost of this project would be only a small fraction of the financial savings to the country. (For precise details about costs of such a project, individuals in positions of leadership may contact Maharishi University of Management in Fairfield, Iowa.) The practical implication of all the research on the Maharishi Effect is that this action-at-a-distance approach provides a remarkably effective but underused preventive factor for reducing crime. Its ability to generate coherence in collective consciousness and thus strengthen informal social control on every level of society is unique in crime prevention; if properly supported, this approach could be a major avenue to reducing crime at the city, state, and even international levels.

NOTE

1. Transcendental Meditation, TM, and TM-Sidhi are registered or common law trademarks licensed to Maharishi Vedic Education Development Corporation and used under sublicense or with permission.

AUTHOR'S NOTE

Address correspondence to David Orme-Johnson, 191 Dalton Drive, Seagrove Beach, FL 32459 (E-mail: davidoj@gnt.net).

Transcendental Meditation in Criminal Rehabilitation and Crime Prevention. Pp. 283-302.

Preventing Terrorism and International Conflict: Effects of Large Assemblies of Participants in the *Transcendental Meditation* and *TM-Sidhi* Programs

DAVID W. ORME-JOHNSON

Maharishi University of Management

MICHAEL C. DILLBECK

Maharishi University of Management

CHARLES N. ALEXANDER

Maharishi University of Management

ABSTRACT This study tested the hypothesis that group practice of the Transcendental Meditation (TM)[1] and TM-Sidhi[1] programs by approximately the square root of 1% of the world's population globally reduces terrorism and international conflict. For 3 periods during 1983-1985, ranging from 8 to 11 days, practitioners of these programs assembled in one place to practice in a group. Data on the numbers of casualties and fatalities due to terrorism were obtained from the Rand Corporation and grouped as five-day aggregates, forming a single time series spanning the 3 assemblies. Data on international conflict were generated from date-blind ratings of news events in the *New York Times* and *London Times* to give comparable blocks for time series analysis before, during, and after each of the assemblies. Time series intervention analyses used the Akaike information criterion to objectively define optimal noise models. The analyses found a 72% drop in terrorism ($p <$ .025) and an average drop of 32% in international conflict (p values from < .005 to < .025) during the assemblies. These results are consistent with similar effects of smaller such assemblies on local populations and suggest that long-term implementation of groups could have a major impact on terrorism and international conflict worldwide.

KEYWORDS Terrorism, international conflict, Transcendental Meditation, consciousness, crime prevention

Terrorism is defined as the unlawful use of force and violence against persons or property to coerce a government or civilian population for political or social objectives (see Title 22 of the United States Code, Section 2656f[d]; U.S. Department of State, 1998). When war is viewed separately from its social and political justifications, it also is fundamentally a type of crime, violating religious and civil codes of moral behavior. War is condoned by society in the furtherance of political, economic, or social objectives. Yet many in society regard this killing and destruction as criminal, particularly when they do not agree with the objectives intended to excuse it.

Strategies for preventing war have fallen into two broad categories: (a) create more weapons, i.e., deterrence theory or peace through strength; and (b) destroy weapons, i.e., disarmament theory or peace through cooperation (Davies & Alexander, in press). Neither approach has been successful. With regards to deterrence, historical studies show that increasing armaments are highly correlated with increased war proneness (Singer, 1986; Gochman, 1990). Significant disarmament in a world of heavily armed antagonists has never been achieved because of mutual mistrust and misperception. In reality, then, no nation today can truly defend itself against destruction; it can only counter-destroy.

Terrorism presents a similar situation: No individual or group can truly protect itself from terrorist attack. The United States (U.S.) counterterrorist policy includes making no concessions and striking no deals with terrorists, bringing terrorists to justice for their crimes, and isolating and applying pressure to states that sponsor and support terrorism to force them to change their behavior. Yet terrorism continues worldwide, with 304 terrorist acts in 1997. As former President William Clinton declared after the terrorist attack in Luxor, Egypt, "Once again, we are reminded of a painful truth: Terrorism is a global threat. No nation is immune. That is why all nations must redouble our commitment to fight this scourge together" (U.S. Department of State, 1998, p. 3).

The theoretical perspective informing the present research, the Maharishi Vedic Science[1] program, is unique in the history of conflict resolution, both in its theory and in the extensive research demonstrating its effectiveness (for reviews, see Orme-Johnson, 1994, in press; Orme-Johnson & Dillbeck, 1987). The theory holds that international conflicts and terrorism, as well as crime and other indices of societal conflict, are fundamentally consequences of stress in collective consciousness (Maharishi Mahesh Yogi, 1977a, 1986a, 1996).

Collective consciousness is defined as the holistic level of a society that arises from and defines the quality of life in the population. Just as the trillions of individual cells in the human body have a holistic level of functioning that is associated with the consciousness of the individual, so, too, the individual members of a society have a holistic level of interaction that may be termed the collective consciousness of society (Maharishi Mahesh Yogi, 1977a). From this perspective, there is a level of collective consciousness associated with each level of social organization, e.g., family consciousness, community consciousness, state consciousness, national consciousness, and world consciousness.

The quality of the collective consciousness of each of these levels arises from the quality of consciousness of its individual members. Reciprocally, collective consciousness influences each individual member. Stress in individual lives, for example, creates stress in collective consciousness, which permeates society and influences everyone's behavior. According to Maharishi Mahesh Yogi (hereafter referred to as Maharishi), when stress in collective consciousness is allowed to accumulate, it not only raises the rates of crime, sickness, and other social problems but also may break out in collective violence, such as wars and terrorism (1986a).

> The basis of terrorism can be understood in this: Whatever may seem to be the cause of the outbursts of terrorism, whatever little excuses there are, these excuses arise on the surface of the human race only from the stress in world consciousness, and stress is not seen until it bursts out. (pp. 83-84)
>
> I don't see any solution to terrorism except creating coherence in world consciousness. No power of the sword can possibly eliminate terrorism. Many governments are involved in promoting terrorism, but there is no direct political, economic, or social measure to stop terrorism in the world except to educate the people to think and act according to natural law and by creating coherence in world consciousness. (p. 162)

Maharishi defines *life in accord with natural law* as life with greater cooperation and mutual support for the diverse objectives of different factions in the population (Maharishi Mahesh Yogi, 1986a). The rationale for the hypothesis that the Transcendental Meditation and TM-Sidhi programs promote thought and action in accord with natural law and create coherence in collective consciousness is that these programs provide the direct experience of the underlying universal field of pure consciousness, the unified field of natural law, which is the source of natural law that structures order and harmony throughout the universe (Hagelin, 1987). Following the principle that the influence of coherent members of a system is proportional to their number squared, it was predicted that as few as the square root of 1% of a population contacting the unified field of natural law through the Transcendental Meditation and TM-Sidhi programs would create a measurable influence of coherence throughout society (Maharishi Mahesh Yogi, 1986a).

Previous research on the city, state, and national levels has indicated that groups constituting the square root of 1% of the population practicing the Transcendental Meditation and TM-Sidhi programs together do reduce crime (Dillbeck, Banus, Polanzi, & Landrith, 1988; Dillbeck, Cavanaugh, Glenn, Orme-Johnson, & Mittlefehldt, 1987; Hagelin et al., 1999; Hatchard, Deans, Cavanaugh, & Orme-Johnson, 1996). These groups also have been found to improve quality of life (Assimakis & Dillbeck, 1995; Cavanaugh, 1987; Cavanaugh & King, 1988; Cavanaugh, King, & Ertuna, 1989; Dillbeck, 1990; Dillbeck & Rainforth, 1996; Orme-Johnson, Alexander, Davies, Chandler, & Larimore, 1988; Reeks, 1991). In addition, these groups reduce armed conflict (Orme-Johnson, Alexander, & Davies, 1990; Orme-Johnson et al., 1988) on the city, state, national, or international levels, depending on the size of the group.

The hypothesis of the present research is that participation in this program by the square root of 1% of the world's population (approximately 7,000 individuals at the time of the interventions) can create a field effect large enough to reduce tension and stress in the whole world population and, thereby, to create measurable reductions in terrorism and international conflict. This is the first research to test the ability of this technology to reduce social violence on a worldwide level.

METHOD

Independent Variable

The independent or intervention variable was the occurrence of large assemblies of participants in the Transcendental Meditation and TM-Sidhi programs. There have been three such large assemblies during which the number of participants approached or exceeded the threshold of participants predicted to produce an influence on a global scale: December 27, 1983, to January 6, 1984 (about 8,000 participants in Fairfield, Iowa); December 28, 1984, to January 6, 1985 (over 6,000 participants in The Hague, The Netherlands); and July 9-17, 1985 (about 5,500 participants in Washington, D.C.). Each assembly involved the twice-daily practice of the Transcendental Meditation and TM-Sidhi programs in large groups; other periods of the assembly were given to lectures and organizational activities. Each of these three assemblies constituted a planned experiment, with hypotheses regarding the predicted effects on conflict and terrorism made formally to scientists and journalists in advance.

Dependent Variables

International Conflict

For each of these assemblies, a separate daily time series was constructed from content analysis of one of the major newspapers that gives extensive coverage to international events–the *New York Times*, which has been widely used as the primary U.S. source for scoring international conflict and civil conflict (e.g., Taylor & Jodice, 1983, p. xvii) or the *London Times*, which has a somewhat broader coverage of European and African events. To meet the requirement of length for time series analysis, each time series covered at least a 2-month period, starting before the assembly began and ending sometime after its conclusion. For each assembly, articles were scored for international conflict using scales derived from Azar's (1980) conflict scale category. The dependent (endogenous) variable of international conflict was constructed from negative events only: The score for a given day was the sum of negative events for that day. For a negative event that involved different actions with various degrees of hostility, the most hostile action was scored. Ambiguity about the occurrence of an event or its duration was resolved by checking the Associated Press and United Press International archives.

Each article was scored by two raters blind to the date of the article. If the difference of the two scores between raters was no greater than one scale unit, the two scores were averaged. If there were larger differences between ratings (less than 1% of the cases), raters discussed the article with a third person until a consensus was reached. Interrater reliability was $r = .88$ for the Iowa assembly, $r = .97$ for the Holland assembly, and $r = .98$ for the Washington assembly. The slightly lower level of reliability for the Iowa assembly probably results from the fact that a different version of the rating scale was used, as described later in this article.

The collection of data on international conflict for the three assemblies was conducted initially in the context of three separate studies. Thus, there were slight variations in the length of the time period, in the method of selecting articles for scoring, and in the scales used. These small differences in methodology should provide a further test of the generalizability or robustness of results. For the Iowa and the Washington assemblies, articles were selected from the first three pages, the News Index, and the News Summary of the *New York Times*. For the Holland assembly, events were selected from the first six pages of the *London Times* or from the first two pages of the *London Sunday Times*. These differences in source, as well as differences in the length of the series for which content analysis was performed, were based on decisions made prior to examination of conflict events, as part of designing the three different intervention studies.

For the Iowa assembly, articles were selected in the following categories: (a) all articles reporting international conflicts in trouble-spot areas; (b) U.S.-Soviet relations pertaining to these conflict areas, to arms limitation talks, to the deployment of arms or missiles, or to any other indications of improved or worsened superpower relations; and (c) any politically motivated civil disturbance or terrorist act anywhere in the world. The scale used for the Iowa assembly was a simplified form of Azar's (1980) conflict scale, in which international and domestic conflicts were combined and in which the negative half of his 15-point scale was reduced to 4 negative scale points ranging from unchanged negative conditions (nonsignificant acts in an area currently undergoing conflict) to strong negativity (full-scale battles). The assessment of conflict was based on 206 articles (76.5% of a total of 269 articles, the remainder of which were judged to describe positive events). Analysis covered a 63-day period from November 26, 1983, to January 27, 1984, which constituted 31 days before, 11 during, and 21 after the assembly (a baseline period of at least 4 weeks before the intervention period was desired for modeling ongoing trends).

The scale used for rating conflict in the Holland and Washington assemblies was the negative half of a 15-point scale modeled on that of Azar. This 7-point scale, which ranged from mild verbal hostilities to full-scale war, combined Azar's International and Domestic Conflict Scale Categories (Azar, 1980) to permit scoring of both domestic and international political violence, since most conflicts include both.

For the Holland assembly, all articles concerning international relations or events in the specified pages of the *London Times* were selected for scoring. The dates of analysis were from November 30, 1984, to February 3, 1985. This comprised 66 days of which 28 days were before, 10 were during, and 28 were after the intervention. During this period, 318 articles were rated as negative events (69.6% of a total of 457 articles, with the remainder containing only events judged as positive).

For the Washington assembly, articles selected from the specified *New York Times* pages were those that met the same criteria listed above for the Iowa assembly. There were 129 days in this series–100 before, 8 during, and 21 after the intervention–covering the period from April 1 to August 7, 1985. Analysis of international conflict is based on 638 negatively scored articles (68.8% of the total of 927 articles, of which the remainder were positive events). Further details on the scales and scoring procedures are available from the authors.

International Terrorism

To increase reliability of the data on international terrorism, because the separate intervention periods were short, the combined influence of all three assemblies was estimated relative to a 2-year control period. A database of all international terrorist events worldwide, the Chronology of International Terrorism (Extract), was obtained from the Rand Corporation (1987). This data included the date of the event, a description of the event, and the number of fatalities and injuries resulting from it. The measure of terrorism used here was the sum of fatalities and injuries. The Rand Corporation data bank was derived from public domain sources by monitoring approximately 100 newspapers, journals, and periodicals. The definition of terrorism used in compiling the database was "violence, or the threat of violence, calculated to create an atmosphere of fear and alarm" (Rand Corporation, 1987, p. 1). All events were international in scope, excluding indigenous (domestic) incidents irrespective of their motivation. Incidents of separatist groups were included only when they took place outside of the country or when aimed at a foreign target within the country. Incidents that occurred in the midst of a war were not included in the data bank. Acts of kidnapping, attacks against installations, hijackings, barricade and hostage events, assassination, and incidents involving significant threats or conspiracies were all included. Hoaxes, arrests or discoveries of terrorists' caches, smuggling, bank robberies, or unsubstantiated threats were not included (Rand Corporation, 1987, pp. 1-2).

To be amenable for time series analysis, the terrorism data required aggregation. This aggregation was necessary because events occurred sporadically rather than continuously. Fatalities and injuries were, therefore, added together into one total, and data were aggregated into 219 five-day periods covering from January 2, 1983, to December 31, 1985. The 5-day interval was chosen to provide the best nonoverlapping fit with the intervention periods. Thus, a time period was not used as an intervention point if it had more than one day outside the dates of the assemblies. There were five intervention points, each of 5-day duration–two for each of the first two assemblies and one for the third.

Data Analysis

The effect of the independent variable on each dependent variable was assessed by time series intervention analysis using the autoregressive integrated moving averages (ARIMA) methodology of Box and Jenkins (1976). This approach allows intervention effects to be accurately estimated while controlling for any serial dependence, trends, or seasonality in the data over time (McCleary & Hay, 1980). In the intervention analysis, the independent variable takes the value of 0 when there is no intervention and the value of 1 during assemblies.

In intervention analysis, the serial dependence of the data is explicitly modeled in a noise model, which serves essentially as the null hypothesis for intervention effects. The finding of a significant intervention effect indicates that a new influence was present at the time of the intervention that could not be predicted from the previous history of the series. It should be noted that this is a very conservative analytical approach. It rigorously controls not only for the past history of the series but also effectively controls, through the noise model, for the influence of unmeasured continuous variables that might be determining the pattern of the series.

The noise model N_t has a form $N_t = [\varphi(B)]^{-1}\theta(B)a_t$, where $\varphi(B)$ and $\theta(B)$ specify autoregressive and moving average parameters, respectively, at various time lags, and where a_t is a series of independent and normally distributed random disturbances. In effect, the noise model removes the serial dependence of the data by modeling it, and the residuals to the noise model (a_t) form independent data points for which usual parametric statistical models are appropriate.

The simplest intervention model is an immediate and continuous effect during the period of the intervention. This is the zero-order transfer function $Y_t = C + \omega_n I_t + N_t$, where Y_t is the endogenous series (dependent variable), C is a possible constant, I_t is the binary intervention series, ω_n is the intervention effect to be estimated at time lag n, and N_t is the stochastic noise model for the endogenous series (McCleary & Hay, 1980, p. 145). In addition to the immediate and continuous effect, it is also possible to model interventions that have either a permanent effect with a gradual onset or an abrupt but temporary effect. These effects are modeled by the first-order transfer function $Y_t = C + f(I_t) + N_t$, where all terms are as previously defined except $f(I_t)$. For the gradual permanent intervention, this term is defined as $f(I_t) = (1 - \delta_1 B)^{-1}\omega_n I_t$, where ω_n is the intervention effect at lag n, and where δ_1 is the rate at which the intervention effect grows; for the abrupt temporary intervention, this term is $f(I_t) = (1 - \delta_1 B)^{-1}\omega_n(1-B)I_t$ (McCleary & Hay, 1980, p. 169). In assessing the three possible forms of intervention–abrupt permanent (zero-order function above), gradual permanent (first-order function above), or abrupt temporary (first-order function above)–the strategy recommended by McCleary and Hay (1980, pp. 168-171) was employed.

To systematize the choice of a noise model, an objective criterion of model diagnosis, the Akaike information criterion (AIC), was utilized (Akaike, 1973). The AIC is a criterion of optimal model choice within a framework of predictive inference for choosing the model most likely to describe another sample of the same process (Larimore, 1983). In this context, the AIC provides the best balance between the opposing goals of parsimony and model fit when evaluating model order and model structure (Larimore & Mehra, 1985), based on the fundamental statistical principles of repeated sampling, sufficiency, and an asymptotic version of the likelihood principle (Cox & Hinkley, 1973). The AIC is defined as AIC = -2 ln(maximum likelihood) + 2m, where ln is the natural logarithm and m is the number of model parameters (Larimore & Mehra, 1985). A lower value of the AIC indicates a better model. The maximum-likelihood term of the AIC can be interpreted as an indicator of fit, while the parameter term can be understood as a penalty for overmodeling.

In order to objectively identify the optimal model as defined by the AIC, the following procedure was used. Scale transformations (to make the data more normally distributed) and differencing transformations (to induce stationarity) were performed if necessary. Initial noise modeling was then carried out, assessing the major seasonal trends of the data and modeling possible intervention effects. On this basis, the intervention model was specified. The intervention and noise models were jointly estimated. Then the noise model was diagnosed using the AIC criterion, with the addition of new parameters guided, in the standard manner, by the autocorrelation and partial autocorrelation functions. At each step of addition, the criterion for which parameter to add, from the set of potential parameters suggested by diagnostic indicators, was the parameter that resulted in lowest AIC over the same set of effective observations (because the AIC is dependent upon sample size, and autoregressive parameters consume larger numbers of observations in estimating these models). The optimal model was then reestimated on the full data set available for that model. From this model, in a stepwise fashion, a set of further additional noise parameters was explored, leading to a set of sequentially nested noise models. This approach provided a reasonable and effective heuristic for searching the set of possible models while minimizing the AIC. Larimore (1983), as noted above, suggests absolute minimization of the AIC as the optimal model criterion. However, small differences in the AIC may correspond to the addition of nonsignificant parameters in the noise model. Therefore, at the point at which the best additional noise parameter led to a parameter estimate that did not reach statistical significance, the difference in AIC between the two models was subjected to a significance test (Larimore, 1986). The difference in AIC for two nested models can be tested by use of a generalized likelihood ratio test, which follows a chi-square distributed with degrees of freedom equal to the difference in the number of parameters in the two models (Larimore, 1986). If the probability value for the test was less than or equal to .05 after rounding to 2 decimal places, the additional parameter was added to the noise model.

Although minimization of the AIC was found to lead to complex noise models, the AIC has the virtue of being an objective indicator of model adequacy and of having a solid statistical foundation, as noted previously. In the case of more complex noise models, the inclusion of parameters in the noise model controls for additional seasonal cycles, thus providing for a more rigorous test of the hypothesis of interest, the effect of the intervention.

Reported *p* values for parameter estimates are based upon two-tailed tests for all noise model parameters and constants, and on one-tailed tests for intervention parameters, because the direction of effect is clearly predicted. Data were analyzed on a VAX 11/780 minicomputer using the BMDP 2T time series program. Two of the assemblies occurred at the end of the year. Therefore, after the major analysis for each variable, a secondary analysis is reported from data of previous years to assess the possibility that the observed results are due to seasonal, year-end effects.

RESULTS

International Conflict

Iowa Assembly

The international conflict series for the Iowa assembly, already in the form of a series of independently distributed random disturbances, required no ARIMA parameters in the noise model. The model for this series was $Y_t = C + \omega_0 I_t + a_t$, where C is a constant (the mean of the series), I_t is the exogenous intervention series, ω_0 is the immediate intervention effect, and a_t is a series of independent and randomly distributed disturbances. This form of the intervention function (zero-order transfer function) indicates an immediate, permanent effect during the assembly period. Both of the parameters were statistically significant, with the series mean C = 7.148 ($t(61) = 13.58$, $p < .0001$, two-tailed) and the intervention effect $\omega_0 = -2.603$ ($t(61) = -2.07$, $p < .025$, one-tailed).

Diagnostic tests indicated the model to be adequate. No autocorrelations or partial autocorrelations were significant at the .05 level from lags 1 to 36. The Ljung-Box test for the joint significance of the observed residual autocorrelations (Ljung & Box, 1978) was Q = 12 for lags 1-24 and Q = 22 for lags 1-36, $\chi^2(22) = 12$, $p > .95$, and $\chi^2(34) = 22$, $p > .90$, respectively, supporting the null hypothesis that random noise disturbances are responsible for the observed autocorrelation function of the residuals (i.e., that all cycles in the data were effectively modeled). The AIC for the overall model had a value of 350.839. The mean decline of 2.603 scale units during the intervention period, from a daily mean sum of scores of negative events of 7.148 during the nonintervention periods, represents a decline of 36.4% in international conflict during the intervention period.

Holland Assembly

The intervention effect for the international conflict time series during the assembly in Holland was specified by a gradual or cumulative permanent effect during the intervention period. The intervention model was thus $Y_t = C + (1 - \delta_1 B)^{-1}\omega_0 I_t + N_t$, where Y_t is the endogenous series, C is a constant, δ_1 is a parameter indicating the rate of growth of the intervention effect, B is a backwards shift operator, ω_0 is the amount of growth at each observation in the intervention period, I_t is the intervention series, and N_t is the noise model. For the present series, the noise model was specified by $N_t = C + (1 - \theta_3 B^3)(1 - \theta_6 B^6 - \theta_8 B^8 - \theta_9 B^9 - \theta_{11} B^{11})a_t$, where θ_i are seasonal moving average parameters, $B^n a_t = a_{t-n}$ (a backwards shift operator), and other terms are as previously defined. All parameters were statistically significant, as listed in Table 1. The noise model was appropriate, as indicated by diagnostic tests. No autocorrelations or partial autocorrelations were statistically significant at lags 1-36. The Ljung-Box test for the joint significance of residual autocorrelations was Q = 12 at lags 1-24 and Q = 19 at lags 1-36, $\chi^2(16) = 12, p > .70$, and $\chi^2(28) = 19, p > .85$, respectively. This supports the hypothesis of random noise disturbances, indicating that all cycles and trends in the data were adequately modeled.

The intervention parameters of $\omega_0 = -.9853$ (level) and $\delta_1 = .9887$ (rate of growth) indicate that the intervention effect was $-.9853$ the first day, $-.9853(.9887)$ the second day, $-.9853(.9887)^2$ the third day, and so on, with the power of the rate parameter increasing by 1 each day. The fact that the rate parameter was close to the upper bound of stability (+1) indicates that the intervention effect increased by almost a constant amount (i.e., increased almost linearly) each day. McCleary and Hay (1980, p. 159) note that this situation may indicate that the intervention period is too short to encompass the equilibrium state of the process (i.e., that the value of δ_1 is, in fact, less than 1). They point out that this explanation is most likely with social science data. Given the short period of the intervention (10 days) the explanation seems most plausible, that the cumulative effect of the intervention grew slowly and had not reached an asymptotic value by the end of the intervention period. To estimate the practical magnitude of the intervention effect in a scale comparable to the intervention parameter in the Iowa assembly (an abrupt constant effect), the average daily effect over the 10 days was calculated. This resulted in a de-

Table 1: International Conflict Holland Assembly Parameter Estimates

Parameter	Variable	Value	*t*(58)
1 ω_0	I_t	−.9853	−2.78[a]
2 δ_1	I_t	.9887	51.24[b]
3 C	Y_t	21.79	160.87[b]
4 θ_3	Y_t	.3472	2.71[c]
5 θ_6	Y_t	.4235	6.06[b]
6 θ_8	Y_t	.4771	5.93[b]
7 θ_9	Y_t	.4994	5.89[b]
8 θ_{11}	Y_t	.5828	7.92[b]

Note: One-tailed: [a]$p < .005$ Two-tailed: [b]$p < .0001$ [c]$p < .01$
AIC = 467.816

crease of 5.24 scale scores, where the scale is the total score of all negative events per day. This represents an average decrease of 24.05% from the trend-adjusted, nonintervention mean (21.79).

Washington Assembly

The intervention model for the third time series of international conflict was $Y_t = C + \omega_2 I_t + N_t$, where terms are as previously defined. This indicates an abrupt permanent effect 2 days after the beginning of the intervention period. The noise model was specified by $N_t = (1 - \varphi_3 B^3 - \varphi_6 B^6 - \varphi_{33} B^{33})^{-1}(1 - \theta_{11} B^{11})(1 - \theta_{22} B^{22})(1 - \theta_{29} B^{29}) a_t$, where φ_i is a seasonal autoregressive parameter for lag i, and other terms are as defined earlier. Parameter estimates and significance values are given in Table 2. The noise model was appropriate, as indicated by the diagnostic tests. The Ljung-Box test for joint significance of residual autocorrelations was Q = 7.5 at lags 1-24 and Q = 17 at lags 1-36, $\chi^2(16) = 7.5$, $p > .95$, and $\chi^2(28) = 17$, $p > .90$, respectively, indicating that the hypothesis of random disturbances was tenable. There were no significant autocorrelations or partial autocorrelations at lags 1-36. The statistically significant intervention effect of −6.60 represents a 34.9% decrease in international conflict during

Table 2: International Conflict Washington Assembly Parameter Estimates

Parameter		Variable	Value	$t(86)$
1	ω_2	I_t	−6.600	−2.50[a]
2	C	Y_t	18.93	41.67[b]
3	ϕ_3	Y_t	.2985	3.18[c]
4	ϕ_6	Y_t	−.2586	−2.77[c]
5	ϕ_{33}	Y_t	−.2807	−3.17[c]
6	θ_{11}	Y_t	.2244	1.97[d]
7	θ_{22}	Y_t	.3014	2.52[d]
8	θ_{29}	Y_t	−.2774	−2.39[d]

Note: One-tailed: [a]$p < .01$ Two-tailed: [b]$p < .0001$ [c]$p < .01$ [d]$p \leq .05$
AIC = 630.541

the intervention period, in comparison to the seasonally adjusted nonintervention mean of 18.93, where the scale is the sum of all scores of negative events each day.

Figure 1 displays the estimated percentage reduction in international conflict associated with each of the three assemblies.

Control Analyses for International Conflict

Two control analyses were performed to assess whether the observed reduced international conflict at the year-end time of the Iowa and Holland assemblies would be found in previous years. The first control analysis used the data on international and domestic conflict in the most recent 5 years of the Conflict and Peace Data Bank (COPDAB), i.e., 1973-1978 (Azar, 1980). To make Azar's 15-point international and domestic scales most comparable to the one used here, only the negative items were used (scale scores 9-15), and the constant 8.0 was subtracted from each scale score to make the scale range from 1-7 in severity of conflict. To use a series of days identical to that of the Iowa assembly analysis and similar to that in the Holland assembly analysis,

Figure 1: Percentage Decrease in International Conflict During Each of the Three Assemblies, as Assessed by Time Series Intervention Analysis of Content-Analyzed News Reports

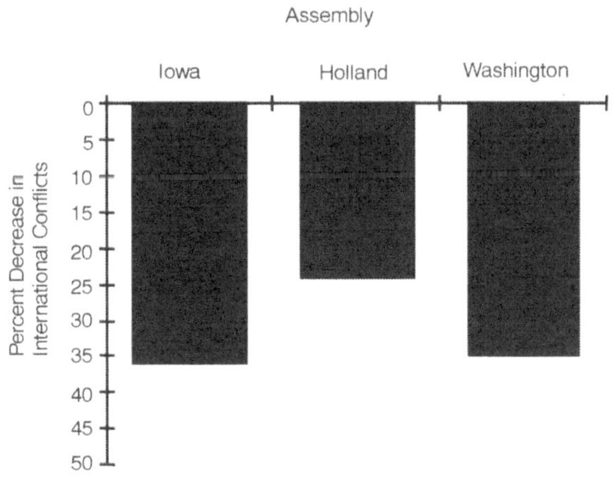

the precise dates used were November 26, 1973, to January 27, 1974, with the same dates used again for 1974-1975, 1975-1976, 1976-1977, and 1977-1978. For each day of the 9-week time series (e.g., all January 1 items of the five time intervals), the scale scores of all items were added together, as was done in the primary analyses reported earlier, to obtain an overall intensity of conflict score for that day of the year totaled across all 5 years. Time series analysis was performed on the series of these overall intensity of conflict scores, constituting 63 observations from November 26 to January 27. Within these dates were 3,493 international and domestic items from the COPDAB file, an average of 55.4 items per day. A mock intervention was constructed with the same dates as the Iowa assembly, December 27 to January 6; these dates were nearly identical to those of the Holland assembly, December 28 to January 6 (one year later).

The COPDAB control series had to be differenced at a lag of one day to achieve stationarity. The AIC-identified noise model for the differenced series was $N_t = (1 - \theta_1 B^1)a_t$, where terms are as previously defined. The intervention model $Y_t = \omega_n I_t + N_t$ was tested for lags n = 0-3 days. At lags zero and one days, the addition of the intervention parameter changed the AIC-identified noise model somewhat, requiring additional noise parameters. For the interventions at lags 2 and 3 days, the noise model remained unchanged. For the lag zero intervention, the noise model was $N_t = (1 - \theta_1 B)(1 - \theta_{21} B^{21} - \theta_{23} B^{23})a_t$, and for the lag one intervention, the noise model was $N_t = (1 - \theta_1 B)(1 - \theta_{18} B^{18})(1 - \theta_{21} B^{21})(1 - \theta_{23} B^{23})(1 - \theta_{36} B^{36})a_t$. Diagnostic criteria were acceptable for all four intervention analyses (lags 0-3). No autocorrelations or partial autocorrelations of residuals were significant in any analysis, and the Ljung-Box test for the joint significance of residual autocorrelations was consistent in each case with the null hypothesis of random noise disturbances, indicating that seasonality and trends were adequately modeled. All noise model parameters were significant at the .05 level, except the parameter θ_{23} in the intervention analysis at a lag of one day, which was significant at the .10 level. (Further details of noise parameter estimates and significance test values are omitted for the sake of space.) The mock-intervention effects did not reach statistical significance, $\omega_0 = 22.70$, $t(58) = 1.19$; $\omega_1 = 29.73$, $t(55) = 1.84$; $\omega_2 = 22.31$, $t(58) = 1.08$; $\omega_3 = 13.81$, $t(57) = 0.67$, where the required two-tailed critical t value is $\pm$ 2.0 for $p = .05$. In fact, the mock interventions indicated that during the years 1973-1978 there was a nonsignificant increase in conflict at the time of the Iowa and Holland assemblies in relation to earlier and subsequent days, rather than a decrease.

Because the COPDAB file does not extend beyond 1978, a second year-end control analysis was performed to assess trends in the year immediately prior to the first (Iowa) assembly. This analysis used a time series based on the *New York Times* during the period November 11, 1982, to January 28, 1983, one year before the first (Iowa) assembly. There were 160 items scored during this period. Scoring was performed in the same way as for the Iowa assembly. The optimal noise model using the AIC criterion was $N_t = C + (1 - \varphi_1 B)^{-1}(1 - \theta_2 B^2 - \theta_7 B^7 - \theta_{25} B^{25})a_t$. Diagnostic criteria indicated that the model was acceptable; the Ljung-Box test was not significant and there were no significant autocorrelations or partial autocorrelations at lags 1-36. The mock intervention was tested at lags zero to three days (as defined above for the COPDAB control analysis). There was an increase in international conflict at each of these lags, which reached significance at lags of 1 and 2 days, $\omega_0 = 2.88$, $t(60) = 1.88$; $\omega_1 = 3.93$, $t(60) = 2.87$; $\omega_2 = 4.13$, $t(59) = 2.83$; $\omega_3 = 2.03$, $t(57) = 1.52$, where the critical two-tailed t value is $\pm$ 2.0 for $p = .05$. The θ_2 parameter of the noise model became nonsignificant for lags one and two and by the AIC criterion the model was better without it, so it was deleted; however, the significance of the mock intervention was similar with or without this parameter. Thus, there is no evidence from either the *New York Times* analysis or the COPDAB file that international conflicts decline during the year-end periods of the assemblies in comparison with surrounding dates. In fact, there appears to be an increase during previous years.

International Terrorism

The time series for terrorism required a natural logarithm transformation for the data to be more normally distributed. This was necessary because several terrorist events resulted in large numbers of casualties and injuries, forming a high upper bound, while the lower bound for the totals of fatalities and injuries was zero. The constant 1 was added to each score prior to log transformation so that the zero values would continue to be defined as zero. Because two of the assemblies occurred at year-end, and a third at midyear, the noise model was diagnosed based upon the autocorrelation function defined at lags 1-84 (420 days or 60 weeks) to look for indications of annual or semiannual seasonality and control for these seasonal influences by including them in the noise model. The intervention model was $Y^*_t = C + \omega_1 I_t + N_t$, where Y^*_t is the log-transformed data series and where other terms are as previously defined. This models a sudden permanent effect at a lag of one, or 5 days (1 data point due to 5-day aggregation) after the onset of the intervention periods. The noise model was $N_t = (1 - \theta_{13} B^{13} - \theta_{22} B^{22} - \theta_{32} B^{32})(1 - \theta_{54} B^{54} - \theta_{55} B^{55})(1 - \theta_{62} B^{62})(1 - \theta_{84} B^{84})a_t$, indicating seasonality at approximately 2, 4, 6, 9, 10, and 14 months (recall that each data point is a 5-day period). The noise model appears adequate. There were no autocorrelations or partial autocorrelations significant at lags 1-84. The Ljung-Box test of joint significance of residual autocorrelations was Q = 19 at lags 1-36 and Q = 44 at lags 1-84, $\chi^2(27) = 19$, $p > .85$, and $\chi^2(75) = 44$, $p > .95$, respectively, consistent with the null hypothesis of random noise disturbances.

All parameters were statistically significant (see Table 3 and Figure 2). McCleary and Hay (1980, p. 174) gave a formula through which the intervention parameter of −1.272 in the natural log metric can be converted directly into a percentage change in the expected value (mean) of the process associated with the intervention. This yields a 72.0% decrease in terrorism 5 days after the onset of the three assemblies.

Control Analysis for International Terrorism

A secondary analysis to assess year-end trends was performed on international terrorism data for the 5-year period beginning March 1978. Daily data on fatalities and injuries were aggregated into 5-day periods and transformed in the natural log metric in a manner identical to the primary analysis. The aggregation began with March 2, 1978, so that the first year-end period came after some baseline, and so that mock-intervention periods were comparable to the year-end assemblies (December 27-31 and January 1-5 of each year). March 1, 1983, was the last day of the final 5-day interval. February 29, 1980, was omitted from the aggregation so that all years had an identical number of days; there were no fatalities or injuries on this day. There were, thus, 365 five-day observations for time series analysis. The noise model, identified for the series by modeling up to lag 36, was $N_t = C + (1 - \varphi_2 B^2)^{-1}(1 - \varphi_8 B^8)^{-1}(1 -$

Table 3: World Terrorism Intervention Analysis Parameter Estimates

Parameter	Variable	Value	*t*(209)
1 ω_0	I_t	−1.272	−2.10[a]
2 C	Y_t	1.802	21.59[b]
3 θ_{13}	Y_t	−.1802	−2.57[d]
4 θ_{22}	Y_t	.1479	2.05[d]
5 θ_{32}	Y_t	−.1618	−2.23[d]
6 θ_{54}	Y_t	.2577	3.29[c]
7 θ_{55}	Y_t	−.1613	−2.07[d]
8 θ_{62}	Y_t	.1987	2.49[d]
9 θ_{84}	Y_t	.1726	2.00[d]

Note: One-tailed: [a]$p < .025$; Two-tailed: [b]$p < .0001$ [c]$p < .01$ [d]$p < .05$
AIC = 785.934

Figure 2: Mean Fatalities and Injuries Due to International Terrorism in Five-Day Aggregates During the Baseline and Intervention (Assembly) Periods

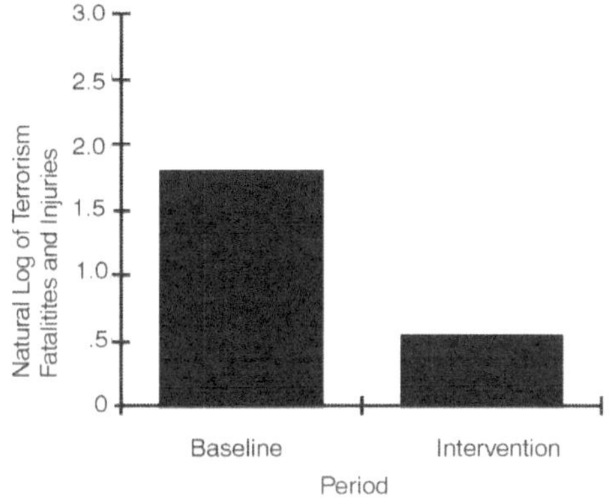

$\varphi_{35}B^{35})^{-1}(1 - \theta_{11}B^{11})(1 - \theta_{36}B^{36})a_t$, where terms are as previously defined. The noise model, although complex, was optimal by the AIC criterion and was adequate in terms of diagnostic tests. There were no significant autocorrelations or partial autocorrelations at lags 1-36. The Ljung-Box test for the joint significance of observed autocorrelations was $Q = 19$ at lag 24, $\chi^2(18) = 19, p > .35$, and at lag 36, $Q = 28$, $\chi^2(30) = 28, p > .55$. This is consistent with the hypothesis of random noise disturbances. All parameters were statistically significant at the .05 alpha level, $C = 1.496$, $t = 12.08$; $\varphi_2 = .2063$, $t = 3.72$; $\varphi_8 = .1159$, $t = 2.03$; $\varphi_{35} = .1748$, $t = 3.13$; $\theta_{11} = -.1335$, $t = -2.33$; and $\theta_{36} = .1216$, $t = 2.02$, where all t-values have 314 degrees of freedom. The model was reestimated adding the mock intervention at either lag zero or one; neither intervention was statistically significant. For lag zero, $\omega_0 = -.0655$, $t(313) = -0.17$; and for lag one, $\omega_1 = -.4440$, $t(312) = -1.15$, where the critical two-tailed t value is $\pm$ 1.96 for $p = .05$. The noise models were still adequate in both cases (details are omitted for space considerations). All noise model parameters were still significant, except that in the case of the analysis at lag one, the φ_8 parameter was $t(312) = 1.92$, $p = .056$. The results of the control analysis, based on the behavior of the variable in previous years, thus indicated that the decrease in international terrorism found during the assembly periods in the primary analysis could not have been expected due to a year-end seasonal effect.

DISCUSSION

As predicted, a statistically significant effect of the large assemblies was observed on both indicators of global conflict. Content analysis of the world news indicated decreases in international conflict associated with the three assemblies of 36%, 24%, and 35%, respectively. A decrease of 72% in casualties and injuries due to world terrorism was found after the onset of the assemblies.

Several of the intervention results may be clarified by discussion. First, unlike the sudden permanent effect on international conflict during the Iowa and Washington assemblies, the form of the intervention effect for the Holland assembly was a gradual permanent one. One possible reason for this is that the Holland assembly used a different source and manner of article selection for content analysis. The *London Times*, the source for this assembly, has a somewhat different coverage of international events than the *New York Times*, which was the source for the other two assemblies. Also, the method of selecting events for the Holland assembly (more from Europe and Africa) did not restrict articles only to recognized areas of international conflict but accepted all articles of international scope. As a result, the data series was less focused on specific international conflict areas and, therefore, may have been less sensitive to immediate changes in these areas. Nevertheless, a positive intervention effect was still found, indicating that the effect is generalizable rather than restricted to a single source or method of sampling. Another possible cause for the gradual intervention effect could be that conflict was quite intense immediately before the beginning of the Holland assembly, particularly in southeast Asia and in Afghanistan-Pakistan. Before the two other assemblies, the level of conflict was not as high.

A second point in the analysis of international conflict concerns the distinctions in the abrupt, permanent intervention effects displayed by both the Iowa and Washington assemblies. The effect of the Washington assembly was found at lag 2 days after the beginning of the assembly, while the effect of the Iowa assembly was immediate. This immediate effect could be related to the fact that the Iowa assembly was, by far, the largest.

A final point deals with international terrorism analysis. The intervention effect for international terrorism was found at lag 5 days (one observation with 5-day aggregation) rather than immediately with the onset of the assemblies. In this analysis, the joint effect of all three assemblies was assessed. Because only the Iowa assembly showed a lag-zero effect on international conflict, some delay in effect for international terrorism might be expected. Also, because the data were aggregated in 5-day periods, even a short time delay in the effect would appear as a 5-day (one observation) lag.

The fact that all of these variables displayed a near-simultaneous improvement indicates that there was a worldwide and holistic influence of reduced tension during the intervention periods. A viable alternative hypothesis for the results of the present study would have to predict both the holistic nature of the changes (a worldwide effect across both conflict variables) and their temporal specificity. The most likely such alternate hypothesis is that because two of the assemblies occurred at the end of the year, the results could be due to some holiday-related effect at that time. This alternative hypothesis appears unlikely for several reasons. The first is that one of the assemblies occurred in midsummer rather than at year-end. Results for this assembly were replicated for international conflict, and this assembly was part of the intervention parameter estimation for terrorism. In addition, the time series analysis for terrorism modeled seasonal cycles up to 84 lags (60 weeks) to explicitly take yearly cycles into account and to ensure that the intervention effects reported would not be due to annual cycles present in the series. Finally, as a direct control, a secondary time series analysis was performed for each variable assessing its year-end behavior in at least 5 previous years. For each of the variables–international conflict and international terrorism–these analyses demonstrated that the magnitude of change found in the present study could clearly not have been expected from the behavior of the variable in previous years. These findings indicate that a general year-end effect is not a viable alternative hypothesis. Indeed, in the case of international conflict, the trend was in the opposite direction.

It is difficult to identify other alternative hypotheses that might account for changes in these variables worldwide during the specific assembly periods. A tenable alternative hypothesis must account for a simultaneous influence on what would ordinarily be considered independent conflicts in different areas (e.g., Latin America, the Middle East, Southeast Asia). Although ad hoc and complex explanations might be attempted, the hypothesis of the present study, while novel, is more parsimonious.

In contrast to the year-end alternative hypothesis and other possible post hoc explanations that do not easily account for the scope or timing of the results, the hypothesis of a rapid onset of the Maharishi Effect on a global scale was predicted, in advance of each assembly, for the variables used in this study. The global reduction in international conflict and terrorism corresponding to or immediately following the onset of the large assemblies of participants in the TM and TM-Sidhi programs strongly supports the theory that generated this research. Furthermore, it extends previous research on this effect to the world scale. The individuals participating in these assemblies were clearly not engaged in behavioral interaction or direct communication with those involved in armed conflict or terrorist acts occurring at multiple locations thousands of miles away. Thus, it appears that the only tenable explanation for an immediate global influence of group practice of the subjective techniques is that this influence is propagated through an underlying field characterized by or capable of interacting with consciousness. On the metropolitan, national, and international levels, this effect has been replicated many times using other conflict variables closely related to terrorism, such as war deaths, war intensity, and crime rates (e.g., Davies & Alexander, in press; Dillbeck, 1990;

Dillbeck et al., 1987, 1988; Hagelin et al., 1999; Hatchard et al., 1996; Orme-Johnson et al., 1988, 1990).

On a practical level, the small number of people required for the effects found here raises the possibility of a global influence of reduced violence through an approach that requires no intrusion in other nations, can be adopted by any country regardless of its governmental system, and involves an insignificant fraction of the defense spending of any major nation. If the principle tested in this research is true, then its continued application on a global level should lead to a significant reduction of conflict around the world. Proposing a growing influence of coherence in the collective consciousness of the world through the cumulative effect of large assemblies such as those studied here as well as the influence of stable groups practicing the Transcendental Meditation and TM-Sidhi programs on several continents, Maharishi Mahesh Yogi predicted in January of 1987 an imminent transition to a more peaceful world, specifying criteria for its achievement that included the ending of international conflicts such as the Iran-Iraq war and a major reversal in U.S.-Soviet relations (*Invitation to Action*, 1987). The outbreak of peace that began to occur in mid-1988–associated with these specific dimensions of international relations–represents a striking transition in world affairs that, despite all commentary, was clearly unanticipated by world leaders and policy makers. An analysis of U.S.-Soviet relations during the period just prior to this transformation (1979-1986), however, indicated that major groups of participants in the Transcendental Meditation and TM-Sidhi programs had a positive influence on relations between the superpowers (Gelderloos, Cavanaugh, & Davies, 1990). In light of the strong findings of the present investigation and consistent results of previous research, we recommend as a next step in researching this phenomenon that a permanent group of approximately 8,000 participants in these programs be established and its effects on international relations and global quality of life be measured.

NOTE

1. Transcendental Meditation, TM, and TM-Sidhi are service marks registered in the U.S. Patent and Trademark Office, licensed to Maharishi Vedic Education Development Corporation and used under sublicense.

AUTHORS' NOTE

Address correspondence to David Orme-Johnson, 191 Dalton Drive, Seagrove Beach, FL 32459 (E-mail: davidoj@emeraldcoast.com).

Transcendental Meditation in Criminal Rehabilitation and Crime Prevention. Pp. 303-318.

SECTION IV: TRANSCENDENTAL MEDITATION IN PRISONS AND PRISON SYSTEMS

The *Transcendental Meditation* Program in the Senegalese Penitentiary System

FARROKH K. ANKLESARIA

The Enlightened Sentencing Project, St. Louis, Missouri

MICHAEL S. KING

Stipendiary Magistrate, Geraldton, Western Australia

ABSTRACT Criminal justice systems in the developing nations of Africa are challenged by a lack of resources for the provision of rehabilitation programs. As a result, they generally experience poor correctional outcomes. Between 1987 and 1989, more than 11,000 inmates and 900 correctional officers and prison administrators in 31 of the 34 prisons in the West African nation of Senegal were instructed in the Transcendental Meditation[1] program. Rule infractions decreased, medical expenses went down 70%, and recidivism dropped from 90% in the pre-meditation period to less than 3% after the program was established. The Senegal project illustrates the significant and positive impact that the use of the Transcendental Meditation program can have on correctional outcomes. It also suggests that the program is a viable rehabilitation approach for use in the criminal justice systems of resource-challenged nations. *[Article copies available for a fee from The Haworth Document Delivery Service: 1-800-HAWORTH. E-mail address: <docdelivery@haworthpress.com> Website: <http://www.HaworthPress.com> © 2003 by The Haworth Press, Inc. All rights reserved.]*

KEYWORDS Transcendental Meditation, Africa, Senegal, criminal justice, offender rehabilitation, prisons

Rehabilitation is the greatest challenge facing the world's corrections systems. In developed countries, billions of dollars have been spent to establish educational, vocational, psychotherapeutic, drug, and other rehabilitation programs in an attempt to rehabilitate offenders. Despite these efforts, recidivism rates remain high. For example, in the United States roughly two-thirds of offenders reoffend and are taken back into custody within three years of release (Beck & Shipley, 1989; Maguire & Pastore, 1995). In addition, since the mid-1970s there has been an ongoing debate in the literature as to the effectiveness of rehabilitation programs. Some criminologists advance the view that rehabilitation programs have generally been ineffective (e.g., Lab & Whitehead, 1989; Lab & Whitehead, 1990), while others posit that the right treatment in the appropriate circumstances has been shown to be effective (Andrews et al., 1990a, 1990b).

For developing countries, the problems are even greater. They face the same challenges concerning recidivism, yet their ability to deal with the problem is further weakened by a lack of resources and by pressing economic, health, and social problems that divert the nation's attention away from the correctional system. Consequently, their ability to introduce rehabilitation programs is severely restricted. This paper is a case study of one African nation's experiment with an innovative approach that has been found by scientific research to be effective in the rehabilitation of offenders. In 1987 the Transcendental Meditation (TM) program was introduced into the entire penitentiary system of the West African nation, the Republic of Senegal.

In addition to the Republic of Senegal, the TM technique has been used in crime prevention and offender and drug rehabilitation programs in the United States, Sri Lanka, Spain, Thailand, India, the Philippines, and other nations (Anklesaria & King, in press). Empirical research in the United States and the Netherlands Antilles has shown that the practice of the TM technique by offenders produces benefits such as: decreased aggression and hostility, decreased anxiety, alleviation of personality disorders, personal growth, decreased recidivism, and improved mental and physical health (for a review, see Hawkins, this volume). Both the theoretical framework behind the use of the TM technique in rehabilitation and prevention and the experimental results obtained so far include psychological, physiological, social, environmental, and spiritual effects. Thus, this technique can appropriately be termed a holistic approach to crime prevention and rehabilitation. In this paper, we will briefly consider the state of corrections and rehabilitation in Senegal, describe the use of the TM program in Senegal, and discuss the implications of this highly successful project.

CORRECTIONS AND REHABILITATION IN SENEGAL

Prior to the introduction of the TM program, Senegal, like many of its neighbors in West Africa, had been unable to introduce rehabilitation programs due to economic pressures. Incarcerated offenders simply languished in prison with little assistance. The healthier prisoners were able to take part in treatments such as work programs, but there was no treatment available for those with psychological or drug problems. In addition, there were no programs for reintegration of prisoners into society or provisions for their employment on release.

WORK-BASED REHABILITATION PROGRAMS

At the Annual Seminar of the Penitentiary Administration in Dakar on February 12-13, 1988, Mr. Ibrahima Sy, the prison governor of the Camp Pénal Prison in Dakar, Senegal's capital city, elucidated previous attempts at rehabilitation in Senegal:

> Some experts thought it was only through work that a man could rediscover his real value and that this might be the best way to rehabilitate a man. This new policy was adopted. It was thus that in Senegal in 1888 a Catholic school–the first of its kind for juvenile delinquents–was established which served as a model for those at Bambey, Richard-Toll, and Nianing and which considerably influenced our homes for maladjusted juveniles. It was thought that the best way to rehabilitate the juvenile offender was to put him to work–work which was generally oriented towards farming. Later, at Camp Pénal Prison, farming, carpentry, masonry, sewing, automobile repairing, and art workshops were set up where inmates could be trained. The idea to use the inmates' skills was favored, and some inmates were even allowed to work outside the prison. It is clear that such a policy has many positive aspects. Indeed, when the inmate is released, he can carry on the trade he has learned and earn a dignified living. Moreover, with the money that he is paid on his release, he can meet his basic needs for a few days following his discharge.
>
> However, experience has shown that this category of inmates, who were thought to be well rehabilitated, constitutes the biggest number of our recidivists. Indeed, not being able to settle down as they wished within society, they end up by coming back to prison where they feel considerably more secure. Moreover, we find that the greatest majority of the long-term inmates of Camp Pénal Prison are people who have stayed in the homes for maladjusted juveniles. These homes are now regarded as the real breeding grounds of delinquents. From all this we can

> infer that work alone is not enough to rehabilitate inmates. We need something more complete, more radical. But what? We often wondered. And finding no answer, we continued to search. (Anklesaria, 1990, pp. 47-48)

It is little wonder that the recidivism rate prior to the introduction of the TM program to Senegal was about 90% one month after being released, according to an estimate made by the director of the Penitentiary Administration of the Republic of Senegal (Anklesaria, 1990). With such conditions, the Senegalese were ripe for the introduction of a rehabilitation program.

THE TRANSCENDENTAL MEDITATION PROGRAM IN THE PENITENTIARY SYSTEM OF SENEGAL

In January 1987, after an introductory lecture given to all the Senegalese prison governors on the benefits of the TM program, the program was introduced on an experimental basis in two of the prisons in Dakar, the capital city. In each of these prisons, the prison officers were instructed prior to the instruction of the inmate population. The TM instructors involved in the project came mainly from French-speaking countries: France, Belgium, Canada (Quebec), and Reunion. All instructions from the teachers in French were translated into Wolof, the national language.

To facilitate any system of prison rehabilitation and to ensure its proper performance by inmates, it is important to have the goodwill, sympathy, and understanding of the prison officers. It is particularly important with a system of rehabilitation that involves an inner, subjective experience such as meditation. It has been found that once the prison officers themselves experience the TM technique and acquire the necessary intellectual understanding of the practice, implementation of the program for the inmates becomes much easier.

The initial period of instruction lasted about one week. Thereafter, both prison officers and inmates met with trained teachers of the TM program once a week in follow-up classes. Both prisons in the capital city encouraged the group practice of the TM program by inmates and prison officers in meditation halls within the prisons. Separate halls for inmates and prison officers were provided in each prison for group meditation and follow-up classes. Follow-up classes included group meditation and discussion of experiences, as well as video and audiotapes discussing the practice. These were translated from English into both French and Wolof.

Observations on the Program in Camp Penal Prison

Mr. Sy summarized his impressions and observations on the impact of this pilot program in his prison:

The results of this program surpassed all my expectations. After one week of practice, I noticed that the backache which tortured me every morning to the point that it prevented me from correctly doing my prayers had simply disappeared. At first I thought it was just a psychological impression, but this was not the case; it was very real, and other good surprises were waiting for me.

Indeed, I felt I was becoming more serene, quieter, more understanding. Today, I more easily accept discussion with the members of my family, particularly with my grown up children. My thoughts are clearer, more precise; it allows me to better understand the instructions of my superiors and to better transmit my orders to my subordinates. Moreover, the latter noticed that I became more relaxed, less grumpy.

Also, we have noticed significant improvements among the prison officers. They now more effectively carry out the mission they are entrusted with. If they ever arrive late for duty, we feel it is unintentional. Among themselves, relations have become better. They treat the inmates in a more humane manner. They are more dynamic.

But the surprise is greatest when we look at the inmates. Everybody knows the atmosphere that always prevailed at Camp Pénal. Very serious incidents have always been part of the pattern of life in this establishment. The reason for this is that this prison takes care of inmates whose sentences range from capital punishment to punishments not less than one year, including life imprisonment. These inmates who considered themselves as "tough guys" or "bosses" were the cause of the almost daily rebellions and fights. These same inmates tell us today that, thanks to the practice of Transcendental Meditation, they sleep better, they smoke fewer cigarettes or have simply stopped smoking, and are no longer obsessed by bad thoughts.

Today, twice a day, without any problems we have about 300 inmates move through the prison in perfect order to reach the meditation hall in the administrative courtyard, which is a considerable distance away from the inmates' dormitories. Only a few months ago it would have been simply unthinkable to move such a large number of inmates in this fashion escorted by only three or four officers because of the serious risk of escapes or uprisings. (Anklesaria, 1990, p. 49)

Inmates Volunteer to Work in City

Mr. Sy also reported on the development of an unprecedented level of inmate participation in cleaning projects around the city:

Taking advantage of this favorable development, we have organized a number of activities which we have named "Operation Clean-Up." This consists of cleaning and improving the city. We collaborate with those departments of public administration who request our help, without asking these latter to pay anything or to supply staff for supervision. Our surprise was still greater when we asked for volunteers from among the inmates for this duty. More than four hundred inmates wanted to go and work, without payment, just for the good of the whole country. This is how the inmates of Camp Pénal, always supervised by a very small number of prison officers, have done work which has been very much appreciated by the civil population, literally "the man in the street," the layman. The inmates did clean-up work all over the city: at hospitals, at many schools and colleges, on the streets of Dakar, and on the highways.

During the work, inmates mingled with the crowd, and never did it occur to them to steal or to commit any reprehensible act, even though opportunities were not lacking. Since the beginning of this operation, in October 1987, up to now [February 1988], we have registered only two escapes. Before the practice of Transcendental Meditation, this number would have been multiplied by at least ten, and the number of infractions made by inmates would have perhaps discouraged us from continuing our work. I have personally noticed that the inmates who are most regular in their meditation are far the best at work. Still better, even those who at the beginning lacked eagerness to do the work are becoming more dynamic as they meditate. *Up to today, not a single meditating inmate released has yet come back to Camp Pénal Prison.*

It has also been noticed, since the introduction of Transcendental Meditation in our establishment, that the number of medical consultations has been reduced by a factor of at least six. The happy consequence is an appreciable decrease in medical expenses and of transportation costs to take the inmates to health care facilities. Even the inmates who were feigning illness to give themselves a day out don't do it anymore. (Anklesaria, 1990, pp. 49-50)

EXPANDING THE PROGRAM

The introduction of the TM program into the two prisons in Dakar from January to April 1987, and into a prison in the nearby city of Thiès in April 1987, were considered pilot projects. The warden of the prison in Thiès conducted an informal pre- and post-TM study looking at rule infractions, behavior of inmates and prison personnel, and health care expenditures (Figures 1 and 2). This study confirmed the results in the other two prisons. In all three prisons, personnel were impressed by the difference after the introduction of the TM program and reported an immediate increase of peace and quiet in the prisons. Colonel Mamadou Diop (personal communication, January 12, 1988), the Di-

Figure 1: Mean Monthly Infractions at Thiés HAC

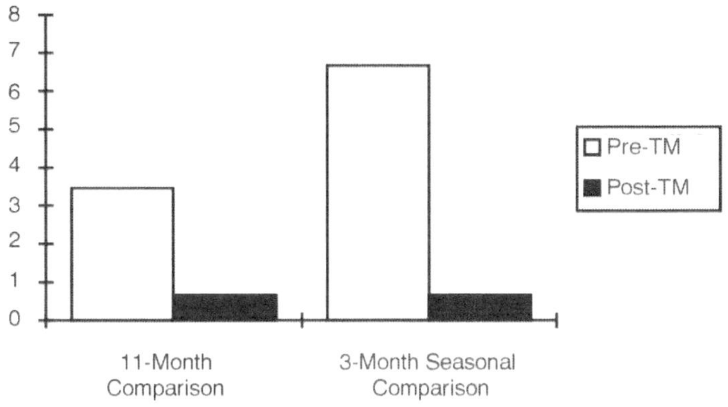

Figure 2: Mean Monthly Medical Consultations at Thiès HAC

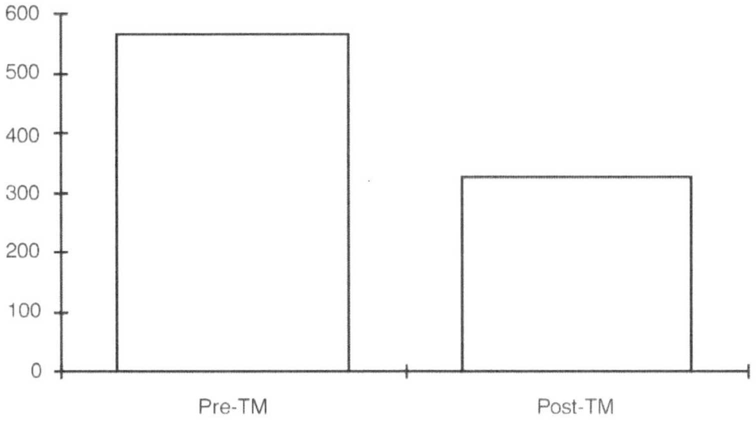

rector of the Penitentiary Administration, said in a message he sent to the founder of the TM program, Maharishi Mahesh Yogi:

> Within a few months of applying your method, it had become apparent to us that your system of rehabilitation had more than confirmed all the theoretical hopes and promises. The time had come to take action. In August 1987, in a letter to the Director of Diourbel Prison, I said this: "The experimental period of this program is now over. The reports from the different prison governors clearly indicate that this new program introduced by the Penitentiary Administration in collaboration with MERU [Maharishi European Research University, a Swiss-based TM organization that implemented the TM program in Senegal] is both reliable and effective. I am now in a hurry to bring these benefits to all the prisons in Senegal."

As a result of the positive impact of the TM program in these prisons, the government of Senegal quickly and conscientiously applied the program to its entire prison system from August 1987 to February 1989. In all, over 11,000 inmates and 900 prison officers were instructed in the TM program. Out of a total of 34 prisons in the country, 31 were involved in the program. Included were maximum security prisons, prison farms, prisons housing both adults and juvenile offenders, and one women's prison. The three prisons not included in the program were located in a remote corner of the country, which made implementation of the program too difficult.

Thiès House of Arrest and Correction: Governor's Report

Decreased rule infractions, decreased medical consultations by inmates, and improvements in the behavior of the correctional staff were reported by Alioune Badara Deme, the governor of the Thiès House of Arrest and Correction (HAC), for a 3-month period following the introduction of the TM Program (A. B. Deme, personal communication, August 4, 1987). The data reported were based on prison records for two periods. The first period is a pre-TM 11-month period from June 1, 1986, to May 4, 1987. Beginning on May 4, approximately 274 inmates and 43 of 51 correctional staff were instructed in the TM technique. The second reporting period is a 3-month post-TM period that began on May 4, 1987, and ended on the day of the report, August 4, 1987. The extended length of the pre-TM comparison period was deliberately chosen to reflect and allow for seasonal influences as noted later in this article.

In the pre-TM period, there were 39 infractions committed by 64 inmates that resulted in placement in a cell, or an overall average of 3.5 infractions by 5.8 inmates per month. In the post-TM period, there were only 2 infractions involving 4 inmates that required placement in a cell, or an average of .67 infractions by 1.33 inmates per month. This represents an overall reduction in infractions of 81%.

A more accurate comparison would be to compare the 3-month post-TM period to a comparable seasonal period the year before, i.e., June through August (the hottest months). Comparing an average of 6.7 infractions per month during this period to the post-TM period gives a reduction in infractions of 90%–only 1/10 as many. Deme (personal communication, August 4, 1987) commented that "our experience in the prison environment reveals that heat in no way contributes to the creation of calm in prison." Thus the dramatic post-TM reduction in infractions during the hottest months is even more significant (Figure 1).

Similarly, during the pre-TM, eleven-month period there were 6,067 medical consultations by inmates, or an average of 552 per month (564 per month during June-August). During the post-TM, three-month period there were 971 medical consultations or a monthly average of 324. Again comparing the comparable seasonal periods, the post-TM reduction in medical consultations was 43% (Figure 2). Deme (personal communication, August 4, 1987) notes the further benefit of the reduction in medicinal/pharmaceutical products used when consultations were reduced, and the consequent reduction in "the cost of these operations to the state budget."

Negative behavior, rule infractions, and absence from post by correctional staff were also evaluated by Deme (personal communication, August 4, 1987). He said that no infractions by staff were reported during the post-TM period, as compared to an average of 2.2 per month during the pre-TM period. There was a reduction in absenteeism of approximately 13% during the post-TM period.

Deme (personal communication, August 4, 1987) concluded, "We have recorded less placement in cell, less administrative punishments, and less consultations at the hospital, where the reserves of medicine are stabilizing. There has indeed been improvement and progress in the various areas of social life at the Thiès HAC."

OBSERVATIONS ON THE NATIONAL TM PRISON PROJECT

The changes observed by the prison administration are mainly in the form of letters and reports sent by the governors of the 31 prisons to prison headquarters in the capital city. Colonel Diop (personal communication, January 12, 1989) summarized the results:

> The first results of this program in Senegalese prisons were really dramatic, as much for their speed to manifest as for their intensity. The reports that one prison director after another sent to me after only a few days or weeks of the application of this program share in common the same amazement and deep satisfaction. These results can be summarized as follows:

a. Inmates:
   - Immediate improvement in sleep–disappearance of insomnia, which was widespread.
   - Very sharp reduction in irritability and aggressiveness.
   - Very sharp reduction in negativity; more confidence in oneself and in the future, more joyfulness.
   - Improvement in relationships between inmates–more openness, better communication, reduction in the number of thefts and diverse types of aggressive behavior.
   - Improvement in health; marked decrease in drug consumption.

b. Staff:
   - More self-confidence and more concern for the inmates.
   - More self-control.
   - Greater conscientiousness.
   - Better health.
   - Less absenteeism and lateness.

c. Prison as a whole:
   - Almost complete cessation of fights between inmates, in the courtyards, and in the rooms.
   - Marked decrease in rule violations by inmates as well as by staff.
   - Decrease in the number of escapes.
   - Sharp decrease in the number of medical consultations–as much as 70-80%.

In another open letter, Colonel Diop (personal communication, November 20, 1991) stated the following about the prison officers under his command:

> Among junior officers and enlisted men, I have also seen a sharp decline in rule infractions, increased maturity, increased personal discipline, a greater respect for superiors, strengthened loyalty and patriotic ideals, better interpersonal relationships, and strengthening of esprit de corps. The above mentioned documentation and findings were made possible on the basis of: reports from the different officers on duty; visits and inquiries that I personally conducted in the field; inspection of the numerous registers, particularly the punishment and medical records; and examination of the management reports. I have also observed these results in the attitude of my close colleagues at work, in their personal testimonies, and also in myself.

Experiences of Prison Governors, Prison Officers, and Inmates

Thousands of experiences were also collected from the prison governors, prison officers, and inmates themselves. These experiences are set out in detail in the book, *New Horizons in Criminology and Penitentiary Science: The*

Maharishi Unified Field Based Integrated System of Rehabilitation in Senegalese Prisons (Anklesaria, 1990). They can be classified into the following major categories:

1. Improvements in physical health: elimination of psychosomatic and stress-related disorders;
2. Improvements in mental health and the strengthening of personality and intellectual capacity;
3. Improvements in spiritual life; and
4. Improvements in behavior while incarcerated.

Given below are some typical experiences in each category:

1. Physical Health

> The most surprising effect is the change that has taken place at night. Previously, the atmosphere was tense, the inmates would talk loudly, shout, and hammer at the bars. Now, the only noise we hear are snores!
>
> –Inmate, Fort B Prison

> TM must be the most effective method against drug abuse, because it helped me to stop smoking marijuana completely! The money I was spending every day for cigarettes or medicines (for my chronic bronchitis, my asthma, and rheumatism) can now be spent in a better way.
>
> –Inmate, Camp Pénal Prison, Dakar

> My headaches are gone. Before TM, one of my shoulder blades would become painful at night. To my surprise, the pain disappeared from the moment I started TM.
>
> –Prison Officer, Thiès

> My ulcer attacks have disappeared. I have had this disease for more than 10 years. I had used all kinds of medicine which had not brought about any improvement.
>
> –Prison Governor, Kaffrine

> We have noticed a sharp diminution in visits to the doctor. Approximately 70% less patients are coming to the prison clinic every day. At night, consultations have stopped completely.
>
> –Papa Aldiaw Gueye, Prison Governor, Saint-Louis

The inmates' medical consultations have become rare since the system was introduced–10 per month now, as compared to 130 consultations per month prior to meditation.

–Yakhya Dieye, Prison Governor, Podor

The first thing that struck me when I started my work here in September 1987 was the number of inmates going for medical consultations–on an average about 13 per day. Since the program was introduced, I have made the objective observation that the number has been progressively reduced, and sometimes as much as two weeks pass by without even a single consultation being recorded.

–Issa Thione, Prison Governor, Bignona Prison

2. Mental Health

I was very impulsive and was reacting without thinking. Now, I take time to think about what I am doing. Therefore my behavior is more positive.

–Inmate, Foundiougne

Since I started Transcendental Meditation, I no longer lose my temper so quickly. After each sitting, my mind is in a state of total peace; nothing disturbs it.

–Inmate, Sébikotane

"What is happening to you Magaye? You are becoming less nervous!" That's what I was told, just four days after starting meditation. I feel great, quite at ease; I am less anxious than before.

–Inmate, Camp Pénal Prison, Dakar

Meditation gives me an inner feeling of well-being which to a large extent eliminates my aggressive character.

–Inmate, Thiès

I have noticed that with TM I can learn my lessons more easily. Previously, I could not study for more than 45 minutes. Now, I can study for up to three hours without feeling sleepy or tired.

–Prison Officer, Camp Pénal Prison, Dakar

3. Spiritual Life

One of the most surprising results of the project has been the enrichment of the inmates' and staff's spiritual life. Before the beginning of the project, some people were wondering whether the program was in accord with the fundamentals of Islam, the main religion of our country. But it became clear very quickly that there was no conflict between Islam and Maharishi's Transcendental Meditation. No one was asked to change his beliefs or to follow any moral code, and meditation altered in no way the prescribed prayer times. Also, a good number of prisoners spontaneously reported that since they had started Maharishi's Transcendental Meditation, they felt a greater peace of mind, which improved the quality of their prayers. With this increased inner calm, they naturally felt inclined to do the five daily prayers as prescribed by our religion. These changes happened without any encouragement either from the Penitentiary Administration or from the teachers of MERU, since instruction into Maharishi's Transcendental Meditation does not imply any moral or religious prescription.

–Colonel Mamadou Diop, Director of Penitentiary Administration

Before meditation, I would rarely pray, and I would get involved with petty things that were not my concern. Now I pray at each prescribed time.

–Inmate, Ziguinchor

Meditation has made me harmonious, patient, wise, purposeful, hopeful, and reserved. It has facilitated the practice of my religion, and I'm very happy about that.

–Inmate, Camp Pénal, Dakar

4. Improved Behavior

Since I started to meditate, I don't feel I am in a prison. I have begun to talk with the inmates as well as with the prison officers, whom I didn't want to see before.

–Inmate, Mbour

With TM, my relationships with others are becoming more cordial. Before, I would get upset over nothing. I feel much better now.

–Inmate, Camp Pénal Prison, Dakar

> Previously, every time I woke up, I was in a terrible mood. Now, it is the opposite. I wake up in the morning in very good spirits. The bad moods and quarrels are over, no rough times anymore. I live in perfect harmony with the inmates of the cell.
>
> –Inmate, Camp Pénal Prison, Dakar

> The atmosphere of the prison is now extremely quiet–it's dead calm!
>
> –Prison Governor, Kaffrine

> Even my family speaks about my being more available to them. In the past, when I had finished my work at night, I would not take the time to stay with the members of my family in the lounge. But since I started, understanding has grown and family affection is strengthened.
>
> –Prison Officer, Camp Pénal, Dakar

> I wish that a larger part of the population could benefit from these courses; I am sure that they contribute towards peace, stability, and social cohesion.
>
> –Inmate, Koutal

RECIDIVISM

Colonel Diop reported that prior to the introduction of the TM program, the rate of recidivism in the correctional system was about 90% *in the first month after release* (Anklesaria, 1990). In contrast, in the last half of 1988, during which 2,390 prisoners were released, there were less than 200 recidivists, of whom not more than 20% were meditators. In effect, the recidivism rate of the meditating prisoners was less than 3% for that period, because most of the recidivists came from the three prisons where the TM program had not been introduced.

It is important to note that these results were not the product of a controlled study and, therefore, must be treated with some reserve. However, Diop (personal communication, January 12, 1989) made the following comment on the reduction in recidivism in his letter to Mr. Anklesaria:

> Considering that there is no structure or scheme for the reintegration of inmates into society, nor is there any provision for work or jobs for those released, it appears that the only possible explanation for this remarkable

drop in recidivism in our country is to be found in the application of your program.

Diop (Anklesaria, 1990) also stated that there was a subsequent reduction in the costs of the prison system, due to the reduced overcrowding resulting from the dramatic reduction in recidivism. These results occurred over the comparatively short period of 2 years.

CONCLUSION

As reported by the Prison Administrator, the Senegal TM prison project brought about an increase in mental and physical health, spiritual practice, and prosocial behavior, as well as a dramatic reduction in recidivism. The introduction of the TM program to the prison system of Senegal was, in the view of the prison governors, so successful that at the Annual Seminar of the Penitentiary Administration in Dakar on February 12-13, 1988, the governor of every prison in Senegal supported a resolution endorsing the TM program (Anklesaria, 1990).

Previous research on the TM program in prisons has shown the practice of the technique to be effective both in the United States and in the Netherlands Antilles, two widely different cultures. The reported success of the program in Senegal adds further anecdotal support for the effectiveness of this rehabilitation approach around the world and indicates the potential benefit that would be available from a nationwide implementation of the TM program in any nation's correctional system.

The Senegal TM program project is unique in African correctional history. For the first time in Africa, a rehabilitation program was made freely available to virtually all inmates in a nation's prison system. We suggest that the results of this program lend support for its introduction into the correctional systems of other nations. Although we do not discount the need for reform of the socioeconomic structure of African society to combat crime, as Kayode and Alemika (1984) propose, the successful use of the TM program in Senegalese prisons suggests it is equally important to promote the development of the full potential of the individual to prevent crime and rehabilitate offenders. We should also bear in mind that Colonel Diop reports dramatic reductions in recidivism during the application of the TM program without any evidence for other causes, such as socioeconomic improvements.

Coyle (1993) suggests that many of the prisons of African nations are unsuited to their cultures, being largely a legacy of colonial times. In addition, he observes, "It is also a very expensive use of scarce resources to take a large group of people out of society, to render them totally unproductive, and then have to feed, clothe and care for them" (p. 1977). Given the positive outcome of the use of the Transcendental Meditation program in the correctional system of Senegal and its application in community-based corrections, we suggest that it would be cost effective for developing nations in Africa and elsewhere to use community-based projects modeled on the Enlightened Sentencing Project for offenders for whom it is appropriate to use a community-based disposition (Anklesaria & King, this volume).

The impressive, positive anecdotal reports on this project demand confirmation from empirical research on the use of the TM program in the correctional systems of Senegal or other African nations, preferably using randomized, longitudinal, controlled designs. Studies of changes in physiology, psychology, and behavior through the practice of the TM program would be possible, given sufficient funding and the use of culture-free or culture-appropriate test instruments. As Arthur (1991) points out, many African correctional systems lack adequate record keeping, and, therefore, empirical studies on recidivism may be difficult. However, even in the absence of the means and resources to conduct empirical or archival research, the implementation of nation-wide TM projects in countries of the African continent and elsewhere will add further valuable anecdotal support for this program.

NOTE

1. Transcendental Meditation, TM, and TM-Sidhi are registered or common law trademarks licensed to Maharishi Vedic Education Development Corporation and used under sublicense or with permission.

AUTHORS' NOTE

Address correspondence to The Enlightened Sentencing Project, 625 N. Euclid Avenue, Suite 228, St. Louis, MO 63108.

Transcendental Meditation in Criminal Rehabilitation and Crime Prevention. Pp. 319-331.

Cost Savings from Teaching the *Transcendental Meditation* Program in Prisons

DAVID L. MAGILL

The Enlightened Sentencing Project, St. Louis, Missouri

ABSTRACT This paper quantifies cost savings to correctional systems and to society resulting from implementation of the Transcendental Meditation (TM)[1] program. Based on results from studies at several maximum-security prisons, including Folsom and San Quentin in California and Walpole in Massachusetts, up to 56% fewer inmates are convicted of new crimes when they are released after beginning the TM program. Furthermore, practitioners of this program are returned to prison up to 45% less often for parole violations or any other reason. These and other effects described in this paper allow the TM program to lower costs. Savings are projected to arise from: (a) reduced recidivism, (b) reduced medical expenses, (c) a more manageable prison environment, (d) improved quality of life for staff, and (e) a reduced crime rate for society. Conservatively, the overall ratio of program cost to total savings is estimated at 1 to 10, with 46% of savings accruing to the correctional system and 54% to the general public. Total savings over 5 years for every 1,000 inmates and 100 correctional officers instructed is estimated at $31.6 million. These projections imply that instructing a substantial fraction of the 6 million people under correctional supervision in the United States would lead to savings in the tens of billions of dollars. *[Article copies available for a fee from The Haworth Document Delivery Service: 1-800-HAWORTH. E-mail address: <docdelivery@haworthpress.com> Website: <http://www.HaworthPress.com> © 2003 by The Haworth Press, Inc. All rights reserved.]*

KEYWORDS Cost savings, criminal behavior, Transcendental Meditation, TM, crime prevention, recidivism

Studies in several corrections systems where the Transcendental Meditation program was taught to prison inmates, probationers, parolees, or staff have produced evidence supporting significant cost savings (Alexander, 1982; Bleick & Abrams, 1987). Both the correctional system and society as a whole benefit. Savings result from reductions in recidivism, maintenance of a more manageable prison environment, reductions in medical expenses, and improvements in the quality of life for staff. Societal savings are predicted to result from reduced recidivism and reduced crime rates when the program is implemented on a large enough scale.

QUANTIFYING REDUCTIONS IN RECIDIVISM

Improved psychosocial functioning in inmates practicing the TM program at Walpole State Prison, a maximum-security institution in Massachusetts, led to studies that examined subsequent recidivism rates (Alexander, 1982; Alexander, Rainforth et al., this volume). Over a 3.5-year period, recidivism (as indicated by return to prison) was 33% lower for practitioners of the TM program than for random samples from four other treatment groups, controlling for relevant demographic variables. Recidivism, as indicated by new conviction rate, was 47% lower.

Two other studies on recidivism were conducted on inmates from the California Department of Corrections. The first found that 259 male felon parolees who had learned the TM technique had 35-45% less recidivism from 1 to 5 years after parole than a closely matched control group of parolees (Bleick & Abrams, 1987). A 15-year follow-up study showed this reduction in recidivism remained at 35-45% for the entire 15 years after release (Rainforth, Alexander, & Cavanaugh, this volume). Prison education, vocational training, and psychotherapy, by contrast, did not significantly reduce recidivism in this population (Bleick & Abrams, 1987).

A large demonstration project in Senegal, West Africa, showed even more dramatic results. Between 1987 and 1989, the TM technique was taught to all inmates in 31 of the 34 prisons; 11,000 inmates and 900 correctional officers practiced the TM technique regularly during the 2-year project. This project differed from those in the U.S. prisons in that all correctional officers practiced the program, and all the inmates in each institution practiced it together. This comprehensive approach appeared to have an even greater effect on recidivism. The results were summarized in a letter from Colonel Mamadou Diop, Director of the Penitentiary Administration:

> . . . in Senegal usually about 90% of the inmates released after serving their sentence come back to prison within 1 month. However, 6 months after 2,000 meditating inmates were released in 1988, we could register less than 40 recidivists (a 2% return rate). . . . Considering that there is no

structure or scheme for the reintegration of inmates into society, nor is there any provision for work or jobs for those released, it appears that the only possible explanation for this remarkable drop in recidivism in our country is to be found in the application of your program. (Anklesaria, 1990)

ASSUMPTIONS USED IN CALCULATING SAVINGS FOR CORRECTIONAL SYSTEMS

On the basis of the findings in U.S. state prisons, we use a conservative estimate of 30% reduction in recidivism for calculating cost savings due to the TM program. Costs and other statistics are based on those for the state of New York. These savings are predicated on a recidivism rate of 42% for return-to-prison within 3 years and assume that those who return to prison will stay in prison for an additional 3 years. Assuming higher comparison rates of return-to-prison or longer prison stays increases the savings; decreasing them decreases the savings. Probation populations, for example, typically have lower recidivism rates (in terms of return-to-prison) than those released from state prisons. Thus, cost savings for probationers will be proportionately less. Mean wages and benefits are based on the average figures for correctional employees in the state of New York. This model assumes a cost of $3,000 per inmate for instruction in the TM program.

EXPECTED COST SAVINGS IN PRISON SYSTEMS FROM TEACHING THE TM PROGRAM TO INMATES

The expected savings for a prison system as a result of teaching the TM program to inmates has two components: reduced costs while in prison and reduced costs associated with reincarceration due to new convictions or due to technical parole violations (see Tables 1 and 2).

Table 1 lists three areas of projected savings for the prison system while the inmates are still incarcerated: reduced staff, reduced health care costs for inmates, and early release. Savings from fewer assaults or riots are also likely when the TM program is introduced for inmates, but we have not attempted to quantify these in this paper.

Reduced Staffing

Studies indicate that inmates practicing the TM program commit fewer infractions of rules and use more of their time in constructive activities (Bleick & Abrams, 1987; Ballou, 1993). Such changes produce a calmer prison environment, and in a calmer environment, fewer staff are needed. For example, if six corrections officers are needed on each shift to supervise 100 inmates, in the

Table 1: Reduced Costs While in Prison

Costs of Incarceration	Savings if 1,000 inmates practice TM
Staffing: $46,830 per year per officer. Source: American Corrections Association Directory, 1997.	Reduction of staff from 330 per 1,000 inmates to 290 per 1,000 inmates, resulting in 40 fewer staff. $1,873,200 saved per year.
Medical Costs: $1,950 per year per inmate. Source: Sourcebook of Criminal Justice Statistics-1997 Chart 1.11.	10% reduction per year per inmate, a savings of $195 per inmate, 11 months. $179,000 saved in the first year.
Incarceration Costs: $25,962 per inmate per year. Source: ACA Directory, 1997.	One month early release per inmate due to decreased rule infractions and increased participation in education and other self-development programs, a savings of $2,163.50 per inmate. $2,163,500 saved per year.
Total Savings for Cohort in Prison	**$4,215,700**

Parameters used in Tables 1 and 2

1. Wages: $36,025
2. Benefits: 30%
3. Medical costs: $1,950
4. Annual cost of incarceration: $25,962
5. Recidivism: Year 1/2/3 – 24%/12%/6%
6. Recidivists serve average of 3 years
7. TM reduces recidivism by 30%
8. Recidivists return, on average, mid-year
9. Cost is $3,000 per inmate
10. Inmates are released one year after instruction
11. 1,000 participants

calmer environment created by practice of the TM program, only five officers might be needed. (This is a suggestion made by the maximum security warden at Lorton Correctional Institution in Washington, DC, during a private meeting in 1992. He specified this level of anticipated staffing change based on the research presented to him.) This reduction will be achieved through natural staff turnover and reduced overtime. (The analysis assumes a decrease from 33 security officers/100 inmates to 29 security officers/100 inmates. For comparison, in state prison systems in the United States, staffing ranges from 13 to 40 per hundred [Camp & Camp, 1993].)

Reduced Health Care Costs

During the TM project in the Senegalese prison system, health care costs were reduced by 70% in the first year of the program (Anklesaria, 1990).

Table 2: Reduced Reincarceration Costs

Costs of Incarceration	Savings if 1,000 inmates practice TM
First Year After Release: 24% of those released are expected to return to prison in the first year after release. Assuming they spend an average of six months in prison this first year, the cost to the state for reincarceration is $3,115,470.	With a 30% reduction in recidivism, the cost of reincarceration drops to $2,180,829. This saves $934,641 in the first year.
Second Year After Release: 12% of those released are expected to return to prison in the second year. Assuming they spend an average of six months in prison this second year, the cost to the state for their reincarceration is $1,557,735. Additionally, the 24% who returned in the first year cost an additional $6,230,940 for their next 12 months stay. Total for the year: $7,788,676.	With a 30% reduction in recidivism, the cost of reincarceration drops to $5,452,073. This saves $2,336,603 in the second year.
Third Year After Release: 6% of those released are expected to return to prison in the third year. Assuming they spend an average of six months in prison this third year, the cost to the state for their reincarceration is $778,868. Additionally, the 24% who returned in the first year cost an additional $6,230,940 for their next 12 months stay, and the 12% who returned in the second year cost an additional $3,115,470. Total for the year: $10,125,279.	With a 30% reduction in recidivism, the cost of reincarceration in year three drops to $7,087,695. This saves $3,037,584 in the third year.
Subsequent Years After Release: The 24% released who returned in the first year spend an additional six months in prison in the fourth year after release. The 12% who returned in the second year spend an additional 18 months in the fourth and fifth years after release. And, the 6% who returned in the third year spend an additional 30 months in the fourth, fifth, and sixth years after release. Total for these years: $11,683,014.	With a 30% reduction in recidivism, the cost of reincarceration in years four, five, and six drops to $8,178,110. Savings for subsequent years: $3,504,904.
Total Savings for Cohort After Release.	**$9,813,732.**

Orme-Johnson's cross-sectional study of 2,000 TM practitioners in a Blue Cross plan in the United States found a 50% reduction in costs (Orme-Johnson, 1987). The longitudinal study of Herron and co-workers of the general Canadian population also found a gradual reduction (10% per year), reaching the 50% level after 5 to 6 years (Herron, Hillis, Mandarino, Orme-Johnson, & Walton, 1996). A conservative estimate of 10% reduction in health care costs is used for the present analysis.

Early Release

Research indicates that the TM program reduces rule infractions and increases participation in educational and other programs (e.g., Dillbeck & Abrams, 1987). As a result of such improvements, current parole policies in many states would permit earlier release. We assume that inmates instructed in the TM program will be released an average of one month earlier.

Reduced Reincarceration Costs

The savings for reduced recidivism are based on the studies of prior releases of all those who learned the TM program in 3 California prisons between 1975 and 1981. Releases from Folsom, Deuel Vocational, and San Quentin showed a 35-40% reduction in recidivism for all reasons and a 40-50% reduction in new convictions (Bleick & Abrams, 1987). The savings are calculated assuming an average of three years for the reincarceration period. (While return sentences for minor violations are often less than 3 years, many of those released return more than once, and recidivists are typically given longer sentences than first-time entrants.) In overcrowded correctional systems, early release and reduced recidivism will produce savings by reducing the number of new prisons that must be built. Such savings will not be apparent, however, unless the program is implemented throughout most of the system. Therefore, savings from reduced need for new prisons were not included in the present analysis.

Discussion of Cost Savings from Teaching TM to Inmates

The total savings for the agency for costs incurred both while the inmates are incarcerated and for their reincarceration would be $14,029,432. (Note: this assumes that those who started the TM program in their first stay in prison produce no savings to the system if they are reincarcerated.) The cost-benefit analysis for the department of corrections for inmates taught the TM program thus shows a savings-to-expense ratio of 4.7 to 1 for each 1-year cohort.

SAVINGS TO PRISON SYSTEMS FROM TEACHING CORRECTIONAL OFFICERS AND STAFF

Prison work is stressful. Prison personnel have higher stress levels than the normal population, resulting in greater cigarette, drug, and alcohol use; higher sick leave rates; higher divorce rates; and higher frequency of heart disease, tension headaches, backaches, ulcers, diabetes, obesity, and other serious psychophysiological problems (ACA, 1983). Studies of stress in correctional systems indicate that the life expectancy of prison employees is an average of

16 years shorter than the general population (ACA, 1984). Because the TM program reduces stress, it is not surprising that evidence indicates it also reduces substance use (Alexander, Robinson, & Rainforth, 1994; Hawkins, this volume), other risk factors for disease (Schneider et al., 1995; Alexander, Schneider et al., 1996), and most other health problems (Orme-Johnson, 1987), with a consequent extension of lifetime (Alexander, Langer et al., 1989; Alexander, Barnes et al., 1996). Table 3 calculates the probable savings for prison systems by teaching the TM program to correctional officers and staff, independent of whether it is also taught to the inmates.

Assumptions Used for Estimating Savings for Teaching Prison Employees

An annual reduction of 10% in health care costs for staff is predicted, reaching a reduction in year 5 of 50% less than staff who do not practice the TM program. This is based on three field studies on medical costs and utilization rates involving several thousand people (Orme-Johnson, 1987; Orme-Johnson & Herron, 1997; Herron et al., 1996). The Herron results were obtained during a 7-year longitudinal study of 599 Canadian participants in the TM program. The two studies found a 10% annual, cumulative reduction in health care costs. The Orme-Johnson study was a cross-sectional study of 2,000 members of a Blue Cross plan who practiced the TM program. Given the high levels of stress in state prisons, a program that greatly reduces stress and promotes a more orderly, peaceful environment in the prison would likely produce even greater savings for prison employees than for the general population. Senegalese prisons, for example, found 50% to 70% reductions in health care costs. Ambulances on nightly standby at Senegalese prisons to handle routine knife fights were sent home when the inmates stopped fighting. Corrections officers and inmates who, prior to TM, were rarely in the same room together, after TM, sat together and closed their eyes during meditation (Anklesaria, 1990).

Additional savings are projected due to fewer worker's compensation claims. Worker's compensation and disability claims are often stress-related or related to assaults. The calm atmosphere of the prison produced by the institution-wide implementation of this program will produce significant reductions in claims of this sort. The reductions we have used in our calculations are modest. They apply, of course, only to new claims.

For the purpose of our estimation, savings per employee are reduced by 60% by year 5. This reduction results from turnover among those who began the program and from attrition in program participation. In either case, the state would no longer receive the benefit of their participation in the program. While the individual officer may continue to benefit after moving to a position outside the prison service, cost savings for the prison system, of course, will stop when an officer leaves. This assumption of 60% reduction is probably excessive, because the 10% annual reduction obtained in the insurance studies cited above was for the entire group that began TM, regardless of whether they

Table 3: Typical Department of Correctional Services Staff Cost-Benefit Analysis

Projected Five-Year Costs Without the TM Program (per Employee)					
	Year 1	Year 2	Year 3	Year 4	Year 5
Major Medical	$3,328	$3,461	$3,738	$4,037	$4,360
Worker's Comp	$1,110	$1,143	$1,177	$1,212	$1,249
Sick Leave	$1,686	$1,737	$1,789	$1,842	$1,898
Training Cost	$435	$448	$461	$475	$490
Total	$6,559	$6,789	$7,165	$7,567	$7,996
Projected Five-Year Costs with the TM Program (per Employee)					
	Year 1	Year 2	Year 3	Year 4	Year 5
Major Medical	$3,012	$2,930	$3,044	$3,230	$3,481
Worker's Comp	$899	$968	$995	$1,061	$1,098
Sick Leave	$1,526	$1,470	$1,457	$1,474	$1,515
Training Cost	$352	$379	$404	$428	$450
Total	$5,789	$5,747	$5,900	$6,193	$6,544
Annual Savings	$770	$1,041	$1,265	$1,374	$1,452
Five-Year Savings	$5,902				
Cost of Program	$1,500				
Savings to Cost Ratio	3.93				
Summary of Parameters:					
Wages	$36,025				
Fringe	30%				
Wage Inflation	3%				
Major Medical Inflation	4%				
Work Comp Factor	3.08%				
Sick Leave Days	9.00				
Length of Service	7 years				
Percentage Factors Applied for TM Program Reductions					
% Continuing	95%	77%	62%	50%	40%
Major Medical	9%	17%	26%	34%	43%
Worker's Comp	20%	20%	25%	25%	30%
Sick Leave	9%	17%	26%	34%	43%
Training Cost	20%	20%	20%	20%	20%

were regular or irregular in their practice, or had discontinued the practice altogether.

Projected 5-Year Costs Without the TM Program

The year-1 costs are estimates using 1996 health care figures from the Missouri Department of Corrections. Applying an inflation factor in each category generates costs for years 2-5. The inflation factors are listed under "Parameters." We have used a 4% annual increase in health care costs, reflecting recent trends (Tokarski, 1999).

The annual personnel training cost of $891 per correctional officer is the estimated total cost of training divided by the average number of officers in a department. We have used a typical seven-year average length of service, which is a 14% annual turnover rate (Camp & Camp, 1993).

Projected 5-Year Costs with the TM Program

The projected 5-year costs with the TM program were computed by subtracting the percentage reduction expected for the expense category and year from the corresponding "without TM" figure. The percent reduction is first multiplied by the "percent continuing" to reflect the fraction of the original population expected to remain employed by the Department and to be continuing the TM program through that year. "Percent continuing" reflects two factors: the staff turnover rate and the rate at which staff discontinue the practice of the TM program.

We assume the average length of service will improve to 8 years, and that on the average, employees leave the prison service mid-year. From surveys of previous TM programs in large corporations and in the Canadian health service, we assume here that 5% of the active TM participants will discontinue the practice each year (Herron et al., 1996). The combination of these two factors (staff turnover and program attrition) produces the estimate of "percent continuing" in a given year. Those not continuing are assumed to yield no benefits to the Department. Note that the 3.9:1 savings-cost ratio accrues even though only 40% of the employees who start the program are expected to be employed by the prison and continuing the practice of TM for the entire 5 years.

Discussion of Cost Savings for Corrections Staff

The savings-to-cost ratio for Department of Corrections staff over a 5-year period is 3.9 to 1. The four areas of savings are listed in the left column of the top part of Table 3. The cost-benefit analysis has four parts: (a) the projected 5-year costs per employee in each area without the TM program, (b) the projected 5-year costs per employee with the TM program, (c) the parameters used, (d) and the percentage reductions applied to the top chart (without TM) to obtain the costs with the TM program. Immediate savings would occur only to the extent that the state is self-insured. By "self-insured," we mean the state assumes the risks for health care expenses. Thus, a state is self-insured in this sense, even when it pays an HMO or insurer to administer its health care program.

SOCIETAL BENEFITS

A number of studies have estimated the annual cost of crime to society as a whole. Of necessity, some of the costs in these studies are speculative. The projected savings are also speculative in that there have been no actual implementations of the TM program in prison systems in the United States on a large enough scale to reduce crime to such an extent that it would be noticed in crime statistics. Since most crime is not reported to police and a large fraction of reported crime does not result in a conviction, one cannot assign a specific percentage of crime to parolees with certainty. Table 4 gives recent estimates for various categories nationwide and what sorts of social savings could be expected. The analysis assumes that a parolee who is not reconvicted of a crime is no longer committing crimes. While this gives police, parole officers, and courts (and parolees) more credit than most of them would willingly accept, it is difficult to justify any other specific number.

Table 4: Societal Costs of Crime

Costs:	
Police, courts, and prisons	$90 billion (*Business Week* 12/13/93)
Private protection	$65 billion (BW)
Property loss	$45 billion (BW)
Economic value of lost and broken lives and medical care for victims	$175 billion (BW)
Urban decay due to those fleeing violence	$50 billion (BW)
Crimes against business	$120 billion (*U.S. News and World Report*, 1/17/94)
Drug abuse (excluding police and incarceration costs)	$40 billion (USNWR)
Driving while intoxicated	$110 billion (USNWR)
Total	$695 billion
Less cost of incarceration	($26) billion
Cost of crime due to "at-large" criminals	$669 billion

Estimating Societal Cost Savings

To estimate societal cost savings, we begin by estimating the total cost of crime for the United States and dividing this by an estimate of the number of people involved in criminal activity (see below). This gives the societal "cost per criminal," (an average, of course, as different classes of crimes have differing costs).

We then apply this cost to the 5-year probability of return to prison. In this model, the "cost for a year" is as follows: "the probability of a person being at-large in that year" times "the cost of being at-large" plus "the probability of being incarcerated in that year" times "the cost of incarceration." We have used a participating population of 1,000 for this estimate.

Estimating the Number of People Involved in Criminal Behavior

It is difficult to determine the number of criminals to whom the cost may be attributed and thereby obtain an "average cost per criminal." However, the number of persons engaged in criminal behavior is certainly larger than the number under court supervision. The Bureau of Justice statistics states that there are 6.3 million individuals under court supervision in the United States (Bureau of Justice Statistics, 2001). There are numerous indicators that the actual number of people committing crimes each year in the United States is considerably more than 6 million. For example, nationwide: (a) only 38% of crimes are reported to the police (Sourcebook of Criminal Justice Statistics–1992, 3.11, 1993); (b) only 130,000 of the estimated 6 million violent crimes in 1990 resulted in felony convictions (USNWR, 1/17/94); and (c) one in four of those arrested for a serious crime are currently on probation or parole (Bureau of Justice Statistics, 1996, 1999). Furthermore, a self-report survey of high school seniors found that in the past year: 4.3% had committed armed robbery, 6% had committed auto theft, 13% had committed aggravated assault, 22% had gotten in trouble with the police because of something they did, and 30% had shoplifted (Sourcebook–1992, 3.70, 1993). Given the above data, we have conservatively estimated that the number of people involved in crime in the United States is twice the 6 million currently under court order, putting the cost of crime per criminal at $55,750 per year.

Calculating the Societal Cost Savings

In calculating the savings to society in Table 4, we assume: (a) everyone who will not return to prison has a zero cost–that is, they do not commit any crimes; (b) everyone who will return to prison has a cost of $55,750 per year from the time he is released until the time he returns to prison; and (c) everyone who returns to prison stays there for an average of 2 years and is then released with the probability of further recidivism outlined as follows. For recidivism (defined as return-to-prison), we have estimated that 24% return in the first year, 12% in the second year, 6% in the third, 3% in the fourth, and 3% in the fifth. The societal savings calculation computes the expected savings for one person released and then multiplies by the number of people initially participating in the TM program.

A further refinement would be to determine to what degree the zero cost assumption might be modified. Even parolees who do not return to prison often have difficulty adjusting after release. They may participate in drug treatment programs, welfare programs, homeless shelters, Medicaid, and receive unemployment insurance. On the other hand, a study of VA veterans who were compulsive gamblers or alcoholics and who learned the TM program showed them to have improved employment status (Bielefeld, 1981). Also, Brooks and Scarano (1985) showed improved employment status among Vietnam veterans being treated in a VA hospital for post-traumatic stress disorder. Improved employment of inmates after release could significantly reduce these other kinds of costs. Further research could compare post-release social program costs of parolees who learned the TM program in prison vs. those who did not. The significant costs associated with gathering statistics on the finances and program activities of parolees have, to date, prevented gathering baseline data we might use for making estimates (Georgia, 1999). Thus, no estimates of such savings are included.

Discussion of Societal Benefits

The analysis in Table 4 computes the expected societal cost over 5 years of releasing an inmate from a typical U.S. state prison system. Table 5 shows the savings for an inmate who has learned the TM program and has been released at the start of year 1. The 5-year societal savings-to-cost ratio for the inmates who have learned TM and have been released is 8.5 to 1.

CONCLUSION

The estimated ratio of benefits to program cost by introducing a program to instruct 1,000 inmates and 100 correctional officers in the TM technique is 10 to 1. The expected benefits total $31.6 million (combining in-prison savings by teaching inmates and correctional officers with societal savings, which includes the savings from reductions in recidivism). The currently stated program cost is $3.15 million. Of the total savings, 46% would be realized directly by the government, while the general public would realize 54%.

Cost-of-crime estimates vary widely, as do the public's perception of crime and the funding allocated to criminal justice activities. Inmate costs and time spent in prison depend on the actions of legislators as well as on the actions of offenders. Thus, the actual cost savings realized from the TM program also will vary. The range of savings estimated in this paper, however, should be

Table 5: Societal Savings per Inmate Released

United States: Societal cost of crime per inmate released at start of year 1; savings with TM

Description:	Yr 1	Yr 2	Yr 3	Yr 4	Yr 5
Recidivism rate	24%	12%	6%	3%	3%
Probability of being at-large, committing crimes	48%	24%	12%	15%	12%
Cost of crime per criminal at-large	55,750	57,423	59,145	60,920	62,747
Probability of being reincarcerated	0%	24%	36%	18%	15%
Cost of incarceration, per person	25,962	26,741	27,543	28,369	29,220
Average annual cost of person released at start of year one	26,760	20,199	17,013	13,952	11,541
Reduction due to TM	30%	30%	30%	30%	30%
Average annual cost after TM	18,732	14,139	11,909	9,766	8,079
5-year cost before TM	89,466				
5-year cost after TM	62,626				
5-year savings, per person	26,840				
5-year savings, 1,000 TM releases	26,839,665				
Cost–1,000 TM inmates, 100 TM correctional officers	3,150,000				
Benefit-cost ratio	8.52				

readily apparent if adopted for a large portion of a state's offenders and criminal justice personnel for 3 to 5 years.

NOTE

1. Transcendental Meditation, TM, and TM-Sidhi are registered or common law trademarks licensed to Maharishi Vedic Education Development Corporation and used under sublicense or with permission.

AUTHOR'S NOTE

Address correspondence to David Magill, Enlightened Sentencing Project, 625 N. Euclid Avenue, Suite 228, St. Louis, MO 63108 (E-mail: davemagill@ltds.com).

REFERENCES

Abrams, A. I. (1989). A follow-up study of the effects of the Transcendental Meditation program on inmates at Folsom Prison. In R. A. Chalmers, G. Clements, H. Schenkluhn, & M. Weinless (Eds.), *Scientific research on Maharishi's Transcendental Meditation and TM-Sidhi program: Collected papers* (pp. 2108-2112). Vlodrop, The Netherlands: Maharishi Vedic University Press.

Abrams, A. I., & Siegel, L. M. (1978). The Transcendental Meditation program and rehabilitation at Folsom State Prison: A cross-validation study. *Criminal Justice and Behavior*, *5* (1), 3-20.

Adey, W. R., & Bawin, S. M. (1977). Brain interaction with weak electrical and magnetic fields. *Neurosciences Research Program Bulletin*, *15*, 104-129.

af Klinteberg, B. (1996). Biology, norms, and personality: A developmental perspective. *Neuropsychobiology*, *34*, 146-154.

Agnew, R. (1985). A revised strain theory of delinquency. *Social Forces*, *64* (1), 151-167.

Agnew, R. (1992). Foundation for a general strain theory of crime and delinquency. *Criminology*, *30* (1), 47-87.

Agnew, R., & White, H. R. (1992). An empirical test of general strain theory. *Criminology*, *30* (4), 475-499.

Ahlström, H. H. (1991). *Transcendental Meditation, adaptation mechanisms and valuations*. Unpublished doctoral dissertation, Maharishi International University, Iowa.

Akaike, H. (1973). Information theory and an extension of the maximum likelihood principle. In B. N. Petrov & F. Csake (Eds.), *Second International Symposium on Information Theory* (pp. 267-281). Budapest, Hungary: Akademiai Kiado.

Akana, S. F., Scribner, K. A., Bradbury, M. J., Strack, A. M., Walker, C. D., & Dallman, M. F. (1992). Feedback sensitivity of the rat hypothalamo-pituitary-adrenal axis and its capacity to adjust to exogenous corticosterone. *Endocrinology*, *131* (2), 585-594.

Alcoholics Anonymous. (1955). *Alcoholics Anonymous*. (2nd ed.). New York: Alcoholics Anonymous World Services.

Alexander, A., Roessler, R., & Greenfield, N. (1963). Ego strength and physiological responsivity. *Archives of General Psychiatry*, *9*, 142-145.

Alexander, C. N. (1982). Ego development, personality and behavioral change in inmates practicing the Transcendental Meditation technique or participating in other programs: A cross-sectional and longitudinal study. (Doctoral dissertation, Harvard University, 1982). *Dissertation Abstracts International*, *43*, 539B.

Alexander, C. N., & Boyer, R. W. (1989). Seven states of consciousness: Unfolding the full potential of the cosmic psyche in individual life through Maharishi's Vedic Psychology. *Modern Science and Vedic Science, 2* (4), 325-371.

Alexander, C. N., & Langer, E. J. (Eds.). (1990). *Higher stages of human development: Perspectives on adult growth.* New York: Oxford University Press.

Alexander, C. N., & Orme-Johnson, D. W. (this volume). Walpole study of the *Transcendental Meditation* program in maximum security prisoners II: Longitudinal study of development and psychopathology. *Journal of Offender Rehabilitation,* 36(1/2/3/4), 127-160.

Alexander, C. N., Barnes, V. A., Schneider, R. H., Langer, E. J., Newman, R. I., Chandler, H. M., Davies, J. L., & Rainforth, M. (1996). A randomized controlled trial of stress reduction on cardiovascular and all-cause mortality in the elderly: Results of 8 and 15 year follow-ups. *Circulation, 93,* 629. Abstract.

Alexander, C. N., Cranson, R. W., Boyer, R. W., & Orme-Johnson, D. W. (1987). Transcendental consciousness: A fourth state of consciousness beyond sleep, dreaming, and waking. In J. Gackenbach (Ed.), *Sleep and dreams: A sourcebook* (pp. 282-315). New York: Garland Publishing, Inc.

Alexander, C. N., Davies, J. L., Dixon, C. A., Dillbeck, M. C., Oetzel, R. M., Druker, S. M., Muehlman, J. M., & Orme-Johnson, D. W. (1990). Growth of higher stages of consciousness: Maharishi's Vedic psychology of human development. In C. N. Alexander & E. J. Langer (Eds.), *Higher stages of human development: Perspectives on adult growth* (pp. 286-341). New York: Oxford University Press.

Alexander, C. N., Druker, S. M., & Langer, E. J. (1990). Introduction: Major Issues in the Exploration of Adult Growth. In C. N. Alexander & E. J. Langer (Eds.), *Higher stages of human development* (pp. 3-32). New York: Oxford University Press.

Alexander, C. N., Heaton, D. P., & Chandler, H. M. (1994). Advanced human development in the Vedic psychology of Maharishi Mahesh Yogi: Theory and research. In M. E. Miller & S. R. Cook-Greuter (Eds.), *Transcendence and mature thought in adulthood* (pp. 39-70). Lenham, Maryland: Rowman & Littlefield Publishers, Inc.

Alexander, C. N., Langer, E. J., Newman, R. I., Chandler, H. M., & Davies, J. L. (1989). Transcendental Meditation, mindfulness, and longevity: An experimental study with the elderly. *Journal of Personality and Social Psychology, 57,* 950-964.

Alexander, C. N., Rainforth, M. V., & Gelderloos, P. (1991). Transcendental Meditation, self-actualization and psychological health: A conceptual overview and statistical meta-analysis. *Journal of Social Behavior and Personality, 6* (5), 189-247.

Alexander, C. N., Rainforth, M. V., Frank, P. R., Grant, J. D, von Stade, C., & Walton, K. G. (this volume). Walpole study of the *Transcendental Meditation* program in maximum security prisoners III: Reduced recidivism. *Journal of Offender Rehabilitation,* 36(1/2/3/4), 161-180.

Alexander, C. N., Robinson, P., & Rainforth, M. (1994). Treating and preventing alcohol, nicotine, and drug abuse through Transcendental Meditation: A review and statistical meta-analysis. *Alcoholism Treatment Quarterly, 11* (1/2), 13-87.

Alexander, C. N., Robinson, P., Orme-Johnson, D. W., Schneider, R. H., & Walton, K. G. (1994). The effects of Transcendental Meditation compared to other methods of relaxation and meditation in reducing risk factors, morbidity, and mortality. *Homeostasis, 35* (4-5), 243-263.

Alexander, C. N., Schneider, R. H., Staggers, F., Rainforth, M., Sheppard, W., Clayborne, M., Kondwani, K., Smith, S., & Murray, P. (1997, July). *Effects of stress reduction on improved quality of life in hypertensive African Americans: A randomized controlled study of Transcendental Meditation and progressive relaxation.* Paper presented at the Twelfth International Interdisciplinary Conference on Hypertension in Blacks, London, England.

Alexander, C. N., Schneider, R. H., Staggers, F., Sheppard, W., Clayborne, B. W., Rainforth, M., Salerno, J., Kondwani, K., Smith, S., Walton, K. G., & Egan, B. (1996). A trial of stress reduction for hypertension in older African Americans (Part II): Sex and risk subgroup analysis. *Hypertension, 28* (2), 228-237.

Alexander, C. N., Swanson, G. C., Rainforth, M. V., Carlisle, T. W., Todd, C. C., & Oates, R. M., Jr. (1993). Effects of the Transcendental Meditation program on stress reduction, health, and employee development: A prospective study in two occupational settings. *Anxiety, Stress, and Coping, 6*, 245-262.

Alexander, C. N., Walton, K. G., & Goodman, R. S. (this volume). Walpole study of the *Transcendental Meditation* program in maximum security prisoners I: Cross-sectional differences in development and psychopathology. *Journal of Offender Rehabilitation*, 36(1/2/3/4), 97-125.

Alexander, V. K. (2000). Charles N. "Skip" Alexander: Spiritual seeker and psychologist. *Journal of Adult Development, 7* (4), 191-192.

Amaral, D. G., & Sinnamon, H. M. (1977). The locus coeruleus: Neurobiology of a central noradrenergic nucleus. *Progress in Neurobiology, 9*, 147-196.

American Correctional Association. (1983). *Correctional officers: Power, pressure and responsibility*. American Correctional Association.

American Correctional Association. (1984). *Stress management for correctional officers and their families* (pp. xi-xii). American Correctional Association.

American Correctional Association. (1995). *Directory of juvenile and adult correctional departments, institutions, and paroling authorities*. Langham, MD: American Correctional Association.

American Correctional Association. (1997). *1997 Directory, juvenile and adult correctional departments, institutions, agencies and paroling authorities*. American Correctional Association.

American Psychological Association. (1993). *Violence and youth* (Volume 1). Washington, DC: American Psychological Association Press.

Andrews, D. A. (1990). Some criminological sources of anti-rehabilitation. *Canadian Journal of Criminology, 32*, 511-524.

Andrews, D. A., & Bonta, J. (1994). *The psychology of criminal conduct.* Cincinnati, OH: Anderson.

Andrews, D. A., Bonta, J., & Hoge, R. D. (1990). Classification for effective rehabilitation: Rediscovering psychology. *Criminal and Justice Behavior, 17* (1), 19-52.

Andrews, D. A., Zinger, I., Hoge, R. D., Bonta, J., Gendreau, P., & Cullen, F. T. (1990a). Does correctional treatment work? A clinically relevant and psychologically informed meta-analysis. *Criminology, 28* (3), 369-404.

Andrews, D. A., Zinger, I., Hoge, R. D., Bonta, J., Gendreau, P., & Cullen, F. T. (1990b). A human science approach or more punishment and pessimism: A rejoinder to Lab and Whitehead. *Criminology, 28* (3), 419-429.

Anklesaria, F. (1990). *New horizons in criminology and penitentiary science: The Maharishi unified field based integrated system of rehabilitation in Senegalese prisons* (p. 159). Vlodrop, The Netherlands: MVU Press.

Anklesaria, F. K., & King, M. S. (this volume). The *Transcendental Meditation* program in the Senegalese penitentiary system. *Journal of Offender Rehabilitation,* 36(1/2/3/4), 303-318.

Anklesaria, F. K., & King, M. S. (this volume). A community-based sentencing program for probationers: The Enlightened Sentencing Project: A judicial innovation. *Journal of Offender Rehabilitation*, 36(1/2/3/4), 35-46.

Anklesaria, F., & King, M. S. (1993a). Developing the full potential of police officers: Maharishi's integrated system of rehabilitation in the Brazilian military police forces. In F. Anklesaria & M. S. King (Eds.), *Scientific research on Maharishi's integrated system of rehabilitation* (pp. 222-229). Fairfield, IA: Maharishi University of Management Press.

Anklesaria, F., & King, M. S. (1993b). The nation-wide implementation of Maharishi's integrated system of rehabilitation in Senegal–A case study. In F. Anklesaria & M. S. King (Eds.), *Scientific research on Maharishi's integrated system of rehabilitation*. Fairfield, IA: MIU Press.

Anklesaria, F., & King, M. S. (Eds.). (in press). *Total rehabilitation: The theoretical basis and practical applications of Maharishi's integrated system of rehabilitation.* Fairfield, IA: Maharishi University of Management Press.

Antelman, S. M., Caggiula, A. R., Knopf, S., Kocan, D. J., & Edwards, D. J. (1992). Amphetamine or haloperidol 2 weeks earlier antagonized the plasma corticosterone response to amphetamine: Evidence for the stressful/foreign nature of drugs. *Psychopharmacology*, *107*, 331-336.

Appelle, S., & Oswald, L. E. (1973). Simple reaction time as a function of alertness and prior mental acivity. *Perceptual and Motor Skills*, *38*, 1263-1268.

Apter, A., van Praag, H., Plutchik, R., Sevy, S., Korn, M., & Brown, S. -L. (1990). Interrelationships among anxiety, aggression, impulsivity, and mood: A serotoninally linked cluster? *Psychiatry Research*, *32*, 191-199.

Arbuthnot, J., Gordon, D. A., & Jurkovic, G. J. (1987). Personality. In H. C. Quay (Ed.), *Handbook of juvenile delinquency* (pp. 139-183). New York: Wiley.

Arlin, P. K. (1989). Problem solving and problem finding in young artists and young scientists. *Adult Development*, *1*, 197-216.

Aron, A., & Aron, E. N. (1980). The Transcendental Meditation program's effect on addictive behavior. *Addictive Behaviors*, *5*, 3-12.

Aron, A., & Aron, E. N. (1989). Rehabilitation of juvenile offenders through the Transcendental Meditation program: A controlled study. In R. A. Chalmers, G. Clements, H. Schenkluhn, & M. Weinless (Eds.), *Scientific research on Maharishi's Transcendental Meditation and TM-Sidhi program: Collected papers, volume 3* (pp. 2163-2169). Vlodrop, The Netherlands: Maharishi Vedic University Press.

Aron, A., Orme-Johnson, D. W., & Brubaker, P. (1981). The Transcendental Meditation program in the college curriculum: A 4-year longitudinal study of effects on cognitive and affective functioning. *College Student Journal*, *15* (2), 140-146.

Aron, E. N., & Aron, A. (1982). Transcendental Meditation program and marital adjustment. *Psychological Reports, 51*, 887-890.

Arthur, J. (1991). Development and crime in Africa: A test of modernization theory. *Journal of Criminal Justice, 19*, 499-513.

Arthur, W. J., & Day, D. V. (1991). Examination of the construct validity of alternative measures of field dependence/independence. *Perceptual and Motor Skills, 72*, 851-859.

Assimakis, P. D., & Dillbeck, M. C. (1995). Time series analysis of improved quality of life in Canada: Social change, collective consciousness, and the TM-Sidhi program. *Psychological Reports, 76*, 1171-1193.

Aston-Jones, G. (1985). Behavioral functions of the locus coeruleus derived from cellular attributes. *Physiological Psychology, 13*, 118-126.

Aston-Jones, G., & Bloom, F. E. (1981). Norepinepherine-containing locus coeruleus neurons in behaving rats exhibit pronounced responses to non-noxious environmental stimuli. *Journal of Neuroscience, 1*, 887-900.

Ax, A. (1953). The physiological differentiation between fear and anger in humans. *Psychosomatic Medicine, 15*, 433-442.

Azar, E. E. (1980). The Conflict and Peace Data Bank (COPDAB) project. *Journal of Conflict Resolution, 24*, 143-152.

Badawi, K., Wallace, R. K., Orme-Johnson, D. W., & Rouzere, A. M. (1984). Electrophysiologic characteristics of respiratory suspension periods occuring during the practice of the Transcendental Meditaton program. *Psychosomatic Medicine, 46* (3), 267-276.

Baer, N., Nidich, S., & Abrams, A. (1989). A comparative study of Maharishi International University and two small private colleges on perceived personal growth, perceived academic atmosphere, and general quality of life. In R. A. Chalmers, G. Clements, H. Schenkluhn, & M. Weinless (Eds.), *Scientific research on Maharishi's Transcendental Meditation and TM-Sidhi program: Collected papers, Volume 4* (pp. 2371-2377). Vlodrop, The Netherlands: Maharishi Vedic University Press.

Bakan, D. (1966). *The duality of human existence.* Boston: Beacon.

Ballou, D. (1977). The Transcendental Meditation program at Stillwater Prison. In D. W. Orme-Johnson & J. T. Farrow (Eds.), *Scientific research on the Transcendental Meditation program: Collected papers, volume 1* (pp. 569-576). Rheinweiler, Germany: Maharishi European Research University Press.

Banquet, J. P. (1973). Spectral analysis of the EEG in meditation. *Electroencephalography and Clinical Neurophysiology, 35*, 143-151.

Banquet, J. P., & LeSevre, N. (1980). Event-related potentials in altered states of consciousness. *Motivation, Motor and Sensory Processes of the Brain, Progress in Brain Research, 54*, 447-453.

Barak, G. (Ed.). (1994). *Varieties of criminology: Readings from a dynamic discipline.* Westport, CT: Praeger.

Baron, R. (1974). Aggression as a function of victim's pain cues, level of prior anger arousal, and exposure to an aggressive model. *Journal of Personality and Social Psychology, 29*, 117-124.

Barr, R., & Pease, K. (1990). Crime placement, displacement and deflection. In M. Tonry and N. Morris (Eds.), *Crime and justice: A review of research, Volume 12* (pp. 277-318). Chicago, IL: University of Chicago Press.

Barratt, E. S. (1959). Anxiety and impulsiveness related to psychomotor efficiency. *Perceptual and Motor Skills, 9*, 191-198.

Barratt, E. S. (1965). Factor analysis of some psychometric measures of impulsiveness and anxiety. *Psychological Reports, 16*, 547-554.

Barriga, A. Q. (1996). *Preliminary evaluation of a social-cognitive model of adolescent problem behaviors.* Unpublished doctoral dissertation, The Ohio State University.

Barriga, A. Q., & Gibbs, J. C. (1996). Measuring cognitive distortion in antisocial youth: Development and preliminary evaluation of the How I Think questionnaire. *Aggressive Behavior, 22*, 333-343.

Barriga, A. Q., Harrold, J. R., Stinson, B. L., II, Liau, A. K., & Gibbs, J. C. (under review). Cognitive distortion and problem behaviors in adolescents. *Criminal Justice and Behavior.*

Barriga, A. Q., Landau, J. R., Stinson, B. L., II, Liau, A. K., & Gibbs, J. C. (2000). Cognitive distortion and problem behaviors in adolescents. *Criminal Justice and Behavior, 27* (1), 36-57.

Baumrind, D. (1985). Familial antecedents of adolescent drug use: A developmental perspective. In C. Jones & R. Battjes (Eds.), *Etiology of drug abuse: Implications for prevention.* (National Institute of Drug Abuse Research Monograph, No. 56, pp. 13-44, DHHS Publication No. ADM 85-1335). Washington, DC: U.S. Government Printing Office.

Beck, A. J. (2000, April). *Prison and jail inmates at midyear 1999.* Publication no. NCJ 181643. Washington, DC: U.S. Department of Justice, Bureau of Justice Statistics.

Beck, A. J., & Shipley, B. E. (1987). *Recidivism of young parolees* (Bureau of Justice Statistics Special Report NCJ-104916). Washington, DC: U.S. Department of Justice.

Benson, H., & Wallace, R. K. (1972). Decreased drug abuse with Transcendental Meditation: A study of 1,862 subjects. In C. J. D. Zarafonetis (Ed.), *Drug abuse: Proceedings of the international conference* (pp. 369-376). Philadelphia, PA: Lea and Febiger.

Bernard, C. (1879). *Leçons sur les phénomènes de la vie commune aux animaux et aux végétaux, Volume 2.* Paris: Baillière.

Bevan, A. (1980). Endocrine changes in Transcendental Meditation. *Clinical and Experimental Pharmacology and Physiology, 7*, 75-76.

Bevan, A. J. W., Young, P. M., Wellby, M. L., Nenadovic, P., & Dickins, J. A. (1976). Endocrine changes in relaxation procedures. *Proceedings of the Endocrine Society of Australia, 19*, 59.

Biaggio, M. K., & Maiuro, R. D. (1985). Recent advances in anger assessment. In C. D. Spielberger & J. N. Butcher (Eds.), *Advances in personality assessment* (pp. 71-111). Hillsdale, NJ: Lawrence Erlbaum.

Bielefeld, M. (1989). Transcendental Meditation: A stress reducing self-help support system in vocational rehabilitation: Do psychologists really belong? Paper presented at the Annual Convention of the American Psychological Association, Los Angeles, California. In R. A. Chalmers, G. Clements, H. Schenkluhn, & M. Weinless (Eds.), *Scientific research on Maharishi's Transcendental Meditation and TM-Sidhi program: Collected papers, vol. 3* (pp. 2123-2127). Vlodrop, The Netherlands: Maharishi Vedic University Press.

Bilchik, S. (2000). *1999 National report series, juvenile justice bulletin: Kids and guns* [On-line]. Available: <http://www.ncjrs.org/html/ojjdp/jjbul2000_03_2/kid3. html>.

Bjork, J., Dougherty, D., Moeller, F., Cherek, D., & Swann, A. (1999). The effects of tryptophan depletion and loading on laboratory aggression in men: Time course and a food-restricted control. *Psychopharmacology (Berl), 142* (1), 24-30.

Black, D. (1976). *The behavior of law*. New York: Academic.

Blackburn, R. (1971). MMPI dimensions of sociability and impulse control. *Journal of Consulting and Clinical Psychology, 37*, 166.

Blackburn, R. (1975). An empirical classification of the psychopathic personality. *British Journal of Psychiatry, 127*, 456-460.

Blackburn, R. (1986). Patterns of personality deviation among violent offenders: Replication and extension of an empirical taxonomy. *British Journal of Criminology, 26* (3), 254-269.

Blackburn, R. (1996). Replicated personality disorder clusters among mentally disordered offenders and their relation to dimensions of personality. *Journal of Personality Disorders, 10*, 68-81.

Blanchard, D. C., & Blanchard, R. J. (1979). Defensive behaviors in rats following septal and septal-amygdala lesions. *Journal of Comparative and Physiological Psychology, 93*, 378-380.

Blanchard, E., Kolb, L., Pallmeyer, T., & Gerardi, R. (1982). A psychophysiological study of posttraumatic stress disorder in Vietnam veterans. *Psychiatric Quarterly, 54* (4), 220-229.

Blasi, A. (1980). Bridging moral cognition and moral action: A critical review of the literature. *Psychological Bulletin, 88*, 1-45.

Bleick, C. R., & Abrams, A. I. (1987). The Transcendental Meditation program and criminal recidivism in California. *Journal of Criminal Justice, 15* (3), 211-230.

Bliss, E. L., Thatcher, W., & Ailion, J. (1972). Relationship of stress to brain serotonin and 5-hydroxyindoleacetic acid. *Journal of Psychiatric Research, 9*, 71-80.

Bloomfield, H. H., & Kory, R. (1976). *Happiness: The TM program, psychiatry, and enlightenment*. New York: Simon and Shuster.

Borland, C., & Landrith III, G. (1977). Improved quality of city life through the Transcendental Meditation program: Decreased crime rate. In D. W. Orme-Johnson & J. T. Farrow (Eds.), *Scientific research on the Transcendental Meditation program: Collected papers, Volume 1* (pp. 639-648). Rheinweiler, Germany: Maharishi European Research University Press.

Box, G. E. P., & Jenkins, G. M. (1976). *Time series analysis: Forecasting and control* (Rev. ed.). San Francisco: Holden-Day.

Braithwaite, J. (1989). *Crime, shame, reintegration*. Cambridge: Cambridge University Press.

Brand, C. R., & Deary, I. J. (1982). Intelligence and inspection time. In H. J. Eysenck (Ed.), *A model of intelligence* (pp. 133-148). New York: Springer.

Brautigam, E. (1977). Effects of the Transcendental Meditation program on drug abusers: A prospective study. In D. W. Orme-Johnson & J. T. Farrow (Eds.), *Scientific research on the Transcendental Meditation program: Collected papers, volume 1* (pp. 506-514). Rheinweiler, Germany: Maharishi European Research University Press.

Brier, N. (1995). Predicting antisocial behavior in youngsters displaying poor academic achievement: A review of risk factors. *Journal of Developmental and Behavioral Pediatrics, 16* (4), 271-276.

Broderick, P., & Lynch, V. (1989). Behavioral and biochemical changes induced by lithium and L-tryptophan in muricidal rats. *Neuropharmacology, 21*, 671-679.

Brooke, S. M., de Haas-Johnson, A. M., Kaplan, J. R., Manuck, S. B., & Sapolsky, R. M. (1994). Dexamethasone resistance among nonhuman primates associated with a selective decrease of glucocorticoid receptors in the hippocampus and a history of social instability. *Neuroendocrinology, 60*, 134-140.

Brooks, J. S., & Scarano, T. (1985). Transcendental Meditation in the treatment of post-Vietnam adjustment. *Journal of Counseling and Development, 64*, 212-215.

Broome, V. J. (1989). *Relationship between participation in Transcendental Meditation and the functionality of marriage.* Unpublished master's thesis, University of Witwatersrand, Johannesburg, South Africa.

Brown, G. L., Ebert, M. H., Goyer, P. F., Jimerson, D. C., Klein, W. J., Bunney Jr., W. E., & Goodwin, F. K. (1982). Aggression, suicide, and serotonin: Relationship to CSF amine metabolites. *American Journal of Psychiatry, 139*, 741-746.

Brown, G., Goodwin, F., Ballenger, J., Goyer, P., & Major, L. (1979). Aggression in humans correlates with cerebropinal fluid amine metabolites. *Psychiatry Research, 1*, 131-139.

Brown, M. (1976). Higher education for higher consciousness: A study of students at Maharishi International University. (Doctoral dissertation, University of California at Berkeley, 1976). *Dissertation Abstracts International, 38*, 649A-650A.

Brown, S.-L., Botsis, A., & Van Praag, H. (1994). Serotonin and Aggression. In M. Hillbrand & N. Pallone (Eds.), *The psychobiology of aggression: Engines, measurement, control* (pp. 27-39). New York: The Haworth Press, Inc.

Browne, G. E., Fougére, D., Roxburgh, A., Bird, J., & Lovell-Smith, H. D. (1989). Improved mental and physical health and decreased use of prescribed and non-prescribed drugs through the Transcendental Meditation program. In R. A. Chalmers, G. Clements, H. Schenkluhn, & M. Weinless (Eds.), *Scientific research on Maharishi's Transcendental Meditation and TM-Sidhi program: Collected papers, volume 3* (pp. 1884-1905). Vlodrop, The Netherlands: Maharishi Vedic University Press.

Browning, D. L. (1986). Psychiatric ward behavior and length of stay in adolescent and young adult inpatients: A developmental approach to prediction. *Journal of Consulting and Clinical Psychology, 54*, 227-230.

Bujatti, M., & Riederer, P. (1976). Serotonin, noradrenaline, and dopamine metabolites in the Transcendental Meditation technique. *Journal of Neural Transmission, 39*, 257-267.

Burch, G., Cohn, A., & Neuman, C. (1942). A study by quantitative methods of spontaneous variations in volume of the fingertip, toe tip, and posterio-superior portion of the pinna of resting, normal, white adults. *American Journal of Physiology, 136*, 433-447.

Burchfield, S. R. (1979). The stress response: A new perspective. *Psychosomatic Medicine, 41* (8), 661-672.

Bureau of Justice Bulletin. (1993). *Drugs, crime and the justice system. National update. Criminal victimization in 1991*. Washington DC: Bureau of Justice.

Bureau of Justice Statistics. (1993a). *Survey of state prison inmates, 1991* (p. 26). Washington, DC: U.S. Department of Justice.

Bureau of Justice Statistics. (1993b). *Sourcebook of criminal justice statistics–1992*. Washington, DC: U.S. Department of Justice.

Bureau of Justice Statistics. (1994). *Sourcebook of criminal justice statistics–1993*. Washington, DC: U.S. Department of Justice.

Bureau of Justice Statistics. (1995). *Sourcebook of criminal justice statistics–1994*. Washington, DC: U.S. Department of Justice.

Bureau of Justice Statistics. (1996, 1999). *Felony defendants in large urban counties*. NCJ-176981, p. 8.

Bureau of Justice Statistics. (1999a). *Drugs and crime facts, 1994* [Online]. Available at www.ojp.usdoj.gov/bjs/drugs.htm.

Bureau of Justice Statistics. (1999b). *Expenditure and employment statistics: Summary findings* [Online]. Available at <www.ojp.usdoj.gov/bjs>.

Bureau of Justice Statistics. (2001). *Corrections statistics*. [Online]. Available at: <www.ojp.usdoj.gov/bjs/correct.htm>.

Buss, A. H., & Durkee, A. (1957). An inventory for assessing different kinds of hostility. *Journal of Consulting Psychology, 21* (4), 343-349.

Buydens-Branchey, L., & Branchey, M. (1992). Cortisol in alcoholics with a disordered aggression control. *Psychoneuroendocrinology, 17* (1), 45-54.

California Department of Corrections. (1999). *About the California Department of Corrections: Fact sheet*. California Department of Corrections Internet Web page (http://www.cdc.state.ca.us/factsht.htm).

Camelia, C. R. T., Alexander, C. N., Hawkins, M. A., Durchholz, C. F., & Walton, K. G. (1995). [Effects of Maharishi's Consciousness-Based approach to rehabilitation on inmates in the Netherlands Antilles: IV. Changes in motivation.] Unpublished raw data.

Camp, G. M. & Camp, C. G. (1993). *The corrections yearbook–Adult corrections*. South Salem, NY: Criminal Justice Institute.

Campbell, D. T., & Stanley, J. C. (1966). *Experimental and quasi-experimental designs for research*. Chicago: Rand McNally.

Candelent, T., & Candelent, G. (1975). Teaching Transcendental Meditation in a psychiatric setting. *Hospital and Community Psychiatry, 26*, 156-159.

Cannon, W. B. (1939). *The wisdom of the body*. New York: Morton.

Carruthers, W., Carruthers, B. J. B., Day-Vines, N. L., Bostick, D., & Watson, D. C. (1996). Conflict resolution as curriculum: A definition, description, and process for integration in core curricula. *The School Counselor, 43*, 345-373.

Cattell, R. B. (1966). The scree test for the number of factors. *Multivariate Behavioral Research, 1* (April), 245-276.

Cattell, R. B., & Vogelman, S. (1977). A comprehensive trial of the scree and KG criteria for determining the number of factors. *Multivariate Behavioral Research, 12* (July), 289-325.

Cavanaugh, K. L. (1987). Time series analysis of U.S. and Canadian inflation and unemployment: A test of a field-theoretic hypothesis. *Proceedings of the American Statistical Association, Business and Economics Statistics Section* (pp. 799-804). Alexandria, VA: American Statistical Association.

Cavanaugh, K. L., & King, K. D. (1988). Simultaneous transfer function analysis of Okun's Misery Index: Improvements in the economic quality of life through Maharishi's Vedic Science and technology of consciousness. *Proceedings of the American Statistical Association, Business and Economics Statistics Section* (pp. 491-496). Alexandria, VA: American Statistical Association.

Cavanaugh, K. L., King, K. D., & Ertuna, C. (1989). A multiple-input transfer function model of Okun's Misery Index: An empirical test of the Maharishi Effect. *Proceedings of the American Statistical Association, Business and Economics Statistics Section* (pp. 565-570). Alexandria, VA: American Statistical Association.

Cavanaugh, K. L., King, K. D., & Titus, B. D. (Eds.). (1989). *Consciousness and the quality of economic life: Empirical research on the macroeconomic effects of the collective practice of Maharishi's Transcendental Meditation and TM-Sidhi program.* Chicago: Midwest Management Society.

Central Bureau of Statistics. (1996). *Statistical yearbook of the Netherlands Antilles.* Willemstad, Curaçao: Netherlands Antilles Government Printing Office.

Chaiken, S. R., & Young, R. K. (1993). Inspection time and intelligence: Attempts to eliminate the apparent movement strategy. *American Journal of Psychology, 106* (2), 191-210.

Chalmers, R. A., Clements, G., Schenkluhn, H., & Weinless, M. (Eds.). (1989). *Scientific research on Maharishi's Transcendental Meditation and TM-Sidhi program: Collected papers, volumes 2-4.* Vlodrop, The Netherlands: Maharishi Vedic University Press.

Chandler, H. M. (1990). Transcendental Meditation and awakening wisdom: A 10-year longitudinal study of self-development. *Dissertations Abstracts, 51* (10), 5048B.

Chandler, H. M., Alexander, C. N., & Heaton, D. P. (2003). Transcendental Meditation and postconventional self development: A 10-year longitudinal study. *Journal of Social Behavior and Personality.*

Chandler, K. (1987). Modern science and Vedic science: An introduction. *Modern Science and Vedic Science, 1* (1), 5-26.

Chen, M. (1984). A comparative study of dimensions of healthy functioning between families practicing the TM program for five years or for less than a year. (Doctoral dissertation, University of Pittsburgh, 1984). *Dissertation Abstracts International, 45* (10), 3206B.

Cherek, D. R., Moeller, G., Schnapp, W., & Dougherty, D. M. (1997). Studies of violent and nonviolent male parolees: 1. Laboratory and psychometric measurements of aggression. *Biological Psychiatry, 41*, 514-522.

Childs, J. P. (1973). The use of Transcendental Meditation as a therapy with juvenile offenders (Doctoral dissertation, University of Tennessee, 1990). *Dissertation Abstracts International, 34* (8), 4732A.

Childs, J. P. (1977). The use of the Transcendental Meditation program as a therapy with juvenile offenders. In D. W. Orme-Johnson & J. T. Farrow (Eds.), *Scientific research on the Transcendental Meditation Program: Collected papers, volume 1* (pp. 577-584). Rheinweiler, Germany: Maharishi European Research University.

Chrousos, G. P., & Gold, P. W. (1992). The concepts of stress and stress system disorders. *Journal of the American Medical Association, 267*, 1244-1252.

Clarke, J.C., & Saunders, J. B. (1988). *Alcoholism and problem drinking: Theories and treatment.* New York: Pergamon.

Clayton, V. P., & Birren, J. E. (1980). The development of wisdom across the life-span: A re-examination of an ancient topic. In B. P. Baltes & O. G. J. Brim (Eds.), *Life-span development and behavior.* Vol. 3 (pp. 103-135). New York: Academic Press.

Cleare, A., & Bond, A. (1995). The effect of tryptophan depletion and enhancement on subjective and behavioural aggression in normal male subjects. *Psychopharmacology (Berl), 118* (1), 72-81.

Coccaro, E. F., Kavoussi, R. J., Cooper, T. B., & Hauger, R. L. (1997). Central serotonin activity and aggression: Inverse relationship with prolactin response to d-fenfluramine, but not CSF 5-HIAA concentration, in human subjects. *American Journal of Psychiatry, 154* (10), 1430-1435.

Cohen, J. (1988). *Statistical power analysis for the behavioral sciences.* Hillsdale, NJ: Lawrence Erlbaum Associates.

Cohen, J., & Cohen, P. (1975). *Applied multiple regression/correlation analysis for the behavioral sciences.* Hillsdale, NJ: Lawrence Erlbaum Associates.

Cohen, M. A. (1990). A note on the cost of crime to victims. *Urban Studies, 27*, 139-146.

Cohler, B. J., Stott, F. M., & Musick, J. S. (1995). Adversity, vulnerability, and resilience: Cultural and developmental perspectives. In D. Cicchetti & D. J. Cohen (Eds.), *Developmental psychopathology: Volume 2, Risk, disorder and adaptation.* (pp. 753-800). New York: Wiley.

Collett, D. (1994). *Modelling survival data in medical research.* London: Chapman & Hall.

Commons, M. L., Richards, F. A., & Armon, C. (1984). *Beyond formal operations: Late adolescent and adult cognitive development.* New York: Praeger.

Congressional Budget Office Report. (1990). *The economic and budget outlook: Fiscal years 1991-1995.* (A report to the Senate and House Committees on Budget Part I). Washington, DC: Congressional Budget Office.

Cook, P. J. (1995). Gun control. In J. Q. Wilson & J. Petersilia (Eds.), *Crime.* San Francisco: ICS Press.

Cook-Greuter, S. R. (1990). Maps for living: Ego development stages from symbiosis to consciousness universal embeddedness. *In M. L. Commons, C. Armon, L. Kohlberg, F. A. Richards, T. A. Grotzer, & J. D. Sinott (Eds.), Adult development volume 2:* Models and methods in the study of adolescent and adult thought. (pp. 79-104). New York: Praeger.

Cooper, M. J., & Aygen, M. M. (1979). A relaxation technique in the management of hypercholesterolemia. *Journal of Human Stress, 5*, 24-27, 1979.

Cooper, R., Joffe, B. I., Lamprey, J. M., Botha, A. Shires, R., Baker, S. G., & Seftel, H. C. (1985). Hormonal and biochemical responses to Transcendental Meditation. *Postgraduate Medical Journal, 61* (714), 301-304.

Copenhaver, J., Schalock, R., & Carver, M. (1978). Para-chloro-D,1-phenylalanine induced filicidal behavior in the female rat. *Pharmacology, Biochemistry and Behavior, 8*, 263-270.

Costa, P., Stone, S., McCrae, R., Dembroski, T., & Williams, R. (1987). Hostility, agreeableness-antagonism, and coronary heart disease. *Holistic Medicine, 2*, 161-167.

Counts, G. (1932). *Dare the school build a new social order?* New York: The John Day Company.

Cox, D. R. (1972). Regression models and life tables (with discussion). *Journal of the Royal Statistical Society, B, 74*, 187-220.

Cox, D. R., & Hinkley, D. V. (1973). *Theoretical statistics.* New York: Dover.

Cox, D. R., & Oakes, D. (1984). *Analysis of survival data.* London: Chapman and Hall.

Coyle, A. (1993). Penal reform: Prisons in Africa. *West Africa*, 3971, 1977.

Cranson, R. W., Orme-Johnson, D. W., Gackenbach, J., Dillbeck, M. C., Jones, C. H., & Alexander, C. N. (1991). Transcendental Meditation and improved performance on intelligence-related measures: A longitudinal study. *Personality and Individual Differences, 12*, 1105-1116.

Crowne, D. P., & Marlowe, D. (1960). A new scale of social desirability independent of psychopathology. *Journal of Consulting Psychology, 24*, 349-354.

Cullen, F. T., & Gendreau, P. (1989). The effectiveness of correctional rehabilitation: Reconsidering the "nothing works" debate. In L. Goodstein & D. L. Mackenzie (Eds.), *The American prison: Issues in research and policy* (pp. 23-44): New York: Plenum Press.

Cunningham, M., & Koch, W. (1977). The Transcendental Meditation program and rehabilitation: A pilot project at the Federal Correctional Institution at Lompoc, California. In D. W. Orme-Johnson & J. T. Farrow (Eds.), *Scientific research on the Transcendental Meditation Program: Collected papers, volume 1* (pp. 562-568). Rheinweiler, Germany: Maharishi European Research University.

Curzon, G., & Green, A. R. (1968). Effect of hydrocortisone on rat brain 5-hydrocortisone on rat brain 5-hydroxytryptamine. *Life Sciences, 7*, 657-663.

Curzon, G., & Green, A. R. (1969). Effects of immobilization on rat liver tryptophan pyrrolase and brain 5-hydroxytryptamine metabolism. *British Journal of Pharmacology, 37*, 689-697.

Dahlstrom, A., & Fuxe, K. (1964). Evidence for the existence of dopamine-containing neurons in the central nervous system. I. Demonstration of monoamines in the cell bodies of brainstem neurons. *Acta Physiologica Scandinavica. Supplementum, 222*, 1-55.

Damasio, A. R., Tranel, D., & Damasio, H. (1990). Individuals with sociopathic behavior caused by frontal damage fail to respond autonomically to social stimuli. *Behavioral Brain Research, 41*, 81-94.

Davidson, R. J., & Schwartz, G. E. (1976). Psychobiology of relaxation and related states. In D. Mostofski (Ed.), *Behavioral modification and control of physiological activity.* Englewood Cliffs, NJ: Prentice-Hall.

Davies, A. O., & Lefkowitz, R. J. (1981). Agonist-promoted high affinity state of the beta-adrenergic receptor in human neutrophils: Modulation by corticosteroids. *Journal of Clinical Endocrinology and Metabolism, 53*, 703-708.

Davies, A., & Lefkowitz, R. (1980). Corticosteroid-induced differential regulation of beta-adrenergic receptors in circulating human polymorphonuclear leukocytes and mononuclear leukocytes. *Journal of Clinical Endocrinology and Metabolism, 51*, 599-605.

Davies, J. L. (1978). *The Science of Creative Intelligence in high schools: Some psychological effects and evidence for reduced use of drugs.* Unpublished manuscript, Maharishi International College, Perth, Australia.

Davies, J. L. (1988). Alleviating political violence through enhancing coherence in collective consciousness: Impact assessment analyses of the Lebanon war. *Dissertation Abstracts International, 49* (8), 2381A.

Davies, J. L., & Alexander, C. N., (in press). Alleviating political violence through reducing collective tension: Impact assessment analysis of the Lebanon war. *Journal of Social Behavior and Personality.*

Davies, J. L., Alexander, C. N., & Orme-Johnson, D. W. (1988). Alleviating political violence through enhancing coherence in collective consciousness: Impact assessment analyses of the Lebanon war. *The Journal of the Iowa Academy of Science, 95* (1), 1. (Also presented at the eighty-fifth annual meeting of the American Political Science Association, September 1989, Washington, DC).

Davies, J., & Alexander, C. (1990). Alleviating political violence through enhancing coherence in collective consciousness: Impact assessment analyses of the Lebanon war. Summary of a paper presented at the 85th Annual Meeting of the American Political Science Association, September 1989. In R. K. Wallace, D. W. Orme-Johnson, & M. C. Dillbeck (Eds.), *Scientific research on the Transcendental Meditation program: Collected papers, Volume 5* (pp. 3260-3262). Fairfield, IA: Maharishi International University Press.

De Witt, N. W. (1954). *Epicurus and his philosophy.* Westport, CT: Greenwood Press.

Denno, D. W. (1990). *Biology and violence.* New York: Cambridge University Press.

Denton, D., Coghlan, J. P., Fei, D. T., McKinley, J., Nelson, J., Scoggins, E., Tarjan, E., Tregear, G. W., Tresham, J. J., & Weisinger, R. (1984). Stress, ACTH, salt intake and high blood pressure. *Clinical Medicine and Experimental Hypertension: Theory and Practice, A6*, 403-415.

Descarries, L., Audet, M. A., Doucet, G., Garcia, S., Oleskevich, S., Seguela, P., Soghomonian, J. -J., & Watkins, K. (1990). Morphology of central serotonin neurons. In P. M. Whitaker-Azmitia & S. J. Peroutka (Eds.), *The Neuropharmacology of Serotonin* (pp. 81-92). New York: The New York Academy of Sciences.

d'Espagnat, B. (1979). The quantum theory and reality. *Scientific American, 241* (5), 158-181.

Dewey, J. (1889/1964). My pedagogic creed. In R. D. Archambault (Ed.), *John Dewey on education: Selected writings* (pp. 427-439). New York: Modern Library.

Dhanaraj, H. (1989). The influence of Transcendental Meditation on cessation of drug use: Some preliminary findings. In R. A. Chalmers, G. Clements, H. Schenkluhn, & M. Weinless (Eds.), *Scientific research on Maharishi's Transcendental Meditation and TM-Sidhi program: Collected papers, volume 2* (pp. 1159-1161). Vlodrop, The Netherlands: Maharishi Vedic University Press.

DiJulio, J. J. (1995). Tougher law enforcement is driving down urban crime. *Policy Review, Fall*, 1995, 12-16.

Dillbeck, M. C. (1983a). Testing the Vedic psychology of the Bhagavad-Gita. *Psychologia, 26*, 232-240.

Dillbeck, M. C. (1983b). The Vedic psychology of the Bhagavad-Gita. *Psychologia, 26*, 62-72.

Dillbeck, M. C. (1988). The mechanics of individual intelligence arising from the field of cosmic intelligence–the Cosmic Psyche. *Modern Science and Vedic Science, 2* (3), 244-278.

Dillbeck, M. C. (1990). Test of a field theory of consciousness and social change: Time series analysis of participation in the TM-Sidhi program and reduction of violent death in the U.S. *Social Indicators Research, 22*, 399-418.

Dillbeck, M. C., & Abrams, A. (1987). The application of the Transcendental Meditation program to correction. *International Journal of Comparative and Applied Criminal Justice, 11* (1), 111-132.

Dillbeck, M. C., & Alexander, C. N. (1989). Higher states of consciousness: Maharishi Mahesh Yogi's Vedic psychology of human development. *The Journal of Mind and Behavior, 10*, 307-334.

Dillbeck, M. C., & Araas-Vesely, S. (1986). Participation in the Transcendental Meditation program and frontal EEG coherence during concept learning. *International Journal of Neuroscience, 29*, 45-55.

Dillbeck, M. C., & Bronson, E. C. (1981). Short-term longitudinal effects of the Transcendental Meditation technique on EEG power and coherence. *International Journal of Neuroscience, 14*, 147-151.

Dillbeck, M. C., & Dillbeck, S. (1987). The Maharishi Technology of the Unified Field in education: Principles, practice, and research. *Modern Science and Vedic Science, 1* (4), 383-482.

Dillbeck, M. C., & Orme-Johnson, D. W. (1987). Physiological differences between Transcendental Meditation and rest. *American Psychologist, 42*, 879-881.

Dillbeck, M. C., & Rainforth, M. V. (1996). Impact assessment analysis of behavioral quality of life indices: Effects of group practice of the Transcendental Meditation and TM-Sidhi program. *Proceedings of the American Statistical Association, Social Statistics Section* (pp. 38-43). Alexandria, VA: American Statistical Association.

Dillbeck, M. C., Assimakis, P. D., Raimondi, D., Orme-Johnson, D. W., & Rowe, R. (1986). Longitudinal effects of the Transcendental Meditation and TM-Sidhi program on cognitive ability and cognitive style. *Perceptual and Motor Skills, 62*, 731-738.

Dillbeck, M. C., Banus, C. B., Polanzi, C., & Landrith III, G. S. (1988). Test of a field model of consciousness and social change: The Transcendental Meditation and TM-Sidhi program and decreased urban crime. *The Journal of Mind and Behavior, 9*, 457-485.

Dillbeck, M. C., Cavanaugh, K. L., Glenn, T., Orme-Johnson, D. W., & Mittlefehldt, V. (1987). Consciousness as a field: The Transcendental Meditation and TM-Sidhi program and changes in social indicators. *The Journal of Mind and Behavior, 8* (1), 67-104.

Dillbeck, M. C., Landrith, III, G., & Orme-Johnson, D. W. (1981). The Transcendental Meditation program and crime rate change in a sample of forty-eight cities. *Journal of Crime and Justice, 4*, 25-45.

Dillbeck, M. C., Orme-Johnson, D. W., & Wallace, R. K. (1981). Frontal EEG coherence, H-reflex recovery, concept learning, and the TM-Sidhi program. *International Journal of Neuroscience, 15*, 151-157.

Dillbeck, M. C., Raimondi, D., Assimakis, P. D., Rowe, R., & Orme-Johnson, D. W. (1989). The longitudinal effects of the MIU curriculum on intelligence and field independence. In R. A. Chalmers, G. Clements, H. Schenkluhn, & M. Weinless (Eds.), *Scientific research on Maharishi's Transcendental Meditation and TM-Sidhi program: Collected papers.* (pp. 2385-2386). Vlodrop, The Netherlands: Maharishi Vedic University Press.

Dillbeck, S. L., & Dillbeck, M. C. (1997). Introduction: Twenty-five years of unfolding knowledge of pure consciousness through Maharishi's Vedic science. *Modern Science and Vedic Science, 7* (1), 1-36.

Dillbeck, S., & Dillbeck, M. C. (1979). The Transcendental Meditation program as an educational technology: Research and applications. *Educational Technology, 11*, 7-13.

Dillbeck, S., & Dillbeck, M. C. (1990). *Interviews with inner-city children* [Videotape]. Fairfield, IA: Maharishi University of Management Press.

Dixon, W. J. (1992). *BMDP statistical software manual*, (Volumes 1 & 2). Los Angeles: University of California Press.

Dodge, K. A., Price, J. M., Bachorowski, J. -A., & Newman, J. P. (1990). Hostile attributional biases in severely aggressive adolescents. *Journal of Abnormal Psychology, 99*, 385-392.

Domash, L. (1977). Introduction to scientific research on the Transcendental Meditation and TM-Sidhi program. In D. W. Orme-Johnson & J. T. Farrow (Eds.), *Scientific research on the Transcendental Meditation program: Collected papers, Volume 1* (pp. 13-31). Rheinweiler, Germany: Maharishi European Research University Press.

Dossey, L. (1989). *Recovering the soul.* New York: Bantam.

Dukes, R. L., & Stein, J. A. (1997). Long-term impact of drug abuse resistance education (DARE). *Evaluation Review, 21* (4), 483-495.

Dupre, L. (1980). The mystical experience of the self and its philosophical significance. In R. Woods (Ed.), *Understanding mysticism*. New York: Image Books.

Durchholz, C. F., Travis, F. T., Camelia, C. R. T., Hawkins, M. A., & Walton, K. G. (1995). [Effects of Maharishi's Consciousness-based rehabilitation on inmates in the Netherlands Antilles: III. EEG and EDA changes.] Unpublished raw data.

Durkheim, E. (1951). *Suicide: A study in sociology* (J. A. Spaulding & G. Simpson, Trans.). New York: The Free Press. (Original work published 1897).

Edwards, D. V. (1990, August). On consciousness-centered social conflict theory: The case of the Maharishi Technology of the Unified Field. Paper presented at the annual meeting of the American Psychological Association, Boston, MA.

Egan, V. (1993). Can specific inspection time strategies be inferred by their latency? *The Irish Journal of Psychology*, *14* (2), 253-269.

Elliott, D., Huizinga, D., & Ageton, S. (1985). *Explaining delinquency and drug use.* Beverly Hills, CA: Sage.

Elliott, G. R., & Eisdorfer, C. (Eds.). (1982). *Stress and human health: Analysis and implications of research.* New York: Springer Publishing Co.

Ellis, G. (1979). *Inside Folsom Prison: The Transcendental Meditation and TM-Sidhi program.* Palm Springs, CA: ETC Publications.

Emrick, C. D. (1974). A review of psychologically oriented treatment for alcoholism: I. The use and interrelationships of outcome criteria and drinking behavior following treatment. *Quarterly Journal of Studies on Alcohol*, *34*, 534-549.

Emrick, C. D. (1975). A review of psychologically oriented treatment of alcoholism: II. The relative effectiveness of different treatment approaches and the effectiveness of treatment versus no-treatment. *Quarterly Journal of Studies on Alcohol*, *35*, 534-549.

Engel, G. L. (1953). Homeostasis, behavioral adjustment and the concept of health and disease. In R. Roy & M. D. Grinker (Ed.), *Mid-century Psychiatry* (pp. 33-58). Springfield, IL: Charles C. Thomas.

Ennett, S. T., Tobler, N., Ringwald, C. L., & Flewelling, R. L. (1994). How effective is Drug Abuse Resistance Education? A meta-analysis of Project DARE outcome evaluations. *American Journal of Public Health*, *84* (9), 1394-1406.

Eppley, K. R., Abrams, A. I., & Shear, J. (1989). Differential effects of relaxation techniques on trait anxiety: A meta-analysis. *Journal of Clinical Psychology*, *45* (6), 957-974.

Eysenck, H. (1977). *Crime and personality*. St. Albans, England: Paladin Frogmore.

Eysenck, H. H., & Eysenck, S. B. G. (1975). *Eysenck personality questionnaire.* San Diego, CA: Educational and Industrial Testing Service.

Farinelli, L. (1989). Possibilità di applicazioni della tecnologia della coscienza in aspetti di medicina preventiva: Una ricerca pilota [Potential application of a technology of consciousness in areas of preventive medicine: A pilot study]. In R. A. Chalmers, G. Clements, H. Schenkluhn, & M. Weinless (Eds.), *Scientific research on Maharishi's Transcendental Meditation and TM-Sidhi program: Collected papers, volume 3* (pp. 1830-1846). Vlodrop, The Netherlands: Maharishi Vedic University Press.

Farrington, D. P. (1989). Early predictors of adolescent aggression and adult violence. *Violence and Victims*, *4*, 79-100.

Farrington, D. P. (1991). Childhood aggression and adult violence: Early precursors and later-life outcomes. In D. J. Pepler & K. H. Rubin (Eds.), *The development and treatment of childhood aggression* (pp. 5-29). Hillsdale, NJ: Erlbaum.

Farrow, J. T., & Hebert, J. R. (1982). Breath suspension during the Transcendental Meditation technique. *Psychosomatic Medicine*, *44* (2), 133-153.

Farwell, L. A. (1996). *Effects of consciousness on a quantum-mechanical process: Evidence for a new conscious unified field paradigm in science.* Paper presented at the annual Conference on Science of Consciousness, Tucson, AZ.

Farwell, L. A., & Farwell, G. W. (1995). Quantum-mechanical processes and consciousness. *Bulletin of the American Physical Society*, *40* (2), 956-957.

Federal Bureau of Investigation. (1996). *Crime in the United States: Uniform crime reports 1996.* Washington, DC: U.S. Government Printing Office.

Federal Bureau of Investigation. (1997). *Crime in the United States: Uniform crime reports 1997.* [Online]. Available at: <www.fbi.gov/ucr>.

Feeley, M., & Simon, J. (1994). Actuarial justice: The emerging new criminal law. In D. Nelken (Ed.), *The futures of criminology* (173-201). London: Sage.

Fehr, T., Nerstheimer, U., & Törber, S. (1977a). A longitudinal study of the effect of the Transcendental Meditation program on changes in personality. In D. W. Orme-Johnson & J. T. Farrow (Eds.), *Scientific research on the Transcendental Meditation Program: Collected papers, Volume 1* (pp. 476-483). Rheinweiler, Germany: Maharishi European Research University.

Fehr, T., Nerstheimer, U., & Törber, S. (1977b). Study of personality changes resulting from the Transcendental Meditation program: Freiburger Personality Inventory. In D. W. Orme-Johnson & J. T. Farrow (Eds.), *Scientific research on the Transcendental Meditation program: Collected papers, volume 1* (pp. 420-424). Rheinweiler, Germany: Maharishi European Research University Press.

Felson, M. (1994). *Crime and everyday life.* Thousand Oaks, CA: Pine Forge Press.

Ferguson, P. C. (1989). An integrative meta-analysis of psychological studies investigating treatment outcomes of meditation techniques. In R. A. Chalmers, G. Clements, H. Schenkluhn, & M. Weinless (Eds.), *Scientific research on the Transcendental Meditation and TM-Sidhi program: Collected papers, volume 3* (pp. 2039-2048). Vlodrop, The Netherlands: Maharishi Vedic University Press.

Ferguson, P. C., & Gowan, J. C. (1976). Psychological findings on Transcendental Meditation. *Journal of Humanistic Psychology, 16,* 51-60.

Ferguson, R. E. (1989a). A self-report evaluation of the effects of the Transcendental Meditation program at Massachusetts Correctional Institution Walpole–a follow-up. In R. A. Chalmers, G. Clements, H. Schenkluhn, & M. Weinless (Eds.), *Scientific research on Maharishi's Transcendental Meditation and TM-Sidhi program: Collected papers, volume 2* (pp. 1156-1158). Vlodrop, The Netherlands: Maharishi Vedic University Press.

Ferguson, R. E. (1989b). The Transcendental Meditation program at Massachusetts Correctional Institution Walpole: An evaluation report. In R. A. Chalmers, G. Clements, H. Schenkluhn, & M. Weinless (Eds.), *Scientific research on Maharishi's Transcendental Meditation and TM-Sidhi program: Collected papers, volume 2* (pp. 1146-1156). Vlodrop, The Netherlands: Maharishi Vedic University Press.

Fergusson, D. M., Lynskey, M. T., & Horwood, L. J. (1996). Alcohol misuse and juvenile offending in adolescence. *Addiction, 91* (4), 483-494.

Fergusson, L. C. (1992). Field independence and art achievement in meditating and nonmeditating college students. *Perceptual and Motor Skills, 75,* 1171-1175.

Fergusson, L., Bonshek, A., & Le Masson, G. (1996). Vedic Science Based education and nonverbal intelligence: A preliminary longitudinal study in Cambodia. *Higher Education Research and Development, 15* (1), 73-82.

Ferris, C. F. (1996). The rage of innocents. *The Sciences, 36* (2), 22-26.

Ferris, C. F., & Grisso, T. (Ed.). (1996). *Understanding aggressive behavior in children.* New York: The New York Academy of Sciences.

Field, G. (1986). The psychological deficits and treatment needs of chronic criminality. *Federal Probation, 50* (4), 60-66.

Field, G. (1998). From the institution to the community: Studies show benefits of continuity of care in reduced recidivism, relapse rates. *Corrections Today, 60* (6), 94-97.

Fischer, K. (1980). A theory of cognitive development: The control and construction of hierarchies of skills. *Psychological Review, 87*, 477-531.

Fischer, K. W., Kenny, S. L., & Pipp, S. L. (1990). How cognitive processes and environmental conditions organize discontinuities in the development of abstractions. In C. N. Alexander & E. J. Langer (Eds.), *Higher stages of human development* (pp. 162-187). New York: Oxford University Press.

Fitts, W. H., & Hamner, W. T. (1969). *The self-concept and delinquency.* Nashville, TN: Counselor Recordings and Tests.

Flavell, J. (1985). *Cognitive development* (2nd ed.). Englewood Cliffs, NJ: Prentice-Hall.

Flavell, J. H. (1970). Cognitive changes in adulthood. In L. R. Goulet & P. B. Baltes (Eds.), *Life-span development psychology: Research and theory.* New York: Academic Press.

Fontenot, M., Kaplan, J., Manuck, S., Arango, V., & Mann, J. (1995). Long-term effects of chronic social stress on serotonin indices in the prefrontal cortex of adult male cynomolgus macaques. *Brain Research, 705* (1-2), 105-108.

Fowles, D. C. (1993). Electrodermal activity and antisocial behavior: Empirical findings and theoretical issues. In J. C. Roy, W. Boucsein, D. C. Fowles, & J. H. Gruzzelier (Eds.), *Progress in electrodermal research* (pp. 223-237). New York: Plenum.

Frank, S., & Quinlan, D. M. (1976). Ego development and female delinquency: A cognitive-developmental approach. *Journal of Abnormal Psychology, 85*, 505-510.

Freeley, M., & Sarat, A. (1980). *The policy dilemma: Federal crime policy and the Law Enforcement Assistance Administration, 1968-78.* Minneapolis, MN: University of Minnesota Press.

Frew, D. R. (1974). Transcendental Meditation and productivity. *Academy of Management Journal, 17*, 362-368.

Friend, K. E. (1977). Effects of the Transcendental Meditation program on work attitudes and behavior. In D. W. Orme-Johnson & J. T. Farrow (Eds.), *Scientific research on the Transcendental Meditation program: Collected papers, volume 1* (pp. 630-638). Rheinweiler, Germany: Maharishi European Research University Press.

Friend, K. E., & Maliszewski, M. (1978). More on the reliability of the kinesthetic aftereffects measure and need for stimulation. *Journal of Personality Assessment, 42* (4), 385-391.

Fuller, R. (1996). The influence of fluoxetine on aggressive behavior. *Neuropsychopharmacology, 14* (2), 77-81.

Ganong, W. F. (1987). *Review of medical physiology* (13th ed.). Norwalk, CT/San Mateo, CA: Appleton & Lange.

Gaylord, C., Orme-Johnson, D. W., & Travis, F. T. (1989). The effects of the Transcendental Meditation technique and progressive muscle relaxation on EEG coherence, stress reactivity and mental health in black adults. *International Journal of Neuroscience, 46* (1-2), 77-86.

Geisler, M. (1978). Therapeutische Wirkungen der Transzendentalen Meditation auf Drogenkonsumenten [Therapeutic effect of Transcendental Meditation on drug consumption]. *Zeitschrift für klinische Psychologie, 7* (4), 235-255.

Gelderloos, P. (1987a). Psychological health and development of students at Maharishi International University: A controlled longitudinal study. *Modern Science and Vedic Science, 1* (4), 470-487.

Gelderloos, P. (1987b). *Valuation and Transcendental Meditation.* Lelystad, The Netherlands: Soma Scientific Publisher.

Gelderloos, P., Cavanaugh, K. L., & Davies, J. L. (1990). The dynamics of US-Soviet relations, 1979-1986: Effects of reducing social stress through the Transcendental Meditation and TM-Sidhi program. *Proceedings of the American Statistical Association, Social Statistics Section* (pp. 297-302). Alexandria, VA: American Statistical Association.

Gelderloos, P., Goddard, III., P. H., Ahlström, H. H. B., & Jacoby, R. (1987). Cognitive orientation toward positive values in advanced participants of the TM and TM-Sidhi program. *Perceptual and Motor Skills, 64*, 1003-1012.

Gelderloos, P., Hermans, H. J. M., Ahlstrom, H. H. B., & Jacoby, R. (1990). Transcendence and psychological health: Studies with long-term participants of the TM and TM-Sidhis program. *Journal of Psychology, 124*, 177-197.

Gelderloos, P., Lockie, R. J., & Chuttoorgoon, S. (1987). Field independence of students at Maharishi School of the Age of Englightenment and a Montessori school. *Perceptual and Motor Skills, 65*, 613-614.

Gelderloos, P., Walton, K., Orme-Johnson, D. W., & Alexander, C. N. (1991). Effectiveness of the Transcendental Meditation program in preventing and treating substance misuse: A review. *International Journal of Addictions, 26*, 293-325.

Gendreau, P., & Ross, R. R. (1987). Revivification of rehabilitation: Evidence from the 1980s. *Justice Quarterly, 4*, 349-407.

Gendreau, P., Little, T., & Goggin, C. (1996). A meta-analysis of the predictors of adult offender recidivism: What works! *Criminology, 34* (4), 575-607.

Georgia. (1999). Parolee supervision. *Georgia Board of Pardons and Paroles executive summary of October, 1996.* [Online]. Available at: <www2.state.ga.us/Departments/AUDIA/index/dept/per/parolee.htm>.

Gergen, D. (1996, March 25). Taming teenage wolf packs. *U.S. News and World Report, 120*, 68.

Gerra, G., Avanzini, P., Zaimovic, A., Fertonani, G., Caccavari, R., Delsignore, R., Gardini, F., Talarico, E., Lecchini, R., Maestri, D., & Brambilla, F. (1996). Neurotransmitter and endocrine modulation of aggressive behavior and its components in normal humans. *Behavioural Brain Research, 81*, 19-24.

Gerra, G., Zaimovic, A., Avanzini, P., Chittolini, B., Giucastro, G., Caccavari, R., Palladino, M., Maestri, D., Monica, C., Delsignore, R., & Brambilla, F. (1997). Neurotransmitter-neuroendocrine responses to experimentally induced aggression in humans: Influence of personality variable. *Psychiatry Research, 66* (1), 33-43.

Gest, T. (1994, January 17). Cost of crime: $674 billion. *U.S. News and World Report*, 40-41.

Gibbons, D. C. (1986). Juvenile delinquency: Can social science find a cure? *Crime and Delinquency, 32* (2), 186-204.

Gibbs, J. C. (1991). Sociomoral developmental delay and cognitive distortion: Implications for the treatment of antisocial youth. In W. M. Kurtines & L. Gewirtz (Eds.), *Handbook of moral behavior and development* (pp. 95-110). Hillsdale, NJ: Lawrence Erlbaum Associates.

Gibbs, J. C., Barriga, A., & Potter, G. (1996). *The How I Think questionnaire.* Unpublished manuscript, The Ohio State University.

Gibbs, J. C., Potter, G. B., & Goldstein, A. P. (1995). *The Equip program.* Champaign, IL: Research Press.

Glaser, J. L., Brind, J. L., Vogelman, J. H., Eisner, M. J., Dillbeck, M. C., Wallace, R. K., Chopra, D., & Orentreich, N. (1992). Elevated serum dehydroepiandrosterone sulfate levels in practitioners of the transcendental meditation (TM) and TM-Sidhi programs. *Journal of Behavioral Medicine, 15* (4), 327-341.

Glueck, B. C., & Stroebel, C. F. (1975). Biofeedback and meditation in the treatment of psychiatric illnesses. *Comprehensive Psychiatry, 16*, 303-321.

Glueck, S., & Glueck, E. (1940). *Juvenile delinquents grow up.* New York: Commonwealth Fund.

Gochman, C. S. (1990). Prometheus bound: The state and war. In C. Gochman & A. Sabrosky (Eds.), *Prisoners of war?* Lexington, MA: Lexington Books.

Gold, S. N. (1980). Relations between level of ego development and adjustment patterns in adolescents. *Journal of Personality Assessment, 44*, 630-638.

Goldstein, D. S. (1995). *Stress, Catecholamines, and Cardiovascular Disease.* New York: Oxford University Press, Inc.

Goldstein, P. J., Lipton, D. S., Spunt, B. J., Belluci, P. A., Miller, T., Cortez, N., Kahn, M., & Kale, A. (1989). Crack and homicide in New York City, 1988: A conceptually based event analysis. *Contemporary Drug Problems, 16* (Winter), 651-687.

Goleman, D. J., & Schwartz, G. E. (1976). Meditation as an intervention in stress reactivity. *Journal of Consulting and Clinical Psychology, 44* (3), 456-466.

Gonzalez-Campoy, J. M., Romero, J. C., & Knox, F. G. (1989). Escape from the sodium-retaining effects of mineralocorticoids: Role of ANF and intrarenal hormone systems. *Kidney International, 35*, 767-777.

Goodman, R. S., Orme-Johnson, D. W., Rainforth, M. S., & Goodman, D. H. (1997). *Transforming political institutions through individual and collective consciousness: The Maharishi Effect and government.* Paper presented at the annual meeting of the American Political Science Association, Washington, DC.

Goodman, R. S., Walton, K. G., Orme-Johnson, D. W., & Boyer, R. (this volume). The *Transcendental Meditation* program–A Consciousness-Based developmental technology for rehabilitation and crime prevention. *Journal of Offender Rehabilitation*, 36(1/2/3/4), 1-33.

Gore, S., Abrams, A., & Ellis, G. (1989). The effect of statewide implementation of the Maharishi Technology of the Unified Field in the Vermont Department of Corrections. In R. A. Chalmers, G. Clements, H. Schenkluhn, & M. Weinless (Eds.), *Scientific research on Maharishi's Transcendental Meditation and TM-Sidhi program: Collected papers, Volume 4* (pp. 2453-2464). Vlodrop, The Netherlands: Maharishi Vedic University Press.

Gorsuch, R. L. (1974). *Factor analysis.* Philadelphia: W. B. Saunders.

Gottfredson, D. C. (1985). Youth employment, crime, and schooling. *Developmental Psychology, 21*, 419-432.

Gottfredson, M. R., & Hirschi, T. (1994). A general theory of adolescent problem behavior. Problems and prospects. In R. D. Ketterlinus & M. E. Lamb (Eds.), *Adolescent problem behaviors* (pp. 41-56). Newbury Park, CA: Sage.

Gottfredson, M. R., & Hirschi, T. (1995). National crime control policies. *Society*, January-February, 30-38.

Graham, R., Peterman, M., & Scarff, T. (1971). *Insights into the Richmond community.* Unpublished manuscript.

Greaves, G. B. (1980). An existential theory of drug dependence. In D. Lettieri, M. Sayers, & H. Pearson (Eds.), *Theories of drug abuse.* Washington, DC: National Institute on Drug Abuse.

Greenberg, D. (1991). Modeling criminal careers. *Criminology, 29*, 17-46.

Greenwood, P. W., Rydell, C. P., Abrahams, A. F., Caulkins, J. P., Chiesa, J., Model, K. E., & Klein, S. P. (1994). *Three strikes and you're out: Estimated benefits and costs of California's new mandatory-sentencing law.* Santa Monica, CA: Rand.

Greiner, T., & Burch, N. (1955). Response of human GSR to drugs that influence the reticular formation of brain stem. *Federation Proceedings, 14*, 346.

Gustafson, R. (1994). Alcohol and aggression. In M. Hillbrand & N. Pallone (Eds.), *The psychobiology of aggression: Engines, measurement, control* (p. 243). New York: The Haworth Press, Inc.

Guyton, A. C. (1991). Blood pressure control–special role of the kidneys and body fluids. *Science, 252*, 1813-1816.

Guyton, A. C. (1996). *Textbook of medical physiology.* (9th ed.). Philadelphia: W. B. Saunders Co.

Hagelin, J. S. (1987). Is consciousness the unified field? A field theorist's perspective. *Modern Science and Vedic Science, 1* (1), 29-89.

Hagelin, J. S., Rainforth, M. V., Orme-Johnson, D. W., Cavanaugh, K. L., Alexander, C. N., Shatkin, S. F., Davies, J. L., Hughes, A. O., & Ross, E. (1999). Effects of group practice of the Transcendental Meditation program on preventing violent crime in Washington, DC: Results of the National Demonstration Project, June-July 1993. *Social Indicators Research, 47*, 153-201.

Hahn, H. R., & Whalen, T. E. (1989). The effects of the Transcendental Meditation program on levels of hostility, anxiety, and depression. In R. A. Chalmers, G. Clements, H. Schenkluhn, & M. Weinless (Eds.), *Scientific research on Maharishi's Transcendental Meditation and TM-Sidhi program: Collected papers, volume 2* (pp. 1030-1036). Vlodrop, The Netherlands: Maharishi Vedic University Press.

Hair, J. F., Anderson, R. E., & Tatham, R. L. (1987). *Multivariate data analysis with readings* (Revised ed.). New York: Macmillan.

Haller, J., Makara, G., & Kruk, M. (1998). Catecholamine involvement in the control of aggression: Hormones, the peripheral sympathetic, and central noradrenergic systems. *Neuroscience and Biobehavioral Reviews, 22* (1), 85-97.

Happel, R. M., & Auffrey, J. J. (1995). Sex offender assessment: Interrupting the dance of denial. *American Journal of Forensic Psychology, 13* (2), 5-22.

Haratani, T., & Henmi, T. (1990). Effects of Transcendental Meditation (TM) on the mental health of industrial workers. *Japanese Journal of Industrial Health, 32* (7), 346.

Hare, R. (1970). *Psychopathy: Theory and research*. New York: Wiley.

Hare, R. D. (1978). Electrodermal and cardiovacular correlates to psychopathy. In R. D. Hare & D. Schalling (Eds.), *Psychopathic behavior: Approaches to research* (pp. 107-144). New York: Wiley.

Harland, A. T. (1995). Introduction. In A. T. Harland (Ed.), *Choosing correctional options that work: Defining demand and evaluating the supply* (pp. xiii-xviii). Thousand Oaks, CA: Sage.

Harland, A. T. (1996). *Choosing correctional options that work: Defining demand and evaluating the supply.* Thousand Oaks, CA: Sage.

Harman, H. H. (1976). *Modern factor analysis.* Chicago: University of Chicago Press.

Harrell, A. (1996). Evaluation of children at risk program: Preliminary findings. *In National Evaluation Conference, National Institute of Justice*, Washington, DC.

Harrell, T. H., Honaker, L. M., & Davis, E. (1991). Cognitive and behavioral dimensions of dysfunction in alcohol and polydrug abusers. *Journal of Substance Abuse, 3* (4), 415-426.

Hartman, B. K., Zide, D., & Undenfriend, S. (1972). The use of dopamine-hydroxylase as a marker for the central noradrenergic nervous system in the rat brain. *Proceedings of the National Academy of Sciences (USA), 69*, 2722-2726.

Harwood, H., Fountain, D., & Livermore, G. (1998). *The economic costs of alcohol and drug abuse in the United States, 1992* (NIH Publication No. 98-4327). Washington, DC: U.S. Government Printing Office.

Hatchard, G. D., Deans, A. J., Cavanaugh, K. L., & Orme-Johnson, D. W. (1996). The Maharishi Effect: A model for social improvement. Time series analysis of a phase transition to reduced crime in Merseyside metropolitan area. *Psychology, Crime & Law, 2* (3), 165-174.

Hauser, S. T. (1976). Loevinger's model and measure of ego development: A critical review. *Psychological Bulletin, 83*, 928-955.

Hawkins, M. A. (1998). Effects of Maharishi's Consciousness-Based approach to rehabilitation with inmates on Curaçao. Doctoral dissertation. Maharishi University of Management.

Hawkins, M. A. (this volume). Effectiveness of the *Transcendental Meditation* program in criminal rehabilitation and substance abuse recovery: A review of the research. *Journal of Offender Rehabilitation*, 36(1/2/3/4), 47-65.

Hawkins, M. A., Alexander, C. N., Travis, F. T., Camelia, C. R. T., Walton, K. G., Durchholz, C. F., & Rainforth, M. W. (this volume). *Consciousness-Based* Rehabilitation of Inmates in the Netherlands Antilles: Psychosocial and Cognitive Changes. *Journal of Offender Rehabilitation*, 36(1/2/3/4), 205-228.

Hays, R. D., Hayashi, T., & Stewart, A. L. (1989). A five-item measure of socially desirable response set. *Educational and Psychological Measurement, 49*, 629-636.

Hazelden Foundation. (1991). *Hazelden news and professional update.* (Available from Hazelden Foundation, CO3, PO Box 11, Center City, MN 55012-0011).

Hebert, R., & Lehmann, D. (1977). Theta bursts: An EEG pattern in normal subjects practicing the Transcendental Meditation technique. *Electroencephalography and Clinical Neurophysiology, 42*, 397-369.

Heilbrun, A. B. (1979). Psychopathy and violent crime. *Journal of Consulting and Clinical Psychology*, *47* (3), 509-516.

Heilbrun, A. B. (1982). Cognitive models of criminal violence based upon intelligence and psychopathy levels. *Consulting and Clinical Psychology*, *50* (4), 546-557.

Henry, B., Caspi, A., Moffitt, T. E., & Silva, P. A. (1996). Temperamental and familial predictors of violent and nonviolent criminal convictions: Age 3 to age 18. *Developmental Psychology*, *32* (4), 614-623.

Henry, J. P., & Grim, C. E. (1990). Psychosocial mechanisms of primary hypertension. *Journal of Hypertension*, *8*, 783-793.

Herrnstein, R. J. (1995). Criminogenic traits. In J. Q. Wilson & J. Petersilia (Eds.), *Crime* (pp. 39-64). San Francisco: Institute for Contemporary Studies Press.

Herron, R. E., Hillis, S. L., Mandarino, J. V., Orme-Johnson, D. W., & Walton, K. G. (1996). The impact of the Transcendental Meditation program on government payments to physicians in Quebec. *American Journal of Health Promotion*, *10* (3), 183-191.

Herron, R. E., Hillis, S. L., Mandarino, J. V., Orme-Johnson, D. W., Walton, K. G. (1996). The impact of the Transcendental Meditation program on government payments to physicians in Quebec. *American Journal of Health Promotio*, *10*, 208-216.

Hicks, J. (1980). Mystical experience as cognition. In R. Woods (Ed.), *Understanding Mysticism*. New York: Doubleday.

Higley, J. D., Mehlman, P. T., Taub, D. M., Higley, S. B., Suomi, S. J., Linnoila, M., & Vickers, J. H. (1992). Cerebrospinal fluid monoamine and adrenal correlates of aggression in free-ranging rhesus monkeys. *Archives of General Psychiatry*, *49*, 436-441.

Hill, H. E., Haertzen, C. A., & Glasser, R. (1960). Personality characteristics of narcotic addicts as indicated by the MMPI. *Journal of General Psychology*, *62*, 127-139.

Hillbrand, M., & Pallone, N. J. (Ed.). (1994). *The psychobiology of aggression: Engines, measurement, control*. New York: The Haworth Press, Inc.

Hindelang, M. J. (1973). Causes of delinquency: A partial replication and extension. *Social Problems*, *20*, 471-487.

Hinton, J., O'Neil, M., Hamilton, S., & Burke, M. (1980). Psychophysiological differentiation between psychopathic and schizophrenic abnormal offenders. *British Journal of Social Clinical Psychology*, *19*, 257-269.

Hirschi, T. (1969). *Causes of delinquency*. Berkeley, CA: University of California Press.

Hirschi, T., & Gottfredson, M. (1983). Age and explanation of crime. *American Journal of Sociology*, *89* (3) 552-584.

Hirschi, T., & Hindelang, M. J. (1977). Intelligence and delinquency: A revisionist review. *American Sociological Review*, *42*, 571-587.

Hjelle, L. A. (1974). Transcendental Meditation and psychological health. *Perceptual and Motor Skills*, *39*, 623-628.

Hodgins, S., Mednick, S. A., Brennan, P. A., Schulsinger, F., & Engberg, M. (1996). Mental disorder and crime: Evidence from a Danish birth cohort. *Archives of General Psychiatry*, *53*, 489-496.

Hoffman, J. P., & Su, S. S. (1997). The conditional effects of stress on delinquency and drug use: A strain theory assessment of sex differences. *Journal of Research in Crime and Delinquency, 34*, 46-78.

Hoffman, P. B. (1983). Screening for risk: A revised salient factor score (SFS 81). *Journal of Criminal Justice, 11*, 539-547.

Hoffman, P. B., & Beck, J. C. (1974). Parole decision-making: A salient factor score. *Journal of Criminal Justice, 2*, 195-206.

Hoge, R. D., Andrews, D. A., & Leschied, A. W. (1996). An investigation of risk and protective factors in a sample of youthful offenders. *Journal of Child Psychology and Psychiatry, 37* (4), 419-424.

Holroyd, K., & Lazarus, R. (1982). Stress, coping and somatic adaptation. In L. Goldberger & S. Breznitz (Eds.), *Handbook of stress: Theoretical and clinical aspects* (pp. 21-35). New York: The Free Press.

Holt, R. R. (1980). Loevinger's measure of ego development: Reliability and national norms for male and female short forms. *Journal of Personality and Social Psychology, 39*, 909-920.

Holt, W. R., Caruso, J. L., & Riley, J. B. (1978). Transcendental Meditation vs. pseudo-meditation on visual choice reaction time. *Perceptual and Motor Skills, 46*, 726.

Hope, T. (1995). Community crime prevention. In M. Tonry & D. P. Farrington (Eds.), *Building a safer society. Crime and justice*, Volume 19. Chicago: University of Chicago Press.

Hunt, W. A., Barnett, L. W., & Branch, L. G. (1971). Relapse rates in addiction programs. *Journal of Clinical Psychology, 27*, 455-456.

Hustmyer, Jr., F., & Karnes, E. (1964). Background autonomic activity and "analytic perception." *Journal of Abnormal and Social Psychology, 68*, 467-468.

Huxley, A. (1945). *The perennial philosophy*. New York: Harpers.

Hyman, R. B., Feldman, H. R., Harris, R. B., Levin, R. F., & Malloy, G. B. (1989). The effects of relaxation training on clinical symptoms: A meta-analysis. *Nursing Research, 38*, 216-220.

Infante, J. R., Torres-Avisbal, M., Pinel, P., Vallejo, J. A., Peran, F., Gonzalez, F., Contreras, P., Pacheco, C., Roldan, A., & Latre, J. M. (2001). Catecholamines in practitioners of the Transcendental Meditation technique. *Physiology and Behavior, 72*, 141-146.

International Criminal Police Organization. (1994). *International crime statistics: 1994*. Lyons, France: Interpol General Secretariat.

Invitation to action: Maharishi's program to create world peace. (1987). Vlodrop, The Netherlands: Maharishi Vedic University Press.

Iyer, V. R. K. (1977). Chairman's opening remarks. In World Government of the Age of Enlightenment, *First World Assembly on Law, Justice and Rehabilitation* (pp. 12-18).

Izzo, R. L., & Ross, R. R. (1990). Meta-analysis of rehabilitation programs for juvenile delinquents: A brief report. *Criminal Justice and Behavior, 1*, 134-142.

Jackson, Y. (1977). Learning disorders and the Transcendental Meditation program. *Dissertation Abstracts International, 38* (6), 3351-A.

Jacobs, B. L. (1986). Single unit activity of locus coeruleus neurons in behaving animals. *Progress in Neurobiology, 27*, 183-194.

Jahn, R. G., Dunne, B. J., Nelson, R. D., Dobyns, Y. H., & Bradish, G. J. (1997). Correlations of random binary sequences with pre-stated operator intention: A review of a 12-year program. *Journal of Scientific Exploration, 11* (3), 345-367.

James, W. (1890). *The Principles of psychology, volumes 1 and 2.* New York: Henry Holt.

James, W. (1898/1977). *Human immortality: Two supposed objections to the doctrine.* Boston: Houghton Mifflin.

James, W. (1902/1982). *The varieties of religous experience.* New York: Penguin.

James, W. (1929). *The varieties of religious experience.* New York: Modern Library.

Jedrczak, A., Beresford, M., & Clements, G. (1985). The TM-Sidhi program, pure consciousness, creativity and intelligence. *The Journal of Creative Behavior, 19* (4), 270-275.

Jedrczak, A., Toomey, M., & Clements, G. (1986). The TM-Sidhi programme, age, and brief test of perceptual-motor speed and nonverbal intelligence. *Journal of Clinical Psychology, 42*, 161-164.

Jennings, W., Kilkenny, R., & Kohlberg, L. (1983). Moral-development theory and practice of youthful and adult offenders. In W. S. Laufer & J. M. Day (Eds.), *Personality theory, moral development, and criminal behavior* (pp. 281-355). Lexington, MA: Lexington.

Jevning, R., Pirkle, H. C., & Wilson, A. F. (1977, November). Behavioral alteration of plasma phenylalanine concentration. *Physiology and Behavior, 19* (5), 611-614.

Jevning, R., Wallace, R. K., & Beidebach, M. (1992). The physiology of meditation: A review. A wakeful hypometabolic integrated response. *Neuroscience and Biobehavior Reviews, 16*, 415-424.

Jevning, R., Wells, I., Wilson, A. F., & Guich, S. (1987). Plasma thyroid hormones, thyroid stimulating hormone, and insulin during acute hypometabolic states in man. *Physiology and Behavior, 40* (5), 603-606.

Jevning, R., Wilson, A. F., & Davidson, J. M. (1978). Adrenocortical activity during meditation. *Hormones and Behavior, 10* (1), 54-60.

Jevning, R., Wilson, A. F., & Smith, W. R. (1978). The Transcendental Meditation technique, adrenocortical activity, and implications for stress. *Experientia, 34*, 618-619.

Jones, C. (1989). The impact of Maharishi's Vedic science based education in higher education: The example of Maharishi International University, *Modern Science and Vedic Science, 3* (2), 154-199.

Jones, C., Clayborne, B. M., Grant, J., & Rutherford, G. (this volume). Attacking crime at its source: *Consciousness-Based* education in the prevention of violence and antisocial behavior. *Journal of Offender Rehabilitation*, 36(1/2/3/4), 229-255.

Jouvet, M. (1972). The role of monoamines and acetylcholine neurons in the regulation of the sleep waking cycle. *Ergebn Physiol, 64*, 166-307.

Judd, C. M., & Kenny, D. A. (1981). *Estimating the effects of social interventions.* New York: Cambridge University Press.

Juhel, J. (1991). Relationships between psychometric intelligence and information-processing speed indexes. *Cahiers de Psychologie Cognitive, 11* (1), 73-105.

Kaiser, H. F. (1956). *The varimax method of factor analysis.* Unpublished doctoral dissertation, University of California, Berkeley.

Kandel, E., Mednick, S. A., Kirkegaard-Sorensen, L., Hutchings, B., Knop, J., Rosenberg, R., & Schulsinger, F. (1988). IQ as a protective factor for subjects at high risk for antisocial behavior. *Journal of Consulting and Clinical Psychology, 56* (2), 224-226.

Kantak, K., Hegstrand, L., & Eichelman, B. (1985). Facilitation of shock-induced fighting following intraventricular 5,7-dihydroxytryptamine and 6-hydroxy-DOPA. *Psychopharmacology, 74*, 157-160.

Kasdin, A. E. (1987). *Conduct disorder in childhood and adolescence.* Newbury Park, CA: Sage.

Katkin, E. (1965). Relationship between manifest anxiety and two indices of autonomic response to stress. *Journal of Personality and Social Psychology, 2*, 324-333.

Katkin, E. (1966). The relationship between a measure of transitory anxiety and spontaneous autonomic activity. *Journal of Abnormal Psychology, 71*, 142-146.

Katkin, E., & McCubbin, R. (1969). Habituation of the orienting response as a function of individual differences in anxiety and autonomic lability. *Journal of Abnormal Psychology, 74*, 54-60.

Katz, D. (1977). Decreased drug use and prevention of drug use through the Transcendental Meditation program. In D. W. Orme-Johnson & J. T. Farrow (Eds.), *Scientific research on the Transcendental Meditation program: Collected papers, volume 1* (pp. 536-543). Rheinweiler, Germany: Maharishi European Research University Press.

Katz, R. (1980). Role of serotonin mechanisms in animal models of predation. *Progress in Neuro-Psychopharmacology and Biological Psychiatry, 4*, 219-231.

Katz, R. (1981). Education as transformation: Becoming a healer among the Kung and the Fijians. *Harvard Educational Review, 51* (1), 57-78.

Kayode, O., & Alemika, E. O. (1984). An examination of some socioeconomic characteristics of inmates of a Nigerian prison. *International Journal of Comparative and Applied Criminal Justice, 8* (1), 85-91.

Kegan, R. (1978). The evolving self: A process conception for ego psychology. *The Counseling Psychologist, 8*, 5-34.

Kegan, R. (1982). *The evolving self: Problem and process in human development.* Cambridge, MA: Harvard University Press.

Kegan, R. (1986). The child behind the mask: Sociopathy as developmental delay. In W. H. Reid, D. Dorr, J. I. Walker, & J. W. Bonner, III. (Eds.), *Unmasking the psychopath* (pp. 45-77). New York: W. W. Norton.

Kember, P. (1985). The Transcendental Meditation technique and postgraduate academic performance. *British Journal of Educational Psychology, 55*, 164-166.

Kenny, D. A. (1979). *Correlation and causality.* New York: John Wiley & Sons.

Kepple, G. (1973). *Design and analysis: A researcher's handbook.* Englewood Cliffs, NJ: Prentice-Hall.

King, J. A. (1996). Perinatal stress and impairment of the stress response: Possible link to nonoptimal behavior. *Annals of the New York Academy of Sciences, 794*, 104-112.

King, M. S. (1997). *Nature's intelligence or human reason? Natural law in Maharishi's Vedic Science and in legal and ethical thought.* Unpublished doctoral dissertation. Fairfield, IA: Maharishi University of Management.

King, M. S. (1999). *Deterrence, rehabilitation and the Enlightened Sentencing Project: Reflections from legal theory.* Paper presented at the conference entitled Innovations in Sentencing: The Enlightened Sentencing Project, Melbourne, Australia.

Klajner, F., Hartman, L. M., & Sobell, M. B. (1984). Treatment of substance abuse by relaxation training: A review of its rationale, efficacy and mechanisms. *Addictive Behaviors, 9*, 41-55.

Klein, D. B. (1984). *The concept of consciousness: A survey.* Lincoln, NE: University of Nebraska Press. (Reference cited is facing the book title page.)

Kobal, G., Wandhofer, R. A., & Plattig, K.-H. (1975). EEG power spectra and auditory evoked potentials in Transcendental Meditation. *Pflugers Archive, Supplement, 359* (191), R 96.

Kohlberg, L. (1969). Stage and sequence: The cognitive developmental approach to socialization. In D. A. Goslin (Ed.), *Handbook of socialization theory and research.* Chicago: Rand McNally.

Kohlberg, L. (1973). Continuities in childhood and adult moral development revisited. In P. B. Baltes & K. W. Sahaie (Eds.), *Life-span development psychology: Personality and socialization.* New York: Academic Press.

Kohlberg, L. (1984). *Essays on moral development, Volume 2: The psychology of moral development.* San Francisco: Harper and Row.

Kohlberg, L., & Kramer, R. (1969). Continuities and discontinuities in childhood and adult moral development. *Human Development, 12*, 93-120.

Kohlberg, L., & Ryncarz, R. A. (1990). Beyond justice reasoning: Moral development and consideration of a seventh stage. In C. N. Alexander & E. L. Langer (Eds.), *Higher stages of human development* (pp. 191-207). New York: Oxford University Press.

Kohlberg, L., Kauffman, K., Scharf, P., & Hickey, J. (1974). *The just community approach to corrections: A manual, Part I.* Cambridge, MA: Moral Education Foundation.

Kosten, T., Mason, J., Giller, E., Ostroff, R., & Harkness, L. (1987). Sustained urinary norepinephrine and epinephrine in post-traumatic stress disorder. *Psychoneuroendocrinology, 12* (1), 13-20.

Kotch, J. B., Browne, D. C., Ringwalt, C. L., Dufort, V., Ruina, E., Stewart, P. W., & Jung, J. W. (1997). Stress, social support, and substantiated maltreatment in the second and third years of life. *Child Abuse and Neglect, 21* (11), 1025-1037.

Kottke, T. T., Battista, R. N., Defriese, G. H., & Brekke, M. L. (1988). Attributes of successful smoking cessation interventions in medical practice: A meta-analysis of 39 controlled trials. *Journal of the American Medical Association, 259*, 2883-2889.

Kramer, D. A. (1990). Conceptualizing wisdom: The primacy of affective-cognitive relations. In R. Sternberg (Eds.), *Wisdom: Its nature, origins, and development.* New York: Cambridge University Press.

Kranzler, J. H., & Jensen, A. R. (1989). Inspection time and intelligence: A meta-analysis. *Intelligence, 13*, 329-347.

Krueger, R. F., Schmutte, P. S., Caspi, A., & Moffitt, T. (1994). Personality traits are linked to crime among men and women: Evidence from a birth cohort. *Journal of Abnormal Psychology, 103* (2), 328-338.

Kruesi, M. J. P., Hibbs, E. D., Zahn, T. P., Keysor, C. S., Hamburger, S. D., Bartko, J. J., & Rapoport, J. L. (1992). A 2-year prospective follow-up study of children and adolescents with disruptive behavior disorders. *Archives of General Psychiatry, 49*, 430-435.

Kuhn, D., & Brannock, J. (1977). Development of the isolation of variables scheme in experimental and "natural experiment" contexts. *Developmental Psychology, 13*, 9-14.

Kundrotas, L. W., & Gregg, R. V. (1977). Urinary excretion of 5-hydroxyindoleacetic acid (5-HIAA) in the rat after immobilaization stress. *Physiology and Behavior, 19*, 739-741.

Lab, S. P., & Whitehead, J. T. (1990). From "nothing works" to "the appropriate works": The latest on the search for the secular grail. *Criminology, 28* (3), 405-417.

Labouvie-Vief, G. (1990). Modes of knowledge and the organization of knowledge. In M. L. Commons, C. Armon, L. Kohlberg, F. A. Richards, T. A. Grotzer, & J. D. Sinnott (Eds.), *Adult development, volume 2: Models and methods in the study of adolescent and adult thought.* New York: Praeger Publishers.

Lacey, J., & Lacey, B. (1958). The relationship of resting autonomic cyclic activity to motor impulsivity. In S. Cobb & W. Pennfield (Eds.), *The brain and human behavior*. Baltimore: Williams and Wilkins.

Lang, A. (1993). Alcohol-related violence: Psychological perspectives. In S. Martin (Ed.), *Alcohol and interpersonal violence: Fostering multi-disciplinary perspectives* (NIAAA Research Monograph No. 24; pp. 121-147). Rockville, MD: National Institute of Health.

Lang, R., Dehof, K., Meurer, K. A., & Kaufmann, W. (1979). Sympathetic activity and Transcendental Meditation. *Journal of Neural Transmission, 44* (1-2), 117-135.

Langan, P. A., & Cunniff, M. A. (1992). *Recidivism of felons on probation, 1986-1989* (Bureau of Justice Statistics Special Report NCJ 134177). Washington, DC: U.S. Department of Justice.

Larimore, W. E. (1983). Predictive inference, sufficiency, entropy, and an asymptotic likelihood principle. *Biometrika, 70*, 175-181.

Larimore, W. E. (1986). *Development of statistical methods using predictive inference and entropy* (Technical Report SSI-1112). Cambridge, MA: Scientific Systems.

Larimore, W. E., & Mehra, R. K. (1985). The problem of overfitting data. *Byte, 10*, 167-180.

LaVoie, A. L. (1984). Embedded Figures Test. In D. J. Keyser & R. C. Sweetland (Eds.), *Test critiques* (pp. 259-265). Kansas City, MO: Test Corporation of America.

Lazar, Z., Farwell, L., & Farrow, J. T. (1977). The effects of the Transcendental Meditation program on anxiety, drug abuse, cigarette smoking, and alcohol consumption. In D. W. Orme-Johnson & J. T. Farrow (Eds.), *Scientific research on the Transcendental Meditation program: Collected papers, volume 1* (pp. 524-535). Rheinweiler, Germany: Maharishi European Research University Press.

Le Clair, D. P. (1977). *Development of base expectancy prediction tables for treatment and control groups in correctional research.* (Paper #124). Massachusetts Department of Corrections.

Le Clair, D. P. (1978). *Societal reintegration and recidivism rates.* (Paper #159). Massachusetts Department of Corrections.

LeDoux, J. E., Cicchetti, P., Xagoraris, A., & Romanski, L. M. (1990). The lateral amygdaloid nucleus: Sensory interface of the amygdala in fear conditioning. *Journal of Neuroscience, 10*, 1062-1069.

Lefebvre, H., Contesse, V., Delarue, C., Vaudry, H., & Kuhn, J. (1998). Serotonin regulation of adrenocortical function. *Hormone and Metabolic Research, 30* (6-7), 398-403.

Lehrer, P. M., Carr, R., Deepa, S., & Woolfolk, R. L. (1994). Stress management techniques: Are they all equivalent, or do they have specific effects? *Biofeedback and Self-Regulation, 19*, 353-401.

Lemieux, A., & Coe, C. (1994). Abuse-related posttraumatic stress disorder: Evidence for chronic neuroendocrine activation in women. *Psychosomatic Medicine, 57*, 105-115.

Levine, P. H. (1976). The coherence spectral array (COSPAR) and its application to the study of spatial ordering in the EEG. In J. I. Martin (Ed.) *Proceedings of the San Diego Biomedical Symposium, 15.* New York: Academic Press, Inc.

Levitsky, D. K. (1998). Effects of the Transcendental Meditation Program on neuroendocrine indicators of chronic stress. (Doctoral dissertation, Maharishi University of Management, 1998.) Ann Arbor, MI: UMI Dissertation Services. (No. 9806955).

Lidberg, L., Ruck, J., Asberg, M., Scalia-Tomba, G., & Bertilsson, L. (1985). Homicide, suicide and CSF 5-HIAA. *Acta Psychiatrica Scandinavica, 71*, 230-236.

Linnoila, M., Virkkunen, M., Scheinin, M., Nuutila, A., Rimon, R., & Goodwin, F. (1983). Low cerebrospinal fluid 5-hydroxyindoleacetic acid concentration differentiates impulsive from non-impulsive violent behavior. *Life Sciences, 33*, 2609-2614.

Linnoila, V. M., & Virkkunen, M. (1992). Aggression, suicidality, and serotonin. *Journal of Clinical Psychiatry, 53* 10 (suppl), 46-51.

Linsky, A. S., & Straus, M. A. (1986). *Social stress in the United States: Links to regional patterns in crime and illness.* Westport, CT: Auburn House.

Lipsey, M. W. (1992). Juvenile delinquency treatment: A meta-analytic inquiry into the variability of effects. In T. D. Cook, H. Cooper, D. S. Cordray, H. Hartmann, L. V. Hedges, R. J. Light, T. A. Louis, & F. Mosteller (Eds.), *Meta-analysis for explanation* (pp. 83-127). New York: Russell Sage Foundation.

Lipsey, M. W., & Wilson, D. B. (1993). The efficacy of psychological, educational, and behavioral treatment: Confirmation from meta-analysis. *American Psychologist, 48* (12), 1181-1209.

Lipton, D., Martinson, R., & Wilks, J. (1975). *The effectiveness of correctional treatment: A survey of treatment evaluation studies.* New York: Praeger.

Ljung, G. M., & Box, G. E. P. (1978). On a measure of lack of fit in time series models. *Biometrika, 65*, 297-303.

Ljunggren, G. (1977). Inflytandet av Transcendental Meditation på neuroticism, medicinbruk och sömnproblem [Influence of Transcendental Meditation on neuroticism, medicine usage and sleep problems]. *Läkartidningen, 74*, 4212-4214.

Loeber, R., & Stouthamer-Loeber, M. (1987). The prediction of delinquency. In H. C. Quay (Ed.), *Handbook of juvenile delinquency* (pp. 325-383). New York: Wiley.

Loevinger, J. (1976). *Ego development: Conceptions and theories*. San Francisco: Jossey-Bass.

Loevinger, J. (1979). Construct validation of the sentence completion test of ego development. *Applied Psychological Measurement, 3*, 281-311.

Loevinger, J. (1984). On the self and mediating behavior. In J. Arnoff & A. I. Rabin (Eds.), *Personality and the prediciton of behavior*. Orlando, FL: Academic Press.

Loevinger, J. (1985). Revision of the Sentence Completion Test of ego development. *Journal of Personality and Social Psychology, 48*, 420-427.

Loevinger, J. (1993). Measurement of personality: True or false. *Psychological Inquiry, 4* (1), 1-16.

Loevinger, J., & Wessler, R. (1970). *Measuring ego development I: Construction and use of a sentence completion test*. San Francisco: Jossey-Bass.

Loevinger, J., Cohn, L. D., Bonneville, L. P., Redmore, C. D., Streich, D. D., & Sargent, M. (1985). Ego development in college. *Journal of Personality and Social Psychology, 48*, 947-962.

Lofholm, N. (1998, July 16). Deadly school violence targeted: Attorneys general to tackle issue. *The Denver Post*, p. B4.

Long, J. V. V., & Scherl, D. J. (1984). Developmental antecedents of compulsive drug use: A report on the literature. *Journal of Psychoactive Drugs, 16*, 169-182.

Luthar, S. S. (1991). Vulnerability and resilience: A study of high-risk adolescents. *Child Development, 62*, 600-616.

Lykken, D. (1957). A study of anxiety in the sociopathic personality. *Journal of Abnormal Psychology, 55*, 6-10.

Lynam, D., Moffitt, T., & Stouthamer-Loeber , M. (1993). Explaining the relation between IQ and delinquency: Class, race, test motivation, school failure, or self-control? *Journal of Abnormal Psychology, 102* (2), 187-196.

Lyubimov, N. N. (1992, May 19-21). Mobilization of the hidden reserves of the brain. [Abstract] Program Abstracts of the 2nd Russian-Swedish Symposium "New Research in Neurobiology," Brain Research Institute, Russian Academy of Medical Sciences, Moscow. (Available from Reprints Office, Psychology Department, M.U.M. 1000 North 4th Street, Fairfield, IA 52557)

MacKenzie, B., & Cumming, S. (1986). How fragile is the relationship between inspection time and intelligence: The effects of apparent-motion cues and previous experience. *Personality and Individual Differences, 7* (5), 721-729.

MacKenzie, D. L. (1997). Criminal justice and crime prevention. In L. W. Sherman, D. Gottfredson, D. MacKenzie, J. Eck, P. Reuter, & S. Bushway (Eds.), *Preventing crime: What works, what doesn't, what's promising* (Report NCJ 165366, pp. 9-1 to 9-76). Washington, DC: U.S. Department of Justice.

MacLean, C. R. K., Walton, K. G., Wenneberg, S. R., Levitsky, D. K., Mandarino, J. V., Waziri, R., Hillis, S. L., & Schneider, R. H. (1997). Effects of the Transcendental Meditation program on adaptive mechanisms: Changes in hormone levels and responses to stress after 4 months of practice. *Psychoneuroendocrinology, 22* (4), 277-295.

MacLean, P. D. (1978). A mind of three minds: Educating the triune brain. In *77th yearbook of the National Society for the Study of Education* (pp. 308-342). Chicago: University of Chicago Press.

MacMahon, B., Pugh, T. F., & Ipsen, J. (1960). *Epidemiologic methods.* Boston: Little, Brown.

Magill, D. (this volume). Cost savings from teaching the *Transcendental Meditation* program in prisons. *Journal of Offender Rehabilitation*, 36(1/2/3/4), 319-331.

Maguire, K., & Pastore, A. L. (Eds.). (1995). *Sourcebook of criminal justice statistics. U.S. Department of Justice, Bureau of Justice Statistics.* Washington, DC: U.S. Government Printing Office.

Maguire, K., & Pastore, A. L. (Eds.). (1998). *Sourcebook of criminal justice statistics* [Online]. Available at: <www.albany.edu/sourcebook>.

Maharishi Mahesh Yogi (1963/1995). *Science of being and art of living.* New York: Meridian.

Maharishi Mahesh Yogi (1966). *Science of being and art of living.* Los Angeles: International SRM.

Maharishi Mahesh Yogi (1968). *The science of being and art of living.* New York: Signet.

Maharishi Mahesh Yogi (1969). *On the Bhagavad-Gita: A new translation and commentary, Chapters 1-6.* Baltimore: Penguin.

Maharishi Mahesh Yogi (1972). *The Science of Creative Intelligence: Knowledge and experience* [course syllabus]. Los Angeles: Maharishi International University Press.

Maharishi Mahesh Yogi (1977a). *Creating an ideal society.* Rheinweiler, Germany: Maharishi European Research University Press.

Maharishi Mahesh Yogi (1977b). Inaugural address. In *First world assembly on law, justice, and rehabilitation* (pp. 20-27). Seelisberg, Switzerland: Age of Enlightenment Press.

Maharishi Mahesh Yogi (1986a). *Life supported by natural law.* Washington, DC: Age of Enlightenment Press.

Maharishi Mahesh Yogi (1986b). *Maharishi's program to create world peace: Removing the basis of terrorism and war.* Washington, DC: Age of Enlightenment Press.

Maharishi Mahesh Yogi (1986c). Unified field based education [lecture delivered July 13, 1985]. In *Life Supported by Natural Law* (pp. 94-101). Washington, DC: Age of Enlightenment Press.

Maharishi Mahesh Yogi (1994). *Vedic knowledge for everyone: Introduction to Maharishi Vedic University.* Vlodrop, The Netherlands: Maharishi Vedic University Press.

Maharishi Mahesh Yogi (1995a). *Maharishi University of Management: Wholeness on the move* (2nd ed.). India: Maharishi Prakashan.

Maharishi Mahesh Yogi (1995b). *Maharishi's absolute theory of government: Automation in administration.* New Delhi, India: Age of Enlightenment Publications.

Maharishi Mahesh Yogi (1996). *Maharishi's absolute theory of defence.* New Delhi, India: Age of Enlightenment Publications.

Maharishi Mahesh Yogi (1997). *Celebrating perfection in education.* Maharishi Vedic University Press, Vlodrop, The Netherlands.

Maharishi University of Management. (1993). *A proven program for our criminal justice system: Maharishi's Transcendental Meditation and corrections.* Fairfield, IA: Author.

Maller, R. A., & Zhou, X. (1996). *Survival analysis with long-term survivors.* New York: John Wiley & Sons.

Malloy, P., Fairbank, J., & Keane, T. (1983). Validation of a multimethod assessment of posttraumatic stress disorders in Vietnam veterans. *Journal of Consulting and Clinical Psychology, 51* (4), 488-494.

Maltz, M. D. (1984). *Recidivism.* New York: Academic Press.

Maltz, M. D. (1990). *SURFIT: Survival fitting and analysis software for industrial, biomedical, correctional, and social science applications.* Department of Criminal Justice and Quantitative Methods, University of Illinois, Chicago.

Marcus, J. B. (1996). *The crime vaccine: How to end the crime epidemic.* Baton Rouge, LA: Claitor's Publishing Division, Inc.

Marcus, S. V. (1977). The influence of the Transcendental Meditation program on the marital dyad. (Doctoral dissertation, California School of Professional Psychology, 1977.) *Dissertation Abstracts International, 38* (8), 3895-B.

Marlatt, G. A., & Gordon, J. R. (Eds.). (1985). *Relapse prevention: Maintenance strategies in addictive behavior change.* New York: Guilford.

Marlatt, G. A., & Marques, J. K. (1977). Meditation, self-control and alcohol abuse. In R. B. Stuart (Ed.), *Behavioral self-management: Strategies, techniques and outcomes* (pp. 117-153). New York: Brunner/Mazel.

Martin, J. (1960). Variations in skin resistance and their relationship to GSR conditioning. *Journal of Mental Sciences, 106*, 281-287.

Martin, S. E. (Ed.). (1993). *Alcohol and interpersonal violence: Fostering multidisciplinary perspectives* (NIH Publication No. 93-3496). Rockville, MD: National Institute on Alcohol Abuse and Alcoholism.

Martinetti, R. F. (1976). Influence of Transcendental Meditation on perceptual illusion. *Perceptual and Motor Skills, 43*, 822.

Martinson, R. (1974). What works? Questions and answers about prison reform. *The Public Interest, 35*, 22-54.

Marzuk, P. M. (1996). Violence, crime, and mental illness: How strong a link? *Archives of General Psychiatry, 53*, 481-486.

Maslow, A. H. (1962). *Toward a psychology of being.* Princeton: Von Nostrand.

Maslow, A. H. (1964). *Religions, values, and peak experiences.* Columbus, OH: Ohio State University.

Maslow, A. H. (1976). *Farther reaches of human nature.* New York: Viking.

Mason, L. I., Alexander, C. N., Travis, F. T., Marsh, G., Orme-Johnson, D. W., Gackenbach, J., Mason, D. C., Rainforth, M., & Walton, K. G. (1997). Electrophysiological correlates of higher states of consciousness during sleep in long-term practitioners of Transcendental Meditation Program. *Sleep, 20* (2), 102-110.

Mason, S. T., & Fibiger, H. C. (1978). 6-OHDA lesion of the dorsal noradrenergic bundle alters extinction of passive avoidance. *Brain Research, 152*, 209-214.

Masten, A. S., & Coatsworth, J. D. (1995). Competence, resilience, and psychopathology. In D. Cicchetti & D. J. Cohen (Eds.), *Developmental psychopathology, volume 2: Risk, disorder and adaptation* (pp. 715-752). New York: Wiley.

Masten, A. S., Best, K. M., & Garmezy, N. (1990). Resilience and development: Contributions from the study of children who overcome adversity. In D. Cicchetti and D. J. Cohen (Eds.), *Development and Psychopathology*, *2*, 425-444.

Maxwell, S. E., & Delaney, H. D. (1990). *Designing experiments and analyzing data: A model comparison perspective*. Belmont, CA: Wadsworth.

McAdams, D. (1979). *Construction and validation of a thematic scoring system for the intimacy motive.* Unpublished doctoral dissertation, Harvard University, Cambridge, MA.

McCarthy, W., & Hagan, J. (1992). Mean streets: The theoretical significance of situational delinquency among homeless youth. *American Journal of Sociology*, *98* (3), 597-627.

McCleary, R., & Hay, R. A., Jr. (1980). *Applied time series analysis for the social sciences.* Beverly Hills, CA: Sage.

McClelland, D. C. (1961). *The achieving society.* New York: Van Nostrand.

McClelland, D. C. (1975). *Power: The inner experience.* New York: John Wiley.

McClelland, D. C., Atkinson, J. W., Clark, R. A., & Lowell, E. L. (1953). *The achievement motive.* New York: Appleton-Century Crofts.

McDavid, J., & McCandless, R. (1962). Psychosocial theory, research and juvenile delinquency. *Journal of Criminal Law, Criminology, and Police Science, 53*, 1-14.

McEvoy, T. M., Frumkin, L. R., & Harkins, S. W. (1980). Effects of meditation on brainstem auditory evoked potentials. *International Journal of Neuroscience, 10*, 165-170.

McEwen, B. (1998a). Protective and damaging effects of stress mediators. *New England Journal of Medicine*, *338* (3), 171-179.

McEwen, B. S. (1998b). Stress, adaptation, and disease. Allostasis and allostatic load. *Annals of the New York Academy of Sciences*, *840*, 33-44.

McEwen, B. S., & Stellar, E. (1993). Stress and the individual: Mechanisms leading to disease. *Archives of Internal Medicine*, *153*, 2093-2101.

McEwen, B. S., Lambdin, L. T., Rainbow, T. C., & De Nicola, A. F. (1986). Aldosterone effects on salt appetite in adrenalectomized rats. *Neuroendocrinology*, *43*, 38-43.

Mednick, S. A., Gabrielli, W. F., & Hutchings, B. (1984). Genetic influences in criminal convictions: Evidence from an adoption cohort. *Science*, *224*, 891-894.

Megargee, E. I. (1972). *The psychology of violence and aggression.* Morristown, NJ: General Learning Press.

Megargee, E. I., & Bohn, M. J. (1979). *Classifying criminal offenders.* Beverly Hills: Sage.

Metzler, C., & Wittenberg. S. (1980). *The development of validated base expectancy tables.* (Paper #160). Massachusetts Department of Corrections.

Michaels, R. R., Huber, M. J., & McCann, D. S. (1976). Evaluation of Transcendental Meditation as a method of reducing stress. *Science, 192* (4245), 1242-1244.

Miczek, K. A., DeBold, J. F., Haney, M., Tidey, J., Vivian, J., & Weerts, E. M. (1993). Alcohol, drugs of abuse, aggression and violence. In A. J. Reiss, Jr., & J. A. Roth (Eds.), *Understanding and preventing violence, volume III: Social and psychological perspectives on violence* (pp. 370-570). Washington, DC: National Academy Press.

Miller, T. R., Cohen, M. A., & Wiersema, B. (1996). *Victim costs and consequences: A new look* (Summary Report Gov. Doc. J28.24/3: v. 66): U.S. National Institute of Justice.

Mills, P. J., Schneider, R. H., Hill, D., Walton, K. G., & Wallace, R. K. (1990). Beta-adrenergic receptor sensitivity in subjects practicing Transcendental Meditation. *Journal of Psychosomatic Research*, *34* (1), 29-33.

Milner, J. S. (1998). Individual and family characteristics associated with intrafamilial child physical and sexual abuse. In P. K. Trickett & C. J. Schellenbach (Eds.), *Violence against children in the family and community* (pp. 141-170). Washington, DC: American Psychological Association.

Moffitt, T. E. (1993). Adolescent limited and life-course-persistent antisocial behavior: A developmental taxonomy. *Psychological Review*, *100* (4), 674-701.

Monahan, R. J. (1975). *Impressions of the Transcendental Meditation technique in an outpatient drug rehabilitation clinic.* Paper presented at the First International Conference on Psychology and the Science of Creative Intelligence, Fairfield, IA.

Monahan, R. J. (1977). Secondary prevention of drug dependence through the Transcendental Meditation program in metropolitan Philadelphia. *The International Journal of the Addictions*, *12* (6), 729-754.

Morgan, W. W., & Rudeen, P. K. (1976). Temporal study of 5-hydroxyindoleacetic acid normalization during recovery from immobilization stress. *Experimental Neurology*, *51*, 259-262.

Morgan, W. W., Rudeen, P. K., & Pfeil, K. A. (1975). Effect of immobilization stress on serotonin content and turnover in regions of the rat brain. *Life Sciences*, *17*, 143-150.

Morley, E., & Rossman, S. (1996). Cities in Schools: Supporting school safety through services to at-risk youth. *Education and Urban Society*, *28* (4), 473-491.

Munck, A., Guyre, P. M., & Holbrook, N. J. (1984). Physiological functions of glucocorticoids in stress and their relation to pharmacological actions. *Endocrine Reviews*, *5* (1), 25-45.

Murray, C. A., & Cox, Jr., L. A. (1979). *Beyond probation: Juvenile corrections and the chronic delinquent*. Beverly Hills, CA: Sage.

Myers, T. I., & Eisner, E. J. (1974). *An experimental evaluation of the effects of karate and meditation.* Final report for the U.S. Army Institute for the Behavioral and Social Sciences, Social Processes Technical Area. Washington, DC: American Institutes for Research.

Nataraj, P., & Radhamani, M. G. (1989). The Transcendental Meditation program and its effects on psychological functions in secondary school students of a rural Indian high school. In R. A. Chalmers, G. Clements, H. Schenkluhn, & M. Weinless (Eds.), *Scientific research on Maharishi's Transcendental Meditation and TM-Sidhi program: Collected papers, volume 2* (pp. 955-962). Vlodrop, The Netherlands: Maharishi Vedic University Press.

National Criminal Justice Reference Service. (2000). Annual report on drug use among adult and juvenile arrestees 1999. In Arrestee Drug Abuse Monitoring Program. Web site: <www.ncjrs.org/pdffiles1/nij/181426.pdf>.

National Institute for Dispute Resolution. (1993). *Facts and information: 1992-1993*. Washington, DC.

Nettelbeck, T. (1987). Inspection time and intelligence. In P. A. Vernon (Ed.), *Speed of information-processing and intelligence* (pp. 295-346). Norwood, NJ: Ablex.

Nidich, R., & Nidich, S. (1988). Improving the social climate of a Philippine secondary school through the practice of the Transcendental Meditation program [abstract]. *Abstracts of papers of the annual meeting of the Mid-Western Educational Research Association*, p. 14.

Nidich, R., Seeman, W., & Dreskin, T. (1973). Influence of Transcendental Meditation: A replication. *Journal of Counseling Psychology*, *20*, 565-566.

Nidich, S. (1989). The Science of Creative Intelligence and the Transcendental Meditation program: Reduction of drug and alcohol consumption. In R. A. Chalmers, G. Clements, H. Schenkluhn, & M. Weinless (Eds.), *Scientific research on Maharishi's Transcendental Meditation and TM-Sidhi program: Collected papers, volume 3* (pp. 2115-2123). Vlodrop, The Netherlands: Maharishi Vedic University Press.

Nidich, S., & Nidich, R. (1987). Holistic student development at Maharishi School of the Age of Enlightenment: Theory and research. *Modern Science and Vedic Science*, *1* (4), 432-468.

Nidich, S., & Nidich, R. (1989a). Increased academic achievement at Maharishi School of the Age of Enlightenment: A replication study. *Education*, *109* (3), 302-304.

Nidich, S., & Nidich, R. (1989b). The Transcendental Meditation and TM-Sidhi program and moral development. In R. A. Chalmers, G. Clements, H. Schenkluhn, & M. Weinless (Eds.), *Scientific research on Maharishi's Transcendental Meditation and TM-Sidhi program: Collected papers, volume 3*, (pp. 2034-2037). Vlodrop, The Netherlands: Maharishi Vedic University Press.

Nidich, S., & Nidich, R. (1992). *Growing up enlightened*. Fairfield, IA: Maharishi International University Press.

Nidich, S., Nidich, R., & Rainforth, M. (1986). School effectiveness: Achievement gains at the Maharishi School of the Age of Enlightenment. *Education*, *107*, 49-54.

Nidich, S., & Orme-Johnson, D. W. (1982). Kohlberg's stage 7, natural law, and the Transcendental Meditation and TM-Sidhi program. In R. A. Chalmers, G. Clements, H. Schenkluhn, & M. Weinless (Eds.), *Scientific research on Maharishi's Transcendental Meditation and TM-Sidhi program: Collected papers, volume 4*, (pp. 2877-2882). Vlodrop, The Netherlands: Maharishi Vedic University Press.

Nidich, S., Ryncarz, R., Abrams, A., Orme-Johnson, D. W., & Wallace, R. K. (1983). Kohlbergian cosmic perspective responses, EEG coherence, and the Transcendental Meditation and TM-Sidhi program. *Journal of Moral Education*, *12*, 166-173.

Nidich, S., Seeman, W., & Dreskin, T. (1973). Influence of Transcendental Meditation on self-actualization: A replication. *Journal of Counseling Psychology*, *20*, 565-566.

Noam, G. G., Hauser, S., Santostefano, S., Garrison, W., Jacobson, A., Powers, S., & Mead, M. (1984). Ego development and psychopathology: A study of hospitalized adolescents. *Child Development, 55*, 184-194.

Noam, G. G., Paget, K., Valiant, G., Borst, S., & Bartok, J. (1994). Conduct and affective disorders in developmental perspective: A systematic study of adolescent psychopathology. *Development and Psychopathology, 6*, 519-532.

Noam, G. G., Recklitis, C. J., & Paget, K. F. (1991). Pathways of ego development: Contributions to maladaptation and adjustment. *Development and Psychopathology, 3*, 311-328.

Noguera, P. (1995). Preventing and producing violence. *Harvard Educational Review, 65* (2) 189-212.

Novy, D. M., Frankiewicz, R. G., Francis, D. J., Liberman, D., Overall, J. E., & Vincent, K. R. (1994). An investigation of the structural validity of Loevinger's model and measure of ego development. *Journal of Personality, 62* (1), 87-118.

Nystul, M. S., & Garde, M. (1977). Comparison of self-concepts of Transcendental Meditators and nonmeditators. *Psychological Reports, 41*, 303-306.

O'Connell, D. F., & Alexander, C. N. (Eds.). (1994). *Self-recovery: Treating addictions using Transcendental Meditation and Maharishi Ayur-Veda.* Binghamton, NY: The Haworth Press, Inc.

Oeting, R. R., & Beauvais, F. (1987). Peer cluster theory, socialization characteristics and adolescent drug use: A path analysis. *Journal of Counseling Psychology, 34*, 205-213.

Office of Juvenile Justice and Delinquency Prevention. (1993). *Comprehensive strategy for serious, violent, and chronic juvenile offenders.* Washington, DC: U.S. Department of Justice.

Office of Juvenile Justice and Delinquency Prevention. (1996). *Juvenile offenders and victims: 1996 update of violence.* Washington, DC: U.S. Department of Justice.

Olson, R. W. (1964). MMPI sex difference in narcotic addicts. *Journal of General Psychology, 71*, 257-266.

Opstad, P. K. (1992). Androgenic hormones during prolonged physical stress, sleep, and energy deficiency. *Journal of Clinical Endocrinology and Metabolism, 74*, 1176-1183.

Orme-Johnson, D. W. (1973). Autonomic stability and Transcendental Meditation. *Psychosomatic Medicine, 35*, 341-349.

Orme-Johnson, D. W. (1977). EEG coherence during transcendental consciousness. *Electroencephalography and Clinical Neurophysiology, 43* (4), E 487.

Orme-Johnson, D. W. (1981). Prison rehabilitation and crime prevention through the Transcendental Meditation and TM-Sidhi program. In L. J. Hippchen (Ed.), *Holistic approaches to offender rehabilitation* (pp. 346-383). Springfield, IL: Charles C. Thomas.

Orme-Johnson, D. W. (1987). Medical care utilization and the Transcendental Meditation program. *Psychosomatic Medicine, 49*, 493-507.

Orme-Johnson, D. W. (1988a). The cosmic psyche: An introduction to Maharishi's Vedic psychology–the fulfillment of modern psychology. *Modern Science and Vedic Science, 2* (2), 113-163.

Orme-Johnson, D. W. (1988b). Topographic EEG brain mapping during yogic flying. *International Journal of Neuroscience*, *38*, 427-434.

Orme-Johnson, D. W. (1992). Theory and research on conflict resolution through the Maharishi Effect. *Modern Science and Vedic Science*, *5* (1-2), 76-100.

Orme-Johnson, D. W. (1994). Transcendental Meditation as an epidemiological approach to drug and alcohol abuse: Theory, research, and financial impact evaluation. *Alcoholism Treatment Quarterly*, *11*, 119-168.

Orme-Johnson, D. W. (1995). Summary of scientific research on Maharishi's Transcendental Meditation and TM-Sidhi Program. *Modern Science and Vedic Science*, *6* (1), 60-155.

Orme-Johnson, D. W. (2000). An overview of Charles Alexander's contribution to psychology: Developing higher states of consciousness in the individual and the society. *Journal of Adult Development*, *7* (4), 199-215.

Orme-Johnson, D. W. (this volume). Preventing crime through the Maharishi Effect. *Journal of Offender Rehabilitation*, 36(1/2/3/4), 257-281.

Orme-Johnson, D. W., & Dillbeck, M. C. (1987). Maharishi's program to create world peace: Theory and research. *Modern Science and Vedic Science*, *1*, 206-259.

Orme-Johnson, D. W., & Farrow, J. T. (Eds.). (1977). *Scientific research on the Transcendental Meditation program: Collected papers, volume 1*. Rheinweiler, Germany: Maharishi European Research University Press.

Orme-Johnson, D. W., & Gelderloos, P. (1988). The long-term effects of the Maharishi Technology of the Unified Field on the quality of life in the United States (1960 to 1983). *Social Science Perspectives Journal*, *2* (4), 127-146.

Orme-Johnson, D. W., & Granieri, B. (1977). The effects of the Age of Enlightenment Governor Training courses on field independence, creativity, intelligence, and behavioral flexibility. In D. W. Orme-Johnson & J. T. Farrow (Eds.), *Scientific research on the Transcendental Meditation Program: Collected papers, volume 1* (pp. 713-718). Rheinweiler, Germany: Maharishi European Research University Press.

Orme-Johnson, D. W., & Haynes, C. T. (1981). EEG phase coherence, pure consciousness, creativity, and TM-Sidhi experiences. *International Journal of Neuroscience*, *13*, 211-217.

Orme-Johnson, D. W., & Herron, R. E. (1997). An innovative approach to reducing medical care utilization and expenditures. *American Journal of Managed Care*, *3*, 135-144.

Orme-Johnson, D. W., & Moore, R. (this volume). First prison study using the *Transcendental Meditation* program: La Tuna Federal Penitentiary, 1971. *Journal of Offender Rehabilitation*, 36(1/2/3/4), 89-95.

Orme-Johnson, D. W., & Walton, K. G. (1998). All approaches to preventing or reversing effects of stress are not the same. *American Journal of Health Promotion*, *12* (5), 297-299.

Orme-Johnson, D. W., Alexander, C. N., & Davies, J. L. (1990). The effects of the Maharishi Technology of the Unified Field: Reply to a methodological critique. *Journal of Conflict Resolution*, *34* (4), 756-768.

Orme-Johnson, D. W., Alexander, C. N., Davies, J. L., Chandler, H. M., & Larimore, W. E. (1988). International peace project in the Middle East: The effect of the

Maharishi Technology of the Unified Field. *Journal of Conflict Resolution, 32* (4), 776-812.

Orme-Johnson, D. W., Clements, G., Haynes, C. T., & Badawi, K. (1977). Higher states of consciousness: EEG coherence, creativity, and experiences of the sidhis. In D. W. Orme-Johnson & J. T. Farrow (Eds.), *Scientific research on the Transcendental Meditation program: Collected papers* (pp. 705-712). Rheinweiler, Germany: Maharishi European Research University Press.

Orme-Johnson, D. W., Dillbeck, M. C., & Alexander, C. N. (this volume). Preventing terrorism and international conflict: Effects of large assemblies of participants in the *Transcendental Meditation* and *TM-Sidhi* programs. *Journal of Offender Rehabilitation*, 361/2/3/4), 283-302.

Orme-Johnson, D. W., Dillbeck, M. C., Alexander, C. N., Chandler, H. M., & Cranson, R. W. (1989). *Time series impact assessment analysis of reduced international conflict and terrorism: Effects of large assemblies of participants in the Transcendental Meditation and TM-Sidhi program.* Paper presented at the annual meeting of the American Political Science Association, Atlanta, Georgia.

Orme-Johnson, D. W., Dillbeck, M. C., Bousquet, J. G., & Alexander, C. N. (1989). The world peace project of 1978: An experimental analysis of the application of the Maharishi Technology of the Unified Field in major world trouble spots: Increased harmony in international affairs. In R. A. Chalmers, G. Clements, H. Schenkluhn, & M. Weinless (Eds.), *Scientific research on Maharishi's Transcendental Meditation and TM-Sidhi program: Collected papers, volume 4.* Vlodrop, The Netherlands: Maharishi Vedic University Press.

Orme-Johnson, D. W., Wallace, R. K., & Dillbeck, M. C. (1989). Longitudinal effects of the TM-Sidhi program on EEG phase coherence. In R. A. Chalmers, G. Clements, H. Schenkluhn, & M. Weinless (Eds.), *Scientific research on Maharishi's Transcendental Meditation and TM-Sidhi program: Collected papers, volume 3.* Vlodrop, The Netherlands: Maharishi Vedic University Press.

Orme-Johnson, D. W., Wallace, R. K., & Dillbeck, M. C. (Eds.). (in press). *Scientific research on Maharishi's Transcendental Meditation and TM-Sidhi program: Collected papers, volume 6.* Fairfield, IA: Maharishi University of Management Press.

Orme-Johnson, D. W., Wallace, R. K., Dillbeck, M. C., Alexander, C. N., & Ball, O. E. (1989). Improved functional organization of the brain through the Maharishi Technology of the Unified Field as indicated by changes in EEG coherence and its cognitive correlates: A proposed model of higher states of consciousness. In R. Chalmers, G. Clements, H. Schenkluhn, & M. Weinless (Eds.), *Scientific research on Maharishi's Transcendental Meditation and TM-Sidhi program: Collected papers, volume 1* (pp. 2245-2265). Vlodrop, The Netherlands: Maharishi Vedic University Press.

Orme-Johnson, D. W., Zimmerman, E., & Hawkins, M. (1997). Maharishi's Vedic Psychology: The science of the Cosmic Psyche. In H. S. R. Kao & D. Sinha (Eds.), *Asian perspectives on psychology* New Delhi: Sage Publications.

Orme-Johnson, R. F. (1987). A unified field theory of literature. *Modern Science and Vedic Science, 1* (3), 323-373.

Orpinas, P., Kelder, S., Murray, N., Fourney, A., Conroy, J., McReynolds, L., & Peters, Jr., R. (1996). Critical issues in implementing a comprehensive violence prevention program for middle schools: Translating theory into practice. *Education and Urban Society*, *28* (4), 456-472.

Orwoll, L., & Perlmutter, M. (1990). Wisdom and the study of wise persons. In R. J. Sternberg (Eds.), *Wisdom: Its nature, origin, and development*. New York: Cambidge University Press.

Ottens, A. J. (1975). The effect of Transcendental Meditation upon modifying the cigarette smoking habit. *Journal of the School of Health*, *45* (10), 577-583.

Overbeck, K. D. (1982). Auswirkungen der technik der Transzendentalen Meditation (TM) auf die psychische un psychosomatische Befindlichkeit. *Psychotherpaie-Psychosomatik Medizinishce Psycyhologie*, *32* (6), 188-192.

Overbeck, K. -D., & Tönnies, S. E. (1989). Some effects of Transcendental Meditation on children with learning problems. In R. A. Chalmers, G. Clements, H. Schenkluhn, & M. Weinless (Eds.), *Scientific research on Maharishi's Transcendental Meditation and TM-Sidhi program: Collected papers, volume 2* (pp. 963-967). Vlodrop, The Netherlands: Maharishi Vedic University Press.

Ozasa, H., Kita, M., Inoue, T., & Mori, T. (1990). Plasma dehydroepiandrosterone-to-cortisol ratios as an indicator of stress in gynecologic patients. *Gynecologic Oncology*, *37*, 178-182.

Palkovits, M., Brownstein, M., Kizer, J. S., Saavedra, J. M., & Kopin, I. J. (1976). Effect of stress on serotonin concentration and tryptophan hydroxylase activity of brain nuclei. *Neuroendocrinology*, *22*, 298-304.

Palmer, T. (1975). Martinson revisited. *Journal of Research in Crime and Delinquency*, *12*, 133-152.

Palmer, T. (1978). *Correctional intervention and research*. New York: D.C. Heath.

Parker, L. N. (1991). Control of adrenal androgen secretion. *Endocrinology and Metabolism Clinics of North America*, *20*, 401-421.

Pascual-Leone, J. (1990). Reflections on life-span intelligence, consciousness, and ego development. In C. N. Alexander & E. J. Langer (Eds.), *Higher stages of human development* (pp. 258-285). New York: Oxford University Press.

Patanjali (1978). *Yoga Sutras*. (R. Prasada, Trans.). New Delhi, India: Oriental Books Reprint Corp. (Original work published 1912)

Paternoster, R., & Mazerolle, P. (1994). General strain theory and delinquency: A replication and extension. *Journal of Research in Crime and Delinquency*, *31*, 235-263.

Paton, S., Kessler, R., & Kandel, D. (1977). Depressive mood and adolescent illicit drug use: A longitudinal analysis. *Journal of Genetic Psychology*, *31*, 267-289.

Patterson, G. R. (1982). *Coercive family processes*. Eugene, OR: Castalia.

Patton, J., Stanford, M. S., & Barratt, E. S. (1995). Factor structure of the Barratt Impulsiveness Scale. *Journal of Clinical Psychology*, *51* (6), 768-774.

Pearson, C. (in press). *The supreme awakening: The unbounded potential within.* Fairfield, Iowa: Maharishi University of Management Press.

Peck, D. L., & Jones, R. (1985). The high cost of Alabama's habitual felony offender act: A preliminary assessment. *International Journal of Offender Therapy and Comparative Criminology*, *29*, 251-264.

Pelletier, K. R. (1974). Influence of Transcendental Meditation upon autokinetic perception. *Perceptual and Motor Skills*, *39*, 1031-1034.

Pelletier, K. R. (1974, April). *The effects of the Transcendental Meditation program on perceptual style: Increased field independence.* Paper presented at the meeting of the Western Psychological Association, San Francisco, CA.

Penner, W. J., Zingle, H. W., Dyck, R., & Truch, S. (1974). Does an in-depth Transcendental Meditation course effect change in the personalities of the participants? *Western Psychologist, 4*, 104-111.

Pepler, D. J., King, G., & Byrd, W. (1991). A social-cognitively based social skills training program for aggressive children. In D. J. Pepler & K. H. Rubin, (Eds.), *The Development and Treatment of Childhood Aggression* (pp. 361-379). Hillsdale, NJ: Erlbaum.

Petersilia, J. (1994). Debating crime and imprisonment in California. *Evaluation and Program Planning, 17* (2), 165-177.

Petersilia, J. Turner, S., Kahan, J., & Peterson, J. (1985). Executive summary of Rand's study, "Granting felons probation": Public risks and alternatives. *Crime and Delinquency, 31* (3), 379-392.

Petrenko, E. V., Orlova, T. V., & Lyubimov, N. N. (1993). Cerebral control of afferent somatosensory projections. *Bulletin of Experimental Biology and Medicine, 116* (9), 1046-1048.

Phillpotts, G. J. O., & Lancucki, L. B. (1979). *Previous convictions, sentence and reconviction.* (Home Office Research Study, No. 53.). Her Majesty's Stationery Office, London.

Piaget, J. (1970). Piaget's theory. In P. H. Mussen (Eds.), *Carmichael's manual of child psychology.* New York: Wiley.

Piaget, J. (1972). Intellectual evolution from adolescence to adulthood. *Human Development, 15*, 1-12.

Piper, E. S. (1985). Violent recidivism and chronicity in the 1958 Philadelphia cohort. *Journal of Quantitative Criminology, 1* (4), 319-344.

Pitts, Jr., F. (1969). The biochemistry of anxiety. *Scientific American, 220* (2), 69-75.

Plutchik, R., & van Praag, H. (1997). Suicide, impulsivity, and antisocial behavior. In D. Stoff, J. Breiling, & J. Maser (Eds.), *Handbook of antisocial behavior* (pp. 101-108). New York: John Wiley & Sons, Inc.

Pope, M. K., & Smith, T. W. (1991). Cortisol excretion in high and low cynically hostile men. *Psychosomatic Medicine, 53*, 386-392.

Prentice, D. A, & Miller, D. T. (1992). When small effects are impressive. *Psychological Bulletin, 112*, 160-164.

Pritchard, D. A. (1979). Stable predictors of recidivism. *Criminology, 17*, 15-21.

Quay, H. (1965). Psychopathic personality as pathological stimulation-seeking. *American Journal of Psychiatry, 122*, 180-183.

Quay, H. C. (1977). The three faces of evaluation: What can be expected to work. *Criminal Justice and Behavior, 4*, 341-354.

Quay, H. C. (1987a). *Handbook of juvenile delinquency.* New York: Wiley.

Quay, H. C. (1987b). Intelligence. In H. C. Quay (Ed.), *Handbook of juvenile delinquency* (pp. 106-117). New York: Wiley.

Quinn, S. (1993, July 18). To the couch, Mr. Clinton! On therapy, the presidential press corps and the sudden need to be nice to Bill. *The Washington Post*, p. C1.

Radin, D. (1998). *The conscious universe.* New York: HarperCollins.

Raine, A. (1993). *The psychopathology of crime: Criminal behavior as a clinical disorder.* San Diego, CA: Academic Press.

Raine, A. (1996). Autonomic nervous system factors underlying disinhibited, antisocial, and violent behavior: Biosocial perspectives and treatment. *Annals of the New York Academy of Sciences, 794*, 46-59.

Raine, A., & Jones, F. (1987). Attention, autonomic arousal, and personality in behaviorally disordered children. *Journal of Abnormal Child Psychology, 15*, 583-599.

Raine, A., Venables, P. H., & Williams, M. (1990a). Autonomic orientation responses in 15-year old male subjects and criminal behavior at age 24. *American Journal of Psychiatry, 21* (4), 424-433.

Raine, A., Venables, P. H., & Williams, M. (1990b). Relationships between CNS and ANS measures of arousal at age 15 and criminality at age 24. *Archives of General Psychophysiology, 2*, 221-225.

Raine, A., Venables, P. H., & Williams, M. (1990c). Relationships between N1, P300 and CNV recorded at age 15 and criminal behavior at age 24. *Psychophysiology, 27*, 567-575.

Raine, A., Venables, P., & Williams, M. (1995). High autonomic arousal and electrodermal orienting at age 15 years as protective factors against criminal behavior at age 29 years. *American Journal of Psychiatry, 152* (11), 1595-1600.

Rainforth, M. V., Alexander, C. N., & Cavanaugh, K. L. (this volume). Effects of the *Transcendental Meditation* program on recidivism among former inmates of Folsom Prison: Survival analysis of 15-year follow-up data. *Journal of Offender Rehabilitation*, 36(1/2/3/4), 181-203.

Ramirez, J. (1989). The Transcendental Meditation program as a possible treatment modality for drug offenders: Evaluation of a pilot project at Milan Federal Correctional Institution. In R. A. Chalmers, G. Clements, H. Schenkluhn, & M. Weinless (Eds.), *Scientific research on Maharishi's Transcendental Meditation and TM-Sidhi program, Collected papers, volume 2* (pp. 1118-1134). Vlodrop, The Netherlands: Maharishi Vedic University Press.

Ranchor, A., Sanderman, R., Bouma, J., Buunk, B., & van den Heuvel, W. (1997). An exploration of the relation between hostility and disease. *Journal of Behavioral Medicine, 20* (3), 223-240.

Rand Corporation. (1987). *Rand chronology of international terrorism (extract).* Santa Monica, CA.

Rankin, J. H., & Kern, R. (1994). Parental attachments and delinquency. *Criminology, 32* (4), 495-515.

Raven, J. C. (1965). *Guide to using the Mill-Hill Vocabulary Scale with the Progressive Matrices Scale.* London: Lewis.

Recklitis, C. J., & Noam, G. G. (1990, August). *Aggression in adolescent psychopathology: Developmental and personality dimensions.* Paper presented at the annual meeting of the American Psychological Association, Boston, MA.

Reddy, M. K. (1989). The role of the Transcendental Meditation program in the promotion of athletic excellence: Long- and short-term effects and their relation to activation theory. In R. Chalmers, G. Clements, H. Schenkluhn, & M. Weinless (Eds.), *Scientific research on Maharishi's Transcendental Meditation and TM-Sidhi pro-*

gram: Collected papers (pp. 907-950). Vlodrop, The Netherlands: Maharishi Vedic University Press.

Redmond, D. E., & Huang, Y. H. (1979). Current concepts. II. New evidence for a locus coeruleus-norepinephrine connection with anxiety. *Life Sciences, 25*, 2149-2162.

Redmore, C. D. (1976). Susceptibility to faking of a sentence completion test of ego development. *Journal of Personality Assessment, 40*, 607-616.

Reeks, D. L. (1991). Improved quality of life in Iowa through the Maharishi Effect. *Dissertation Abstracts International, 51* (12), 6155b, Maharishi International University.

Reiss, A. J., & Roth, J. A. (Eds.). (1993). *Understanding and preventing violence: Volume I.* Washington, DC: National Academy Press.

Rest, J. R. (1975). Longitudinal study of the Defining Issues Test of moral judgement: A strategy for analyzing developmental change. *Developmental Psychology, 11*, 738-748.

Rock, M. (1975). Self-reflection and ego development. (Doctoral dissertation, New York University, 1975). *Dissertation Abstracts International, 36*, 3066B.

Rolf, J., Masten, A. D., Cicchetti, D., Neuchterlein, K. H., & Weintraub, S. (Eds). (1990). Risk and protective factors in the development of psychopathology. Cambridge, MA: Cambridge University Press.

Rose, M. (1996). Tougher discipline, safer schools. *American Teacher, 80*, 10-12.

Rosen, A. S., & Nordquist, T. A. (1980). Ego development levels and values in a yogic community. *Journal of Personality and Social Psychology, 39*, 1152-1160.

Rosenthal, R., & Rubin, D. B. (1982). A simple, general purpose display of magnitude of experimental effect. *Journal of Educational Psychology, 74*, 166-169.

Roslund, B., & Larson, C. A. (1979). Crimes of violence and alcohol abuse in Sweden. *International Journal of the Addictions, 14* (8), 1103-1115.

Ross, R. R., & Fabiano, E. A. (1985). *Time to think: A cognitive model of delinquency prevention and offender rehabilitation.* Johnson City, TN: Institute of Social Sciences and Arts.

Roth, R. (1987). *Transcendental Meditation.* New York: Donald I. Fine.

Roth, R. (1994). *Maharishi Mahesh Yogi's Transcendental Meditation* (Rev. ed.). New York: Primus.

Royer, A. (1994). The role of the Transcendental Meditation technique in promoting smoking cessation: A longitudinal study. In D. F. O'Connell & C. N. Alexander (Eds.), *Self recovery: Treating addictions using Transcendental Meditation and Maharishi Ayur-Veda* (pp. 221-239). Binghamton, NY: The Haworth Press, Inc.

Rubin, D.B. (1976). Inference and missing data. *Biometrika, 63*, 581-592.

Rubinstein, J. L. (1977). Case study: Office of Evaluation. In S. O. White & S. Krislov (Eds.), *Understanding crime: An evaluation of the National Institute of Law Enforcement and Criminal Justice.* Washington, DC: National Academy of Sciences.

Rutter, M. (1987). Psychosocial resilience and protective mechanisms. *American Journal of Orthopsychiatry, 57*, 316-331.

Rutter, M. (1990). Psychosocial resilience and protective mechanisms. In J. Rolf, A. S. Masten, D. Cicchetti, K. H. Nuechterlein, & S. Weintraub (Eds.), *Risk and protective factors in the development of psychopathology* (pp. 181-214). New York: Cambridge University Press.

Sadava, S. W. (1975). Research approaches to illicit drug use: A critical review. *Genetic Psychology Monograph, 91*, 3-59.

Samenow, S. E. (1984). *Inside the criminal mind.* New York: Random House.

Sampson, R., & Groves, W. B. (1989). Community structure and crime. *American Journal of Sociology, 94* (4), 774-802.

Sampson, R., & Laub, J. (1993). *Crime in the making.* Cambridge, MA: Harvard University Press.

Sapolsky, R. M. (1990). Adrenocortical function, social rank, and personality among wild baboons. *Biological Psychiatry, 28*, 862-878.

Sapolsky, R. M. (1992). *Stress, the aging brain, and the mechanisms of neuron death.* Cambridge, MA: The MIT Press.

Sapolsky, R. M. (1996). Why stress is bad for your brain. *Science, 273*, 749-750.

Sapolsky, R. M., Krey, L. C., & McEwen, B. S. (1984a). Glucocorticoid-sensitive hippocampal neurons are involved in terminating the adrenocortical stress response. *Proceedings of the National Academy of Sciences, USA, 81*, 6174-6177.

Sapolsky, R. M., Krey, L. C., & McEwen, B. S. (1984b). Stress down-regulates corticosterone receptors in a site-specific manner in the brain. *Endocrinology, 114*, (1), 287-292.

Sapolsky, R. M., Krey, L. C., & McEwen, B. S. (1986). The neuroendocrinology of stress and aging: The glucocorticoid cascade hypothesis. *Endocrine Reviews, 7* (3), 284-301.

Sapolsky, R. M., Zola-Morgan, S., & Squire, L. R. (1991). Inhibition of glucocorticoid secretion by the hippocampal formation in the primate. *Journal of Neuroscience, 11* (12), 3695-3704.

Sarbin, T. R., & Adler, N. (1970). Self-reconstitution processes: A preliminary report. *The Psychoanalytic Quarterly, 57*, 4.

Scharf, P., & Hickey, J. (1976). The prison and the inmates' conception of legal justice: An experiment in democratic education. *Criminal Justice and Behavior, 3*, 107-122.

Schecter, H. E. (1977). A psychological investigation into the source of the effect of the Transcendental Meditation technique (Doctoral dissertation, York University, 1977). *Dissertation Abstracts International, 38* (7), 3372B.

Schenkluhn, H., & Geisler, M. (1977). A longitudinal study of the influence of the Transcendental Meditation program on drug abuse. In D. W. Orme-Johnson & J. T. Farrow (Eds.), *Scientific research on the Transcendental Meditation program: Collected papers, volume 1* (pp. 544-555). Rheinweiler, Germany: Maharishi European Research University Press.

Schlitz, M. (1996). Intentionality and intuition and their clinical implications: A challenge for science and medicine. *Advances: The Journal of Mind-Body Health, 12* (2), 58-65.

Schmidt, P., & Witte, A. D. (1989). Predicting criminal recidivism using 'split population' survival time models. *Journal of Econometrics, 40* (1), 141-159.

Schmidt-Wilk, J., Alexander, C. N., & Swanson, G. C. (1996). Developing consciousness in organizations: The Transcendental Meditation program in business. *Journal of Business & Psychology, 10* (4), 429-444.

Schneider, R., Staggers, F., Alexander, C., Sheppard, W., Rainforth, M., Kondwani, K., Smith, S., & King, C. (1995). A randomized controlled trial of stress reduction for hypertension in older African Americans. *Hypertension, 26* (5), 820-827.

Schroedinger, E. (1958/1967). *What is life? The physical aspect of the living cell & mind and matter.* Cambridge, England: Cambridge University Press.

Schwartz, E. (1989). The effects of the Transcendental Meditation program on strength of the nervous system, perceptual reactance, and auditory threshold. In R. Chalmers, G. Clements, H. Schenkluhn, & M. Weinless (Eds.), *Scientific research on Maharishi's Transcendental Meditation and TM-Sidhi program: Collected papers* (pp. 1926-1927). Vlodrop, The Netherlands: Maharishi Vedic University Press.

Schwarzschild, B. M. (1985). Anomaly cancellation launches bandwagon for superstring theory of everything. *Physics Today, 38,* 17-20.

Sechrest, L., White, S. O., & Bronn, E. D. (Eds.). (1979). *The rehabilitation of criminal offenders: Problems and prospects.* Washington, DC: The National Research Council, National Academy of Sciences.

Seeman, T., Singer, B., Rowe, J., Horwitz, R., & McEwen, B. (1997). Price of adaptation–allostatic load and its health consequences. *Archives of Internal Medicine, 157* (Oct. 27), 2259-2268.

Seeman, W., Nidich, S., & Banta, T. (1972). Influence of Transcendental Meditation on a measure of self-actualization. *Journal of Counseling Psychology, 19,* 184-187.

Sellin, T., & Wolfgang, M. E. (1964). *The measurement of delinquency.* New York: Wiley.

Selman, R. L. (1978). Socio-cognitive understanding. In T. Lickona (Ed.), *Moral development and behavior.* New York: Holt, Reinhart & Winston.

Selye, H. (1936). A syndrome produced by diverse nocuous agents. *Nature, 138,* 32.

Selye, H. (1974). *Stress without distress.* Philadelphia: Lippincott.

Selye, H. (1978). *The stress of life.* New York: McGraw-Hill.

Sgoifo, A., de Boer, S., Haller, J., & Koolhaas, J. (1996). Individual differences in plasma catecholamine and corticosterone stress responses of wild-type rats: Relationship with aggression. *Physiology and Behavior, 60* (6), 1403-1407.

Shafii, M., Lavely, R. A., & Jaffe, R. D. (1974). Meditation and marijuana. *American Journal of Psychiatry, 131,* 60-63.

Shafii, M., Lavely, R. A., & Jaffe, R. D. (1975). Meditation and the prevention of alcohol abuse. *American Journal of Psychiatry, 132,* 942-945.

Shafii, M., Lavely, R. A., & Jaffe, R. D. (1976). Decrease in cigarette smoking following Transcendental Meditation [Abstract]. *MERU Journal, 24,* 29.

Shear, J. (1990). *The inner dimension: Philosophy and the experience of consciousness* (Volume 4). New York: Peter Lang.

Shecter, H. (1977). The Transcendental Meditation program in the classroom: A psychological evaluation. (Doctoral dissertation, York University, Toronto, 1977). *Dissertation Abstracts International, 38B,* 3372-3373.

Sherman, A. D., & Petty, F. (1980). Neurochemical basis of the action of antidepressants on learned helplessness. *Behavioral and Neural Biology, 30,* 119-134.

Sherman, A. D., & Petty, F. (1982). Additivity of neurochemical changes in learned helplessness and imipramine. *Behavioral and Neural Biology, 35,* 344-353.

Sherman, L. W. (1997a). Conclusion: The effectiveness of local crime prevention funding. In L. W. Sherman, D. Gottfredson, D. MacKenzie, J. Eck, P. Reuter, & S. Bushway (Eds.), *Preventing crime: What works, what doesn't, what's promising*. Washington, DC: National Institute of Justice.

Sherman, L. W. (1997b). Thinking about crime prevention. In L. W. Sherman, D. Gottfredson, D. MacKenzie, J. Eck, P. Reuter, & S. Bushway (Eds.), *Preventing crime: What works, what doesn't, what's promising*. Washington DC: National Institute of Justice. [On-line]. Available: <http://www.ncjrs.org/works/chapter2.htm>.

Sherman, L. W., Gottfredson, D. C., MacKenzie, D. L., Eck, J., Reuter, P., & Bushway, S. D. (1997a). *Preventing crime: What works, what doesn't, what's promising. Research in brief* (Report No. NCJ-171676). Washington, DC: National Institute of Justice. (ERIC Document Reproduction Service No. ED 423 321)

Sherman, L. W., Gottfredson, D., MacKenzie, D., Eck, J., Reuter, P., & Bushway, S. (1997b). *Preventing crime: What works, what doesn't, what's promising* (Report No. NCJ 165366). U.S. Office of Justice Programs.

Sherman, L. W., Gottfredson, D., MacKenzie, D., Eck, J., Reuter, P., & Bushway, S. (Eds.) (1997c). *Preventing crime: What works, what doesn't, what's promising*. Washington, DC: National Institute of Justice. [On-line]. Available: http://www.ncjrs.org/works

Silverman, A., Cohen, S., & Shmavonian, B. (1959). Investigation of psychphysiologic relationships with skin resistance measures. *Journal of Psychosomatic Research*, *4*, 65-87.

Singer, J. D. (1986). Research, policy, and correlates of war. In O. Osterud (Ed.), *Studies of war and peace*. Oslo: Norwegian University Press.

Smart, Y. (1979). *An analysis of recidivism rates among residents released from Massachusetts correctional instititutions in 1977*. (Paper #182). Massachusetts Department of Corrections.

Smith, J. C. (1975). Meditation as psychotherapy: A review of the literature. *Psychological Bulletin*, *82*, 558-564.

Smith, J. C. (1976). Psychotherapeutic effects of Transcendental Meditation with controls for expectation of relief and daily sitting. *Journal of Consulting and Clinical Psychology*, *44*, 630-637.

Snarey, J., Kohlberg, L., & Noam, G. (1983). Ego development in perspective: Structural stage, functional phase, and cultural age-period models. *Developmental Review*, *3*, 303-338.

Snyder, J., & Patterson, G. (1987). Family interaction and delinquent behavior. In H. C. Quay (Ed.), *Handbook of juvenile delinquency* (pp. 216-243). New York: Wiley.

So, K.-T. (1995). Testing and developing holistic intelligence in Chinese culture with Maharishi's Vedic psychology: Three experimental replications using Transcendental Meditation. *Dissertation Abstracts International*.

So, K.-T., & Orme-Johnson, D. W. (2001). Three randomized experiments on the holistic longitudinal effects of the Transcendental Meditation technique on cognition. *Intelligence*, 29(5), 419-440.

Spence, K. (1958). A theory of emotionally based drive (D) and its relation to performance in simple learning situations. *The American Psychologist*, *13*, 131-141.

Spergel, I. A. (1966). *Street gang work: Theory and practice*. Reading, MA: Addison-Wesley.

Spielberger, C. D., Gorsuch, R. L., & Lushene, R. E. (1970). *STAI manual for the State-Trait Anxiety Inventory (self-evaluation questionnaire).* Palo Alto, CA: Consulting Psychologists Press.

Spitzer, R. C., & Endicott, J. (1975). *Schedule for affective disorders and schizophrenia.* (2nd ed.). Biometric Research, New York State Psychiatric Institute.

Sprinthall, N. H., & Mosher, R. (Eds.). (1978). *Value development as the aim of education.* Schenectady, NY: Character Research.

Stanford, M. S., & Barratt, E. S. (1992). Impulsiveness and the multi-impulsive personality disorder. *Personality and Individual Differences, 13* (7), 831-834.

Steffenhagen, N. R. (1980). Self-esteem theory of drug use. In D. Lettieri, M. Sayers, & H. Pearson (Eds.), *Theories of drug abuse.* Washington, DC: National Institute of Drug Abuse.

Stein, K. B. (1968). The TSC Scales: The outcome of a cluster analysis of the 550 MMPI items. In P. McReynolds (Ed.), *Advances in psychological assessment* (Volume 1). Palo Alto, CA: Science and Behavior Books.

Stephanopoulos, G. (1999). *All too human: A political education.* New York: Little, Brown.

Sterling, P., & Eyer, J. (1988). Allostasis: A new paradigm to explain arousal pathology. In S. Fisher & J. Reason (Eds.), *Handbook of life stress, cognition and health* (pp. 631-651). New York: John Wiley & Sons, Inc.

Stern, J. (1966). Stability-lability of physiological response systems. *Annals of the New York Academy of Sciences, 134*, 1018-1027.

Stern, J., Stewart, M., & Winokur, G. (1961). An investigation of some relationships between various measure of galvanic skin response. *Journal of Psychosomatic Research, 5*, 215-223.

Sternberg, R. J. (Ed.). (1990). *Wisdom: Its nature, origins, and development.* New York: Cambridge University Press.

Stone, E., Eqawa, M., & Colbjornsen, C. (1989). Catecholamine-induced desensitization of brain beta adrenoceptos *in vivo* and reversal by corticosterone. *Life Sciences, 44*, 209-213.

Suarez, V. W. (1989). The relationship of the practice of Transcendental Meditation to subjective evaluation of marital satisfaction and adjustment. In R. A. Chalmers, G. Clements, H. Schenkluhn, & M. Weinless (Eds.), *Scientific research on Maharishi's Transcendental Meditation and TM-Sidhi program: Collected papers, volume 2* (pp. 1184-1199). Vlodrop, The Netherlands: Maharishi Vedic University Press.

Subrahmanyam, S., & Porkodi, K. (1980). Neurohumoral correlates of Transcendental Meditation. *Journal of Biomedicine, 1*, 73-88.

Sullivan, M. (1995). New directions for research in the prevention and treatment of delinquency: A review and proposal. *Adolescence, 30*, 1-17.

Sullivan, P. J. (1975). A curriculum for stimulating moral reasoning and ego development in adolescents. (Doctoral dissertation, Boston University, 1975). *Dissertation Abstracts International, 36*, 1320A.

Swaim, R., Oetting, E., Edwards, R., & Beauvais, F. (1989). Links from emotional distress to adolescent drug use: A path model. *Journal of Consulting and Clinical Psychology, 57*, 227-231.

Sykes, G. M., & Matza, D. (1957). Techniques of neutralization: A theory of delinquency. *American Sociological Review, 22*, 664-670.

Tart, C. T. (1975). *States of consciousness*. New York: Dutton.

Taub, E., Steiner, S. S., Weingarten, E., & Walton, K. G. (1994). Effectiveness of broad spectrum approaches to relapse prevention in severe alcoholism: A long-term, randomized, controlled trial of Transcendental Meditation, EMG biofeedback and electronic neurotherapy. In D. F. O'Connell & C. N. Alexander (Eds.), *Self-recovery: Treating addictions using Transcendental Meditation and Maharishi Ayur-Veda* (pp. 187-220). Binghamton, NY: The Haworth Press, Inc.

Taylor, C. L., & Jodice, D. A. (1983). *World handbook of political and social indicators* (3rd ed., Volume 1). New Haven, CT: Yale University Press.

Taylor, M., & Creelman, T. (1967). PEST: Efficient estimate on probability function. *Journal of the Acoustic Society of America, 41*, 782-787.

Tellegen, A., & Atkinson, G. (1974). Openness to absorbing and self-altering experiences ("absorption"), a trait related to hypnotic susceptibility. *Journal of Abnormal Psychology, 83*, 268-277.

Tennant, F. S. (1985). *Primer on neurochemistry and drug dependence*. West Covina, CA: Veract.

Thierry, A. M., Fekete, M., & Glowinski, J. (1968). Effects of stress on the metabolism of noradrenaline, dopamine and serotonin (5HT) in the central nervous system of the rat (II) modifications of serotonin metabolism. *European Journal of Pharmacology, 4*, 384-389.

Throll, D. A. (1989). The effects of the Transcendental Meditation technique upon adolescent personality. In R. A. Chalmers, G. Clements, H. Schenkluhn, & M. Weinless (Eds.), *Scientific research on Maharishi's Transcendental Meditation and TM-Sidhi program: Collected papers, volume 2* (pp. 1087-1095). Vlodrop, The Netherlands: Maharishi Vedic University Press.

Tittle, C., & Logan, C. H. (1973). Sanctions and deviance: Evidence and remaining questions. *Law and Society Review, 7*, 371-379.

Tjoa, A. (1975). Meditation, neuroticism, and intelligence: A follow-up. *Gedrag: Tijdschrift voor Psychologie [Behavior: Journal of Psychology], 3*, 167-182.

Tobin, P., & Guerra, N. (1994). *What works in reducing adolescent violence: An empirical review of the field*. Boulder, CO: Center for the Study and Prevention of Violence.

Tobler, N. S. (1986). Meta-analysis of 143 adolescent drug prevention programs: Quantitative outcome results of program participants compared to a control or comparison group. *Journal of Drug Issues, 16*, 537-568.

Toch, H., & Adams, K. (1986). Pathology and disruptiveness among prison inmates. *Journal of Research in Crime and Delinquency, 23* (1), 7-21.

Tokarski, C. (1999). Health care inflation set to resume. *Between Rounds*, February/March 1999.

Torbert, W. R. (1994). Cultivating postformal adult development: Higher stages and contrasting interventions. In M. Miller & S. Cook-Greuter (Eds.), *Transcendence and mature thought in adulthood: The further reaches of adult development* (pp. 39-70). Lanham, MD: Rowman and Littlefield Publishers.

Travis, F. (1979). Creative thinking and the Transcendental Meditation technique. *The Journal of Creative Behavior, 13* (3), 169-180.

Travis, F. T. (1990). An empirical test of Maharishi's junction point model of states of consciousness. *Modern Science and Vedic Science, 4* (1), 43-56.

Travis, F. T. (1994). The junction point model: A field model of waking, sleeping, and dreaming, relating dream witnessing, the waking/sleeping transition, and Transcendental Meditation in terms of a common psychophysiologic state. *Dreaming, 4*, 91-104.

Travis, F. T., & Orme-Johnson, D. W. (1990). EEG coherence and power during Yogic Flying. *International Journal of Neuroscience, 54*, 1-12.

Travis, F., & Pearson, C. (2000). Pure consciousness: Distinct phenomenological and physiological correlates of "consciousness itself." *International Journal of Neuroscience, 100*, 77-89.

Travis, F., & Wallace, R. K. (1997). Autonomic patterns during respiratory suspensions: Possible markers of Transcendental Consciousness. *Psychophysiology, 34*, 39-46.

Travis, F., & Wallace, R. K. (1999). Autonomic and EEG patterns during eyes-closed rest and Transcendental Meditation (TM) practice: The basis for a neural model of TM practice. *Consciousness and Cognition, 8*, 302-318.

Turnbull, M. J., & Norris, H. (1982). Effects of Transcendental Meditation on self-identity indices and personality. *British Journal of Psychology, 73*, 57-68.

Tyack, D. (1974). *The one best system: A history of American urban education.* Cambridge, MA: Harvard University Press.

U. S. Census Bureau. (1998). *Statistical abstract of the United States: 1998.* Washington, DC: U.S. Government Printing Office.

U. S. Census Bureau. (1999). *Statistical abstract of the United States: 1999.* Washington, DC: U.S. Government Printing Office.

U. S. Department of Health and Human Services. (1991). *Drug abuse and drug abuse research: The third triennial report to Congress from the Secretary, Department of Health and Human Services.* Rockville, MD.

U. S. Department of Justice. (1996). *Crime in the United States: Uniform crime reports.* Washington, DC: U.S. Government Printing Office.

U.S. Department of State. (1998). *Patterns of global terrorism, 1997.* Washington, DC: U.S. Government Printing Office.

United Kingdom Prison Service. (1994). *Prison Statistics, England and Wales.* London: Government Printing Office.

van den Berg, W. P., & Mulder, B. (1976). Psychological research on the effects of the Transcendental Meditation technique on a number of personality variables. *Gedrag: Tijdschrift voor Psychologie, 4*, 206-218.

Vaux, A., & Ruggiero, M. (1983, April). Stressful life change and delinquent behavior. *American Journal of Community Psychology, 11* (2), 169-183.

Veit, C. T., & Ware, J. E. J. (1983). The structure of psychological distress and well-being in general populations. *Journal of Consulting and Clinical Psychology, 51* (5), 730-742.

Verbeuren, T. J. (1989). Synthesis, storage, release, and metabolism of 5-hydroxytryptamine in peripheral tissues. In J. R. Fozard (Ed.), *The Peripheral Actions of 5-Hydroxytryptamine* (1-18). New York: Oxford University Press.

Vickers, D., Nettelbeck, T., & Willson, R. J. (1972). Perceptual indices of performance: The measure of "inspection time" and "noise" in the visual system. *Perception, 1*, 263-295.

Waddock, S. A. (1995). *Not by schools: Sharing responsibility for Americans' education reform.* Westport, CT: Praeger.

Waldrop, M. M. (1985). String as a theory of everything. *Science, 229*, 1251-1253.

Wallace, R. K. (1970a). Physiological effects of Transcendental Meditation. *Science, 167*, 1751-1754.

Wallace, R. K. (1970b). The physiological effects of Transcendental Meditation: A proposed fourth major state of consciousness. Doctoral thesis, Department of Physiology, School of Medicine, University of California at Los Angeles, Los Angeles, California, U.S.A. In D. W. Orme-Johnson & J. T. Farrow (Eds.), *Scientific research on the Transcendental Meditation program: Collected papers* (pp. 43-78). Rheinweiler, Germany: MERU Press.

Wallace, R. K. (1986). *The Maharishi Technology of the Unified Field: The neurophysiology of enlightenment.* Fairfield, IA: MIU Neuroscience Press.

Wallace, R. K. (1993 The physiology of consciousness. Fairfield, IA: Maharishi International University Press.

Wallace, R. K., & Benson, H. (1972). The physiology of meditation. *Scientific American, 2266* (2), 84-90.

Wallace, R. K., Benson, H., & Wilson, A. F. (1971). A wakeful hypometabolic physiologic state. *American Journal of Physiology, 221* (3), 795-799.

Wallace, R. K., Mills, P. J., Orme-Johnson, D. W., Dillbeck, M. C., & Jacobe, E. (1983). Modification of the paired H reflex through the Transcendental Meditation and TM-Sidhi program. *Experimental Neurology, 79*, 77-86.

Wallace, R. K., Orme-Johnson, D. W., & Dillbeck, M. C. (Eds.). (1990). *Scientific research on Maharishi's Transcendental Meditation and TM-Sidhi program: Collected papers, volume 5.* Fairfield, IA: Maharishi International University Press.

Walton, K. G., & Levitsky, D. (1994). A neuroendocrine mechanism for the reduction of drug use and addictions by Transcendental Meditation. *Alcoholism Treatment Quarterly, 11* (1/2), 89-117.

Walton, K. G., & Levitsky, D. K. (this volume). Effects of the *Transcendental Meditation* program on neuroendocrine abnormalities associated with aggression and crime. *Journal of Offender Rehabilitation*, 36(1/2/3/4), 67-87.

Walton, K. G., & Pugh, N. D. C. (1994). [Correlation between 5-HIAA excretion and measures of aggression, anger, anxiety, depression, and leadership ability.] Unpublished raw data.

Walton, K. G., & Pugh, N. D. C. (1995). Stress, steroids, and "ojas": Neuroendocrine mechanisms and current promise of ancient approaches to disease prevention. *Indian Journal of Physiology and Pharmacology, 39* (1), 3-34.

Walton, K. G., Alexander, C. N., Camelia, C. R. T., Hawkins, M. A., & Durchholz, C. F. (2001). *Effects of Maharishi's consciousness-based approach to rehabilitation on inmates in Netherlands Antilles: II. Changes in biochemical indicators of stress.* Unpublished manuscript.

Walton, K. G., Cavanaugh, K. L., & Pugh, N. D. (in press). Effect of group practice of the Transcendental Meditation program on biochemical indicators of stress in non-meditators: Causal analysis of a field theory of consciousness. *Journal of Social Behavior and Personality.*

Walton, K. G., Pugh, N. D. C., Gelderloos, P., & Macrae, P. (1995). Stress reduction and preventing hypertension: Preliminary support for a psychoneuroendocrine mechanism. *Journal of Alternative and Complementary Medicine, 1* (3), 263-283.

Wandhofer, A., Kobal, G., & Plattig, K. -H. (1976). Shortening latencies of human auditory evoked brain potentials during the Transcendental Meditation technique. *Zeitschrift fur Elektroenzephalographie und Elektromyographie EEG-EMG, 7,* 99-103.

Warner, T. Q. (1986). Transcendental Meditation and developmental advancement: Mediating abilities and conservation performance (Doctoral dissertation, York University, 1986). *Dissertations Abstracts International, 47* (8), 3558B.

Warshal, D. (1980). Effects of the Transcendental Meditation technique on normal and Jendrassik reflex time. *Perceptual and Motor Skills, 50,* 1103-1106.

Weatherburn, D., & Lind, B. (1997). On the epidemiology of offender populations. *The Australian Journal of Psychology, 49* (3), 169-175.

Weekes, J. R., & Morison, S. J. (1993). Offender typologies: Identifying treatment-related personality characteristics. *Forum on Corrections Research, 5,* 10-12.

Wells-Parker, E., & Bangert-Drowns, R. (1990). Meta-analysis of research on DUI remedial interventions. *Alcohol, Drugs and Driving, 6,* 147-160.

Werner, O. R., Wallace, R. K., Charles, B., Janssen, G., Stryker, T., & Chalmers, R. A. (1986). Long-term endocrinologic changes in subjects practicing the Transcendental Meditation and TM-Sidhi program. *Psychosomatic Medicine, 48,* 59-66.

West, D. J., & Farrington, D. P. (1973). *Who becomes delinquent?* London: Heinemann Educational.

White, H. (1997). Alcohol, illicit drugs, and violence. In D. Stoff, J. Breiling, & J. Maser (Eds.), *Handbook of antisocial behavior* (pp. 511-523). New York: John Wiley & Sons, Inc.

White, J. L., Moffitt, T. E., & Silva, P. A. (1989). A prospective replication of the protective effects of IQ in subjects at high risk for juvenile delinquency. *Journal of Consulting and Clinical Psychology, 57* (6), 719-724.

White, J. L., Moffitt, T. E., Caspi, A., Bartusch, D. J., Needles, D. J, & Stouthamer-Loeber, M. (1994). Measuring impulsivity and examining its relationship to delinquency. *Journal of Abnormal Psychology, 103* (2), 192-205.

White, R. W. (1967). Competence and the growth of personality. In J. H. Masterman (Ed.), *The ego, science, and psychoanalysis* (pp. 42-49). New York: Grune and Stratton.

Whitehead, J. T., & Lab, S. J. (1989). A meta-analysis of juvenile correctional treatment. *Journal of Research in Crime and Delinquency, 26* (3), 276-295.

Widom, C. S. (1978). An empirical classification of female offenders. *Criminal Justice and Behavior, 5* (1), 35-52.

Wigner, E. (1967). *Symmetries and reflections.* Amherst, MA: OxBow.

Wilkinson, L. (1989). *SYSTAT: The system for statistics.* Evanston, IL: SYSTAT.

Wills, T. A., & Schiffman, S. (1985). Coping and substance abuse: A conceptual framework. In S. Shiffman & T. A. Wills (Eds.), *Coping and substance abuse.* Orlando, FL: Academic.

Wilson, H. (1980). Parental supervision: A neglected aspect of delinquency. *British Journal of Criminology, 20*, 203-235.

Wilson, J. Q. (1994). What to do about crime. *Commentary, 98* (3), 25-34.

Wilson, J. Q. (1995). Crime and public policy. In J. Q. Wilson & J. Petersilia (Eds.), *Crime* (pp. 489-510). San Francisco: Institute for Contemporary Studies Press.

Wilson, J. Q., & Herrnstein, R. J. (1985). *Crime and human nature.* New York: Simon & Schuster.

Winer, B. J. (1971). *Statistical principles in experimental design* (2nd ed.). New York: McGraw-Hill.

Winquist, W. T. (1977). The Transcendental Meditation program and drug abuse: A retrospective study. In D. W. Orme-Johnson & J. T. Farrow (Eds.), *Scientific research on the Transcendental Meditation Program: Collected papers, volume 1* (pp. 494-497). Rheinweiler, Germany: Maharishi European Research University Press.

Winter, D. G. (1973). *The power motive.* New York: Free Press.

Witkin, H. A., Dyk, R. B., Faterson, H. F., Goodenough, D. R., & Karp, S. A. (1974). *Psychological differentiation: Studies of development.* Potomac, MD: Lawrence Erlbaum.

Witkin, H. A., Oltman, P. K., Raskin, E., & Karp, S. A. (1971). *Manual for the Embedded Figures Tests.* Palo Alto, CA: Consulting Psychologists Press.

Witkin, H. A., Price-Williams, D., Bertini, M., Christiansen, B., Ramirez, P. K., & Van Meel, J. (1974). Social conformity and psychological differentiation. *International Journal of Psychology, 9*, 11-29.

Wolfgang, M. E., Thornberry, T. P., & Figlio, R. M. (Eds.). (1987). *From boy to man, from delinquency to crime.* Chicago: University of Chicago Press.

Wysong, E., Aniskiewicz, R., & Wright, D. (1994). Truth and DARE: Tracking drug education to graduation as symbolic politics. *Social Problems, 41* (3), 448-456.

Yochelson, S., & Samenow, S. E. (1976). *The criminal personality. Volume 1.* New York: Jason Aronson.

Yochelson, S., & Samenow, S. E. (1977). *The criminal personality . Volume 2.* New York: Jason Aronson.

Yoder, B. (1990). *The recovery resource book.* New York: Simon & Schuster.

Zamble, E., & Porporino, F. J. (1990). Coping, imprisonment, and rehabilitation: Some data and their implications. *Criminal Justice and Behavior, 1*, 53-70.

Zhang, Y. (1991). Inspection time correlation with IQ in Chinese students. *Personality and Individual Differences, 12* (3), 217-219.

Zuckerman, M. (1964). Perceptual isolation as a stress situation. *Archives of General Psychiatry, 11*, 255-276.

Index

Absenteeism, reduced, 311
Addiction, effects of TM program, 10
Adrenergic receptors, 82
lower percentage of high-affinity beta-adrenergic receptors in long-term practitioners of the Transcendental Meditation program, 83
Aggression
decreased, 9,14,128,144,149, 152,154
neuroendocrine abnormalities and, 68-71
Akaike information criterion, 283
Alarm or stress response, 77
Alcohol, cigarette, and illicit drug usage, reduced, 11,243
Alcoholics Anonymous (AA), 112
Aldosterone, 83
normalization of salt intake and kidney function with practice of the TM program, 85
Alexander, Charles Nathaniel (Skip), 1,2,27,181-203,205-228, 283-302
doctoral dissertation on rehabilitation of prisoners
cross sectional study, 97-125
longitudinal study, 127-160
recidivism study, 161-180
In Memoriam, xxxi-xxxvi
model of human development, 11-16
States of Consciousness Inventory (SCI), 4,29,98,108,121,137, 145,148,149,150
synthesis of Western developmental theory and Maharishi's Vedic Science, 11-26
Allostasis and allostatic load, 71-73
Alpha-2-adrenoceptors, responsible for the start and maintenance of aggression, 69
Anklesaria, Farrokh, 27,35-46,303-318
Anxiety, decreased, 3,9,54-56,59,98, 121,128,144,149,154,183
Athletic performance, improved, 14
Attrition, 153
Autonomic balance and stability, increased, 3,9,92
Azar's (1980) conflict scale category, 287

Barratt Impulsiveness Scale (BIS), 212
Behavioral Inventory (BI), 213
Beta-adrenoceptors, associated with fine tuning of aggression, 69
Box-Jenkins autoregressive integrated moving averages (ARIMA) time series analysis, 267,289
Boyer, Robert, 1-33
Brahmananda Saraswati, 254
Buss-Durkee Hostility Inventory (BDHI), 212

Camelia, Carl R.T., 205-228
CASH (Can Anyone Save Humanity) Drug Rehabilitation, 113,127, 134,150,151,152,154
Catecholamines, 68

and the Transcendental Meditation program, 83
epinephrine, 69
norepinephrine, 69,77
and locus coeruleus, 77
Causal analysis, 269
Causes of crime, 5,260,
biobehavioral influences, 5,68-71,99
psychosocial influences, 5
risk factors, 49-50
social-environmental factors, 5
stress, xxi-xxii, 71-79
Cavanaugh, Kenneth L., 181-203
Chi-square test for differences in proportion, 167
Choice reaction time, faster, 14
Christian groups, 113,127,135,151,155
Chronology of International Terrorism, 289
1% Cities, 268
Clayborne, Mawiyah, 229-255
Cognitive-developmental theory, 223
Cognitive development, increased, 121
Cognitive flexibility, improved, 14
Coherence proportional to the number of coherent elements squared, 266,286
Collapse of the wave function, 262
Collective consciousness, 31,265,285
and modern physics, 262
in the social sciences (Gustav Fechner, William James, Emile Durkheim), 261
idealist tradition and connection of human beings on the level of consciousness, 261
increasing coherence in, 264-281
College of Natural Law, 271
Communicativeness, increased, 128,129,131
Community-based rehabilitation project, 35-46
Compliance to treatment, 142,223,226
Compulsive behavior, reduced, 89
Consciousness-based approach to criminal rehabilitation, 4-11, 100-101,205,208,235-237
Consciousness-based Education, 229-255
Consciousness-Based faculty development program, 237
prevention-oriented health education program, 237
research related to criminal risk factors, 237
Science of Creative Intelligence (SCI), 237
principles of, 248
with at-risk students, Newark, NJ, Washington, D.C., 250-252
and reduced teacher burnout as measured on Maslach Teacher Burnout Inventory, 251
Content analysis of major newspapers, 277
COPDAB file, 296
Cosmic consciousness (see Maharishi's Seven States of Consciousness)
Cost effectiveness, 280
Cost reduction, 318
Cost savings, 319-331
Costs of crime, 201
Costs of crime prevention programs, 258
Costs of incarceration, 182
Counseling groups, 127,134,150,151, 152,154
Countries in which the Transcendental Meditation program has been implemented in criminalsettings, 304
Creating coherence for the national government, 272
Creativity, increased, 14
Crime prevention, 232-235,260,305 (also see Consciousness

Based Education, Maharishi Effect)
Criminal rehabilitation, research on the Transcendental Meditation program and, 53-57
Cross-lagged panel correlation, 269
Curaçao federal prison, Netherlands Antilles, 205-228
  methods, 208-217
  results, 217-222
    cognitive distortion, reduced, 221-222
    intelligence related measures, improved, 222
  discussion, 222-227

Defining Issues Test, 107
Deme, Alioune Badara, governor of the Thiès House of Arrest and Correction, Senegal, 310
Department of Legal Medicine (DLM) Counseling, 114
Depression, reduced, 15,226
Developmental psychology, 12
DHEAS (dehydroepiandrosterone sulfate) and the ratio of DHEAS to cortisol, 85
  decrease with age, 86
  increased with practice of the Transcendental Meditation program, 86
Dillbeck, Michael C., 283-302
Diop, Colonel Mamadou, Director of the Penitentiary Administration, Senegal, 310, 311,315
Drop-out rates, low, 142
Drug rehabilitation (see CASH)
Durchholz, Christian F., 205-228

Ecology of crime, 240
Education programs in rehabilitation settings, 113,186
EEG coherence, 6,129,241,266
Effectiveness of rehabilitation programs, enhancement of, synergistic interaction, 179,193,196,200
Ego-development (see also self-development)
  in Maharishi University of Management alumni, 246-247
  Loevinger's scale (the SCT), 3,4, 29,98,101-103,119-120,128, 129,131,155-158
  outcomes for TM program and controls, 15,104,143-159
Enlightened Sentencing Project, 35-46
  probationers' experiences, 42-43
  judges' observations, 43-44
Enlightenment, 3 (also see Maharishi's Seven States of Consciousness)
Experience of transcendental consciousness as the solution to crime, 264-267
External formal social control (e.g., police and prison programs, control of criminogenic commodities), research, 259

Factor analysis of test measurements, Walpole I cross-sectional study, 116-117
Field effects of consciousness, 262-281 (also see Maharishi Effect)
Field independence, increased, 14,122
Fluid intelligence, growth of, 14
  in Cambodia and China, 247
Folsom State Prison, 181-203
Fourth state of consciousness (see Maharishi's Seven States of Consciousness)
Frank, Paul R., 161-180

Freezing of the autonomic nervous system, 94

Galvanic skin response, GSR (sympathetic skin response, SSR), 81-82
  lower frequency of spontaneous GSRs during practice of the TM technique, 81,89,92
Geer, Gerald T., xxx-xxxvii
Glass effect sizes and phi coefficients (tetrachoric correlations), 168
God consciousness (see Maharishi's Seven States of Consciousness)
Goodman, Rachel S., 1-33,97-125
Grant, James D., 161-180,229-255
Group Embedded Figures Test, 107,214
Group therapy, 186

Hagelin, John, xxvii-xxix
Hawkins, Mark A., 47-65,205-228
Health care costs, reduced, 322-323
5-HIAA (5-hydoxyindoleacetic acid)
  aggression, anger, anxiety, and depression associated with lower excretion, 80
  leadership ability associated with higher excretion, 80
  lower levels in cerebrospinal fluid of criminals, 68
  higher urinary levels in individuals practicing the Transcendental Meditation program, 79
Hierarchy of levels of the mind, 11
Homeostasis, 71-72
Hostility, decreased, 9,14,54,56
How I Think Questionnaire (HIT), 213
Hypertension, reduced, 9
Hypothalamic-pituitary-adrenocortical (HPA) axis, aggression, and hostility, 68-71,78-79,83-86
  ACTH (adrenocorticotropic hormone), 70,78
  cortisol, 70,78,83-86
  hippocampus, portion of the limbic system associated with functioning of HPA-axis, 78
  stress-induced changes in, 78-79
Impulse expression, normalized, 226
Incarceration rate, United States, 48,162
Informal social control, 260-261
  employment, 260
  home nurse visitations, 260
  job training, 260
  parent-training strategies, 260
  school-based programs that work, 260
Inmates volunteer to work in city, 307-308
Insomnia, reduced, 9
International conflict, percentage decrease during three assemblies, 295

Jones, Christopher, 229-255
Just Community Schools, 248,249

King, Michael S., 35-46,303-318
Knower, process of knowing, and known, 7
Knowledge is structured in consciousness, 246
Kohlberg, Lawrence, 156
  moral reasoning scale, 3
  stages of moral development, 17,20

Lactate, blood levels, 82
Learning and memory, improved, 14
Levitsky, Debra K., 67-87
Lie scale, 121,137,140,141,144, 148,149-150,209,222
Ljung-Box test, 292,293,294,296, 297,299

Local culture, independence of, 279
Loevinger (see ego-development)
Loevinger's theory of self-development, 17-20
London Times, 287
Longitudinal Study of Transcendental Meditation program and prison rehabilitation, 127-160
Long-term goals developed in prison inmates, 131

Magill, David L., 319-331
Maharishi Effect, crime reduction, and societal well-being, 31, 257-281
  Extended Maharishi Effect, 257
    Canada, improved quality of national life (1972-1986), 276
    Ideal Society Campaign, improved quality of life, 273-274
    Israel (1983), decreased war, improved quality of life, 274-275
    Merseyside England, decreased crime (1978-1991), 271-272
    Metro Manila, improved quality of life (1984-1985), 271
    Metro Manila Region, decreased crime (1979-1981), 271
    Puerto Rico, decreased crime (1984), 274
    Union Territory of Delhi, India, decreased crime (1980-1981), 270
    U.S., decreased index of homicide, suicide, and motor vehicle fatalities (1979-1985), 275-276
  Washington, D.C., decreased crime (1981-1983), 271
  Washington, D.C., decreased crime (1993), 272-273
  Global Maharishi Effect, 277,283-302
    Holland assembly, decreased international conflicts, 292-294
    Iowa assembly, decreased international conflicts, 292
    Washington assembly, decreased international conflicts, 294-295
    terrorism, decreased (1983-1985), 276-277,284-286,297-298
Maharishi Mahesh Yogi, 2,14,37, 208,236,254,264,279,302
Maharishi School of the Age of Enlightenment, 247-249
  achievement of students, 248-249
  research on students, 248
Maharishi's Seven States of Consciousness, 3,5,11, 12,13,21-24
  1. sleep, 129
  2. dreaming, 129,137
  3. waking, 129,137,140,145, 148-150,154
  4. transcendental consciousness (also called pure consciousness), 5,6,7,9,13,15, 21,129,136,155,257,264
  5. cosmic consciousness, 12,22-23, 137,148,156
  6. refined cosmic consciousness (God consciousness), 12,23, 137
  7. unity consciousness, 12,23-24, 137,148
Maharishi University of Management (formerly Maharishi International University), 246
  longitudinal research on undergraduates, 246-247
Maharishi Vedic Science, 2,11,12,264
Mason, the Honorable David C., xxi-xxiv, 27,36

Mass discharge (global activation of the sympathetic nervous system), 77
Maximum security prisoners, rehabilitation, 97-203
  Folsom 15-year follow-up, 181-203
    subjects and data collection, 184-185
    data analysis, 185-189
    results, 189-196
      primary recidivism outcomes, 189-194
      recidivism graded according to offense severity, 194-195
    discussion, 196-201
  Walpole cross-sectional study, 97-125
    subjects, 106-107
    measures, 107-109
    design, 110-111
    programs, 111-114
    results, 114-122
      avocational business involvement, increased, 122
      cognitive and moral development, 120-121
      demographic outcomes, 114-116
      ego development, higher scores, 119-120
      Embedded Figures Test, increased field independence, 122
      negative effect, reduction of, 121
      postconceptual experience scores on SCI higher, 121
      psychopathology, decreased, 117-118
      TAT intimacy motivation and need for power measures, 122
    discussion, 123-125
  Walpole longitudinal study, 127-160
    subjects, 130-132
    programs, 133-136
    measures, 136-138
    procedures, 138
    statistical design, 138-141
    results, 141-154
      increased self-development, 127,143-148,152
      increased postconceptual experience, 128, 148-149,152
      decreased schizophrenic symptoms, 128,149
      decreased aggression, decreased trait anxiety, lie scales, 128,149-150,152
    discussion, 155-159
  Walpole study, reduced recidivism, 161-180
    methods, 165-169
    results, 169-172
    discussion, 172-179
Medical expenses, prison, decreased, 303,309,311
Mental Health Inventory (MHI), 212
Meta-analyses
  effectiveness of rehabilitation programs, 99,163,176,198
  Transcendental Meditation program and increased basal skin resistance, 81-82
  Transcendental Meditation program and reduced blood lactate levels, 82
  Transcendental Meditation program and self-actualization, 15,95, 104
  Transcendental Meditation program and substance abuse, 10,243
  Transcendental Meditation program and trait anxiety, 65

Transcendental Meditation program, physiological responses, vs. eyes closed, 6
Transcendental Meditation program vs. other techniques, 9,65
Mill Hill Vocabulary Scale, 107
Misery Index, 242
Misleading scale, 128,137,141,148
MMPI (Minnesota Multiphasic Personality Inventory), 28,53,89
Modifiable criminogenic risk factors, 179
Moore, Richard M., 89-95
Moral reasoning, 94,131,156
Muslim groups, 113,127,135-136, 150-154

Natural law, 25-26
action in accord with, 248,254,285
influence of attention on, 263
Netherlands Antilles, TM program prison rehabilitation in, 205-228
Neuroendocrine
abnormalities associated with crime, 68-71
systems mediating adaptation, 67
Neuroticism, decreased, 9
New York Times, 287
Noise model, 289
Number of people victimized by crime annually in the United States, 163

Object-referral consciousness, 7,16
Obsessive thoughts, reduced, 89
Orme-Johnson, David W., xxx, 1-33, 89-95,127-160,257-302

Parole officers and families, instruction in the Transcendental Meditation program, 45
Peak experiences, 24
Personal Orientation Inventory (POI), 15,62
Piaget, Jean, 2,12,13,16-17
stages of human development, 16-17
Plant Problem, the, 107
Police effectiveness, improved, 265
Political and Community Caucus Groups, 114
Positive affect, increased, 15
Postconceptual experience (see Alexander's States of Consciousness Inventory)
Post-traumatic stress disorder, 77,78
relief from, 10,15, 63,330
Principled moral reasoning, 121
increased, 14
Prison rule infractions, decreased, 3, 14,183,303,309,311
Prisons in the U.S. where the Transcendental Meditation program has been taught, 243-244
Prison wardens and guards, experiences with the TM program, 245,312-316
Program integrity, value of program support structure, 175-176
Progressive Matrices Test, 107
Protective factors of criminal behavior, 207,259
Psychasthenia, decreased, 89,93
Psychopathology, decreased, 8,29, 55,127,130,136,162
Psychopaths, 70
Pure consciousness (also see Maharishi's Seven States of Consciousness)
definition of, 7
experiences in the Western tradition, 235-236

Rainforth, Maxwell V., 161-228
Random assignment studies, 183
Ratio of program cost to total savings, 319
Reachout, 113
Recidivism, 14,29,30,32,48,50,55, 56,161-203,245,303,306, 316-317
  background variables associated with, 169-170
  predictors of, 168
Refined cosmic consciousness (see Maharishi's Seven States of Consciousness)
Reincarceration costs, reduced, 324
Reincarceration rates, comparison among programs, 171-172
Relapse rates, 48,50
Relations between the superpowers, positive influence on, 302
Resilience, 9-10,87
  strengthening consistent with research on the Transcendental Meditation program, 87
Respiratory suspension, 129
Responsible attitude and behavior, increased, 128,129,131
Restful alertness, 6,7
Rigidity, reduced, 89
Risk factors of criminal behavior, 8, 47,49-50,230,259,279
  physiological, psychological, sociological, and alcohol and drug abuse, 238-243
Risk factors of disease, reduced, 325
Risk factors of poor development, 9
Rutherford, George, 229-255

Salient factor score, 185
San Quentin, 245
School-based approaches to crime, 233-235
  constraint and punishment, 233-234
  social services (e.g., mentoring, counseling, after-hour programs), 234
  curricula enhancement (e.g., conflict resolution, personal skills, law, violence prevention training, peer mediation, anti-drug and anti-gang components), 234-235
School climate, 242
School success factors, 230
School violence, 31,230
Self-actualization, 15,20
Self-development (see ego development)
Self-esteem scale (SE), 213
Self-monitoring, 128,129,131
Self-referral consciousness, 7,16 (also see Maharishi's Seven States of Consciousness)
Self-reflective, 129
Self-respecting, 128,129,131
Self-selection, 198
Senegal, Republic of, 32,303-318
  experiences of administrators, officers, and inmates, 312-316
  results in, 311-312
Sensory-motor performance, improved, 13
Sentence Completion Test of Ego Development, 107,136
Serotonin (5-hydroxytryptamine, 5-HT), 8,68,75-77
  aggression associated with, 68
  increased metabolism associated with the Transcendental Meditation technique, 76
Shankaracharya tradition, 254
Simplest form of human awareness, 257
Smoking, reduced, 64
Social costs of criminal conduct and substance abuse, 48,328

Social disorganization theory, 240
Social introversion, decreased, 89
Social stress index, 273
Social variables known to influence crime, 269
Special Hospitals Assessment of Personality and Socialization (SHAPS), 98,109,116,121, 136
Split population model, 187
Staffing, reduced, 321
STAI (Spielberger's State Trait Anxiety Inventory), 53, 54,55,61,62,137
Standard Metropolitan Statistical Areas, U.S., 270
States of Consciousness Inventory (SCI, see Alexander, Charles Nathaniel (Skip))
State Stress Index, 8
State-Trait Anxiety Inventory, 109
Strategies for preventing war, 284
Stress, xxi-xxii, 37,67,71,73-75,178, 254
  coping skills, xxii, 38
  hormones, 8,75-79,130
  normalization of, 8-9,79-86,129, 130,133,134,232
  stress-induced neuroendocrine abnormalities associated with aggression and crime
    serotonin systems, 75-77
    catecholamine systems, 77-78
    HPA axis, 78-79
  TM program's effects on stress-induced neuroendocrine abnormalities associated with
    aggression serotonin systems, activity increased, 79-80
    catecholamine systems, activity reduced, 81-83
    HPA axis, activity normalized, 83-84
    aldosterone and kidney function, 85
    DHEAS and ratio of DHEAS to cortisol, 85-86
Stress index, 8,240
Substance abuse, 3
  reduced substance abuse and addiction, 9-11,58-64
  substance use, research on the Transcendental Meditation program and, 58-64
  substance abuse and crime, 10
Superstring theory, 264
Survival analysis, 181
Sy, Mr. Ibrahima, prison governor of the Camp Pénal Prison, Dakar, Senegal, 305
  experiences, 307
Sympathetic nervous system (SNS), 77
  Transcendental Meditation program and, 81

Tellegen Absorption Scale (TAS), 108
Terrorism, 276-277,284,289
  international, decreased fatalities and injuries due to, 299
Thematic Apperception Test (TAT), 98,109
  Intimacy Motivation, 122
  Need for Power, 122
Time series analysis, 267,283
Total savings after release for a cohort of 1,000 inmates practicing the TM program, 323
Transcendental consciousness (see Maharishi's Seven States of Consciousness)
Transcendental Meditation (TM) program, 2
  comparison with other procedures, 10,15
  cost effectiveness, 33
  description of program, 6,111,133, 236

effectiveness of program, 157
mechanics of the practice, 6-7
origin and nature of, 5-6,177
physiological changes during, 6, 129-130
regularity of practice of and results, 92,117
rehabilitation of maximum security prisoners with, 97-203
related to the causes of drug and alcohol abuse, 237-244
related to the sociology of criminal behavior, 242
research reviews, 51-64,164, 237-244,265
Transcendental Meditation (TM) program and:
belief systems and lifestyles, 39
desire, 14
ego, 15
feelings, 14-15
functional capacity of the mind, 14
intellect, 14
levels of the mind, 13-16
mind, 14
rehabilitation programs
Folsom State Prison, 181-203
La Tuna Federal Penitentiary, 28,89-95
Massachusetts Correction Institution at Walpole, 97-203
Netherlands Antilles, 205-228
Senegalese Penitentiary System, 303-318
twenty-five programs summarized, 53-64
research, general, 51-52
Transcendental Meditation (TM) Sidhi program 3,31,236
amplitude of cortical and brainstem responses to somatosensory stimuli, increased, 266
distribution of brain response to sensory input, wider, 266
research, general, 267-281
sociological research on, 241-243
Transcendental Meditation (TM) technique, 1
subjective experiences
at-risk students, 250-252
prison officials, inmates, 311-316
higher states of consciousness (see Alexander, States of Consciousness Inventory, Maharishi's Seven States of Consciousness, and Pure consciousness)
Transcending
description of, 6-7,129
dual process of with stress normalization in rehabilitation, 129
physiological correlates of, 79-86, 129-130
subjective measure of, 130
Transfer function approach of time series analysis, 271
Travis, Frederick T. 205-228

Unfreeze development, 2,155
Unified field of all the laws of nature, 26,257,264
United States incarceration rate, 162
Unity consciousness (see Maharishi's Seven States of Consciousness)

Vanillylmandelic acid (VMA), 82
Vedic tradition, 5,129,136,158,236, 254,278
Vocational training, 186
Von Stade, Christopher, 161-180

Wallace, Robert Keith, 6
Walpole prison, 95-180

Walton, Kenneth G., 1-33,67-87,
97-125,161-180,205-228
Workers' compensation claims, fewer,
326
World terrorism intervention analysis,
298

Yoga Sutras of Patanjali, 278
Yogic flying and maximum EEG
coherence, 267

Zhang's Inspection Time Test,
214-215